CW00819558

BLUE NIPPON

AUTHENTICATING JAZZ IN JAPAN

E. Taylor Atkins

Duke University Press

Durham and London 2001

© 2001 Duke University Press
All rights reserved
Printed in the United States of America on acid-free paper ∞
Typeset in Scala by Keystone Typesetting, Inc.
Library of Congress Cataloging-in-Publication Data appear
on the last printed page of this book.

Lyrics to "The Tokyo Blues" reprinted with permission of
Ecaroh Music. Lyrics to "Trouble in Mind" reprinted with
permission of Universal Music Publishing Group.

For the ladies in my life,
Zabrina Marie and Gabriella Rose

CONTENTS

LIST OF ILLUSTRATIONS

ACKNOWLEDGMENTS

Country roads in the American South are mystical and inspiring. Robert Johnson met a Gentleman at the intersection of two such roads, bartering his soul for dexterity on the guitar, and music has never been the same. Fortunately, the Gentleman with whom I conversed on a road in Puryear, Tennessee, doesn't make deals.

In the summer of 1990 I was taking a dusk-time, post-supper stroll along the road to my grandparent's house (we called it "walkin' your dinner off"). In another month I was to commence graduate studies in Japanese history, and on that night I was plagued by the self-doubt and uncertainty that all prospective graduate students in the humanities feel if they've been paying attention to the world at all. My problem was that I had music in my head all the time, not shōguns and such. That evening I pleaded for some way to integrate my passion with the only obvious career choice for someone whose talents are limited to academic pursuits. A month later I was enrolled in Ronald Toby and David Plath's Japanese pop culture seminar—when this idea was delivered to me. I never even considered anything else. Some of my mentors may have worried that I enjoyed it too much, but that was the only reason it was worth doing.

To our beloved Ma, who taught us how to pray on country roads: we miss you.

This book is the product of many people's generosity, insights, and efforts. While I am quite happy to share credit for its successes with the many people who assisted me, I insist on monopolizing blame for its shortcomings.

This project could not possibly have succeeded without the generous cooperation of the jazz musicians, historians, critics, and aficionados who shared their experiences, knowledge, and collections with me. The names of individuals I interviewed are listed in the References section, but I would like to make special mention of Isono Teruo, Segawa Masahisa, Ueda Sakae, Uchida Kōichi, Dr. Uchida Osamu, the late Yoshida Mamoru and his sister Takako, and the late Yui Shōichi for their kind assistance. The American scholars who pioneered Western-language research in this field, Sidney Brown, Elizabeth Sesler-Beckman, George Yoshida, and Larry Richards, were exceptionally generous with their materials and knowledge, and I owe them much gratitude for blazing significant trails. Larry's talent for finding documents relating to the early history of jazz is matched only by his generosity in sharing them.

Special thanks to Elizabeth Maclachlan for tipping me off to the "Buddhist Jazz Funeral"; to Kōno Tamaki, Odaka Megumu, Noguchi Kōichi, and Satō Tsukasa of the Inter-University Center for Japanese Language Studies for assisting with translations of texts and taped interviews; to Iwata Mizuho, Yasumi Takashi, and the rest of the staff at the Japan–United States Educational Commission (JUSEC) for smoothing the transition to life in Japan; to the late Koyama Hachirō ("Buddy") and his wife Tsuneko for their hospitality and generosity during our two-year stay in their rental house in Yokohama; to Mr. Horita Akio and Ms. Ueki Yoshiko of the Ōsaka City Archives for advice on dance-hall-related materials; to Mr. Sugiura Takeshi of the Okazaki Mindscape Museum for assistance with the Uchida Osamu Jazz Collection; the staff of the Okazaki City Library for hospitality and listening space; to Dr. Itō Kuniharu for generously donating a number of valuable videos from his collection; to NIU Media Productions / Imaging for great work; and to Yoshida Emi for obtaining a rare and lovely duo recording by Takayanagi Masayuki and Ino Nobuyoshi that I had foolishly passed up too many times.

I want to make special mention of the Sugiura family of Okazaki, without whose assistance and hospitality this project would have been the poorer. Introduced to me by a mutual friend, the Sugiuras invited me to spend several days in their home, without knowing me from Adam, and immediately made me feel comfortable. We spent countless hours in what I dubbed their *jazu jinja* ("jazz shrine"), listening to and discussing music, food, and just about everything else (is there anything else?). They introduced me to "Doctor Jazz," Uchida Osamu, and handled negotiations that enabled me to use Dr. U's jazz collection in Okazaki. They also introduced me to eel and red miso ("the brand His Majesty the Emperor eats"), as I introduced them to gumbo and soul food. Of the many gifts this project has provided me personally, their friendship is easily the one I cherish most.

Initial research and writing (1993–96) was funded by a Fulbright Grant, a University of Illinois Graduate Research Fellowship, and an Andrew W. Mellon Dissertation Fellowship. Additional research in the summer of 1998 was possible thanks to grants from the Northeast Asia Council of the Association of Asian Studies and the Graduate College of Northern Illinois University. I was unable to take advantage of a postdoctoral fellowship from the Japan Society for the Promotion of Science, but wish to acknowledge their willingness to support this project. Thanks also to the helpful staff at the following libraries: Min'on Music Library, National Diet Library, the prefectural libraries of Kanagawa, Kyōto, and Ōsaka, and the city libraries of Yokohama, Tokyo, Kōbe, Ōsaka, and Okazaki.

From this project's inception, Jeffrey Hanes, Ronald Toby, and David Plath offered both encouragement and penetrating yet constructive criticism. Kevin Doak contributed at a later stage with similar enthusiasm and insight. A number of other friends and colleagues commented on all or portions of the manuscript at various stages of preparation: Michael Auslin, Sundiata Djata, Laura Driussi, Gregory Guelcher, Samuel Kinser, Narita Ryūichi, Matthew Norman, George Spencer, Torii Yusuke, and Stephen Vlastos. I received valuable feedback at several venues at which I presented my work: the Ph.D. Kenkyūkai in Tokyo; the Midwest Conference on Asian Affairs in St. Louis and Champaign; the Social Science Research Council's Joint Council for Japanese Studies Dissertation Workshop at Asilomar in Monterey, California; the University of Victoria's Japanese Popular Culture and Asian Pop Culture conferences; the University of Iowa's Center for Asian and Pacific Studies Seminar; Northern Illinois University's Department of History Brownbag Seminar; the Midwest Japan Seminar at the University of Nebraska–Lincoln; the Indiana University East Asian Studies Center Colloquium; and the 44th Annual Meeting of the Society for Ethnomusicology in Austin, Texas.

Ken Wissoker, Katie Courtland, Leigh Anne Couch, and Justin Faerber of Duke University Press have been exceedingly kind and helpful, and I benefitted also from the comments of two anonymous referees for the Press. Excerpts of this book have been published in the journals *positions: east asia cultures critique* and *Japanese Studies,* and as a chapter in *Japan Pop: Inside the World of Japanese Popular Culture* (M. E. Sharpe), and are reproduced here in revised form with permission. All the editors (Tani Barlow, Judith Snodgrass, and Timothy Craig, respectively) and referees deserve my thanks for their comments.

My family, Bill, Barbara, and Kirby Atkins, provided a home environment in which the arts and intellectual work were valued, and thus contributed enormously to the realization of this project. My wife Zabrina has contributed characteristic patience, intelligence, good judgment, and sense of adventure, while holding our lives together during my prolonged physical and mental absences. There is no better way to describe the depth of my love and admiration for her than to say that she is my hero. Throughout the writing of this book, our daughter Gabriella Rose has never failed to remind her papa where his priorities should lie and why he was writing it in the first place. Finally, I want to thank the musicians whose performances I witnessed during the course of research, for proving that soul has no skin color and no passport.

Author's note: All quotations and paraphrases in the text that are not footnoted come from personal interviews conducted by the author. Please refer to the References section for dates and locations of personal interviews. Transliteration of Japanese names and words follows the standard Hepburn system. Unless otherwise indicated, all translations from Japanese or French are my own. In most cases Japanese proper names are in Japanese order, with the surname first.

BLUE NIPPON

Scenes from the Jazz Scene

Mix Dynamite. Is it a description or a command? Both, perhaps, and only incidentally a band name; but also an unwitting Zen riddle (kōan) inducing sudden and shocking enlightenment, like the monk's bamboo cane across the shoulders. . . .

As the sounds of swing fade in the October twilight, borne by Yokohama's sea breezes to destinations unknown, my companions and I decide to Mix Dynamite. The Sharps and Flats Big Band have just finished a swinging set on board an ocean liner docked in the harbor. An all-day jazz tour of the port city is coming to a close, but we have a taste for one more band. What we had heard throughout the day had been familiar, usually pleasing, utterly professional, if never earth shattering. One more band, we agree, to cool us out, send us home mellow. We climb the stairs to a loft dubbed Airegin (Nigeria spelled backwards) after Sonny Rollins's tune—a comparatively normal appellation in a country where jazz bars bear playful names such as Down Home, Jazz Inn Something, Relaxin' at Daddy, Dig, Dug, 4 Why Y, Place Where Lee Konitz Plays, Tom, Rug Time, Jum Jam, Coltrane Coltrane, and Fan Fan.

The joint is cramped beyond belief, youthful jazz buffs sitting shoulder to shoulder like commuters on Tokyo's famously congested trains. Jazz giants share wall space with black children from a Harlem street scene—"Jazz Mobile Here Today!"—but real live foreigners invite curious glances, if not quite stares. Okay, cool, so the gaijin want to Mix Dynamite. Of course, they have no idea what they're in for.

Chattering ceases as the big bass player, with a Charlie Haden face and a Charlie Mingus body, saunters to the front. Sweat moistens his forehead and T-shirt as he rakes a metallic rattle across the strings of his instrument. The pianist reaches inside the body of the piano to jerk on its strings. The drummer, thin, wiry, and shorn, joins in the cacophony, followed by tenor sax and trombone. The audience is lifted from its seats and mangled in midair by music (is that what it is?). Sonic shrapnel stabs my brain, which is up way past its bedtime already. As if there's not enough to look at already, the coup de grâce: there's a dude sitting in front of me with a monkey on his shoulder. He looks like he just left the con-struction site—filthy shirt and dusty split-toed boots—and he's already been to the well a number of times. Smiling to reveal a dearth of front teeth, he pulls out a battered trumpet and blows, sounding like a diseased goat. He reaches to his left and wrestles the drink from another listener's hand, lets the monkey have a sip, then downs it.

The music is constructed through chain reaction. The cacophony suddenly stops and the horn players engage in a jagged a cappella duel, trying to break one another up. That monkey gets nervous, and leaps on my shoulder on his way to the bar. "OOOIIIII!" the monkey man screams between horn bleats. The burly tenor man, Katayama Hiroaki, cracks up before he can blow. Katayama knows who it is messing with him.

The audience is still floating when bassman Ino Nobuyoshi reins in the wild horses he unleashed with a solid groove tethered to our navels. The band pulls it together for the majestic theme of Ino's "Yawning Baku." The audience has tumbled from its hovering position to fall deep in the gutbucket. Funky as you wanna be. Before it's all over we've all been to church, sung "Amazing Grace," maybe even handled some snakes. Mix Dynamite owns this crowd: we hang on to every shard of sound they fire at us and ride them as they speed to some mysterious zone we know is there but rarely visit. This ain't no cocktail lounge, jack: piano man rocking so much he gonna smack his head on the keyboard, monkey man making his own music that he just got to share with everyone around him. Here you let all that mess hang out. Beyond these walls is a jaded, materialistic society in advanced stages of moral decline. But if you come up in here you better love and believe in something. The outer realm is pensive and plastic, a place where people speak of their livelihoods and wellbeing bursting in a bubble. Here you sit around the table with your jazz family and dig into heaping helpings of spontaneity, soul, ecstasy, and fun. "Man," my friend Eric said as we slapped hands after the show, "they need this music." They? WE need it, brother, Lord knows we ALL need it. Plenty Plenty Soul. Go ahead on, Mix Dynamite.

I am ashamed to admit how low my expectations for Japan's jazz were when I went there on a Fulbright in 1993. They had been lowered by what I read

going in, all of which suggested I could *study* this stuff in a detached manner, but would remain unmoved by its paltry charms. Akiyoshi Toshiko's
music hinted that I might be wrong, but nonetheless I was prepared to po-
litely demur on the quality and originality of jazz "made in Japan." Frankly
speaking, wasn't part of the attraction of the topic—to colleagues, friends,
family, even fellowship and search committees—the whole superficially oxy-
moronic quality of "jazz in Japan"? Isn't part of the appeal of rock bands
such as Shōnen Knife and Guitar Wolf in the United States that they subvert
the imagery of Japanese to which we've grown accustomed? When the
media saturates us with images of demure Japanese ladies and uptight
salary men, there is visceral satisfaction in watching and hearing Japanese
get funky. If their society insists on conformity as severely as we've been led
to believe, then iconoclasm, ingenuity, and rebellion are that much more
significant, not to mention entertaining.

Mix Dynamite slapped me and spanked me and opened my mind to the
possibility that jazz could be real in Japan, that it could be more than a super-
ficial bauble demonstrating urbane sophistication and faux hipness, but rather
could fill holes in people's lives that empowered them to scream out in joy and
anguish. Lady Day, Mingus, Rahsaan, Duke, Ornette—all these cats had taught
me that's what the music was supposed to do for us. And these folks here in Japan
knew that. Hearing jazz in Japan made me reconsider most everything I thought
I knew about these people and this music.

Subsequent prowlings in Japan's jazz clubs confirmed my enlightenment experience. Raw emotionalism, exuberance, showmanship, and integral audience participation are de rigueur at the annual "2.26" performance
by the postmodern jazz band Stir Up! February 26 is not only the mutual
birthday of three of the performers (saxophonist Hayasaka Sachi, pianist
Yamashita Yōsuke, and drummer Tsunoda Ken), but also the fateful day on
which young army cadets attempted a coup to topple the party government
in 1936. The "2.26" concert slyly invokes the energy and chaos of that
violent day through sound, while subverting the misguided ultranationalist
idealism of the cadets with an irreverent party ethos. The 1995 edition we
witnessed brought to mind the days when jazz music was inseparable from
the dance, when instrumental soloists and jitterbuggers and lindyhoppers
fed one another ideas as a matter of course. Hayasaka contorted her body as
she eked smears and bleats from her horn, urged on by guest percussionist
Senba Kiyohiko's battery of electronic drums and squeeze toys, while audience members punctuated the music with physical and vocal interjec-
tions. People can climb walls at "2.26," and they do. I wondered how some
of those dapper, upright artistes currently canonizing jazz would respond if
their audiences acted that way.

Granted, this is not the kind of behavior Japanese jazz fans are known for, and more sedate experiences are most certainly available. Japanese are famous students and evangelists of the music. Some seek relaxation in jazz, others little more than unobtrusive background to accompany the more urgent tasks of romance or *nominikeishon* (frank conversation facilitated by massive quantities of alcohol). But there are also those for whom jazz is a passion, a cathartic exercise, and a spiritual communion between musician and listener. Jazz appreciation of this intensity must be learned and cultivated like the mental discipline of Zen. There are even "temples" where the aspiring aficionado is inculcated in perceptive appreciation of the music and its history: the famous jazz coffeeshops (*jazu kissa*). These unique establishments are celebrations of funky, soulful iconoclasm, but they have their own brand of discipline. The house rules posted at Jazz Position Onga-kukan in Tokyo's Shibuya ward state:

> Welcome. This is a powerful listening space. Please 'dig' your jazz. We ask that you observe silence while the music is playing.

The hardcore jazz coffeehouses are not places at which to socialize, conversationally, at least. Rather, they are places where one is socialized, evangelized, and indoctrinated into the mental discipline of jazz appreciation, and to a deeper understanding of the music's message and spirit.[1]

This should not imply that Japan lives up to its reputation as "jazz heaven," laurels conferred by American and European commentators who bemoan the music's status in the land of its birth. To read some accounts, one would assume that everyone in the East Asian archipelago not only knows who Charles Mingus, Billie Holiday, and Bill Evans are, but give a damn. It is a seductive myth, though, which seems quite tenable when one observes firsthand the sophistication and enthusiasm of jazz aficionados. Yet it is all too easily disabused when one steps out of their warm company. The jazz presence on radio is minuscule, on television virtually nonexistent. Pop-rock and sentimental *enka* ballads rule; even rock-derived musics have been more successfully incorporated as native vernacular music than jazz has. Granted, the nostalgic evocations of best-selling author Murakami Haruki, who relies on jazz and American popular music to transport readers on a sentimental journey to an innocent age before economic Godzilladom, only work because his audience is savvy to the musical references. Murakami's fiction reverberates with song: "All of his works somehow embody that ballad-like quality that marked the jazz music of the early 1960s. And, through that quality, he has captured part of what it meant to be a young Japanese during that time."[2] The effectiveness of Murakami's musical sentimentality among his urban readership indicates that modern Japan shares a

1. Signboard for Chigusa, Japan's oldest *jazu kissa*, located in Noge-chō, Yokohama. The original building was destroyed in Allied air raids in 1945, but proprietor Yoshida Mamoru rebuilt on the same lot in the late 1940s, when Noge-chō was a major black market site. Yoshida died in 1994; as of 1998 his sister Takako and a small group of regulars were keeping Chigusa open. Photo taken by the author in 1994.

common musical heritage with the United States: "Slow Boat to China" and "The Girl from Ipanema" evoke nostalgia on both sides of the Pacific. Nonetheless, jazz remains foreign to most Japanese, and thus the "jazz community" represents a bizarre alien (at best, hybrid) subculture virtually unintelligible to the masses.

The Hip and the Square

I believe that Hemingway, in depicting the attitudes of athletes, expatriates, bullfighters, traumatized soldiers, and impotent idealists, told us quite a lot about what was happening to that most representative group of Negro Americans, the jazz musicians—who also lived by an extreme code of withdrawal, technical and artistic excellence, rejection of the values of respectable society. They replaced the abstract and much-betrayed ideals of that society with the more physical values of eating, drinking, copulating, loyalty to friends, and dedication to the discipline and values of their art.—Ralph Ellison, *Going to the Territory*

"Jazz community" is a term coined by Alan Merriam and Raymond Mack in 1960 to include audiences as well as performers in jazz sociology, to demystify jazz subcultures, and to critique the famed alienation and hostility of musicians toward outsiders: "The specific character which sets the jazz community apart from all other occupational groups, then, is that not only do the professionals constitute a group, but their public is included in it."[3] In later incarnations the jazz community has been defined as a subculture or a "mode of being in the world"—with its own ideologies, rituals, aesthetic principles, linguistic practices, symbolic meanings, and social, racial, and economic hierarchies—whose very identity is premised either on de facto racial segregation or on the uniqueness of the music itself.[4]

Broadly speaking, Japan's jazz community bears strong resemblance to the sociological profiles of other national jazz communities. Most musicians in the early part of the century came from working-class backgrounds and were trained in bands-for-hire or the military. A significant few came from Japanese society's upper crust, cutting their teeth in college bands. The jazz audience in the golden age of the dance halls, the 1920s and 1930s, by and large represented the educated, urban professional class. Dance halls were not inexpensive entertainment venues, so the fan with little money relied on recordings and the occasional movie theater "attraction band" for a jazz fix. The sociological profiles and class backgrounds of jazz musicians, and perhaps to a lesser degree those of audiences, changed substantially in the postwar era. As the American public's valuation of jazz as a "serious musical form" increased, recruitment into the occupation "from a middle-class base" increased, as did the musicians' level of musical and extramusical education. As jazz's aesthetic status shifted from "popular entertainment" to "art music," the socioeconomic profile of jazz aficionados was also elevated.[5]

In their original theory, Merriam and Mack acknowledged generational, stylistic, and regional "cliques and inner circles" that essentially fractured the jazz community. Generally speaking, Japan's jazz community is simply mad about stylistic and racial categorization, which guarantees its own fragmentation. While the average fan prefers the hard bop of the 1950s and 1960s, or contemporary music that sounds similar, there are connoisseurs who care only for Dixieland, for the "white, West Coast" sound, or for African American pianists. The markers of difference between specializations may seem inconsequential to anyone but the connoisseurs—but that is what makes them connoisseurs. Japan's culture industry makes it easy for consumers to cultivate iconoclastic identities by providing ever more specialized niches that satiate increasingly specialized tastes. Fan clubs, newsletters, chat rooms, and even *jazu kissa* facilitate the jazz community's fragmentation by catering to these peculiar tastes, though more stylistically inclusive umbrella organizations such as the Hot Club of Japan persist.

The overwhelming majority of jazz aficionados have always resided in major cities such as Tokyo, Yokohama, Nagoya, Ōsaka, and Kōbe; they have advanced educations; they are affluent enough to afford the technology and entertainment venues through which to enjoy a hobby that does confer a degree of sophistication and status. Most were socialized as "jazz buffs" in college. Although they represent prosperous strata of Japanese society, members of the jazz community revel in their own (real or imagined) marginality. So strongly do so many jazz aficionados identify with their heroes—who, as "blues people," Amiri Baraka noted, were doomed to perpetual marginality within American society—that cultivating an image as an eccentric "oddball" (*kawatta hito*) is analogous to finding one's own distinctive "voice," "bag," or "grove," an infinitely more rewarding path than "slumming with the squares." (The irony of any nonconformist ethos, of course, is that self-styled iconoclasts inevitably conform to *some* alternative mode established by someone else, often a media-manufactured superstar.) But because the very historical marginality of African Americans in most political and social contexts has become a defining element of their aesthetic systems and cultural practices, one must acknowledge the "hegemony of the marginal" in those systems and practices.[6]

"Marginality," though conferring authenticity, also implies a lack of the economic, political, and educational resources necessary for "participation, or exercise of roles, in either a general or a specific area or in given spheres of human activity . . . which are considered to be within the radius of action and/or access of the individual or group."[7] This clearly does not characterize Japan's jazz audience en masse, for it comprises some of Japan's most elite people: the urban salaried worker, the educated professional, the self-styled cosmopolitan. The jazz community's presumed marginality can be used to obscure its involvement in the construction and diffusion of nationalistic ideologies, an involvement which I argue is quite deep. We assume that subcultures exist in unambiguous opposition to everything for which the dominant or hegemonic culture stands, that they challenge "the principle of unity and cohesion" and contradict "the myth of consensus." Dick Hebdige warns against emphasizing "integration and coherence at the expense of dissonance and discontinuity,"[8] but it is just as dangerous to understate a subculture's extensive economic, cultural, political, and social stakes and connections in the power structure.

Some people are clearly more marginal than others, finding in something like jazz a vehicle for personal liberation from the rigid hierarchies and expressive constraints that modern capitalist society imposes. The individual who undertakes the risky venture of opening a jazz coffeehouse publicly disdains profit, thus rebelling against the materialistic fetishes that define personal success in contemporary Japan. The collector who pours most of his or her salary into hi-fi stereo equipment, cover charges, and jazz albums often sacrifices more common leisure activities such as travel or *pachinko* (a pinball game). The musician who spends hours a day practicing, who performs for less than transportation expenses, and who will be lucky to record for a small independent label, is as distant from the secure corporate salaryman ideal as one can be. In cocktail conversation, four young professional women told me that it may be kind of "cool" (*kakko ii*) for women their age to hang out and smoke at jazz bars, but that in general there is a "dark" (*kurai*) image of people going to these places alone and listening seriously to the music in a trancelike state. In spite of the fact that most of the jazz folk I met were very sociable, they do seem to have a reputation as being socially awkward loners—*otaku*, in contemporary parlance—obsessed with an all-consuming and alien hobby.

The Japanese jazz community is distinctive enough to have its own peculiar rituals for burying its dead. On a blistering afternoon in June 1994, I attended what can only be described as a Buddhist jazz funeral for jazz writer Noguchi Hisamitsu at Tokyo's Gansenji. The Christian hymn "Just a Closer Walk with Thee" wafted over the overflow crowd of grievers sweltering in their black mourning garb, giving way to the more jubilant "When the Saints Go Marching In." It was admittedly a surreal spectacle for someone who had grown up singing these hymns in a Southern Baptist church; I could just hear the deacons at Puryear (Tennessee) Baptist Church hollering sacrilege. But the blending of two established funeral traditions was an appropriate farewell for an artist and music critic who spent his life promoting American popular culture in Japan. Rooted in West African secret societies, French martial processions, and African American fraternal organizations, the jazz funeral in Japan was transformed into a paean to a life lived between two nations. According to musician and historian Danny Barker, the jazz funeral was a custom among the black working class, "a diehard cult of some of the musicians and a few of their followers" whose social relationships centered in Bourbon Street bars. The collective effort by the bar membership to send their deceased comrade off "with music" reinforced solidarity and collective identity within the small community.[9] In like manner, the incorporation of the jazz funeral into a Buddhist mourning ritual signified the Japanese jazz community's collective identity and its destiny as a bridge between two worlds.

Of course, artists in general and musicians in particular occupy ambivalent positions in practically all societies. "The artist, particularly the poet, is both cursed and blessed," Sarah Spence remarks.

> Inhabiting a place between earth and sky, man and God, the artist's axial coordinates are both the most sacred and the most profane. S/He has access to truths that we much desire to know and are terrified of, at the same time. We endow him/her with sacred properties and then exile her/him beyond the limits of our conscious existence. We do this because of the knowledge s/he has or may have; we do it because s/he knows the most intimate parts of our souls—that which is most us, and that which we resist most strenuously.

In his classic *Anthropology of Music,* Alan Merriam described a cross-cultural "pattern of low status and high importance, coupled with deviant behavior allowed by the society and capitalized upon by the musician." But if "the musician is distinguished by certain kinds of social behavior, so is his audience." The devoted aficionado may try to pass in the straight world, or may publicize membership in the jazz community with berets, facial hair, or T-shirts with jazz faces, challenging social compulsions toward conformism "obliquely, in style."[10]

Of course, such challenges often go ignored: having spent several months immersed in a community of people for whom "there is no god but jazz," I was sobered to that community's invisibility when my former host family, devoted *enka* fans who live in a small town outside of Ōsaka, tried to convince me that "Japanese don't listen to jazz." This is perhaps true enough in contemporary Japan, where jazz is but one of a staggering number of cultural products from which consumers may choose to entertain themselves. But the historical evidence presented in the following chapters indicates that for most of this century jazz has hardly been of peripheral concern. On the contrary, the raucous sounds of jazz reverberated within a nation that many envisioned as a virtuously self-contained household, threatening to explode the walls, bust out the windows, and tear the roof off the sucker.

The Theme

Since the early twentieth century, American music has enjoyed immense popularity and sparked much controversy in Japan. There is ample historical evidence testifying to the prominence of jazz in Japanese urban cultural life, for nearly as many years as the music is old. As in America, jazz has been both loved and reviled in Japan, but rarely has it been regarded as insignificant. This book explores the reasons for the Japanese fascination with jazz, and describes the dilemmas faced by Japanese artists struggling to liberate themselves from foreign models and working to define individual and collective standards of creativity. It challenges some of our most inveterate myths about Japan, about the evolution and "universality" of jazz, and about the relationship between race, cultural authenticity, and creativity. It provides a model for understanding the motivations and frustrations, the behavior and artistic development, and the social roles of creative artists in modern Japanese history. Finally, it enters the contemporary debate about race and authenticity that has rendered the jazz world yet another battleground in the "culture wars."

Scholars are increasingly aware of the value of historical and ethnographic studies of Japan's popular culture. In recent years there have been numerous collections of essays on various aspects of Japanese pop culture,[11] not to mention increasingly copious fan-oriented publications on topics such as "Japanimation." But there are far fewer focused, scholarly, and in-depth treatments of particular topics within this new field. In contrast to cinema or advertising, music in particular remains one of the most underutilized sources for and subjects of broader historical inquiry. Historians would do well to borrow one of the basic premises of ethnomusicological research: that one can understand a given society or culture through the study of musical sounds, performance, aesthetics, training, and instrumentation. Jazz provides an ideal and fascinating case study for the importation, assimilation, adaptation, and rejection of American popular culture and the identity anxieties such processes provoke.

Unlike the handful of previous histories of jazz in Japan, my study recontextualizes the music within that country's contentious modern history. I portray jazz not as a benign art that simply captivated the popular consciousness, but rather as a site of contestation where competing aesthetic and social values, definitions of modernity and of self, and standards of artistic originality vied. I argue that the Japanese fascination with jazz throughout the century has been precisely because the music encapsulated and represented these struggles over identity and creativity in a way no other single art has. My theoretical base is a conception of popular culture as a realm of contestation and negotiation, where producers and consumers, artists and audiences confer and dispute identities, aesthetics, and social mores.[12] This approach provides not only new perspectives on major themes in modern Japanese history, but also a conceptual framework for the study of jazz in other non-American contexts. It is my hope that the result will be a new outlook on Japan's seemingly incessant debates on modernity and identity as well as a better understanding of how jazz transformed global culture.

Identity politics and resurgent ethnic nationalism (as if it ever went away) have profoundly shaped contemporary conceptualizations of jazz, affecting everything from the racial composition of bands to our narratives of jazz history. There is an obsession with identifying and filtering the "pure" or "authentic" core of the music from the eclectic and multiracial contexts in which it was actually created. More often than not, the lines drawn between "authentic" and "inauthentic" correspond closely with markers of ethnic difference. The irony is that such racialist conceptualizations of "authenticity" undermine the music's pretensions as a "universal language," rendering it yet another marker of insurmountable ethnic difference. Here I challenge these widespread notions by highlighting the contributions of individual Japanese jazz artists to the idiom, and by recounting the historical, racial, and commercial obstacles and pressures they have had to surmount to do so.

There is much cultural capital, racial pride, and national prestige invested in jazz: the music has been an integral part of the image that the United States projects of itself abroad, and of the image that African Americans in particular promote among themselves and others in their legitimate efforts to redress erasure of their contributions from history. Though many nineteenth-century Americans despaired of ever making a significant national contribution to world culture, late-twentieth-century Americans are convinced that the music created by descendants of Africans on American soil represents a unique gift to the world. Jazz has thus become an integral element in a self-aggrandizing narrative of American ingenuity, dynamism, and creativity. This means that throughout its history Japan's jazz community has had to locate itself in an aesthetic hierarchy that explicitly reflects and reinforces asymmetries of power and cultural prestige in the Japan-U.S. relationship by placing American jazz artists at the apex as "innovators" and non-Americans at the bottom as "imitators." Because the essentially American character of jazz is regarded as so incontestable, aesthetic distinctions between authentic and inauthentic practitioners are made to seem natural, even by Japan's own culture industry: the commercial marketing and presentation of jazz performance by the indigenous entertainment industry reinscribes Japan's artistic and cultural subordination. Exceptional artists—motivated by an explicit cultural nationalism, by "purely" artistic interests, or most often by both—have protested this situation, in the process creating highly original music.

The model I present here for understanding jazz in Japan is rooted in the most salient characteristic of that country's jazz community, a consistent ambivalence about the authenticity of its own jazz expressions (an ambivalence similar in nature to that with which several generations of white

American and European jazz musicians have grappled). Based on racialist conceptualizations of authenticity, this ambivalence motivated some prominent jazz artists to develop what I call "strategies of authentication" to legitimate jazz performed by Japanese. These include interpreting and attempting to replicate the exact sounds of American jazz as well as the social and cultural contexts (e.g., the "hipster scene") in which jazz is produced; asserting the basic affinity of the "colored races" (the Japanese as "yellow negro"); sojourning in America or in interwar Shanghai as a rite of authentication; and efforts to "indigenize" or "nationalize" jazz by incorporating textures, instruments, or aesthetic principles from traditional musics, thereby creating what some believed to be a national style of jazz, "which foreigners cannot imitate." The authenticating strategies described in this book were developed to counter powerful psychological, institutional, and sociocultural forces that have continually cast doubt on the authenticity of the art of Japanese jazzers, as "jazz" and as "Japanese."

The product of archival research and fieldwork in Japan and the United States, including interviews conducted in the mid-1990s with musicians and aficionados representing each generation and occupation within Japan's jazz community, *Blue Nippon* makes use of oral, documentary, literary, pictorial, cinematic, and musical source materials from Japan, the United States, and Europe to reconstruct the social, artistic, and intellectual history of jazz as a mass and subcultural phenomenon in Japan. It tells the story of jazz in Japan through the voices of the people who created it and responded to it. Chapter 1 introduces the concepts of "authenticity," "jazz in Japan," and "Japanese jazz." The second chapter discusses the role of jazz in the transformation of Japan's modern entertainment industry, arguing that the music enabled Japanese to have an authentic "modern" experience comparable to that of other "cultured" nations, taking the reader into the neon-lit world of "modern boys" and "modern girls," and reproducing sensationalistic eyewitness accounts of the dance halls and cafes that kept modernites entertained and incited debate in the decades before World War II. Chapter 3 follows up with an analysis of the debates that jazz sparked and conceptualizations of jazz as the aural expression of modernism, which many believed threatened existing social and aesthetic mores. I go on to describe how those conceptualizations manifested themselves in forms of social control that affected all of Japan's entertainment industry. Chapter 4 diverges from existing portrayals of the wartime jazz community as a besieged dissident group whose art was officially proscribed as "enemy music"; it reconstructs the hidden history of how jazz musicians survived this ban by playing "jazz for the country's sake," crafting a nationalistically correct jazz in an attempt to preserve their avocation and assimilate within a society mobilized for war. The fifth chapter explores the attractions of jazz for a generation of rebellious postwar youth whose inherited value system had been discredited by the war and Occupation reforms. In the context of national reconstruction and expanding entertainment and leisure pursuits, jazz appealed to a generation whose inherited value system had been shattered, yet jazz remained beholden to American-defined standards of artistic originality and authenticity. Chapter 6 discovers the roots of Japan's emergence as a significant source of jazz artistry in the 1960s and 1970s in a second push for an identifiable national style of jazz. In the neonationalist cultural efflorescence inspired by student-led protests against U.S. hegemony in East Asia and facilitated by Japan's rise to economic prominence, jazz artists and aficionados sought a self-referential aesthetic that would render comparisons to American jazz standards moot. In the Postlude, I explore how tensions over authenticity, creativity, and identity persist in a contemporary scene sorely divided between a neo-bop revival movement and a tenacious avant-garde dedicated to irreverent exploration.

Keeping Time: Studying Jazz in Japan

Burton Peretti, author of two cultural histories of jazz in the United States, has recently written what few in the field of jazz studies have been willing to admit:

> Jazz historiography has long been a pleasurable, vaguely discursive enterprise, disconnected from the highly empirical project of the academy, perhaps more interested in a good story than in uncovering the past "as it essentially was." . . . Interviews by journalists, critics, and fans, while often irresistibly entertaining, have also been adulatory and superficial. In book form, many interviews and sketches are often called "jazz history," but they are designed mainly to present uncritically the words of jazz's creators and admirers, as if this task alone resulted in the writing of history. . . . Of course, academic historians share the blame, since they have ignored jazz for decades and have deprived jazz history of their empirical expertise.[13]

Academic scholars with an interest in jazz have most likely read recreationally in what one of my mentors derisively refers to as the "jazz buff" literature, struggling (with varying degrees of success) to overcome its mythic excesses and hagiographic tendencies. In a 1974 essay Phillip S. Hughes attempted to draw a distinction between "jazz critics and historians," whose primary interest was "jazzmen of artistic importance," and "sociologists of jazz," who are "not interested in the artistic merit of the people they study." But Hughes conceded a "lingering influence of the appreciative (or 'normative') attitude among sociologists. It seems that even when we aim for detachment, it is difficult to shake off the legacy of our socialization into the mythologies and mystique of jazz, which for most of us precedes our professional socialization." "Let us secularize jazzmen," Hughes beseeches. "It will surely not detract from our enjoyment of their artistic product to do so. Sociologists should be students of the 'jazz myth,' not its bearers."[14]

Such calls for methodological eclecticism and demystification have led to a handful of important studies, which have been particularly instructive on social receptions of jazz, musical communities, cultural and musical hybridity, and the improvisational process, but which are only beginning to dislodge prevailing practices and perspectives that privilege hagiography and canon building, discographical ephemera, racial politics, stylistic evolution, and national mythmaking.[15] Notably absent from such reform efforts are exhortations for the systematic investigation of a world of jazz activity beyond U.S. borders. With a handful of exceptions, jazz historiography has consistently failed to look overseas for jams of consequence. Those studies of jazz in non-American contexts which do exist tend to be almost purely descriptive, though S. Frederick Starr's and Michael Kater's respective studies of jazz in the USSR and Nazi Germany are exemplary history in my judgment. (Both, however, choose to focus more on the relationship between jazz and state ideology than on aestheticized authenticity.)[16]

I mentioned earlier that most of my informants were dumbstruck by the notion of anyone, let alone an *American*, studying jazz history in Japan, but there indeed have been moments, however brief and fleeting, at which Japanese acknowledged that jazz music actually had a history in their country. Although a couple of jazz pioneers composed brief overviews or autobiographies as early as the 1930s, the 1960s and 1970s witnessed a relative flood of oral histories, memoirs, nostalgia concerts, and compilations of vintage recordings, apparently surprising many who were convinced that native jazz could be no older than the Occupation era. The leading jazz monthly *Swing Journal* occasionally published photographic retrospectives and commemorative essays prior to the late sixties, but it was a new quarterly, *Jazz Critique* (*Jazu hihyō*, founded in 1967), which first published oral history projects and rap sessions about the music's origins and significance in Japan.[17] Since the mid-1990s, there has been another surge of interest in history, of which this study is most certainly a beneficiary. Both reflective "moments" can be characterized as periods in which pride in the domestic product is unusually high, thus contributing to regenerated interest in its historical roots.

The first major "boom" in the study of domestic jazz history occurred in the mid-seventies, most certainly tied to a more general nostalgia for the pre–World War II era. Veteran jazz musicians who had long since retired or retreated to the security of Ginza cabarets or studio orchestras capitalized on this "Japanese jazz renaissance," producing numerous comeback concerts and albums. Neophytes were taken aback by the flood of historical recordings that confirmed the nation's jazz heritage.[18] Critics Segawa Masahisa, Yui Shōichi (1918–1998), Noguchi Hisamitsu (1909–1994), and Honda Toshio, as well as musicians Uchida Kōichi and Ōmori Seitarō wrote popular histories and produced massive reissue projects that brought prewar and early postwar jazz recordings back into circulation.[19] Since the 1980s there have been a plethora of "jazz coffeehouse memoirs," elegies to the jazz cafe that document the personal conversion experiences or "jazz epiphanies" of individual aficionados (as well as the joys of "hi fi" audio).[20] Saitō Ren's Kishida Prize-winning play *The Shanghai Advance Kings* (*Shanhai bansukingu*, 1979), loosely based on the experiences of trumpeter Nanri Fumio and other Japanese jazzers in 1930s Shanghai, brought jazz history to an even wider public and led to the publication of another oral history in 1983. There are also a handful of biographies of well-known jazz artists, of which Ueda Sakae's painstakingly researched biography of legendary pianist Moriyasu Shōtarō is the most eloquent and evocative portrait of the first postwar decade's jazz scene yet composed.[21] Written primarily for a specialized audience of jazz converts, these early histories are rich in detail and the frequently titillating lore of jazz folk, but neither maintain pretensions to scholarly distance nor offer ethnographic, musicological, or sociological analysis.[22] The pioneering Western scholar of jazz in Japan is Professor Sidney Brown of the University of Oklahoma, a scholar of Meiji-era political history who used the Japanese jazz histories and his own interviews with musicians such as Sera Yuzuru, Moriyama Hisashi, and Shimizu Jun to write a series of conference papers and produce a documentary film on the subject. Two masters theses, composed by Elizabeth Sesler-Beckman and Larry Richards respectively, explore the problem of Japanese creativity in the jazz idiom, and the gap between prewar conceptualizations of jazz and the music itself.[23]

In writing this book, to my knowledge the most comprehensive history published in any language thus far, I have drawn from and synthesized elements from prior studies, collected and analyzed many previously un- or under-utilized sources, and introduced a conceptual framework that makes the topic immediately relevant to Japanese cultural studies, ethnomusicology, and jazz studies. The search for authenticity is but one dimension of the jazz experience in Japan, not to mention one whose importance has varied historically. Nevertheless, discourses of authenticity are crucial to Japanese conceptualizations of jazz, to the social positioning and artistic development of creative people, and to the cultural identity crises that mark Japan's twentieth-century experience.

I get paid to be a teacher and scholar of Japanese history, so one of my interests is the impact of jazz, as a symbol ascribed with "affective or cultural meaning,"[24] on Japanese self-conceptions, social values, and cultural preoccupations and amusements. As a longtime collector, student, disc jockey, and underachieving player of jazz music, I bring my interest in the actual creation of musical sound and the construction of aesthetic systems to the table as well. In crafting what is inherently an interdisciplinary work with many potential audiences, I must ask the reader's indulgence. Readers from the respective fields of Japanese history, ethnomusicology, or jazz studies will approach this book with varying expectations, which I have tried to anticipate and accommodate to the best of my ability, but there are doubtless points on which some specialists will crave elaboration. I expect, for instance, that scholars of music will desire more musicological analysis or biographical information, while historians of Japan will wish for rather less. I am likewise more interested in the specific artistic behaviors and aesthetic values of Japan's jazz musicians and fans than in the larger processes of industrial cultural production or theories of globalization, though I do not deny the relevance of such lines of inquiry and make frequent mention of the impact of cultural hybridization and commercial considerations on artistic behavior.[25] I hope that I have found a middle ground that best serves the interests of all potential audiences.

I have attempted to balance good storytelling with sophisticated analysis, both of which I believe to be crucial elements to the finest historical writing. When academic history omits or diminishes the lore and real-life experiences of its human subjects it loses not only its capacity to attract, fascinate, and instruct its audience, but also its soul. While abstract concepts such as "authenticity" and "identity" enhance our comprehension, this book is also a collection of stories about people moved by musical sound to do extraordinary things, often against the conventional wisdom or accepted values of their society. Here I use these stories to tell another: a tragic success story, if you will, of underacknowledged artistic accomplishments achieved in spite of considerable social and ideological obstacles. In crafting this story I have inevitably been compelled to be selective, and many readers will no doubt be disappointed to find little information here on well-known and important artists such as guitarist Watanabe Kazumi, pianist Ozone Makoto, trumpeter Tiger Okoshi, clarinetist Kitamura Eiji, saxophonist Abe Kaoru, and countless others. That suggests to me that there are still many stories remaining to be told and much more music left to be heard.

Whenever I think I may have overstated the prejudice against jazz "made in Japan," someone makes a remark that convinces me that such sentiments are alive and well. At the April 2000 meeting of the Midwest Japan Seminar at the University of Toronto, at which Sidney Brown debuted his documentary, one participant claimed that, based on his experience walking into a bar or two in Tokyo, the Japanese "haven't got it." My retort is that he walked into the wrong bar. One can just as easily find jazz musicians in the United States—some with major label recording contracts—who "haven't got it." Conversely, there are Japanese who have "got it" and have "had it" for a long time. They may not be "typical," but neither were John Coltrane or Sidney Bechet, and that is why we remember them.

It should be clear that I am extremely critical of ethnonational notions of authenticity and the unequal power relations that determine and confer authenticity. However unintentionally, uniform, self-contained categories such as "black jazz," "white jazz," or "Japanese jazz" are socially constructed concepts that inevitably diminish the accomplishments of individual artists who through imagination and discipline transform their personal experiences and visions into musical sound. Anyone who seriously listens to and studies jazz music must realize that these racialized categories hold no water: for instance, Stan Getz, regarded as exemplary of a "white" style, was influenced most profoundly by African American swing artist Lester Young, and then in turn inspired Eddie Harris, progenitor of the supposedly "black" style known as soul jazz. Still, I realize that these racialized categories merit study rather than outright dismissal. They exist for a reason, and their persistence at a time when identities are increasingly fluid suggests that there is still much to ponder regarding the aesthetics and culture of jazz, for which the study of jazz beyond U.S. shores will prove instructive.

I realize, however, that some readers will find my own credibility for this venture lacking: some will ask, what right does a white academic have to confer authenticity on Japanese jazz artists, to argue that they can be the real thing? Many would no doubt consider my case stronger if I were black, and neither postmodernist posturing nor earnest wishing are likely to dissipate such skepticism. Americans of European descent are rarely welcome weighing in on authenticity in cultural categories associated with Americans of African descent, as ethnomusicologist Ingrid Monson acknowledges in her book *Saying Something*:

Since whiteness tends to be a sign of inauthenticity within the world of jazz, the appeals of white musicians [or writers] to universalistic rhetoric can be perceived as a power play rather than genuine expressions of universal brotherhood. If jazz is one of the few cultural categories in which being African American is evaluated as "better" or more "authentic" than being non-African American, a white musician's appeal to a colorblind rhetoric might cloak a move to minimize the black cultural advantage by "lowering" an assertive African American musician from his or her pedestal to a more "equal" playing field. It is this rhetoric that provokes African Americans to take more extreme positions on ethnic particularity.[26]

To charges that I am diminishing the importance of African Americans as creators of jazz music by seeking acknowledgment of Japanese (and other non-American) contributions to the art and validation of the meanings they have found in it, I can only respond that it is out of respect for my own African American musical heroes that I do so. It seems to me a magnificent accomplishment to create an art and a culture so potentially inclusive and open to revision that anyone can contribute authentically to it, if its performers and advocates will only allow it be so.

CHAPTER ONE

THE JAPANESE JAZZ ARTIST AND
THE AUTHENTICITY COMPLEX

AKIYOSHI TOSHIKO: *How do you play the blues that way?*
How can I learn to play them so authentically?

HAMPTON HAWES: *I play the blues right because I eat collard*
greens and black-eyed peas and corn pone and clabber.

AKIYOSHI [sighs]: *Where can I find that food? Do I have to go*
to the United States to get it?

HAWES [laughs]: *All you need is the feeling. If you have the*
feeling, you could eat Skippy peanut butter and play the blues
right. And if you don't have that feeling, you could eat collard
greens and all that so-called Negro food all the time and sound
corny.—quoted in Nat Hentoff, *The Jazz Life*

I was born with Eric Dolphy for a father, and Billie Holiday for a
mother. So in my alto performances, I must somehow surpass
Eric Dolphy. That is my duty.—saxophonist Abe Kaoru, quoted
in Morita Yūko, *Abe Kaoru, 1949–1978*

While touring Japan in 1977, some members of the Art
Ensemble of Chicago made the following indelicate if
not ungracious remarks: "We have listened to performances by Japanese groups, but they are making music
that stands atop Afro-American traditions. So it is not
original." "Only black people's music has progressed
with the times," the AEC musicians continued. "In the
past we (black people) made music in Africa. We were
making music in times of slavery. With the times it
has progressed in different forms. Our (black) music
moved with the world. If you (Japanese) don't start
from this, you'll never create original work. It takes five
hundred years." Now, while many Japanese jazz fans

must have had no quarrel with this statement, others took it as well as a poke in the eye.[1] A similar response met saxophonist Branford Marsalis nearly two decades later when he made the following remark in the December 1993 issue of *Playboy*, in reply to a query regarding his band's popularity in Japan:

> The Japanese, for whatever reason, are astute in terms of [jazz's] history and legacy. Unlike many other people, they have identified jazz as part of the American experience. But I don't think they understand it most times, especially at my shows. They just stare at us, like, "What the hell are they playing?" But they come to hear me anyway. It's almost like classical music: Somebody told them it's necessary and that we're good. So they come and scratch their heads and clap and they leave. The audiences are strange when you play those big concert halls. The clubs are much hipper and the club owners are great. They'll take care of you. They take you out to eat, and they'll even get a great-looking girl for you if you want one. I've declined.[2]

While the Art Ensemble's statement questioned the authenticity of jazz *performed* by Japanese, Marsalis's remarks challenged the much-heralded Japanese understanding and *appreciation* of jazz, arguing that they are superficial at best. Coming as they did in the wake of a torrent of American invective against Japan ("Japan bashing"), Marsalis's comments (and similar remarks made later by saxophonist Kenny Garrett) wounded a substantial number of devoted jazz fans, who recognize that Japan has done more than its part to keep this art alive and viable in the merciless 1990s marketplace.

Who made the statements was as important as what was said. The Art Ensemble is the product of 1960s black militancy in the arts; Marsalis and Garrett are major figures in a new generation of African American jazz artists with a somewhat politicized view of jazz, its history, and its future. It is unfair to portray the predominantly black "Young Lion" movement (of which the Marsalis brothers and Garrett are leading lights) as a monolith, but it nevertheless has acquired a reputation for obsessing about authenticity and for equating that virtue with African American ethnicity. Thus to many Japanese jazz fans, who by virtue of their chosen hobby are for the most part unusually well-informed and sensitive to racial injustice in the United States, Branford Marsalis and Kenny Garrett's statements sounded uncomfortably like the popular T-shirt slogan "It's a black thing, you wouldn't understand."

Some responded angrily: "The reason that audiences are cheerless at your [Marsalis's] concerts is because they know 'this guy's not putting himself into it,'" Terajima Yasukuni, owner of the Meg jazz coffeehouse in Kichijōji, retorted. To Garrett, who had criticized Japanese fans for being too conservative in their tastes, Terajima said mockingly: "He says, 'it's strange that records with standards sell better [in Japan] than our personal originals . . . do these people really understand jazz?' It's *because* we understand jazz that we buy records with standards on them. What is so 'personal'? You write boring originals with stupid melodies. . . . Try to write a melody better than a standard. We're all waiting for that." Other responses were more coolly analytical. In an essay in the intellectual journal *Gendai,* Murakami Haruki argued that, given Marsalis's base of support within a militant, "aggressive" black middle class for whom racial pride is paramount, the saxophonist's remarks were to be expected: "If Branford Marsalis had said in an American interview that 'Japanese are a wonderful audience who understand jazz as well as we black people do,' he probably would have been booed down harshly by his supporters in his home country." But Murakami conceded that Marsalis may have had a point: he urged Japanese who listen to jazz, rap, or blues to appreciate them as more than music, and to "pay a bit more attention to the totality of the history and culture of black people in America."[3]

Certainly there are many American jazz artists who vociferously dispute the opinions of Marsalis and Garrett. The liner notes to Cannonball Adderley's 1963 LP *Nippon Soul* noted "a special quality that Japanese fans bring to adulation of their heroes, an intensity of feeling that many jazz artists have said they often experience as a physical sensation when they perform for Japanese audiences." "[The Japanese] treat jazz as a high class art form," drummer Donald "Duck" Bailey has said. "They know, they really know about jazz. . . . They knew more about me than I knew about myself." In his liner notes to the 1988 live album *Pick Hits,* guitarist John Scofield complimented Japanese fans for their "understanding and appreciation": "When we play in Tokyo we always think the audience is a little more sophisticated than in other places, a little more 'in tune' with what we're trying to do." Expatriate pianist Tom Pierson also rejects Marsalis's statement: with a sense of wonderment that years of experience have yet to erase, he tells of Japanese fans who treat him "like a soccer star" and kiss his hands in gratitude for his music. In his autobiography, Miles Davis remembered warmly the reception he received on his first visit to Japan in 1964, in spite of his rather inauspicious entrance:

> Flying to Japan is a long-ass flight. So I brought coke and sleeping pills with me and I took both. Then I couldn't go to sleep so I was drinking, too. When we landed there were all these people to meet us at the

airport. We're getting off the plane and they're saying, 'Welcome to Japan, Miles Davis,' and I threw up all over everything. But they didn't miss a beat. They got me some medicine and got me straight and treated me like a king. Man, I had a ball, and I have respected and loved the Japanese people ever since. Beautiful people.[4]

Ultimately the accuracy of Marsalis's and Garrett's allegations about audiences is less important than the assumptions that produced them and the reactions they elicited. The angst that the Marsalis-Garrett controversy engendered in many Japanese jazz devotees was rooted in their historical ambivalence or "complex" about the authenticity of their own jazz culture. The implication that jazz, a music that has touched them deeply, was not really theirs but someone else's was understandably frustrating, for not only were the remarks made in the wearisome context of "Japan bashing," but they also forced many Japanese to rethink the various attempts they had made to "authenticate" or legitimate the meanings jazz held for them and the music they produced themselves. Many had grown comfortable with the idea that jazz was a "universal language," and that one's appreciation of jazz was as unique as an artist's "voice." Many felt that their very obvious preference for the music of *black* American artists showed that they were "down," that they *understood.* Now they were being told that they had missed something, that the meanings they found in jazz were not real, and that their efforts to study, collect, and support the music had amounted to no more than a superficial comprehension.

We might regard the AEC and Marsalis-Garrett controversies as nothing more than examples of the dissonance between artists' and audiences' expectations: artists, the conventional wisdom goes, want to press forward into hitherto unknown realms of expression, while audiences want to hear what they already know they like. On the other hand, we might view them as additional manifestations of the contemporary Japanese obsession with their image abroad. One can scarcely watch the television news in Japan without seeing the results of some poll taken among people in foreign countries, which asks them to sum up their impressions of Japan in ridiculously simplistic terms. But these controversies were also the product of particular historical experiences. The respective uproars were products of the Japanese jazz community's special history of negotiating and defining its own identity in relation to Japan and America. They challenged the dominant narrative of the jazz community's history, which traced a linear development of artistic progress from "imitation" of American models to "innovation" of original, *Japanese* music. In sum, the controversies seemed to invalidate, or at best render ineffectual, a consistent, century-long campaign to authenticate jazz in Japan.

Ain't Nothin' Like the Real Thing:
The Authenticity Fetish

If we think of "jazz" not only as a music but as a relatively self-contained and identifiable culture, we are unlikely to discover other cultures as consumed with the idea of authenticity. It is an obsession that potentially undermines the rhetorical universality of jazz, as expressed here by *Down Beat* contributor Michael Bourne in 1980: "Jazz, more than ever before, is a universal language. Around the world, more than the classics, more than rock and roll, jazz has become a universal language, what all music is supposed to be, especially among the young. The spirit of jazz has endured even when outlawed."[5]

Though authenticity by definition favors the particular over the universal, it is interesting to note, as have Ingrid Monson and Charley Gerard, that universalist and particularist rhetorics coexist in jazz discourse, often in the same person. "An individual speaking to an interlocutor who underplays the role of African American culture in the music . . . might choose to respond with ethnically assertive comments," Monson observes. "In a context in which something closer to racial harmony prevails, a musician might choose to invoke a more universalistic rhetoric."[6]

What does *authenticity* mean? It appears that there is no authentic definition of *authenticity*: it is so malleable a trope that each author can and does construct a plausible definition appropriate to virtually any historical or artistic subject. While there seems to be general agreement that the idea of authenticity was invented as a peculiarly modern response to the perceived erosion of particularized heritages and identities in an era of globalization, there is otherwise a considerable diversity of definitions and applications. Anthropologists investigating how authentic Third World cultures represent themselves to First World tourists, or how historical sites and artifacts are presented to the public, have defined the concept as verisimilitude, credibility, originality (as opposed to a copy), or authoritativeness. For ethnomusicologists, *authenticity* means preserving the social contexts of performances, original performance practices, and the spiritual and cultural meanings of music—in other words, accurately representing unfamiliar "world musics" in a manner faithful to their original contexts. Edward Bruner adds that authenticity implies that someone has the power or authority to "authenticate" a representation; the concept of authenticity thus privileges one voice as more legitimate than another. Musicologist Peter Kivy's analysis of authenticity as an aesthetic standard in music suggests roughly two conceptions: "historical authenticity" (authorial intention, contemporary sound, and contemporary performance practice—the kind of authenticity valued by practitioners of "early music"); and "personal authenticity" (emotive "sincerity," expressiveness, or assertiveness). Kivy acknowledges that one kind of authenticity necessarily entails sacrifice of the other: "Personal authenticity comes into conflict with a composer's performing intention or wish, even though the composer may have intended personal authenticity as well." Philosopher Joel Rudinow offers yet another aesthetic definition of the term as "a species of the genus credibility . . . [whose] most precise, formal, and fully institutionalized application in the artworld is to distinguish from the forgery a work 'by the author's own hand.' . . . More broadly, less precisely, but in an essentially similar way, 'authenticity' is applicable to the artifacts and rituals which are a culture's 'currency,' conferring value on those 'acceptably derived' from original sources. . . . In such applications authenticity admits of degrees."[7]

In keeping with established practice, here I adapt and refine the term *authenticity* to reflect its meaning(s) in the jazz culture. Authenticity in jazz, as in other folk arts, implies that an artist must possess specific qualities—educational background, life experience, ethnic heritage, motivations, or artistic vision—which confer upon the artist the *right* not only to work unchallenged in a particular medium, but to establish the standard by which all others working in that medium will be judged. Those who are influenced by such work may be deemed "authentic" or "inauthentic" depending either on how closely they adhere to the aesthetic standards enshrined in the "original," or how closely their personal profiles match the specific experiential, ethnic, or motivational qualities of the "original's" creator. The standards for determining authenticity may change or be contested, yet some such standard is always in operation and its power is significant.

Authenticity, in this sense, is aestheticized as a criterion in the judgment of taste. Conceptualized thusly, it rather resembles what Pierre Bourdieu has called the "aesthetic disposition" in the reception of art: "Any legitimate work tends in fact to impose the norms of its own perception and tacitly defines as the only legitimate mode of perception the one which brings into play a certain disposition and a certain competence. . . . [A]ll agents, whether they like it or not, whether or not they have the means of conforming to them, find themselves objectively measured by those norms." But whereas Bourdieu (with reference to José Ortega y Gasset) describes an aestheticism in the "legitimate" arts that actively distances itself from human emotions and realities—favoring "form over function"—jazz and other folk or "black expressive" forms value precisely those human qualities that constitute lived experience: earthiness, funk (bodily odor), pain, anger, carnality, and joy. Neither an aristocracy nor a bourgeoisie with aristocratic pretensions establishes these aesthetic norms, but rather a historically despised underclass—whose aesthetic values are then interpreted, translated, codified, and communicated by bourgeois bohemians (jazz critics) who explicitly reject the value system in which they were brought up. These aesthetic values, ideally rooted in real life experience, represent a standard of authenticity that holds for all who would dare engage in the creative activity in question.[8]

Authenticity and originality are "paramount" in the aesthetics of jazz, and charges of "imitativeness, insincerity or inauthenticity" are the most "devastating" that a jazz artist can suffer.[9] There are a number of standards by which jazz performers are judged for authenticity: they are expected to defy commercial pressures, revere "the tradition," and "pay dues" as a journeyman or "scuffling" musician. Theoretically, every jazz aficionado would agree that Kivy's notion of "personal authenticity" is the major criterion for superlative jazz performance. In the real world, however, preoccupied as it is with issues of race and power, what we might call "national authenticity" and "ethnic authenticity" often have more operational power, perhaps because they are easier to determine "objectively" than personal authenticity. In any case, jazz is regarded as an authentic folk expression of quintessentially American values (although since many regard American values to be universally acceptable, that fact does not necessarily disqualify jazz as a "universal language"). In pianist and educator Billy Taylor's racially neutral language, jazz is "America's classical music." "The equation of jazz and America is easy enough to figure," Robert G. O'Meally writes:

> Jazz is freedom music, the play of sounds that prizes individual assertion and group coordination, voices soloing and then (at their best) swinging together, the one-and-many *e pluribus unum* with a laid-back beat. . . . For all its abstruseness, jazz is an insistently democratic music, one that aims to sound like citizens in a barbershop or grocery line, talking stuff, trading remarks. . . . According to the jazz/democracy perspective, in the growing blueprint society that is the United States we are all improvisers, making it up as we go along and depending on flexibility and resiliency—both hallmarks of the music—to make our way together.[10]

Yet O'Meally concedes that "while some hear in jazz these broad American themes, others hear in it the essence of black particularity, mystery, and memory: blackness traced in rhythm and tune back to the Old World of Africa." The racial or ethnic element to the virtue of authenticity has held strong currency ever since the days when French critics such as Hughes Panassié held up Louis Armstrong as an "instinctive" musical genius, a musical "noble savage." Simply put, it is no mystery that many regard African American ethnicity as a basic precondition of authentic jazz expression. Musicians and critics of diverse ethnic backgrounds concur with

Ralph Gleason's famous assertion that "the blues is black man's music, and whites diminish it at best or steal it at worst. In any case they have no moral right to it."[11] The "black music ideology" first articulated in the 1960s by Amiri Baraka, Frank Kofsky, Stanley Crouch, and others contends that the blues, the root of jazz and other musical genres, is "not an idiom made up of rules that can be taught and transmitted like any other musical form. . . . [T]he blues is not just a music but a world view. The blues is not something that African Americans *do* but how they *live*. They are *blues people*." Even though the blues has perhaps been dislodged in contemporary music by funk and dance music, the ideology continues to resonate in the work of hip-hop critics and authors like Rickey "Uhuru Maggot" Vincent, whose *Funk: The Music, the People, and the Rhythm of the One* (1996) asserts that "Funk is the means by which black folks confirm identity through rhythm, dance, bodily fluids, and attitude. . . . The idea and the importance of funk comes from the depths of black American life, particularly that aspect of black America which never got around to integrating. . . . The impulse of The Funk rests deep in the 'Souls of Black Folk' (to borrow from W. E. B. Du Bois). . . . One might even claim that it is the funky nature of black Americans that is the salvation of this nation." Rudinow reflects that in the age of political correctness such assertions of racial essentialism and cultural ownership seem "paradoxically to be both progressive and reactionary."[12]

The jazz culture is usually regarded as relatively exemplary in terms of race relations, and veteran musicians such as the late Doc Cheatham (who once said "I don't know what they mean by black music. I have never seen any black music. I've seen black notes on white paper") are appalled by the racial polarization of the jazz world at the end of the twentieth century. But today that world has become another battleground in the culture wars, prized turf to be secured and defended in the seemingly unending struggle to define and preserve essentialist notions of culture and identity. Working bands "voluntarily segregate" themselves; young black musicians have become marketable emblems of racial pride; and even institutions such as the National Endowment for the Arts American Jazz Masters Fellowships and Jazz at Lincoln Center are accused of "Crow Jim" (or "reverse racist") tendencies. Wynton Marsalis, artistic director of the Lincoln Center program, has retorted that "the great innovators in jazz have been African American and . . . it is necessary to spotlight the top rung first before moving on to the lesser contributions of whites."[13]

Dissonance in historical perspective underlies this debate: historically speaking, which "race" *created* jazz, and therefore *owns* it? Although in recent years a number of writers have responded to racial polarization by attempting to document significant contributions to the art's development by nonblack artists (examples include James Lincoln Collier's *Jazz: America's Theme Song*, Gene Lees's *Cats of Any Color*, and Richard M. Sudhalter's *Lost Chords: White Musicians and Their Contribution to Jazz, 1915–1945*), the "melting pot" metaphor expressed by Dan Morgenstern of the Rutgers University Institute of Jazz Studies is hotly contested. "I see jazz as an American music which came into being through the interaction between different musical cultural elements," Morgenstern says. "And what was so fascinating about jazz was the mixture of European and African and Latin American and, you know, all kinds of Native American, all these elements coming together and out of that came a new music." By contrast, saxophonist Archie Shepp dismisses this view: "This is my music. I want to make that clear. . . . In my estimation, so-called jazz music is founded on African American blues idioms. Now what did Western music give to the blues? Except to give the people who sang it the blues?" After all, Leadbelly once said, "Never was a white man had the blues, cause nothin' to worry about." Put even more succinctly, what Morgenstern calls "interaction" and "mixture" Amiri Baraka regards as the "Great Music Robbery."[14]

For any Japanese performing or identifying with a musical genre typically characterized as "black"—jazz, soul, reggae, funk, Afro-Cuban, rhythm and blues, or gospel—ethnic authenticity and credibility are major issues ("Japanese rap? Makes as much sense as Polynesian polkas, right?").[15] Suggestions that Japanese cannot be authentic jazz performers because of their lack of ethnic authenticity are prolific, but these musicians' "personal authenticity" has often been maligned as well by Japanese and non-Japanese alike. Evaluations of the personal authenticity of Japanese jazz artists are too often rooted in common assumptions about the derivative nature and inherent uncreativity of Japanese people. In *The Penguin Guide to Jazz on CD, LP and Cassette*, British critics Richard Cook and Brian Morton simultaneously acknowledge the existence of these unflattering stereotypes, while shamelessly and gleefully using them to critique recordings. A review of Duke Jordan's *Kiss of Spain*, featuring the rhythm team of Ino Nobuyoshi and Togashi Masahiko, states, "It would be nice to say that the Japanese rhythm section had managed to defy the stereotype and play relaxed, swinging jazz. Alas, no; not a hair out of place, not a cue missed, but hardly swinging." Of keyboardist Akagi Kei, the authors note, "Like a lot of Japanese, he has a secure technique and a slightly chill delivery." A review of bassist Peter Kowald's *Duos: Europa America Japan* singles out the Japanese participants for abuse: the music "works fine with the Westerners, but there are inevitable difficulties with the Japanese players . . . [rooted in] basic aesthetic philosophies . . . most of the [Japanese] espouse a kind of violent synthesis between great formality of diction and very disruptive abstraction." A

Charles Mingus recording from 1971 is spoiled by a "typically well-coached but utterly uninspired Japanese band" (Miyama Toshiyuki's New Herd). Even Japanese audiences are not immune from criticism: according to Cook and Morton, two of Scott Hamilton's live albums are marred by "the irritation of a relentlessly self-congratulatory Japanese audience (who applaud themselves every time they recognize a standard)." Kōdansha's authoritative *Japan: An Illustrated Encyclopedia* does Japanese jazz artists no better service, but rather neatly sums up the stereotypes and prejudices with which many view jazz in Japan:

> One Western genre that has firmly established itself within the Japanese music scene is jazz. Japan is home to an important and highly profitable market for jazz, boasting numerous clubs, some of the best jazz magazines in the world, and a steady core of avid fans. Major international jazz figures play extensively in Japan's clubs and concert halls. The flourishing scene has also produced native musicians like saxophonist Watanabe Sadao, regarded as the patriarch of Japanese jazz, Hino Terumasa, and Watanabe Kazumi, and jazz fusion groups Casiopea and T Square. Yet while many of Japan's jazz artists display marvelous technical ability, few display any real originality.[16]

Yasumi Takashi, a jazz pianist who played in the University of Minnesota Jazz Band and currently works for the Japan–United States Education Commission, regards his own improvisations as nothing more than an assemblage of licks he has heard by American artists. He admits to a certain prejudice against Japanese jazz artists, claiming that they have masterly technique but express themselves poorly through improvisation. His prejudice against native artists was hardly unique, judging from the number of times even the most generous and cooperative of my informants laughed at the idea of an American historian studying jazz in Japan. They often asked why I would "go to the trouble" of coming to Japan to study jazz, when I'm from the "jazz homeland" (*jazu no honba*). Most insist that Japanese have contributed nothing of substance to the music and therefore merit little attention, especially from an American. (Incidentally, the prejudice against nonblack, non-American musicians applies to European artists as well: as Jean-Phillipe André noted in an 1989 exposé in France's *Jazz Magazine*, even French musicians are the "wrong" ethnicity for Japanese jazz audiences.)[17]

However, an alleged failure to meet criteria of ethnic and personal authenticity as defined by Americans is only part of the Japanese jazz artist's dilemma. Historically speaking, jazz performers and aficionados have also had to answer to another standard of authenticity: that of native Japanese culture itself. From the perspective of the social mainstream, jazz has always been and remains not only an alien culture but a paramount example of American cultural imperialism, which actively contributes to the erosion of indigenous social and aesthetic norms. Insofar as modern Japanese history is largely the tale of a struggle to locate and preserve the purity and integrity of a native culture that is imagined to be definable and uniform, people who found particular appeal in jazz music have struggled to define their identities according to (at least) two very different standards. For most of the twentieth century, in fact, jazz folk were singled out as inimical to the national project of nurturing and preserving Japan's cultural "essence," even if that essence was subject to constant reformulation as circumstances dictated.

Well before the crash modernization and "internationalization" programs and the assault by "intrusive" Western cultures and technologies in the last two centuries, Japanese struggled to define the parameters of "Japaneseness." For centuries prolific and perceptive students of ideas and institutions from continental Asia, Europe, and the United States, Japanese have thus often fixated on identifying a native core essence. One contemporary manifestation of this tendency was the best-selling mass market and academic literature of the 1970s and 1980s known as "discourses on the Japanese" (*Nihonjinron*), which testified to the uniqueness and purity of an unchanging "Japanese culture." Proponents argue that Japan's geographical isolation engendered "unique" systems of social relations, cultural values, and aesthetic sensibilities. Japanese and Western scholars have reacted by demonstrating that "Japanese culture" is an artificially coherent and misleadingly monolithic category of relatively recent pedigree, contrived to suppress the very real differences, innovations, variations, complexities, and conflicts that have driven modern Japanese history. Yet even if it is a "phantasm," the *idea* of "Japanese culture" has proven irresistible, durable, and compelling, as the popularity of *Nihonjinron* literature suggests.[18] Its ideas are so commonplace as to have permeated respectable social scientific and even physiological scholarship: the pioneering sociologist of mass culture Katō Hidetoshi argues that "Japanese popular culture is unique, and its research methodology requires that special consideration be given to this singularity," while Tsunoda Tadanobu describes functional differences between Japanese and "Western" brains in his best-selling treatise.[19]

When publicized abroad, *Nihonjinron* notions make Japanese look not only racist but ridiculous. But the premises of these ideas—that there is a genetically determined and therefore immutable, *proprietary* relationship between race and culture, and that cultures possess definable, pure, and uniform essences—pass for conventional wisdom virtually everywhere.

They most certainly inform the ideology of jazz as "black music." Although several scholars have demonstrated that one of the legacies of imperialism is the inherent heterogeneous hybridity of all "cultures"—indeed, one can argue that such was the case well before imperialism—and that "cultures" have no identifiable essences that hold meaning for all individuals, the power of "race thinking" and of notions of definable cultural quintessence remain undisturbed. In both the Japanese and black American nationalist cases, such ideologies are constructed in response to political and economic marginalization (both real and imagined) and fears of cultural dilution or extinction (again, both real and imagined). Their veracity may be questionable in coldly rational terms, but their power is not. They are basic to identity formation and empowerment efforts. They are also pivotal to understanding the process by which omnipresent art forms such as jazz are transmitted, received, and evaluated. Still, as Edward Said has suggested, we need not accept this situation in perpetuity: "No one can deny the persisting continuities of long traditions, sustained habitations, national languages, and cultural geographies, but there seems no reason except fear and prejudice to keep insisting on their separation and distinctiveness, as if that was all human life was about."[20]

Jazz in Japan and "Japanese Jazz"

Over the past several years I have often been asked, "Does Japanese jazz sound different?" It is a question that innocently assumes not only the homogeneity of "Japanese jazz" but also the "naturalness" of non-American performers incorporating traditional indigenous musics into their jazz. Ethnomusicologist Timothy Taylor has remarked that non-Western musicians "face constant pressure from westerners to remain musically and otherwise premodern—that is, culturally 'natural'—because of racism and western demands for authenticity."[21] Many Western critics complain of non-Western artists "selling out" their traditions, while applauding the "creative choices" exercised by artists such as Paul Simon or Peter Gabriel, who appropriate (and copyright) non-Western musics. In her research on contemporary fashion, sociologist Lise Skov notes a similar compulsion to categorize the work of Japanese fashion designers as examples of a "profound 'Japaneseness.'" Designer Yamamoto Yōji at first embraced but later resisted the "orientalist" expectations of Western fashion mavens: "There is no nationality in my clothes. . . . My clothes shouldn't have any nation. But when I came to Paris I realized, and I was pushed to realize, that I am Japanese because I was told 'You are here representing *mode japonaise.*'" In response to Kawakubo Rei's challenging early-eighties designs, many European fashion critics tried to make sense of her work through reductive inferences about the influence of Zen aesthetics. But, Skov contends, Kawakubo's "Comme des Garçons garments have rarely carried any overt allusions to either a particular culture or a specific historical situation. Kawakubo has tended to empty her clothes of any recognizable connotations." While "certain forms of Japanese aesthetics" may influence aspects of Kawakubo's work, Skov argues, it is necessary to prevent "the innovative and provocative features of her design from being reduced to mere reiterations of stereotypical aspects of 'Japanese aesthetics.' "[22] Other examples of the compulsion to locate contemporary art forms within a unitary trajectory of Japanese art and aesthetics are abundant, particularly in studies of cinema and *anime*. It matters little that Japanese filmmakers, painters, poets, and composers have drawn on multinational sources of inspiration to create work that they view as universal; they continue to be pigeonholed as quintessentially Japanese.

This compulsion appears in previous studies of jazz in Japan, although the authors rarely feel a similar compulsion to defend their assertions with evidence. (A typical example is Richard Ichirō Mayeda's hedging statement, "Japanese jazz is jazz tinged with a Japanese flavor. I believe this is true, but it is difficult to prove without considerable technical detail that would be of little interest to the average reader.") Elizabeth Sesler-Beckman's thesis argues more forcefully for the existence of a distinctive Japanese variation of the jazz idiom (and presents comparative musicological evidence to "prove" her contention):

> The Japanese musicians that emerged [between 1965 and 1970] were often playing a highly emotional and many times extreme music which did not, on the face of it, reflect such traditional Japanese values as love of order or quiet tranquility. Yet it is my hypothesis that this musical movement represents the highest form of Japanese expression and that it is, in fact, a powerful example of Japanese culture flowering through the form of American jazz. It is here that a national Japanese jazz style emerges, and it is here that Japanese musicians have found the juncture where imitation of old forms has become something truly new and innovative. Musicians such as Hino [Terumasa], Yamashita [Yōsuke], Togashi [Masahiko], and Satoh [Masahiko] have successfully captured not just the trappings of traditional Japanese musical forms but the actual essence of *what it is to be Japanese* within their musical improvisations.[23]

While shooting footage for his documentary film *Tokyo Blues: Jazz and Blues in Japan,* Craig McTurk told the *Japan Times* that "there are palpable differences in Japanese jazz." "If jazz is an international language, every country has its own dialect. In Japan some people leave more space in the music. You could call it the Zen approach to music, sort of like less is more."[24] (In consultations during the postproduction phase of McTurk's film, I pointed out that Zen is a rigorous spiritual practice that is as alien and unnatural an approach to life to most Japanese as it is to most Americans. I had never met a jazz musician who had studied Zen, let alone self-consciously incorporated its aesthetic principles into performances. Furthermore, respect for space is nothing unique to any one country or philosophy, as the musics of Thelonious Monk, Miles Davis, the Art Ensemble of Chicago, and Sun Ra attest.)

While a handful of Japanese jazz artists indeed have elected to "Japanize" jazz, most others understandably resent the assumption that this is the only legitimate creative avenue open to them. Pianist Kikuchi Masabumi ("Pooh") indignantly recalled an encounter in the sixties with saxophone colossus Sonny Rollins, who reportedly lectured, "Because you all are Orientals your mission is to tie Oriental music to jazz."[25] As an artist whose authentic jazz credentials were above reproach (and who spent a great deal of time studying traditional Japanese religion and art), Rollins must have felt he was in a position to suggest directions for potential Japanese exploration. Failure to follow such sage advice put at risk the acknowledgment of Japanese artists by one of the masters. But Rollins is not alone in his preconceptions. While watching a live performance of percussion-heavy Afro-Cuban music in Chicago, a colleague once asked me if Japanese performed music in such a style. When I told him about talented percussionists I had seen—Yahiro Tomohiro and Senba Kiyohiko, and the world-famous Japanese salsa band Orquestra de la Luz—he shook his head. "They shouldn't do that. They've got their own wonderful traditions."

Paradoxically, those very "wonderful traditions" have been looked upon as the source of both Japanese failures *and* successes in the jazz idiom. For instance, traditional modes of transmission/education and of social organization within Japanese artistic communities are often said to contribute to a lack of spontaneity, creative assertiveness, and imaginative exploration. On the other hand, some of the Japanese jazz artists who have received the most international praise are those who conspicuously draw on their heritage to incorporate textures and aesthetic principles associated with traditional Japan, thereby creating what many have imagined to be a recognizable "national dialect."

The persistent illusion that Japan is a "nation of imitators," psychologically incapable of originality and socialized to devalue creativity, is a stereotype that far too many Japanese believe themselves, one which hardly does justice to the artistic legacies of Murasaki Shikibu, Chikamatsu Monzaemon, Kurosawa Akira, Sesshū, Kawabata Yasunari, Bashō, and Akiyoshi Toshiko. It is, in fact, a stereotype of relatively recent pedigree, rooted in the Japanese state's persistent efforts since the mid-nineteenth century to achieve parity with the Western nations by studying and following their examples. The "imitator" stereotype remains powerful today: it is at the heart of frictions between Japan and the United States over technology transfers, and underlies calls for national education reform. It also explains why Japan's most accomplished and popular jazz artists are identified as "the Japanese version" of someone else—"Japan's Satchmo" (Nanri Fumio), "Japan's Sonny Rollins" (Miyazawa Akira), and "Japan's Gene Krupa" (George Kawaguchi).[26]

The "nation of imitators" is an offensive stereotype, but it is rooted in some very real historical and social realities: the consensual value of conformity in Japan; the education system's willful failure to encourage critical thinking; the historical legacy of centuries of "cultural borrowing"; and the primacy of the "school" (iemoto) in Japan's artistic and musical tradition. "The West believes in the personality," musicologist Eta Harich-Schneider has written. "The East believes in the school. A work of art is evaluated in the West by its degree of independence and originality; in the East as a perfect specimen of a type." To achieve the aesthetic ideal of "a perfect specimen of a type," music education (including the popular Suzuki violin method) has for centuries focused on mastery of "form" (kata), which theoretically leads to the pupil's understanding of the internal principles. Christine Yano argues that kata continues to be relevant in karaoke singing: "It is a frankly mimetic activity . . . [giving rise to a kind of] individualism which is highly patterned, relying upon the fixedness of the form more than the originality of expression. A karaoke singer in Japan is not singing as Hideo Tanaka (pseudonym) but rather as Hideo-Tanaka-in-the-form-of-Kitajima-Saburō (well-known enka singer)." Patterned "kata of music, text, gesture . . . makes the expression culturally safe and understandable."[27] According to this line of argument, the process by which "new or imported forms of mass culture often acquire a dō, or specific way,"[28] explains the historical tendency for some Japanese jazz artists to strongly identify with the style of a particular American master, to the extent of even embracing a reputation as the "Japanese version" of that master. While some artists attribute these labels to simple-minded and even hostile critics—pianist Sugino Kichirō complains that "they're always calling some Japanese musician the 'Japanese Coltrane' or the 'Japanese Miles Davis.' They won't let the young people who are creating original music have any credit for it"—keyboardist Satō Masahiko concedes that there was a time in the late fifties and early sixties when Japanese musicians meeting for the first time asked one another, "By the way, who are you imitating?"[29] Sugita Kuniko, a language teacher who played saxophone in a modern jazz combo at Waseda University, told me about how her bandmates staunchly identified themselves as disciples either of Sonny Rollins or of John Coltrane, debating the saxophonists' relative merits ad nauseum.

Several people whom I interviewed insisted that something strongly akin to the old *iemoto* system governs social practices in the jazz community. As with other occupations in premodern Japan, artistry was an inherited trade. The *iemoto* system consists of real and fictive kinship relations between masters and hereditary or "adopted" disciples who trace their "lineage" to the founder or head of the *iemoto*. Examples of arts, trades, and crafts governed by this system include *ikebana* (flower arranging), tea ceremony, gangsters, martial arts, painting, calligraphy, music, theater, archery, incense burning, mathematics, and dancing. Traditionally the *iemoto* master's authority in setting standards for style, content, and behavior is unquestioned. Disciples are not free to reinterpret a style that is assumed to have achieved inner perfection; rather they master established techniques through "unconscious imitation," through slow, secretive oral lessons that heighten the "superiority and mystery" of the master's authority. The disciple begins as an apprentice, then is accredited as a member of a fictive family. The disciple even assumes a new name (*gō*), using the school's name as a surname and the root of the master's name in the personal name. With this name is conferred the prestige of the master's school, and the disciple owes unflinching loyalty and service to it, in exchange for professional promotion by the master. Disciples are ranked by years of accreditation, skill, and closeness to the master. They are not to compete among themselves but rather engage in mutual aid throughout their professional careers.

I have no evidence to suggest that Japan's jazz community has ever been anywhere near this formal in structure, but there clearly are band apprenticeships and hierarchies of musicians and aficionados based on age, ability, and experience. Some have found them to be so formal and powerful as to be suffocating. Hinata Toshifumi, a keyboardist and enormously successful composer of television and film music, claimed that the dominance of this "apprentice system" (coupled with a general feeling that nonblacks cannot play jazz authentically anyway) was behind his decision to get out of jazz. After an intense education at Boston's competitive Berklee school, he returned to Japan and found it hard to gig without connections to certain prominent individuals. There are ramifications to ignoring the etiquette of *iemoto*-like relations: jazz writer Segawa Masahisa described the immensely popular pianist Ōnishi Junko as a "rebel" who often gets in trouble for her lack of backstage manners, consistently failing to make the obligatory deferential greetings to older musicians. Finally, two alums of Waseda University jazz bands, Sugita Kuniko and Anzai Takeshi, describe an environment in which the hierarchical relationships between upperclassmen (*senpai*) and underclassmen (*kōhai*), and between students and "old boys" (*OB kai,* band alumni) were basic. Anzai was the head (*gakuchō*) of the accomplished Waseda High Society Orchestra when I met him in 1994. At rehearsal, he was accorded much respect and many bows from his bandmates, but the actual running of the rehearsal was delegated to another student. None of the band members are music majors; there is no faculty advisor and no formal class in jazz theory or pedagogy. Rather, High Society is a club entirely run by extremely self-motivated students. The veterans take responsibility for initiating the newcomers in the intricacies of improvisation, arranging, jazz history, and aesthetics. But as with *iemoto,* the maintenance of High Society's international reputation so as not to let the "old boys" down is of paramount importance. A grueling practice regimen (at the expense of schoolwork, naturally) ensures the preservation of the tradition. (As of 1994, High Society had toured the United States five times and performed in India, China, and Sweden.)

I do not wish to dismiss lightly the residual influence of *kata* and *iemoto* in contemporary Japanese aesthetic practice, but modern transformations of aesthetic and social mores limit their value in understanding jazz culture in Japan. Such systems are neither peculiar to Japan nor antithetical to practices in the jazz world. Harich-Schneider's East-West formulation in particular understates the fact that Western aesthetic *practice* (if not theory) often rewards formula or technical virtuosity at the expense of artistic "originality" or "soul." "Originality" and "soul" themselves are problematic and difficult to judge. As George Clinton's lampooning song "What is Soul?" suggests, the aesthetic virtue of "soul" can just as easily be used to perpetuate comical stereotypes of black Americans as to exalt their artistic achievements. Moreover, what some listeners regard as "original" may be little more than the manipulation of old tricks in new ways. The process of extemporaneous performance has been demystified by cross-cultural studies, which demonstrate that structure, formulae, and extensive preparation are as basic to improvisation as to composition.[30] Even the most "original" of jazz artists betray the influence of *somebody* in their own work, and all "original" jazz artists are recognizable for melodic and rhythmic signatures on which they fall back at every performance. Every serious student of the music begins by listening to, transcribing, analyzing, and replicating the improvised solos of the masters. This is and has always been basic to jazz education, whether formal or informal.

Furthermore, the differences between *iemoto* and the jazz world's aesthetic and social hierarchies are more of degree than of kind. As the music has developed over time, jazz has subdivided into stylistic schools or sects, founded by a few exceptional musicians whom all other musicians within the style revere. Apprenticeships with name bands, such as Art Blakey's Jazz Messengers or Betty Carter's trio, confer legitimacy in much the same way that Japanese *iemoto* do. All young jazz artists are expected to demonstrate familiarity with and master the musical lessons of Parker, Ellington, Monk, and a few select others: to achieve credibility in the contemporary jazz scene, it is said, one must "deal with the Duke." Mastery of the now-mainstream language of bebop—the ability to "play changes"—is considered essential before a musician can legitimately explore alternative avenues of expression. (Ornette Coleman's refusal or inability to "play changes" makes him suspect to many aficionados, some forty years after he burst on the scene.) In reality, this is not much less constricting than the traditional music training regimen in Japan: in both cases, there are masters, there are students, there are established curricula and practice procedures, and there are expectations of individual achievement within those boundaries. Jazz musicians, no more or less than musicians in other traditions, face the paradox of appearing to be in "the tradition" while still doing their "own thing."[31] It is thus indefensible to argue that the Japanese have a peculiar penchant for identifying a " 'perfect' way of doing things," conducive to the development of flawless technique and formula rather than to individual expression and novelty.[32] Tom Pierson, a pianist and composer who abandoned New York City for the safer streets of Tokyo in 1991, turns the stereotype of the "imitative" Japanese on its head in his critique of the neoconservative Young Lions ("kittens," in his words): he calls Wynton Marsalis "a Japanese jazzman, in the worst sense of the word."

If "Japanese tradition" is of limited value in explaining the alleged "defects" in jazz performed by Japanese, might it account for its successes? There are those who would say yes, some of whom were quoted earlier. Japanese jazz artists who have incorporated instruments, repertoire, and textures from indigenous traditional musics have certainly garnered attention that might otherwise have eluded them. But "Japanese jazz" (a term I use here exclusively to denote the concept of a national style of jazz peculiar to Japan) is more than a cynical concession to audience demands for exoticism.[33] Historically speaking, the idea of a singular Japanese national style of jazz was constructed as an authenticating strategy to assuage the various dilemmas the Japanese jazz community has faced. Japan as a nation has invested considerable effort in the cultivation of a distinctive national cultural identity, and this effort finds expression no less in the jazz community than in other artistic communities and subcultures. The Japanese jazz community has historically regarded itself as a distinctive entity within the jazz world, an island nation unto itself, and has framed its identity in a way that is consonant with ideologies of the ethnic and cultural exceptionalism of the Japanese nation. This sense of separation from the jazz "mainstream" (which runs, of course, in the United States) is physically manifested and thus normalized in the record store bins, where albums by Japanese artists are invariably clustered together at the end of the jazz section, and in distinct readers' and critics' polls for Japanese and non-Japanese artists (with virtually no crossover of Japanese into the "regular" polls). The jazz community often speaks of "Japanese jazz" as a coherent whole, with specific objectives, shared shortcomings, and developmental strategies that echo the rhetoric of national development employed by government and industry. Through the idea of a national style, Japanese jazz artists have attempted to resolve the following quandaries: what are the expressive possibilities of an "American" art in a non-American culture? Does a performer surrender his or her national or ethnic identity when performing jazz? Or is it possible to express that identity *through* the "American" art of jazz? If so, does such expression constitute a unique national style? Can such a national style be considered authentic jazz?

Creating a "Japanese jazz" is just one of several authenticating strategies I have identified in my research. It is clear that the strategic paradigms used by performers and aficionados to authenticate jazz in Japan have been variegated and rooted in the demands of particular historical moments. These paradigms inevitably resound in the music of particular eras. Recordings from the decades immediately following the world wars indicate that musicians were listening closely to and attempting to replicate the feats of America's jazz giants. But recordings from the years of the Pacific War or from the late 1960s onward demonstrate a willingness to tinker with jazz, to "indigenize" it, and even to forge a distinctive national style. Clearly the authenticating strategies and aesthetic imperatives shifted with historical developments, particularly those that involved Japan's self-conceptions and political and cultural relationship with the United States. In the 1930s enterprising *jazumen* sought authenticity in the seedy "jazz frontier" of Shanghai; in the 1950s they mingled conspicuously with black American GIS and shot heroin backstage; and in the 1980s their quest led them to Boston's Berklee School of Music (where Japanese comprise some 10 percent of the student body) and apprenticeships in American bands. But a national style promised to be the most effective strategy, in that it would resolve all aspects of the authenticity complex: it would demonstrate Japanese creativity and personal authenticity, reverse the jazz community's alienation from the native cultural mainstream, and render moot comparisons to an ethnic standard of authenticity established in America.

All too well aware of the value of individual creativity in jazz, many Japanese artists naturally have been uncomfortable as "the Japanese version" of their American heroes. Veteran saxophonist Oda Satoru admits that he was bothered when he was billed as "Japan's Lester Young" at a performance in Ireland, but sighs that it was the most convenient way to "label" him for an audience unfamiliar with his work. He was much more pleased when another European festival described his music as "Asian jazz" in its promotions. One solution to the discomfort of being recognized as the *kagemusha* ("double") of an American jazz giant has been to transform the perceived ethnic "disadvantage" into a vehicle for an allegedly unique Japanese expression within the jazz idiom, something that would distinguish the music of Japanese artists from that of Americans. The result, it was argued, would be an inimitable national style of jazz that would express the "Japanese essence," a music that would be recognizably Japanese and constitute a unique contribution to the collective jazz oeuvre.

The desire to assert a Japanese national identity through music was by no means unique to jazz. In fact, proponents of a national style of jazz could and did look for musical and philosophical inspiration from a number of classical composers, such as Takemitsu Tōru (1930–1996), Miki Minoru, Yuasa Jōji, and Akutagawa Yasushi, who were groping toward similar goals. Hillary Tann describes this effort as a "search for a voice within a universal musical language" and an important motivating force in contemporary Japanese music. Judith Ann Herd depicts a "neonationalist" tradition whose stated goal was the establishment of "an independent voice" free from "European cultural imperialism."[34] As I describe in Chapters 4 and 6, similar movements to liberate Japanese artists from their obsession with American models distinguish the late thirties and early forties and the late sixties in Japan's jazz history.

There are those within Japan's jazz community who may invoke the "universal language" metaphor—the ideal that jazz is a music unique in its capacity to speak to and for all peoples—yet who still feel that Japanese are the "wrong" ethnicity to perform authentic jazz. Ironically, the same racialist premises can be and have been invoked to assert the creation of a jazz that only ethnic Japanese could create, which "foreigners cannot imitate." The late Yui Shōichi, a prominent jazz critic who expounded at great length on the subject of a national style, highlighted the ambiguity in a statement quoted by Sesler-Beckman: "Jazz has gone from a national [American] music to an international music and now is *both national and international.* Japanese jazz was born in the sixties and represents a uniquely Japanese expression. We are now in some ways more spiritual and more technically advanced than Westerners." Jazz is an international music in that all nations have jazz; but, as Yui explained elsewhere, each country has developed its own distinctive national tradition and sound, and therefore jazz constitutes a form of national expression and a mark of national difference. (In his *Jazz in Black and White,* Charley Gerard demonstrates a similar comfort with this ambiguity when he states that "Jazz is somehow able to be both an African-American ethnic music and a universal music at the same time, both an expression of universal artistry and ethnicity.")[35] In later years Yui would refer to this conceptualization as "jazz nationalism."

What do Japanese consider to be Japanese jazz? There are about as many definitions as there are jazz musicians and fans in Japan. For some, Japanese jazz represents the fusion of the improvisatory, harmonic, and rhythmic elements of jazz with native pentatonic scales, folk melodies, or instrumentation. Such musical experimentation first occurred in the mid-to-late 1930s, but has continued sporadically throughout the decades. One of the most successful representatives of this approach is the bamboo flute (*shakuhachi*) master Yamamoto Hōzan, who has almost singlehandedly brought a new timbre to the tonal palette of jazz. Many proponents of a national style have pointed to Yamamoto as the ultimate example of an original artist who expresses "the Japanese heart" in a way that foreigners could not hope to emulate. But traditional Japanese musics such as court music (*gagaku*) and folk songs (*min'yō*) are no more linked to ethnicity than are jazz or Western classical music. Japanese jazz musicians have repeatedly confessed that mastering the vocabularies of indigenous musics did not come naturally to them, but rather required considerable effort, in spite of their supposed ethnic "advantage." Moreover, a number of non-Japanese—from John Coltrane, Tony Scott, and Charlie Mariano, to Herbie Mann, John Kaizan Neptune, John Zorn, and Jamaaladeen Tacuma—have successfully incorporated Japanese folk melodies and instrumentation into their music. If "Japanese jazz" is no more than a musical fusion, it hardly constitutes an inimitable national style that comes naturally to Japanese and is impossible for foreigners to replicate.

Yet the fusion of traditional Japanese musics with jazz strikes many proponents of a national style as too gimmicky and does not begin to do justice to their concept of "Japanese jazz." For them, there is something much more intangible, even mystical, that distinguishes jazz performed by Japanese artists: a Japanese artist playing Tin Pan Alley tunes on the Western piano unconsciously expresses his or her ethnic identity as much as an improvising *koto* player does, they say. As cited in Chapter 6, Yui Shōichi and percussionist Togashi Masahiko, among others, have highlighted the importance of "space" (*ma*), the relatively long, pregnant intervals between notes, as a distinctive feature of Japanese jazz. When challenged with the rebuttal that Thelonious Monk, Miles Davis, and many other non-Japanese artists have accorded a great deal of respect to space in their music, they respond that the Japanese "sense of space" is unique because it is spontaneous and "unconscious" rather than calculated for effect.

Aside from space, there are supposedly other ephemeral characteristics that make Japanese jazz distinctive. Saxophonist Oda Satoru has coined the term "yellow jazz" to connote an as yet undeveloped style, using what he calls Asian techniques, sounds, scales, and spirit, which Japanese and other Asians "have in their blood" and should develop further. Another conceptualization comes from stereo dealer Sugiura Shūichi and his wife Hitomi, activist jazz fans who reside in Okazaki outside of Nagoya. The Sugiuras insist that when they listen to a jazz performance they can identify the ethnicity of the performer. (I am often asked if I ever tested them, and while it was tempting, I came to the conclusion that proving or disproving their "ethnic listening" skills would serve no purpose.) For them, Japanese jazz is moodier and less energetic than American jazz. They believe that Japanese are basically a sad people (this from some of the most cheerful people I know) and that the sadness reflected in song forms such as *enka* colors their jazz. Through the common language of jazz, the Sugiuras say, Americans and Japanese express themselves in ways that are determined by their respective backgrounds and that will be understood by their respective audiences. Shūichi used colors to illustrate his conception: jazz is red, Japanese culture is white, and Japanese jazz is pink.

It should be acknowledged that Japanese jazz as a coherent national style is not a concept accepted by most jazz aficionados, but even those who scoff at the idea feel that jazz as played by Japanese is subtly different, usually with the added implication that it is ultimately inferior to the American product. Sugiura Shūichi asserts that Japanese do not have the physical power to play jazz like Americans so they must play their own way. Segawa Masahisa contends that the "inferior" physique, lack of power, and lung capacity of Japanese accounts for the lack of any "powerful" trumpeters in Japan's jazz pantheon. But the problems do not end at the front line: "Japanese rhythm sections are often much weaker," pianist Imada Masaru has said. "Japanese are very tight, but Americans are more relaxed, more jazzy." Saxophonist Inagaki Jirō cites experiences playing with Bud Shank and Lionel Hampton in which he and other Japanese musicians, operating on what he calls "Japanese time," played their parts too early compared with their American counterparts. Inagaki's son Masayuki adds that the Japanese rhythmic sense is impaired: they cannot play behind the beat or the chord for fear of "messing up." Elsewhere Inagaki is quoted as saying, "Japanese just can't match the quality of the American players. They can read music well, and pick up on concepts quickly. But the individual musicians don't devote themselves to their instruments and their music like the Americans do. We've produced a few top players in this country. . . . But I don't think we'll ever catch up."[36]

Finally, there are those who believe that the very idea of a national style is inimical to the individualistic aesthetic principles of jazz, if not outright ridiculous. Avant-garde saxophonist and Stir Up! bandleader Hayasaka Sachi is one of many who regard jazz as a music in which individual creativity is the only determining factor and national or ethnic origin have no bearing. Pianist and Mix Dynamite leader Itabashi Fumio believes that "Itabashi jazz," not "Japanese jazz," should always be his first concern. Then there is Isono Teruo ("Terry"), a drummer, DJ, critic, former club owner, and former USIS employee, who scoffs at the very idea of "Japanese jazz." It's all American music, he says, adding, "Japanese have no originality." I asked Isono what he would say to musicians like Satō Masahiko and Togashi Masahiko, who at one point in their careers made the creation of Japanese jazz their missions. He offered the following words of advice: "It's impossible. It's unnecessary. Just quit it."

Three decades after the last major push for a national jazz voice, one must conclude that this particular authenticating strategy has failed to convince the average aficionado, as have all other authenticating strategies. A 1989 piece in *Japan Update* portrayed a jazz scene that was uncommonly harsh for native artists:

> Ironically, it's Japan's love of this American idiom that drives most young musicians away from their own dreams. The music, to too many in Hayasaka [Sachi]'s potential young audience, just doesn't seem "authentic" unless it's played by Americans. The craze is for performers from the U.S., who therefore naturally demand the highest prices they can get—much more, "sometimes ten times as much," than most could command in their own home country—and thereby drain the coffers of performance and recording fees that might go to Japanese musicians.
>   . . . The paucity of jobs and money fosters a strange irony in which young Japanese musicians leave the richest jazz market in the world—Japan—to find work and to study in America, home of the musicians who are making all the money.

. . . Why play for pennies, standing before audiences who think that in Japanese jazz, they're hearing only second-best imitations? Because they love it.[37]

Indeed, if I have hammered home the idea that Japanese are convinced of their own inauthenticity, it must be conceded that they have continued to play this music. I know of some performers for whom the authenticity complex has proven artistically and professionally crippling, but for the vast majority of players its power cannot match their love for the art and their determination to understand it, feel it, and express themselves through it. It might even be argued that in some cases the authenticity complex has given them more incentive to pour their whole selves into the creative process, to peer deeper into themselves and into their imaginations than they might have otherwise. Inagaki's contention that individual musicians in Japan "don't devote themselves to their instruments and their music like the Americans do," is rather unfair, for those Japanese who have succeeded artistically and commercially could not have overcome the psychological, racial, and commercial obstacles described above without such devotion. "When I started it was the utmost compliment if you were told that you sounded exactly like an American jazz musician," trumpeter Hino Teru-masa maintains in Craig McTurk's documentary *Tokyo Blues*, "But nowa-days, if you're told that you sound like someone else, it's a criticism."

In the interest of challenging these widespread assumptions about cul-tural authenticity, I present the experiences of Japan's jazz artists and afi-cionados with the intention of asking the reader to consider the possibility that Japanese too might be "blues people"—in Baraka's sense of folk who not only play music but live it. In the 1960s Japanese made the case that there must be an indigenous musical analogue to the blues because both Japanese and people of African ancestry shared a history of oppression by whites. But that is far too simple and problematic an equation, and is not what I mean by my suggestion. If blues-based music is, as Baraka, Cornel West, and others insist, an *outlook* or "mode of being" as much as an expressive idiom, then one can make a case for Japanese who identify strongly with such music. In *Tokyo Blues* pianist Yamashita Yōsuke charac-terizes jazz as a "kind of gift for people living in the twentieth century." "As I got involved in jazz I gradually realized that jazz has the greatest possibility as a musical expression. . . . The greatest thing about jazz is that every musician can play in his own style with improvisation. When I realized this essential fact . . . I could play with various musicians of different fields only if their music has a sense of improvisation." People like Hino and Yama-shita defied significant social pressure and outright suppression to formulate a distinctive ethos and lifestyle that danced to a jazz beat. In a society which they feel severely limits creativity and public displays of emotion, Japan's real blues people live for individual self-expression and the yet unmade and unheard sound, and jazz is their chosen vehicle for such discovery. It is to their stories that we now turn.

CHAPTER TWO

THE SOUNDTRACK OF MODERN LIFE:
JAPAN'S JAZZ REVOLUTION

Japan is jazz mad. . . . It has practically become everybody's
business to know something of jazz in order to keep in touch with
the spirit of the times.—Uenoda Setsuo

In the autumn of 1919 a Japanese college student
strolled the streets of Chicago, searching for a new
sound. Kikuchi Shigeya (1903–1976), Keiō University
student and son of a member of the Japanese parlia-
ment, had accompanied his father Kikuchi Takenori to
the United States for the First International Labor Conference in October 1919, then lingered behind to travel
around the States. A friend studying at the University
of Michigan had piqued the young pianist's curiosity
with tales of some "queer bands" in the U.S. The location and timing of Kikuchi's quest were fortuitous, for
he wandered a city that a flood of entertainers from the
Crescent City had transformed into the new jazz capital
of the world.[1]

Kikuchi's search ended when he stumbled upon a
group of black musicians that seemed to fit the description "queer band." "When I was staying at the Congress
Hotel in Chicago I was able, unexpectedly, to hear a real
jazz band at a street theater. I was also able to hear a
three-piece jazz band at a vaudeville show near Michigan Avenue." Kikuchi later recounted how the drummer twirled and threw his sticks into the air, the pianist
played with his back to the keyboard, and a beautiful
dancer performed acrobatic feats to the musicians' jamming. He marveled at the solo "breaks," the "noisy"
ensembles that followed these solo outbursts, and the
precision with which the band ended the performance.
"It was quite an acrobatic performance—I was scared
out of my wits. . . . So *this* is jazz!"[2]

The following day Kikuchi rushed to a record store

and asked to hear some jazz records. "The clerk made a strange face and said, 'What'll become of you if you listen to jazz? I have plenty of better records, so buy those. You should leave those jazz records alone.'" But Kikuchi insisted, and the clerk brought out three records by the Original Dixieland Jass Band, including "Tiger Rag," "Ostrich Walk," and "Skeleton Jungle." Kikuchi listened to make sure they were exactly like the music he had heard the previous night and, "feeling like I was taking the devil's road," bought them. He would take these records back to Japan in 1920, where he gathered some acquaintances at the "Bunjunsha" in Tokyo's Ginza district to listen to the records and discuss the music.[3] Kikuchi spent the rest of his life trying to replicate the sounds he heard on the streets of Chicago and on those records, and over the next several decades countless others would follow in his footsteps, trying to master "that sound."

It seems that the word *jazz* first appeared in Japanese print in the summer of 1920, in a sheet music periodical featuring a photo of four men posing with drums, guitar, violin, and banjo, with the caption "Tokyo Jazz Band."[4] By 1929 the word *jazu*—connoting a staggering variety of musical styles, meanings, images, and values—was in the headlines and on everyone's lips;[5] in the tense years leading up to Japan's invasion of China, a "Jazz Age" was in full swing. Jazz, along with American movies, fashions, and professional sports, evoked a new ethos of carefree cosmopolitanism, playful subversion, and "erotic grotesque nonsense" (*ero guro nansensu*). Though certainly marginal from the perspective of Japan's rural majority and official elites, jazz was at the very heart an escapist entertainment culture that prospered in spite of—perhaps because of—the economic travails and nationalist agitation of the day. Moreover, as a commercial product, popular music such as jazz helped transform Japanese society into a mass consumer culture.[6]

The early history of jazz in Japan is as shrouded in the fog of legend and dim memories as are the origins of the music itself, yet there are a variety of perspectives from which to peer into the fog. One approach is to identify macrotrends and historical processes that characterize the early twentieth century: the inclusion of Japan in post–World War I economic and security arrangements; the integration of the world's entertainment markets; the growing popularity of international leisure travel; and the development of mass-produced recording technology. Another approach is to focus on the contributions of foreign visitors or visionary Japanese "pioneers" to the popularization of an alien music. This latter approach entails reliance on memoirs and oral accounts, which are often inherently unverifiable if not tainted by weak memory or attempts at self-glorification. Yet, as a number of scholars who use oral materials have pointed out, legends, lore, and lies can

be as instructive as unassailable eyewitness accounts of "fact." "The importance of oral testimony may often lie not in its adherence to facts but rather
in its divergence from them," Alessandro Portelli writes. "Where imagination, symbolism, desire break in . . . the credibility of oral sources is [thus] a
different credibility." Imagination, memories, and impressions are as valuable as verifiable events or facts in the study of oral accounts, for "psychological truth" often explains more than "objective truth." Thus historians using
oral evidence must pay attention not only to the "facts" and events described
but also to the language, the shape and themes of the informant's narrative,
and the social contexts and interactions in which these narratives are formulated.[7] In any case, there is little else to go on: the memories and lore of
Japan's first jazzmen are virtually the only "documents" we have for re-
searching the embryonic jazz culture before domestically produced recordings and periodicals devoted to popular music appeared in the late twenties
and early thirties.

Another caveat: it is crucial to remember two important points about the
word *jazz* when investigating the cultural history of the early twentieth
century. First, if one applies the current, accepted musicological criteria for
defining "jazz" as a style—with distinctive aural characteristics such as
"swing," improvisation, and subtleties of pitch identified as "blues" sonorities—little of the music that Japanese (or Europeans and Americans, for that
matter) knew as "jazz" in the twenties and thirties would qualify. In fact,
most of the music unproblematically labeled "jazz" in the first half of the
twentieth century is no longer considered to be a part of the "jazz tradition."
Thus a musicologically formalist approach is ahistorical at best, for the
relative importance of musicological criteria such as swing, blue notes, and
improvised solos has changed with the music. The word *jazz* simply has not
retained a consistent musicological meaning, and it seems best for historians either to conform to contemporary definition(s) that held sway in the
time periods under scrutiny, or to formulate definitions "based on a sociocultural analysis of jazz rather than on its internal aesthetics."[8] The second point is that in the interwar period the word *jazz* could and did refer to a
number of different things: when one scans a variety of period source
materials it becomes clear that "jazz" could refer specifically to popular
music, social dance, or other forms of American popular culture sweeping
Japan after World War I; yet it also connoted a new set of social mores,
fashions, gender relations, and consumer practices otherwise known as
"modernism" (*modanizumu*). Jazz allowed Japanese to experience an authentic "modernity" that placed them squarely in the politically and culturally prestigious company of elite Western nations.

As we stroll the noisy, neon-lit streets of the interwar jazz community, it should be borne in mind that Japan's Jazz Age coincided with a time of political, social, cultural, and economic volatility, which fed a gnawing uneasiness over the perceived erosions of traditions and the rising prominence of America in Japanese cultural life. The jazz culture's development occurred within a context of, and thus was decisively shaped by, expanding state power in the realms of thought, art, and behavior.[9] Moreover, since the music itself represented entirely new ways of viewing the world, interacting with others, and inflaming the passions of the self, it is fair to say that Japan's jazz culture was hardly peripheral but rather at the very heart of the turbulence and controversy of the times. Many Japanese feared revolution in the twenties and thirties, while others advocated it. Legislation and "thought police" seemed effective in squashing proletarian revolution; but what, people asked, might be done about the jazz revolution?

Changing Tunes

There is a strange little film called *Jazz Warlord* (*Jazu daimyō*, 1986), based on Tsutsui Yasutaka's story, that portrays a fanciful, anachronistic vision of how jazz was introduced to Japan. Three emancipated American slaves wander aboard a ship bound for Asia, winding up in Japan in time for the political upheaval known as the Meiji Restoration. Wielding instruments and jamming on "Maple Leaf Rag" ad nauseum, the trio are interrogated by a regional warlord with musical inclinations of his own, who is also preoccupied by the political turmoil around him. Finally, with rebel forces seizing his domain and drunken mobs, confused by the political bedlam and chanting *ee janaika* ("ain't it grand?"), tumbling into his castle, the warlord and his retinue join their foreign guests in an apocalyptic, orgiastic jam session, with clarinet, trombone, cornet, percussion, *koto, shamisen,* and abacus—daring the world to end *right now.*

Needless to say, it did not quite happen that way.

Japanese have a historical reputation for prolific cultural appropriation and the adaptability of their customs, language, religions, arts, and philosophies to foreign modes. Significant contacts with outsiders, as well as indigenous social and political upheavals, are also reflected in transformations of Japanese musical styles, known collectively as *hōgaku*. *Hōgaku* rarely stood independently of religious ritual, dance, or literature;[10] thus music inevitably mirrored changes in beliefs, language, and politics. *Gagaku*, the elegant court music derived from Chinese and Korean models, symbolized not only the cosmopolitan ethos of the day, but also the expanded power and authority of the imperial court in the Nara period (710–784). The diffusion of esoteric and salvationist Buddhist sects in the medieval period contributed to the development of new bodies of music, such as choral chants (*shōmyō*) and sung prayers based on sutras. The vogue for spartan Zen aesthetic principles among the medieval warrior elite found expression in the austere refinement and prolific use of space that characterize *nō* theater music. On the other hand, the rise of an urban merchant caste with a thirst for bombastic spectacle and novelty was expressed musically in the explosive capabilities of *kabuki* theater music, with drummers clattering sticks on the floor to accompany onstage action. The *enka* or *sōshi bushi* of the 1870s and 1880s, sung on street corners and in political plays, expressed the satirical, antigovernment ideologies of the "Freedom and People's Rights" activists. Each major shift in Japanese life and thought thus had musical accompaniment.

In the nineteenth and twentieth centuries two successive waves of musical importation—the first from Europe, the second from North and South America—signaled Japan's national efforts to win respect and parity in a world order dominated by the Western nations. By the time Japanese began wrestling with jazz (part of the second wave of musical Westernization) in the 1920s, they relied on musical skills instilled during the first such wave. It is possible that the Japanese music education system, based on Western models since the early Meiji period (1868–1912), helped Japanese musicians learn jazz more easily, since they were already accustomed to Western instruments, notation, harmony, and theory.[11] On the other hand, jazz musicians' accounts suggest that such thorough inculcation of European classical techniques and philosophies could hinder as often as facilitate ear training and comprehension and mastery of jazz sonorities, syncopated rhythms, and improvisation. Indeed, accomplished section musicians who could read scores well were plentiful in the decades before World War II, but only a handful made efforts to develop their talents as improvisers. Jazz thus represented a challenge to a music culture whose values had been thoroughly refashioned, in quite recent memory, to reflect the technical and aesthetic standards of European composed music.

Japan was but one of many countries whose musical standards were deliberately and officially refashioned in the age of imperialism. The global diffusion of Western music cannot be separated from the narrative of the European powers' imperialist encroachments in Asia and Africa. Richard Kraus contends that Western music, rather than acting as a benign art with "universal" appeal, was one of the most powerful elements of cultural colonization: "Beyond its European heartland, [Western] music's considerable aesthetic attractions are reinforced by the West's political and economic domination of the world." The adoption of Western music in the non-Western world thus occurred in the context of blatantly unequal relationships of power.[12] In India, Africa, and Southeast Asia, colonial pressures and "civilizing" policies imposed by the imperialist powers led to the standardization of Western music. From the perspectives of colonized peoples, Western music was associated irrevocably with the might of the colonizers.

Even Japan, which never suffered actual colonization yet was subjected to imperialist pressures (particularly a system of unequal treaties), voluntarily enacted public policies favoring Western music. The aim was to demonstrate Japan's "civilization and enlightenment," and to achieve cultural parity with the Western imperialist powers. Ethnomusicologists have long bemoaned the homogenizing effects of Westernizing policies such as Japan's on the diversity of the world's musics; they argue that policies favoring Western music endanger the continued development and survival of indigenous musics. Admittedly, this "cultural imperialism" thesis—in which musical diffusion occurs in one direction, from the powerful to the weak, overpowering, displacing, and even destroying local flavors—overlooks the "internal dynamics of resistance and opposition" that enable indigenous musics to adapt quite healthily and even to acquire aesthetic respectability and public sponsorship.[13] Nevertheless, it is certainly no accident of history that the basic music educational standards in most countries are based on Western models.

Christian missionaries first introduced Western music to Japan as early as the mid-sixteenth century, but it was not until the late Edo period (1853–1868), when persistent efforts to open Japan to international trade succeeded, that Western music made a lasting impact.[14] The American recognized for "opening" Japan, Commodore Matthew C. Perry, also introduced Japan to music based on "African-American" models. When Perry returned to Japan in 1854 to conclude a treaty, the two delegations each offered entertainment. On 27 March, in return for a *sumō* demonstration, Perry invited the Japanese delegation aboard the flagship *Powhatan* for an exhibition that crewman Edward McCauley dubbed an "Ethiopian performance." The official record of the Perry expedition described the event:

> After the banquet, the Japanese were entertained by an exhibition of negro minstrelsy, got up by some of the sailors, who, blacking their faces and dressing themselves in character, enacted their parts with a humor that would have gained them unbound applause from a New York audience even at Christy's. The gravity of the saturnine Hayashi was not proof against the grotesque exhibition, and even he joined with the rest in the general hilarity provoked by the farcical antics and humorous performances of the mock negroes.[15]

There were, of course, black crewmen among the American delegation, but the introduction of "black music" to Japan was mediated through whites (a pattern that would remain in place in the Jazz Age).[16] It is possible to overstate the significance of this one event, but some scholars argue that the minstrel performance made a lasting impression on the Japanese: that the "distorted caricature" of black people as a "subjected race" and as "comic jester[s] and quintessential entertainer[s]" would continue to characterize Japanese attitudes toward people of African descent and the products of their culture.[17]

It would be another seventy years before Japanese had significant contact with the music of black Americans,[18] but in the meantime the Meiji government sponsored a systematic program to incorporate classical and martial musics of European pedigree as part of its "civilization and enlightenment" agenda. The Meiji government's motivation for adopting Western music as the standard for the nation's military and educational system was part of the larger program of importing Western culture and technology in order to achieve parity with the Western nations and renegotiate unequal treaties. But music was more than a mere trapping affixed to impress the West. Having observed the apparent effects of music on the "national spirits" of Westerners, policymakers in Meiji Japan believed music (specifically, music based on Western standards) was necessary for the success of a modern nation. "Western music was regarded not as an art," Ury Eppstein argues, "but as a means to an end for pragmatic purposes: the modernization of the military and then of the educational system. Music was valued as a factor conducive to the establishment of discipline and to raising morale in the army and navy, and to the spiritual and physical health and character formation of school pupils." Furthermore, music was an essential element of the "ceremonial style of governance" that the Meiji leaders cultivated, as they sought to emulate and surpass the pomp and pageantry of European and North American courts and governments.[19]

It was perhaps appropriate, therefore, that no single group made more of an effort to exploit the potential spiritual effects of music that the Japanese military, the ultimate extension of the new government's power. In the late nineteenth century, the Imperial Army and Navy took the most initiative in the appropriation of Western music, performing the first public concerts of Western music for Japanese audiences, creating a body of patriotic music (including the emperor-centered national anthem *Kimigayo*), and training most of Japan's non-elite musicians and music educators until the middle of the twentieth century. It was a military band which provided the music for Japan's first Western-style social dance, a national "coming out" party celebrating the state's "Europeanization policy" and the "excellence of Japanese culture and Japanese women" at Tokyo's famed Rokumeikan in 1883.[20]

Following the military's lead, the architects of the national education system moved to incorporate Western music into its curriculum. In 1875 the government sent Izawa Shūji (1851–1917), a civil engineer and educator, to the United States to observe music education in the primary schools. Izawa and his American advisor Luther Whiting Mason (1828–1896) compiled collections of songs for primary schoolchildren, with Japanese lyrics and Western melodies, notation, and instrumental accompaniment. They viewed this approach as a "middle course . . . blending Eastern and Western music [to] establish a kind of music which is suitable for the Japan of today."[21] This "middle course" presaged other deliberate attempts to "blend" Western and Japanese musical traditions to create a "national music" (including movements to indigenize jazz), but few artists from the traditional music sphere were included in the policymaking process. The result, William Malm contends, was "the training of generations of Japanese youth to a harmonically oriented music [that] has created a series of mental blocks which shut out the special musical potentials of traditional styles."[22] By the time the first generation of Japanese jazzmen started their training, they were virtually alienated from the traditional art music of their forebears. Future efforts by Japanese composers and jazz musicians to incorporate elements from traditional musics (hōgaku) required extensive study for which their backgrounds in Western music had not prepared them.

Aside from the military and the schools, most Japanese commoners were exposed to Western music through advertising.[23] As businesses increasingly relied on live bands to attract customers in the early twentieth century, commercial bands not only offered employment to professional musicians (at a time when there were no permanent symphony orchestras in Japan), but also exposed many Japanese to Western-style music for the first time. The earliest commercial brass bands, known as jinta (precursors of later chindonya or "ding-dong bands"), walked the streets advertising everything from makeup and toothbrushes to beer and tobacco. Uchida Kōichi's oral history research indicates that several early jazzmen with experience in jinta claimed to have worked for less legitimate enterprises, such as gangster-run street vendors known as tekiya. One early jazz writer described jinta musicians improvising in a manner resembling the "break" in traditional jazz, where the band stops momentarily while a soloist embellishes the music.[24] In this respect they may have resembled the New Orleans brass bands of roughly the same period that eventually evolved into jazz bands. It is unclear, however, whether or not former jinta bandsmen who later studied jazz improvisation felt any sense of comfort or familiarity with the concept.

Jinta started fading from view in the 1910s, following the repression of street activity after the Russo-Japanese War, the financial panic of 1908, and the increasing use of the print media for advertising.[25] They were super-seded by department store youth troupes (*shōnen ongakutai*) and so-called *bandoya* (bands for hire), many of which produced future jazzmen. From the founding of the Mitsukoshi youth troupe in 1909 until the dissipation of such bands in the 1920s, department store music schools provided free training for youths and employed them to perform in or around the stores to attract customers. Many future classical, popular, and jazz musicians graduated from these youth troupes. *Bandoya* performed similar functions but were independent businesses, often run by former military bandsmen, training and providing bands for movie theaters and galas. The department store youth troupes and *bandoya* were an alternative for musically inclined youngsters who lacked both the social standing and the finances to go to elite conservatories such as the Tokyo School of Music.[26] Most of Japan's journeyman musicians—in the classical, jazz, and popular fields—were products of these organizations, and went on to employment in hotel ball-rooms or salon orchestras aboard ocean liners.

The increasingly heavy traffic of musicians of various nationalities across the Pacific in the 1910s was central to the diffusion of American popular song forms such as ragtime and fox-trots.[27] Starting in 1912 the Tōyō Ship-ping Company (TKK) hired salon orchestras to entertain passengers on vessels departing Yokohama and Kōbe for San Francisco, Seattle, Hong Kong, Manila, and Shanghai. When in American ports, Japanese musicians learned as much as they could about the latest American music, attending dance parties and concerts, collecting instruments and sheet music, and receiving instruction in ragtime and dance music directly from American musicians. "Jazz follows the flag," a *New York Times* writer stated. "Ships freighted with jazz—'Made in America'—form the newest product of export to the Orient. Cargoes of jazz are laden on all vessels passing through the Golden Gate. To the Orient they sail, carrying the jazziest song hits, the latest dance steps and the phonograph records, stopping sometimes to un-load some the cargo of choice tunes at Honolulu."[28]

Violinist Hatano Fukutarō (1890–1974) insisted, "I've never had much to do with jazz," but his group was at the forefront of the importation pro-cess.[29] In a 1971 interview he recalled his maiden voyage to San Francisco in 1912:

> The Golden Gate Bridge and the Bay Bridge were not yet there at that time; rather, the broken down buildings and roads were striking and desolate, even though six years had passed since the 1906 earth-quake . . . At the Sherman Clay Music Store, which we had rushed into on the guidance of the head of the [Tōyō] music school, we were thrilled

when we saw scores and instruments from America. Since, by chance, the store clerk was a bassoonist in the San Francisco Symphony, he knew about salon dance music, and divided the songs that were popular at the time into "dinner music" and "dance music" and taught us how to play them. Even now that sixty years have passed, I can't forget that kindness.[30]

Throughout the 1910s and 1920s ocean liner bands continued to bring written scores and recordings into Japan, occasionally performing the new music for Japanese audiences at classy hotels in Yokohama and Kōbe. In the years before transnational entertainment conglomerates and their formalized distribution networks, this more informal route laid the groundwork for the widespread diffusion and acceptance of American popular music in Japan and the rest of Asia.

Another trend of tremendous significance to the diffusion of jazz was the booming popularity of social dance. Following the Rokumeikan party of 1883, music and social dancing had remained the province of foreigners and the Japanese elite until well into the twentieth century. But with economic prosperity and the rise of a new urban middle class in the 1910s, "music was liberated from the salons to the streets." Domestic production of musical instruments, phonographs, and recordings soared, and remained relatively steady in spite of the postwar recession.[31] By the middle of the Taishō period (1912–1926) "dance fever" (*dansu netsu*) had struck Japan's urban middle class. Social dances for couples, such as the one-step, two-step, and fox-trot, became necessary skills for the upscale "modernite." "The Japanese are jazzing by day and by night," a *Metronome* correspondent reported.

> The "foreign craze" trips merrily on its way through the sacred traditions of Nipponese etiquette and of the home. . . . Girls and young married women manage the intricate steps of the jazz in tabi and zorii with surprising ease.
>
> . . . Foreign dancing undoubtedly has come to stay. It is much in evidence in Tokio [sic] and has spread into Yokohama, Osaka and Kobe, although not to any extent outside of the big cities. The majority of dancers are foreign-trained students, who got the spirit of the dance by contact with Western life. What will be the effect upon national life is a problem occupying many thinking Japanese. In the main they approve of it—with reservations. That is, they approve of the social principle it involves, of bringing young people together in a more informal way.
>
> . . . When one considers that almost every plane of thought is thus reversed [in Japan], it is surprising how well the alien toe has been made to trip. . . . [Still] it must never be forgotten that while the enter-

prising progressives of Nippon imitate us they do so only to get the gold of our civilization and add it to their own. . . . They are always and eternally Japanese, and in their hearts feel the same superiority over us as we do toward them.

Another American writer, Burnet Hershey, toured the world to report on jazz in distant climes from Cairo to Calcutta, from Bangkok to Beijing. His account of jazz in the Japanese capital region around the time of the 1923 Kantō Earthquake is worth quoting at length:

> Japan really is the crossroads where jazz ends and ragtime begins. . . . I was in Yokohama only a few hours when I heard the call of the West—a jazz band tuning up, or getting out of tune, in the Grand Hotel. In this most European of Japanese cities there are half a dozen jazz bands. One European troupe, led by an ex-U.S. Navy bandmaster, dispenses ragtime at the leading hotel. The others are Japanese groups who, with that marvelous faculty for imitating the Occident, manage to organize some semblance of jazz.
>
> Here the youth of Japan toddle with their favorite Miss Yaki-San or Mlle. Cherry-Blossom, arrayed in her finest kimono and gaudiest obi, her black hair greasier than ever. In the picturesque background of paper lanterns such as only the Japanese in Japan can hang, and in a setting of doll-house, papier-maché balconies and toy gardens, they glide and tango. I watched them and marveled at their adroitness, their natural grace. I danced with a little cat-eyed butterfly in a gold-red kimono embroidered with dragons and bats. Broadway would have raved about her.
>
> One thing I found astonishing—how, with all the quick steps required by jazz, these dancers, men and women alike, were able to keep on their sandals, caught to their feet only by the insertion of the sandal-band. Not a slipper was lost.
>
> Japanese jazz bands are veritable orchestras. The Japanese evidently figure if a four-piece band can make so much noise how much better and more American is it if the number of pieces are multiplied. So we find a twenty-five piece orchestra attempting jazz in Tsurumi.
>
> In Tokio [sic], at the Imperial Hotel, destroyed by fire a few weeks ago, they held three dances a week. A Japanese band supplied the music there for a while, substituting one atrocity after another for what they call "jahss." The Americans call them "joss" bands.[32]

Hiraoka Shizuko, the wife of a Tokyo restaurateur who had become enamored of social dancing during a tour of Europe and America, capitalized on the craze by opening Japan's first commercial dance hall, the Kagetsuen, in Yokohama's Tsurumi district in March 1920.[33] As the decade progressed, social dancing at hotel ballrooms and commercial dance halls became much more popular and accessible throughout Japan's major cities, with Ōsaka becoming the unchallenged locus of "dance fever" in the mid-twenties. Ōsaka establishments such as Cottage set national trends, such as the so-called "ticket system," whereby male customers brought tickets for a whirl with a professional female "taxi dancer" (Russian or Japanese) employed by the dance hall.[34]

The popularity of social dance among Japanese urbanites and the advent of the commercial dance hall were of primary importance to the introduction and popularization of jazz in Japan, for in the interwar period social dance and jazz were practically synonymous. The music prospered and suffered as social dance did. Moreover, it was in the commercial dance hall that the jazz community—musician and audience—came together. Early jazz was a participatory music, in which the spontaneous interaction between performer and listener (or dancer) contributed to the shape of the music.[35] In interwar Japan, the only sanctioned place where this crucial interaction could occur was the commercial dance hall. As the 1920s progressed and local governments imposed boundaries on live jazz performance and social dance, musicians and dancers were confined to the dance halls. We may rightly locate the "origins" of jazz in Japan in the commercial dance hall, where the jazz community developed its own separate identity.

But there were also individuals who noodled around with the new music informally in their parlors before building up the courage to play in public. Among these was Kikuchi Shigeya, whose encounter with a Chicago jazz band is the earliest known by a Japanese. A hunger to learn more about jazz inspired another trip to the United States in 1924, when he purchased a collection of Jelly Roll Morton piano transcriptions and caught performances by Duke Ellington and Red Nichols.[36] Kikuchi shared his passion with some Keiō schoolmates, the sons of Baron Masuda Tarō and heirs to the Mitsui *zaibatsu* (corporate conglomerate), at whose Gotenyama mansion American guests and music were fixtures. The Masudas studied jazz by comparing homemade recordings of their own performances to American records. Kikuchi, himself struggling to learn jazz piano, reported that the Masudas' jazz performance was quite advanced: "They were playing real American jazz, the [Masuda] girls were singing as a trio, and the piano performances by Yoshinobu and Sadanobu were good for the time."[37] Bassist Kami Kyōsuke (1902–1981) wrote that the Masuda brothers (Katsunobu, Yoshinobu, Takanobu, Tomonobu, and Sadanobu—the "five Nobus") started playing jazz after the 1923 Kantō Earthquake, when Katsunobu returned from his studies at the University of Pennsylvania "with a trombone and a whistle." Around 1925 the Masudas befriended Dōmoto Takaji, a Japanese-American Amherst College graduate and heir to a "canned fruit" company, who played trumpet with a band of foreigners residing in Yokohama and Tokyo. Dōmoto lived in the Masuda mansion and coached three of the Masuda brothers in a dance band known as the Collegians (later the Keiō Red and Blue Jazz Band), which played parties in the American embassy, the Morrison House in Kamakura, and the Yokohama New Grand Hotel.[38] Although none of the Masudas pursued careers in music, Kikuchi praised them as "pioneers": "Since at the time it took several years to learn this much about jazz technique, I make special mention [of the Masuda brothers] as the pioneers of Japanese jazz, especially jazz piano, who probably started studying at the same time or earlier than I."[39]

Some historians have made much of the idea that the members of Japan's highest social class embraced jazz, the music of America's lowest social class. The irony is appealing, if perhaps overstated. There were a few amateur and collegiate bands in the capital region—Keiō's Red and Blue band and Hōsei University's Luck and Sun Jazz Band are the best known—whose personnel consisted of "college pals and good-for-nothing sons of the wealthy."[40] But in the early and middle twenties the real center of jazz activity was unquestionably western Japan, particularly Ōsaka and Kōbe, and the musicians who were most zealous about jazz were the products of the unambiguously nonelite department store youth troupes and *bandoya*. In this Kansai region jazz was not the province of the elite, but rather of the burgeoning urban middle class who supported and patronized the prosperous dance hall and cafe industries. In Kansai we find yet another strand of the narrative of jazz's popularization in Japan, to which the involvement of the capital's elite was peripheral.

"Japan's Chicago"—Ōsaka Jazz

Most historians attribute Ōsaka's cultural prominence in the 1920s to the effects of the devastating Kantō Earthquake of 1 September 1923, which thoroughly leveled the Tokyo entertainment districts of Shinjuku and Asakusa, where most professional musicians worked in movie houses, theaters, and the popular Asakusa Opera.[41] But this is only a partial explanation at best, for it virtually ignores the Kansai region's rich tradition as a major cultural center since the Edo period: Ōsaka, after all, was where the great puppet plays of Chikamatsu Monzaemon (1653–1725) were written and performed, and though political authority had since shifted eastward, Ōsaka's persistent importance as a commercial and industrial center guaranteed its

continued status as a locus of entertainment and cultural pursuits. Moreover, the region was much more cosmopolitan in the early twentieth century than is usually acknowledged, due to the heavy traffic of passenger
liners from around the world. The destruction of Tokyo and Yokohama in
1923 and the subsequent westward exodus of artists, writers, intellectuals,
and musicians may have hastened Ōsaka's rise as the capital of mass entertainment in the 1920s, but it did not cause it. As the center of American-
inspired mass entertainment culture, Ōsaka—"the America of Japan," in
the disparaging words of Ōya Sōichi (1900–1970)—was ripe for jazz.[42]

Musicians who fled the ravaged capital did so for a compelling reason:
there was an unprecedented demand for their services in the movie theaters, dance halls, and cafes of Ōsaka's Dōtonbori entertainment district, an
"architectural cocktail" that provided fertile soil from which Japan's early
jazz community sprouted. "Dōtonbori slumbered during the day to awaken
at dusk with a kaleidoscopic display of neon lights and a mad crush of
pleasure seekers."[43] Dubbed by a 1923 survey of leisure patterns of Ōsaka's
"highest class entertainment spot"—"bourgeois" as opposed to "proletarian" Sennichimae—the district boasted the "most advanced arts," and
was a place where "the true popular culture of a new age" flourished. Its
pleasures were trendy and cosmopolitan, and well beyond the reach of most
Ōsakans' entertainment budgets. "The average joes hang around the fronts
of Dōtonbori's big theaters," the survey reported, "just looking at the decep-
tive high-art posters, then after taking some pleasure from them, pass on
through to Sennichimae, where they demand cheap and actual amusement."[44] Good-time "modern boys and girls" were drawn to the district's
renowned Five Theaters and its ubiquitous dance halls and cafes (which,
although modeled on the French *café*, were more closely akin to what we
know as "bars").[45] Actually, cafes and dance halls were often indistinguishable: following the example set by the Naniwa bar Cottage, Ōsaka cafe
owners remodeled their businesses as dance halls, creating such legendary
early jazz spots as Paulista, Union, and Parisian; and when the dance halls
were banned by city ordinance in 1927, several reverted back to cafes. As
competition grew increasingly fierce (between 1924 and 1927 the city of
Ōsaka alone boasted twenty dance halls), proprietors of such establishments
abandoned recorded music in favor of the visual spectacle and high-decibel
appeal of live bands. On these bandstands Japan's first jazz musicians struggled with the music that was taking the world by storm. Hattori Ryōichi
remembered Dōtonbori as Japan's "jazz mecca."

> At that time, Union, Bijin-za, Paulista, and the Akadama Eatery that
> came into Dōtonbori, took the initiative by hiring Filipino jazz bands

[to play] cafe jazz. Cafes progressed to cabarets and music halls, and at every door was written in big letters "Jazz Performances Nightly," with the principal repertoire being "Song of Araby," "My Blue Heaven," "Titina," "Mon Paris," and "Kimi koishi."

At that time, Nanri Fumio and Taniguchi Matashi, who were sixteen or seventeen, came to Dōtonbori from the Takashimaya Youth Band, and joined the best bands in the dance halls and cabarets. Even today these young pioneers of Japanese jazz are topics of conversation.

On summer nights Dōtonbori would be crowded for the "ship boarding," in which movie stars and stage actors appearing at the Five Theaters would come down to parade through Dōtonbori. Cheers would rise up from both banks [of the Dōtonbori river] and from the bridge, jazz would erupt, cheering boats of beautiful cafe waitresses would compete, and dances and shows on the water along with fireworks would commence. . . . [T]he river would be painted in five colors with the neon lights. . . . I want to say that Dōtonbori, which raised many jazzmen, was truly the Japanese jazz mecca.[46]

A half-hour's train ride from Ōsaka, the port city of Kōbe boasted plenty of its own entertainment facilities, many catering to the city's foreign residents. American bands occasionally played "one-night stands" at Kōbe's magnificent Oriental Hotel while in port, but Kōbe's top resident bands were from the Philippines. In the 1910s and 1920s Filipino bands were the most in demand for ocean liner gigs, and contributed much to the diffusion of American popular and jazz music in Asian port cities such as Shanghai, Manila, and Hong Kong. "Filipino orchestras are the interpreters of jazz on the Pacific Ocean liners," the *New York Times* reported. "Where music is concerned, the Filipinos are known as the Italians of the East. Add their own barbaric musical strain—a blend of Oriental and Spanish 'ear culture'—and you get an idea of their adeptness with the torturous instruments of jazz." Several Japanese musicians have asserted that the first jazz they ever heard was performed by Filipino bands in Kōbe.[47] Saxophonist and composer Hattori Ryōichi (1907–1993), who led a band of Filipinos called the Manila Red Hot Stompers in the mid-1920s, testified to the influence of Filipino jazzmen: "They were weak readers, but their musical sense and performance technique were amazing. It could be said that they were the 'parents' who raised Japanese jazzmen." Maeno Kōzō (1897–1977), an early jazz saxophonist, recounted his efforts to learn the art of "faking" (improvising) from Filipino jazzmen:

Around that time, when I couldn't improvise easily, there were no chord names yet, and I did not understand theoretically why one "fakes." What I relied on were jazz records and I imitated those as best I could. It was a period of frustration because I couldn't understand the point of receiving instruction and a theoretical explanation from Filipino performers considering the language handicap. It was later, around 1929 or 1930, that improvisation gradually began to be performed by Japanese musicians.[48]

There appear to be virtually no in-depth studies of the processes by which Filipinos were acculturated to American popular and dance music in the early twentieth century ("Didn't everyone learn from American records?" asks star clarinetist Raymond Conde, who came to Japan in 1934 to study medicine before embarking on a successful musical career yet downplays the influence of his countrymen on Japan). Nonetheless, Filipinos retained throughout the twentieth century a reputation in Pacific Asia as premier entertainers. Japan's earliest jazzmen certainly regarded musicians from the Philippines as the closest link to America that they could hope to have in the 1920s.

While cities in postwar Europe and even the USSR attracted substantial numbers of black and white American jazz performers,[49] direct contact between American and Japanese jazzmen was decidedly rare in the 1920s. There are a few sketchy accounts of American jazz bands in Japan in the 1920s. American businessman William Kildoyle—who, in the words of one newspaper, played jazz piano "like a barefoot Negro"—led a band called the Tokyo Jazz Hounds and performed with a banjoist on a very early radio broadcast in 1925. Although the newspaper predicted that "because this is the very first jazz band in Japan, [Kildoyle]'s name will certainly occupy a quite important position in Japanese music history,"[50] he has been all but forgotten in the oral record. There is little more information about another band known either as the Dixie Minstrels or the Original Dixielanders. Filipino clarinetist Vidi Conde claimed that the Original Dixielanders toured Japan in 1926–27, performing traditional jazz standards such as "Tiger Rag," "Twelfth Street Rag," and "Shine." "Most of the Japanese were stupefied," he recounted, "and because they didn't clap or do anything, we could only think, 'these are people who have no idea what they're seeing or hearing.' " The Dixie Minstrels, a band from Hawai'i that recorded for Nippon Columbia in the late twenties, had a lineup identical to that of the Original Dixielanders. Led by trumpeter Bob Hill, the Minstrels toured Japan with "tap dancers and rollerskaters" and performed at an exposition at Tokyo's Ueno Park in March 1928, offering many Japanese their first taste of New Orleans-style jazz.[51]

Trumpeter Obata Mitsuyuki (1909–1960) and reedist Ashida Mitsuru (1910–1967) recalled a more extended and influential encounter with an

American pianist during their tenure with the Tenkatsu Ichiza vaudevillian magic troupe. Today this musician is known only by the Japanese phonetic approximation of his name, "Okunesu," but he is believed to have come to Japan in 1925 as a member of a four- or five-piece Chicago-style jazz band ("a true Dixieland band," in bassist Kami Kyōsuke's estimation) recruited by the Tenkatsu troupe during a U.S. tour.[52] Ashida Mitsuru was playing at the Zebra Club in Kōbe's Mitsunomiya district when he was recruited to join the Tenkatsu jazz band soon after the troupe's return to Japan in April 1925:

> That was around the time that the Tenkatsu Ichiza returned from its American tour and brought five American jazz musicians, but unfortunately all of them left Okunesu behind and returned to their country . . . Okunesu asked [pianist] Kikuchi Hiroshi to assemble some Japanese jazz musicians. I don't know the details [after that], but we formed one band with Obata Mitsuyuki (trumpet), me (alto sax), Kawano Masaaki (tenor sax), Katō Kazuo (drums), a Mr. Nara (violin), and Kikuchi Hiroshi (piano), and went on tour with Tenkatsu Ichiza. Okunesu was a Chicago-style musician, and taught us about Chicago jazz. Then we became familiar with jazz performance methods, harmonic progressions, improvisation, rhythm, and how to take "breaks". . . . Okunesu's teachings about jazz performance were very helpful. Okunesu coached the band and appeared as a featured soloist. Sometime in 1926, at the peak of the Tenkatsu show's popularity, he returned to the U.S.[53]

Okunesu's pupils Obata and Ashida, who could claim a closer connection to the source of jazz than most of their colleagues, would eventually perform in Japan's earliest professional jazz bands, including that of the most vocal claimant to the coveted title of "father of Japanese jazz." Ida Ichirō (1894–1972), a violinist, banjoist, and bandleader, was certainly the most aggressive in asserting his own role in popularizing jazz in Japan. His jazz autobiography (serialized in the periodical *Variety* in the late 1930s) recounts years of struggle to win recognition for a music that was despised by respectable society.[54] Whether Ida was the visionary he claimed to be is open to debate; nevertheless, even those of his contemporaries whom Ida mortally offended credited him with the "professionalization" of jazz in the early twenties. It is not clear what distinguished his Laughing Stars and Cherryland Dance Orchestra from other dance bands of the period—his repertoire contained none of the traditional jazz standards associated with New Orleans and Chicago, nor did he devote much attention to improvisation—so it may be the case that referring to his groups as the "first jazz bands" in Japan is merely convenient.

Ida started his musical career at age sixteen when he entered the Mitsu-koshi Youth Band in 1910, and spent several years in dance and salon orchestras, including the Kagetsuen dance hall's first house band and ocean liner bands. Ida wrote that he and his bandmates received "coaching," at company expense, from the bandmaster at the St. Francis Hotel in San Francisco, learning such "jazz numbers" as "Dardanella" and "La Vida." In March 1922 Ida joined the Takarazuka Revue, an all-female musical theater that remains popular with theatergoers. Ida commenced his jazz studies with a rehearsal band of seven bandmates and received permission to pre-sent the new music during intermissions at Takarazuka performances. But when the rest of the orchestra threatened to resign because they "couldn't work with fellows playing vulgar, non-music like that jazz," Ida resigned in the spring of 1923, stung by his "narrow-minded," "self-righteous," and "cowardly" colleagues.[55]

By May 1923 Ida and three comrades (Takami Tomoyoshi, Yamada Kei-ichi, and Iwanami Momotarō) formed the Laughing Stars. The band lived and rehearsed in a rental house, with the sponsorship of Kōbe's Kitao Mu-sic Shop. During its short lifespan, the band performed at dance parties throughout Kōbe and Ōsaka, with Ida exhorting his sidemen to play like the foreign dance bands they heard at Kōbe's Oriental Hotel. The band stayed together a scant two months. Ida contended that the group disbanded in July 1923 for economic reasons (he claimed to have sold his piano to pay his sidemen their shares), but Takami attributed the Stars' dissolution to more personal reasons: things soured when Ida married a woman with whom his sideman Yamada was in love.[56]

As he drifted between Tokyo and Ōsaka in the mid-twenties, Ida all but gave up on jazz: "Having lost all hope in my future with jazz music, I sold or gave away all of my cherished jazz scores and . . . felt relieved."[57] But by 1925 he had assembled a jazz "attraction band" that performed at theaters and amusement parks throughout the Kansai, and which eventually became the Saturday night house band at the Paulista dance hall in Ōsaka. When the Paulista's owner, a gangster named Yoneyama, threatened Ida with a sword for switching sidemen, the group fled to the Union dance hall, where it adopted the name the Cherryland Dance Orchestra around 1926.

In the absence of recordings, it is difficult to determine what the Cherry-land Dance Orchestra sounded like. Japanese historians have rather casu-ally labeled it a "Dixieland band,"[58] but the band's repertoire consisted almost exclusively of hit tunes by the self-styled "King of Jazz," Paul White-man, which represented a distinctive stylistic shift away from the wildly rhythmical and polyphonic, chaotic order of New Orleans and Chicago jazz. Saxophonist Maeno Kōzō claimed that "when we were at Union we listened to the Paul Whiteman band's records every day and got a feeling for them, and we studied jazz techniques such as vibrato." In my interview with Cherryland pianist Taira Shigeo, he repeatedly insisted that the band "did not improvise at all," but rather played from written arrangements and took turns noodling around with a song's melody. One jazz critic (who admittedly never actually *saw* the band) surmises that Cherryland solos were not examples of "perfect adlibbing," but what little liberties the soloists did take were "epoch-making."[59] Again, it is not clear what distinguished Ida's band from its competitors. It may very well be the case that other bands (particularly Maeno Kōzō's early Ōsaka groups) were of comparable ability and stature, but have been lost in the oral record amid Ida Ichirō's self-aggrandizing bluster.

The Cherryland Dance Orchestra's profitably year-long tenure at Union coincided with the zenith of the Kansai dance craze in mid-twenties. Commercial dance halls were almost always packed with customers, even when the halls raised entrance fees to ¥1. The phenomenon might have expanded (in early 1927 there were over fifty requests for new dance hall permits), but city and prefectural ordinances effectively shut down the Ōsaka halls in 1927.[60] The immediate provocation for the imposition of constraints was the failure of the dance halls to honor the period of mourning for the Taishō emperor, whose death was announced on Christmas Day in 1926. By order of the Home Ministry (Naimushō), New Year's parties were to be canceled and all music emanating from movie theaters, dance halls, and cafes was to be suspended for a six-day period.[61] The Ōsaka dance halls obeyed the order, but wasted no time reopening when the official mourning period ended. Their haste to resume what was already considered to be questionable activity aroused the ire of city officials, who on 25 March 1927 enacted severe restrictions: all guests had to register their names and addresses; guests could not sit with the "taxi dancers"; no alcohol was permitted; and no dating outside the hall was allowed.

When enforcement of the regulations proved difficult, the city elected to shut down the dance halls for good on 26 December 1927. The announcement received fairly little attention outside of the jazz community—it earned only a brief mention on page five of the *Ōsaka Asahi*'s Christmas edition—indicating that jazz and social dance were still of marginal concern to most Ōsakans. "It has come to pass that Ōsaka's two dance halls, Union and Paulista, will finally extinguish their gaudy appearances, except for the twenty-fifth [Christmas Day]," the paper reported coolly. "Union . . . will shut down voluntarily, . . . and from the twenty-sixth will become a bar, retaining its employed dancers and musicians, while Paulista is currently conferring with its employees."[62]

The Ōsaka regulations represent the beginning of a series of official actions that would attempt to hamper jazz activity throughout the interwar period. Ōsaka's municipal government did not target jazz music specifically, but rather the activity of social dancing, which involved the very public physical contact of the sexes. Still, the dance hall ban had an effect on musicians similar to that of the Kantō Earthquake four years earlier: loss of employment, resulting in an eastward exodus. Several dance halls opened along the Hanshin route from Ōsaka to Kōbe to fill the void. But many musicians, including Ida Ichirō, decided to return to the reconstructed capital, where a new urban culture hospitable to jazz was emerging from the ruins of the earthquake.

Of course, what was "new" to Tokyo was not necessarily new in other regions of Japan. "Modern" entertainments such as dance halls, cafes, musical revues, and jazz bands, all but unknown in the capital region during the post-earthquake reconstruction phase, had established histories in western Japan. The famous Ginza bars and cafes came to be celebrated in dozens of novels, popular songs, and movies, though they were often dismissed by connoisseurs as gaudy clones of the older Ōsaka establishments. Novelist Tanizaki Jun'ichirō (1886–1965), whose contempt for Tokyo is legendary, noted: "To be sure, Osaka cafes with their noisy bands are somewhat vulgar; but no one could possibly call these cramped little places [in the Ginza] in the smallest degree elegant." . . . "The Osaka kind may be vulgar," he added, "but they do at least require a certain investment. These Tokyo ones do not . . . such places have sprung up like bamboo shoots after a rain." Tanizaki was one of the few writers, artists, and intellectuals who, having fled Tokyo for Ōsaka following the 1923 disaster, did not return to the capital.[63] Following the Ōsaka dance hall ordinances of 1927, the musicians who had learned jazz in the Kansai joined the stream of artistic talent that returned to the capital.

Jazz historians like to say that Ida Ichirō and the Cherryland Dance Orchestra, penniless and looking like "miserable beggars" when they arrived at Tokyo station, "brought" jazz from Ōsaka to Tokyo in April 1928.[64] Cherryland was indeed the toast of Tokyo's popular music community, playing a two-week-long, extended engagement at Mitsukoshi Hall for capacity crowds, and later appearing at the Asakusa Electric Hall as the Shōchiku Jazz Band. Amateur musicians who had been playing dance parties in the capital region for several years were reportedly spellbound.[65] But it would be misleading to attribute Tokyo's fascination with jazz to the influence of one band. Rather than *starting* a trend, Cherryland capitalized on the general growth of Tokyo's popular music scene, as reflected in the proliferation of commercial dance halls and the emerging commercial power of a hit-oriented recording industry. Besides, the band's existence was too short to make much of an impact: by the summer of 1928, the Cherryland musicians had gone their separate ways, attracted by more profitable opportunities at every turn. Ida blamed his pianist Taira Shigeo for leading a mutiny that took the Cherryland sidemen to Asakusa's Tameike Dance Hall,[66] but Taira insisted in our interview that he accepted Tameike's invitation with Ida's blessing, and that his bandmates simply wanted to tag along and so deserted their leader. Ida attempted to keep the band going by recruiting musicians such as star trumpeter Nanri Fumio (1910–1975) from Ōsaka—no one in backwards Tokyo could play his music—but in 1929 he quit bandleading for good and joined Polydor Records as house composer and arranger.

Ida entered the record business at an opportune moment. At the end of the 1920s, there were several major recording companies in Japan, the most prominent of which—Polydor, Nippon Columbia, and Nippon Victor—were supported by foreign capital. These companies marketed import records of classical and popular music from America and Europe, but in the late 1920s they initiated domestic production of popular music and created the Japanese song genre known as *ryūkōka* (literally "popular song"). One style of *ryūkōka* was the "jazz song" (*jazu songu*), which Larry Richards defines loosely as "Western-style songs with accompaniment by Western instruments": either American Tin Pan Alley tunes with lyrics translated into Japanese or original Western-style songs by Japanese composers and lyricists.[67] The early formula for jazz songs was established with the simultaneous release of "My Blue Heaven"/"Song of Araby" by two record companies in 1928. In a scenario unimaginable in our day of copyright laws and exclusive contracts, Nippon Columbia and Nippon Victor released the same coupling of songs by the same vocalist, Futamura Teiichi, at roughly the same time.[68] Both versions were enormous hits and set the standard for future cover versions of American songs with Japanese lyrics. Representative jazz song recordings featured polished arrangements, improvisational restraint, and lightly accented rhythms. Yet within that formula all types of North and Latin American and European popular styles—Tin Pan Alley tunes, "symphonic jazz," tango, rumba, *chansons*, and Hawaiian music—were fair game. Standard jazz band instrumentation was often supplemented with shimmering vibraphones, Hawaiian slack-key guitars, and violin sections. Jazz song lyrics were invariably romantic, impressionistic, and maudlin (thus presaging modern *enka*), with "apparently no sequence of thought and sentiment between the lines."[69]

Neither the warm reception accorded to the Cherryland Dance Orchestra nor the popularity of the first jazz song records prepared anyone for the sensational and controversial record "Tokyo March" ("Tokyo kōshinkyoku," 1929), the anthem for the modernist generation. The release of the first sound motion picture (an American musical short entitled *Marching On*) in 1929 and the popularity of erotic musical productions such as the Asakusa and Takarazuka revues contributed to the increased visibility of jazz in Japan. Yet the simple mention of the word *jazz* in the lyrics of a song as sensational and controversial as "Tokyo March"—which sold over three hundred thousand copies in its first year—was perhaps the primary impetus propelling jazz into the national spotlight.[70]

> Dancing to jazz, liquor in the wee hours.
> And with the dawn a flood of tears for the dancer . . .
> Vast Tokyo is too small for love,
> Fashionable Asakusa, secret trysts . . .
> Long-haired Marxist boys, ephemeral love of the moment . . .
> Shall we see a movie, shall we drink tea, or rather shall we run away on the Odawara Express?

Composed by Nakayama Shinpei with lyrics by Saijō Yaso, a poet and professor of French literature at Waseda University, "Tokyo March" featured a jazzy rhythm track arranged by Ida Ichirō and the vocals of the conservatory-trained Satō Chiyako. Nippon Victor ingeniously promoted the record by distributing one thousand free copies to bars and cafes throughout Tokyo.[71] Targeting these establishments was a brilliant marketing strategy, for "the song has a firm grip on the sensational aspect of Tokyo night life," as Uenoda Setsuo observed, "which is an everlasting source of nightmare for parents."[72] The song's visibility (or audibility) was increased through an early example of "tie-in" marketing: the song inspired a serialized novel and became the theme song for a film by renowned director Mizoguchi Kenji.

The beat alone was provocative enough for some people, but lyrical references—"dancing to jazz," "drinking liquor," "rush hour," "ephemeral 'red love' of the moment," romantic trysts—aroused the "profound distrust [of] educational and social workers, policemen and parents." That was the censored version: lyrical references to "long-haired Marxist boys" were snipped out because, following the mass arrest of communists in April 1929, they were a bit *too* timely. The song was banned from airplay on Japan's national radio network, which had already severely limited popular music programming in its broadcast schedule. This action inspired a series of editorials in the *Yomiuri* newspaper about the potentially harmful effects of "Tokyo March" and other popular records, in which lyricist Saijō directly confronted an executive of the JOAK (later NHK) radio network concerning the network's refusal to air the song. The spokesman for JOAK, Iba Takashi, defended the decision as a public obligation to "protect" school kids from the lyrics' immoral influence.[73]

Thus, after years of seething within the entertainment districts of Ōsaka and Kōbe, jazz finally burst into the public consciousness of the nation. The ensuing debates (discussed in greater detail in the next chapter) indicate that issues of public morality and cultural identity were at least as urgent as matters of taste. Jazz was not merely a music to be accepted or reviled, but rather a metaphor for Japan's participation in global cultural trends. The larger issue of whether Japan should allow itself to be engulfed by a wave known alternately as "modernism" or "Americanism" provided the subtext for these discussions. In the meantime, seemingly oblivious to all of this, musicians, entertainers, and entrepreneurs continued to take the music to the people, in the process creating a jazz industry that prospered despite public agitation and economic woes. Drummer Jimmy Harada (1911–1995) reflected that hard times in the "real world" made jazz all the more popular:

> Starting with the New York stock crash in 1929, the world fell into depression, and it's said that there were over three million unemployed people—it got to the point that because of frost damage [to crops], young girls in the Tōhoku [northeastern] region were turned out to sell their bodies. We speak of a Heisei recession [in the 1990s], but it can't compare to the recession of that time. Under these conditions, the reason that the dance halls prospered must be that people forgot the bad times and had some fun for a while. You could say that the times demanded it.
>
> For that reason alone jobs for us performers increased. . . . In 1930 I would go up to Tokyo [with my bandmates] and after working the afternoon at Florida Dance Hall in Akasaka, we'd turn right around and rush back to the Carlton Dance Hall in Yokohama's Bashamichi and work the night.[74]

Historians often attribute the economic crash to the freewheeling careless-ness, frivolity, and public apathy of America's Jazz Age; conversely, in Japan the Jazz Age may very well be attributed to the economic travails of the day.

Japan's Jazz Age

Japan's Jazz Age began just as America's was ending. The year of the stock market crash in America, which in many ways signaled the coda of Fitz-gerald's Jazz Age, was the same year that witnessed Japan's most intense engagement with jazz to date. Owing in large part to the furor over "Tokyo

March," by 1929 jazz was in the headlines, editorials, and literature, and on the radios and turntables in Japan's most fashionable cafes and night spots. The initial media barrage about jazz would soon subside, in part because jazz had in a relatively short time entrenched itself firmly as part of the "soundscape"—or, in Ōya Sōichi's words, the "cacophony"—of modern urban life.[75]

Japan's Jazz Age was a period of intense excitement, prosperity, and institutional and artistic creativity within the jazz community. It was a period in which musicians were in high demand, domestic and imported jazz recordings were widely available, opportunities for travel abroad were numerous, and new institutions—dance halls, jazz coffeehouses, studio and house bands, and a jazz press—appeared. Jazz even provided the soundtrack for Japan's first domestically produced "talkie," *The Madame and the Wife* (1931), the story of a married playwright who gets involved with the "modern girl" next door and her jazz band.[76] But the emerging public profile of the jazz culture was met by increasingly hostile counter-trends: the widening diplomatic rift with the Western world, the growth of nationalist expression in the arts, the expanding imperialist presence in East Asia, and the usurpation of political power from the parties by the military. In other words, the entrenchment of the jazz culture within Japan's mass entertainment industry only added to the tensions of the era and provoked a more virulent response from the music's critics. In the face of these attacks the jazz community demonstrated resilience and resourcefulness, and just kept on dancing.

Dance Hall Days

Throughout most of the interwar period, live jazz band performances were limited almost exclusively to movie theaters and commercial dance halls. But with the advent of talking pictures—a trend bitterly opposed by theater musicians and silent film narrators (*katsuben/benshi*)[77]—dance halls eventually enjoyed a virtual monopoly on live jazz and dance music. This was crucial in two respects: first, in the absence of viable alternative sites for jazz performance, the legal pressures and commercial modus operandi of dance halls determined the ways that the music developed in Japan; second, the association of jazz with an enterprise as controversial as dance halls assured that the "respectable" public would regard the music with suspicion and even antipathy. Public outcries against the scandalous behavior that went on in dance halls spurred police crackdowns, modeled on the Ōsaka ordinances, in several municipalities—and suppression of dance halls necessarily entailed suppression of jazz.

2. With a banner proclaiming "Romantic Night," dancers sway to the sounds of Metropolitan Isawa and His Light Swingers at one of Yokohama's many dance halls in 1933. Photo courtesy of Mainichi Shinbun.

Dance halls' "ticket system" and limited business hours significantly influenced the performance styles of interwar jazz musicians. In addition to the fifty-*sen* admission fee, dance halls sold tickets, each good for one dance with a "taxi dancer." Dancers and musicians alike were motivated by management to keep those tickets circulating. While dancers sold (and received commissions on) ¥2 booklets containing ten tickets, musicians were responsible for playing as many *short* songs as possible, for the more songs they played the more tickets were sold. Whisking through each tune in two to three minutes, bands usually performed between forty and fifty songs before calling it a night at eleven P.M.[78] Needless to say, semiannual contract renewals depended on a band's ability to move tickets as well as dancers.

With brevity thus rewarded, extended "jamming," "stretching out," and improvisation were effectively discouraged in the dance hall context, and the lack of legitimate, alternative after-hour venues inhibited informal jam sessions for Japanese jazzers. Their American counterparts developed the post-gig jam session, at which musicians could experiment and improvise free of commercial demands and dancers' requests. The jam session has been called a jazz musician's "ritual of purification, . . . a self-cleansing by the reaffirmation of his own esthetic values."[79] Such sessions occurred at smaller clubs with permissive managers and flexible hours, but such condi-

3. "Taxi dancers" await ticket-bearing customers at the Ginza Dance Hall, Tokyo, September 1933. This image suggests not only the massive scale dance hall operations could assume, but the strict regulations governing them: city ordinances proscribed dancers from fraternizing with customers and mandated physical separation. In theory, a three-minute whirl with one of these women was strictly business. Photo courtesy of Mainichi Shinbun.

tions were virtually absent in Japan in the twenties and thirties. According to saxophonist Nagao Masashi, what is now known as "adlibbing" was called "faking" back then, and entailed little more than selectively plagiarizing favorite licks from records or from foreign visitors such as alto saxophonist Tommy Misman. A few talented players—trumpeter Nanri Fumio, trombonist Taniguchi Matashi, Ashida Mitsuru, guitarist Tsunoda Takashi, and Filipino émigrés Raymond Conde and Francisco "Kiko" Reyes (1906–1993)—developed confident, inspired solo voices in spite of these conditions, but they were exceptions in a music industry in which improvisational prowess was commendable yet by no means obligatory. In short, the legal constraints and economic demands entailed in dance hall work shaped decisively the form and content of jazz performances in Japan.

The symbiosis between jazz and social dance also had ramifications for public perceptions of the music. The Ōsaka ordinances of 1926 and 1927 made nationwide headlines and significantly established the parameters of later discourses on public morality. However, initially Ōsaka's dance hall ban had the immediate effect of stimulating the proliferation of dance halls elsewhere. While some Ōsaka entrepreneurs complied by reverting their dance halls back to cafes, other simply stepped outside the city limits or to surrounding prefectures (Kyōto, Hyōgo, and Nara) and built new ones. Customers and musicians followed in droves. "It is still the case that dance halls are not allowed in Ōsaka," Kitao Ryōnosuke wrote in his 1932 book *Modern Ōsaka*. "However, anywhere in Ōsaka, if you mention the name of a hall, right away a taxi will run you toward the Hanshin National Railway [connecting Ōsaka and Kōbe]. That is how prevalent dance halls are along the rail line in Hyōgo [prefecture]." He counted as many as five halls between Kuise and Nishinomiya, each catering to specialized clienteles of "gentlemen," students, and "professionals." He even characterized one place in Nishinomiya as "family-oriented." With after-hours jamming essentially proscribed, night after night Kansai musicians and dancers apparently made their final hour together as memorable as possible. Kitao remarked that dance halls did not really feel like dance halls until the wee hours. "At eight o'clock, a ticket good for one dance, which up to now had been ten *sen*, skyrockets to twenty. . . . Bodies joined, the time has come to inhale the scent of face powder." Closing was at midnight, but "on summer nights when it really gets going, when one can really dance, when the real dance hall experience occurs, is the one or two hours from around ten or eleven o'clock [until closing]."[80]

Jazz and social dance obviously did not disappear in Kansai as a result of the Ōsaka proscription, yet nevertheless, significant numbers of dance hall proprietors, musicians, dancers, and dance instructors abandoned Kansai altogether for the newly rebuilt capital region,[81] thereby rekindling a social dance craze that the earthquake had all but interrupted. The Kagetsuen in Yokohama was razed in the disaster, so in the mid-twenties the dance-mad in the Tokyo area settled for dance lessons or private parties with recorded music. They also congregated at several dozen neon-lit watering holes known as *chabuya* ("chop shops") in Yokohama's Honmoku district.[82] These pleasure palaces, originally the exclusive play spots of Yokohama's foreign residents, indulged every imaginable physical pleasure, with food, drink, rooms (and women) for rent, and recorded music for sing-alongs and dancing—imagine a restaurant, tavern, nightclub, *karaoke*, love hotel, and bordello all under one roof, a one-stop Dionysian fantasy. Jimmy Harada recalled "expending his youth" in *chabuya*, and Uchida Kōichi characterizes them as favorite after-hours hangouts for jazz musicians and affluent Tokyo playboys. For a time *chabuya* figured prominently in the popular arts: they provided an erotic setting for Murata Minoru's 1924 Nikkatsu film *Night Tales of Honmoku*, starring the vampish Sakai Yoneko; a *chabuya* woman was the model for Tanizaki Jun'ichirō's vixen Naomi in his serialized novel *A Fool's Love*; and the 1937 hit "Separation Blues" was conceived in a *chabuya*. Less welcome attention came in 1931 when a League of Nations Inspection Committee investigating the international sale of women paid Honmoku a visit.[83]

People with a keener interest in *dancing* were sated in the late 1920s when a glut of new commercial dance halls opened in the Tokyo area. In other cities, as well, the popularity of dance halls eventually surpassed that of more traditional forms of entertainment: in order to compete with the modern "erotic service" offered by dance hall girls and cafe waitresses, even geisha added tangos and fox-trots to their list of artistic accomplishments. "With their traditional Shimada-style coiffures jiggling, [so-called *dansu geisha*] were wildly popular as they tangoed with their equally modern customers in Pontochō."[84] While many Japanese decried the decline of indigenous debaucheries, one American spectator sniffed that it was all for the better:

> The whole geisha business ought to be done away with, as it is a menace to the home. Whether the geisha be moral or immoral she is in the position of the "other woman," and one trained to be amusing at that, which puts the home-making wife at a disadvantage. Therefore it would seem the part of wisdom for the intelligent Madame Kimono to learn to jazz with her husband and his friends, and not to leave the important business of entertainment to a professional class.[85]

The prediction that social dancing would promote couples going out together proved to be groundless, for "nice girls" and "good wives" did not go to dance halls—why should they, when the dance halls provided female partners for the men anyway?

For a while, as "dance fever" became ever more contagious, it must have seemed that Tokyo was remaking itself in Ōsaka's image. Ōya and Tanizaki both noted the "Ōsaka-ization of Tokyo,"[86] and like the Ginza cafes that Tanizaki scorned as pale imitations of the Western version, some of Tokyo's first dance halls were merely transplants from the Kansai. Ōsaka's famous Union Dance Hall opened a Tokyo branch in 1927 in Ningyō-chō, celebrating with a Christmas party attended by dignitaries and celebrities of stage and screen. House band drummer Izumi Kimio, himself an émigré from Kōbe, recalled the easterners' backwardness: "There were still a lot of dancers who couldn't dance well, so [saxophonist] Takami Tomoyoshi, who was good at it, coached them step by step during the intermission, and became real popular with the women."[87] Of course, as the dance halls migrated east the suspicions surrounding them tagged behind: police who issued a permit to Yawata Kiyoshi, owner of the Nichibei ("Japan-America"), strongly advised that he refrain from labeling his establishment a "dance hall."[88] Naturally he ignored this advice, recognizing perhaps that the dance hall's precarious respectability was part of its draw.

These were the fat days when, in spite of the Depression, dance halls were a relatively safe investment. A survey published in a dance magazine in 1937 recorded thirty-nine major halls outside of Tokyo (not to mention seventeen in Japanese colonial territories abroad), from Chiba, Yokohama, and Kawasaki, to Niigata, Beppu, Kōbe, and even the ancient capitals of Nara and Kyōto.[89] Obviously expansion was highly concentrated within the megalopolis along Japan's coastal industrial (Tōkaidō) belt. One was hard pressed to find dance halls in the hinterland, where the economic crisis was felt most acutely—thousands of rural tenant farmers were reduced to eating tree bark, so an evening spent in a posh dance hall seemed unimaginably frivolous for them. Dance halls thus became potent symbols of the widening cultural gap between urban and rural Japanese, a gulf that ultranationalist leaders exploited skillfully in their rise to political prominence.

Admittedly, at a time of such severe privation lavish dance halls made easy targets of themselves. Ginza Dance Hall boasted a revolving bandstand, while the most opulent and celebrated establishment of Japan's Jazz Age, Ballroom Florida (named after a Parisian dance hall), took up the entire third floor of Akasaka's Tameike Hall.[90] Large halls such as Ginza, Florida, and Teitoza in Tokyo employed more than one hundred taxi dancers apiece, bringing the total number of professional female dancers (in Tokyo and vicinity, presumably) to nearly eight hundred, according to a 1933 survey.[91] Florida was known for contracting elite foreign bands to play the night shows, and Douglas Fairbanks, Charles Chaplin, and other celebrities from the worlds of politics and entertainment entered their names on its police-mandated guest register. Florida developed such a reputation that it was not a gig that just any foreign musician could count on getting: "Any band which goes out to Japan must be good," American correspondent Burton Crane advised *Metronome* readers. "There's no sense taking out a bunch of boys who can't cut the stuff well enough to get by [in America]. . . . Japanese employers aren't dumb and they don't buy bands on hearsay. They'll have friends in the United States listen to your outfit before anything is signed."[92]

While foreign bands would remain a staple during Florida's golden years, after 1930 the best native bands, such as Kikuchi Shigeya's group, performed matinees for early-bird dancers.[93] At most other, less acclaimed dance halls, of course, Japanese bands headlined. The dance hall craze propelled Japan's most talented musicians into the ranks of high-paid entertainers, at a time when unemployment afflicted college-educated people nationwide. Bassist Watanabe Ryō (1903–1976), leader of the Hōsei University Luck and Sun Jazz Band, recalled that while many of his classmates cast about in vain for jobs, he landed his first paying gig at Tokyo Union soon after graduation: "I was invited to turn pro by [Union bandleader] Yamada Waichi, and performed at Union for ¥60 [a month] immediately after leaving Hōdai in the spring of 1928. That summer I was transferred to Maeno Kōzō's band at Union in Ōsaka Ebisubashi, [working] for ¥105. In the end I returned to Tokyo again, and made ¥315 in Yamada's band. That was a time when there were no jobs, even if you graduated from college."[94] Jimmy Harada recalled making nearly twice the starting salary of a college-educated corporate employee, and music writer Horiuchi Keizō has estimated that dance hall musicians made as much as ¥200 to ¥300 a month at a time when ¥50 was considered a good income.[95]

Swing, Swing, Swing: Jazz Entertainment

In the public imagination, the dance hall was the entertainment venue most commonly associated with jazz. But one can imagine that, at a time when ¥50 a month was considered a good wage and ¥2 bought only a half-hour's worth of dancing, it was not a venue that most people could afford. However, the burgeoning recording, radio, film, and theater industries made jazz more accessible to a wider public and created more opportunities for musicians to work and hone their craft. Among the alternatives available to jazz lovers was the jazz coffeehouse (*jazu kissa*), where customers could enjoy the latest imported and domestic recordings for the price of a cup of coffee. "It was our coffeehouses," one proprietor maintained, "that spread jazz, the music of the upper classes, among the masses."[96]

The *jazu kissa* seemed rather tame when compared to the glamorous mystique and cutting-edge danger of the dance hall, yet it became one of the Japanese jazz community's most distinctive and resilient institutions. According to Yoshida Mamoru (1913–1994), proprietor of Yokohama's "Swing and Hot Jazz Chigusa" since 1933, the jazz coffeehouse was an amalgamation of elements from different types of early-twentieth-century businesses offering food, drink, music, and so-called "erotic service": "milk halls" specializing in milk and cake; Western-style coffee shops serving coffee and tea; and cafes and *chabuya*, which provided phonograph music and attractive waitresses. Specialized "music coffeehouses," with record collections of particular musical genres such as European classical, tango, *chansons*, Japanese pops, and jazz, appeared in the late twenties and early thirties. The first to specialize in jazz was probably Tokyo's Blackbird in 1929.[97]

Brown Derby, Brunswick, Duet, Maison Rio, and Duke—these were among the glittery names that adorned *jazu kissa* in the Jazz Age. Jazz coffeehouses cultivated reputations and clienteles based on the strength of their record collections and sound systems, or on the beauty of their waitresses or "record girls." Elite establishments developed resourceful means for acquiring imported records (which, as "luxury items," were subject to a 10 percent duty): for instance, Yoshida beseeched sailors bound for the United States to buy American records for Chigusa. Record shops with strong stocks of imported jazz, such as jazz writer Muraoka Tadashi's (1897–1963) Rhythm Company, were another source. The latest titles were prominently advertised in coffeehouse windows, to draw customers with a hunger for the new: records by Red Nichols, Tommy Dorsey, Duke Ellington, Count Basie, and especially Benny Goodman were sure draws. Although some of these artists were available on domestically produced releases, the foreign labels lent that special aura of authenticity, so the most prestigious jazz coffeehouses stocked only imports.[98] Of course, few entertainment venues in Japan have dared to neglect the erotic element entirely and the fancier jazz coffeehouses were no exception. They hired young women in evening wear for customers' visual stimulation, as well as to tend the phonographs and take requests. In the time-honored tradition of Yoshiwara bordellos, which advertised star courtesans through the art of the woodblock print, *jazu kissa,* cafes, and dance halls used snapshots of their record or "sign girls" (*kanban musume*), waitresses, and taxi dancers in their advertising. The most glamorous of these women became minor celebrities, with gossip columns detailing their exploits in popular music magazines.[99]

What is perhaps most significant about jazz coffeehouses is the role they played in the musical education of several generations of jazz musicians and aficionados in Japan. Even in the postwar years when jazz was more prolific on the radio, the coffeehouse remained the most important place to study and acquire a jazz vocabulary. Musicians in the interwar period were quick to realize the value of the jazz coffeehouse. "We couldn't hear new records except in jazz coffeehouses and if we didn't hear them soon, we thought we'd be behind the times," tenor saxophonist Matsumoto Shin (1908–1978) remarked. "So we went to coffeehouses all the time."[100] While Matsumoto may have overstated the unavailability of records to musicians— with dance and studio work at the wages already mentioned, musicians were hardly too poor to buy phonographs and records—the fact remains that coffeehouses, whose raison d'être was staying on top of the latest trends in popular music, were invaluable resources of aural and even printed information. In their off-hours musicians haunted *jazu kissa,* soaking in the sounds of their American heroes, occasionally notating entire solos and arrangements, and eventually taking these lessons with them to the gig.

Ear training is not necessarily a perfect method, but it is considered a crucial skill in jazz. Most jazz musicians agree that one does not learn to play from any book. At any rate, Japanese of the twenties and thirties had few alternatives to an aural method. As demand for news from the American music world rose in the 1930s, Japanese publishers did respond with books and new types of music magazines, less scholarly and more star-driven than those stuffy classical journals that prevailed in the 1910s and 1920s yet appealing to a jazz and dance audience. Readers could turn to Shioiri Kamesuke's *Jazz Music* (1929), a translation of Paul Whiteman's *Jazz*, or a 1936 vernacular primer on jazz theory and individual instrumental techniques for basic musicological analysis and history.[101] Hard-core fans pored over imported copies of *Downbeat, Metronome,* and *Melody Maker,* but there were also a handful of new vernacular magazines that ran translations of articles from the foreign press, reviews of foreign records, and the latest dance steps from abroad, in addition to features, ads, and gossip from the domestic front.[102] These magazines carried the voices of a new generation of music writers and critics specializing in jazz and dance music, including Muraoka Tadashi (whose articles and reviews under the romanized pen name "TAY MURAOKA" were occasionally published in English), illustrator Noguchi Hisamitsu, and Nogawa Kōbun (1900–1957). Using the nom de plume Ōi Jazurō (大井蛇津郎, a pun meaning "let's jazz a lot"), Nogawa became known as Japan's foremost jazz researcher and writer, earning the respect of artists as a lyricist and translator, producer and promoter, disc jockey, and arranger. One thing that struck me about Japan's jazz community is the sense of mutual purpose, respect, and even close friendship between musicians and critics, to the point that musicians address writers as *sensei.* This, of course, is in stark contrast to the usually hostile relationship between musicians and critics in America. The consensus seems to be that Nogawa Kōbun set an example in this respect. At any rate, Noguchi Hisamitsu regarded him as a courageous advocate of jazz at times when "prejudice and contempt toward jazz were terrible."[103] Nonetheless, as Kikuchi Shigeya would note in the postwar years, the dearth of instructional materials in the interwar period made an aural education fundamental for many.[104]

In many respects, the late twenties and early thirties were a boon to musicians interested in popular, jazz, and dance styles. Although some five thousand musicians nationwide are believed to have lost theater work with the advent of talking pictures, those who were willing to adapt to popular tastes found more than adequate compensation working in dance halls, theatrical revues, and movie and recording studios.[105] It was not uncommon for the most talented and industrious musicians to work two or more such gigs at a time, making records during the day and accompanying dancers at night. Neither was it uncommon for them to move on a whim, in what was by all accounts a seller's market: "At that time," Hattori Ryōichi joked, "if a musician had one arm he had a job."[106] With high demand for musicians' services in most larger cities and in Japanese territories abroad, the musical life could be as stable or mercurial as desired. From the band-leader's perspective, it could be difficult to keep a group together, but there were almost always replacements waiting in the wings.

Japan's earliest jazz records featured accompaniment by amateur groups such as the Red and Blue Jazz Band and the Cosmopolitan Novelty Orchestra, or by freelance pickup bands. But as demand for more hit records skyrocketed, stable studio orchestras were created to ensure consistent quality and steady production of popular and jazz songs. The best known of these by far was the Nippon Columbia Jazz Band, an ensemble with an incomparable musical reputation and a relatively stable lineup. Founded in October 1929 by company president L. H. White (with the recruiting aid of Japanese American playboy Dōmoto Takaji), the band consisted of the most talented jazzmen in the nation: old pros from Kansai (trombonist Taniguchi Matashi, pianist Taira Shigeo, saxophonists Takami Tomoyoshi and Ashida Mitsuru, trumpeters Obata Mitsuyuki and Nanri Fumio, and drummer Tanaka Kazuo) joined forces with the capital region's top collegiate and amateur bandsmen (bassist Watanabe Ryō, banjoist Sakai Tōru, and bassist/conductor Kami Kyōsuke) to form a true all-star lineup, capable of swinging, sweetening, or jazzing up any arrangement that came their way. As evidenced on dozens of hit records, the band's strength was its versatility, for it might be called on for a barn-burning swinger, a passionate tango, or a maudlin ballad of separation and lost love. The ensemble was without question the toast of the industry, with monthly wages ranging from ¥200 to ¥250 in the early days.[107] Following promotional gigs in Korea, Manchuria, and Tokyo's Union Dance Hall, the original members parted ways in 1931, but by October of the following year a new Columbia Jazz Band was in the studio recording more hits. The CJB was capable of playing the most intricate arrangements with precision, but what set it apart from the competition was the presence of Japan's most adept soloists—guitarist Tsunoda Takashi and occasionally Nanri—who could enliven even the most mediocre date. Joining forces with Kikuchi Shigeya's matinee band, the CJB moonlighted at Ballroom Florida as Kikuchi and His Florida Boys, and for one year kept the dancers moving at Japan's most grandiose dance palace.[108]

If an aspiring musician could not find employment in one of the five major recording studio orchestras, there were also a number of so-called "symphonic jazz" orchestras that performed for radio broadcasts, movie soundtracks, and theatrical revues. Musicians no longer willing to "sacrifice their livelihoods for classical music" could join the Corona Orchestra, the Photo Chemical Laboratory (PCL) Studio Orchestra, or the Tokyo Broadcast (NHK) Orchestra.[109] The symphonic jazz style—created by James Reece Europe and popularized by Paul Whiteman—became associated in Japan with Kami Kyōsuke, "the Japanese Paul Whiteman." A veteran of 1920s amateur bands and a graduate of Tokyo Imperial University, Kami quit as conductor of the Columbia Jazz Band in 1930 to study composition at UCLA, where he rented a house in "the middle of the Negro town" (a fact he doubtless accentuated to embellish his authenticity) and occasionally performed on contrabass with the Pasadena Symphony.[110] He returned to Japan in 1932 with a bundle of jazz primers and Whiteman arrangements for broadcast on the JOAK radio network with the Corona Orchestra. Although Japanese musicians had been performing Whiteman's music in small groups for years, Kami presented that music in the grandiose context for which it was originally intended. "When I introduced symphonic jazz in Japan, everyone was surprised," Kami recounted. "Everyone stared in wonder: 'is jazz really this good?!' I was surprised, too. . . . It so happened that I returned to Japan at a time when jazz was at its worst or most decadent. . . . It was said that [Whiteman] was the 'Jazz God,' that he took jazz from the dance hall to the concert hall. . . . He was quite a hero back then."[111] At Hibiya Hall on 29 July 1932, Kami conducted the Corona Orchestra in the successful Japanese premiere of, appropriately, Gershwin's *Rhapsody in Blue*. Kami then took his style of music to the big screen as leader of the PCL orchestra. According to jazz trombonist Taniguchi Matashi (who joined PCL in late 1932 and would become its musical director after its takeover by Tōhō studios in 1937), PCL contained an odd mixture of symphonic musicians and jazzmen, who were collectively responsible for composing and performing movie music.[112]

Life was generally good for jazz and popular musicians: unlike most Japanese in the early 1930s, they could expect either to find steady work at lucrative salaries, or to change jobs capriciously. A select few even enjoyed celebrity status. A resemblance to Gary Cooper was said to have made Ashida Mitsuru an object of female adoration. In a well-publicized scandal, trumpet ace Nanri Fumio's playing so enraptured one young woman that she committed suicide when her feelings were not reciprocated.[113] But in general musicians were overshadowed by the singers and dancers whom they accompanied. As sexualized "objects of visual display,"[114] jazz singers (particularly females) enjoy a popularity that often eclipses their own musical talents, let alone that of their accompanists. Few musicians could hope to share the spotlight with the glamorous and exotic vocalists and dancers who populated interwar Japan's stages and screens.

It should come as no surprise that several of Japan's most popular jazz singers were not Japanese. The unlikely star Burton Crane, a financial writer for the *Japan Advertiser,* had a smash hit with his debut record "Show Me the Way to Go Home"/"Drunk Last Night" (April 1931) and thus earned the sobriquet "the Rudy Vallee of Japan."[115] In an interview in 1961, Crane described his rise to stardom:

> In those days, there was a great fad of foreignism. All the youngsters would go along—they'd been reading Henri Murger's *Scenes de la Vie de Boheme:* the story on which *La Boheme* was based. They'd been reading that, and they used to go along, the men with long hair and the girls with bobbed hair, arm in arm, which in 1925 was considered very daring in Japan. . . .
>
> Before I left Japan, I had a rather unusual experience which came in handy later. In my efforts to learn spoken Japanese better, I used to go out to the bars. The office of the *Japan Advertiser* . . . [closed] at 11 P.M., and the bars closed at 12, so that I just had time to go to a nearby bar for one half-litre bottle and maybe 45 minutes of practice in conversational Japanese. The bars [cafes] had just sprung up. They had started about 1927–28. I hadn't been very conscious of them until I got back in 1929, and then found that the young men who had joined the paper during my absence were more fluent in Japanese than I. I was a little ashamed of it, because I had a much larger vocabulary than they. So I began splitting away from them, not going to the bars with them but going alone, so that I could talk to the waitresses and practice. I would be the only one and they would have to talk to me. They taught me to sing some Japanese songs, and before long they were asking me to sing some American songs, which I translated into Japanese, and did sing. Word of this came to Columbia Gramophone Co., and before long I was chivied into making a couple of records, which accidentally became overnight hits. My second record was a big hit, as well as the first. . . .
>
> So I became something of a national character, and made a couple of appearances on the Japanese stage, with the permission of course of B. W. Fleisher, the publisher of the *Japan Advertiser.* . . .
>
> I appeared at the Dotumbure Sochikuza with the Choshku Girls Opera Company. Oh, heavens, that must have been 25 days. Then I appeared at the Osaka Gaikicho as master of ceremonies with an American jazz band. I sang as well.[116]

Another American singer who made quite an impression was Midge Williams (1908–?), a twenty-five-year-old black American who came to Japan with pianist Roger Segure and her three tap-dancing brothers, following a

4. The multitalented Japanese American jazz entertainer Alice Fumiko Kawabata, 1935. Photo used with permission of Segawa Masahisa.

stint at the Canidrome Ball Room in Shanghai. After an audition with Florida bandleader Kikuchi, the Williams party performed for five days at Florida in late January 1934, and later at the Teikoku Hotel and Kokka Dance Hall. The following month Williams recorded several jazz songs (in Japanese and in English) with the Columbia Jazz Band, including "Dinah" and "St. Louis Blues," two tunes of which Japanese jazz fans and musicians never seemed to tire. Williams's extended stay made a lasting impression on jazz singers and musicians, who marveled at her "feeling and expression" and "smart, polished improvisatory sense." Singers Mizushima Sanae and Shimizu Kimiko, who were performing at Florida in a Boswell Sisters-style chorus, recalled that Williams generously taught them jazz vocal techniques between sets.[117]

Yet the most famous jazz vocalists were undoubtedly the Japanese American singers who recorded and performed in Japan. Frustrated by racial barriers that prevented them from breaking out of menial work and into the American entertainment industry, in the early thirties talented *nisei* ("second-generation," Americans of Japanese ancestry) started migrating from San Francisco, Los Angeles, and Seattle to their parents' homeland, where recording companies and musical revues eagerly hired them. *Nisei* singers—Helen Sumida, Tadashi "Tib" Kamayatsu (1912–1980), crooner Rickey Miyagawa (1911–1949), and his sister Miyagawa Harumi ("the best jazz singer"), Helen Honda, the nasal-voiced Taft Beppu, singer and hula dancer Betty Inada, trumpeter and vocalist Moriyama Hisashi (1910–1990), pianist Charlie Kikugawa (1907–1993), and "the amber-colored Josephine Baker," Alice Fumiko Kawabata—became stars of stage, screen, and song. The amazingly limber Kawabata, who was sixteen when she arrived in Yokohama in 1932, determined "to teach her audiences what to appreciate, to show them that jazz was not necessarily vulgar," was producing her own musical revue within a year of her arrival, and became one of interwar Japan's most beloved and most versatile entertainers.[118]

Even popular homegrown vocalists such as Dick Mine (1908–1991) and Awaya Noriko could not compete with the luster of the *nisei* singers, in part because their American nationality imparted an aura of authenticity to

5. Nisei crooner Rickey Miyagawa fronts the massive Photo Chemical Lab (PCL) symphonic jazz orchestra, ca. 1937. Kami Kyōsuke, the self-styled "Paul Whiteman of Japan," conducts. Photo used with permission of Segawa Masahisa.

them. (Given the phrase *bata kusai,* "reeking of butter," applied to these singers and other things American, perhaps "odor" is more appropriate than "aura.") Native familiarity with American culture, many contended, was a crucial precondition for "real" jazz talent: "Jazz is America's national music," one Japanese writer maintained. "It is the rhythm of Americanism. . . . Jazz musicians must live in America's cities, and must make America's language and customs their own. This is the greatest reason why the jazz orchestras of Berlin and Paris have not developed even a little."[119]

The ostensible reason that record companies sought *nisei* singers was that they could sing jazz songs convincingly in both English and Japanese. Many jazz songs were sung at least partially in English, and purist jazz audiences made (and continue to make) the rather unreasonable demand that Japanese vocalists sing with correct pronunciation. But bilingualism alone does not explain the popularity of the *nisei* singers. Japanese audiences were attracted to *nisei* entertainers because they were ethnically Japanese and yet still foreign and exotic: "living oxymorons."[120] In a sense, the familiar ethnicity of these entertainers provided a bridge between Japanese audiences and the exotic world of American culture and jazz. Japanese ethnicity made audiences feel more familiar or comfortable with these entertainers, yet their American upbringings and habits not only made them objects of curiosity and fascination, but also "authenticated" them as jazz artists. As Americans, they were assumed to have a familiarity with jazz that geography denied Japanese nationals. It was argued that the rhythmic sense and phrasing of the *nisei* singers were closer to those of Armstrong and Holiday than to those of Japanese vocalists, and recordings do bear this out: compare Nakano Tadaharu's on-the-beat crooning on "Side By Side" (1938) with the rhythmic liberties and bluesy inflections on Taft Beppu's "St. Louis Blues" (1934).[121] The *nisei* singers were thus held up as unofficial arbiters of authenticity, entertainers whose nationality conferred a degree of authority which Japanese nationals were assumed not to possess. This aura of authenticity contributed to their popularity, and thus to that of jazz in Japan.[122]

Despite—perhaps because of—bad times, entertainment seems to thrive. There never seems to be a shortage of people who can scrape together the money to have a good time. For the upper and middle classes, at least, jazz was an appealing diversion, and Japan's jazz community profited accordingly. There was the ever-present specter of police control and harassment by right-wing secret societies, but the bands played on. Still, sword-wielding paramilitary hotheads could wreck a good party. When local and national officials, police, or right-wing vigilante groups made things hot at home, a number of musicians, dancers, and entrepreneurs sought more temperate climes where they could jam in peace. Fortunately for them (if not for Chinese and Koreans), Japan's rising imperialist profile on the Asian continent provided just such a haven: Shanghai. Just as "underdeveloped" Asia represented a frontier of opportunity for Japanese industrialists and military adventurism, Shanghai represented a "jazz frontier" for Japanese entertainers. No portrait of Japan's Jazz Age would be complete without an excursion across the sea to imbibe the glittery decadence of "Asia's jazz mecca."

Shanghai: The Jazz Frontier

In 1921, an eighteen-year-old trumpeter named Saitō Hiroyoshi (1903–1981) left his Ōsaka home, telling his parents that he was going to Tokyo. Instead, he boarded a boat bound for China and disembarked at Shanghai, where he played for four years in a multiethnic band at the Olympic Theater. Saitō thus established the "Shanghai sojourn" as an act of adolescent rebellion and a rite of (musical) passage. By the time Saitō returned to Japan in 1925, dance halls and cabarets owned by and catering exclusively to Japanese riddled the foreign settlement in Shanghai, providing entertainment for a growing Japanese population that was presumably permanent. These first Japanese dance halls in Shanghai employed Filipino bands with a few token Japanese members until the number of Japanese musicians in Shanghai made all-Japanese bands feasible.[123]

Because Shanghai was, for Japanese as well as for Westerners, a mythical place renowned for debauchery and danger, I have referred to it as a "jazz frontier": it was contested terrain where disparate cultures came together, a treaty port that extraterritoriality agreements had rendered virtually lawless, a liminal world where one tested one's mettle and came away transformed. The term *jazz frontier* was not actually used by Japanese. I have coined it after a close reading of the imagery, language, and thematic content of the jazz community's folklore and oral accounts, which describe all the romance, danger, and personal transfiguration that are fundamental to frontier experiences.

Proper frontiers beckon to and challenge prospective "pioneers," compelling them to develop and rely on survival skills rendered dormant by "civilization." The individual on the frontier encounters hostile natives, lawlessness, adventure, and romance; he conquers the frontier to yield personal fortune and cultivate survival skills and character—I say "he" because, on the symbolic level at least, the frontier is a hypermasculine environment, to which women are "brought" along to perform supporting roles. Ultimately, the symbolic frontier, as it appears in the mental map of the "pioneer," is terrain to be conquered and appropriated, to be put to personal use, in an effort to cultivate character, talent, and wealth.[124] Shanghai was such a place for the Japanese jazzman looking for personal and artistic authentication.

If we understand the frontier as an amalgamation of geographical and temporal circumstances, transformative effects, and symbolic meanings, it is difficult to conceive of a better descriptive term than *frontier* for portraying the Chinese treaty port in the early twentieth century. In the years between the world wars, Shanghai was virtually *everyone's* "frontier," the colonial playground for transients from over twenty nations. It was a truly cosmopolitan space where, in the words of one observer, "races mingle but never merge."[125] "Shanghai sojourners," semipermanent residents "whose loyalties fluctuated between attachment to native place and . . . a new identity as *Shanghai ren* (Shanghai people)," comprised a community (or, more correctly, a collection of communities) rendered "turbulent, unruly, and crime-ridden" by the treaty principle of extraterritoriality. Vice was Shanghai's most profitable commodity—prostitution was the single largest employer of female labor in Shanghai, and one in thirty residents "sold sex for a living."[126]

Among these "Shanghai sojourners" were a number of musicians, singers, stage and taxi dancers, and cabaret and dance hall proprietors of Japanese nationality and ethnicity, entrusted with entertaining the Japanese settlement in the Hongkew district (which boasted between twenty and thirty thousand residents in the mid-1930s).[127] Shanghai was their playland, their refuge, their frontier.

In many respects the "jazz frontier" was fundamentally different from other frontiers: this is a geographic zone of cultural interaction, but not between *native* and *invading* populations. On the jazz frontier the culture that mediates the interaction, jazz, is not indigenous to the zone; the populations that are interacting are *all* invaders (Americans, Japanese, Russians, Filipinos, etc.); and the natives (the Chinese) are really peripheral to the interaction. But the jazz frontier is more idea than place, the product of the Japanese jazz community's collective imagination, and thus a frontier by virtue of its meaning rather than its location or inherent transformative powers. For Japanese musicians, Shanghai represented a rite of authentication and initiation into the jazz culture, an alternative experience, and a stepping stone to fame and fortune in the homeland's entertainment industry.

Moreover, I use the term *jazz frontier* because it not only evokes the romance and lawlessness of Shanghai street life, but also highlights the city's status as contested terrain in the early twentieth century. Like all frontiers, Shanghai was pried open by a succession of invading armies, entrepreneurs and big business, and peripheral support groups (such as entertainers). Sheltered by the umbrella of Japan's imperial presence in China, jazz musicians enjoyed relative artistic and personal freedoms while they entertained the troops, financiers, and bureaucrats who were subjugating the Asian continent. They played roles analogous to the wandering minstrels, the honky-tonk pianists, and the saloon girls on the American frontier—marginal, perhaps, to the process of expansion, yet quite essential to the morale of the "expanders."

Through the medium of oral history—in which the "living source" is given complete editorial and interpretive license to determine "what really happened"—Japan's jazz community distances itself from the larger context of Japanese imperialism and portrays its experience in Shanghai as an innocent romp. But, clearly, there would have been no party in Shanghai had there not been a pernicious Japanese imperial presence already in place. Seen in this light, Japan's jazz frontier looks less like an extended party or fling and more like the ill-gotten booty of Japanese imperialism.[128]

The "opening" of Japan's jazz frontier in Shanghai was facilitated by the considerable expansion of leisure travel across the Pacific and the resulting diffusion of American popular music. In the interwar period America gradually displaced Europe as the principal cultural influence in Asia, securing its hold through the spectacle of motion pictures and the rhythmic power of American dance music. As noted earlier, some Japanese musicians took full advantage of the heavy transpacific traffic and visited the so-called "home of jazz" (*jazu no honba*). But there were many more with similar inclinations who were unable to make that particular voyage. Those with an interest in jazz thus searched for an alternative site, someplace geographically accessible yet musically and culturally closer to "the source." The growth of a cosmopolitan society in Shanghai, not to mention the steadily expanding Japanese political and economic presence in China, made the port city a logical choice.

By the late 1920s and 1930s Shanghai had a firm reputation as the "Asian jazz mecca." "The Temple of Temples where his Pagan Highness Jazz is worshipped in the Orient is Shanghai—'Paris of the East,'" the *New York Times* reported in 1923. "There in the exotic atmosphere of the gay and cosmopolitan, in that city which is a mixture of the familiar and the strange, jazz has come to mean Shanghai. Shanghai without jazz, without its night clubs, without its ballrooms crowded with diplomats, business men, tourists and that ever picturesque rabble of European fortune hunters, adventurers and derelicts cluttering the gay cities of the East, would not be Shanghai. Jazz is the very essence of its existence." Hundreds of lavish dance halls, casinos, cabarets, and nightclubs catered to a "large and affluent population of Western bachelors."[129] Ernest O. Hauser's *Shanghai: City For Sale* (1940) provides an evocative portrayal of Shanghai night life (from the Western bachelor's perspective, of course):

> You drifted into one of those cabarets, an hour or so before midnight, you chose your table not too far from the floor, and you looked them over: the pretty Chinese girls with their slit silk dresses and with too much rouge on their soft cheeks; the glorious Russians with their décolleté evening gowns—Chanel and Molineux models, if you did not look too closely; the stupid and touchingly attractive Koreans; the slightly simian half-castes; the quick and clever Japanese. . . . And you bought your ticket and danced with them, and if you invited one of them to your table, you had to pay something extra and the girl had apple cider that turned into champagne on your chit. But if you wanted to go home with her, she would have to ask the management first. . . . And you might wind up in "Blood Alley," where you went to get as much local color as possible, among the drunken soldiers and sailors of the armies and navies of the world.[130]

This vibrant night life attracted dancers and musicians from around the world to Shanghai.[131] The American composer and arranger Claude Lapham drew attention to the fact that the late-night carousings of Shanghai's "night people" enjoyed jazz accompaniment: "I can assure you on the word of an observant musical globetrotter that the Orient is MORE interested in jazz than all of Europe with the exception of England." Lapham incited a minor sensation when he told readers of *Metronome* that "China needs American bands."

> Shanghai represents a Seventh Heaven for the jazz musician. . . . It far outshines Paris in many respects, especially in appreciation of jazz. Here there are also no labor restrictions whatever, good money and easy life prevail—in fact, many American jazz bands have been imported from America, and what happens—the liquor and the beauty of the Chinese charmers—(I can personally rave about the latter, but never the former)—gets them.[132]

The scenario was not as rosy as Lapham portrayed it (as a series of rebuttals pointed out),[133] but there were, nonetheless, enough American musicians in Shanghai to attract ambitious Japanese with an interest in jazz. It was the closest access to American performers that Japanese would have before 1945.

In essence, the Shanghai sojourn represented an opportunity to circumvent the pattern of learning jazz indirectly from scores and records, in other

words, to learn by living the "jazz life." Learning by ear or eye may have enabled aspiring Japanese jazzmen to replicate jazz sonorities, rhythms, and
improvised solos, but provided little if any understanding of the theoretical
intricacies of rhythm, melody, and harmony that would allow them to apply
the language of jazz in original ways themselves. Living the "jazz life" in
Shanghai, however, in close proximity with some established jazz masters,
enabled them to learn jazz performance more directly, and to master and
apply jazz techniques with the powers of their own imaginations. The jazz
luminaries who resided in Shanghai included Teddy Weatherford (1903–
1945), a progressive pianist who had played with Erskine Tate and Louis
Armstrong and who resided in Shanghai in the late 1920s.[134] Weatherford's
informal "pupils" included such Japanese stars as drummer "Shanghai"
Yamaguchi Toyosaburō (1905–1970) and trumpeter Nanri Fumio, both of
whom convinced their countrymen that Shanghai was the place to go to
learn how to "play for real." "Teddy Weatherford, who was at a high-class
foreigners' club, came by to hear me play," Nanri recounted. "He asked me,
'Who'd you learn from?' and when I said 'Louis Armstrong's records,' he
said, 'I've played with Louie. Come over to my hotel.' . . . He showed me blue
notes and tenth chords. It was the best lesson."[135] American bands maintained a strong presence in Shanghai into the 1930s (Lapham counted
twenty American bands in 1936), and continued to draw ambitious Japanese with a taste for blue notes and syncopation. "If it's jazz you want, go to
Shanghai!" became the Japanese jazzman's equivalent to Horace Greeley's
exhortation "Go west, young man!"

However, Shanghai was more than a musician's "woodshed": it also represented a place where youthful romantic fantasy was played out, where the
chase was more fun than the capture, where the social rules governing
public intercourse between the sexes held little sway. "Deceiving the ladies
in four/four time" (*Onna damasu mo fōbiito*), as drummer Jimmy Harada
put it, was part of the total Shanghai experience.[136] The classic, romantic
scenario for the voyage to the "jazz frontier" entailed a male musician and
a female dancer running off together, shirking responsibility, shocking
friends and family, but eventually returning to Japan in glamorous triumph.
The romance of this image wanes when one considers that musicians actually received bounties or financial advances from dance hall owners as a
reward for bringing female dancers with them from Japan. Thus there was
as much avarice as romance behind the standard pickup line "Let's run
away to Shanghai together!" (*futari de Shanhai e nigeyō*); the musicians
most accomplished at this delicate art of persuasion were dubbed "advance
kings" (*bansukingu*).[137] The awkward social implications of this arrangement are illustrated in the following confession by clarinetist Ōkawa Kōichi,

who was in Shanghai from 1938 to 1941: "I was married at the time, but I had a dancer I liked on the side and we went to Shanghai together. When we got there the dancer said to me, 'We can get by just fine on my earnings, so you send all of your income to your wife in Japan.' "[138]

Music and hormones saturated the Chinese port's piquant air, but Shanghai was not without its travails, which only added to the romantic mystique of the "jazz frontier." Japanese faced fierce competition for jobs from nationalities with better "musical reputations," such as Filipinos and Americans, and earned only a fraction (sometimes as low as one-thirtieth) of the pay that musicians from other countries commanded.[139] Nanri Fumio related his experience of poverty in the pursuit of art: "Of course, when I was listening to [Weatherford] play I couldn't work, so I found a day job, but even with that I had no money—I'd pick up radish leaves at the market and boil them by burning old newspapers, and for three or four days that'd be all I'd eat. Even now when I see a daikon radish I remember my Shanghai days and wax nostalgic."[140] In Nanri's testimony, we find poverty romanticized and exalted as the crucial "dues-paying" experience which "authentic" jazz artists are expected to endure.

Japanese also faced the antipathy of the locals. Anti-Japanese sentiment exploded in violent demonstrations by Shanghai students and workers in May 1925, and grew ever more hostile as the aggression of the Japanese military in China persisted.[141] Legend has it that jazz singer Mizushima Sanae (1909–1978) responded to the increasingly hazardous climate of the 1930s by donning Chinese clothing and "passing" as a native. She adopted the stage name Daria Sagara and sang jazz and tango songs (occasionally in Spanish) with a mixed band of Chinese and Filipinos. The ruse worked for about a year, until one night when a Japanese in the audience remembered her from her days as the "mama-san" of a Tokyo coffeehouse and blew her cover, compelling her to return to Japan in 1936.[142]

A sojourn on the "jazz frontier" was dangerous, perhaps, yet not without rewards. Those musicians, singers, and dancers who dared to undertake this risky venture enjoyed prestige as "Shanghai returnees" (Shanhai gaeri) when they returned to Japan. The very word Shanghai conferred a degree of authenticity for which people who merely copied records could not hope. "Shanghai returnees" were said to have learned from the source, to have "paid their dues," to be real jazumen. In the interwar period, a sojourn on the "jazz frontier" of Shanghai represented one such authenticating experience, comparable to that which Boston's Berklee School of Music promises young Japanese musicians today.

Artistic authentication, adolescent rebellion, greed, and romance were not the only motivations for fleeing to the "jazz frontier." Nanri Fumio and others have mentioned the increasing pressure of city ordinances, the police, and right-wing activists on the dance hall culture in Japan as another impetus for making the voyage to China. Around 1929, Nanri claimed, "ruffians with samurai swords came to harass the dance halls every night. I couldn't put up with that, so I went over to Shanghai, not knowing whether I could survive."[143] Nanri's comment highlights the cultural tensions of the era, tensions which the dance hall culture, the very heart of interwar Japan's jazz community, felt most acutely. Business was so good that the halls raised admission fees to slow down the flow of customers; yet local ordinances, police, and right-wing paramilitary groups constantly challenged the dance halls' social legitimacy and contained the industry's expansion. The response of some jazz musicians, dancers, singers, and dance hall proprietors was to escape this tense situation by going overseas.

It is ironic that the expansion of Japan's empire in East Asia provided the very "safe havens" to which they could flee. Shanghai is but one example: following the establishment of the colony/puppet state Manshukuo in 1932, some prominent jazz musicians, singers, and dancers followed thousands of "pioneers" to make their fortunes there. (When Nanri Fumio worked at the Peroke dance hall in Dairen, he made ¥500 a month, at a time when ¥1,000 would buy a house with a garden in Tokyo.)[144] Japan's "jazz frontier" thus expanded apace with Japan's imperial presence in Asia, and the theoretically subversive jazz subculture profited accordingly. But Manchuria, while certainly viewed as a frontier by many Japanese in the thirties, lacked the symbolic significance of Shanghai: Shanghai offered a stage on which to act out adolescent romantic fantasies; a chance to make (and squander) fortunes (Nanri Fumio and trombonist Shūtō Isamu both made enviable fortunes in China, yet admitted returning to Japan broke, having exhausted their money partying).[145] It was also a sanctuary from the suppression of the jazz culture in the homeland and, above all, an authenticating experience, which transformed musicians, dancers, and singers into *jazumen*, with all the prestige, fame, and fortune that such status entailed.

The "closing of the frontier," or the point after which a particular geographical or cultural zone no longer constitutes a "frontier," is a perennial topic of debate among historians. The closing of the jazz frontier, however, is unambiguous. With the Pacific War and, eventually, the Chinese Communist takeover, Shanghai's reputation as a lawless, cosmopolitan playground for the world's great powers declined drastically. Although during the war there was still a substantial Japanese presence in the city—tied even less ambiguously to Japan's military, political, and economic expansion in the region—the entertainment districts withered amid slogans such as "frivolity is the enemy." The Japanese-owned dance halls in Shanghai, to which a number of musicians and dancers fled following the domestic dance hall ban of November 1940, were shut down in December 1941. Needless to say, Japanese musicians were unwelcome in establishments outside of the Japanese concession. For them the "jazz frontier" was essentially closed.

The concept of the "jazz frontier" provides us with a broad theme to characterize the oral testimony of Japan's interwar jazz community. In oral accounts of Shanghai, we can detect the jazz musician's belief in the primacy of American models, the hunger for "authenticity," and the desire for a place where the jazz culture could thrive independent of political pressures. All of these things could be found and attained only on the "jazz frontier," a place of mythical status that Japanese themselves created in Shanghai. But the term *jazz frontier* also reminds us that Shanghai was the site of an invasion and of intense cultural encounters. It recontextualizes the jazz community's fantasy land within the larger framework of Japanese expansion on the Asian continent, a connection about which the oral record is disingenuous. After all, those artists who were unwilling to tolerate the intervention of police and government in their lifestyles and artistic aspirations were quite eager to take advantage of, and profit from, Japan's pernicious profile in East Asia.

For most, however, a Shanghai sojourn was not intended to be permanent, but rather a temporary rite of passage that added an aura of authenticity and marquee value to their names. Artists who returned from a Shanghai sojourn were virtually guaranteed a privileged status within the burgeoning jazz and entertainment industry of the homeland. But it was also a refuge from the home islands, where jazz had become a major point of contention in ongoing discussions about the integrity of Japan's very identity.

Authentic Modernity

In his influential book *Imagined Communities,* Benedict Anderson argues that a sense of temporal simultaneity, a feeling of shared time that transcends regional boundaries and is engendered by print and electronic media, is a crucial precondition for building national communities.[146] One might argue that the same precondition is necessary for the creation and maintenance of *inter*national communities. In the early twentieth century Japan was regarded by many as part of such a community, the "modern" industrial nation-states which had emerged victorious from the Great War. Japanese foreign policy followed the dictates of the catchphrase "cooperative diplomacy," and an emerging urban middle class made lifestyle and consumption choices similar to those made by their counterparts in the West, symbolizing the simultaneity of time that guaranteed Japan's inclusion in such a community of nations. Although there was hardly consensus on the matter, many believed, or at least hoped, that Japan was experiencing modernity concurrently with the elite European and North American nations. The introduction and development of jazz music in Japan was, for many, most emblematic of this sense of sharing in the modern moment. Jazz allowed Japan's self-styled modernites to experience an authentic and simultaneous modernity though they might never see or directly experience the rest of the modern world.

This made jazz the latest example of a well-worn pattern of musical appropriation in Japanese history: as they had done with Chinese and Korean court musics in the seventh and eighth centuries, and with European classical and martial music in the nineteenth, Japanese borrowed music in part to remake their own civilization, and in part to impress outside observers. There were of course significant differences, in terms of both motivation and of process. Continental Asian and European classical musics were appropriated by Japan's most elite classes and circulated virtually exclusively among them; such musics indeed signified and reinforced their separation from the unwashed masses. On the other hand, jazz and popular dance musics from Latin America, the United States, and Europe were not only imported and promoted primarily by nonelite urban commoners, but were disseminated by mass media technologies that made them readily available to a broader public, namely the newly prosperous urban middle classes with a bit of money to blow and a hankering for authentic modern exotica. Japan's first jazz enthusiasts may not have been of the humblest origins, but they represented only a sub-elite at best, newly empowered to initiate processes of cultural appropriation.

Though not the all-consuming and sometimes debilitating obsession it would be for successive generations, the authenticity of their music was not unimportant to Japan's first generation of jazz musicians. Those like Ida Ichirō, Nanri Fumio, and Kami Kyōsuke, whose résumés boasted of forays to jazz's "homeland" (*honba*) or its Asian "frontier" (Shanghai), enjoyed elite status in Japan's jazz and entertainment communities. *Nisei* entertainers like Kawabata Fumiko and Moriyama Hisashi, uniquely qualified to mediate between the native/familiar and the foreign/exotic, likewise lent an enviable and inimitable aura of authenticity to the jazz entertainment of the 1930s. Yet, as described in Chapter 4, there was also a desire to authenticate jazz in Japan as identifiably, even prescriptively, *Japanese,* a desire that became increasingly marketable and politically correct as a Japan "spiritually mobilized" for war slipped from its admittedly precarious stance as an elite "modern" nation and charted its own course as an international rogue and pariah.

TALKIN' JAZZ: MUSIC, MODERNISM, AND
INTERWAR JAPAN'S CULTURE WARS

It goes without saying that jazz is the modern person's dance music. It is the music of the modern people of Japan, of France, of America, of the world. Those of us who breathe the modern air and live in the present day should at least understand this jazz music.—Japanese advertisement, 1929

Jazz originally was the accompaniment of the voodoo dancer, stimulating the half-crazed barbarian to the vilest deeds. The weird chant, accompanied by the syncopated rhythm of the voodoo invokers, has also been employed by other barbaric people to stimulate brutality and sensuality. That it has a demoralizing effect upon the human brain has been demonstrated by many scientists.—Ladies Home Journal, 1921

The fact is that jazz transforms people into drunkards and sex maniacs, drives them mad, and causes civilized people to fall to the level of the African jungle. Because of [jazz] it is a fact that divorce is increasing; it is also a fact that hothouse virgins [onshitsu no shojo] are maturing "too fast"; and generally speaking it is also a fact that the revolution in male-female relationships was brought about by jazz.—Murobuse Kōshin, *Gaitō no shakaigaku*, 1929

On 7 November 1933 Tokyo police arrested twenty-four-year-old dance instructor Tamura Kazuo for embroiling a number of prominent families in a major sex scandal. The "Ginza Hall Incident," which earned a four-column headline, a photograph, and a half-page of coverage in the *Tokyo Asahi*, mingled adultery with rhythmic music and dancing to titillate and scandalize the public. Introducing himself to new conquests as Eddie Cantor (a popular American entertainer), the prolific paramour used his "beauty" and "winks, which women find appealing," to "infatuate" and seduce not only cafe waitresses and *geisha,* but also the wives and daughters of physicians, corporate executives, and social elites from Tokyo, Ōsaka, and Chiba—all the while shacking up with a waitress from the Black Cat Cafe (Cafe Kuroneko).

Although Tamura might easily be dismissed as a "typical gigolo," what could account for the actions of the "idle rich women" (*yūkan jogun*)? "Is the instructor bad?" the headline queried, "Or are the madams bad?" The scandal heightened apprehension about a general decline of moral standards, from which social elites no longer seemed immune, and raised concern about the "defectiveness" of substantial control measures already in place.[1] A genre of trashy novels set in dance halls—of which Mori Shigetarō's *The Age of Dance Hall Erotic Pleasures* (1932) is representative—peddled a sensationalized and unfavorable image of jazz and social dance as "Western" and "hedonistic," while newspapers fanned the flames with more real-life dance hall scandals such as the "Pink Incident" (also 1933). For some, incidents such as the Tamura scandal were alarmingly predictable in an age of rising rates of divorce, illegitimacy, and juvenile delinquency, an age that positively gloried in the excesses of "modernism."[2] Why feign shock, they would ask, when young women and men are allowed to embrace each other tightly and move suggestively to the primitive beat of foreign music?

Such scandals provided ample fodder for those who found the seeds of the destruction of Japanese civilization in the cinematic spectacle, the gender-bending fashion, and the pulsating beat that was modernism. Noting that the misbehavior of rebellious "modern girls and boys" was accompanied by a jazzy soundtrack, writers and advertisers seized on the most sensational and titillating aspects of the jazz subculture and used them to shape public perceptions of the music and its social effects. "The emergence of a spectacular subculture is invariably accompanied by a wave of hysteria in the press," Dick Hebdige has written in his influential *Subculture: The Meaning of Style.* "This hysteria is typically ambivalent: it fluctuates between dread and fascination, outrage and amusement. . . . In most cases, it is the subculture's stylistic innovations which first attract the media's attention."[3] The result of such publicity in interwar Japan was a prolonged, alternately composed and hysterical public discussion about jazz, social dancing, and popular entertainment that rivaled the intensity of contemporaneous debates in the United States. But whereas puritanical Christian morality and racial hatred informed the American controversy, in Japan no less than a nation's cultural identity and sense of self was at stake.

The introduction and proliferation of jazz in Japan coincided with a pivotal moment in that nation's relations with the rest of the world. Japan's military participation in the Great War had been limited to seizing German territories in East Asia and the Pacific, but its role was acknowledged as a supplier of nonmilitary goods to the Allies. By virtue of being on the "right side," Asia's preeminent power was thus included (as an unequal partner, of course) in the community of victor nations and achieved an unprecedented degree of political, economic, military, and cultural integration with that community. Relative parity within the Western international system had seemed a distant dream to the directors of Japan's modernization campaign in the late nineteenth and early twentieth centuries, yet there was little celebration for having achieved a long-sought national goal. The haughty racism so evident in American and European diplomacy toward Japan—manifested in the rejection of a "racial equality" clause in the Versailles Treaty and in American restrictions on Japanese immigration—only heightened the sense that Japan's membership in the elite club of modern nations was only grudgingly acknowledged, and that its best efforts to play the game by Western rules would not change that. There was also a sense that the drive to emulate and rub shoulders with the Western powers had been conducted at the expense of Japan's own national identity. Such fears had been prevalent at least since the 1880s, but the importation of new technologies and forms of culture and entertainment in the 1920s made the complete obliteration of indigenous social and aesthetic values a foreseeable and imminent possibility.

In the years between the world wars, Japan was essentially torn between "cosmopolitan" and "nativist" impulses: on the one hand, the period of "Taishō democracy" was characterized by electoral party politics, "cooperative diplomacy," leftist activism and public ideological debate, and a burgeoning entertainment culture conspicuously based on foreign models; on the other hand, the same era witnessed the flowering of a politicized cultural traditionalism and militancy among "agricultural fundamentalists," artists and writers, the military, and the state.[4] Popular culture became a primary arena for this contest, for the producers and consumers of mass entertainment freely tested and toyed with the "imported arts" (hakurai geinō), adopting some, abandoning others, or even adapting them to create "nationalistically correct" variations. The popularization of jazz in the interwar period was part cause and part consequence of the cosmopolitan impulse, but the nativist impulse guaranteed that the music's popularity would not go uncontested.

While it would be a stretch to suggest that jazz was a preeminent cause of Japan's early-twentieth-century crisis of values and cultural identity, jazz and social dance upped the ante by intensifying and polarizing national discussions on these issues. For both champions and opponents of cosmopolitanism, jazz was emblematic of Japan's integration and participation in modern culture, and its social and aesthetic ramifications significantly heated ongoing debates over a nation's soul.

It should be noted that "jazz debates" and consequent social control efforts were virtually a universal phenomenon in the post–World War I years. If Americans could not agree on the aesthetic and social ramifications of jazz, Europeans and Asians could hardly be expected to do so, especially given their ambivalence toward the growing prevalence of American ideas, technologies, and entertainments in all other facets of life. The tensions exposed by jazz and the subcultures that embraced it were common to Europe and Japan. Many self-styled "modernites" in London, Paris, Moscow, and Berlin seized on jazz as a symbol of youth emancipation from "Edwardian values." Pretensions to universality to the contrary, jazz was not universally welcomed in Europe, but rather encountered vehement resistance, on aesthetic and social grounds, at a time when peoples around the world were struggling to craft and preserve essentialist definitions of their national selves. Tensions were particularly acute in Germany, where the popularity of jazz in the twenties compelled the fledgling Nazi Party to target jazz as an "alien culture" detrimental to indigenous German values. Another extreme example would be the USSR, where official opinions of jazz changed with each political shift—was it bourgeois music, produced by the capitalist record industry, or was it the legitimate and revolutionary folk expression of an oppressed minority?[5] Even France and Britain, where jazz became all the rage, were not completely immune from such controversies. Clearly, in the 1920s jazz was conspicuous evidence for the emergence of an Americanized global culture, and thus was a favorite target of nationalist assaults wherever a trumpet bent a blue note.

Ultimately concerns over the nation's cultural identity and its status in the new world order provided the subtext for Japan's early experience of jazz. The widely held belief that jazz music itself was not a mere byproduct but rather an *agent* of cultural transformation—engendering what social critic Ōya Sōichi called a "culture of the senses"—was born from anxieties that many Japanese felt regarding their nation's ever-shifting self-image. In the early-twentieth-century Japanese are said to have lived a "double life," a "mixture of the imported and the domestic, . . . at best an expense and an inconvenience, . . . and at worst a torment, leading to crises of identity and such things." But "double life" does little to convey the anguish that afflicted intellectuals and artists who actively sought definitions of personal and national selves.[6] Amid the anxious excitement of the age, Japanese seized upon jazz as a symbol and a root cause of their country's increasing intimacy with the Western world and the concomitant erosion of "traditional" culture. It would be nearly a decade after the music's introduction to Japan before these conceptualizations would become fully developed and articulated, but with the release of the controversial record "Tokyo March" in 1929, the Japanese jazz debates began in earnest.

Just as Japanese jazz artists closely monitored musical developments in the United States, so did Japanese writers eavesdrop on the American jazz controversy—in critiquing an alien art, the alien's opinions were valuable source material—so there are a number of overlapping and recurring themes between the two national discussions. A word should be said, therefore, about the one American whose ideas and music may have shaped Japanese conceptualizations of jazz more than any other individual's. In contemporary jazz scholarship, Paul Whiteman (1890–1967), the self-styled "King of Jazz," epitomizes the white man who exploits a racist marketplace to claim credit for and profit from a diluted version of a black American art form.[7] The current resentment against Whiteman is well expressed in the song "Jazz Thing" from Spike Lee's 1990 film *Mo' Better Blues*. Gangstarr's Guru raps:

> Its roots are in the sound of the African,
> Or should I say the mother, bringing us back again,
> From the jungle on the Congo,
> It came with a strong flow and continued to grow.
> Feet moved to the beat of the timbalo,
> Now dig the story and follow,
> For then it landed on American soil,
> Through the sweat, the blood, and the toil,
> It praised the Lord and shouted on chain gangs.
> Pain they felt but it helped them to maintain. . . .
>
> . . . Now listen, see,
> The real mystery is how music history
> Created Paul Whiteman or any other white man,
> And pretended he originated,
> And contended that he innovated
> A Jazz Thing.
> Schemin' on the meanin' of a Jazz Thing.[8]

Most concerned parties thus portray Whiteman as someone who not only deliberately obscured the original Africanisms in jazz music but took credit for its charms. I certainly have no stomach for defending Whiteman's artistry, but historians should not allow current (and ever-changing) aesthetic prejudices to blind us to Whiteman's importance as an icon of the interwar era whose musical and intellectual influence was, for a time, unequaled. Whiteman's "symphonic jazz," which "combined dance music with just a dash of hot jazz and the trappings of the classical music concert to make his music palatable to the masses,"[9] made him pivotal to the public acceptance of jazz, thus paving the way for the popularity of swing music in the thirties and forties.

In any case, to the general American populace symphonic and "hot" jazz together represented a single cultural movement with profound social significance.[10] In his autobiography *Jazz*, published in 1926, Whiteman himself unapologetically promoted a vision of jazz as cultural revolution:

> In America, jazz is at once a revolt and a release. Through it, we get back to a simple, to a savage, if you like, joy in being alive. While we are listening to jazz, all the artificial restraints are gone. We are rhythmic, we are emotional, we are natural. . . . The world seems brighter, troubles don't weigh so heavily, the natural joy and delight there is in just being alive comes to the surface. That is a good experience. After it, one goes back to everyday affairs rid of the pressure of the suppressed play spirit, refreshed and ready for work and difficulties. This, it seems to me, is the great value of jazz in American life.[11]

Whiteman's music and writings are especially important in the study of jazz history in Japan because his records and repertoire were the single greatest influence on the first generation of Japanese jazzmen. In later years, when Whiteman was attacked as a fraudulent "King," his Japanese counterpart Kami Kyōsuke defended his music as the "flow of the times."[12] Beyond his musical influence, Whiteman's ideas about jazz and his own role in the music's history were available to Japanese readers through a translation of his autobiography. Natsukawa Tarō's translation *Jazo*, published in September 1929, became the primary source of information and citations for Japanese writers commenting on jazz. The respected journal *Central Review* (*Chūō kōron*) described it as "one of the books of the century, in which the commendable, courageous American pioneer spirit thrives."[13]

Whiteman may not have been the only recognized authority on jazz in Japanese eyes, but he was unquestionably the dominant one. Today, when definitions of jazz are highly contested, it is difficult to imagine one person's vision being so thoroughly paramount. Whiteman's legitimacy as the "King

of Jazz" went unchallenged until the 1930s witnessed an emerging consensus among European jazz critics that "real" jazz was "black."[14] Mainstream media and recordings exported to Japan were bound to reflect
Whiteman's hegemony in the 1920s. At that time, the American recording
industry was nearly as segregated as public facilities in the American South.
So-called "race records" featuring African American performers were marketed almost exclusively to black people through black-owned media such
as the *Chicago Defender.* Very few "race records" or recordings of "hot jazz"
appear to have reached Japan in the 1920s: in their personal accounts virtually none of the early Japanese musicians cite King Oliver, Louis Armstrong's Hot Five and Hot Seven, Bessie Smith, Jelly Roll Morton, Fletcher
Henderson, or even "hot" white artists such as the ODJB, the New Orleans
Rhythm Kings, or Bix Beiderbecke as influences. Whiteman, on the other
hand, was ubiquitous, providing the inspiration and repertoire for Japan's
Cherryland Dance Orchestra and other contemporaneous groups. While
the connections between jazz and the black American experience were
generally known in the abstract, for most members of Japan's jazz community Whiteman and white men were more readily accessible.[15] In sum,
Whiteman's musical "synthesis" and ideological pronouncements provided
the foundation for Japanese conceptualizations of jazz in the 1920s. Japanese social critics and aesthetes modeled their arguments on Whiteman's,
yet modified them in an attempt to elucidate the meanings of jazz for
contemporary Japan.

There were two basic categories of discourse: "aesthetic" debates about
the music's artistic merits or defects; and "sociocultural" debates dealing
with the music's effects on behavior and customs, and its ramifications
for Japan's cultural identity. The aesthetic controversy—of immense importance to the international classical music establishment in the early
twentieth century—was almost the exclusive province of specialized music
periodicals. The sociocultural controversy, however, received mainstream
media attention, thus enlightening a broad audience about the magnitude
of jazz's influence. In weighing the various positions taken, it is difficult,
perhaps misleading, to characterize them as anything other than inconclu-
sive or ambivalent. Scholars of the jazz debates in America and elsewhere
tend to classify the debaters as "pro" or "con," "advocates" or "detractors."
But a significant number of Japanese commentators attempted, at least, to
adopt a detached stance in their writings, in an effort to *explain* the jazz
phenomenon rather than promote or denigrate it. As part of their project of
"scientifically" and dispassionately documenting and interpreting the social
and cultural upheavals of their day, they discussed jazz as a pivotal and
defining element of modern lifestyles.[16]

This is not to suggest that they did not have opinions about jazz's aesthetic value or social impact. Many did have strong feelings, which inevitably colored their essays. Yet their arguments are not easily reducible to "pro" or "con." Nomura Kōichi's essay "In Praise of Jazz Music," published in *Music World* (*Ongaku sekai*) in 1929, illustrates this point. While Nomura insisted that jazz was by no means a "pure, high art," he suggested that jazz had a useful artistic role to fulfill, for it exposed many Japanese to Western music for the first time. Public curiosity about jazz would eventually evolve into an appreciation for the Western classical tradition, which would in turn be beneficial to Japan's cultural refinement: the "Jazz Age," he contended, would enable Japan to become more literate in Western music and ultimately to produce "our own Beethoven and Schubert." Authentic jazz be damned, but jazz could make for authentic *classical* music in Japan.[17] In the final analysis, Nomura did not allow a clear aesthetic prejudice against jazz to inhibit his capacity to appreciate it as a potentially beneficial artistic movement.

Jazz and Modernism

The underlying assumption for both the aesthetic and social discourses was the irrevocable association of jazz and modernism, a cultural wave that swept Japanese cities in the twenties and thirties and engendered its own prolific controversies. This association was the overarching theme of the numerous essays on jazz: specifically, Japanese commentators were fascinated, repulsed, or attracted by what they perceived as jazz's transformative powers, its ability to alter the physical environment, customs, and moral codes and render them "modern." There was general consensus on one other point: that jazz was far too important a cultural trend to go unexplained and misunderstood. Celebrants of the modernist revolution advocated awareness of jazz because their ethos dictated that all new trends be embraced, but even those who expressed chagrin about jazz urged readers to acquire some knowledge of it, if only for the defense of cherished values. This theme of the grave necessity for an awareness of jazz would remain a constant in Japanese discussions of jazz for the next few decades.

Numerous Japanese historians have traced the origins of modernism in Japan to the Kantō Earthquake of late summer 1923, which decimated what remained of old Edo/Tokyo and caused a "revolution in urban life." Whether the disaster engendered a sense of progressive hope or a rationale for fatalistic decadence, most agree that a technologically "modern city" arose in the capital,[18] and that the arts and entertainment assumed new significance. "The people [who survived] the disaster were not only starved for food," as one historical account puts it, "they hungered for music, for print media, in other words, for culture. In this way the starvation for culture made Japanese more aware of the importance of culture."[19] The content, distribution, and audience of the emerging culture of modern Tokyo was noticeably different from those of old Edo. A new middle class of educated, salaried urbanites with the time, money, and desire for leisure and entertainment facilitated the development of a mass culture that valued "erotic grotesque nonsense" (ero guro nansensu). Cafes, dance halls, radio, movie theaters, revues, Western clothing and coiffure, and popular music were among the pleasures of young urbanites. The "new" culture (which, as noted earlier, was mostly old hat to hip Ōsakans) was dubbed "modernism" (modanizumu), a term that for Japanese implied the primacy of American images and models,[20] yet was quite distinct from the state-directed "modernization" efforts of the Meiji period: whereas modernization implied scientific positivism and capitalist rationalism, modernism suggested images of "lightness, frivolity, cheerfulness, and the new."[21]

"Modernism"—a "revolution in the era of cataclysms"—is an amorphous term that encompasses any number of early-twentieth-century artistic and cultural trends, including primitivism, cubism, dadaism, atonality, and abstract expressionism. Signaling the wider acceptance and even normalization of avant-garde sensibilities, European modernism was politicized aesthetics with no "clear political consequence." It "explored new levels of experience, new realms of being, new physical and intellectual technologies. . . . Speed, abstraction, montage, collage, stream-of-consciousness, the twelve-tone row—all were new modes of representation designed to capture new visions of the world." Modernist arts demanded new ways of seeing, hearing, and thinking to be appreciated; they made jarring shocks to the system artistically reputable. (In fact, Tyrus Miller contends that, in its disregard for formalist mastery and aesthetics and its integration with the social world, interwar modernism was in essence "protopostmodernist.")[22] No single art captured the fascination with primitivism, the flirtation with atonality, and the fast pace and repetitive rhythms of modern life better than jazz, a music that virtually all contemporary commentators (and subsequent historians) agreed expressed the very essence of modernism.

The rise of modernist culture in Japan also indicated a noticeable shift away from the adoption (and adaptation) of European models and toward the preeminence of American influence.[23] Wilsonian democratic ideals were well-received among democratic intellectuals and activists, but by the mid-twenties the American influence on Japanese political thought had proven less enduring than the American impact on Japanese business management, lifestyles, and popular culture. Syncopated dance music, automobiles, professional sports, and movies from America served as quintessential symbols of modernism, and as the primary conveyers of modernist images and ideals, they shaped Japanese conceptions of modern lifestyles.[24] Japanese intellectuals and writers were cognizant of the growing prominence of America in Japanese cultural life and pondered its ramifications. "Already no one doubts that America rules today's world," Murobuse Kōshin wrote in 1929. "These days Europe has lost its ruling position in all respects. . . . What is ruling our lives today? How about that circular building? How about that cinema? That jazz? That radio? That Ford? How about the financial world view? Sports? . . . Americanism is becoming a principle of our lives." Ōya Sōichi likewise equated the diffusion of automobiles, airplanes, radio, jazz, sports, finance capital, and independent journalism with the emerging cultural prominence of Americanism.[25]

But for many, modernism represented more than the importation of American lifestyles and fashions: it also signaled the erosion of traditional aesthetic and moral values, political conduct, and social interaction, particularly between the sexes. Social critics noted a seemingly dramatic transformation of morals, manners, fashions, and entertainments, collectively termed "customs" (*fūzoku*). Not a few Japanese observers, like their American and European counterparts, perceived a strong link between the values and customs of modernism and jazz music itself, which for many represented "another manifesto of cultural revolution."[26] In Japan the word *jazu* became a synonym for modernist *fūzoku*. In fact, a Japanese verb was coined to describe "jazzlike" activities and attitudes: *jazuru* ("to jazz"), as defined in the *Dictionary of Modern Words* (1930), meant "to make merry with jazz, to mess around, to talk rubbish, to be noisy, to live without cares dancing nonsensically, like jazz."[27]

The people most guilty of "jazzing" were the *moga* ("modern girl"), whose fashions, indecorous behavior, and liberated sexuality were inspired by the flapper and other female images from the American cinema, and her "foppish" companion the *mobo* ("modern boy").[28] As the icons of the era, the *moga* and *mobo* represented not only the rebellious attitudes of many well-off urban youth, but also the fears of the guardians of traditional culture and morality. The *moga*, especially, was castigated in the media as a "glittering, decadent, middle-class consumer who, through her clothing, smoking, and drinking, flaunts tradition in the urban playgrounds of the late 1920s."[29] But the *moga* and *mobo*'s worst transgressions by far were those that challenged the dominant cultural rules governing gender roles and sexual activity. One advocate of modernist sensibilities conceded that "what brings a bad reputation to the modern girl is chiefly her relation with the other sex." As early as 1917 the writer Inage Sofū had worried that the

Taishō era would witness the "feminization of masculine beauty" and the "masculinization of feminine beauty."[30] The *moga*'s "masculine" assertiveness and the *mobo*'s affected "dandiness" seemed only to confirm such fears. As we shall see, several Japanese writers contended that the new liberal attitudes toward sex and gender relations were partially due to the influence of jazz. The important point is that, as in France, the United States, and elsewhere, jazz became a "signifier" of modernism, "an assemblage of representations commonly read into the music."[31] The prevalent image of the *mobo* and *moga* lazily strolling arm-in-arm through the Ginza, as jazz songs emanating from innumerable cafes beckoned to them, symbolized the emergence of a new, foreign moral and aesthetic sensibility.

It Swings, But Is It Art?

For connoisseurs and performers of European classical music, putting jazz in its proper place on the aesthetic hierarchy was a mission of considerable gravity. To these critics, the foreignness of jazz was hardly an issue—after all, they were defending not *hōgaku* but the European classical tradition, which by that time had established itself as a tradition in Japan, if of a more recent pedigree. There is a discernible vexation with the spotlight shifting from artistic, European "high" culture to commodified, American "pop" culture, expressed in explicitly classist terms that reflect the importance of European classical culture as an emblem of refinement and status in Japan. Jazz, they grumbled, was "low class," "vulgar," "noisy," "non-music."[32]

Such elitist rhetoric expressed not only the upper-crust aesthete's distress for the cultural health of society, but also the mundane yet very real anxieties of classically trained musicians and critics who feared the implications of what was widely acknowledged as a musical revolution. Would the jazz band, they worried, make the orchestra obsolete? As one commentator put it, the jazz band symbolized the American ethic of rational efficiency because it could generate as much noise as an orchestra with a smaller number of musicians.[33] Another writer sounded a more insensitive note: in contrast to the "white-haired old men" whom most people envisioned playing Beethoven, jazz "demands youth. It demands youth overflowing with joy and power. One person does not stagnate with one instrument. One person handles many different instrumental [roles]. This is impossible for the white-haired old man who plays Beethoven. Jazz's instruments are young people. One must be young. Long live youth [*wakamono banzai*]!"[34] The Takarazuka orchestra's revolt against Ida Ichirō's jazz performances in the early twenties was almost certainly motivated by this mixture of perturbations—employment anxiety, concerns for artistic purity, and fear of

(musical) revolution. The orchestra's musicians were skeptical of Ida's motivations for playing jazz, which they dismissed as purely commercial. "The
jazz music movement is, of course, not a pure art movement," one writer
scoffed. "It is probably better to say that it is a profit-making show business
movement of professional musicians."[35] It is interesting to note that most
early jazzmen would have agreed with this admittedly cynical evaluation.
With the current campaign to enshrine jazz as a respectable "fine art" in full
swing, it is easy to forget that most of the trailblazers regarded themselves as
entertainers whose primary responsibility was to get the dancers moving,
the liquor flowing, and the libido surging.

There is no question that the classical music establishment harbored
considerable resentment and even disgust for jazz, but the new music was
not without its champions. There were writers and musicians who found
aesthetic merit in jazz, particularly in that of Whiteman, whom they credited with translating jazz "noise" into "music." An early advocate was
Horiuchi Keizō (1897–1983), one of the country's most prolific and respected music critics. As an engineering student at the University of Michigan in the late 1910s and early 1920s, Horiuchi sent a communication to a
Japanese music periodical describing his impressions of a jazz performance: "In the end, a jazz band is an orchestra that makes noise. It is hardly
related to music."[36] But, as Larry Richards has noted, Horiuchi's opinions of
jazz softened considerably. By 1923 Horiuchi was analyzing the music seriously, and within two years he admitted to a nostalgic yearning to hear the
music again: "In fact I had intended to form a jazz band in Tokyo, but since
I've not found any suitable musicians I'm giving up. It saddens me that my
only means of contact with jazz is the phonograph." By 1928 Horiuchi had
succeeded in assembling a band at JOAK (now NHK) for radio broadcasts,
and in later years he would translate lyrics for many jazz song recordings.[37]

Horiuchi defended jazz's aesthetic worth by explaining its artistic "progress" under Whiteman's guidance. The first jazz he heard was an "unmusical," "violent" performance by "incompetents" who didn't even use sheet
music, he wrote, but his first impression was rectified by Whiteman's emergence: "[He] was the person who started arranging jazz songs beautifully as
music. . . . When I heard his jazz band in New York in 1919 I changed my
thinking toward jazz. . . . At last artistic songs in a jazz style are being
created. The highest class jazz was the music composed for performance
[not dance music]: that was 1924's *Rhapsody in Blue*. . . . Now the tones in
jazz are never unmusical. A performance by an excellent jazz band will give
complete artistic satisfaction." Whiteman demonstrated that jazz need not
be low-class dance music: rather, it too could be an edifying art if exaggerated syncopation, "unmusical" sonorities, and improvisation were elimi-

nated, and if jazz could be "liberated from the practical purposes of dance music" and be rather a music "that aims for pure artistic expression, and generally is no lower than the standards of contemporary musical technique." Improvisational prowess did not impress Horiuchi: "In the past [jazzmen] made up their parts spontaneously, but in the last four or five years, that is, since the appearance of Paul Whiteman and his influence, correctly arranged parts are played from memory."[38]

It is ironic that virtually every musical characteristic to which Horiuchi objected is held up today as a defining element of distinguished jazz performance. With his jazz criticism so thoroughly steeped in the aesthetic values of the classical connoisseur, he was certainly a queer advocate of jazz. His sensibilities inclined him to admire the "synthesis" of symphonic jazz and to believe that this was the highest stage to which the music could aspire. But as the lyricist for numerous jazz songs and the person responsible for first broadcasting jazz on the radio, he was usually in the position of defending popular music against accusations of depravity, as he did in a newspaper editorial on the "Tokyo March" controversy.[39] Horiuchu's position would become even more ambiguous in the thirties and forties, when his voice joined a cacophony calling for the eradication of jazz.

Horiuchi's influence led to the 1929 publication of the first vernacular book of serious jazz analysis, by his pupil Shioiri Kamesuke (1900–1938). In addition to describing jazz's origins, blues, instrumentation, arrangement, rhythm, and piano techniques, Shioiri contributed to the lionization of Whiteman: "If it were not for Paul Whiteman's creative powers, jazz would have ended as a simple fox trot." Whiteman's innovations, rooted in the European gift for melody, "liberated" jazz from its origins in "barbarism," Shioiri insisted.[40] If jazz had aesthetic merit, it was due to Whiteman's efforts to trim the "unmusical" elements and create a more sophisticated style.

It is obvious from such writings that classical aesthetics invariably colored perceptions of jazz, leading either to outright contempt for the music, or to a preference for melodious, classical-*sounding* variations of jazz. Even more favorable essays made explicit an aesthetic prejudice against improvisation and syncopated rhythms (jazz "put the sin in syncopation"). There is also a not-so-subtle undercurrent of elitism and even racism in such remarks: few Japanese failed to note the origins of jazz among a despised minority in the United States, and even those who found artistic merit in jazz qualified their assertions by insisting that an originally "barbaric" music had been suitably sanitized for respectable consumption. It is, of course, not likely that most of these writers had actually heard "hot" jazz, but rather more likely that they relied on American descriptions soaked in classical pretension and the venom of racism. In any case, even Japanese advocates of jazz made it clear that without the civilizing efforts of Svengali Whiteman, jazz was a cheap, boisterous tramp, an unmelodious, ridiculously rhythmical, miserable excuse for music. The bias against rhythm was particularly pronounced, rooted not only in a classical aesthetic sensibility but also in mistrust of the effects that rhythm could have on the body and social behavior. The ambivalence toward rhythm was a theme that both music writers and social critics evinced in their respective discussions of jazz.

The Sociology of the Streets

Shioiri Kamesuke, Horiuchi Keizō, and other music writers were not content merely to dissect jazz musicologically and situate it within a Eurocentric aesthetic hierarchy. They did not hesitate to enter the fray when it came to speculating on the sociological import of the music in Japan. They joined Ōya Sōichi, Kawabata Yasunari (1899–1972), Gonda Yasunosuke (1897–1951), and other chroniclers who documented the emergence of the modernist culture and attributed it to the seductive powers of jazz, collectively presenting a portrait of "modern life" (*modan raifu*) in which the sounds of jazz were always within earshot. As the crucial soundtrack to the urban fantasy of "modern life," *jazu* was part of the general vocabulary by the early 1930s: it popped up in literature, scholarly social criticism, the popular media, or wherever the encroachment of America on Japanese cultural life was the topic of conversation. Kawabata's 1929 novella *The Asakusa Crimson Gang*, based on the author's observations of Asakusa street culture, incorporated jazz into its vision of modernity: "eroticism, nonsense, speed, and humor like the current events cartoons, jazz songs and women's legs." Ōya, for whom modernism was little more than the aping of American lifestyles, identified a "social stratum" of people who "lived imported modernism through movies, jazz music, dance, and sports." Others noted that the speedy, automated, competitive American lifestyle was based on the tempo of jazz.[41] A sensational ad for the fifteen-volume series *Ultramodern Jazz Literature of the World's Great Cities* declared: "Struggles for political power, disarmament conferences, . . . bankruptcy, the sale of chastity, adultery, abandoned children, domestic quarrels, airplane and automobile crashes, gambling swindles, murder, factory closings, unemployment, . . . strikes—all these events are performed to jazz accompaniment."[42]

But jazz was more than mere background music for modern lifestyles. Rather, jazz itself embodied the modern, contributed qualitatively to modern life, and through its transformative nature affected people's behavior and the environment of urban lifestyles. Like their American counterparts, Japanese observers regarded jazz as no less than "a language and an experience that conveyed change—not merely an aspect of culture affected by change."[43] "Jazz is the music of the modern populace," Horiuchi wrote. "Our lives and thoughts are reflected here [in jazz]. We should not ask if it is right or wrong. Jazz is here. Around the world the desires of today's people are poured into jazz. Denying jazz music is tantamount to denying the present day."[44]

Intellectuals depicted jazz as an international wave sweeping the civilized world, a timely portrayal in the heyday of Japanese cosmopolitanism. In previous decades it had become something of a national custom to ride such waves, to assume that Japan closely followed a path of progress blazed by the West, and that resistance was, in any case, either foolishly self-defeating or hopelessly futile. Such a course, governed by "scientific" laws of social evolution and technological progress, offered Japanese the teleological comfort of seeing their own future in Western countries. In the grand tradition of steam engines, telegraphs, and electricity, jazz was thus regarded as an international global trend that need not be—indeed, could not be—resisted. Depending on one's perspective, it was either comforting or alarming to witness the same trends in other countries. "Jazz is international," music writer Matsuyama Sueyoshi argued. "Wherever one goes it appears to be prevailing." Horiuchi assured skeptics that "jazz music is the modern popular music of cultured countries." "Like it or not," an observer of cafe culture sighed, "the time has come when jazz is venturing into the world." "Jazz is contagious," Uenoda Setsuo declared, "and . . . Orientals are not immune from this international fad any more than Europeans." Jazz, Shioiri proclaimed, "is the modern person's dance music. It is the music of the modern people of Japan, of France, of America, of the world. Those of us who breathe the modern air and live in the present day should at least understand this jazz music."[45] Jazz thus signaled Japan's cosmopolitanism and its arrival in the modern Western world.

Jazz was flexible enough a metaphor to represent in musical terms either the transformations that created and defined modern society, or the revolt against those changes. Kathy Ogren's analysis of the American jazz debates characterizes the Japanese discourse equally well: "All commentators strongly identified [jazz] with change and with the emergence of modern sensibility, despite a lack of consensus on the benefits or ills associated with the music."[46] Jazz was said to be the musical embodiment and even a cause of the fast pace, mechanization, noise, libidinal liberation, adolescent rebellion, and amorality (or immorality) that characterized modern life. A

6. "Dai Tokyo no jazo—
The Jazz-Band of Tokyo,"
from *Asahigurafu*
2 Nov. 1927.

1927 collage in *Asahigraph* entitled "The Jazz-Band of Tokyo" is a striking illustration of the symbolic associations jazz greedily accrued in Japan.[47] It is a picture often used to depict reactions to urbanization and concomitant environmental changes that occurred in interwar metropolises. A conductor stands in the center of the picture, reading a score and waving a baton. A swirl of images surround him, apparently paying no heed to the conductor's efforts to bring order to the "performance." The images include an electric streetcar, a steam engine, a whistle-blowing policeman, a street vendor, a tractor, a street entertainer, and an automobile, each with its own racket rendered in onomatopoeia. "Jazz," here treated as a metaphor for the dissonant, mechanical urban noise, is portrayed as a disorganized hodgepodge of sound. In Japanese mass media, the word *noise* (*sōon*) was often used to describe jazz's sound and, conversely, the word *jazz* was synonymous with *noise*. Hosokawa Shūhei regards the *Asahigraph* collage as indicative of jazz becoming an indistinguishable part of the "soundscape" of post-earthquake Tokyo. The noise of reconstruction in the capital "made people feel the real chaos of the collapse of Meiji and Taishō morality and ways of life. It is not without reason that that noise sounded like the new music—jazz and symphonies." The word *jazz* came to represent not only dance music but also the constant, indecipherable noise generated by machinery, phonographs, and radios.[48] On this point, classical music enthusiasts were likely to agree that jazz was more akin to noise than to music.

The "noise" with which jazz was associated was most often described as mechanical. The rapid mechanization of Japanese industry and society during the wartime boom and following the earthquake was one of the most conspicuous changes of the early twentieth century. Commentators used the word *jazz* to describe the rhythms, tempos, and sounds of the various new machines that changed the aural environment of the city. Shioiri Kamesuke defined modernism as "machinism" (*kikaishugi*), which he viewed as a trend conceived in the United States and the USSR and imported to Japan. With its "random, mechanical rhythm," he wrote, jazz was the "musicalization of American rationalism and efficiency." Moreover, because a small jazz band, with each member performing several instruments, was capable of producing the "same results" as a much larger symphony orchestra, the jazz band symbolized the American ethic of rational efficiency.[49]

But most commentators were not oblivious to the dual nature of jazz: it could be both primitive and modern, old and new, "savage and civilized." "Associated with primal sources (wild, erotic passions) and with technology (the mechanical rhythm of brushed drums, the gleaming saxophone)," jazz not only represented mechanization and efficiency, but was the clarion call of rebellion against soulless materialism and pragmatism.[50] Rhythmic jazz was the music of the body, the crucial link to the primitive: "Jazz gives the body the pleasant movement of rhythm," Horiuchi wrote. "Modern people demand rhythm." Murobuse Kōshin argued that jazz, as the music of "the people" rather than of the intelligentsia, rejected science and intellectualism. Jazz represented "emotion as opposed to reason," and constituted a "humanist revolt against machinism, a savage revolt against the high-speed civilization."[51] It was exactly the primitivist appeal of jazz performance that worried some Japanese observers, who in essence portrayed the "primitive" jazz ethic as a root cause of the misbehavior of the *mobo* and *moga*.

The "emotional," "irrational," and "popular" nature of jazz concerned those Japanese writers predisposed to distrust the morality of the "masses." In particular, they worried about the influence of jazz and social dancing on gender relations and sexual morality. In this regard they often repeated the concerns of the self-appointed arbiters of morality in the U.S. jazz debates. Of course, they did not base their arguments on the Judeo-Christian moral codes that informed the American critique of jazz, but many Japanese commentators nonetheless echoed the puritanical rhetoric of their American counterparts when it came to issues of gender, women's liberation, and sexuality. In Japanese portrayals the sexual play and gender ambiguities that were so visible in the streets, cafes, and dance halls were closely linked to jazz, if not *caused by* jazz. Kawabata Yasunari uses the "Ginza Jazz Dance" to highlight the "gender fluidity" of *The Asakusa Crimson Gang*'s cross-dressing protagonist Yumiko:[52]

> The changes of costume are so rapid that breasts are openly displayed in the process.
> And now we have Number 6, "Jazz Dance. Ginza."
> On a street the width of a sash; Sailor trousers, false eyebrows,
> An Eton crop. What fun! Swinging the snakewood! Silk hat at an angle, black velvet vest, red string necktie, collar opened whitely, a thin stick under an arm—it is of course an actress impersonating a man. Her legs are bare.[53]

In Kawabata's sensationalized depiction of Asakusa, jazz is more than mere accompaniment to the dance: the author's choice of the word jazz, in the same year that "Tokyo March" propelled that word into the modern vocabulary, was a deliberate one, for no single word captured the culture of nudity, gender ambiguity, and play for its own sake better than *jazz*. Androgyny and commodified sexuality were, of course, not unprecedented in the land of the *onnagata* (female impersonator in *kabuki* theater) and licensed prostitution, but acceptable transgressions of gender laws historically had been much more open to men than to women. In the jazzy culture of modernism women seemed to transgress the gender boundaries and codes of sexual behavior as freely as men.[54]

The *moga*—as portrayed via Kawabata's Yumiko and Tanizaki Jun'ichirō's vixen Naomi (*A Fool's Love*)—was identified as the principal transgressor of these taboos. The media stereotypes of the *moga*—"Japanese version" of the American flapper, eroticized cafe waitress or "taxi dancer," or shameless flirt toying with men's libidinal urges—are well documented. Contemporary explanations of the *moga*'s misbehavior have yet to receive scrutiny. But such "explanations" are offered in the jazz debates, where participants suspected jazz as the primary stimulant. "America's teenage girls are said to mature 'too fast' due to jazz's frenzied influence," Murobuse Kōshin warned in his 1929 book *The Sociology of the Streets*. "Jazz makes people into drunkards and sex maniacs, drives them mad, and causes civilized people to fall to the level of the African jungle. Because of [jazz] it is a fact that divorce is increasing. . . . [I]t is also a fact that the revolution in male-female relationships was brought about by jazz." Murashima Yoriyuki (1891–1966), author of *The Cafe: Palace of Pleasure* (1929), shared Murobuse's concerns about the influence of jazz on sexual morality. Murashima maintained that in America jazz substituted for alcohol as a stimulant during Prohibition:

"People felt like they were drunk without liquor." Cafe proprietors in Japan, eager to indulge their customers' every fantasy and craving, added "this strongly stimulating music" to the already provocative mix of beautiful waitresses (*jokyū*) and alcohol. Murashima contended that jazz "causes the listener's reason to evaporate and destroys his will; instead his daydreams recur, and his animalistic sexual desires rise." As the destroyer of carnal inhibitions and stimulator of hormonal ecstasy, jazz was obviously more than background music.[55]

None of the music critics or essayists cited above openly called for government or police intervention to control or contain the emerging jazz culture. They were concerned about jazz's social implications and put forth hypotheses, based on teleological observations of America and considerable fieldwork within domestic street culture, regarding the social and cultural significance of jazz in Japan and the modern world. But those very assertions and hypotheses, even if originally put forth in the (dis)interest of "social science," provided an intellectual base on which apparatuses of social control could be justified and constructed. Commercial dance halls were from their inception subject to stringent regulation to prevent their numbers from exceeding the official capacity to supervise them. Immutably entangled with "erotic service," social dance, and raunchy popular song lyrics, perhaps jazz's guilt was primarily one of association. Although the music itself was not explicitly singled out as an object of state control until after Pearl Harbor, it is clear that an ample consensus suggesting that jazz stimulated public immorality had already emerged a decade earlier.

Of course, Japan boasted a venerable history of businesses that commodified female companionship and indulged the affluent male customer's every sexual fantasy and sensual pleasure: too much very well known history and lore would have to be swept under the rug before Japanese could convincingly adopt a puritanical posture. To those with nativist proclivities, then, what made the modern cafe and its jazz more objectionable than the traditional *geisha* house and its *nagauta* was little more than the conspicuously "foreign" character of such entertainments. Moreover, traditional forms of erotic entertainment had proven their manageability, having been contained within officially sanctioned and licensed, semiprivate places for centuries. The brothels, theaters, and teahouses constituting early modern erotic service more or less recognized their "proper place," spatially, socially, and culturally. The boundaries of pleasure quarters such as Kyōto's Shimabara, Edo's Yoshiwara, and Ōsaka's Shinmachi were clearly marked with earthen walls, moats, and monitored entrances.[56] By contrast, in the 1920s and 1930s social conservatives, nationalists, government officials, and police fretted that the unruly, "foreign" jazz culture did not or would not recognize the "public transcript" that guaranteed the integrity of such boundaries.[57] The challenge for them was to determine new limits that a mass media phenomenon such as the jazz culture would observe. *Central Review*'s American correspondent Hata Toyokichi reported that even in the United States there were stringent laws circumscribing social dance and jazz activity: "One must not think that the troubles [associated with social dance] are limited to restrictive Japan." Even Wisconsin imposed boundaries on jazz and social dance, he noted.[58] But it became clear that the integrity of those boundaries was easily compromised in the new era of media technologies. The media's fascination with and penchant for sensationalizing jazz culture made confinement within socially sanctioned borders unimaginably difficult. In a world of newspapers, magazines, records, movies, and radio, how could one hope to confine something as sensational as jazz? Moreover, national coordination was necessary to prevent the spurts of growth experienced in Kansai and in the capital resulting from Ōsaka's 1927 dance hall ban. Finally, law enforcement officials and censors had to cope with the jazz community's seemingly boundless ingenuity for circumventing each new restriction they handed down. Musicians, dancers, and proprietors discovered that, with delicacy and cunning, it was possible simultaneously to obey the letter and violate the spirit of any law directed at crashing their party.

The power of jazz to arouse and titillate may have been a cause of chagrin to some, but it could be appealing and even useful to others, particularly advertisers: depending on the target market, images associated with modernism, social dance, jazz, and wild times could be quite effective for selling products or drawing customers. Japanese advertisers were becoming particularly adept at creating desire and manipulating behavior through the use of potent imagery, and they found that *moga, mobo,* cigarettes, booze, and saxophones were appealing to the new urban consumer class (Ōya's "modern stratum"). It is, of course, impossible to gauge accurately and comprehensively how prevalent images of jazz were, but two collections of graphic design and advertising, *Great Compilation of Commercial Ad Design* (1936, reprinted in 1989) and *Japanese Modern: Graphic Design between the Wars* (1996),[59] suggest that they were quite popular with advertisers and consumers. In addition to numerous posters, magazine and newspaper ads, and matchbook covers featuring top-hat-wearing *mobo* and flapperlike *moga* images, both collections include ads featuring identifiable jazz musicians. Banjos, saxophones, and caricatures of black minstrel entertainers appeared in advertising for a variety of products and businesses. A print ad for Regal Pomade features a typical icon, a tuxedo-clad saxophonist, blowing vigorously with grotesquely inflated cheeks of Gillespian proportions. Advertisers plainly sought to create a sense of desire for modern lifestyles, entertainments, and arts, iconographically equating them with urbane sophistication and thus promoting the ideals (such as they were) of modernism. For a time, at least, such strategies worked, until the intellectual climate encouraged advertisers to use restraint with modernist imagery and, rather, adopt more nationalistic themes and symbols.[60]

Jazz and Japan's "Culture Wars"

The 1930s was a tumultuous decade in Japanese history, witnessing the steady erosion of electoral party control over the government and the military, brutal suppression of left-wing political groups, military adventurism in Asia, withdrawal from the League of Nations and from international arms control treaties, and domestic terrorism designed to destabilize the party government. Rising rates of juvenile delinquency, divorce, illegitimacy, and other social ills alarmed many Japanese. Advocates of reform, from militant terrorist to nativist intellectual, felt threatened that "external pollution" would contaminate the very essence of indigenous culture and thus legitimized militant action.[61] They advocated not only significant changes in political and economic structures but also a profound transformation (or "restoration," as they put it) of culture and society through the purging of Western cultural influences.

At first glance, it may appear ironic that the height of the Japanese jazz community's prosperity coincided with the nationalist upheaval of the thirties; but it actually makes a great deal of sense, since the jazz community itself provided an easy target on which the diverse conservative, fascist, and nativist movements of the day could agree to concentrate their fire. Government officials, militarists, agrarian fundamentalists, and advocates of native arts differed in their visions for the nation, but they could usually reach a consensus that the jazz culture was disruptive to those visions. For many, the dance hall and the community that supported it represented the ultimate examples of the spiritual and moral decay that modernism and American materialism and individualism supposedly instigated. With the nation facing so many internal and external challenges, it must have seemed offensively frivolous for leisure and entertainment to consume so much attention and economic resource. Moreover, the prosperity of the dance hall culture only intensified existing resentments over disparities of wealth and privilege: why should effete urbanites be allowed to blow several days' wages dancing the night away when their country cousins were starving in their villages or dying on the frontiers of northeast Asia? The various writings on jazz cited earlier lent credence to these discomfiting impressions and thus provided an intellectual foundation for social control measures taken by law enforcement, municipal governments, and eventually the national state.

As noted earlier, the dance hall was the primary target of harassment and legal suppression. If the tough economic times make the interwar jazz and dance community's prosperity seem remarkable, the persistent scrutiny and interference of local and national officials make it even more so. The specter of social control dogged the social dancer's every step and reflected the specific concerns over public morality raised in the jazz debates. In 1928 national attention focused on Kōbe, to see how the port city would deal with swarms of dance refugees from Ōsaka and a sizable foreign population determined to fight for its right to party. The Hyōgo prefectural government's November 1928 code, designed to prevent degradation of "morals," thus set the standard that police and municipal governments would emulate nationwide.[62] The regulations required proprietors, dancers, and instructors to apply for permits and to register with the police their names, addresses, birth dates, occupations, and (in the case of married dancers) spousal consent. Furthermore, Hyōgo set up architectural and zoning restrictions: dance halls could not be located in basements or higher than the third floor of any building; no extraneous rooms or internal locks were permitted; and halls were not allowed within one hundred meters of government buildings, residential neighborhoods, shrines and temples, hospitals, or schools.

The code extended minute control over employees' and customers' behavior: no one under age eighteen was allowed to enter the halls; dancers and customers were seated separately and were barred from fraternizing; alcohol was prohibited; drunks and "people with infectious diseases" were not permitted to enter; "obscene words and deeds" were proscribed; and halls were to close at eleven P.M. "The public morals of the dancers were subject to great scrutiny," dance instructor Hara Kiyoshi recollected. "Each girl had a time card on which she had to write down the hour and minute she left the hall and the exact time she arrived home, with her parents' seal affixed when she got there. The next morning she had to show that to the manager at the hall and get his seal too."[63] The requirement that all customers register their names, occupations, and other personal information every time they entered a dance hall also contributed to a sense that "jazzing" was suspicious (if not criminal) behavior that required constant police vigilance.

Four days after Hyōgo's restrictions were announced, Tokyo's Metropolitan Police Board fired a preemptive strike against "dance fever" in the capital with its own code, threatening those who failed to adhere to any of its twenty-two articles with revocation of permits and shutdowns, and reserving the right of unannounced inspections by undercover officers to guarantee compliance.[64] It is clear that such regulations favored larger halls and discouraged the smaller operations that could not meet the stringent requirements.[65] Unable either to meet the code or to compete with the famous large halls' massive amounts of capital, prime locations, stunning decors, top bands, attractive dancers, and police connections, smaller dance halls withered in a competitive, even hostile, climate. After all, it was simply easier for the police to monitor fewer, larger halls. Yet neither the strict regulations nor periodic harassment by right-wing groups hindered the profitability of dance halls, or discouraged an increasing number of entrepreneurs from applying for permits in the early 1930s. One Ōsaka writer observed, "Of all the institutions in the gay quarters, dance halls have become one excellent way to do business."[66]

The most detailed and evocative contemporary account of dance hall culture from the perspective of dancers and patrons that I have yet encountered, in Kitao Ryōnosuke's 1932 *Modern Ōsaka*, suggests that the regulations did little to correct the improprieties they were designed to address. The essay appears on the surface to be a detached description in keeping with other "scientific" studies of modernism at the time. Yet, like other writers whom Miriam Silverberg has dubbed "ethnographers of modernity," Kitao apparently could not resist the urge at once to titillate his audience and to fan the flames of moral outrage. His bizarre portrait of dance halls in Hyōgo and Ōsaka prefectures juxtaposes nude women, uniformed students, shiftless foreigners, and lusty couples locked in scandalously tight embraces, camel-walking and foxtrotting and tangoing the night away.

Some joints reminded Kitao of public baths: after checking one's hat and coat at the door and stripping, one went in and saw "many naked women moving about." "With the dim, gloomy lighting, and sound of the band echoing eerily, somehow it felt at first like the bathroom of a spa. . . . Hmm, shall I warm myself a bit?" Immediately thereafter he noted, "At the halls one happens to see that the number of students, who are legally banned [from dance halls], is quite large. They wear their school uniforms and caps. Just when you think that they are only male students, you see female students inside [as well]. At any given hall, the prices for afternoon and evening tickets are different, yet even when evening comes the student regulars do not leave."[67] Kitao went on to offer minute descriptions of the taxi dancers' bodies, noting in particular how slender they all were and that they did not "look Japanese." "Women with body odor don't sell well to Japanese, but sell to many foreigners. Foreigners don't play around long, but three of them will [show up and] buy ten dance tickets, fool around with a woman to their heart's content for ten or fifteen minutes, then quickly withdraw." At one point the author referred to the dancers, sitting demurely in their white dresses waiting for a patron's come-hither wink, as "prostitutes" (shōgi), and suggested that some halls were prepared to accommodate a patron's desire for a more private dance. Yet even if a customer's inclination was simply for a whirl on the dance floor, "[he] is really holding the woman's body," Kitao emphasized. "It is a dangerous thing. . . . [for] the body warmth of a solemnly embraced wife or daughter to revive in the heads of gentlemen memories of the touch of a woman of the gay quarters."[68]

Kitao's was apparently one of the less hysterical accounts of dance hall culture to appear in the thirties, but with its imagery of naked women and predatory paramours mingling with schoolchildren, it clearly provided enough fodder to enrage moralists. As pressures on the dance halls increased, one music critic warned that the jazz musician and aficionado's dependence on the dance hall endangered the music's future in Japan. Funabashi Yōji lamented, "In Japan today [1935], the jazz life cannot maintain its economic independence separate from the dance hall," which was subject to shutdowns and suppression by the authorities at any so-called "time of crisis." He advocated that "as a principle, jazz bands as a group should move out" of the halls and find alternative, less vulnerable venues. Aware that jazz and dance musicians did not have the most laudable of social reputations, Funabashi scolded them for making two to three times more money than most people, yet failing to manage it responsibly. "I have seldom heard talk of saving . . . it seems that there are many wasteful people"—indeed, jazz musicians such as trumpeter Nanri Fumio and trombonist Shūtō Isamu have confessed to squandering considerable fortunes living the fast life. Disgusted with such behavior, Funabashi reproved: "If they save a little every month, and with that common fortune organize to buy necessary scores, recordings, and music magazines, and have a general rehearsal even twice a week, they will be able to [create] a style as a band and earn recognition; without vainly bluffing they should majestically insist upon their value as an individual band." Such financial responsibility and independence from the constricting demands of the dance halls would not only rehabilitate the public image of musicians, but enable them to "create good jazz in Japan."[69]

Funabashi's call for prudence and his warnings about the dangers of continued reliance on the dance halls proved prophetic. To the average worker with few employment options, the stereotypical jazz musician with plenty of work who nevertheless continued to drift from job to job for personal reasons, who usually blew his large salary at watering halls and dens of iniquity, and then had the nerve to borrow advances (bansu) against his wages, and who fraternized shamelessly with the "taxi girls" with whom he worked, was hardly a commendable figure. Trashy novels and newspaper reports of scandals involving dance halls fanned the flames of discontent throughout the thirties. As Nagai Yoshikazu points out, the jazz and dance industry rarely even tried to respond to such media vilification, but rather devoted its energies to mastering the latest steps or debating the relative merits of English or French dancing. Rarely did jazz musicians or dance hall advocates directly address the legal and social pressures they faced.[70] Perhaps they sensed that the ideological climate made it increasingly unlikely that their pleas would find sympathetic ears.

What did the public really think of dance halls? According to Shigeta Tadayasu, there was too broad a spectrum of opinions to indicate more than a general consensus that some sort of control or containment mechanism was necessary. Shigeta's *Theory and Reality for Policing Customs* (1934), a comprehensive guide to the rationale for and implementation of control over everything from cafes, brothels, amusement parks, eateries, and film, to public baths, teahouses, inns, advertising, and "general manners," recorded a variety of opinions on dance halls and categorized them. There were those, the author noted, who detected no harmful effects in social dancing as an entertainment, and therefore perceived no need for the police to be concerned. Indeed, because liquor was forbidden in dance halls and because dancers and patrons were seated separately, Shigeta contended, "morals within the halls are rather good compared to cafes and bars. Because of the various scandals spread by the newspapers and such, there are many people who think dance halls are bad places, but such is not the case. There are various problems outside the halls, but what goes on inside is not what the public imagines." Contrary to Kitao's sensational exposé of what went on behind the dance hall's closed doors, Shigeta insisted, the regulations were appropriately stringent and appeared to be working. Nevertheless, most opinions suggested varying levels of discomfort with dance halls: some felt that "since foreign customs such as social dancing were not akin to Japan's pure and beautiful customs, it should be banned with firmness"; others contended that social dancing was intended for personal enjoyment between family and friends, and that the commodified ticket and taxi dancer system was thus "not truly social dancing"; finally, others opined that it was "too early" to introduce social dancing into the private household suddenly, and that therefore social dancing should be left to the dance hall "pros" because "if the proper controls are applied there is little harm."[71]

All of these perspectives suggested that there was a consensus for *some* form of control of social dancing, in order to quarantine any malignant influence emanating from the dance hall. Although Shigeta noted that social dance was "by no means limited to upper-crust society" any longer, there were still more people who did not go to dance halls than there were those who did (he cited a January 1933 survey stating that on a good day nearly five thousand people went to dance halls, presumably in Tokyo).[72] Those with no stake in the jazz and dance community usually supported police efforts to contain a conspicuously "foreign" and "hedonistic" subculture. Public outcries and reports of scandalous behavior had the predictable effect of instigating more police control. Local law enforcement could and eventually did refuse to issue more dance hall permits after the initial growth spurt of the late twenties and early thirties. Large numbers of permit applications continued to pour in, but now were routinely rejected. Alternative venues, such as dance schools or even modified private homes, represented the bulk of further growth in the industry in the 1930s.

It seems fair to say that, as primary instigators of Japan's "culture wars," jazz music and dance were singled out as targets in an ideological turf battle. It is misguided to portray jazz culture as the target of an extremist, lunatic fringe; rather, it provoked in a broad and diverse population a sense that the viability and integrity of Japanese society and culture were threatened. As 1920s-style "cosmopolitanism" lost credibility as a national ethos, 1930s-style "culturism" (*bunka shugi*) won adherents from a variety of social spheres. After a brief flirtation with cosmopolitanism, many Japanese intellectuals and artists sought a return to what they imagined traditional indigenous culture to be, and to a spirituality supposedly obscured by modernism's sensual physicality. Renowned novelist Tanizaki Jun'ichirō was representative of this intellectual current: having experienced "modern" Western-style pleasures himself, he later mocked the superficial adoption of a Western veneer in *A Fool's Love* and *Some Prefer Nettles*. He and others advocated a revival of a spiritual and aesthetic sensibility that they maintained was unique to Japan and made it superior to Western accomplishments.[73] It might be argued that *culturism* is just a more polite term for *fascism*, especially if we accept the definition of the latter term as a "cultural movement" obsessed with the "folk," cultural authenticity, and national community.[74] What is important to acknowledge is that moderate intellectuals seeking national spiritual renewal are as representative of culturism/ fascism as militant jingoists, hotheaded cadets, thought police, and terrorists: all shared a nightmare of cultural and aesthetic atrophy as terrifying to them as the potential loss of oil sources was to the Imperial Navy.

Critiques of jazz continued to find expression in both aesthetic and sociological discourses. As anyone familiar with the eleventh-century novel *The Tale of Genji* can attest, matters of aesthetics and taste have often functioned as a legitimate basis for social and political criticism in Japan. In this grand tradition, taste issues were at the heart of critiques of modernism, which seemed appropriate given the importance placed on image and appearance in modernism: modernism was thus critiqued virtually on its own terms.[75] In their campaign to excavate, formulate, and articulate a representative indigenous aesthetic, some well-known writers seized on jazz as the antithesis of the refined artistic sensibilities of the Japanese people. Kuki Shūzō (1888–1941), whose 1930 essay "The Structure of '*Iki*'" spoke with scriptural authority of an authentic indigenous aesthetic, dramatized the fundamental incompatibility of jazz with Japan's aesthetic virtues: "The facial expressions characteristic of *iki* have no relation at all to the Western vulgarities, including winking an eye or puckering up the lips to play jazz."[76]

Other critics worried more about the social effects of jazz than aesthetic degradation. They expressed discomfort with the selfish "individualism" that the American art of jazz was believed not only to represent but to promote. This was an increasingly common theme as the nation became embroiled in war and demands for national unity and the suppression of individuality became more strident. Others, such as Ōya Sōichi, set the stage for later condemnations of "decadent" modernism and a struggle to edify and elevate the "spirit" rather than indulge and gorge the "senses."

> If bourgeois literature is a literature of the emotions, and proletarian literature is a literature of the will, it can be said that the literature of the modern stratum is a literature of sensuality. Modern life's center of gravity is in the senses.
> Modern life is a type of consumptive economics, the aim of which is to satiate the senses. . . . There are no "ideals" in modern life. That is because those who live within this [modern] social stratum think that having "ideals" is insignificant. There is no "morality" in modern life. That is because they know well the classist nature of "morality." . . . It is a world of sensuality.[77]

Advocates and detractors alike concurred that jazz stimulated suggestive physical activity: it did not appeal to the mind or the spirit, but rather to the body. Japan's long tradition of sensual indulgence (of which Kuki's *iki* was itself representative) notwithstanding, jazz seemed to have a distinctly less edifying, objectionably boorish quality incompatible with supposedly more refined, traditional erotic sensibilities.[78] Writers such as Ōya, Murobuse Kōshin, and Murashima Yoriyuki had effectively ascribed to jazz the power to make people abandon their sexual inhibitions in revolutionary ways.

Japan versus the West; authentic traditionalism versus inauthentic modernism; group-ism versus individualism; spirituality versus sensuality: these were the polarized discursive categories that shaped Japanese conceptualizations of jazz and set the conditions by which the music was embraced or rejected. It is also fair to say that jazz was among the most important catalysts of these debates. As fans and detractors both conceded, jazz was too *loud* to tune out, too provocative to ignore in a nation that was rethinking the essence and boundaries of its own culture.

Even as late as 1935 (when it no longer seemed politic to do so), Muromachi Jirō opined in a dance periodical that jazz was an indispensable element of life in modern times. Referring to the "modern" nations collectively as "we" and "us," he contended that people in the postwar world demanded a more "stimulating and powerful" music than previous generations had to "satiate our senses." Muromachi mentioned Duke Ellington's performance before enthusiastic audiences in Paris to prove that "jazz is their true art, the fountain of their lives. Classical music, then, has finally receded from the realities of our lives." "Do we not," he queried, "actually sense the motion of our lives in the sound of the saxophone? . . . This music was born from our lives, and shapes the content of our lives."[79] But by explicitly framing his conception of jazz as symbolic of cultural and historical similarity between the West and Japan, the essayist was some years behind the times, swimming upstream against an intellectual current that promised to wash away cosmopolitan modernism and all of its trappings. Fundamental differences from the West, and alternative, authentically indigenous definitions of "modernity,"[80] were increasingly regarded as among Japan's virtues, so associating jazz with modernism in the mid- to late thirties was a defensive strategy best avoided.

A mere one year later, another dance magazine carried a roundtable discussion with a very different message. Ikeda Yasukichi, head of the Tokyo Metropolitan Police Board's "Morals" division, was among the discussants. Participant Fujimura Kōsaku insisted that the "national conditions [*kokujō*] of Japan are quite different from those of foreign countries, and I think it is wrong for our dance community to take in all Western things as they are. I think that even if we take the [Western] form we should make a spiritually Japanese style." In response, another discussant sang, "Even if I learn the dance of another country, in my heart is the Japanese spirit," to a round of applause.[81] The roundtable was held on 20 February 1936, six days before fourteen hundred troops from the Imperial Army's First Division fanned out through Tokyo, assassinating politicians and army commanders, seizing government and police buildings and the prime minister's residence, and calling for their comrades to join in the mutiny and protect the glory of the emperor from the indignities heaped upon him by foreign powers. This shocking coup attempt was peacefully defused through imperial intervention, but most historians agree that Japan had turned a corner, moving toward confrontation with the Western powers as well as with the legacies of its own recent, cosmopolitan history.

The Jazz Revolution

Japan's early experience of jazz closely resembled the "jazz encounters" of other nations: at every stop on its global adventure, jazz excited youth, incited debate, and, as a metaphor for a feared American cultural hegemony, inspired nationalist reactions. Transmitted via new mass-media technologies of radio, recordings, magazines and newspapers, and moving pictures, jazz's apparent ubiquity in the interwar period made it a likely candidate for the first truly international art form. Jazz's ability to elicit such powerful emotional responses in audiences around the world was revolutionary. But its "racial" origins within a predominantly black underclass, its eventual appropriation by a predominantly white bourgeoisie, and its status as a symbol of "uniquely American" values and modes of behavior also aroused consternation in countries where national self-determination and efforts to define "pure" ethnic identities were priorities. Some Germans under the Weimar regime danced to jazz, while others targeted jazz as a polluting element in national cultural life. In the USSR the Communist Party struggled to achieve consensus on whether jazz was bourgeois or proletarian. In France jazz was appropriated by political radicals and artistic avant-gardists in their struggle against a bourgeois society that, in their view, repressed individual expressive freedoms and marginalized art. Our comfortable characterization of jazz as a "universal language" fails to do justice to the conflicts the music ignited around the world in the first half of the century.

Jazz's unsettling presence in Japan elicited responses similar to those in other countries, but there were some important differences. In Japan, jazz was linked much less obviously to avant-garde movements in the arts and literature or with left-wing radical politics than was the case in European countries, where the music's engagement with radical politics was more explicit. Jazz was "the new signifier for bohemian life" in interwar Europe; leftists detected in jazz "musical evidence of social reform and [racial] integration."[82] By contrast, in Japan modernism in general and jazz in particular were decidedly apolitical—indeed, the implied connection between jazz and radical politics in the lyrics of "Tokyo March" ("dancing to jazz . . . Marxist boys with long hair") was perhaps the only link that the general public might have recognized, and the excision of that lyric from the final recording ensured that most people would never even perceive such a connection. Those writers and artists who engaged jazz in their work usually employed it as a metaphor for modernist eroticism or to provide provocative background settings.

Although other scholars might see it differently, my reading of modernism and jazz culture suggests that it was more spectacle than political revolt in the traditional sense, committed more to a rather vague sense of personal liberation than to any particular dogma or agenda. *Modanizumu* was not so much a system of beliefs as a plethora of commodities: the "revolutionaries" were consumers, armed with hairstyles, short skirts, pulp novels, and phonograph records; *modanizumu* was not something you believed in, but rather something you wore or listened to. The "revolution" with which modernism and jazz were associated did not aim to undermine Japanese capitalism or overthrow the emperor system, but rather instructed adherents in new sensual and aesthetic experiences, and new modes of social interaction and diversion. Its challenge was to the social rules for public behavior, attire, gender relationships, and speech, not to political privilege or economic injustice—the *mobo* and *moga*, merrily spending daddy's money for their own entertainment, were indeed the products and beneficiaries of political privilege and economic injustice. Yet whether or not overtly political intent is discernible, the political *consequences* of modernist/jazz "customs" (*fūzoku*) are most obvious. Jazz musicians and aficionados may have regarded themselves as politically disinterested, but their critics were quick to equate the act of dancing with subversion. In the eyes of rightist detractors, at least, the personal was political.

Another noticeable difference between the early jazz experiences of Japan and Europe was the lack of a Japanese analogue to the *négrophilie* that was a defining element of modernism and jazz culture in Europe, particularly in France. Besides the allegedly "magical" power of African sculptures which spellbound Cubist and Fauvist artists, black icons such as "the jazzman, the boxer (Al Brown), the *sauvage* Josephine Baker" fascinated interwar Parisians. There was a sense among many European artists and intellectuals that the simple, primitive culture of black people represented the antidote to civilization's evils and evoked the spirit of a new age. From the perspective of the primitivist connoisseur suffering a "crisis of values" in the postwar era, black people's childlike naturalness and assumed "lack of intelligence and civilization" were "virtues, not vices."[83] Japanese seem to have acknowledged a black contribution to modernism: "The blood of black people [*kuronbō*] has crept into the art worlds of Europe and America," Hata Toyokichi wrote in *Central Review*. "Black melodies and black lifestyles have certainly invaded contemporary lifestyles [throughout] the world. . . . Due to jazz music, black blood has already become our blood."[84] But the ubiquitous, exaggerated caricatures of black people, beckoning from countless posters promoting jazz events in Europe, do not seem to have been as prevalent in Japan's early jazz culture. One obvious reason for this difference is that there were far fewer (and much less well known) black musicians performing jazz in Japan in the 1920s than there were in Europe. It also seems quite natural that "primitivism" held less appeal to a non-Western nation that had spent the last half-century trying to demonstrate its "modernity," than it did to a jaded, war-torn European society whose "civilized" values were called into question by a conflict of unprecedented scale and savagery. For whatever reason, Japan's own experience of *négrophilie,* and the equation of blackness with authentic jazz expression, would come much later.

Repeating Riffs

While my focus here has been on Japan in the twenties and thirties, it seems appropriate at this point to note that a number of the same themes and issues raised in the interwar jazz discourses would recur in the immediate post–World War II era, when jazz was essentially reintroduced to Japan by U.S. Occupation forces. The equation of cosmopolitan modernity with American-style democracy and lifestyles, as well as the sense that, like it or not, some knowledge of jazz was imperative in the modern world, indicate that conceptualizations of jazz had undergone less radical transformations than had the music itself. This thematic continuity is particularly visible in Nogawa Kōbun's *The Music of Modern Man: Jazz* (1949), the structure and focus of which mirrors closely Shioiri Kamesuke's *Jazz* of exactly twenty years earlier. Like Shioiri's book, Nogawa's prefaces musicological and sociological explanations of jazz with a grand statement about the music's role in shaping international and domestic culture in the modern era; and like his predecessor, Nogawa stressed the "inseparable" relationship between jazz and modern America's mechanized society.[85]

Other postwar writers emphasized jazz's affinity with the Occupation's mission of democratization and the historical moment of "modernity." In the Occupation era that word had shed most of the negative (if not the West-centric) connotations it had acquired during the war, and was again regarded as a positive national goal. As the quintessential modern music, jazz was more relevant than Western classical music to the sunny optimism of modern lifestyles. "We Cannot Live without Jazz," poet Fujiura Kō proclaimed. "People in the age of radio, airplanes, atomic bombs and the like cannot disregard jazz by saying that this stimulating sound is vulgar. . . . Jazz is already in our bodies. It is already moving in our veins. . . . It is fun. It is happy. It is beautiful." In the years following the official "jazz ban," the return of jazz to public airwaves signaled the nation's newfound freedom. "There is a well-known saying that 'jazz and freedom go hand-in-hand,'" bassist and broadcaster Honda Toshio noted, "and in fact, in Japan and Europe after the Second World War, jazz and freedom *did* come hand-in-hand." Critic Noguchi Hisamitsu argued that in spite of continued prejudice against jazz, "no one can deny that somehow [jazz] is the music that has lived in the everyday lives of twentieth-century people." Noguchi described jazz as a "democratic music" with a "modern character." "Jazz is not a music imposed by America: it is the music of a new age that appeals to something in the emotions of twentieth-century man."[86]

Occupation-era discussions, like the interwar debates, claimed that the presence and popularity of jazz in Japan confirmed the nation's status as a partner in the "free world" community of nations. As their predecessors had argued that jazz was "international music," postwar writers purveyed the notion of jazz as a "universal music." "The fever for jazz is not a phenomenon observable only in Japan," Noguchi remarked. "It is neither the music of one American region, nor Negro folk music, but . . . is becoming a global music." "As the accompaniment to active modern lifestyles," Nogawa reiterated, "jazz has sunk strong roots not just in America but in South America, Russia, and of course Europe. And it is now entering Japan with a rapid energy." Composer Mayuzumi Toshirō noted, paradoxically, that "in the end jazz has become a cosmopolitan national music," symbolizing "common traits between Negroes and people throughout the world."[87] In an era that many still regard as "Japan's second opening to the world,"[88] the "universal," cosmopolitan nature of jazz was played up, squaring nicely with America's cold war stance that its own culture and values were "universal" and beloved throughout the world.

Having asserted jazz's importance as an international culture relevant to Japan's own modernization and democratization, postwar commentators echoed their interwar predecessors by stressing the imperative necessity for a true understanding of jazz. "It is meaningful for many reasons that Japanese, as cultured people, listen to, understand, and try to grasp the essence of jazz," Nogawa urged. As Japanese embarked on a determined effort to attain an American standard of living, they could not afford to dismiss or misunderstand jazz. "Everything is being rationalized, to such an extent that cultured people around the world now aspire to the living standard of American cultural life. Jazz exists as one of the alphas of American cultural life. This is a fact that Japan, rising from the ravages of war and defeat and standing as a cultured country, cannot ignore."[89]

Again, even those whose enthusiasm for jazz was tempered, or those who

perceived something ominous in jazz's influence on postwar society, advocated knowledge of it. This was particularly true during the early fifties'
"Jazz Boom," which witnessed the proliferation of jazz broadcasts, concerts,
and coffeehouses. A 1953 newspaper article described the fad in language
that echoes accounts of two decades earlier: "Fans [of the jazz boom] are
making their parents cry and becoming the objects of criticism from social
psychologists. . . . Recent jazz concerts have gone beyond 'enthusiastic,' and
are halfway maniacal. It's not that fans, primarily high school and college
students, are listening to jazz; they are literally going wild over the sound.
And the bands are 'blowing' to respond to audience demands." Musicologist Sonobe Saburō, who argued that "the popularity of jazz is one manifestation of [American] colonialism," conceded that because "[jazz is] the
popular music that satiates youthful energy, is filled with a modern sensibility, and overflows with rich human emotion," it should be "well studied."
The renowned social psychologist Minami Hiroshi, in a popular women's
magazine, lent the aura of "science" to his contention that jazz had a "narcotic effect" on young people. His admonishment that concerned parents,
"who reject jazz [yet] know nothing about it," "investigate a little more to
find out what is bad about [jazz]," was motivated by a clear desire to "protect" young people from its influence. The author's concerns centered on a
statement he attributed to a teen-aged jazz fan: "It's great, because when
you listen to and watch jazz, at that moment you can live without thinking."
"Sadly, many young people do not want to think about reality," Minami
lamented, "and if they are listening to jazz all the time they gradually lose
the habit of quietly thinking about things. . . . The suspension of thought is
the result of jazz's psychologically narcotic effect."[90] Friends and foes of jazz
alike thus repeated riffs that had aired a few decades earlier, indicating that
concerns about the effects of modernity on an authentic Japanese identity
were not alleviated by the Occupation.

Of the thematic similarities spanning pre– and post–World War II jazz
discourses, this idea that jazz *mattered* is crucial. The music's Japanese aficionados appear always to have had a missionary's enthusiasm for spreading the jazz gospel, so it is not surprising that they would insist on its
importance. But it is clear that even detached observers and outright opponents of jazz music and social dance acknowledged a revolutionary potential that warranted attention, if not vigilance. Ideas, information, and issues
from America's own public jazz debates plainly had an impact on the content of the Japanese discussion, but it is evident that Japanese brought their
own tastes, anxieties, and frustrations to the table. The principal impulses
behind conversations on jazz were the desire to account for the seemingly
dramatic shifts in domestic behavior, morality, and popular consciousness

and to ascertain Japan's position within the international cultural sphere. If essays on jazz proved that Japan was indeed a "modern" nation, questions were then raised about the sacrifices made to attain such status and even its desirability. As "part and parcel of the American civilization that has been pouring into the country with irresistible force,"[91] jazz represented either the integration of Japan into an emerging "global" culture or the gradual and unwelcome erosion of authentic traditional culture, or both.

Needless to say, the ideas about jazz discussed in this chapter collectively had a substantial impact on the Japanese jazz community's economic and social life, artistic inspirations, technical development, and creative aspirations. By shaping the public consciousness of jazz as an inauthentic alien and erotic art that induced the jarring moral and behavioral changes of modernism, commentators, however unintentionally, provided intellectual grounds for the creation of social control mechanisms whereby the jazz community's influence could be contained. When the jazz community's response came, it was a musical one. Fearful for the very survival of their culture by the mid-thirties, jazz musicians and aficionados actively sought ways not only to circumvent the law and deflect hostility, but also to integrate with the hegemonic order—by making jazz Japanese.

CHAPTER FOUR

"JAZZ FOR THE COUNTRY'S SAKE": TOWARD A NEW CULTURAL ORDER IN WARTIME JAPAN

Unfortunately, I have to admit that I did not have the courage to resist in any positive way, and I only got by, ingratiating myself when necessary and otherwise evading censure. . . . Because of my conduct, I can't very well put on self-righteous airs and criticize what happened during the war. . . . In wartime we were all like deaf-mutes.—Kurosawa Akira, *Something Like an Autobiography*

There is a ten-year blank in Japanese jazz history, from 1940 to 1947, '48.—Yoshida Mamoru, "Daremo shiranai Nihon jazu shi (2)"

How funny to listen to jazz music on the night before going out to kill the jazzy Americans!—kamikaze pilot Oikawa Hajime, quoted in *Fifty Years of Light and Dark: The Hirohito Era*

In the middle of Japan's "Great Holy War," the legendary singer Awaya Noriko, home from a tour entertaining Japanese troops in Southeast Asia and strutting down the Ginza with a fresh manicure and heavy lipstick, was accosted by a member of the Patriotic Women's Association. "In these times," the woman scolded, "luxury is the enemy!" "Hey, this is my preparation for battle!" Awaya retorted. "Can I go on stage with unkempt hair and an unpainted face? A singer's stage makeup is no more a 'luxury' than a soldier's helmet is!" In an interview years later Awaya explained, "Many people performed in military uniform or *monpe* [pajamalike work pants]. But the people who came to hear me were looking for dreams. I couldn't appear on stage in monpe. That would be depressing for me and my audience." But she did not characterize her actions as subversive: "I had no such logic. It was just my character. I do things when I want to do them and if I don't want to . . . I don't."[1]

In her rejoinder to the self-righteous patriot's admonishment, Awaya essentially portrayed herself as a "patriotic entertainer" whose gaudy-glam style abetted rather than subverted Japan's "holy crusade." During the war, permanent waves and cosmetics were indeed proscribed through government edict and peer pressure, but Awaya certainly made a case for persisting with her beauty regimen. The encounter and Awaya's response bring to light a relatively unexamined aspect of Japan's wartime experience: the *positive* roles that artists created for themselves in a society where free artistic expression was considered dangerous. For centuries, Japanese artists and entertainers had attempted to navigate the treacherous waters mined by ever-evolving political circumstances, and arts such as *kabuki* theater bear the marks of government-mandated "refinement."[2] In many respects, jazz and other modern art genres were bound to undergo a similar "modification" during the years of modern Japan's greatest cataclysm. Call it opportunism, hypocrisy, or prudence: to Japanese artists who lived through the Pacific War, it was called surviving or getting by.

Most readers will find it surprising that jazz maintained any sort of presence in wartime Japan. Conventional wisdom certainly suggests that jazz, the most quintessentially "American" of popular arts that seized the Japanese imagination in the early twentieth century, disappeared from the face of the archipelago, victim of a state-mandated "total jazz ban" (*zettai jazu kinshi*). Jazz musicians, fearing the omniscient eyes and probing tentacles of the military police (*kenpeitai*), must have tooted their horns discreetly, if at all, we are told. Oral testimonies by jazzmen who lived through the war rarely if ever contradict this vision, but rather echo those of countless other Japanese who regard the war as a time of personal suffering. Jazz musicians and aficionados describe how a draconian police state deprived them of their livelihood, now and then peppering their remarks with occasionally comic tales of sedition and noncompliance.[3] It is worth quoting at length a representative statement that illustrates what jazz artists remembered about their wartime experiences and how they narrated them. The following account is taken from Matsuzaka Hiro's roundtable interview with trumpeter Nanri Fumio, drummer Okuda Munehiro, and saxophonist Matsumoto Shin, published in *Jazz Critique* in 1972. Matsuzaka's introductory remarks state:

> On December 8, 1941, there was a declaration of war against both America and Britain, and through violent compulsion all the orches-

tras and artist collectives were ordered to disband in succession; as far as songs were concerned, dull songs, limited to military songs [gunka], popular songs [ryūkōka] suitable to the emergency situation, and folk songs [min'yō], circulated, but what remained in the hearts of the masses of course leaned toward the sorrowful songs that had been sung since the old days.

Matsuzaka then queried his informants about their wartime experiences.

MATSUZAKA: What happened to the musicians after the dance halls closed in the autumn of 1940?
OKUDA: There were some who quit performing, others who got draft notices, everyone was already scattered. As for light music bands, there were the Shōchiku Light Music Orchestra, Sakurai Kiyoshi and his band, Nagauchi Tadashi and his band, Moana Glee Club, Kaida Katsuhiko's band, Okuda Munehiro and his band, and that was about it.

Because I was contracted to Polydor Records, I went out with other Polydor artists in a movie attraction band. Even after we got into the war, the big movie theaters in the six major cities still always had attraction bands between films. We went on several provincial tours with [singers]. And comfort tours for the troops.

There was something interesting that happened in Ōsaka. The police stopped me, and when I asked why they said, "When we counted earlier you hit your cymbal sixty times. You hit it too many times, and that's Anglo-Americanish," so I called an officer to come back and watch tomorrow, and he said, "If you perform mixing in military and folk songs there's no problem"—but the previous day when the police came to the theater I had occasionally played flashy drum solos on "Yagi-bushi." That was Sugii Kōichi's arrangement.

After that . . . my draft notice came [Okuda was then ordered to form a comfort band]. . . . But when we were moving from Harbin [Manchuria] to the south the transport ship we were riding was sunk and we were thrown out into the sea and suffered much.
MATSUZAKA: Mr. Nanri, was the reason you returned from Dairen [Manchuria] because the dance halls were closed by the war?
NANRI: In the autumn of 1940, dance halls were closed in Dairen and in the hinterland. When I went to Dairen in 1936, it was at the height of the Manchurian Railway boom and the economy was good . . . it was the most prosperous period of my life. . . .

When I returned to Japan there were no dance halls, so I joined the Shōchiku Light Music Orchestra and we made the rounds at such places as the Asakusa Electric Hall and the National Theater.

MATSUZAKA: At that time you could still play jazzy stuff, right?
NANRI: At that time you could, but after December 8, 1941, it became enemy music [*tekisei ongaku*] and we absolutely could not play it. It was okay to play German and Italian songs because of the alliance, so we played "O Sole Mio" and "Two-Headed Eagle" in a jazz style, but it seemed that everything sounded like jazz to the police and they told us our performance method was bad. Even if we were told that, though, we couldn't stop or we wouldn't eat. That was something I fought throughout. When we performed for the troops we played military songs and pop songs as jazz. We fooled them a lot, and we were quite busy! Later I entered the army and because my regiment was in Okinawa, most of my peers died in the war.[4]

I asked similar questions of Raymond Conde, a Filipino clarinetist who performed for shortwave radio propaganda broadcasts directed at Allied troops. I naturally assumed that Conde's experiences as a foreigner and a jazz performer would be particularly poignant. But his replies to my queries were relaxed, dispassionate, and rather uninformative, if delivered with his ever-present smile.

Until the mid-nineties, at least, memories of World War II that dealt with anything other than personal loss and hardship were actively suppressed.[5] A perusal of any standard biographical dictionary reveals that a whole generation of people left blank spaces in their biographies, which coincide with the war. One need not have committed war crimes and atrocities to be reticent with reminiscences of wartime life. "To see ordinary Japanese in World War II as simultaneously victims and victimizers offends our conventional sense of morality," John Dower has written, "but is nonetheless an important step toward recognizing that the great war in Asia was a tragedy for everyone involved."[6] Japanese are often taken to task for failing to sustain a resistance movement analogous to the one in Nazi Germany. But does failure to resist necessarily constitute complicity? Does periodic compliance negate the occasional subversive act? It is clearly fairer and more accurate to acknowledge that small acts of subversion and compliance occurred on a daily basis, that even the most selfless patriot was capable of hoarding rationed food for the family, and that even the most reluctant of imperial subjects could contrive a way to fight the hated enemy.

Our common approaches to cultural life in wartime society have been to recite the many formal and informal limits on artistic expression; to regard all artistic products of such circumstances as aesthetically compromised and therefore unworthy of attention;[7] and to commemorate those courageous few who suffered explicit persecution rather than sacrifice their creative autonomy. But, as will become clear in this chapter, the history of jazz in wartime Japan demands that we find new approaches that do justice to the social and cultural complexities of the time. How were disparate social groups to achieve consensus and integration during the "national emergency"? What were the role and status of the artist? How were the limits on the artist's creativity to be decided, and who would decide them? Does the production of art that shapes or reinforces popular conceptions of national exceptionalism constitute war responsibility?

These are questions that apply to all of the arts, but there are more specific questions related to jazz and the issues of authenticity with which this book is concerned. For a couple of decades, America had been the sole referent of authentic jazz for Japanese. Now that war with America had commenced, and contact with American jazz masters assuredly severed, how could the music develop? Was it possible for Japanese to formulate their own collective voice within a jazz or jazzlike idiom? Did the war thus represent an unprecedented opportunity to create something new and self-referentially authentic, something unifying rather than divisive, something quintessentially Japanese? Contemporaneous evidence suggests that, while they might have denied it later, some musicians and writers answered these questions with a decisive affirmative. It is worth emphasizing that, whereas S. Frederick Starr and Michael Kater depict attempts to "nationalize" jazz in the USSR and Nazi Germany, respectively, as state-inspired and state-directed, in Japan endeavors to create a "national music" (kokumin ongaku) were often made as responsive yet autonomous creative decisions by the artists themselves.[8]

In wartime Japan jazz was indeed a topic of much discussion and subject to extreme measures of control, but many people recognized that it was also ideally suited to certain wartime purposes. Recognizing that jazz and popular dance music had sunk roots too deeply for a "total jazz ban" to be plausible, music experts and policymakers (often the same people) envisaged a new jazz that contributed positively to the reformation of national cultural life and to the war effort. Without necessarily embracing an anti-American, expansionist, or fascist ideology and supporting the conflict wholeheartedly, Japan's jazz community made a painstaking effort to find a positive role for itself and its music in wartime society. The jazz of this period, usually referred to as "light music" (keiongaku) or "salon music" (saron myūjikku), represented a compromise that would satisfy state censors, cultural nationalists, audiences starved for diversion, and jazz musicians who had traditionally merely replicated the latest American trends. Given the circumstances, performing "jazz for the country's sake" (kuni no tame no jazu)—on "comfort tours" for soldiers and munitions workers, on records for a public in dire need of cheering up, or on shortwave radio propaganda broadcasts—was a task gladly undertaken by Japan's jazz community.

"Japanese Jazz" and "Cultural Renaissance"

Late one evening in 1937, the same year that war erupted between Japan and Nationalist China, Hattori Ryōichi was downing a drink in a seedy Yokohama *chabuya*. Something about the neon lights, the background music, the customers' flirtatious yet desperate merrymaking, and the sounds of the nearby harbor struck him as strangely moving, even sad. Gifted as a songwriter, Hattori was inspired to express those feelings in music. He was convinced that the blues was the only effective musical form for capturing the dank, dark mood of Honmoku, but it could not be the same blues that evoked Mississippi cotton fields and chitlin-circuit juke joints. Working with his lyricist Fujiura Kō (1898–1979), he mused, "I don't think that the blues, such as W. C. Handy's 'St. Louis Blues,' is the monopoly of black people. Don't you think that a Japanese blues in Japan, an Oriental blues, is quite possible?"[9] Hattori encountered difficulty pitching the idea to his record company and to his chosen chanteuse, tango and chanson singer Awaya Noriko, but his persistence resulted in the hit "Farewell Blues." By 1938 a "blues" fad was in full swing. The theme of "Farewell Blues" was hardly remarkable: like any number of Japanese popular songs from that time and since, it described lost love in a specified, evocative setting. But the *idea* of the "Japanese blues" must have been compelling. Hattori's audacious effort to nativize a music that most people then and since have regarded as peculiar to black Americans was a pivotal, if not entirely unprecedented, moment in the history of Japanese popular culture.

It was also timely, for it coincided nicely with similar nativist movements in other art media of the 1930s, collectively dubbed a "cultural renaissance." A sense of the exceptionalism of Japanese moral and aesthetic values infused the work of painters, composers, poets, novelists, and filmmakers who were devoted to the sacralization of Japan and its cultural identity. They actively resisted what they regarded as contaminating influences from European culture through their art; they questioned the application of amoral industrial modernity to Japan; and they sought at once to reestablish contact with the continental Asian roots of Japanese culture and to assert Japan's suitability for regional leadership.[10] Fine arts and mass media served these purposes by selling emperor souvenirs, inserting patriotic themes in advertising, disseminating romanticized images of "exotic" peoples within Japan's empire, and sanctifying "cultural traditions." Defining the "Japanese essence" through art and folklore was an "institutionalized activity" in the 1930s. Even Kurosawa acknowledged the movement's effects: "The Japanese have rare talents. In the midst of the war it was the encouragement of the militarist nationalist policies that led us to a fuller appreciation of traditions and arts, but," he added, "this political sponsorship is not necessary."[11]

In some respects, Hattori's jazz homage to Japaneseness dovetailed nicely with these artistic currents; in others, it differed sharply. Unlike many nationalist artists, Hattori and other jazzmen who followed his example should not be characterized as cultural xenophobes. Theirs was a decidedly cosmopolitan ethos, starved for musical stimulation from any source, East or West. They simply added Japan to the list of possible sources of inspiration. Nor were they prepared to abandon the rhythmic base, instrumentation, or sound of a jazz band. The undeniable preference for American jazz continued unabated, with swing hits by Benny Goodman, Artie Shaw, and Count Basie gaining popularity. Hattori and others who set out to "indigenize" jazz may have shared assumptions about the uniqueness of the Japanese spirit, aesthetic sensibility, and emotional tendencies. By appropriating melodies, lyrical themes and symbols, and sometimes entire songs for jazz arrangement, they hoped not only to sell records on the domestic market (this motive cannot be overlooked), but to expand the expressive possibilities of jazz to include the allegedly singular culture of Japan. But they originally had no intention of *limiting* their work to such expressions.

The central figure in the Japanification of jazz, Hattori Ryōichi, had been a fixture of Ōsaka's vibrant mid-twenties jazz scene, performing in the Izumoya Youth Band, saxophonist Maeno Kōzō's dance band, the Manila Red Hot Stompers, and the Ōsaka Philharmonic Orchestra, before moving on to arrange and compose for Taihei Records and study with Russian conductor Emmanuel Metter (1884–?), a disciple of composer Nikolay Rimsky-Korsakov and refugee of the Russian Revolution who had been hired to conduct the Ōsaka Philharmonic. Hattori was among the few jazz musicians who remained behind when others deserted Ōsaka for the capital in the late 1920s, but he too headed east when his company, Nittō Records, moved its operations to Tokyo in 1933. After a brief tenure in the Tokyo Union house band led by *Shanhai gaeri* Kikuchi Hiroshi (1902–1954), Hattori retired his saxophone and devoted more time to composition. In 1936 Hattori joined Nippon Columbia, the preeminent "jazz song" factory, as house composer and arranger, thus starting a long association that would earn him the sobriquet "Japan's Cole Porter."[12]

When Hattori's nativized blues hit the record bins, he reinvigorated the eclectic genre known as "jazz songs." Since the first records of 1928, jazz songs were most often translated versions of American Tin Pan Alley hits: vocalists invariably sang the lyrics in both Japanese and English, stepping aside for instrumental breaks (usually prearranged but occasionally improvised). Songs selected usually reflected the public's taste for themes of "love and homesickness,"[13] yet jazz songs continued to be regarded as "imported culture" (hakurai geinō). The paucity of original Japanese compositions within the jazz song genre in the early thirties most certainly contributed to this lingering foreignness; it did not help that Japanese versions often competed with the original versions on the market (either imported or pressed domestically by multinational corporations such as Columbia and Victor). Yet within a few years, a handful of composers and arrangers emerged to reinvent the genre as a nativist voice in jazz, for a market increasingly receptive to prescriptive notions of Japaneseness.

For Hattori, creating Japanese jazz usually meant writing arrangements of traditional folk songs for jazz band, or composing original compositions with native themes or associations. In his autobiography Hattori wrote, "With 'The Mountain Temple Priest,' I ventured to emphasize the rhythm and maintain a jazz style. But that would not have been enough to make a hit. I think it worked because I chose a folk song, a handball song that everyone knows. In other words, the fact that I aimed at a Japanese jazz, within the jazz idiom, led to its success. The same can be said of my blues. The plan was for a Japanese blues that used the emotions of Japanese people as material."[14]

Hattori stated his motives for mining the folk repertoire in blatantly commercial terms: his job, after all, was to sell records that Japanese consumers would buy, while still retaining his artistic interest in jazz. It seems that Hattori never relinquished the belief that his music was essentially "jazz," whether "Japanese" or not, and neither did he cease to seek musical inspiration from wherever possible. He and the few others who followed his example never lost faith in a cosmopolitan artistic outlook that included Japan as one among several potential sources of inspiration. The composition that best represents his vision, "The Mountain Temple Priest" (1937), which "successfully applies a female chorus to a jazzified ancient Japanese melody," is cited by Segawa Masahisa and others as proof of the existence of a truly "Japanese jazz" in the interwar era.[15]

Hattori's jazz arrangements of Japanese folk songs established a precedent that a few composers and arrangers at other record companies imitated and that deeply influenced the "light music" that even virulent nationalists considered acceptable in the late 1930s and early 1940s. His influence on other composers and arrangers was direct, for he personally tutored future competitors from other labels in harmony, music theory, and arranging—at informal, all-night sessions in his own home. Pianist Taira Shigeo and clarinetist Sano Tasuku took their lessons from the master to Nippon Victor, where they too jazzed Japanese material. (It bears repeating that most of the music under consideration here would not be considered "jazz" by our contemporary standards, but I am using the more musicologically expansive definition[s] in currency at the time.)

Columbia may have resisted Hattori's "Japanese blues" initially, but as war broke out on the Asian continent, Japan's recording industry became increasingly receptive to popular music that met the standards of the regime's campaign to "spiritually mobilize" the populace for total war. Jazz records that celebrated Japanese exceptionalism or promoted pan-Asian brotherhood fit the bill, for a while at least. In September 1937 each record company voluntarily halted production of controversial popular songs, and increased production of military songs.[16] As the government and armed forces stepped up rhetoric about Asia's common cultural and racial heritage and mutual grievances against the Western colonial powers, to justify the war in China, a handful of jazz artists produced records for a public receptive to the idea of pan-Asian brotherhood. They demonstrated that even they could comply with spiritual mobilization goals, by producing patriotic "jazz" marches and jazz treatments of Asian folk songs. As the Japanese military used Western military technology in an attempt to unify East Asia under its own aegis, so Japanese musicians used Western music to promote the vision of a common Asian heritage. The ambiguity is visible in the very titles "Canton Blues," "Jazz Rōkyoku," and "China Tango."

Historians have typically described this musical shift as an attempt to "deceive" the authorities or to fend off pressure from government censors.[17] But there is no evidence to suggest that artists were cajoled by their record companies or by the authorities into adopting Chinese material for propagandic reasons. Rather, the project must have seemed appropriate at a time when the notion of Asian unity under Japanese leadership was considered a worthy goal. The public response was quite favorable, either because the music was artistically rewarding, or because jazz aficionados perceived that nativized jazz was a safe, officially acceptable alternative as American jazz came under increasingly fierce attack.

Hattori, his pupils Sano and Taira, and Sugii Kōichi (1906–1942) were the most prolific producers of "Asianified jazz." Hattori and Sugii, in particular, were well versed in various types of music and, with exquisite timing, turned to the Chinese folk repertoire just as the "China Incident" degenerated into a quagmire. Very little is known about Sugii, and Hattori's autobiography barely mentions his China songs, so we have no record of their sudden interest or respective motivations for jazzing Chinese music. Hattori's "China period" commenced as soon as he returned from a tour to entertain Japanese troops in the spring of 1938. His songs appeared on

Columbia records, Shōchiku stage shows, and Tōhō motion pictures that either borrowed Chinese melodies or employed Chinese settings. His songs certainly capture the romantic ambivalence that colored Japanese perceptions of their Asian neighbors at that time: for all the talk of a common Asian heritage that necessitated postcolonial unity, images of Asians in mass culture often made them seem queer and exotic, charmingly backward and even desperate for Japanese guidance. Again illustrative of popular entertainers' involvement in valorizing and "selling" the Japanese colonial project, the lyrics to Hattori's "Shanghai Souvenir," "Nanjing Souvenir" (both 1938), "Canton Blues," and "China Tango" (both 1939) evoke a romantic playland worlds away from the carnage of Shanghai and Nanjing:

China Tango, a song of dreams,
Red paper lanterns sway, swinging to the wind, swinging to the song,
In a swinging, darkening Chinese town.
China Town, a moonlit night, China Tango, faint as a dream,
A street vendor's flute fades, and the distant red lights, and the blue lights, as well
The forelocks of young girls,
The night grows late, without dreariness.

China Tango, a song of the night
In the deep night sky, damp with fog, damp with song
Suzhou is great! The junk boats,
China Town, a moonlit night, China Tango, faint as a dream.
The rouge windows on the street corner, damp with blue jade balls,
In the forelocks of young girls, the shadows, too, are fun,
As the night grows late.[18]

Hattori could be even more blatantly patriotic, as suggested by his hit songs "I Love Japan," "Jazz Rōkyoku" (both 1938), and "Patriotic March" (1939) (none of which are included in the definitive three-cd Hattori anthology issued in 1989).

Clarinetist Sano Tasuku produced similar pieces as an arranger for Polydor, King, and Nippon Victor. Guilty, perhaps, of lèse-majesté for boasting to an interviewer, "I was the first to really jazzify folk songs and perform them onstage," Sano demonstrated his debt to Hattori by arranging (in occasional partnership with Taira Shigeo) a number of Japanese folk songs and shamelessly patriotic ditties for Victor during the late 1930s, with titles such as "Hinomaru March" (1938), "Japanese Emotions," "Pacific March," and "Hero of the Sea" (all 1939). If Hattori was one of the foremost peddlers of jazzy imagery of China, Sano was the same for Southeast Asia. His hit "Java

Mango Vendor" (1942) was one of several songs he composed based on impressions of South Sea cultures he culled from newspaper accounts and photographs of Japan's conquest of the region (although Sano would eventually see occupied Southeast Asia firsthand as a member of an orchestra entertaining troops).[19]

Sano was also responsible for a 1942 suite, entitled *Songs around the World*, that is intriguing on several levels. For one thing, it was released on four sides, a double-record set, at a time when materials for phonograph records were becoming increasingly scarce. This was a practice reserved primarily for classical music, used in jazz only in exceptional cases (most notably Duke Ellington's *Reminiscing in Tempo*), suggesting that King Records felt considerable confidence in the release. The contents, however, are more fascinating in light of the conventional narrative about the fate of jazz in wartime Japan. Sano arranged for the King Light Music Orchestra a collection of folk songs from Japan, China, Italy, and Germany, as well as England, Hawaii, and the United States. On this piece, "O Sole Mio" and "Sakura Sakura" join "My Old Kentucky Home" and "Aloha." The arrangement veers from passionate tango to thundering swing, from light waltzes to schmaltzy string passages. Sano deliberately set East Asian melodies over Argentinean rhythms or bombastic American swing, thus further decentering the identity of the music. The Japanese folk melodies are randomly located in the piece, given no more privileged or reverent a treatment than the others. For jazzmen such as Sano, perhaps, Japan was still part of "the world," not outside or above it. Clearly, as late as 1942, months after the first official denunciations of jazz had been issued, it was possible not only to produce music that drew on eclectic—even enemy—sources, but to jazz those sources, as well.[20]

It is no mean musical feat to meld aharmonic Japanese melodies to jazz and blues harmonies and rhythms, and it does not always come off. I would venture that no one was more accomplished at this delicate task than Sugii Kōichi, whose rarely cited work holds up brilliantly to contemporary standards of jazz performance. A graduate of Tokyo Imperial University, he had studied classical piano since childhood but developed a particular interest in tango and popular music while stationed in Buenos Aires as an employee of an Ōsaka shipping company.[21] A self-taught, enthusiastic student of various folk musics, Western classical music, jazz, and even American cartoon soundtracks, Sugii spent the mid-thirties performing on accordion and bandore, singing, and arranging for Sakurai Kiyoshi's tango orchestra before joining King Records as a staff arranger in 1938. Over the next three years he masterminded the King Salon Music Series, an ambitious collection of thirty songs (fifteen records) consisting primarily of Japanese and

Chinese folk songs arranged for jazz band. Star jazzmen such as Nanri Fumio and the Filipino brothers Vidi and Raymond Conde lent their improvisatory talents to the dates, creating what must certainly be the most significant early jazz masterpieces "made in Japan."

Sugii reportedly reached a fairly wide audience for his music via recordings, radio broadcasts, and theater performances (Okuda Munehiro's testimony cited earlier states that Sugii's arrangements were used on his "light music" tour). His strongest charts are distinguished from those of his contemporaries by a rhythmic rawness that evokes memories of Ellington's "jungle period," and by Sugii's seemingly endless palette of tonal colors (a trait he shared with Ellington and Akiyoshi Toshiko).[22] An early death robbed Japan of one of its premier jazz talents: Sugii was hospitalized on the day that Japan attacked Pearl Harbor, and died in April 1942 at the age of thirty-six. Sano Tasuku contributed four more swing arrangements for the King Salon Music Series before the project was shelved in 1942. The series under Sugii and Sano's guidance demonstrated that one could continue to write and record music that was identifiably jazzy during the war period, while still expressing and purveying the officially sanctioned (if somewhat contradictory) visions of Japanese exceptionalism and Asian cultural unity. Like Hattori Ryōichi, they added "Asian" colors to their respective palettes at a time when demonstrations of pan-Asianism not only ingratiated them with prospective censors but also sold like hotcakes.

It should be noted that in the late thirties American swing à la Goodman captivated far more Japanese jazz aficionados than "Asian jazz" ever could. But the music of Hattori, Sano, and Sugii was very much a product of its time, well suited for a nationalistic climate. They could pay homage to Japan's cultural heritage and mission in Asia, and thereby authenticate their jazz as both original and as Japanese, without explicitly rejecting the very prominent American influence in their music. As U.S.-Japan relations worsened, however, that was not good enough. Even Hattori met criticism for the "decadence" of his music and lyrics, and it became clear that even the production of explicitly patriotic songs would not soothe rabid foes of the jazz and dance subculture. The previous chapter demonstrated that jazz music and jazz people represented the exact opposite of everything that virulent nationalists valued. The continued presence of jazz in Japan—nativized or otherwise—was inimical to their own vision of a national culture free of foreign influence. Yet, as discussed below, the complete eradication of jazz and Euro-American culture proved impossible, and the work of the "Asian jazz" composers came to represent the only real precedent for a national popular music that could be used to define Japan's national character as well as actually fight the enemy. The musical innovations of the late

1930s, the effort to authenticate their music as native by creating a Japanese jazz, demonstrated that the jazz community had the potential to contribute positively to the culture of a people at war. With a little guidance.

War on the Jazz Community

The war on jazz began in earnest shortly after the Marco Polo Bridge incident of 7 July 1937, drawing on an arsenal of ideological weaponry accumulated over a decade. The announcements of the National Spiritual Mobilization campaign in September 1937 and the National Mobilization Law in March 1938 gave the Home Ministry the authority to intervene in the jazz and dance industry, authority that had heretofore been the province of local law enforcement.[23] Critics of dance halls were cheered that their worst fears would be abolished through national policy, as the Home Ministry stated its unambiguous position at the outset: "The existence of dance halls and dance schools, which rebel against our national conditions (kokujō), disturb [our standards of] womanhood, encourage frivolity in our youth, and exert not a little bad influence on the nation's public morality, [is] truly undesirable."[24]

People within the jazz community may have scoffed at the idea that they were a threat to the moral fabric of society, but they had to adjust to a very real change in their circumstances. During the early years of the jazz controversy, members of the community had generally been remiss in responding to charges of immorality and cultural subversion, but now they made frantic efforts to demonstrate their willingness to spiritually mobilize. Members of the dance industry hurriedly organized their first nationwide advocacy group, the All Japan Dance Hall League, and petitioned the Home Ministry and the police with a "New Policy" that earned them a temporary reprieve. Under these new regulations, "professional female dancers" and "adult male customers" were the only legally sanctioned couples that could engage in social dancing.[25] In addition, guests had to register their names, ages, and addresses upon entering the halls so that the police would have a record of dance hall customers for future reference. (Actually some municipalities had enacted such measures much earlier.) To further demonstrate their patriotism to the public, dance halls advertised that all of their taxi dancers were enlisted in either the Patriotic Women's Association or the Women's National Defense Association. Taxi dancers were paraded before the press on visits to Yasukuni Shrine (where the spirits of Japan's war dead are enshrined), or hosting a special "Night for Comforting the Imperial Army."[26] Some musicians, taxi dancers, and managers who could not cope with the new policy fled to Shanghai, Dairen, or other East Asian destinations where

7. Professional dancers from Tokyo's Kokka (National Flower) Dance Hall take a break from military drills with the Patriotic Women's Association (*Aikoku Fujin Kai*), 18 January 1938. In spite of their military attire, these women retain some *moga* proclivities, with their cigarettes and (soon to be outlawed) perms. Photo courtesy of Mainichi Shinbun.

the atmosphere was, for a time, less constricting. But most continued to work in the dance halls at home, hoping that conspicuous displays of patriotism would deflect further suppression.

Their efforts proved fruitless. Well before hostilities between Japan and the United States formally began, jazz was labeled "enemy music," and local and national law enforcement did not hesitate to harass dance halls and other establishments that featured jazz. Police dropped in at jazz coffeehouses on a whim and scolded customers as they sipped their coffee: jazz was a "decadent drug," they bellowed, insisting it corrupted anyone seduced by its siren song. "Hidden jazz" (*kakureta jazu*) records—usually Sugii Kōichi's Salon Music Series—enabled a few jazz coffeehouses to weather the storm, for in spite of the undeniably jazzy instrumentation and swing, the Japanese titles on the labels were often enough to satisfy the police that nothing decadent was afoot.[27]

The dance halls were not so lucky. By 1939 dance halls began closing for lack of business, as social censure effectively inhibited customers from patronizing them. With the slogan "luxury is the enemy" on everyone's lips, the entire entertainment industry faced harsh regulation to rid it of frivolity, and the dance halls were singled out for impending elimination. The fateful year for the dance halls was 1940—the same year that Japan entered the Tripartite Alliance with Nazi Germany and Fascist Italy, celebrated the Empire's 2,600th anniversary, and announced its vision of a Greater East Asia Co-Prosperity Sphere. A nationwide dance hall ban was announced effective on the first day of November. Even halls that had already closed their doors opened for the "Sayōnara Dance Night" on Thursday, 31 October 1940. Dance halls nationwide were packed with customers, reportedly three to five times the normal size of a weeknight crowd, jostling and pushing one another to get in. For the final, tearful encore, "The Light of the Firefly" ("Auld Lang Syne"), male customers (who outnumbered taxi dancers) embraced and danced with each other.[28]

Masaki Hiroshi, a lawyer and publisher of the small, independent, leftist magazine *From Nearby* (*Chikaki yori*, published from 1937 to 1949), mentioned jazz prominently in his facetious critique of the state's xenophobic (and hypocritical) attempts to dismantle the *ero guro nansensu* culture of modernism:

> A ban on dance halls, a ban on permanent waves, a ban on using the national flag in advertisements. Prohibitions and more prohibitions: It is just as if the people had all been placed in a reformatory.
>
> Jazz is noisy, neon lights hurt my eyes
> I favor things Japanese, a four-and-a-half mat room
> Drink, drink your fill—if it's saké
> Drink and then to a tumble with the closest whore
> This is the pure and noble spirit of Japan.[29]

Masaki's sarcasm was in stark contrast to the conciliatory attitude with which representatives of the jazz and dance hall industry petitioned the state for leniency. Neither approach, however, stemmed the state and the public's determination to rid Japan of what they viewed as contaminating elements.

Mobilizing Culture

With the dance halls closed and the jazz coffeehouses under constant surveillance, it appeared to many that jazz was doomed in Japan. The boom had gone bust: the economic effect on musicians was comparable to that of the "talkie" revolution a decade earlier. But it turned out that even in a world without dance halls musicians had an important role to play in the New Order. Few would argue that popular music was not an important tool in the spiritual mobilization of the people; on the contrary, there was unanimous consensus on the potentially positive spiritual, physical, and emotional effects of music. Its capacity to corrupt was at least matched by a capacity to edify. It has been argued that in capitalist societies, music is more a diversion from work life than "a profound social issue . . . to be judged with solemn gravity."[30] Communist and fascist regimes, on the other hand, regard art as indispensable to the education, indoctrination, and socialization, and morale of citizens.[31] In authoritarian societies passive entertainment has no place and art can never afford to be irrelevant: it is not a "luxury or pastime, a pleasant embellishment of life," but rather a "vital part of the very nerve center of the social organism," which must be used "to integrate every single individual into the fabric of the state."[32] It was thus crucial to control music and all of the arts through a combination of official censorship, professional restraint, and social censure. Moreover, Japan's leadership advocated the creation of a "national music" designed to "appeal to the people's sentimentality and reinforce cultural norms in people's minds."[33] The Ministry of Education publication "The Way of Subjects" accentuated the importance of relevancy in the arts:

> Unless a country is systematized even in time of peace, so that the total war of the state and the people is displayed, the country is predestined to be defeated before taking to arms. If the state structure is disjointed, and political factions bicker, and economics is left to the ideas of individuals and to free competition, and cultural enterprises, including science, art and others, do not contribute to the state interest, and thought runs against polity and demoralizes the popular spirit, such a state will be a state only in name. . . . It is an urgent matter for Japan to realize the establishment of a structure of national unanimity in politics, economics, culture, education, and all other realms of national life.[34]

To establish and maintain such control, the Home Ministry relied on people familiar with the respective arts to design and enforce professional standards and laws, and to actuate a culture that inspired patriotic fervor and martial spirit among the emperor's subjects. This was the message delivered by Ashida Kunio, head of the Imperial Rule Assistance Association (IRAA, Taiseiyokusankai) Culture Bureau, at an arts and culture conference in December 1940 in Tokyo. "Until now the concept of 'culture' has been based on ethics, science, and aesthetics, but the culture of tomorrow must be tinged with a correct and meaningful politics on top of that," Ashida admonished the 650 scholars, literati, publishers, and artists in attendance. "Politics and the new culture cannot be thought of as separable."[35] Attendees formed the Japan Literature and Arts Central Committee, entrusted with the duty of creating and enforcing professional guidelines that would "improve the collective will" of artists and audiences during the time of crisis.

People in the music business were thus called into service to clarify and perform the appropriate role of music in the New Order. Mobilizing music was a difficult endeavor that would prove to require constant reconsideration and refinement, and a painful task that inevitably put many people in the awkward position of publicly rethinking and refuting prior opinions and beliefs. Jazz critics who had written about and promoted the music for two decades now denounced "enemy music" in their wartime essays. Musicians who had spent their entire careers emulating American music publicly condemned the unfortunate influence it had exerted on indigenous culture. It is unclear how many jazz musicians joined patriotic organizations such as the Japan Music Culture Association and the Japan Record Music Culture Association, but as with other patriotic arts and literary organizations, membership often meant the power of self-policing, not to mention professional survival.[36] A contemporary newspaper article lists jazz writers Horiuchi Keizō and Nomura Kōichi and musicians Hattori Ryōichi, Raymond Hattori, and Kami Kyōsuke as members of one such organization responsible for drafting policies for the elimination of Anglo-American music.[37] Hattori Ryōichi's autobiography is silent on the matter.

Under the guidelines of thought control and apostasy established in the 1925 Peace Preservation Law, no Japanese was beyond redemption: communists, anarchists, even hedonistic jazz musicians were promised reintegration into the emperor's harmonious flock if they pledged to toe the line. "Through each one fulfilling his portion is the harmony of the community obtained," the Ministry of Education publication *Fundamentals of Our National Polity* (1937) instructed. "To fulfill one's part means to do one's appointed task with the utmost faithfulness *each in his own sphere*. . . . Harmony as in our nation is a great harmony of individuals who, by giving play to their individual differences, and through difficulties, toil and labor, converge as one. Because of [individual] characteristics and difficulties, this harmony becomes all the greater and its substance rich. Again, in this way individualities are developed, special traits become beautiful, and at the same time they even enhance the development and well-being of the whole."[38] The promise of assimilation and official recognition may not have reconciled the jazz community to the loss of its beloved music, the very core of its identity and values, but there was certainly value in cutting one's losses and attending "one's appointed task" within one's "own sphere."

With experienced musicians in charge of "cleaning up" the music world, there were no illusions about the formidability of the task. In spite of the rhetoric, they evidently recognized that "sweeping away" jazz from popular entertainment was virtually impossible. Therefore, those entrusted with the daunting project initially drew up relatively loose and abstract standards that assumed a basic unavoidable jazz influence on popular music. They placed their hopes in genres they called "national music," "salon music," or, most frequently, "light music." The term *light music* was coined in the early years of the war to connote an acceptable form of primarily instrumental music that was, in actuality, not so different from the dance music, "symphonic jazz," and nativized jazz of the previous decade. Put another way, *light music* was the acceptable term at a time when *jazz* was taboo: there was little real difference between the "new" edifying version and the "old" decadent one. With the mandate of "eradicating the enemy's music," the designers of musical standards advocated little more than superficial or cosmetic changes in the music. Since the process of designing the new standards remains a mystery, we are left to wonder if the rather vague and innocuous guidelines constitute an act of resistance to the mandate or a concession to reality.

A "realist" perspective is expressed in an anonymous police report entitled "An Opinion Regarding the Control of Jazz Music," published in July 1941, and worthy of extended commentary here.[39] The stated purpose is to clarify the difficult distinctions between light music and jazz for nonspecialists, and thus to contribute to an effective censorship policy. Acknowledging that "within the genre called light music today, there is quite a lot of music that should belong in the so-called jazz category," the report maintained that "the establishment of a music policy as one facet of a culture policy has become essential," and that a viable distinction between jazz and tolerable popular music was an important element of such a policy (348).

The report briefly outlined the historical development of the music in America and Japan and justified criticism of jazz by citing the early opposition to the music in America. "There are some who say that even today jazz has not lost the sense that, because of its Negro origins, it is an uncultured, maddening noise." The report called jazz "unharmonious," "non-music," and "a musical ghoul," because of its excessive syncopation and melodic liberties. Jazz was an "extremely Americanized music" that captured the essence of the "unruly national character" of a country "that has no tradition whatsoever" (348). Jazz came to Japan at a time when "the trend in our country was to unconditionally swallow whole the products of European and American civilization," and prospered with the rise of the dance halls. "Hot" and "swing" jazz, "obscene" jazz songs, and "gloomy" blues and tango contributed to a "decadent" and "unhealthy" popular music in the early thirties. The report attributed the "foppish sarcasm" of Japanese dance bands and singers who imitated American styles to the "bad influence of jazz" (348–49).

Why was jazz so popular around the world? Because "today's people who live within the noise of modern culture . . . require a life music besides an appreciation [art] music. Jazz fulfills that demand." The supposed appropriateness of jazz to the modern historical moment complicated efforts to extirpate the music completely. Jazz's influence had so permanently altered modern musical performance techniques and instrumentation that it was impossible to discuss modern music while ignoring jazz. Nevertheless, the author contended, it was entirely appropriate for "other nations which maintain a special national pride" to problematize the presence of the "Americanized" music within their borders. "Just as Germany has examined jazz in the past, in our country as well it is necessary to use strict and fair judgment. Especially nowadays, in a period of surging intentions to establish an independent, new culture suitable to our national characteristics, it is proper and essential" (349).

But rather than repeating empty slogans about eradicating jazz, the report suggested an alternative, perhaps more realistic approach: "A music policy *will not be settled simply by expelling so-called jazz music.* Rather, we must make it our business to find the advantages of jazz music, to enlighten the people's love of music, to provide musical leadership to the masses" (349, emphasis mine). The report conceded that "even in America in the last few years the noise and obscenity that were thought to be characteristic of jazz have been cleared away, and there has been a trend to make the music symphonic and create melodious works. . . . [A]ctually, the music that has been imported or created in our country lately wipes out the colors of the past and creates a new healthy sense." This "light music" promised to save popular music from "noisy," "obscene," "decadent" jazz. "If we take out those unhealthy elements, and can render it into a music that is light, cheerful, and healthily sweet, making a very simple popular music, that would be fine" (350).

The police report went on to elucidate how this might be accomplished, first by outlining the structure and instrumentation of jazz (including the "lascivious" sound of the saxophone), then by specifying the elements to eliminate to create healthy light music. Jazz, the writer asserted, was not so much a *type* of music as a *method* of arranging music. Therefore, if one merely changed the arrangement (which usually entailed de-emphasizing the rhythm and playing the melody "properly"), one could easily convert a piece to "excellent pure music" (353). Music that "should be excluded as much as possible" included: "(1) Music with a riotous rhythm that loses the beauty of the melody; (2) Music that causes lascivious and lewd emotions; or (3) Decadent or ruinous music that causes idleness." On the other hand, music with the following characteristics was acceptable: "(1) Music with melodies that accentuate the characteristic ethnicity of each country; (2) Nimbly merry music (that is not merely riotous); (3) Joking light music; and (4) Lyrical music." The report concluded, "Light music (in the broad sense) that most easily comforts the everyday exhaustion of the minds and bodies of us modern folk plays an important role, and in this time of crisis it is considered proper to accept types of well-meaning jazz, which is more effective than enjoying unhealthy and relatively time-consuming traditional Japanese music [hōgaku], as one form of simple pleasure" (354).[40]

This document calls into question the popular notion of a wartime "total jazz ban," and indicates that people in positions of authority were willing to consider the possibility that jazz had something to offer the popular music of the New Order. The report demonstrated that taming jazz to national purposes was a more realistic and constructive goal than obliterating it. Since jazz already had a hold on certain segments of the population (primarily well-off urban youth), the authorities' aims were better served by controlling it rather than eliminating it altogether. As long as the undesirable elements were removed, jazz, under the guise of "light music," had the potential to become an effective instrument for constructing a healthy new national culture.

It is interesting to note that the author's belief that "jazz" was merely a form that could be divested of its original sensuality and imbued with a "Japanese substance" hearkens back to the Meiji-era paradigm of wakon yōsai, or "Japanese essence, Western science." The debate over whether it was possible or desirable to adopt Western science and technology, remove them from their original basis in Western value systems, and infuse them with an essentialized "Japanese spirit," reached a new intensity during the war years.[41] But the paradigm remained something of an article of faith for those who were advocating a position for jazz in wartime society. Their case essentially rested on the fragile notion that form and content were separable, and that such a thing as "Japanese content" even existed. Just as a Japanese pilot used Western technology to fight the Western foe, it was argued, designated elements of jazz music, cleansed of polluting immorality and rendered expressive of the "Japanese spirit," could serve the national purpose equally well. Moreover, the musical experiments of the late 1930s, which attempted to express a Japanese ethnic and cultural identity through the jazz idiom, seemed to offer empirical justification for a jazz that would not only garner official sanction but contribute positively to soothe and enlighten the people. The surprisingly lenient, if problematic, jazz policy proposed in the 1941 police report thus exemplified principles for cultural architecture enshrined in Fundamentals of Our National Polity: "Our present mission as a people is to build up a new Japanese culture by adopting and sublimating Western cultures with our national polity as the basis, and to contribute spontaneously to the advancement of world culture."[42] The shopworn *wakon yōsai* strategy was thus applied to ensure jazz's continued survival in Japan.

Yet the prospects for jazz's continued presence dimmed considerably following the attack on Pearl Harbor and the concomitant intensification of hostile anti-American rhetoric. The war with America inaugurated a series of official proclamations ostensibly eradicating jazz from Japanese soil. The Home Ministry's Information Bureau issued the first such proclamation within weeks of the Pearl Harbor attack, announcing a "total shutting out of Anglo-American music, and a clean sweep of jazz. . . . [M]ost of it is vulgar and dull, and [the bureau] stated clearly the need to sweep away the decadent, inflammatory, noisy American jazz that is not suitable for wartime."[43] It is inaccurate to state, as so many previous accounts do, that there was a single, enforceable jazz ban in place throughout the war years. As the conflict dragged on, the authorities were compelled to design ever more detailed guidelines in response to blatant noncompliance with government directives and public complaints from citizens who wanted harsher action against the jazz community. Restrictions were imposed incrementally over a period of some years, with each new amendment attempting through more specificity to address violations of previous measures, though enforcement remained haphazard, even lax. A few musicians speak of being scolded for infractions, but I have encountered no record of actual arrests for performing jazz. Most often, enforcement was left to social censure or the occasional police lecture. In sum, the harsh, sweeping official rhetoric is hardly an accurate gauge of actual conditions in the jazz community.

One of the earliest and most scathing denouncements of jazz came from the pen of a writer who had spent the previous two decades promoting jazz in his country: Horiuchi Keizō, director of the Japan Music Culture Association. Within a month of the beginning of the Pacific War, his diatribe on the evils of jazz and American music, entitled "The New Course of Music Culture in the Great East Asian War," appeared in *Music Companion* (*Ongaku no tomo*), carefully omitting references to his personal role in the popularization of jazz.

> It goes without saying that music should encourage daring, patriotism, and courage in the people, enrich them and give them hope, and support their lives in time of war. At this point in time it is especially incumbent upon those of us in the music business to use all means possible to render public service through our music. To fight America and England, we must wipe out any feelings of closeness to them. The

tolerant Japanese character has by and large uncritically accepted the culture of all countries . . . Fortunately there is almost nothing to learn from America and England in terms of music, but even if there was, in these times we should avoid familiarity with their music.

. . . Most Anglo-American music was born of capitalism, liberalism, individualism, and profitism. Even if hostilities with America and England had not begun, it is clear that such music is undesirable in Japan today. We hereby advocate the elimination of Anglo-American music.

We believe that it is proper to avoid even Hawaiian music and the music of Native Americans and black Americans—which is the music of ethnic groups oppressed by [white] Americans and therefore is of no concern to us—as the music of the enemy. Besides, there is no need for Japanese today to perform the music of oppressed [ethnic] nations or of [ethnic] nations with no state. Jazz has already been suppressed. There is no other Anglo-American music worthy of taking up.

Horiuchi's wartime manifesto did not stop at condemning the enemy music, but rather outlined a comprehensive plan for the nation's music community that would ensure its positive participation in the war effort. Horiuchi urged composers to write patriotic songs and lyricists to "give the people hope and brightness." He admonished musicians performing traditional music to "re-create" their "abstract" art to make it accessible to the people. He recommended changes in the ways music was presented to the public, arguing that "many people do not have the time or money for performances" as currently presented; musicians should bring music "closer to all the people" as an act of "public service." Finally, he called for scholars to research the music of East Asia and to provide "musical leadership for East Asia." "We must move together with the Imperial Army and win."[44]

Horiuchi's statement was one of the most spirited yet in its denunciation of jazz, but less shrill voices were still audible. At the Symposium on Overcoming Modernity sponsored by *Literary World* (*Bungaku kai*) in July 1942, the prominent classical composer Moroi Saburō (1903–1977) expressed a much more nuanced opinion that in many respects echoed the perspective of the July 1941 police report cited earlier. Moroi (who also was head of the Japan Music Culture Association for a time) acknowledged the "sensory stimulation" that modern music offered, but suggested that it was still possible to restore "an art of the spirit." He noted a difference in "feel" between Western music and Eastern music, but rather than champion the "modernization" of traditional Japanese music, Moroi advocated a compromise approach that entailed expression of the "Japanese spirit" through Western composition and instrumentation. Thus musicians could creatively "overcome modernity" in music.[45] Moroi's proposal, based on the realistic assumption of unavoidable Western influence on Japanese music, suggested that modern Western music still had a place in a Japan embroiled in a "holy war" against the preeminent Western powers. The key was to tap the creativity of native composers and musicians whose mission was to inject Japanese spirituality into Western musical structures that, for better or worse, had permanently displaced traditional indigenous musics. Although Moroi's comments were intended to address composed classical music, his approach was similar to suggested strategies for dealing with jazz, the quintessential "modern music." But moderate approaches such as Moroi's did not have the virtue of making for good soul-stirring propaganda.

Rebels with a Cause

Now that war with America was no longer hypothetical, the authorities assumed a hardened public attitude toward jazz on Japanese soil. But enforcement and compliance remained haphazard and, at most, jazz musicians merely had to exercise more prudent judgment. In fact, political circumstances had made discretion an occupational necessity for years before the Pacific War began, so jazz folk had become quite accomplished at the delicate art of subtle subversion. Saxophonist and bandleader Nagao Masashi told me that he would get together with a couple of friends to play jazz, shutting the windows even during sizzling hot weather to keep anyone from overhearing their subversive jamming. "A lot of our recording jobs were things like military songs," pianist "Kiko" Reyes, who joined the Nippon Columbia studio orchestra in 1940, recalled, "but when it was break time, we'd close the door and everyone played jazz. Even after the dance halls shut down, there were these 'Light Music Concerts' sometimes at Hibiya Hall or the Japan Youth Hall, and we played jazz there." Reyes later joined an all-star attraction band called the Shōchiku Light Music Orchestra (SLMO), founded in September 1941, which boasted some of the top jazzmen of the dance hall era. The band's drummer, Tanaka Kazuo, reported "cheating" by playing jazz arrangements and improvisations on Italian, German, and Japanese songs, or by translating American popular tunes such as "These Foolish Things" and singing them in Japanese.[46] The clarinetist, Raymond Conde, told me that since the police could not distinguish composed passages from improvised ones, "we improvised in a classical way."

Jazz fans also flouted the state's initial efforts to ban jazz. John Morris, a British teacher of English at Tokyo Imperial University until mid-1942, noted that coffeehouses and cafes featuring recorded jazz showed restraint following the first anti-jazz announcements, but gradually started playing the records again, at ever-increasing volumes, as they "began to realize that the police could not distinguish between Duke Ellington and Mozart."[47] The police may have possessed tin ears, but other patriotic citizens did not and complained about the lack of restraint the jazz community was demonstrating, seemingly thumbing its nose at official pronouncements. One letter to a newspaper editor complained about a so-called "Light Music Concert" at a college in the capital: "In spite of bad weather, the concert hall was full of young men and women . . . but nearly all the performances were swing and jazz. No doubt about it, it was a jazz concert. I expect that with the beginning of the war against America and England, performance of the music of enemy nations was prohibited. . . . [I]s it the case that jazz performed under the name 'light music' goes unhindered?" The writer hoped that stronger controls on music would eliminate these blatant infractions: "I want to wipe out this unhealthy music that floods the bars, coffeehouses, and movie theaters." Another reader, noting with alarm the continued availability of American records, reported witnessing the owner of a record store in Tokyo's Kanda district recommending John Philip Sousa records to a customer looking for "lively" children's music. "These days radio and music organizations are denouncing the enemy's music completely. There is no law that exempts records. The authorities concerned should either demand that record store owners voluntarily turn over these records, or take measures to ban their sale or seize them."[48]

In response to such complaints and to the intransigence of some jazz aficionados, on 13 January 1943 the Information Bureau and Home Ministry reiterated the national campaign to "sweep away American and English music from our homes and streets," this time presenting a list of some one thousand American and English songs, "including most jazz music," for banishment. Possession, sale, and performance of the designated records were prohibited, and live performances of songs from the list proscribed. Records—with catalog numbers meticulously notated—were to be turned over "voluntarily" to the police or the Japan Recorded Music Culture Association immediately, but in some cases the records would be confiscated to discourage cafes and coffeehouses, in particular, from ignoring the law. "In the light music category, the only foreign music that will remain will be European music such as that of Germany and Italy." In addition to "flippant," "frivolous," "materialistic," "decadent," and "lascivious" jazz, "songs with Anglo-American dullness, even if they are composed in Japan" were forbidden.[49] The record ban was followed five months later by a recommendation from the Music Culture Association to ban the sale and performance of all Anglo-American sheet music, "whether jazz or not."[50]

This renewed effort to abolish jazz from the Empire was part of a larger campaign to "clean up" not only the moral content but also the language of wartime culture. That is to say, Anglo-American music was suppressed not only because of its decadence, but also because it perpetuated the undesirable use of the English language in Japan. Throughout the war sporadic efforts to displace "the main foreign language in Japan" extended from name changes to the removal of signs, from clumsy changes in baseball terminology to the contrivance of ponderous names for musical instruments. Jazz singer Dick Mine reverted to his given name Mine Tokuichi; Raymond Conde and "Kiko" Reyes, both of whom became Japanese citizens, adopted the names Raymond Yoshiba and Tazawa Yoshikazu, respectively; Jimmy Harada (whose father was English) changed to Harada Jōji; Japanese American singer Betty Inada became Fukuda Fumiko; and Bucky Shiraki adopted the "powerful" name Shiraki Chikara.[51] Record companies followed suit in February 1943: Nippon Columbia revived its 1920s name Nitchiku, King Records became Fuji Onban, Nippon Victor became Great East Asia (Dai Tōa), and Polydor took the name Victorious War Cry (Shōkō).[52] English musical terms that had been used for nearly a century were replaced with clunky Japanese equivalents: the musical scale (do are mi . . .) was Japanified (ha ni ho . . .); the trumpet mute became known as a "weak sound device" (jakuonki), "saxophone" became "bent metallic flute" (kinzoku seihin magari shakuhachi), and the word "trombone" was replaced by "sliding bent long gold trumpet" (nukisashi magari kin chō rappa).

The graceless attempts to alter the language indicate the difficulty of the task of rooting out jazz. It was still legal to possess and play any jazz records that did not appear on the government's list, and apparently there were quite a few. Some private collectors, cafe and coffeehouse proprietors, and musicians simply refused to turn over their precious records for the token government reimbursements (ten to twenty sen per disc). Another problem was that the confiscation of records was sometimes supervised by collectors themselves. As a representative of the Yokohama Music Coffeehouse League, Yoshida Mamoru was charged with the unenviable task of collecting the banned records from that city's music coffeehouses. But from his own collection of around sixty-five hundred records, Yoshida only turned in five hundred, hiding the remaining records in a pantry on the second floor of his shop. While some might regard it as a way to do in the competition, Yoshida characterized this relatively innocuous action as "one form of protest."[53]

It did not help matters that, since so many American songs had been translated into Japanese, a number of tunes were of uncertain origin. Special committees were established to study such problem songs, but it is worth recounting an incident involving Prime Minister Tōjō Hideki (1884–

1948) to illustrate the magnitude of the problem such committees faced. When Kamiyama Keizō of the Japan Musicians' Association informed the prime minister that "Auld Lang Syne" (known as "Light of the Firefly" in Japanese) was forbidden, Tōjō went from shock to depression and finally anger. "This is completely outrageous. I've never heard of such an order," he stormed. " 'Auld Lang Syne' is sung by everybody right from elementary school, so the song is completely Japanese, isn't it?" Kamiyama later wrote, "I do not know if he was really unaware of the decision or just pretended that he really was unaware of the decision. A despot is not always able to keep an eye on everything."[54] Clearly, even the prime minister was not above rationalizing to rescue a favored song.

The "Light Music Revolution": Music as Self, Music as Weapon

The previous chapter examined the ways that jazz figured into Japanese definitions of self and other, signifying the moral and aesthetic depravity of American culture and the consequent debasement of Japanese ethical and artistic values. During the war jazz retained its symbolic importance—if its "modern" character was no longer considered a virtue—as evidence of the untraversable cultural chasm between Japanese and Americans. Many Japanese regarded the war against the so-called ABCD powers (the Americans, British, Chinese, and Dutch) as no mere conflict over turf and resources, but rather as a holy struggle to cleanse the nation's soul of contamination and preserve its most sacred and beautiful elements. The war challenged the Japanese people to abandon nearly a century of assumptions about Japanese backwardness in relation to the West, and to develop heretofore untapped "spiritual" resources in order to create a new cultural order that could serve as an alternative developmental model for the rest of Asia. The popular and classical music communities perceived their mission as a creative puzzle that required immediate solution: how to define and celebrate Japan's heritage musically, while inspiring the public to greater sacrifice and fervor for the emperor's holy crusade. Vilifying Anglo-American music was not enough; something new and positive must be created, something relevant and unfrivolous yet popular and inspiring, for a time of national crisis.

Official definitions of "Japanese values" portrayed the nation as a harmonious, indivisible family with the emperor as patriarch. Social harmony, loyalty and filial piety, martial spirit (*bushidō*), self-effacement, and assimilation were principal virtues. By contrast, "Americanism" designated any number of attributes that were by extension "not Japanese": materialism, "worldly desires," hedonism, corrupt "Jewish capitalism" and the primacy of "almighty dollar," machines, individualism, the principle of balance of powers, and democracy.[55] Wartime commentators drew on a wealth of Japanese and American rhetoric describing jazz as sensual rather than spiritual, sexual rather than intellectual, debased rather than edifying, the product of Jewish capitalism rather than the songs of oppressed peoples. Tragically, Japan and other Asian nations had been corrupted by the "obnoxious" virus of Americanism, but with determined effort Japan, Asia's new de facto colonial master, could disinfect the region. A newspaper report on Japanese efforts to "aid" the Philippines stated, "What America has pursued in the way of elevating the living conditions of the native inhabitants was far from being satisfactory, as besides her work in their Americanization through culture and education, it seems that she did not forget to lead them to pleasure seeking and self-indulgence. The quality of her films and jazz music was further aggravated by the method of her education."[56] For the wartime Japanese readership, there was little that evoked the depravity of American values and lifestyles better than jazz.

These themes were expressed in a comprehensive rationale for the record ban published in the Home Ministry and Information Bureau's joint organ *Weekly Information (Shūhō)*. The record ban had been necessary to "sweep away" a music "that expressed the [American] national characteristics of frivolity, the supremacy of materialism, and the overwhelming sense of triviality." The abolition of "vulgar, decadent, lascivious, noisy" jazz did not constitute the end of popular music, but rather its "purification."[57] Other critics charged that Anglo-American music had nothing substantial to offer Japanese audiences, so why bother with it? Japan, besides having a "substantial musical tradition" of its own, was allied with the great "musical nations" of Italy and Germany, and therefore could learn nothing from the "Anglo-Saxon nations, which have not really been blessed with a musical heritage."[58] "Fortunately, our enemies America and England are not at all 'exceptional countries' when it comes to music," one writer contended, "and thankfully, erasing Anglo-American music from this world will cause good musicians no pain."[59]

No little ink was expended discounting jazz as the product of a shallow, materialistic society. That was too easy. Creating something new that expressed prescriptive ideals for the Japanese people—something that at once diverted them from their dreary existence yet moved them to greater sacrifice—was the more daunting task. Realizing that the creation of "a music culture that is stronger than that of Anglo-America" was necessary "in order to fight America and England with our own music,"[60] commentators usually agreed that traditional music (*hōgaku* or *gagaku*) did not capture or inspire the popular imagination, nor did it elicit much in the way of fighting spirit. Military songs and "healthy" light music, regardless of their Western origins, were the most effective types of music for moving the masses, so to speak, and therefore required substantial creative attention from native musicians, lyricists, and composers. There were those who maintained preferences for the European classics (especially those of Germany and Italy), but even they conceded that most people were not familiar with classical music and therefore required a vernacular music that edified and inspired them. Domestically produced light music thus was the vehicle with the most potential. "Composers should use the popularity of light music effectively," jazz pianist Wada Hajime argued, "and create an excellent people's music for Japanese."[61]

According to N H K's vice president in charge of music, Maruyama Tetsuo, it was important to distinguish between American jazz, with its "saccharine melodies and decadent lyrics," and Japanese light music that was "pretty and rhythmical." "I think there's a problem with saying that everything about jazz is bad," he added. "I think it's necessary to erect clear limits between America-style jazz and the light music that is performed in Japan." In contrast to jazz, which he dubbed a "fanatical music" used by "Jewish capital" to "manipulate the Japanese people," Maruyama glibly defined "light music" as "music that one can enjoy listening to lightly."[62] While this definition did little justice to the difficult and highly subjective task of distinguishing light music from jazz, Maruyama's basic point was that American jazz was the enemy and that domestically produced light music *by definition* lacked jazz's defects.

In essence, the "light music revolution"[63] that was deemed essential to the viability of wartime culture was an officially sanctioned continuation of the late-thirties effort to develop a national style, a Japanese jazz. It represented the acceptance of the Hattori/Sugii formula, once a peripheral movement in the jazz community, as the solution to the nation's musical problems. By the early to mid-forties, the creation of Japanese jazz was nothing less than a sacred duty, and a way for jazz musicians to continue working with public approval. Admonished to "write pieces with Japanese feeling,"[64] musicians were *forced* to be *liberated* from the spell of American jazz and to create Japanese jazz, the wave of the future. The "light music revolution" also entailed a reformation of the ways that music was presented, performed, sold, bought, and appreciated. Many believed that music should be a form of public service that consoled the people who made daily sacrifices for the war and inspired them to greater productivity and patriotism.

Jazz artists were not alone in their struggle to formulate productive and relevant roles for their art. Visual artists painted war scenes or countless views of Mt. Fuji and "rising suns." The Literary Patriotic Association sponsored the collection and publication of patriotic poems, while member writers produced a steady stream of best-selling war novels. The motion picture industry, which "had never developed a war genre" prior to the late 1930s, produced films that celebrated "purity" of character and Japan's victimization within the cutthroat international environment. A ballet company produced a "Decisive Aerial Warfare Ballet" as "an artistic contribution to the national drive for heightening the air consciousness of the people."[65]

While praising these efforts in other media, music writers (some of whom apparently had adopted pseudonyms, presumably so their earlier associations with jazz would be obscured) believed that music had a special power to inspire and move the people, and exhorted composers and musicians to exploit that power in their work. They insisted that the arts should be an integral part of the daily struggles of wartime life and could, moreover, contribute to a decisive military and cultural victory over Anglo-American civilization. To achieve such victory, people in the music world had to "make music into a weapon."[66] The first issue of *Music Culture* (*Ongaku bunka*), published in December 1943, suggested changes in the content, purpose, and performance of music that would integrate art into wartime society.[67] One author urged that composers and musicians not only had to rid their art of contaminating Anglo-American elements, but to study Japanese folk song forms and incorporate them into a new, creative art that promoted a "sense of commonality among the people." *Music Culture* editor Horiuchi Keizō expressed the need for greater consolidation in the music world. He celebrated the newly simplified structure of the music information press, advocated standardization of an appropriate repertoire, and admonished bands to join the Japan Music Culture Association or "cease" their operations. In another column, musicians and music writers offered their suggestions on "how music could be used to destroy America and England."[68] They envisioned themselves marching to front lines with the emperor's troops, firing at the enemy with their horns, lobbing folk melodies like grenades, ensuring a glorious victory and a validation for their art.

"Jazz for the Country's Sake"

The irony of fighting America with its own music was not lost on some Japanese. Before embarking on a suicide mission to the South Sea Islands, a twenty-three-year-old kamikaze pilot, Oikawa Hajime, penned the customary letter of farewell, remarking bitterly, "Who do you think I am; a fool who has come to realize how dear this thing life is only three days before my death? A rainy day gives me another day of survival today—a bonanza. . . . My co-pilot is sound asleep beside me. Could this silly face of his be the face of a war-god tomorrow? How funny to listen to jazz music on the night before going out to kill the jazzy Americans! How funny, too, is the servant who just came up to me to ask how many beds he should make tomorrow!"[69]

Apparently, even in the military, jazz was not far out of earshot. Coffeehouse proprietor Yoshida Mamoru, who was drafted and sent to central China in 1942 (though, as a consummate *mobo* garbed in German pants and jacket, and Italian or American shoes, he was a rather "strange soldier"), recalled that his commanding officer let him listen to records by the English drummer Joe Daniels in the adjutant room. "I think that my attachment to jazz," he mused, "my unwillingness to let go of that sound no matter what I had to do if I had a chance to hear it, brought me good luck." Reedist and New Herd big band leader Miyama Toshiyuki believes the navy was even more lenient than the army: whenever sailors engaged in singing contests, he claims, "I sang jazz." Jazz critics Yui Shōichi and Segawa Masahisa certainly did not let naval service keep them from listening to banned records, and there is evidence of many hidden record collections and a substantial black market for 78s.[70]

In some ways, military service made contact with jazz more likely, for military men had access to shortwave radio, a privilege denied civilians. Vocalist Oida Toshio and tenor saxophonist Oda Satoru both told me of hearing jazz while serving as sailors in the Imperial Navy. Oida, a radio monitor who had been entranced by American entertainment since before the war, used to listen to shortwave broadcasts of American music on the sly. Oda, who had never heard jazz before, was startled by the music when he encountered it on a U.S. shortwave broadcast in his ship's gun room in 1945. As a navy bandsman he had been trained in European classics, in which his saxophone played a limited role (even more so when new edicts restricting saxophones were issued the previous year). Hearing the prominence of his instrument in jazz was a revelation to him: "So *that*'s how it's done!"

Jazz was also audible from officially sanctioned and ubiquitous "comfort tours" that entertained troops, sailors, and munitions workers through Japan and its empire. (One editorial advocated placing bands in munitions factories because "it is clear that entertainment is linked to productivity.")[71] Entrusted with raising the morale of soldiers abroad and the people at home, bands such as the Shōchiku Light Music Orchestra and NHK's New Order Rhythm Orchestra were considered crucial to the war effort, and kept a few of Japan's best-known musicians employed in service to their country.[72] The "enemy's music" had found a niche.

Service in patriotic associations was another way to contribute positively.

Well acquainted with the "enemy's music," jazz writers and musicians helped shape government policies toward jazz, determined what songs were of Anglo-American origin, and designed measures to banish them. But self-policing had its weaknesses. Hattori Ryōichi told of performing "Tiger Rag," one of the tunes appearing on the banned song list that he had helped draw up. As staff arranger for NHK's "Light Music Hour" program, Hattori slipped the New Orleans standard in with a program of German and Italian music. When asked, "Isn't that American jazz?" Hattori replied, "No, this is a courageous Malayan song about tiger hunting. If you listen you'll realize that there are a lot of sounds that resemble a tiger's roar. I think it's perfect for this time of crisis."[73] It is impossible to judge the veracity of the story, but assuming that it is true, Hattori subverted policies that he himself helped to design. The irony would be lost on the reader of his autobiography because his personal involvement as a policymaker is not mentioned, while his clever sedition receives ample treatment.

If the role of jazz people in wartime music policymaking remains obscure, the literature on one aspect of the jazz community's cooperation in the war effort has gotten a comparatively great deal of publicity: the participation of jazz musicians in the "strategic broadcasts to the enemy" (taiteki bōryaku hōsō) that were conducted by NHK. Well before the war NHK had developed a number of clumsily produced and ineffective foreign-language shortwave broadcasts under the joint aegis of the Foreign Ministry, the Information Bureau, and the Imperial army. In late 1942, following the devastating loss at Midway, a few Allied prisoners of war with radio experience were drafted to produce better broadcasts.[74] Early programs focused on bogus "news" reports about invented Japanese victories and Allied defeats, but with the inauguration of the "Zero Hour" program on 1 March 1943, NHK began incorporating recorded and, later, live music of American pedigree into their radio propaganda, with the aim of demoralizing Allied troops. American popular music and jazz was interspersed with suggestive comments from nasal-voiced female announcers: "Wouldn't you California boys like to be at Coconut Grove tonight with your best girl? You have plenty of Coconut Groves, but no girlies"; or "I wonder who your wives and girl friends are out with tonight. Maybe with a 4F or a war plant worker making big money while you are out here fighting and knowing you can't succeed."[75] The commentary was more entertaining than demoralizing to Allied troops, but the music kept them tuning in to shows such as "Zero Hour," "Humanity Calls," "The Postwar Call," and "Australian Hour" throughout the last two years of the war. The Allies took the bait—jazz—but the message did not hook them.[76]

As the production of records fell off in the latter stages of the war, live performances were the only way to play "jazz for the sake of the country."[77] In 1944 top jazz musicians from the Columbia Jazz Band and Shōchiku Light Music Orchestra formed one band that performed on Sunday afternoons on the "Sunday Promenade Concert," while the New Order Rhythm Orchestra organized by jazz critic Nogawa Kōbun performed for other broadcasts.[78] Moriyama Hisashi (who renounced his American citizenship during the war), Tib Kamayatsu, and other Japanese Americans were enlisted to sing and rewrite the lyrics of popular tunes to mock the Allies and undermine their will to fight.[79] Since the live broadcasts were shortwave and Japanese were forbidden to listen to shortwave radio, theoretically there was little danger that a domestic audience would be corrupted by the malignant transmissions. The Allied soldiers loved them, though, and after the war members of the NHK propaganda bands enjoyed preferential treatment when U.S. servicemen's clubs hired Japanese musicians to entertain American troops.

Much is made of the irony that a state-run radio studio was the only place where Japanese could legally play jazz.[80] But given the dominant conceptions of jazz as a music capable of corrupting its listeners, advocates of jazz as a weapon to weaken Allied resolve were at least philosophically consistent: if jazz was the ultimate example of American depravity, it stood to reason that Japan could undermine Allied resolve and discipline by inundating enemy troops with jazz. Regardless of the intent, however, apparently the easiest part of the NHK program was the recruitment of jazz musicians. When word about the job spread through the jazz community, a number of musicians enthusiastically offered to play "jazz for the sake of the country" for NHK. Since the end of the war, no one admits to feeling like an accessory to a failed and immoral crusade, and a few participants claim to have known nothing at all of the broadcasts' ultimate purpose. Perhaps the convictions of Japanese war criminals and Japanese Americans such as Iva Toguri d'Aquino and Moriyama Hisashi encouraged caution. "There was nothing we could do about war," Conde has explained. "We had nothing to do with the political aim of demoralizing enemy forces. We only wanted to do jazz."[81]

The propaganda broadcasts represented an act of desperation as the tide of the war shifted in favor of the Allies. It became more difficult to motivate an increasingly despondent populace to adhere to the seemingly endless stream of edicts about how it should behave. To "rid light music of the stink of jazz," which apparently lingered despite past efforts, the Japan Music Culture Association issued in April 1944 meticulous guidelines for the instrumentation and sound of light music orchestras. It ordered the cessation of standard jazz and Hawaiian band instrumentation, banned the banjo, steel guitar, ukelele, and jazz percussion instruments, limited the number of saxophones in a band, outlawed the trumpet mute, and proscribed the use of microphones in performance sites holding less than twenty-five hundred people.[82] This final edict had little relevance at a time when musical performances were increasingly rare in Japan anyway. As the victims of incendiary bombings rummaged through the ruins of their neighborhoods searching in vain for relatives and friends, as they mourned the "glorious sacrifices" of their fathers, sons, and brothers at the front or at sea, as they prepared for the seemingly inevitable invasion of their homeland by the foreign devils, what little music remained available, even the officially sanctioned popular songs, military songs, and marches, became noticeably more despairing and "almost decadent."[83] Losing the ukelele was no big deal.

In the wake of Japan's surrender, the late summer and fall of 1945 was chaotic and fearful for most Japanese. Thoroughly convinced by government propaganda of the brutality and rapaciousness of Americans, they feared that the worst was still to come. But people with an interest in jazz were heartened when broadcasts of jazz and popular music resumed on NHK, which had for years broadcast only military songs and German and Italian classics. On 23 September, the U.S. armed forces' station WVTR (now FEN, Far East Network) began broadcasting jazz and American pops for the troops who came to Japan as part of the Allied Occupation. With the beginning of the Occupation, jazz musicians experienced an unprecedented demand for their services that enabled many of them to maintain a standard of living well above that of most Japanese in the late forties.

Taming Jazz

It must be concluded that the Japanese state's all-out war on jazz was only vaguely conceived at best and imperfectly executed. In this respect, the Japanese experience in the late 1930s and early 1940s mirrored that of the Soviet and German regimes of the same period, where jazz "proved far easier to denounce than to eradicate." In the USSR, the Communist Party's positions on jazz had been volatile and erratic. Jazz was condemned as bourgeois American music, and a number of jazz musicians were actually executed in the purges of 1937–1938; but jazz was also one idiom through which the Party circulated "mass songs." In 1938 the State Jazz Orchestra of the USSR was formed in an attempt to create a "Soviet Jazz": "The campaign to rid the Soviet Union of jazz thus culminated with the nationalization of swing music by the government." Following the German invasion of June 1941, jazz, the music of the USSR's American ally, was welcomed as "a release from the bloody drudgery of war" with the government's full approval. "For all its Americanisms, jazz was more nearly acceptable to the ultranationalists in wartime than at any other time in the decades preceding and following the fighting."[84]

In Germany, Hitler and Goebbels had vilified what they called "Nigger-Jew" jazz even before the Nazis assumed power in 1933. "It was in jazz," according to Erik Levi, "more than any other style of music, that the Nazis could achieve a true integration between their ideology of racism and their aesthetic opposition to modernism." But German policies against jazz have been characterized as "half-hearted," undermined by the desire to "bolster the impression of benevolence" by "supplement[ing] the negative policy against old-style jazz with a positive one toward the creation of a new-German idiom, a sort of 'German jazz.'" Unlike the Japanese case, there were a number of German musicians (whom Michael Kater calls "jazz victims") arrested or persecuted by the Nazis for playing jazz. But the continued existence of a popular music that was only superficially different from jazz, in Kater's words, "illustrates the improvised nature of a dictatorial regime whose alleged totalitarianism was neither seamless nor inevitable."[85]

A similar conclusion can be advanced regarding Japan. All three of these authoritarian regimes engaged in simultaneous and failed efforts to evict jazz from their shores and to de-Americanize it to serve national purposes. The Japanese state made numerous pronouncements about eradicating jazz, relying on a mobilized populace more than on the police apparatus, and exhorting the jazz community to police itself and design its own professional standards for healthy popular music. Enforcement was left largely to self-restraint and fear of social censure. Japan's jazz community obviously was unable to carry on as it had before, but neither did it cease to exist.

The jazz community's response to state pressure entailed a musical compromise: jazz could remain in Japanese society, could even be made useful to the war effort, if it could be *made authentically Japanese*. Thereby the jazz community could carve out a constructive role for itself within the New Order, something which its early association with frivolous and decadent modernism had prevented. It goes without saying that individual jazz aficionados demonstrated varying degrees of enthusiasm and effort in their new roles as cultural architects, but in their various guises as music policymakers, soldiers and sailors, "comfort" bandspeople, and broadcasters of propaganda, members of the jazz community were active in defining the new national culture and their place therein.

An Aesthetic Revolution?

As we have seen, jazz kept a toe-hold in Japan, albeit in a contrived, cosmetically altered form called "light music," essentially an officially sanctioned continuation of the "nativized" jazz of the late thirties. Light music was a compromise that neither the jazz community nor the state found wholly satisfactory, but which provided a common ground whereon jazz musicians could continue working "for the sake of the country" with grudging state approval. By fusing Japanese folk material with acceptable ingredients from jazz in the time-honored tradition of the *wakon-yōsai* formula, the jazz community's cultural architects envisaged a popular music that captivated the public the way jazz had and yet contained a "Japanese spirit." Historians have tended to view the light music of this era with contempt, as a consequence of unidirectional pressure from a draconian police state. But it is possible to conceive of wartime jazz in a more positive, if paradoxical, light: the crisis mentality of the authoritarian state and the flowering of cultural nationalism in the late thirties and early forties challenged Japanese musicians for the first time to authenticate their jazz without reference to American standards. In so doing, they not only served the national purpose, but also remained true to the jazz aesthetic's insistence on innovation.

Those of us who live in Western democracies are loath to acknowledge the possible creativity or aesthetic merit of art produced in authoritarian or nationalistic societies (as if the Western democracies were strangers to nationalism and patriotic art). Anything that represents less than the unrestrained, politically liberated vision of the artist, we pretend, is propaganda and by definition unworthy of our consideration.[86] This prejudice blinds us not only to the fact that all artists communicate ideological messages, but to the very real, formal and informal restrictions on artistic expression in the so-called democracies: anyone applying for National Endowment for the Arts funds nowadays would be foolish not to consider the prejudices of the U.S. Congress in designing a project. Besides, to deem "authoritarian art" unworthy of history's attention on the basis of aesthetic prejudice is to ignore potentially valuable source material for historical research.

That said, with the exception of Sugii Kōichi's masterly jazz arrangements of Asian folk songs, I do not wish to make a case for the artistic merit of wartime jazz, but rather to highlight the potential this period had for Japanese creativity within the jazz idiom, and to demonstrate the significance of turning away from American precedents. Societies embroiled in crisis are indeed repressive, but they can also be dynamic and remarkably creative. Social change occurs at dazzling speed; social groups that were previously mutually hostile achieve unprecedented degrees of rapproachement and integration. The Pacific War offered two unprecedented opportunities to Japan's jazz community: an opportunity to achieve a degree of social legitimacy; and a chance to transform jazz itself, to create indigenous standards of authenticity that did not require an American referent. The degree to which they succeeded in either endeavor is debatable. Rhetorically, at least, musicians had an exalted status in wartime society, as those entrusted with edifying and comforting a war-weary populace. But the fact that their mission demanded constant reiteration indicates consistent failure to measure up to their responsibilities as defined by the authorities. Moreover, the fact that increasingly detailed regulations were handed down throughout the war indicates compliance was grudging and inconsistent. Jazz musicians had their purpose, perhaps, but true integration within the social order remained elusive, the way jazz people seem to like it.

It is difficult to judge the music of this period in the absence of a representative number of recordings. Recordings of wartime jazz have not fared well in the postwar period. They are practically never reissued (although the Paddle Wheel Records series *The Legendary Japanese Jazz Scene,* produced by Segawa Masahisa, promises a volume entitled *Salon Music*); the consensus is that they will not sell well and are not worth the effort. They are stigmatized as the products of Japan's lowest hour. But, based on what is available, it is possible to speculate that there was a range of artistic hits and misses, with Sugii's King Salon Music Series representing the apex of wartime jazz and insipid propaganda such as Hattori's "I Love Japan" as the nadir. What is most significant about the musical experiments of the wartime jazz community, more significant than their aesthetic merits or lack thereof, is the attempt to abrogate the referential aesthetic that held American jazz aloft as *the* exemplar simply to be emulated. Few musicians realized its promise, but the challenge to foster domestic creativity within the jazz idiom was a novel approach for an artistic community perennially preoccupied with the achievements of the American jazz masters.

But this new, self-referential authenticity was short-lived. With defeat at American hands came a much deeper sense of Japanese inadequacy in the realms of politics, economics, and culture, a feeling that was not conducive to creative self-assertion. After the war jazz musicians were hired by the hundreds to entertain American troops who wanted to hear familiar sounds from home. Mastery of American models thus became crucial to Japanese musicians' survival. Moreover, the stylistic and social revolution in jazz that produced bebop reinforced a sense of Japanese backwardness. The key to authentic jazz expression, it would be argued, was to study and master the new American style, and to create a cultural lifestyle analogous to that of the bebop "hipster" in Japan. The irony is that with the coming of democracy and new social freedoms in the postwar years, Japanese jazz musicians were not really "free" to be creative. Stifled not only by the demands of the gig but also by a severe lack of confidence in their own technical faculties and legitimacy as jazz artists, they spent the next two decades trying desperately to "catch up" to American jazz. When viewed from that perspective, the war years, a period that virtually all jazz musicians and fans remember as a "dark age," probably held more creative promise than the so-called "golden age" that followed.

CHAPTER FIVE

BOP, FUNK, JUNK, AND THAT OLD DEMOCRACY BOOGIE: THE JAZZ TRIBES OF POSTWAR JAPAN

Walkin' down the Ginza

I heard someone blowin' a cadenza.

They were playin' bebop, and people were drinkin' up some booze.

Well, the music hit me

As hard as a case of influenza.

I'm so glad because they played the Tokyo Blues

I'll take teriyaki.

Please pass me another glass of sake.

Japanese people love music and jazz is what they choose.

Well, I've got to go now.

I'll miss that good old sukiyaki.

I'm so sad because I got the Tokyo Blues.

—Horace Silver, "The Tokyo Blues" (1962)

You look real funky today!—Japanese TV announcer
to fashion show model, early 1960s

More Scenes from the Jazz Scene

It is 1953 and the Big Four are on top of the world. Over the course of a two-week engagement at the Asakusa International Theater in September, some one hundred thousand fans throng to hear the band perform its bombastic versions of "Flying Home" and "How High the Moon." They play in gymnasia and primary school lecture halls throughout Japan. On tour in the northern island of Hokkaidō, the group is guaranteed ¥400,000 per show—twice the fee paid to their competitors—in addition to airfare and board in the finest hotels. Fans are assured spectacle as well as music. "The jazz magazines carried critical reviews," George Ka-

waguchi conceded forty years later, "but what we did was all by forced calculation. There are only four people on a big stage for those theater performances. For the enjoyment of the spectators, we thought it was important to move around and into the audience sometimes."[1] So the Big Four put on a show: "Sleepy" Matsumoto turns upside down on the floor while wailing on his tenor sax, Ono Mitsuru shoulders his upright bass and struts around the stage, and George Kawaguchi tosses and spins his drumsticks, beats on the stage floor, and sends his fans into a frenzy with extended, orgiastic drum solos. The theater seats are superfluous: the fans jump and scream, rush the stage, and in the words of one newspaper, "make their parents cry."

It is two years later, 28 September 1955, and a typhoon rages through the Japanese capital. In the jazz coffeehouse Duet, the hippest bebop pianist in Japan is hanging out with his bandmates from the Double Beats. Tonight his frail, pale, scholarly countenance appears even more delicate. Moriyasu Shōtarō bids his friends good night, picks himself up wearily, and ventures out into the rainy darkness. Half an hour later he stands on the platform of Meguro station battling his demons: artistic frustration, addiction to speed, unrequited love. Jobs are hard to come by if you're unwilling to back a singer, and no one wants to hear that crazy music that you can't even dance to. The train whistle blows.

Trouble in mind, I'm blue,
But I won't be blue always . . .
I'm gonna lay my head on some lonesome railroad line,
Let that two-nineteen train ease my worried mind.

Moriyasu leans forward. His identity is not known for five days.

"The Confusion Era"

Postwar Japan was a society whose very value system had been shattered. Tenets of Japanese nationhood—the unbroken line of divine emperors, patriarchal Confucian ethics, the sense of invulnerability engendered by a glorious martial heritage, and the essential spiritual unity of the Japanese people—had been hammered home for several generations from school age through adulthood. These tenets had proven to be alternately unifying and divisive, and leftist agitation and the flirtation with cosmopolitan modernism in the twenties and thirties seriously threatened their hegemony; but for millions they had been a guiding philosophy, a source of comfort, and the core basis of identity. The Allied Occupation thoroughly discredited these core elements of Japanese cultural identity, initiating not merely structural reform but also no less than a fundamental revolution in "the Japanese psyche." During "the confusion era" Japanese were compelled to engage in intense self-reflection on the nature and viability of indigenous culture, as they eked out tenuous livings among the war ruins. Until August 1945 Japanese culture itself—that unique and superior blend of traditional spirit and modern science—was regarded as a model that promised to liberate Asia from the shackles of debilitating backwardness and colonization. But as the dark clouds of war lifted, Japanese culture became the scapegoat for an unprecedented catastrophe. Through an analysis of indigenous culture and its inherent defects, with the express aim of explaining the rise of an authoritarian state and the imperialist brutality of the previous years, Japanese self-consciously resumed the interrupted journey toward an ideal of modernity as defined by American expectations and accomplishments.[2]

In this chapter, through the stories of postwar Japan's jazz artists and aficionados, I explore how the production and consumption of jazz—both as mass cultural commodity and as subcultural ethos—were decisively shaped in the first two postwar decades by institutional, psychological, and sociocultural impulses set in motion by the Occupation. By "production" I mean the production of musical sound on the bandstand as well as the packaging and marketing of jazz as a commodity; by "consumption," or reception, I mean the received meanings and consequent appeal (and distaste) jazz held for consumers of culture and self-proclaimed rebels. In the context of national reconstruction and expanding entertainment and leisure pursuits, jazz appealed to a generation whose inherited value system had been pummeled, yet the reputed "art of freedom" remained manacled to American-defined standards of artistic originality and authenticity. And for many Japanese, jazz music remained irrevocably the song of the conqueror, inextricably linked to everyday displays of American night.

Japan's jazz community—producers and consumers alike—was not untouched by the structural transformations, cultural self-reflection, and reformative spirit that distinguished the early postwar era, but it had to contend too with the radical transformation of the music itself. What was known as "jazz" in the late 1940s was virtually unrecognizable to most Japanese. Jazz was essentially reintroduced to Japan in bebop, cool, and progressive guises, collectively known as "modern jazz." At a historical moment at which the nation was ostensibly renouncing "feudal" values and rejoining the ranks of the modern democratic capitalist countries, it was not insignificant that the term *modern* was so widely used to describe the new musics. Just as the destruction of the patriarchal household system and the adoption of universal suffrage were regarded as evidence of progress into modernity, modern jazz was said by its creators and its champions to be a sophisticated advance in the music's evolution from whorehouse entertainment to art music.

But the modern jazz revolution of the mid-forties and the ensuing stylistic ruptures in subsequent decades also fortified existing assumptions about
American superiority and Japanese backwardness in the art. Before World
War II American jazz had been an undeniably attractive model to emulate,
but it had been one of many sources of inspiration; even indigenous musics
bubbled in the font of ideas. But in the postwar years, a period in which the
nation's fate allegedly depended on its abilities to "catch up" to an American
standard of living, there was a noticeably heightened sense of urgency to
"catch up" to an aesthetic standard set exclusively by American jazz artists.
Moreover, once it appeared that Japanese artists such as Akiyoshi Toshiko,
Sleepy Matsumoto (1926–2000), and Watanabe Sadao had successfully
"caught up" to American swing stars and beboppers, more changes in
American jazz—toward the "funky" and the "free"—sent Japanese scram-
bling to catch up yet again. The point is that for some two decades after the
Occupation "liberated" Japan, the jazz community remained shackled to a
standard of authenticity that privileged the American exemplar. Rather than
a "liberated" artistic community committed to an exploration of the unknown and the unprecedented, we find a community in the teleological
conundrum of having its artistic future mapped out by others: its aesthetic
was referential; its art was quite deliberately derivative and its customs
contrived; its faith in its own creative powers was too often obscured by its
infatuation with American examples.[3]
    It is perhaps impossible entirely to avoid invoking the views of the promi-
nent literary critic Etō Jun when making such statements. Etō famously
critiques postwar literature as "warped" by the Occupation's censorship policies and imposed Americanisms internalized by Japanese writers. Though
Etō's blatantly nationalistic indignation makes his views vulnerable to attack, John Dower's conclusions regarding Occupation-era censorship suggest that they are not entirely without validity: "Can anyone really believe
that no harm was done to postwar political consciousness by a system of
secret censorship and thought control that operated under the name 'free
expression' . . . ? This was not a screen for weeding out threats to democracy
(as official justifications claimed), but rather a new chapter in an old book of
lessons about acquiescing to overweening power and conforming to a dictated consensus concerning permissible behavior."[4] Now, jazz musicians
were not subject to censorship per se, but when they first took the bandstand in 1945 they performed stock arrangements imported from the States,
and when they took requests they were told to "play Bird." As long as they
made their livings entertaining Americans, American music would monop-
olize their artistic attentions.
    Still, it is fair to ask precisely what made the postwar jazz community in

general so deferential to American examples, so timid about charting its own artistic course, even years after the Occupation ended. Was it a genuine feeling of inferiority wrought by the humiliating experience of defeat and occupation? Was it a genuine lack of technical proficiency? Was it a belief that the jazz idiom was somehow static and sacred, not to be tampered with? Was it the constant and rapid transformations of American jazz styles, repertoire, and aesthetics? Was it the demand of audiences, American and Japanese, that the music sound authentically American? Or was it a lack of confidence in the ability of Japanese to be creative and yet still "authentic" within the boundaries of a "foreign" art? And why does Etō Jun have no counterpart among jazz critics, bemoaning the bypassed paths toward a creative, authentically indigenous music?

Certainly the production of jazz was significantly impacted by institutional factors such as entertainment facilities for U.S. servicemen and artistic production companies, both of which assured uniformity of musical product and conformity to marketable American standards. But psychological factors were decisive as well. At a time when so much deemed "traditional" or "indigenous" was being disavowed, there was little interest in Japanizing jazz, as there had been in previous years. With crushing defeat a recent memory, it was much more respectful, prudent, and lucrative to master the new, modern forms of the music, however daunting. Regardless of rhetorical efforts to envisage jazz as a "universal" music, the possession of no single nation or culture, the association of jazz with the craved cultural, political, and economic might of the United States was too conspicuous to ignore. Thus for the postwar generation of producers of jazz, the dominant strategy of authentication was to replicate the sounds of American jazz and the contexts from which they emanated.

For whom was such jazz produced? The primary consumers were younger Japanese in search of a new ethos to replace the "traditional" one that led their parents down a destructive path. In the first two postwar decades jazz existed in parallel universes, as mass culture and as underground subculture; yet in both cases its appeal was rooted in an ethos of rebellion and anomie traceable to "the confusion era" and the disparagement of the inherited value system. Throughout the fifties and sixties jazz was fairly prominent on the concert stage, big screen, and radio, as well as at upscale cabarets. It cannot, then, be regarded as purely an underground phenomenon. Much like American entertainment in the fifties, postwar Japanese pop culture adopted a voyeuristic posture toward underground street culture, expressing thinly veiled disdain for teenaged punks and "bad girls" while pimping their images with lurid glee. Until rockabilly stole its thunder in the late fifties, at least, jazz was a key ingredient in any artistic portrayal of wayward youth. It was a mass phenomenon to be sure, but only by virtue of the peephole through which it leered at a fascinatingly raunchy underground of self-destructive and promiscuous youth tribes (*zoku*). In a society whose moral core had ruptured, such outcast renegades could be heroes.

The Occupation Blues and "That Old Democracy Boogie"

A mixture of awe and revulsion, deference and anger, elation and grief: there may be no better way than a juxtaposition of antonyms to describe the feelings with which Japanese received their conquerors in the mid-1940s. John Dower's monumental study *Embracing Defeat: Japan in the Wake of World War II* repeatedly highlights the paradoxical, even "surreal," nature of the relationship between the conqueror and the vanquished and their respective aspirations. Isoi Gijin's retrospective novel *We Had Those Occupation Blues* gives this ambivalence literary expression. Protagonist Saigo Hirobumi is the son of a well-off Hokkaidō family whose fortune is dispossessed by Occupation land reforms, so he is forced to look for work at the General Headquarters of Occupation forces. The "relaxed attitude" of his supervisor Colonel Steve makes Saigo "uneasy." He is repulsed by the "slovenliness" of this military officer at their initial meeting, at which the colonel "leaned back and put his feet up on the table and began to puff on a cigarette, humming a jazz tune." But the job at GHQ forces Saigo to adjust not only his attitudes but his tastes: "When he first heard jazz, he told himself something: the country had been defeated and this was his part-time job, so he would just have to listen to the Americans' jazz. He listened only because he had to. But at some point, who knows when, he became inordinately fond of jazz."[5] Isoi's portrayal conveys the sense that jazz remained a foreign music for many, irrevocably associated with the offensive conquerors and thus never entirely out of earshot. But necessity transforms Saigo's tastes.

Daniel J. Perrino, a musician with the University of Illinois Dixieland band "Medicare 7, 8, or 9," tells a story that suggests the soothing effect music could have on the sometimes tense relationship between occupiers and occupied. Perrino was in Japan for eighteen months right after the war, assigned to set up operations in the northernmost island of Hokkaidō for the Supreme Commander of Allied Powers (SCAP). His general encouraged his troops to seek out Japanese with similar interests, and Perrino was relieved of some of his duties to put together a show band. One day the band was on a crowded train bound for Sapporo and required an extra car just to carry the instruments. Japanese passengers, forced to stand as the instruments took up the seats, glared at the Americans. The band's guitarist was discussing a musical matter with a horn player, and they started playing. Perrino says the atmosphere on that train changed instantly as the other riders started digging the music. The band members got off in Sapporo bearing not only their instruments but gifts the Japanese passengers had given them.

It would be needlessly provocative and unfair to state that jazz in particular and Americana in general were rammed down the throats of hapless Japanese audiences—the conquerors were neither that powerful nor that baleful, and the conquered not that easily manipulated. But it would also be naive to imagine the popularization of American entertainment in postwar Japan outside of the matrices of naked power that the United States wielded over its vanquished former foe. For several years after Japan's surrender, visible manifestations of American power dominated the landscape (indeed, in Okinawa and mainland base towns, they still do). People who lived through the Occupation still talk about how "cool" (*kakkō ii*) the Americans appeared, speeding around recklessly in their jeeps, wearing sunglasses, and striding proudly through town, dwarfing the Japanese around them. I cannot count the number of people I have met who launched into such reminiscences when they learned I was an American. The sight of such power has left an indelible imprint on their minds. The visible power of the American occupiers was even more potent in contrast to the misery in which millions of Japanese lived for nearly a decade after the surrender. Even in prosperous times, Japanese often speak of a feeling of "yearning" (*akogare*) for American lifestyles; how much more intense the feeling must have been in the context of defeat and privation.

Surprisingly, perhaps, American troops who arrived on Japan's shores in the late summer of 1945 are remembered rather fondly. They became known not for the atrocities the government had warned its citizens were inevitable (and which did occur on a rarely acknowledged scale), but for the benign gifts they brought: candy, gum, and jazz. We have seen that the music had already acquired a number of symbolic associations over the previous decades, but in the early postwar period jazz came to represent the cultural power of the victor. Jazz blared from Occupation-controlled media and from the entertainment districts set up for the American troops. The Japanese government, on behalf of SCAP, hired hundreds of Japanese entertainers to perform for American troops and for "democratic propaganda" on the airwaves. Perhaps, as Isoi suggested, there *was* no escaping jazz. But the music proved seductive enough that millions of Japanese did not object.

Recognizing that, in the early months at least, radio would be the single most important vehicle for information and entertainment, SCAP moved quickly to control its programming content. Japan's public radio network, NHK, fell under the aegis of SCAP's bureau of Civil Information and Education (CIE), becoming the Occupation authority's principal voice to a Japanese audience. The programming was filled with "democratic propaganda" intended to "promote democratic thinking and international goodwill," reflecting SCAP's aim of fundamentally "reeducating" and "remolding the Japanese mind."[6] Starting in the autumn of 1945 with veteran tenor saxophonist Matsumoto Shin and his New Pacific Orchestra's program *New Pacific Hour* on NHK, radio broadcasts blending music with American-style optimism and democratic ideals provided the sonic backdrop for life in the ruins. Japanese music lovers also tuned in to the U.S. Armed Forces station WVTR to hear the latest American country, pop, and jazz music. Programs such as *Gems of Jazz* and *Honshū Hayride* hit the airwaves along with shows starring Kid Ory, Harry James, and Frank Sinatra. Countless jazz aficionados begin their personal narratives with the epiphany of hearing jazz for the first time on WVTR or NHK.[7]

Thus far I have discovered no documentary evidence conclusively stating that CIE authorities believed jazz programming on NHK and WVTR would democratize Japan, but there is ample circumstantial evidence to postulate that such was indeed the case. The Occupation was nothing if not deliberate in all of its cultural policies. At the earliest planning stages, the U.S. Office of Strategic Services recommended that radio provide "enough customary entertainment to divert some Japanese hostility from the occupying forces."[8] Documentary evidence suggests that CIE poured more energy into information programming than arts and entertainment, but the radio code enacted on 22 September set comprehensive directives for news, drama, poetry, comedy, variety shows, lectures, talks, announcements, and advertising. The official history of the Occupation states:

> The great over-all aim of the United Nations, to make certain that Japan would not again become a threat to the peace and security of the world, entailed the establishment of a government based on democratic concepts and designed to guarantee and promote basic human rights and freedoms. . . . To aid Japan's democratic development, all available media of public information were to be used to acquaint the people with the history, institutions and cultures of democratic nations. The Supreme Commander was directed to establish such minimum controls and censorship as he found necessary for purposes of security and the furtherance of his mission. . . .
>
> In accord with the tradition that music was out of place in times of

mourning or disasters, programs at first included no music but some diverting interludes soon became necessary to relieve the heavy concentration on news broadcasting. On 23 August the customary calisthenics hour was resumed with musical accompaniment, marking the return to more normal programming. On 1 September the second network was reactivated to provide greater variety and recreation and on the following day occupation advice and direction began.[9]

Yet SCAP, which often was and still is accused of using undemocratic means to achieve democratic ends, was nonetheless sensitive to the pitfalls of dictating what kind of music the Japanese could perform and listen to. Following the dissolution of the wartime Japan Music Culture Association on 27 September, SCAP announced that it "would not attempt to influence program making when 'the matter of musical judgment' might be a factor . . . [since] the attempt to control Japanese musical selection would be as undemocratic as anything the Japanese have done [in the past]." Listener polls were monitored for suggestions on entertainment, educational, and cultural programs. "The broadcasting of both western and traditional Japanese music was encouraged and an early Sunday afternoon amateur hour became increasingly popular," one such survey stated. "Quiz programs achieved great popularity with musical request programs rating only slightly less high." The CIE officials assumed that Japanese listeners would be ecstatic about the return of American music to the airwaves. In fact many were, Marlene Mayo's research contends, "but listeners consistently complained about the heavy diet of occidental songs."[10]

Official inhibitions about imposing particular styles of music on Japanese audiences masked an underlying assumption that exposing them to American culture ultimately contributed to the fulfillment of Occupation objectives. The authorities' efforts to saturate Japan with Americana are well documented. For instance, SCAP film policies admonished filmmakers to show kissing scenes, heretofore taboo in Japanese movies, in order to "force the Japanese to express publicly actions and feelings that heretofore had been considered strictly private" (Japanese audiences referred to these gratuitous displays as "kissing movies"). In 1948 SCAP also approved a royalty deal that allowed the Columbia and Victor recording companies to press and sell records by U.S. artists through their Japanese subsidiaries (though at that time few Japanese could afford to buy something as frivolous as a phonograph record anyway). Columbia University sociologist Herbert Passin, a former CIE official, recalled other "idiosyncratic interpretations of 'democratization.'" "I remember meeting young military-government officers in the provinces who were absolutely convinced that square dancing was the magic key to transforming Japan into a democratic society."[11] Likewise, jazz critic, DJ, and drummer Isono Teruo, who worked for the United States Information Service (USIS, CIE's successor) in the 1950s, insists that his employers staunchly believed that jazz and baseball would democratize Japan. Professor Sidney Brown has found evidence that CIE itself sponsored "jazz record concerts" for the public at its Yokohama facility.[12]

Perhaps the best evidence suggesting a faith in the utility of jazz as "democratic propaganda" is the U.S. government's promotion of the music among nonaligned countries during the early years of the cold war, with explicitly stated foreign policy objectives. Goodwill jazz tours were first suggested by Congressman Adam Clayton Powell Jr., who exhorted the State Department to send "fewer ballets and symphonies abroad, and put more emphasis on . . . Americana." According to reports in the *New York Times,* there was considerable public pressure on the State Department to recognize and exploit the propagandic potential of American popular music in Africa, the Middle East, Southeast Asia, and Latin America. "America's secret weapon is a blue note in a minor key," a *Times* reporter argued. "A careful student of the subject soon learns that the United States' most potent weapons in winning the goodwill of the Asians are its motion pictures and its jazz. What makes these two weapons so potentially effective in the 'cold war' is that the Communists cannot match them." Voice of America producers were quite vocal in advocating a conspicuous and positive jazz presence in their broadcasts, which "could demonstrate much more powerfully and subtly than propaganda that jazz represents democracy in many forms." The resulting campaign transformed musical revolutionaries such as Dizzy Gillespie, Count Basie, and Louis Armstrong into quasi-official ambassadors to "countries where communism has a foothold."[13] These blatant calls to deputize jazz in the service of U.S. foreign policy aims reveal a set of assumptions about the democratizing effect of American pop culture that likely informed CIE's decision to broadcast American popular music and jazz in occupied Japan. Indeed, Japan was often cited as proof of the success of the "old democracy boogie." "[Geisha are] doing the *Samisen Boogie,"* *Time* reported in 1949, "a red-hot indication . . . that Japan was *jazzu-crazy.*"[14]

Today jazz may be remembered as the music that wafted from the radio to relieve the suffering of postwar life and hearten the rebuilding effort, but at the time it was known as music for the entertainment of U.S. troops. The Occupation promoted jazz performance not only on the airwaves but in entertainment facilities, located in requisitioned buildings or military bases, which were for the exclusive use of American military and civilian personnel. Ironically the Japanese government, which had so vehemently vilified jazz mere months earlier, had a hand in promoting the music by establishing the Recreation and Amusement Association (RAA) within a week of the surrender. The Home Ministry's stated desire was to "welcome" Allied troops by providing for their musical and sexual "comfort" and entertainment—"jazz and women for American soldiers," as the saying went—but the RAA was really conceived as a preemptive strike to protect "respectable" women from anticipated mass rapes at the hands of occupying forces. The government staffed the RAA by recruiting widows, orphans, Korean and Chinese "comfort women," and "professional" women from the pleasure and entertainment quarters to "serve the country by servicing the GIs."[15] The rapid spread of venereal disease among American soldiers who took advantage of the RAA's services prompted SCAP to close all RAA sexual facilities in March 1946.

The RAA also established a nationwide network of cabarets, dance halls, beer halls, and nightclubs with live musical entertainment for the exclusive use of Occupation forces. (Eventually, night spots run by Japanese and U.S. civilians and American military personnel replaced government-run joints.) Officially classified as Officers' Clubs (OC), Non-Commissioned Officers' (NCO) Clubs, Enlisted Men's (EM) Clubs, and Civilian Clubs (CC), these entertainment facilities were also segregated racially. Particular styles of music were appropriate to each type of club: usually the white OCs favored dance music in the Glenn Miller–Guy Lombardo vein while the black EM clubs went for bebop or rhythm and blues. To complicate matters further, if one got a gig at a club with a particularly high concentration of white servicemen from the American South, proficiency in the somewhat less familiar "hillbilly" or country-and-western styles was essential.[16] Thus Japanese hired to perform at these clubs necessarily developed styles and repertoires appropriate to the clientele.

More often than not playing from stock arrangements provided by the military, Japanese musicians were frequently criticized for being exceptionally unimaginative. "Unfortunately, [Japanese performers] are mere imitators," the leading jazz writer Nogawa Kōbun wrote in Swing Journal in 1951, "and it seems that there is not yet one person with something original."[17] Yet Nogawa's harsh evaluation overlooked the economic tyranny of the job, which dictated that musicians copy and master particular styles of music familiar to the American audiences whom they were entertaining. Still, tenor saxophonist Inagaki Jirō rates not only the creativity but the basic musicianship of that era as exceptionally poor. Playing in a servicemen's camp dance band as a high school sophomore, he dismisses the music they produced as pathetic. Yet the Americans for whom they played tend to be more generous in their recollections of the caliber of performance. In

Kawasaki Hiroshi's elegy to the enlisted men's clubs, George Kawaguchi recalled that standards were high but the rewards were worth the risk of failure: if you played poorly, the GIs stomped the floor and yelled "Get out!" but if you were good you played encore after encore.[18]

With millions of Japanese out of work, destitute, and on the verge of starvation, those in the entertainment field were blessed to work at all, let alone make as much as they did. "While Japanese office workers are clamoring for a 3,000 yen basic wage," the *Japan Times* reported in 1948, "average musicians receive about 20,000 yen monthly from dance halls with one sideman reportedly getting as much as 50,000 yen." "I was still a student," clarinetist Fujika Kōji mused, "but I was making a salary man's monthly pay in one or two nights, and living the delicious life of royalty and nobility."[19] Men who had received their first real musical training in the Imperial Army and Navy were demobilized with little but their clothes and instruments, yet also with marketable skills. Star jazzmen such as vocalist Oida Toshio, clarinetist Miyama Toshiyuki, and tenor saxophonists Oda Satoru, Hara Nobuo, and Miyazawa Akira were among those who made the switch from military marches to swing and bop. Young women, often deprived of male providers by the war, could easily find marginally respectable work as taxi dancers in the servicemen's clubs. Within weeks of the war's end, musicians and dancers were working again, providing for their families and rebuilding their material lives much more rapidly than most of their fellow citizens.

This is not to say that life was peachy for anyone who could play an instrument or cut a rug, for there was considerable variation in the quality of life for entertainers. Those with established reputations as jazz and dance band musicians often had a distinct advantage finding work and being handsomely compensated. Saxophonist Hashimoto Jun recalled sharing a table with American officers, partaking of a full-course dinner, and receiving tobacco and chocolate whenever the New Pacific Orchestra played officers' clubs. New Pacific commanded such respect because most of its members had participated in NHK's shortwave propaganda broadcasts during the war, amusing and entertaining Allied soldiers and sailors in the Pacific theater in the latter years of the war. Rather than charging these musicians with war crimes, U.S. servicemen rewarded them for their skills with premier jobs.[20] Another veteran who found advantage in prior celebrity was pianist Kikuchi Shigeya, leader of the top dance band of the 1930s, who was recognized rummaging through the ruins of Nagoya in October 1945 and invited to assemble a band for the Trocadero servicemen's club. In Ōsaka, drummer Iiyama Shigeo (1910–1976) gathered former members of the wartime Shōchiku Light Music Orchestra in January 1946 to form the

Gay Six, a house band for the American cabaret Kabuki.[21] Clearly, the marquee value that veteran jazz stars carried through the war enabled them to enjoy a success that was quite alien to most other Japanese in the bleak months of the early Occupation.

However, such royal treatment did not extend to everyone. One of the most enduring images of the immediate postwar years was the sight of hundreds of musicians sitting around at major train stations with their instruments, "waiting for the man" to drive up and offer them gigs in pickup bands. At the stations no-name military bandsmen sat with former and future stars saxophonist Kawaguchi Yasunosuke, bassist Watanabe Shin, pianist Akiyoshi Toshiko, and even the self-styled "father of Japanese jazz" Ida Ichirō, all praying that when the trucks pulled up their instruments would be called. "We need two trumpets, a drummer, a bass . . ."; the barkers would holler, and like the day laborers of contemporary San'ya and Kotobuki-chō, the musicians piled into the trucks and rode off to the gig. Sight-reading one's way through a stock chart was a valuable skill in such a context, but improvisation was more often than not unnecessary—this was fortuitous, for "ad libbing" was still a foreign concept to most. After an evening accompanying jitterbugging GIs, the next day found most musicians at the station again, waiting around for the next job. For those who did not break into the big time, this numbing routine continued until the end of the Occupation in 1952.[22]

While the number of "day labor musicians" loitering at stations may have looked overwhelming, it is stunning to note that by most accounts there was still not enough talent to meet the demand. In order to accommodate the demand of servicemen's clubs and Japanese dance halls and cabarets, some three hundred and fifty bands were required on a nightly basis in Tokyo alone. Apparently, some pretty terrible bands managed to fleece the system by charging fees well beyond their worth and capabilities, until an audition and ranking system (in place from April 1947 to March 1952) put an end to this problem. Nogawa chaired a panel of judges from the Japan Musicians' Union, which traveled throughout the country auditioning and ranking Japanese bands and assessing pay scales. There were six rankings (Special A and Special B, then A through D), with the highest ranks earning top performance fees based on American Federation of Musicians wage scales. Musicians were paid by Procurement Demands exchangeable for cash, a system that essentially made them government employees hired to entertain Occupation troops and civilian personnel. The ranking system was hardly objective and incorruptible: since many of the judges were themselves bandleaders, their own bands tended to dominate the Special A rankings and thus the highest pay scales. For instance, Kikuchi Shigeya and

8. Yokosuka, still the site of a U.S. naval base, commemorates with three statues Japanese musicians who entertained U.S. servicemen during the Occupation. Photo taken by the author in 1995.

米軍クラブ仲間の同窓会
協賛 社日本音楽家協会 日本音楽家ユニオン 後援 株ジャズワールド

9. Musicians and singers who entertained U.S. servicemen in the Occupation era, many of whom became the biggest names in postwar pop culture, assemble for a final group picture at their gala reunion party at Tokyo Kaikan, 30 October 1994. Photo taken by the author.

Kami Kyōsuke, both judges on the ranking committee in 1949, held Special A rankings as conductors. Bands earning Special A rankings included Kami's Ernie Pyle Orchestra, Ōno Tadaosa's Gay Stars, Gotō Hiroshi's Dixielanders, Watanabe Hiroshi's Stardusters, Bucky Shiraki's Aloha Hawaiians, and Matsumoto Shin's Ichiban Octet. All these bandleaders were themselves judges.[23] Such abuses aside, the ranking system also guaranteed that bands would aspire to and maintain a performance standard with reference to American aesthetic criteria. "Originality"—that ill-defined bugaboo of jazz aesthetics—may indeed have been rewarded, but most certainly must have paled in comparison to facility at replicating what the GIs already knew they liked.

Jammin' with the GIs

The role that the Occupation and the Korean War played in promoting jazz among the general public in Japan, via radio and entertainment facilities, cannot be overstated. The same can be said of the influence that American servicemen of varying talent exerted directly on Japanese artists. Though not entirely over, the days of vicarious contact with American jazz artists through their records, magazines, or a brief sojourn on the "jazz frontier" were rapidly ending, as Japanese found a handful of jazz giants in their midst, in many cases more than willing to share their knowledge of the new styles of jazz. From the late forties through the fifties, a stream of American jazz artists continued to trickle into Japan: saxophonists Walter Benton, Harold Land, Hal Stein, Oliver Nelson, and Frank Foster, drummer Ed Thigpen, bassists Nabil Marshall "Knobby" Totah and Chris Eastlake, trombonist Dick Nash, pianists Jack Coker, Jodie Christian, Hampton Hawes, and Eddie Costa all mingled with Japanese artists while in the service. Les Brown's Orchestra and Oscar Pettiford's Swing Jamboree performed for troops on USO-sponsored tours, but found time to party and jam informally with their Japanese counterparts and instruct them either with advice or by example.[24] These were just the "name" artists; untold numbers of less well known but capable jazzmen found their ways to the East Asian archipelago. Japanese jazz musicians particularly remember a couple of soldiers, pianists Lt. Norbert de Coteaux and Joe Nesbud (both names are approximated from the Japanese phonetic spellings), who hung out at Yokohama bebop spots and taught the leading Japanese boppers. Uchida Kōichi's research makes most prominent mention of de Coteaux (whom Isono Teruo says "looked like Joe Frazier"). A regular at Yokohama's 400 Club, de Coteaux was a close friend to Akiyoshi and taught the Red Hot Boys' pianist Moriyasu Shōtarō (1924–1955) some technical aspects of bop giant Bud Powell's music. But Ueda Sakae's biography of Moriyasu argues that Nesbud's was the more pivotal influence on Japan's premier bebop legend.[25]

We know a bit more about two other American boppers who left important legacies in Japan: multi-instrumentalist Lt. James T. Araki (1926–1992) and Hampton Hawes (1928–1977). While interned with his family at the Gila River Detention Center in Arizona, Araki performed in the Music Makers band with fellow detainees, mastering trumpet, clarinet, alto saxophone, and guitar. He was drafted out of college to serve in the U.S. Army and sent to his parents' homeland to work as a translator at the war crimes tribunal. In his spare time Araki studied bebop theory and performance techniques, which he went on to share with native musicians. His compositions and arrangements were recorded in August 1947 at the first "modern jazz" recording session in Japan—performed, ironically, by an all-star band of established "trad" and swing musicians thrown together for the date and dubbed the Victor Hot Club.[26] The following year Araki and Nogawa Kōbun organized a bebop study group and "rehearsal band" to perform Araki's original compositions and arrangements in Tokyo. Araki returned to the United States in October 1949; after a brief stint performing with Lionel Hampton, Araki embarked on a successful career as a scholar of Japanese literature at the University of Hawaii at Manoa. He returned to Japan often throughout his career, occasionally jamming with his old friends (and arranging a recording session in 1959),[27] and in 1991 was awarded the Order of the Rising Sun, Fourth Class, for his contributions to the study of Japanese literature and to the promotion of jazz in Japan. George Yoshida, a drummer and historian who played with Araki at the Military Intelligence Language School at Fort Snelling, Minnesota, remarks that Japanese and Japanese American musicians all called him *kami-sama* ("God").

Hampton Hawes, an important bebop pianist from California, was stationed in Yokohama from 1953 to 1954 as leader of the 289th Army Band. Compared to his contemporary bop keyboardists Bud Powell and Thelonious Monk, Hawes's music had a noticeably churchy feel that prefigured the accessibly bluesy pianistic preaching of Horace Silver. Nevertheless, his rootsier style of bebop apparently did not catch on among Japanese artists for some time. That is probably because, as related in his candid autobiography *Raise Up Off Me*, Hawes spent more time hunting down his next heroin fix than playing music (saxophonist Inagaki Jirō told me that Hawes "came to Japan with two stripes on his sleeve and left with none"). "Uma-san"— *uma* means "horse" in Japanese, the nickname being a pun on the Japanese pronunciation of "Hawes" and on the slang term for heroin—had already gigged with Charlie Parker and Dexter Gordon, made a handful of recordings with Shorty Rogers and the Lighthouse All-Stars, and appeared in

10. Lt. James T. Araki in 1948. Japanese credit this multi-instrumentalist and future distinguished scholar of Japanese literature with introducing them to bebop. Photo courtesy of Janet Araki.

Down Beat polls before his tour of duty in Japan, but apparently few Japanese were familiar with his music.[28] Nevertheless, he quickly gained influence as the foremost apostle of Parker's musical (and pharmaceutical) gospel among Japanese jazz musicians (one of my informants provided a lively mimetic description of Hawes teaching him how to shoot up). Lurking the streets of Yokohama in search of his heroin fix, Hawes encountered "the baddest strung-out whore on the block," and asked her:

> "What's your name?"
> "Be-bop."
> "What're you talkin' about, you don't know nothin' about any bebop."
> "I know who Bird and Dizzy are."
> "Now how could you know them, sittin' way over here all your life eatin' rice 'n shit?" Excited and nervous, I said, "You've never had any black-eyed peas, you don't know anything about any goddamn blues," totally naive, you dig, about across-the-sea lines of communication in this field.

Hawes marveled at Japanese knowledge of and enthusiasm for bebop: "These Asians knew about Bird and Dizzy and Bud and all the time I'd

11. Jammin' with the GIs. From left: Raymond Conde, J. Baker, Taniguchi Matashi, Jimmy Araki, Yoda Teruo, and "Shanghai" Yamaguchi Toyosaburō. Photo used with permission of Segawa Masahisa.

thought nobody past 52nd Street [New York] or Central Avenue [Los Angeles] could possibly be hip to them." Hawes wrote that "Be-bop" showed him around the local jazz spots, including the Harlem Club, a Yokohama club managed by American Ray Bass, where a young female pianist was performing. "That little chick in a kimono sat right down at the piano and started to rip off things I didn't believe," Hawes recollected, "swinging like she'd grown up in Kansas City." The pianist was Akiyoshi Toshiko, and the encounter marked the beginning of her ascension as a major jazz star. Curiously, Akiyoshi's 1996 autobiography *Living with Jazz* omits all mention of Hawes and de Coteaux, rather crediting Oscar Peterson and Flip Philips with her "discovery" at the Tokyo coffeehouse Tennessee.[29]

Countless lesser-known soldier-musicians haunted Japan's jazz spots and jammed with the natives. Drummer Raymond Knabner, who did a tour in Japan and Korea in 1952–54, wrote me a letter describing his experience sitting in with the popular Six Joes for a New Year's Eve Armed Forces Radio Service (AFRS) broadcast in 1952. The Japanese musicians he met were, he writes, "greatly gifted, quite creative, and [displayed] a definite ability to learn." In another personal correspondence bassist Phil Morrison (who was stationed at Shiroi Air Force Base from 1954 to 1956) writes, "Some folks might have had a problem with the fact that [Japanese boppers] sounded so much like Bud and Bird (I didn't!)." Chicago pianist Jodie Christian, an airman in Japan from 1954 to 1955, remembers walking into clubs and hearing Japanese pianists play just like him, but rather than criticizing them for being derivative he regards it as a gesture of gratitude: " 'I'm playing like you to thank you for being here.' " Christian maintains that he got to play with a caliber of musicians that he would not have been able to play with in the States.

> They played well! They played better than me! And playing with them kind of got me up, too. . . . They were very helpful, too. They'd help you in any kind of way they could. And just being able to play and earn money was a big help to me, 'cause you're in the service and you get paid once a month, and you're always broke by the end of the month. Here I was earning money when everybody else was broke. So that was a big thing. And like I said, getting up on the tunes, tunes I'd never played before, tunes that I thought about, "how would I play this tune, how would I fit in with Bird?" And here I was with Bird [Watanabe Sadao]! . . .
> Their thinking was, he [Christian] come from where it's really happening, or where it started, so he's authentic. And I'm looking at them and say, well, they're on the ball, they got it, and I can learn from it.

A handful of working bands included Japanese and American members. Walter Benton and Hal Stein provided a two-tenor front line for the Cozy Quartet, a group whose piano chair Jodie Christian occupied when Akiyoshi was visiting her father's burial site. George Nakama, a noncommissioned officer, blew alto sax and introduced bebop tunes as a regular member of the Ichiban Octet. Informal "sitting in" was an even more frequent, if not always welcome, occurrence: there were many unskilled GIs who arrogantly shouldered their ways onto the bandstand. In an interview on National Public Radio's *Jazz Profiles*, Akiyoshi remarked:

> There were professional players [who were] drafted, and they were in service in either Korea or Japan, and of course they are all looking for a place to play. And the musicians' world is very small, so they would say, "Well, go to Toshiko's group and you can always [sit] in." . . . Say, 1954 or five or so, everybody's always coming and sitting in . . . and of course when you're young, I was in my middle twenties, you're kind of cocky, and I got tired of everybody coming and sitting in, somebody who doesn't even play well but because they're American they think they can play. Someone would say, "Hey, can I sit in?" and I'd say, "Sure,"

and I'd play really fast, "Fine and Dandy" or something like that, "Get Happy," and if they can't make it I'd say, "Come later." Sure, that's what I used to do.[30]

The arrogance Akiyoshi observed appears to have been much more widespread among GI jazzmen than Jodie Christian's unpretentiousness. Hawes, who muscled in on countless sessions, later characterized his tour in Japan as "a period of isolation" in which his "musical personality took its definite shape." "I couldn't be influenced by anybody then," he says in the liner notes to his third trio LP, "because I couldn't hear anybody."[31] Hawes's later expressions of admiration for Japanese musicians—like those of others—focused on their ability to recognize, appreciate, and replicate "the real thing," of which he was representative. He never conceded the possibility that he might have something to learn from his Japanese counterparts; if indeed his ears were more open to suggestion at the time, he would not admit it in his recollections. For Hawes and most other U.S. musicians, the real "scene" remained in the States, and noodling around with the natives was a way to develop their own gifts in what they perceived to be a less judgmental and self-conscious setting.

Jazz Booms

Historians of jazz in Japan tend to look on the early 1950s as a golden age, the era of the "unprecedented Jazz Boom" (kūzen jazu būmu). It is tempting to portray the Jazz Boom as merely the fabrication of nostalgic jazz aficionados who imagine a pre–rock and roll utopia, when young people actually listened to jazz, when jazz was truly popular music. But the media recognized the phenomenon as it occurred, making it more legitimate than a wistful hindsight projection. "Jazz mad" teenagers crammed some of the biggest concert halls in Japan's major cities, screaming, clapping, and stomping in homage to their heroes who beat and blew onstage. For performers such as the Big Four, the Six Lemons, Peggy Hayama, or Oida Toshio, it must certainly have been the heady high point of their respective careers. But it also frightened and outraged others, in much the same manner that jazz had inspired controversies some twenty years earlier. There thus seems to be a need to dispel some of the mystique of the Jazz Boom, not only to comprehend its appeal to postwar Japanese youth, but also to understand its limitations and contradictions.

What is usually referred to as the first Jazz Boom was a short-lived fad— lasting from 1952 to 1954 at the longest—that witnessed a rash of jazz coffeehouse (jazu kissa) openings, the resuscitation of social dancing, and the music's heightened visibility in movies, radio, television, stage productions, and concert halls.[32] Jazz critic Yui Shōichi remarked in our conversation that it was not really a "jazz boom" but an "imported entertainment boom" (*hakurai geinō būmu*), of which jazz (broadly defined, he was quick to add, to include everything from Doris Day to rockabilly) was merely a part. I too find it constructive to define the phenomenon more broadly and discuss its intersections with the growth of mass entertainment in postwar Japan. The Jazz Boom as a mass culture trend might be regarded as part cause and part consequence of the fascination with youth and adolescent rebellion, the desire for lifestyles with ample time for leisure, and the maturation of Japan's mass culture industry.

The explosive growth of mass entertainment acted as one herald of Japan's recovery from the ravages of war. The war on the Korean peninsula hastened Japan's recovery and reintegration into the world economy; Japanese enterprises and consumers, less absorbed with acquiring basic needs and financially able to spend money on leisure and entertainment, rebuilt the infrastructure for a thriving mass culture. The end of the broadcasting monopoly meant that private radio stations could compete with the public radio network (NHK), and they did so by airing commercial popular music. By the late fifties there were some thirty regular programs broadcasting live and recorded jazz performances around the country, such as NHK's *Rhythm Hour,* Radio Tokyo's *English Hour,* Radio Kōbe's *Jazz Room* and *Jazz Stars,* Voice of America's *Jazz Club,* and Radio Ōsaka's *Dixieland Jazz Club.* Also LP recordings, extremely rare and prohibitively expensive for most of the first postwar decade, became more readily available to the average consumer by the mid-fifties. Powerful new artistic production companies began to displace record companies as the principal force in popular music in the early fifties, assuming control over "all production aspects of a song and over all who were involved in its creation."[33]

These production companies—of which the mighty Watanabe Productions, founded by the jazz bassist Watanabe Shin, was most identified with jazz—rapidly concocted new ways to market jazz to a young audience. Watanabe and rival companies appear to have been most inspired by the success of American jazz artists, who in the final year of the Occupation began crossing the Pacific for the express purpose of performing for Japanese audiences. Gene Krupa, the drummer who powered Benny Goodman's hit recording of "Sing, Sing, Sing," brought his trio (with tenor saxophonist Charlie Ventura and pianist Teddy Napoleon) to Japan in April 1952. Gamely omitting mention of May Day protesters who pelted his entourage with rocks during an anti-American demonstration, Krupa told *Down Beat,* "It was the most tremendous thing I've ever experienced. Man, we saw nothing but cameras. Every time you turned around a dozen bulbs went off. I'd like to go back." He managed to do so the following year, as a member of Norman Granz's all-star revue Jazz at the Philharmonic (JATP). Ella Fitzgerald, Oscar Peterson, Roy Eldridge, Ben Webster, Benny Carter, Ray Brown, and other jazz giants were welcomed in November 1953 with a parade through Tokyo's Ginza district and played a series of successful concerts. Japan's jazz world was enthralled again when Louis Armstrong arrived a month later, performing for packed houses and graciously jamming with Nanri Fumio, Moriyama Hisashi, and other Japanese who had idolized him for decades.[34]

Armstrong, Krupa, and JATP were renowned not just for their musicianship but also for their showmanship. They were not afraid to play to the crowd; they were engaging and flashy, hard-blowing and hard-hitting, cultivating an "open jam" vibe at their shows. If most bebop artistes found accessibility beneath them, this trio of acts represented jazz's warmer side. They were ideal for creating a mass following for the music, and they were exemplary models for a group of Japanese musicians determined to leave the servicemen's clubs behind and go for the big time. Watanabe Productions and similar companies went to great pains to replicate the drama and ambience of these tours: they placed jazz performances in the concert halls rather than the ballrooms, adroitly assembled all-star packages that guaranteed ample spectacle as well as music, and targeted youthful consumers hungry for a good show and a cathartic experience.

Yet the Jazz Boom had its limits. Though many narrative accounts maintain that the up-tempo, bright outlook of American jazz and pops provided the optimism and energy necessary for the process of resurrecting the nation,[35] the era's best-loved popular songs continued to be those in the vernacular that bore some barely discernible Western musical influence, such as Namiki Michiko's monster hit "The Apple Song" (1945) and Kasagi Shizuko's recording of Hattori Ryōichi's "Tokyo Boogie Woogie" (1947). The U.S. press's self-congratulatory depictions of a whole country gone "jazu-crazy" notwithstanding (indeed, Inagaki Jirō maintains that jazz "boomed" only in Tokyo), the vast majority of Japanese were slow to abandon the ambivalence toward the music that they had nursed for decades. The singing prodigy Misora Hibari, who enjoyed her first hit in 1949 at the age of twelve, spoke more immediately and eloquently to the concerns of most Japanese than did Charlie Parker.

What popularity the music enjoyed among the general public was due in part to the revival of social dancing, to which the fate of jazz had heretofore always been tied. Sidney Brown cites several articles from the *Nippon Times* testifying to the renewed vitality of social dance, which for some exemplified "liberation from rigid wartime restrictions" and "initiation into a new democratic life." Neighborhood associations and labor unions actively promoted social dancing—allegedly with the aim of improving factory efficiency—and even the Japanese Communist Party argued for its utility in "fighting decadence and 'sexualism,' which the ruling class is using to weaken the struggle of the masses."[36] Although legislators and even the emperor's younger brother Takamatsu were spotted in dance halls, and the Ministry of Education endorsed dancing as "healthy recreation," conservative media continued to view social dancing as an activity devoted to "lewd pleasure and ruthless profit," totally inappropriate for the sober task of rebuilding the nation. "Ease and indolence will not enable a defeated nation to break through the impending crisis to rebuild our country," Prime Minister Katayama Tetsu was quoted as saying in the *Nihon keizai*. In the context of national humiliation and suffering, social dance was an indulgent luxury whose main practitioners were "the illegitimate children of the inflation economy who suddenly became rich, the black marketeers, the illegal gentlemen concealing their commodities."[37] But with the old Home Ministry dismantled and the Occupation authorities actively promoting American entertainment, grumbling anti-jazz voices were backed with little muscle.

At roughly the same time that Benny Goodman, Artie Shaw, and Count Basie were forced to disband their large orchestras, conceding commercial defeat to star singers and small combos, audiences in the American officers' clubs and Japanese ballrooms were basking in the luxurious reverberations generated by colossal dance bands. Prewar ensembles averaged ten pieces, but in the late forties enormous dance orchestras, boasting string sections, were twice that size. Bearing names both sunny and odd—such as the Stardusters, Asmanians, Sharps and Flats, Colombians, Swing Masters, Gay Stars, Swing Orpheans [*sic*], Lucky Puppy Orchestra, Blue Sky Orchestra, Swing Youth, Music Benders, and Blue Coats Orchestra—Japanese dance orchestras made Glenn Miller, Les Brown, Artie Shaw, Ray Anthony, and Guy Lombardo their idols. Nanri Fumio's Hot Peppers and Raymond Conde's Gay Septette (based on Goodman's small combos) represented more modest dance-oriented ensembles that were quite popular with both American and Japanese audiences.

Within a year of the surrender, Marigold in Ginza, Grand Tokyo in Shinjuku, and numerous other dance halls, cabarets, and dance schools opened throughout the country. In an early manifestation of what anthropologist William Kelly has called the "metropolitanization of the countryside," rural Japanese, mostly bypassed by the dance boom of the previous decade, started jitterbugging, too. Dance fever swept even rustic Nagano prefecture, the *Nippon Times* reported: "Government employees are now frolicking in the prefectural assembly hall to the tune of catchy dance numbers."[38] Periodicals devoted to social dance reappeared on newsstands after nearly a decade's absence; even *Swing Journal*, world-renowned for a puristic editorial stance favoring "mainstream" jazz as art music, began its life in April 1947 as a periodical devoted to both "Swing Music and Dance." "From now on the dance fan must at the same time understand and appreciate swing music. At this opportunity we decided to publish *Swing Journal* as a general magazine in which [swing and dance] are inseparable." Until Nogawa Kōbun managed around 1950 to push the periodical's editorial policy toward an artistic appreciation of "real jazz," several issues of the magazine were devoted almost exclusively to the latest dance steps.[39]

Given their historical cohesion, the eventual divorce of jazz from social dance was at least modestly revolutionary. It was also quite deliberate. The separation demanded that people around the world rethink their prior assumptions and conceptualizations of jazz, to recognize its spiritual and aesthetic potential as well as its well-established sensual proclivities. Jazz as capital-A "Art" required musicological and sociological redefinition. This was the task of jazz writers, who took it up with missionary zeal. Organizations such as the Hot Club of Japan sponsored "record concerts," a practice adopted from SCAP's Civil Information and Education Bureau, at which old and new jazz records were played and commented upon by critics and studious fans. Founded in 1947, the Hot Club billed itself as an "internationally-known pure jazz studies group" and invited participants to "Enjoy Real Jazz." Its stated mission was to foster analysis, discussion, and appreciation of recorded jazz as both a historical archive and as a continually evolving art. At Hot Club meetings, aficionados developed and refined their aesthetic sensibilities, openly discussing what made classic jazz performances great, how the music had changed, and what avenues it was likely to take in the future. In the coming years similar organizations were created in Ōsaka, Nagoya, Kyōto, and elsewhere.[40] The Hot Club meetings I attended in Tokyo in 1995 might be characterized both as events of reverent, academic formality and sobriety, and as lighthearted affairs at which any fan could be DJ for a day, sharing a beloved jazz moment with sympathetic *jazu nakama* ("jazz pals"). Such Hot Clubs gave the world *jazu otaku* (jazz geeks), whose passion and command of jazz ephemera have become legendary.

Through these gatherings and periodicals such as *Swing Journal*, Japanese aficionados in the late forties and fifties contended that jazz was best relocated from the ballroom bandstand to a setting appropriate to art music, namely the concert hall. Starting in August 1949, the staff of *Swing Journal* organized a series of thirty-three monthly Swing Concerts at Yomiuri Hall in Tokyo, featuring a variety of bands but with increasing emphasis on "modern jazz." Planners hoped that the concerts would not only facilitate the improvement of the participating bands, but also cultivate the audience's tastes and foster the acceptance of jazz as a legitimate concert music. To borrow Lawrence Levine's term for describing changes in cultural presentation in the United States, these self-described "serious" aficionados "sacralized" live *and* recorded jazz performance, re-presenting the music in a context where quiet awe and reverence were more appropriate than participatory rowdiness and frolicking.

The new critical establishment that advocated dignified arenas for jazz was thus dumbfounded by the "jazz concert boom" of the early fifties, which encouraged audience behavior that subverted the "serious" aficionados' sacralizing intentions. The unprecedented number of jazz concerts that companies such as Watanabe Productions promoted throughout the country drew capacity crowds not of studious aesthetes, sitting on their hands with stoic discipline and devotion, but rather of boisterous youths, egging the musicians on to ostentatious displays of instrumental prowess. The critics certainly welcomed the wider exposure the music was getting, but stopped short of endorsing the hype surrounding it. In spite of their best efforts to clean up the music's image, jazz was once again most visible to the general public as little more than a vehicle for transcending inhibitions. "Fans are making their parents cry and becoming the objects of social psychologists' criticism," the *Mainichi shinbun* reported in August 1953. "Recent jazz concerts have gone beyond 'enthusiastic' and are halfway maniacal."

Urban youth were most susceptible to the music's charms. A 1954 survey of 214 jazz concert attendees revealed that the vast majority of the audience was between the ages of seventeen and twenty-three. Only eight attendees were between the ages of twenty-six and fifty; perhaps surprisingly, given the predominance of males among contemporary *jazu otaku*, the survey found the gender ratio to be practically equal. In an article on folk musicians in Niigata prefecture, the Austrian ethnomusicologist Eta Harich-Schneider noted, "Young people, particularly the intellectual, ambitious young students, have lost interest in these cultural survivals and prefer the jazz programmes from Radio Japan to the quaint ballads and songs of olden times which the blind street-singers have to offer." Chagrin over the younger generation's inattention to cultural heritage was matched by persistent apprehension about the psychological effects of jazz music. Recall the citation in an earlier chapter, first published in a prominent women's magazine, in which the eminent social psychologist Minami Hiroshi demonstrated the "narcotic effect" jazz had on teens' brains: "If they are listening to jazz all

the time they gradually lose the habit of quietly thinking about things. . . .
The suspension of thought is the result of jazz's psychologically narcotic
effect." His observations about the increasingly automized and amoral
functioning of the modern mind—and the culpability of jazz in that process—is echoed in the following passage about "whilers" (nagara-zoku), or
people engaged in two tasks simultaneously:

> For example, it is night and you are sitting alone at your desk with a
> textbook open. And you try to concentrate on your lessons, but the
> aftermath of modern daily life with its many stimuli is whirling around
> you even now when you are alone, and you just can't settle down. . . . So
> you switch on the radio, and without seeming to listen you begin to
> hear the late-late jazz program. And then the rhythm of the music
> appropriately puts a part of your self to sleep and banishes excessive
> worry and longing; and riding to its pace as though mounted on a belt-
> conveyor, your studies begin to advance a little as though they were
> automated.[41]

Clearly, the old notions about what this music was capable of inducing had
not been extinguished with the fires of war; the increased jazz presence in
mass entertainment had not alleviated, but rather aggravated, parental anxieties. As in previous decades, municipalities and law enforcement addressed public trepidation with efforts to contain the jazz community's
activities and influence—though such measures were relatively modest
compared to pre–World War II actions. For instance, local and national
governments made clear aesthetic distinctions when levying taxes on concert tickets. In the late fifties the tax on tickets was 20 percent for classical
concerts but 50 percent for jazz and popular music. Diet members and the
Finance Ministry justified the discrepancy by saying that classical music was
art and jazz was entertainment. Curiously, tango concert tickets included a
tax of 30 percent, and if a jazz band included violin and accordion, as in
most tango ensembles, they were likely to get the same rate. But when
singer Peggy Hayama performed a semiclassical program, the audience was
charged the 50 percent rate because she was regarded as a "jazz singer."
Until 1954, these taxes were levied locally, so anyone going to see Louis
Armstrong or JATP paid a 50 percent tax in Tokyo and 20 percent in Ōsaka.
The tax structure's clear favoring of "art" over "entertainment" may have
been annoying, but crackdowns on nightlife were more ominous. In August 1964 a Tokyo municipal ordinance virtually eliminated after-hours
music making by making it illegal for jazz coffeehouses to operate after
eleven P.M.[42] For many, jazz remained a thorny "social problem."
    It seems that the association of jazz with the military and cultural might

of the Occupation authorities was a double-edged sword, legitimating the music for some and discrediting it for others. As expressed perhaps most effectively in film, jazz was the sonic representation of America's intrusion into the nation's cultural life. In many respects, Kurosawa's "unabashedly didactic" postwar cinema lauded the Occupation's cultural engineering project as it occurred. Yet the soundtrack to his 1948 film *Drunken Angel* (*Yoidore tenshi*) dramatizes the "disturbance of indigenous culture" and the "erosion of self [wrought by] the Americanization" of Japan: placid classical guitar vies with a raucously blaring jazz score, resounding off the cesspool that serves as the film's principal metaphor. In this film and 1952's *To Live* (*Ikiru*), the director locates jazz in sleazy, filthy ghettos populated with swaggering gangsters, coquettish taxi dancers, prostitutes, black marketeers, and gamblers.[43] Though hardly a xenophobic guardian of social and aesthetic traditions, Kurosawa expressed the continuing apprehension that many Japanese felt toward the music and the wholesale cultural transformation it portended, by deliberately associating jazz with the criminal opportunism that poisoned postwar society.

But it was precisely this dangerous aura, and the inevitable parental frustration it engendered, that made jazz such an attractive product to a generation trained to condemn its forebears' values as feudal. Throughout the fifties, popular "teen sex" films bearing titles such as *Jazzy Girls, Cheers to the Jazz Girls!*, and *Youthful Jazz Girls* (the key elements of the formula are obvious) maintained a public association of jazz with adolescent rebellion, illicit sex, mobsters, and frivolity.[44] The most famous example would be the seedy, gangster-infested jazz dystopia portrayed in Inoue Umeji's hit *The Boy Who Calls Storms* (*Arashi wo yobu otoko*, 1957), starring film idol Ishihara Yūjirō (1934–1986) as "tough guy drummer" Kokubun Shōichi. The film (which features performances by Watanabe Shin's Six Joes, drummer Shiraki Hideo, and singer Oida Toshio) is a mesmerizing snapshot of a sordid and competitive entertainment world, in which musicians and even jazz critics consort with gangsters. Kokubun's mother rebukes him when he lands a gig with the Six Jokers at a ritzy Ginza cabaret, chastising him for cavorting with mobsters. Rivalries for stardom—in this case as poll-topping drummer, sought by the upstart Kokubun and the established star Charlie Sakurata (Oida)—are as likely to be settled in dark alleys as on the bandstand. Kokubun, already roughed up once before a "drum battle" with Sakurata, stops in mid-solo and begins to sing, thus earning accolades as the "singing drummer" and dethroning his rival. But after his poll victory still fails to impress his mother, Kokubun goes on a drunken binge that makes him vulnerable to a serious attack by the mobsters backing Sakurata. The young drummer's hand is deliberately smashed with a rock and his dreams of fame wither, as his brother Eiichi's career as a "legitimate" composer and conductor begins to soar.

With the American film *Blackboard Jungle* (1955), featuring Bill Haley and the Comets' "Rock around the Clock," rock 'n roll displaced jazz as the music of choice for representing adolescent rebellion onscreen. Beginning in 1956 Japan's analogous *taiyōzoku* ("sun tribe") film genre, of which Ishihara was the unquestioned star, adopted a rock soundtrack to underline the indulgences of a spoiled and wild generation of beachcombers, surfers, and hot rodders. Mark Schilling defines the *taiyōzoku* as "rudderless youths who had grown up in the chaos of the early postwar years and were contemptuous of prewar values, but had only American-style hedonism to put in their place. Instead of dying for the emperor or slaving for the company, like their fathers and older brothers, they preferred to cruise the Ginza looking for girls . . . or head off to the beach."[45] Perhaps even the opening musical sequence of *The Boy Who Calls Storms*—in which an Elvis clone shimmies and shakes in front of a rhythm-and-blues band—suggests jazz's impending obsolescence in film.

These films documented a loss of decorum among Japanese youth, which had been actively fostered at jazz performances in the fifties. Jazz concerts encouraged an ethos of spontaneous and unbridled self-expression, within the ostensibly solemn context of the concert hall. Keenly aware of this, Watanabe Productions engineered the concert boom with the newest name bands in its stable: Yoda Teruo's Six Lemons, Watanabe Shin's Six Joes, the Midnight Suns, the Crazy Cats, and the monstrously popular Big Four. Each band had its own emphasis, but all tended to blend elements of swing and modern styles with a hard-blowing, "cutting contest," jam session feel—it was actually dubbed "blow jazz" (*burō jazu*)—creating an accessible mode that thrilled teens. Fans never failed to cheer soloists on, the *Mainichi* noted, and the musicians obliged with trademark bombast.

Never had a jazz act known as much widespread fame as the first incarnation of the Big Four (drummer George Kawaguchi, saxophonist Matsumoto Hidehiko, pianist Nakamura Hachidai, and bassist Ono Mitsuru). Kawaguchi was heir to a family legacy steeped in music: his father Yasunosuke (1896–1952) lived a musical double life as a classical violinist and jazz saxophonist, and his grandfather had been a musician of the Muraoka *iemoto* before moving to the Kawaguchi house of Niigata prefecture. Yasunosuke was, according to his son, one of the real-life "Shanghai advance kings"; after nearly a decade of performing in dance halls in the capital and the Kansai, in 1932 he left his family to go to Manchuria, which the previous year had been wrested from Nationalist China and established as a puppet state under de facto Japanese control. Six-year-old George and the rest of the family joined him in Dairen the following year, and Yasunosuke would take his son with him on gigs in Shanghai. "It is unfortunate that I do not have an exact memory of it," George wrote in his serialized memoir, "but at this time I saw with my own eyes the performances of black jazzmen from the mother country [America]. I am not conscious of it, but watching from the side the basic movements of drumming, the way of holding the sticks and moving the feet, was very useful to me when I began playing drums myself later."[46] George made his professional debut in his father's band immediately after the war, performing for the Soviet officers whose troops occupied Dairen, before finally evacuating to the home islands in 1947.

With the sounds of Gene Krupa's solo on "Sing, Sing, Sing" thundering in his brain, the twenty-year-old drummer wasted little time locating gigs in the U.S. servicemen's clubs in Yokohama. He gained experience with the Asmanians and Conde's popular Gay Septette before venturing out on his own to found "a superband of only young Japanese." When the lineup for the Big Four was announced in 1952, all observers agreed the band would be a monster. They virtually never played small venues, opting rather for opulent concert stages and weekly broadcasts on Radio Tokyo. Even the critics who tended to disparage the Big Four's bluster conceded that its musicianship spoke well for jazz's indigenous development: *Swing Journal*'s Kubota Jirō cited the band as evidence of the "certain and delightful fact that our country's jazz musicians have improved."[47]

With the newspaper headlines reading "The world is truly in an age of jazz fever," Kawaguchi and company were on top of the world, threatened only by the trickle of visiting jazz acts from the States, who easily topped native artists in terms of pure spectacle. Japan's jazz stars were not immune, however, to the pressures of celebrity, which made their world notorious for volatility. "A jazz band's profile rises and falls, changing like a cat's eyes," the *Mainichi* noted:

In this [jazz] world three-month-old data is of absolutely no use. One band quarrels over money, for instance, prompting its excellent drummer to leave. So that band, with no other recourse, eyes another band's good drummer and lures him away. Because it is a harsh world of survival of the fittest, where a band declines with any loss in talent, excellent players must be in place at all times to secure a fixed income.... What's more, since there are no limits as with baseball teams, the situation is such that [jazzmen] keep creating new bands with like-minded colleagues.

In what at the time must have seemed like a massacre, the two most popular bands, the Six Lemons and the Big Four, both disbanded in March 1954.

Sleepy Matsumoto checked into a hospital for drug rehab, while Kawaguchi and Ono reportedly wearied of the personal rivalry over female fans that their good looks generated. An attempt to combine the remains of the two bands—into the All-Star Six Lemons—lasted only ten months, but Kawaguchi would assemble new editions of the Big Four to perform for the popular radio program *Torys Jazz Game*. The first jazz artist to receive the Minister of Education's 1980 Prize in the Popular Arts and the 1988 Purple Ribbon Medal, the drummer continues to lead a hard bop unit known as the New Big Four Plus One.[48]

With the breakup of the biggest name bands, the concert boom eventually flamed out, but that did not necessarily mean the exit of jazz from the public eye. Jazz maintained a profile in popular entertainment, in part due to the comic band Crazy Cats, led by drummer Hana Hajime and vocalist Ueki "Harry" Hitoshi. Boasting that they represented the *"musekinin* [irresponsible] soul of the sixties," the band got its start in the waning years of the first Jazz Boom as the Cuban Cats in 1955, but soon made a name for itself by inserting slapstick gags between songs (a schtick apparently lifted from another huge act, Frankie Sakai and the City Slickers). As self-styled "hipsters" engaged in buffoonish "jazz play," the group appeared prolifically on television shows such as *Soap Bubble Holiday*, in James Bond satires such as *LAS VEGAS Free-for-All* (*Kurējii kōgane sakusen*, 1967) and *MEXICAN Free-for-All* (*Kurējii mekishiko daisakusen*, 1968), and in Ueki's famous "Irresponsible" (*musekinin*) series of film parodies on the life of the beleaguered corporate worker. (Schilling notes, "In the uptight world of 1960s corporate Japan, [Ueki] Hitoshi represented a welcome breath of fresh air. Even worker bees, it seemed, could dream of making easy honey.")[49] For our purposes, the Crazy Cats are significant for capitalizing and purveying an image of jazz musicians as clownish, slang-slinging ne'er-do-wells. Their audience rewarded the Cats with a longevity of which very few Japanese acts can boast.

As Dick Hebdige, Tom Frank, and many others have documented, the producers of mass culture thrive and reinvigorate their products by appropriating the most titillating and comical surface aspects from folk cultures and subversive countercultures.[50] The Jazz Boom can be viewed as the result of a similar process. It marketed a frightening yet undeniably titillating rebellious ethos and nihilistic "normlessness" begat by the cultural reform agenda of the Occupation era. As Japanese struggled to rebuild shattered lives in a world in which the black market and gangster justice had become commonplace, they cast about for a value system to replace the nationalistic fervor and imperial paternalism that the Occupation sought to destroy. The popular arts reflected the audience's confusion, fear, and prurience in this bewildering era. But in its obsession with spectacle, the Jazz Boom obscured and trivialized the economic and artistic travails of a legitimate underground devoted to the mastery and personalization of a complex musical language and mode of expression.

Granted, the borders between the Jazz Boom and the jazz underground were permeable. Kawaguchi and bebop's creepy genius Moriyasu Shōtarō hung out at the same coffeehouses, while Sleepy Matsumoto was equally comfortable on the concert stage with the Big Four and in the after-hours joints jamming with the scufflers. But in many ways the vibe was different: the music, the venues, the aesthetic, the pay, the jazz life were practically inverted in comparison to one another. Kawaguchi and his confreres were interested in putting on a show: they were content to play familiar songs in a style that their audience found accessible, to prance and pose, beat and blow. They were ambassadors for a music that many still regarded as alien. Moriyasu, Akiyoshi, and their bebop disciples, on the other hand, would turn down gigs rather than play music they thought beneath them. They were willing to sacrifice their mental, financial, and physical health in romantic pursuit of a difficult art that either moved them profoundly or at least superficially impressed them. Dr. Uchida Osamu, a prominent jazz producer and writer, commented on the distinction: "George Kawaguchi was a popular person who simply imitated jazz, yet did nothing with originality. He is quite distinguished for increasing the number of jazz fans, but in those days when people thought that what George Kawaguchi was playing was jazz, Moriyasu was aiming for the real thing."[51]

The charismatic, flamboyant Kawaguchi was a genuine teen idol, a movie star and a major concert draw. On the several occasions that I saw him perform, I caught some sense of the frenzied enthusiasm he once inspired in his fans. In addition to his musical gifts and sense of fun, Kawaguchi is a master showman who has his audience well-trained: during his obligatory ten-minute solos on his theme song, Gene Krupa's "Drum Boogie," his ritual includes periodically looking up from his kit to grin and snatch another wave of applause. His fans always oblige, feeling a sense of contribution as they goad their hero on to further displays of virtuosity. At a performance at the 1994 Yokohama Jazz Promenade, a gentleman two seats to my left, who looked the right age to have been a teenager in the drummer's heyday, beat imaginary drums in imitation of the star's drum solo. Finally, unable to contain himself any longer, he yelped "George!"

Those who scuffled in Kawaguchi's shadow had different motivations. A desire to understand and master American accomplishments, and to authenticate themselves as legitimate jazz artists, compelled them to search for the musical and extramusical keys to replicating classic American jazz performances. "When we started playing at the American bases," pianist Imada Masaru relates, "we could see the kinds of attitudes that American servicemen had. We saw how the musicians would play with drinks on-stage, for example. Very quickly we picked up this as well as the music."[52] Closer study of the American jazz life and intimate contact with practicing American jazzmen inevitably heightened awareness of racial and cultural issues affecting jazz performance. An emerging consensus equated African American ethnicity with authenticity of jazz expression, and insisted that cultural contexts comparable to those within which African American art-ists worked were necessary preconditions for authentic jazz. Japanese jazz aficionados therefore appropriated customs, language, and fashions as well as music. For some, narcotics and post-gig jam sessions, "rituals of [aes-thetic] purification,"[53] were as crucial to playing bop as were bass drum bombs and altered thirteenth chords. These attributes and practices made jazz aficionados a spectacle, even a "social problem," in the eyes of the mainstream. But that was precisely the point: only a culture as spectacular and marginal as that of American black people, Japanese hipsters reasoned, could create pure jazz.

To Bop or Not to Be . . .

A cardinal principle of most jazz history is that the music has maintained an enduring, identifiable core identity throughout its evolution, and that its development has been guided by some mysterious yet consistent inner logic.[54] "Bop was the logical outgrowth of swing," Will Friedwald has writ-ten, "just as swing and the big band era had been the natural progression from the classic jazz of the '20s." This metanarrative of a "logical" or "natu-ral" progression of jazz styles not only undervalues the agency of the artists responsible for stylistic innovation, but also understates the intense contro-versies provoked by those changes. Cab Calloway, Louis Armstrong, and Eddie Condon were outspoken in their opposition to bebop in the 1940s, just as boppers were hostile to the "free" music of Ornette Coleman, John Coltrane, and Sun Ra in the 1960s. "I don't know what he's playing," Dizzy Gillespie said of Coleman in 1960, "but it's not jazz." Thelonious Monk added, "Man, that cat is nuts!"[55] Not too many years earlier, both men caught heat as impertinent revolutionaries; if someone as catholic in his tastes as Gillespie, or someone as loopy as Monk, made such statements, something deeper than a "logical progression of styles" is afoot. "Moldy figs" who accepted revolutionary shifts in the music as "natural," such as Coleman Hawkins, Ella Fitzgerald, or Sonny Rollins, were the exception. Disparaging remarks about each new movement are reprinted often, yet oddly enough do little to dislodge the evolutionary narrative. But such indictments indicate that the "logic" of jazz history has been imposed in hindsight.

It seems that a more historically sensitive perspective on these so-called "stylistic shifts" is to view them as profound, even earth-shattering upheavals, constituting new "musics" rather than variations of a music with an essentially unitary nature. (The same should also be said of the various musics that are lumped together as "classical music" in common parlance.) Such eruptions changed the way people heard, thought about, evaluated, and performed music. Yet the ruptures are not merely or purely musical, but social and cultural as well: "Any analysis of bop that ignores either the nuances of musical language or the political context for its creation is manifestly incomplete," Scott DeVeaux states in *The Birth of Bebop*. The musics known collectively as "jazz" developed in different contexts, appealed to different audiences, and bore different messages. If hot jazz, as Jelly Roll Morton made clear, was an unapologetically bawdy entertainment best presented in black honkytonks and bordellos, swing was the self-consciously sanitized version presented to a mass white audience and performed in dance halls. Bebop distanced itself from both contexts and audiences, and presented itself as an "art music" for a more intellectual audience in small clubs and on concert stages. With bebop, too, came the notion that the artist's responsibility was to play what had never been played before, to take the music into uncharted realms through "continuous innovation." Armstrong realized the social and economic ramifications of the bop revolution better than most jazz historians have since: "Everybody's trying to do something new, no one trying to learn the fundamentals first. All them young cats playing them weird chords. And what happens? No one's working."[56]

I make these points to accentuate how bebop, or *modan jazu*, as it was just as often called, perplexed Japanese musicians. Having won the freedom to play their beloved jazz openly in less circumscribed contexts than ever before, Japanese were truly bewildered to discover that the music had passed them by. And with the bebop ethos of "continual innovation," the music was guaranteed to change again, necessitating constant vigilance and study to stay current. As had been the case in the United States, bebop transformed the social and economic contexts in which jazz performance was presented in Japan, displacing dance halls and giving birth to swanky cabarets, coffeehouses, and after-hours dives for which there had been few if any prewar precedents. Moreover, though Nogawa surely exaggerated when he stated that "all the older musicians have given up and only younger musicians are playing modern jazz," bebop segmented or "genrified" Japan's jazz community, accentuating generational differences with stylistic allegiances. In the interwar period there had been a relative uniformity of experience and repertoire among *jazumen,* but with the modernization of the music musicians aligned themselves within increasingly well-defined stylistic categories: Dixieland, swing, or modern. Even within the modernist camp, there were distinctions between those who favored a "cool," "white," Lennie Tristano–George Shearing approach, a "progressive," Stan Kenton style, and those who characterized themselves as "funky," "black," Charlie Parker–Sonny Stitt devotees. Whenever a well-known artist switched allegiances, it became news in the jazz press: for instance, not long after Krupa's Japan tour with saxophonist Charlie Ventura, *Swing Journal* reported that Sleepy Matsumoto was moving from a Stan Getz-inspired "cool" approach to a more aggressive attack modeled after Ventura, Sonny Stitt, and Gene Ammons.[57]

Knowledge of bebop became an occupational necessity for those Japanese who, by stroke of fate, wound up performing in clubs for African American servicemen. There, audiences were likely to demand that the band "play bebop!" or query, "Hey man, do you known any Bird?" It was a trial by fire for young Japanese musicians, many of whom were still in high school, to master the intimidating harmonic alterations, displaced rhythmic accents, breakneck tempos, and convoluted melodies that distinguished bop from dance musics. They relied on imported records, the rare bebop method book, or the occasional generosity of American beboppers stationed in Japan to get them through. Trombonist and composer Ōmori Seitarō recalls that his friend Dick Charles ordered Stan Kenton scores from America for use in Ōmori's Bold Head Orchestra, but Kenton's "progressive jazz" arrangements were more readily digestible for reading musicians than Charlie Parker's improvisatory flights or Kenny Clarke's off-beat bass drum "bombs."[58]

Japan's first beboppers were refugees from dance orchestras or popular combos, intrigued by the newer frontiers of modern jazz. They occasionally caught the latest sides by Parker, Gillespie, or Powell (recorded on "V-Discs," the only union-approved recordings made in the United States during the American Federation of Musicians-sponsored strikes in 1942–43 and 1948) on wvtr.[59] The new sound caught on well enough that by the late 1940s a handful of groups were vying for the mantle of "Japan's first bebop band." Saxophonist Nagao Masashi used the name Bebop Ace (coined by Nogawa Kōbun) for his new dance band in April 1948, but by his own admission the band did not actually play in the bebop style. Matsumoto Shin claimed the distinction for his Ichiban Octet (1948–1952), but though his was an accomplished swing and dance combo, the band's integration of the modern jazz styles was rather tentative. Two Yokohama-based combos,

Clambake 9 and Gramercy 6, were most successful in honing a convincing bop sound on the bandstands of the port city's black servicemen's clubs.

In January 1948 members of the Swing Orpheans dance orchestra became bored playing dance music and formed the Clambake 9 (CB 9), making the rounds of Yokohama black clubs such as Zanzibar, New Yorker, and Golden Dragon. The band's ace in the hole was its handsome drummer Shimizu Jun, by all accounts the Japanese percussionist most fluent in bop polyrhythms and offbeat accents. *Swing Journal* named CB 9 "Japan's first bop band" in 1950, and called on the group when it needed a native bop band to introduce the new music to young Japanese at its monthly Swing Concerts. Reviewers commended the band for its zeal but criticized it for indulging in twenty-minute solos and choosing tunes that were "too difficult" for performer and listener alike. The flashy combo, plagued by frequent personnel changes and a reputation as a "dope band," broke up in 1951. They never recorded during their heyday, but reunited for the all-star reunion album *Jazz on Flame* (1976), to which they contributed a rather sloppy performance.[60] In contrast to CB 9's reputed wildness, the Gramercy 6 represented bop's "cooler," less volatile side. Originally a college band after the manner of Benny Goodman's swing combo, the band shifted gears in the spring of 1949 as a cool bop band modeled after Miles Davis's "Birth of the Cool" nonet and George Shearing's band. Its popularity with the Japanese jazz public surpassed that of CB 9: Gramercy 6 gigged in Japanese concert halls as well as American servicemen's clubs, recorded a couple of sides for Nippon Victor, and even appeared in the film *The Route to America with You* (*Kimi to yuku Amerika kōro*, 1950). However, competition between the bands remained friendly, and in 1950 they even joined forces to found the Bop Men Club, a free workshop open to anyone wanting to study the music.[61] The sextet, like its nonet rival, disbanded in 1951.

Though bebop can hardly be said to represent the mainstream of Japan's jazz community in the late forties and early fifties, it provided the foundation for the increasingly strident arguments for jazz as serious art music. Eavesdropping on the rancorous discord in the American jazz press, Japanese jazz aficionados debated the evolutionary model of jazz history that regarded bebop and "progressive" jazz as aesthetic advances, increasingly distant from dance and closer to art music.[62] Nogawa Kōbun, his day's foremost jazz aesthete, wrote, "Nowadays [jazz] is widely performed for movies, stage shows, radio, and for appreciation rather than for dancing. . . . As a music [jazz] has not yet developed into a complete form, but gradually continues to develop and progress without rest, and no one knows where it will go." But, although many jazz fans fretted that older styles would simply "disappear," the acceptance of bebop as an evolutionary advancement did not go uncontested. Jimmy Araki himself testified regretfully that audiences were hostile to bop. Nanri Fumio, the self-styled "Japanese Satchmo," defiantly asserted, "I only play Dixie"; besides, he argued, Japanese were physically unable to play bebop because their bodies were not strong enough to play high notes, and "bop without high notes is like *sashimi* without *wasabi*." But, while striving to accommodate the views of fans of traditional jazz, the core of the critical establishment had reached a consensus in the Occupation's later years that bop and related styles represented jazz's arrival as a significant art music suitable for "appreciation" (*kanshō*) rather than dancing.[63]

As noted above, converts to this viewpoint developed a variety of strategies for presenting jazz to new audiences in contexts quite distinct from the old commercial dance halls. Jazz coffeehouses (*jazu kissa*) also reflected the change in attitude, becoming the primary "schoolhouse" where serious jazz fans were socialized into a deeper aesthetic appreciation of jazz. Compared to their relatively opulent predecessors, with their glamorous "sign girls" and exquisite interiors, the jazz coffeehouses of the postwar era were generally more spartan, offering little more than beverages and recordings of "pure jazz" for the serious connoisseur and the studying musician. Financially unable to buy their own records (which cost anywhere from ¥2500 to ¥4000 apiece), aspiring boppers haunted jazz coffeehouses such as Chigusa in Yokohama, Combo in Tokyo, and Combo in Nagoya, where they repeatedly listened to American records and painstakingly transcribed what they heard on paper. Tokyo's Combo, located in Yūraku-chō, was a cramped haven for the most serious of modern jazz enthusiasts. Inagaki Jirō, who collected records for Combo, recalls that the room accommodated only ten or twelve people at a time, but was usually packed with musicians studying recordings. Likewise, Chigusa, located in the heart of Yokohama's black market district of Noge, was the principal study hall for the bebop musicians attempting to answer their African American audience's demands for Bird and Diz. Nagoya had its own "record *kissa*," also known as Combo, which owner Kuno Jirō (1933–1976) eventually converted into a live house. Decorated with stills from Western movies, a large fish tank, and Japanese *shōji* (paper sliding doors), Nagoya's Combo became a hangout for Japanese and American musicians looking to jam (or to shoot up), according to Uchida Osamu. He lists Johnny Hodges, Clark Terry, Sonny Stitt, Philly Joe Jones, and Paul Chambers as among Combo's guests.[64] Establishments such as these were central institutions in Japan's jazz community, functioning as the primary sources of printed and recorded information on the music at a time when few Japanese were affluent enough to amass record collections and hi-fi stereo systems.

As Nogawa steered *Swing Journal* toward a "jazz-as-art" editorial policy, diagrams of the latest dance steps were displaced by articles on the origins, harmonic structures, rhythm, and phrasing that distinguished bebop. In truth, the underground bebop coterie of which Akiyoshi Toshiko and Moriyasu Shōtarō were the acknowledged leaders had little more than the enthusiastic support of jazz writers in *Swing Journal* and *Music Life* to sustain it. While groups like the Big Four toured the country's theaters, Akiyoshi's Cozy Quartet was losing small club engagements regularly over her stubborn refusal to play dance music or pop songs with a vocalist. Toiling in the shadows of the Jazz Boom, if ever in the mass culture industry's voyeuristic eye, scuffling boppers organized their own jam sessions, honing their skills before a sympathetic audience of peers and subverting the artistic production companies' grip on music making. They invented their own brand of "hipster lingo," usually borrowing and modifying English terms or inverting Japanese words. The simple inversion of words—analogous to "pig Latin," perhaps—was particularly popular: "Chigusa" became "Kusachi," *onna* (woman) became *naon*, and so forth. Other usages toyed with foreign loan words: *avec* ("date"), "moose" ("girl," from *musume*), *otsu mata* ("what's the matter"), and *wakaru kenji yo* ("I dig you, man").[65]

The inversion of words suggested an inversion (or subversion) of dominant values, as Albert Goldman notes: "The values of the normal world are defiantly inverted in the world of jazz: *bad, terrible* and *tough* are synonyms for excellence, while *sweet* and *pretty* are terms of disparagement." Amiri Baraka, himself a self-styled "hipster" in his youth, wrote of the subculture in his *Blues People:*

> In a sense the term *cultists* for the adherents of early modern jazz was correct. The music, bebop, defined the term of a deeply felt nonconformity among many young Americans, black and white. And for many young Negroes the irony of being thought "weird" or "deep" by white Americans was as satisfying as it was amusing. . . . It was a cult of protection as well as rebellion. . . . The white beboppers of the forties were as removed from the society as Negroes, but as a matter of choice. The important idea here is that the white musicians and other young whites who associated themselves with this Negro music identified the Negro with this separation, this nonconformity, though, of course, the Negro had no choice.[66]

Similarly, Japanese beboppers had a *choice* to isolate themselves from what they regarded as the inanity and conformity of mainstream society and the entertainment industry: in doing so they often took self-destructive paths, but always in the interest of authenticating their art.

I once asked writer Ueda Sakae what struck her most about the bebop jazz subculture. She knew very little about jazz before commencing re-search for her authoritative biography of Moriyasu Shōtarō, but having interviewed a significant number of jazz folk by this point, she was in a position to reply that the instability of both professional and personal lives amazed her. Musicians seemed to join and leave bands often and casually: for instance, tenor saxophonist Miyazawa Akira ended his memorably fruit-ful association with Moriyasu to join Akiyoshi's Cozy Quartet, ostensibly for a "change of environment" to help him "develop as an improviser." Further-more, Ueda noted that divorce rates were astonishing. Many couples—usually male instrumentalists and female singers or dancers—met through jazz, but were torn apart by the jazz life. The women almost invariably abandoned the entertainment profession, while the men pursued the ample opportunities for philandering which that life presented. Disc jockey Shima Yukio, the *English Hour* host whom Ueda and I interviewed jointly, also commented at length on the remarkable divorce rate among jazz artists: "Musicians are no good!" In the end, for Ueda the volatility that jazz artists seemed almost to welcome into their lives was in striking contrast to the stability that, in her view, most other Japanese covet.

The inverted lifestyles and jargon, and the informal, musician-initiated jam sessions, effectively distinguished the bebop culture from mainstream popular music, but nothing symbolized its estrangement from the "squares" more than narcotics. The subject of drug use in the Japanese jazz community appears to be much touchier than it is in the United States. Most Japanese and Americans who played jazz in Japan in the 1950s maintain that they never witnessed a significant degree of drug abuse. Yet contemporary news reports often tell a different story. It was a compelling enough problem to warrant repeated expressions of rebuke in *Swing Journal,* which periodically restated its strong editorial stance against narcotics and publicly chastised busted musicians for damaging the jazz community's collective reputation. (The high profile arrests of American jazzmen Philly Joe Jones, Charli Persip, Elvin Jones, Curtis Fuller, and Tony Williams for narcotics possession while touring Japan in the 1960s did not help that reputation, either.)[67] Apparently, it was a problem peculiar to boppers: Oda Satoru and Raymond Conde, both of whom doggedly identify themselves as swing musicians, explicitly linked the increasing use of drugs to stylistic changes in the music. Oda told me that he "resisted bebop," which "destroyed jazz" because it was too complicated yet unstimulating. Bebop was so difficult that musicians resorted to drugs to deal with its complexities: "My music doesn't require drugs, because it's easy listening." Conde concurred, referring to drug use as a "crazy and expensive" habit appropriate to bebop's superficial "style" and vacuity of musical content.

The most prevalent narcotics were heroin, marijuana, and philopon, a drug widely distributed to soldiers, pilots, and factory workers during the war to prevent sleep, and increasingly used by students preparing for exams and entertainers in the postwar period. Rampant long-term use led to widespread addiction (reportedly 800,000 addicts in 1949) and eventually to legal restrictions of the drug in Japan.[68] Heroin had special significance, for it was bop legend Charlie Parker's drug of choice. The vain effort to "play like Bird," to achieve the numbed high many believed was a key to Parker's imaginative flights, motivated aspiring boppers around the world to try the drug. "Heroin was tailor-made for inducing a sense of emotional distance, a central tenet of the hipster ethic," Harry Shapiro has written; "the feelings are not euphoric or high in the active sense, but cool and detached." A number of writers have also argued that alienated white musicians used drugs and music to authenticate themselves as artists in a "black" idiom: "If for black musicians heroin symbolized the flight from white society, for white musicians it symbolized the flight *towards* black society. To enter the closed world of the jazz community white musicians had to transcend the distinct disadvantage (in this one respect) of not being black." Moreover, Nat Hentoff has contended, addiction, "aside from proving how much hipper [musicians] were than the squares, also provided a rationalization for failure." It only became less hip when people started dying.[69]

Tenor saxophonist Sleepy Matsumoto reportedly received his moniker from American GIs because of the impassive, drowsy expression he wore while high on heroin. Drummer Shimizu Jun also struggled with heroin addiction in the 1950s, and published a frank autobiographical account in 1961 that gives some indication of the attractions drugs held for Japanese musicians. Shimizu first encountered narcotics while performing in the black soldiers' clubs in Yokohama during the Korean War:

> Nowadays, some ten years after the war, no matter where you search anywhere in Japan, it is impossible to find a place that has the Negro's uniquely powerful odor and rhythm like that club did. . . . [T]hat rhythmic activity even made me hallucinate that I was in Africa. Among the Negro soldiers, who were smoking cigarettes while drinking in the jazz in the corner [of the room], was this one guy, my friendship with whom was the first step toward my misfortune.
>
> At that time one black soldier, to be friendly, gave me some kind of strange cigarette . . . with drugs mixed in with it. That soldier carefully taught me how to smoke that cigarette. . . . While I was in a hazy state, he rattled off, one after the other, the names of first-rate jazzmen who

were drug users. At that point, I fell into the illusion that I, too, could become their equal as a player. . . . I set out to immerse myself among the first-class jazzmen through drugs.

My obsession with black people was fanatical. There were these brothers named Brown at the Mitsukoshi Hotel where civilians stayed, and they let me share their room for half a year. It made me happy when I'd be walking down Ginza Boulevard and sometimes I'd be teased by some girls, "Hey, you stink like a nigger!" [anata nandaka kuronbo kusai wa].

. . . I think it was natural that I found my beloved drug, the Great Jazz Teacher, strangely appealing. . . . Another appeal was that no matter how many hours I played I never felt tired. . . . When I was doing drugs, ideas that I couldn't believe were mine would gush out like a fountain. Perhaps for a moment, [drugs] liberated [me to overcome] the inadequacies of feeling and technique which usually suppressed my subconscious rhythmic sense.

. . . Within one or two months I had become a true junkie. When that happened there was no duty or emotion. Every day I was demanding drugs, and being consumed by drugs. In addition, I had to be careful of the cops. . . . Since I'd become something inhuman, I had no desire for anything in life other than drugs. . . . I entered the hospital repeatedly, five times or more . . . it's an undeniable fact that the temptations are great, especially for us jazzmen, when one compares the nature of our work to other jobs. I think that, among the jazzmen obsessed with [heroin], there were not a few who felt a momentary thrill while playing [high].

Those who don't know drugs say of us jazzmen, "they're weak-willed," or "they're cowards who rely on drugs to be satisfied with their playing." I think that is surely so.[70]

Shimizu's obsessions with drugs and with black people mirror similar feelings, already noted, among other nonblack jazz musicians. However vicariously, Shimizu sought (and found) the quintessential "jazz life"—that constant struggle to study and master the art, scuffle and get paid, and satiate a drug fix. Bird's widely quoted statement that "if you don't live it, it won't come out of your horn" transformed self-destructive lifestyles into the kind of hard luck "dues-paying" crucial to artistic legitimation, resulting in authentic music. Even as far away as Japan, Parker's gospel resounded with a disaffected generation of artists and aficionados determined to try anything that would authenticate their art.

Few people are as knowledgeable about—and as willing to discuss—the issue of drugs as Dr. Uchida Osamu, the Japanese jazz community's de facto surgeon general. His profession made him uncomfortably familiar with the more destructive tendencies of the jazz culture. He tells, for instance, of sixteen-year-old drummer Togashi Masahiko's flight from Tokyo drug charges to Nagoya, where he holed up in the second floor of the Combo *jazu kissa* and contemplated suicide. He also describes vibraphonist Sugiura Yōzō's victory over an infamous drug addiction: Sugiura took out an ad in a jazz publication apologizing to the public for his actions, then quit the music business to open a snack bar in Roppongi, where he and other recovering addicts helped one another rehabilitate. (Sugiura came back in 1965 and was still onstage in the mid-1990s, performing regularly at his own Jazzmen Club in Yokohama.)[71] Uchida explains the drug issue in this way: Japanese musicians were young and did not know right from wrong. They observed American GIs and musicians and thought they needed to use drugs to become good musicians. When they reached the point at which they wanted to quit (usually following a period of incarceration), they came to "Dr. U" for treatment. He describes "cold turkey" as his favored method. With so many musicians hanging around, police in Uchida's hometown of Okazaki came to suspect the physician of actually *supplying* them with narcotics: jam sessions at his home studio often included undercover officers in the audience. Once Uchida was summoned to the police station three days in a row for questioning; when he finally replied that he had to work in his clinic, one officer told him, "Look, I've got a gun . . . ," thus ending the conversation. Uchida concludes that the image of the jazz junkie was so prevalent that anyone associated with musicians was suspect. He reiterates that with so many of their jazz heroes abusing drugs, it was natural that young, impressionable, and frustrated musicians would take it up. He concedes that even he started drinking sweet port wine to "look cool" like the black GIs he saw in Nagoya and Tokyo.

Perhaps no individual artist better personified the personal, artistic, social, and economic tensions plaguing the bebop subculture than Moriyasu Shōtarō, if only because his life ended prematurely by his own hand. Moriyasu's significance extends beyond his considerable prowess as a player, for by taking his own life in a fit of artistic and personal frustration, he provided Japan with a tragic and mythic figure, something which all jazz cultures create. He was the "Japanese version" of the tortured creative genius whose single-minded devotion to his own art inhibited his ability to make it beyond the "dues-paying" stage. Legend has transformed Moriyasu into the archetype of Neil Leonard's "afflicted jazz giant . . . cast in the role of psychotic genius, consumed prematurely by his fidelity to the ideals of the jazz world and posthumously reborn in myth to symbolize them."[72] Before Akiyoshi

Toshiko's "discovery" and successful journey to America, Moriyasu was the person on whom the aspirations of Japan's jazz community rested, whose talent promised to liberate Japan's jazz community from its deferential position in America's shadow.

Moriyasu graduated from Keiō University and, after a brief and unhappy period as a refrigerator salesman, took up music professionally during the Occupation-inspired "entertainment boom" of the late 1940s. Inspired initially by Teddy Wilson, Moriyasu began to explore Bud Powell's music around 1950 while performing at Yokohama's 400 Club with the Red Hot Boys. While most other pianists were studying Lennie Tristano and George Shearing's "cocktail bop," Moriyasu was deconstructing every bebop record he could lay his massive hands on, transcribing not only melodies but solos, bass lines, drum fills, and harmonic progressions, resulting in piles of musical scores.[73] Moriyasu was also a reliable presence at the occasional Yokohama jam sessions that brought Japanese musicians together with American GIs such as Hampton Hawes, Hal Stein, and Walter Benton. (Although they certainly must have met, Hawes never mentions Moriyasu in his autobiography.) Before long he was regarded as the most accomplished bopper in Japan, whose awesome technique and odd personal habits intimidated many musicians and audiences. But he found a musical soul mate in tenor saxophonist Miyazawa Akira, resulting in a brief but inspiring period of exploratory music making with the Four Sounds. As the music's commercial profile sharply rose during the years of the first Jazz Boom, the jazz media commended bands like the Four Sounds and the Cozy Quartet for refusing to "go commercial" and for pursuing the "Negro spirit" of "pure jazz."[74]

No jazz legend is without a body of myth suggesting "prophetic charisma," eccentricity, and an "otherworldly vision," and Moriyasu Shōtarō was no exception.[75] The word "apparition" (*maboroshi*) has become irrevocably associated with him. His pale, sickly countenance suggested a salaried office worker rather than the hippest pianist in Japan. But he must have had a bit of the showman in him, for he was known to play the piano sitting beneath the keyboard with his back to the instrument, essentially playing the piano backwards. His hands were said to be so large that he could play tenths effortlessly.[76] The fact that he was recorded only once, in an unofficial capacity, certainly adds to the mystique surrounding him. The all-night jam session of 27–28 July 1954 at Yokohama's Mocambo club (intended to celebrate Shimizu Jun's release from drug rehab) was recorded by young Iwami Kiyoshi, who would later become a sound technician for Nippon Television. When the tapes were released as LPs twenty-two years later, pianist Hank Jones was among those who expressed surprise and admiration that Japan had produced such an original and talented musician as early as the 1950s.[77] In the last months of his life Moriyasu started exhibiting strange and unstable behavior. Still, his suicide on the rainy night of 28 September 1955 was a profound shock. Miyazawa Akira's eulogy to his musical soul mate mourned the loss of a "genius born of effort."[78]

The story of Japan's other leading bopper has a much happier ending and promised the realization of the Japanese jazz community's ardent quest for legitimation. Akiyoshi Toshiko was born in Liaoyang, Manchuria, in 1929, to an upper-middle-class home in which European classical music and nō theater music were both heard in ample doses. Although her father dabbled as a nō performer and her sister Michiyo played shamisen, the youngest daughter Toshiko chose piano as her instrument in the second grade. After the war her household evacuated to Beppu in northeastern Kyūshū in August 1946. To help the family make ends meet, the sixteen-year-old answered a local dance hall's notice for a pianist, making the transition from classical to popular styles while on the job. Within two years she had secured a Tokyo gig and emigrated to the capital—showing up unannounced at the doorstep of her former Beppu bandmate Oda Satoru—determined to pursue the jazz life. Initially a devotee of Teddy Wilson's music, by the early 1950s she had become entranced by Bud Powell's version of "Body and Soul" and studied his music meticulously. Although opportunities for female instrumentalists were extremely limited, Akiyoshi found work with the Ichiban Octet, Blue Coats, Gay Stars, and Six Lemons before founding the Cozy Quartet in 1952. She was a tough, professional, and uncompromising bandleader, an unlikely position for someone of her gender in the male-dominated jazz world. Her protégé Watanabe Sadao recalled receiving an onstage scolding soon after joining her band: when he was unable to sight-read his way through Akiyoshi's transcription of Charlie Parker's "Moose the Mooche," she berated him, "If you're a pro, you have to be able to play it right off." But Watanabe added that she was just as likely to treat him to a steak dinner after an exemplary performance.[79]

In November 1953, acting on a tip from Hawes, JATP pianist Oscar Peterson ventured out to a Ginza coffeehouse to hear Akiyoshi and was immediately impressed. Hawes and Peterson's praise convinced Norman Granz to record her immediately. At an all-night session at Radio Tokyo studios, Akiyoshi recorded sixteen songs with Ray Brown, Herb Ellis, and J. C. Herd, thus earning the accolades that would lead to a scholarship for composition studies at the prestigious Berklee College of Music in Boston a few years later. The Japanese jazz community was stunned and pleased that one of its own had attracted the admiration of American jazz masters, although few would have picked Akiyoshi as the obvious candidate. Renowned for a stubborn artistic integrity that often cost her work and fame, Akiyoshi vaulted from the category of "no-name pianist" to instant, if limited, celebrity as the jazz community's "Cinderella."[80]

As an Asian and a woman fluent in the language of modern jazz, Aki-yoshi was regarded as a novelty in American jazz circles when she arrived in the United States in January 1956 (she has often remarked—accurately, in my view—that she faced three significant hurdles to her acceptance as a legitimate jazz musician: her race, her nationality, and her gender). In keep-ing with the exoticism that propelled her celebrity, she almost invariably performed in kimono. She appeared on television with Steve Allen (May 1956) and on *What's My Line* (it is interesting to contrast her overwhelmed, smiling shyness at that time with her ultra-cool, sunglassed demeanor to-day), took *Down Beat*'s Blindfold Test, performed at the Newport Jazz Fes-tival, won *Mademoiselle* magazine's Mlle Merit Award, and recorded for jazz impresario George Wein's Storyville label. In the liner notes to her soph-omore album Wein described his new protégé as "pretty as a lotus flower, as gentle and sweet as [a] cherry blossom, and as vigorously articulate at a piano keyboard as a swing-time Padarewski. . . . Jazz at the moment is Toshiko's career, her sole and overwhelming interest, an interest so com-plete as to blot out all others . . . maybe later will come life and love."[81]

But such patronizing remarks could never obscure Akiyoshi's obvious determination and drive. Upon graduation she married Berklee faculty member and alto saxophonist Charlie Mariano and led New York-based bands featuring her own compositions. The diminutive woman likened to a lotus flower and cherry blossom was not afraid to stand up to the gargan-tuan (and frequently violent) bassist Charles Mingus during her stint in his band in the early sixties. During a performance of "Fables of Faubus," which includes a vocal call-and-response section, trombonist Jimmy Knepper told Mingus biographer Brian Priestley that Akiyoshi answered the bassist's "Name me someone who's ridiculous" with "*You're* ridiculous, *I'm* ridicu-lous, we're *all* ridiculous!" then sat down at the piano and carried on.[82]

Akiyoshi's gender may have made her an unlikely savior for a jazz com-munity groping for artistic legitimation, but her personality and talent in fact made her ideal for the job. Unlike many of her colleagues, she was able to translate her understanding of the jazz aesthetic's demands for orig-inality into action, by avoiding any moves that would deny her control of her own career, leading her own bands, choosing her own repertoire, and, in-creasingly, playing her own compositions. Once she made her splash in the Stateside scene, she realized that the only way to earn real respect—not just patronizing curiosity—was to continue to write and to lead bands. Her success awakened jazz aficionados in Japan and elsewhere to the possibility that non-Americans had something to say through and about the idiom. But ambition is not often admired in women, and Akiyoshi met apathy, if not outright resistance, when in later years she tried to take a leadership position among her countrymen by shaking them out of their artistic doldrums.

In a Funk

In January 1961 drummer Art Blakey and the Jazz Messengers, arguably the leading proponents of "funky hard bop" jazz, tore through Japan like a force of nature. In retrospect, most historians of Japanese jazz refer to the tour as "epoch-making." The Blakey tour not only put the word *funky* on everyone's lips as an all-purpose word of praise, but also instigated a cavalcade of American jazz masters that was known at the time as the *"rainichi* (literally 'come to Japan') rush." From 1961 to 1964, the peak of the *rainichi* rush, some seventy-five jazz and popular music acts from America performed in Japan: Thelonious Monk, Sonny Rollins, Horace Silver, Duke Ellington, Helen Merrill, Dave Brubeck, George Lewis, and Eddie Condon were among those hot on Blakey's heels. The British jazz critic Leonard Feather, reporting on a massive package tour billed as the World Jazz Festival, quoted an American booking agent: "All my artists want to go to Japan, and all these [Japanese] promoters want to buy them; so naturally I'll sell them to whoever will pay the best price." "Thank God for Japan!" another agent exclaimed. "It's turning out to be a second Nevada."[83]

Japanese jazz audiences enthusiastically welcomed their American heroes, but the effects of the *rainichi* rush on native musicians were mixed. Many regarded the exposure to and interaction with American jazz masters as a much-needed stimulus for Japanese musicians. Blakey, Julian "Cannonball" Adderley, Lionel Hampton, and others touring the East Asian archipelago enthusiastically jammed with and inspired their Japanese counterparts. Hampton purposefully took an incomplete band to Japan in the spring of 1963, augmenting it with seven Japanese musicians selected through an audition. He dubbed this "pioneering East-West" aggregation the Asiatic-Harlem band. "I have some trombone and trumpet players who could easily play with anybody in the States," Hampton boasted. "And I have a piano player, I don't know his name, but he just sits in the corner and roars. . . . We do it with soul."[84]

But native musicians seeking to generate interest in their own work could find the *rainichi* rush as frustrating as it was stimulating. They could not hope to compete with name American bands for the hearts and money of Japanese jazz fans. With foreign musicians glutting the market and monopolizing the fans' attention, the growing indifference to the Japanese jazz scene was reflected in *Swing Journal*'s flagrant editorial turn away from domestic coverage in the early sixties, and in a precipitous drop in the number of concerts featuring native artists. In Europe musicians' unions had always offered significant and marginally effective opposition to such influxes of American talent. Yet when Feather inquired about the Japanese union's reaction, jazz writer Yui Shōichi replied, "It is a voluntary organization; nobody is obliged to join it. So musicians have no protection against these invasions by foreign musicians." When Feather queried him about the union's actual function, Yui scoffed, "They send congratulations to a musician when he is married, and condolences and a contribution to his funeral."[85]

Thus the *rainichi* rush, while universally remembered fondly as a major and positive turning point in the history of jazz in Japan, might just as easily be regarded as the nadir of a general malaise that had set in within the jazz community since Moriyasu's suicide, the sudden implosion of the Jazz Boom, and the defection of a mass youth audience to rockabilly.[86] There were some positive institutional trends in the late fifties: new jazz coffeehouses continued to open, some featuring live performances to fill the vacuum wrought by the jazz concert bust; a general upswing in urban nightlife, reflecting the effects of Japan's so-called Jinmu economic boom, benefited combos and big bands alike; interest in jazz on college campuses (inspired by Dave Brubeck's campus tours in the United States) rose steadily; furthermore, King Records began to demonstrate a sustained interest in recording and marketing indigenous jazz at home and abroad.[87] Yet in spite of these developments there was an unprecedented degree of soul-searching about the "catch up" aesthetic that had dominated postwar jazz. Artists and critics wondered aloud how to combat the overwhelmingly derivative impulses of indigenous jazz, how to terminate the cycle of imbibing and regurgitating each new American trend, and how to fashion something truly creative and original within the jazz idiom.

Unquestionably, the most positive energy within the jazz community emanated from *jazu kissa*. By the late fifties virtually every major city had at least one such establishment, each spreading its jazz gospel with verve. Just as every jazz artist searches for a personal sound, each coffeehouse took great pains to carve out a distinctive identity. In large metropolises such as Tokyo and Ōsaka it was possible for the discriminating hipster to locate a joint that specialized in New Orleans jazz, swing, or the various schools of modern jazz. Some offered a spartan menu of recorded music and coffee, while others served alcohol and hired live bands. The first to take the latter course (from September 1953) was Ginza's jazz mecca Tennessee, whose mama-san Hayashi Chisasshi had enough clout in the jazz community to carry on an open feud with the mighty Watanabe Productions. "Nurturing no-name artists at Tennessee and sending them on to the entertainment world is my pride and reason for living," Hayashi stated. "Truly, it is the 'Tennessee Music School,' the 'Talent Training Place,'" one journal acclaimed. "Mama [Hayashi] is now planning a new music mixing modern jazz and rockabilly."[88]

Particularly messianic *jazu kissa* proprietors put on periodic "educational" programs for the public, at which prominent jazz experts discussed jazz history or the latest American records. American correspondents, accustomed to the "usual clutter of tables and clatter of highballs," were stuck by the studious atmosphere of Japan's jazz joints. "Japan's hipsters sit in desklike seats set in rows of two, railroad style, sipping their drinks in scholarly contemplation and rarely speaking, as jazz, either recorded or live, engulfs them in smoky parlors. Girls in the crowd affect tight toreador pants; the boys are mighty sharp in Ivy League coats and peaked caps pulled down tight to their dark glasses." It was hardly a profitable enterprise—and by the early sixties one was as likely to hear rockabilly as bebop at some *jazu kissa*—but somehow jazz coffeehouses carried on and remained a central presence and source of energy in Japan's jazz community for another couple of decades.[89]

Another ray of hope was the King Jazz Series of LPs featuring native talent, inaugurated in 1956 under the direction of jazz critic and drummer Kubota Jirō. Albums featuring working groups and all-star conglomerations in concert, studio, and nightclub "jam session" contexts received an unexpectedly enthusiastic response from Japanese fans, thus inspiring other record companies to follow suit. Aware that these recordings would be regarded as representative of their creative world, the King series producers encouraged musicians to record as many original compositions and arrangements as possible. Saxophonist and bandleader Saijō Takanosuke credited the King project as "fantastic incentive that we've never had until now."[90] Perhaps the primary beneficiaries of series such as King's were young composer/arrangers such as Miho Keitarō, Maeda Norio, and Yamaya Kiyoshi. All were employed as staff arrangers for TBS television when they formed the Modern Jazz Meeting of Three in April 1959 (in emulation of composer Mayuzumi Toshirō's Contemporary Music Meeting of Three) and put on a handful of concerts featuring their own compositions and arrangements. All three were inspired by the "West Coast sound" of Shorty Rogers, Bill Holman, and Stan Kenton, and created a tapestry of rich, dark textures and polished, jaunty dynamism within that idiom.[91]

Excitement over the King Jazz Series reached its zenith when the company sealed a distribution agreement with the London Records subsidiary of

Britain's Decca company. But foreign reaction to jazz "made in Japan" was decidedly unenthusiastic: the LPS tended to confirm rather than dispel stereotypes of Japanese as able imitators and poor creators. A *Gramophone* review of a live all-star recording stated that "jazz sounds exactly the same in London and Tokyo. . . . The depressing difference, of course, is that the record purports to present Japanese jazz at its best." Aside from an admirable performance by Suzuki Shōji's Rhythm Aces, "The remaining tracks are painfully dull. Akira Watanabe's group plays rather weedy modern jazz, while Toru Mori . . . leads a plodding Dixieland band. The two big orchestras . . . never rise above the level of second-rate palais bands."[92] By the early 1960s the King Jazz Series had petered out with little fanfare.

The hype about an imminent burst of revolutionary creativity in the jazz community in the late fifties and early sixties was short-lived and unconvincing; neither could it mask the economic and aesthetic dilemmas that plagued jazz artists. By the early sixties many *jazu kissa* had closed or abandoned live music—or just live jazz. By most tallies there were probably only three coffeehouses featuring live jazz in Tokyo in the early sixties, and they were low-paying gigs. Decent-paying jobs were available if one was willing to play in a recording or broadcast studio band, backing singers and TV stars or recording movie soundtracks. While such work facilitated musical versatility in rock, jazz, Latin, country and western, or Japanese pops, it rarely allowed for the harmonic or rhythmic "stretching out" necessary for modern jazz improvisation and composition. Given the obvious fan disinterest in the homegrown product, it was increasingly difficult to cut a hardcore jazz record, put on a concert, or even keep a band together. Frustrated by the tension between the jazz aesthetic's demand for originality and the economic realities of the music business, many just gave up, losing their artistic commitments to jazz.

The situation utterly demoralized Akiyoshi Toshiko and her husband Charlie Mariano when they returned to Japan for two years in the midsixties. Mariano wrote a correspondence published in the U.S. magazine *Jazz:*

> The unfortunate aspect of this situation is that the Japanese jazz musician does not have the incentive or the competition that inspires the scuffling American musician. Furthermore they do not have the necessary outlets for scuffling—there are always places in New York where a musician can work for at least a little "bread," and there are also a great many more recording opportunities.
>
> The attitude here is therefore, "there's no sense in improving, we have all the work we can handle (such as it is), and there's no place to play jazz anyhow!"

... Toshiko and I have been conducting a workshop band, thinking that it would give the jazz players a chance to experiment and exchange ideas. But the sessions have been constantly plagued by absenteeism and a general apathy. One cat merely said, "Well, everyone has to make money."

Mariano's frustrations stemmed from a genuine faith that "jazz can be created in Japan, which means, one of us can come up as a new stream of jazz creator in the future . . . there is a lot of potential here as evidenced by the jazz success of musicians like Akira Miyazawa, Sleepy Matsumoto, and Sadao Watanabe."[93] But their faith in Japanese musicians' potential could not overcome the very real problem of making a living in a depressed domestic jazz market, so the Marianos decided to return to the United States in February 1965. The retreat was especially bitter for Akiyoshi, who had long expressed a desire to return to her homeland and foster the maturation of jazz. She was widely quoted as saying that jazz in Japan was inferior to that of Europe and lacked "guts," an opinion with which many concurred but nevertheless resented. Akiyoshi's failure to light a fire under the Japanese jazz world—not to mention reports that she had burned bridges by saying "Goodbye forever, Japan"—was emblematic of her alienation from it. Acknowledged as "one of the top pianists in the American jazz world," she had come to be regarded as an outsider by many Japanese musicians and fans: in the early sixties the press even adopted the practice of spelling her name in *katakana*, a custom usually reserved for foreign names. But her return to the States was also symbolic of the Japanese jazz community's failure to support its best. In a report on the Marianos' departure, *Swing Journal* (which, by ignoring domestic jazz in its pages, was itself part of the problem) lamented, "It is unfortunate that superior jazz players cannot make a living in their own home country."[94]

It did not bode well for the progress of indigenous jazz that, following the death and departure of the country's premier modernists, the most widespread and marketable jazz format in the late fifties was the clarinet-vibraphone combination based on Benny Goodman's swing combo from twenty years earlier.[95] Perhaps nothing symbolized the jazz community's infatuation with American models better than the appropriation of geographic terminology peculiar to the United States to describe differences in musical style in Japan: within the modernist camp, musicians aligned themselves within an imagined dichotomy between "West Coast" and "East Coast" schools. As Sleepy Matsumoto described the difference, West Coast ("white") jazz was "intellectual" and East Coast ("black") jazz was "emotional."[96]

Nor did the persistent practice of labeling native musicians as the "Japa-

12. Akiyoshi Toshiko jams at a "sayonara" concert sponsored by the Yamaha Jazz Club, Nagoya, 17 January 1965. Discouraged by the scene in her homeland, she would soon return to the United States. Photo used with permission of Dr. Uchida Osamu.

nese versions" of their primary American idols facilitate conceptualizing indigenous creativity. Keyboardist Satō Masahiko once described the late fifties and early sixties as a period when "Japanese jazzmen were pretending to be someone else [and] there was no shame in it"; musicians meeting for the first time often greeted one another with the question, "By the way, who are you imitating?"[97] Inagaki Jirō similarly depicts a jazz culture prone to fads, recounting how he and his colleagues latched on to each new development and player that emerged in the U.S. jazz scene. When Sonny Rollins's first records arrived, Inagaki says, all the Japanese tenor players followed his lead, deserting earlier attachments to Stan Getz and Sonny Stitt. When Inagaki would tell fellow players that he still dug Stitt, they would reply, "Isn't that stupid?" Inagaki himself would be known as the "Japanese John Coltrane" in the early sixties because he took an interest in Trane while his contemporaries were still digging Rollins; he has since been praised for his "foresight." Again, what is significant here is that Inagaki, by his own admission, was not necessarily doing anything "new," but had simply switched to a more "progressive" influence. I would not suggest, as Inagaki and Satō seem to, that this compulsion to imitate was uncritically or casually viewed as natural or desirable; indeed, my research in postwar jazz criticism suggests that the practice was regarded as troubling yet difficult to terminate. Admittedly, some of the best jazz ever produced in the United States was being made at precisely this time: we are talking about the era in which Rollins, Coltrane, Charles Mingus, and Miles Davis were turning out one classic performance after the other, and Cecil Taylor, Ornette Coleman, Jimmy Giuffre, and Sun Ra were just unveiling their "New Thing." These artists were testing the melodic, harmonic, and rhythmic boundaries of the idiom, taking the music into unrecognizable directions. With so daring and impressive a body of work requiring digestion, in combination with the economic constraints mentioned above, it is understandable that Japanese felt there was little room or time left for comparably inventive projects.

Commentators subjected indigenous jazz to intense analysis, searching for musical and institutional inadequacies that prevented parity with the American jazz masters. One common diagnosis detected deficiencies in Japanese players' "rhythmic sense" (*rizumu kan*).[98] Others blamed infrastructural deficiencies, such as the dearth of suitable space for jam sessions or the lack of a supportive recording and entertainment industry. Not everyone was convinced of the situation's bleakness. Moriyasu, Akiyoshi, Miyazawa, Matsumoto, and Watanabe Sadao were heartening proof that "originality," the key to parity, was not entirely unimaginable. One musician commented: "We are still very young, very imitative. . . . We lack original arrangers—so many of the men who write for our bands and combos do nothing but copy Americans. But as our technical proficiency expands it encourages the younger men to experiment with ideas. That applies to individual musicians as well as to writers. In another five or ten years we may have something really good of our own."[99]

A growing number of foreign observers added their "expert opinions" to the project of diagnosing the Japanese jazz community's ills. Japanese have historically been obsessed with foreign opinion of their country, and American and European jazz critics' comments were assiduously collected, translated, and scrutinized.[100] Virtually all foreign commentators expressed a belief in the potential that Japan's jazz world demonstrated, but cautioned that serious changes in structure and attitude were prerequisites to realizing such promise. The enthusiasm and knowledge displayed by Japanese jazz aficionados struck all foreign commentators. The German critic Joachim Berendt remarked: "Japanese interest in jazz is amazing. One asks oneself if all the thousands of young Japanese who listen to jazz all day long in the jazz cafes of Tokyo can possibly understand what they hear. Do they go merely because it's fashionable? If they do, they certainly have better manners than their American and European contemporaries; they don't talk during the performances. They just sit and listen with that concentration of which only the Japanese seem capable." Berendt was also impressed by jazz fans' openness to continuing developments in the music: "The

furious discussions that Ornette Coleman has caused in the West are un-
thinkable in Japan. . . . Tradition and avant garde are not contradictions in
Japan."[101] Leonard Feather wrote that the Japanese jazz audience was characterized by a "lack of deep interest in the homegrown product," and a
tendency to "naturally equate authenticity with the Negro." Feather was
frustrated by the racialist discourse in evidence at a panel discussion on
"Jazz and Race" he attended while in Tokyo. Though impressed by the
Japanese critics' familiarity with the work of African American writers such
as James Baldwin and Amiri Baraka, he objected to Kubota Jirō's dichotomi-
zation of "Negro vs. white jazz." "The old argument about whether or not it
is possible to distinguish a Negro from a white musician on a blindfold-test
basis was again brought up. While conceding that musical style differences
seemingly racial in origin were traceable to social conditions, the Japanese
critics continued to talk along Negro vs. white lines."[102]

Japanese were most interested in knowing whom foreign commentators
regarded as the best musicians in the country—Sleepy Matsumoto, Miyazawa Akira, Watanabe Sadao, and Shiraki Hideo invariably topped such
lists. But all foreign critics chided Japanese musicians in general for being
overly derivative. Pianist George Gruntz, who toured Japan with Helen
Merrill in February 1963, complimented Japanese musicianship ("It was
amazing to be able to rehearse what were different charts in a really comparatively short period of time and then have them played well"), but remarked on the paucity of talented soloists. He attributed this to institutional
deficiencies: "There are no places to go to just play. There are lots of clubs,
but no real jazz ones. Most of the jazz seems to be played on record in the
coffee houses. And surprisingly, I never heard any of the musicians invite
each other to any kind of session. Apparently that kind of thing isn't done."
Berendt stated: "On the average, the technical standards of Japanese jazz
musicians are higher than those of European jazz musicians. . . . They play
well; they don't lack ideas; they are very smooth, even persuasive; but they
lack that characteristic that European esthetics long have defined as 'inev-
itability': a musician must play 'his music' and no other." Mariano was
characteristically blunt: "I wish that the Japanese players would not be so
over-awed by the Americans. They are so much so that they don't realize
what beauty there is in Japanese music. It's one thing to be influenced,
everyone is influenced by other people and experiences, but it can't end
there. . . . It is not the truth until you forget about your Gods and just express
yourself."[103]

These assessments by foreign commentators should not be read uncritically. One problem is that they dealt almost exclusively with the Tokyo
modern jazz scene, virtually ignoring other regions such as the Kansai

region, where for some reason Dixieland jazz, in particular, had a substantial following. Moreover, although foreign observers unanimously expressed faith in Japanese "potential," they were often condescending in tone and occasionally betrayed the influence of commonly held stereotypes of the Japanese as able imitators and poor creators. But I quote them at length here because, significantly, there was a remarkable degree of agreement between foreigners' evaluations of the early-sixties jazz situation and those of Japanese commentators. "There are a few misunderstandings," *Swing Journal*'s editors wrote in preface to translations of Mariano, Feather, and Berendt's respective articles, "but in general they have reported on our country's jazz world accurately and appropriately."[104] Since the Occupation years, Japanese critics, musicians, and fans had historically set great store on what foreigners had to say about their jazz. Now, as real, extended contact between the Americans and Japanese jazz communities was being established, the Japanese became extremely self-conscious. Pride in the handful of Japanese stars who commanded international esteem was offset by embarrassment over the infrastructural and aesthetic impediments to parity.

The early sixties' "funky boom" proved to be a setback, in that it solidified an already emerging consensus, which Feather noted, that *only* black American musicians could play this music authentically and well.[105] In effect, a new racial-aesthetic hierarchy was established: whereas three decades earlier Japanese writers presented Paul Whiteman's explicitly unfunky music as the evolutionary "musicalization" of "wild" black jazz, now so-called "black jazz" (*kokujin jazu*) was regarded as the ultimate artistic achievement in the idiom, a standard to which white Americans, Europeans, and Japanese all aspired. The belief that real jazz is "black" was potentially devastating to the cherished goal of authenticating Japanese jazz: if the allegedly innate and superior "Negro rhythmic sense" was a prerequisite for authentic, soulful jazz performance, then Japanese had no hope. I will elaborate on these points in the following chapter, but it will suffice at this moment to note that, while the postwar Japanese jazz community indulged in considerable self-flagellation for its derivative impulses, it is difficult to tell if Japanese jazz critics and musicians were excoriating themselves for imitating Americans, or for imitating the *wrong* Americans. It was said that with a few exceptions—Akiyoshi, Moriyasu, Watanabe—Japanese musicians primarily imitated white American musicians, particularly Benny Goodman, Lee Konitz, George Shearing, and Dave Brubeck, and thus missed the "black" spiritual core of the music. The act of imitating itself was acknowledged as a severe handicap ("almost all of our country's jazzmen are lacking in individuality . . . [T]hey need to master the vocabulary of jazz and quit forgetting to express *themselves*"),[106] but the *source* that Japanese imitated was portrayed as a bigger problem. The aesthetics of "catch up" thus remained fundamentally unchallenged well into the 1960s.

Catching Up

Oda Makoto echoed a familiar theme when he remarked in a 1962 *Atlas* article that Japan's was a "hybrid culture." "We are disgusted by it," he added, "but it is ours and we have no alternative but to start from where we are. Our third generation suffers, but we feel that something extraordinarily different, strong and great will probably emerge from this hybrid culture." Granted, similar observations had been made frequently for nearly a century by 1962, but before the midcentury cataclysm cultural contact had usually occurred at a safe distance and on strictly controlled terms. After 1945 contact with foreign civilizations was much more intimate and often out of Japanese hands to manipulate. Well after the notorious proclamation of the "end of the postwar" in 1956, Japanese were still living in a society thoroughly transformed by the intimate contact with American culture provided by the Occupation, and grappling with the ramifications of its "hybrid culture."[107]

Japan's modern history has been characterized by a persistent belief in Japanese backwardness vis-à-vis Europe and America, and a perpetual national effort to "catch up" with the West. In the late nineteenth and early twentieth centuries this mode of thinking and operating could be attributed to Japan's fear of Western imperialism and to its anxious international position as the West's pupil and Asia's instructor in the ways of modernity. Humiliating defeat and occupation only magnified the intensity and urgency of the "catch up" ethos. Bereft not only of deeply held ideological and moral principles rooted in the patriarchal social structure and the emperor system, but also of the basic material necessities for sustenance, many Japanese in the postwar period aspired to the standards of lifestyle, political conduct, economic might, and cultural power demonstrated by their conqueror. They often rejected imposed solutions in favor of more familiar ones, but the goal nonetheless was to regain the nation's dignity by following a developmental path blazed by the United States. Given this ethos and the bitter experience of the war and reconstruction, it is not surprising that the Japanese jazz community mirrored the national obsession with "catching up." Even the nihilistic youth countercultures or "tribes," because of their reliance on American imagery and symbols of rebellion, reflected another aspect of the official "catch up" ethos.

The perennially introspective Japanese jazz community was well aware that "catch up" constituted a betrayal of the aesthetic ideals of jazz, but continued simultaneously to reprove itself for imitating and for not imitating well enough. But several more years were to pass before aggressive efforts to express "Japaneseness" through jazz, as a new standard for self-legitimation, would be posed as the solution for extricating the jazz community from the quagmire of slavish imitation. Such efforts would occur in a much prouder, more self-assured, economically successful Japan, a nation with a much more coherent and favorable concept of "national culture" as an asset rather than as a liability.

Following his tenure as Japan's dictator of democracy, General Douglas MacArthur stated in congressional hearings that "measured by the standards of modern civilization, [the Japanese] would be like a boy of twelve as compared with our development of forty-five years." Jazz critic Ōkura Ichitarō doubtless had this notorious remark in mind when he wrote in 1959 that the Japanese jazz world was still a "twelve-year-old child" when compared to the United States.[108] But twelve-year-old children have a habit of growing and maturing, and a new generation of jazz musicians determined to achieve artistic adulthood turned to familiar rhetoric and symbols of national exceptionalism to spur the process along.

CHAPTER SIX

OUR THING: DEFINING "JAPANESE JAZZ"

When I sang my American folk melodies in Budapest, Prague,

Tiflis, Moscow, Oslo, the Hebrides, or on the Spanish front, the

people understood and wept or rejoiced with the spirit of the songs.

I found that where fortunes have been the same, whether people

weave, build, pick cotton, or dig in the mines, they understand

each other in the common language of work, suffering and

protest. . . . Many of the old folk songs which are still young today

echoed the terrific desire to escape bondage, such as the Negro

protest song, "How long must my people weep and mourn." . . .

When I sing "let my people go," I can feel sympathetic vibrations

from my audience, whatever its nationality. It is no longer just a

Negro song—it is a symbol of those seeking freedom.—Paul

Robeson, quoted in *Paul Robeson Speaks*, ed. Philip S. Foner

"What about British jazz? Have we got the feeling?" "If you're

talking about technique, musicianship, I guess the British can be

as good as anybody else. But what do they need to play jazz for?

It's the American Negro's tradition, it's his music. White people

don't have a right to play it, it's colored folk music. When I was

learning bass with Rheinschagen he was teaching me to play

classical music. He said I was close but I'd never really get it. So I

took some Paul Robeson and Marian Anderson records to my

next lesson and asked him if he thought those artists had got it.

He said they were Negros trying to sing music that was foreign

to them. Solid, so white society has its own traditions, let 'em

leave ours to us. You had your Shakespeare and Marx and Freud and Einstein and Jesus Christ and Guy Lombardo but we came up with jazz, don't forget it. . . . British cats listen to our records and copy them, why don't they develop something of their own?"

—Charles Mingus, *Beneath the Underdog: His World as Composed by Mingus,* ed. Nel King

We should create a music that only Japanese can play.

—Satō Masahiko, in *Swing Journal,* August 1970

In 1980 Akiyoshi Toshiko took first place in each of the Big Band, Composer, and Arranger categories in *Down Beat* magazine's readers' poll.[1] By that time, Japan had attained recognition as an economic and technological colossus, producing home electronics and automobiles comparable or superior to those produced in America. Akiyoshi's coronation as the "Triple-Crown Queen" of jazz seemed further proof that Japan could best the Yanks on their own turf. The occasion was of such magnitude that the general media joined the jazz press in the celebration. All Japanese, jazz fan or not, could bask in the glow in Akiyoshi's achievements. Although she had been estranged from the Japanese jazz community for nearly three decades, the composer's victory was as much a national victory as a personal one, signaling the end of the decades-old effort to "catch up" to the standards of American jazz: a multiple first-place win in jazz's most prestigious polls indicated that Japan had not merely "caught up" but had surpassed its former model.

Moreover, by the time of Akiyoshi's win Japan had become widely acknowledged in U.S. and European jazz circles as "jazz heaven," a place where fan enthusiasm, support, and appreciation for an undervalued art was unparalleled. Even the French, renowned for their fondness for the music, proclaimed Japan the "nouveau paradis du jazz." In the era of "Japan as Number One" (as Ezra Vogel's provocative 1979 book was entitled), when economists wagged their fingers at U.S. industry and labor for failing to match Japanese quality and efficiency, U.S. and European jazz critics bitterly noted that Japanese jazz fans shamed their American counterparts with their depth of knowledge, commitment of resources, and level of enthusiasm.[2] *Jazz Journal International* correspondent Fukuhara Haruhiko contended in 1978 that "Japanese record stores have the greatest selection of jazz albums in the world"; by the mid-1980s industry estimates rated Japan as the largest per capita market for jazz LPs. "The tremendous growth of jazz activity in Japan has been a phenomenon of recent years whose repercussions have registered on an international level," Fukuhara wrote. "The jazz record market in Japan is astonishingly buoyant—the range of repertoire available being greater than anywhere else in the world; the club and concert scene is burgeoning . . . ; and Japan is producing jazz musicians of international calibre. . . . The fact that the latest edition of Leonard Feather's *Encyclopedia of Jazz* lists 20 Japanese musicians is an indication of the progress Japan has made in terms of native jazz talent."[3] Indeed, from the late sixties onward, Japanese jazz artists were performing to considerable acclaim throughout Europe, South America, Southeast Asia, the Soviet Union, and the United States. All of this recognition engendered an unprecedented interest in the music's history in the East Asian archipelago, a trend that coincided with the public memorialization of the social history of prewar and early postwar Japan, known as the "Shōwa boom."[4]

Japan's jazz aficionados have continued to yearn for a more conspicuous and positive role for jazz in mainstream society ("Unfortunately, it must be said that when compared to Europe and America, the social value of jazz in Japan is still low," a 1972 *Swing Journal* writer lamented);[5] yet by the 1970s jazz had carved a comfortable and relatively stable niche for itself within Japan's prosperous entertainment market and the country had earned an international reputation as both a major consumer and producer of jazz recordings. (Even established European and American jazz artists, unable to obtain record deals in their home countries, recorded for Japanese labels such as East West and DIW.) Although historically, as we have seen, jazz had enjoyed attention in the spotlights as a mass culture phenomenon, by the 1970s jazz had yielded its capacity for "booms" to rock, Japanese pops, and so-called New Music (akin to what we know as "singer-songwriter"), settling comfortably as a specialized interest or "hobby" (*shumi*) that appealed primarily to a more highly educated, cosmopolitan segment of society.

It has been noted that Japan's "post-postwar" mass culture fragmented in the wake of the "high speed" economic growth campaign, resulting in the "diversification and differentiation of consumer 'masses' " and the creation of "micromasses." Marilyn Ivy paraphrases "new consumer culture theorists" like Fujioka Wakao who observe that "to stimulate consumer demand, producers have been compelled to appeal to (and create) highly targeted, diversified, and nuanced types of consumer desire," and inspire "discriminating consumption" to replace the "undifferentiated," boom-susceptible masses that characterized Japan's urban popular culture in the first couple of decades after the war.[6] While the jazz community might justifiably be dubbed a "micromass," it was itself fragmented into even smaller units. All "producers" within the jazz community—from record companies to festivals and jazz clubs to *jazu kissa*—accommodated consumers with increasingly divergent tastes: consumers with particular stylistic preferences; those whose interest in jazz was more nostalgic than thrill-seeking; those with interests in discographical minutiae; or fans with a particular affection for live "happenings." For several decades now, it has been possible to shop around for and select a personalized jazz experience in Japan's incomparably diverse and kaleidoscopic culture market.

If the recognition of Akiyoshi Toshiko as a major talent confirmed Japan's growing international reputation as a prominent producer and consumer of jazz, it also legitimated efforts by Japanese artists to define their own original voices and identities through the construction of a recognizable national style of jazz. The most prominent and ear-catching works in Akiyoshi's oeuvre were those regarded to be quintessentially "Japanese." Masterpieces such as "Kogun" and "Minamata," which highlighted Akiyoshi's talent for incorporating traditional Japanese instruments, vocal techniques, and melodic elements into powerfully swinging and richly textured big band arrangements, distinguished her work form that of other jazz composers and sealed her reputation. Jazz critics in Japan and abroad, unbothered by the pitfalls of cultural reductionism, hailed her work as expressive of an essentialized "Japaneseness," overlooking the fact that "orientalized" pieces like "Kogun" constituted a relatively small proportion of her oeuvre. Nevertheless, critics and aficionados portrayed Akiyoshi as representative of a Japanese jazz community that had achieved international recognition by exploiting its allegedly "unique cultural heritage" to carve out its own niche within the jazz idiom.

The idea of "Japanese jazz," as developed in the 1960s and 1970s, meshed nicely with the national hubris engendered by Japan's spectacular rise to economic prominence. In the immediate postwar era, indigenous culture and social structures were regarded as impediments to the cherished goals of modernity and prosperity. But the era of economic ascendancy witnessed an "introspection boom" and the wide circulation of theories of cultural exceptionalism, theories that emphasized the "positive" attributes of interdependency, consensus, diligence, and cohesiveness, which allegedly allowed Japan's economy to function like a well-oiled machine. For proponents of "Confucian capitalism," these "national character" attributes purportedly explained Japanese economic might and the dramatic improvements in standards of living, productivity, and competitiveness.[7] Post–World War II "theories of the Japanese" (which were disseminated to a wide readership via best-selling trade paperbacks and scholarly treatises) also reflected continuing anxieties over the sanctity of a cultural identity threatened by international political and economic integration. This neonationalist (the "neo" serves to distinguish it from the militaristic ultranationalism of the early twentieth century) expression also represented an overt protest against American political, military, and cultural hegemony: in part, such theories were designed to distinguish Japan from its principal referent, which had lost much of its moral credibility by attempting to resuscitate a dying colonial system in Southeast Asia.

A tiny but prominent circle within the jazz community created art that reflected these burgeoning neonationalist sensibilities. Although this coterie counted a handful of musicians, fans, and critics from the Occupation generation among its members, the primary energy came from a younger, more politicized, and creatively self-assertive generation of jazz musicians, who openly questioned their forebears' penchant for merely "imitating" American jazz (although they were most conspicuously influenced by the American and European avant-garde movements in jazz and composed music) and embarked on an adventurous quest for independent voices within the idiom.[8] One vocal fringe within this movement advocated the creation of a national style. By using jazz to assert an allegedly unique Japanese sensibility and identity, they felt that they could finally create their own self-legitimating standards of authenticity and contribute something unprecedented to the jazz idiom.

In what was arguably the greatest nationalist mobilization of the arts since the state-initiated campaign of the Pacific War, segments of the jazz community joined other artistic communities in a broader search for a "Japanese voice" in the arts. In the summer of 1960, millions of people swarmed the Diet building in Tokyo to protest the renewal of the U.S.-Japan security treaty. The failure of what Japanese call the Anpo movement frustrated and galvanized left-wing nationalists in the arts—avant-garde writers, post-New Theater playwrights and actors, dancers and choreographers, composers and instrumentalists, and New Wave filmmakers—to create explicitly political art that rejected themes and modes of representation derived from the West.[9] These movements were inherently hostile and predictably divisive: New Wave filmmakers such as Ōshima Nagisa publicly lambasted the elder statesmen of Japanese film, and made movies that were so dark and dense that audiences were encouraged to stay home in the warm glow of their television sets. The jazz community was no different. There was no consensus that the development of a native voice in jazz was a constructive goal, and thus support of the young avant-garde was tentative at best. (Critic Aikura Hisato reportedly left *Swing Journal* over the magazine's persistent Americentric editorial policy and neglect of native artists.) Even those for whom a national style and an indigenous standard of authenticity were paramount were bedeviled with contradictions, as they ultimately sought approval from abroad to legitimize the "Japanese voice" in jazz. Experimental blends of jazz with traditional forms of Japanese music, as performed abroad by Shiraki Hideo (1933–1972), Hara Nobuo's Sharps and Flats, and Akiyoshi Toshiko, pandered to Western audiences' "orientalizing" expectations and provided the approval that Japanese jazzmen had so long craved.

Still, the sixties and seventies witnessed what was arguably Japan's most prodigious flowering of domestic creativity to date in the jazz idiom. The national reputation for skillful imitation has yet to evaporate entirely, but by the 1970s a number of globe-trotting Japanese musicians had garnered well-deserved reputations as jazz originals. From Watanabe Sadao's forays into pop, Latin American, and African musics, and Akiyoshi's masterly blend of Asian musical textures with an Ellingtonian approach to composition and arranging, to Yamashita Yōsuke's energetic and startlingly original approach to improvisation, a number of Japanese jazz musicians demonstrated a newfound and hard-won confidence that was conducive to creativity. This chapter explores the roots of that confidence, highlighting the coincidence of a resurgent cultural nationalism and an unprecedented willingness to stretch the boundaries of the jazz idiom. It is clear that the protest against foreign-imposed standards of authenticity rested on assumptions of essentialized "Japaneseness." Starting in the late 1960s, well-known musicians such as keyboardist Satō Masahiko and percussionist Togashi Masahiko, critic Yui Shōichi, and some jazz aficionados (such as Terui Akira, the owner of the Johnny jazz coffeehouse in Rikuzentakata City, Iwate prefecture, which specializes in jazz records by Japanese artists) all struggled to define the constitutive elements of a Japanese style, and argued that the creation of such a style was a responsibility that artists must carry to fruition.[10]

Did jazz musicians necessarily have to incorporate musical elements or themes from an essentialized "Japanese cultural heritage" to be original? In other words, was the construction of a "Japanese jazz" the only way that Japanese could create original and authentic jazz and be true to the jazz aesthetic? These are the issues with which a prominent minority in Japan's jazz community wrestled from the mid-1960s onward. We are mostly familiar with the solutions developed by international superstars such as Akiyoshi Toshiko, Yamashita Yōsuke, Kikuchi Masabumi, and Watanabe Sadao. But I would like to take this opportunity to shine the spotlight on two revered yet little-known figures—actually, virtually unknown outside of Japan's jazz community—who presented these challenges to a generation of young musicians and equipped that generation with a set of aesthetic and social principles for facing up to them.

The pages of *Swing Journal*'s December 1960 issue were filled to bursting with stories and photographs anticipating Art Blakey's upcoming Japan tour, so perhaps it is little wonder that the flamboyant pronouncement below occupied merely a corner of the magazine's regular news section. The announcement is attributed to the founders of the Jazz Academy and was treated rather diffidently by the *SJ* editors, as if it were the product of kooks with overactive imaginations and delusions of grandeur.

> They [the Jazz Academy] say that their aim is not something that ex-
> presses only one part of human emotions, like funky soul jazz, but
> something that is more expressive of all human emotions; they want to
> perform a music that sings positively of the joys of life. They say that
> their first responsibility is to raise up jazz spiritually. To that end, it
> is important that all the group's members be one in their thought; if
> we are in agreement on our goal spiritually, won't our own "riffs"
> gradually emanate within our improvisations? Such is Mr. Takaya-
> nagi's opinion.[11]

It is unfortunate that *SJ* and other music periodicals failed to follow up on this story, for in their eagerness to show photos of Art Blakey and Horace Silver eating sukiyaki with geisha they missed the opportunity to chronicle the birth and maturation of Japan's avant-garde. Foreign critics, too, missed the opportunity. Their ambivalent assessments of jazz in Japan in the early sixties (quoted at length in the previous chapter) focused on the more estab-lished older generation of musicians and on the tepid concert, nightclub, and cabaret scenes. All thus overlooked a significant youth movement that was occurring within the cramped, unglamorous confines of jazz coffee-houses in Nagoya, Tokyo, and Yokohama. If an observer as sympathetic as Charlie Mariano had been privy to this underground activity, his comments on the state of jazz in Japan might have been more sanguine. But at the height of the funky boom, "Mr. Takayanagi" and company could hardly hope to compete with the spectacle of Sonny Rollins meditating in a Zen monastery.

As it is, what information we have about the Jazz Academy and its various offshoots consists of the published and oral recollections of participants and observers, a single jam session recording, some photographs, and Dr. Uchida Osamu's unreleased reel-to-reel tapes documenting the music, po-etry, and rhetoric of the participants.[12] It is clear that bassist Kanai Hideto and guitarist Takayanagi Masayuki ("Jo-Jo," 1932–1991) founded the Jazz Academy at a time when Japanese jazz artists were marginalized in their own country, when older artists with established reputations monopolized the few jobs that did exist, and when domestic jazz was unfavorably scrutinized and compared to the wave of American jazz talent pouring into Japan. The Jazz Academy thus constituted a protest movement of musicians and fans motivated by both institutional and aesthetic concerns to fundamentally change the ways that improvised music was created, learned, presented, performed, and appreciated.

Like most art movements, there was a generational shift at the base of the jazz avant-garde, with the Occupation-era veterans deliberately handing the baton to younger artists. Kanai and Takayanagi cut their teeth in U.S. servicemen's clubs in the latter years of the Occupation and had remained fixtures of both the underground bebop and the upscale cabaret and concert scenes throughout the 1950s. Jo-Jo had played with vibist Sugiura Yōzō's New Direction Quartet, jammed with Moriyasu Shōtarō, and even joined George Kawaguchi's Big Four + 1 briefly. Kanai had plucked bass for Nanri Fumio's Hot Peppers and the "cool" Westliners, before a pivotal meeting with Duke Ellington in 1964 encouraged him to begin formal study of classical and baroque music to "correct some bad habits." But the jazz movement that the veterans Takayanagi and Kanai instigated in 1960 derived its primary energy from musicians and fans barely out of their teens. Unlike the Occupation-era generation of musicians, who enjoyed ample opportunities to hone their craft in the ubiquitous American service clubs, dance halls, and cabarets, the up-and-coming youngsters of the early 1960s were deprived of an infrastructure that encouraged or allowed them to develop and perform improvised music at all, let alone original music. By scrapping for performance sites, producing their own concerts of original compositions, engaging audience participation, and often playing for free, the members of this youth movement circumvented the established customs and venues that sustained the more established jazz stars and attracted an affluent clientele.

But the new generation not only posed an institutional challenge to the order of things in Japan's jazz community: it also questioned the aesthetics of imitation and "catch up" that had guided the Occupation-era generation. To be sure, members of the Jazz Academy found compelling inspiration in American jazz—particularly that of Charles Mingus, Sun Ra, John Coltrane, and Ornette Coleman—but they combined this influence with an interest in contemporary classical music, minimalism, and the experiments of John Cage, focusing on the development of original compositions, poetry, and "free" improvisations, all with an audacity with which few of the previous generation could identify.

The Jazz Academy began life as a quartet consisting of Takayanagi, Kanai, pianist Kikuchi Masabumi, and drummer Togashi Masahiko, performing in Yokohama jazz coffeehouses from January 1961. Since its performances proved too provocative for most coffeehouse owners and customers, the Jazz Academy was rarely able to play the same venue twice. Takayanagi soon succeeded in negotiating a regular slot at a *chanson* coffeehouse in Tokyo's Ginza district, the Ginparis, where the band performed, usually gratis, on Friday afternoons. (If enough listeners attended a performance, musicians might take home between ¥200 to ¥400 each, enough to buy a drink after the gig.) The organization expanded and evolved rapidly in the coming months, as Takayanagi expressed a desire to transform the Jazz Academy from a band to a "music studies group" open to musician and nonmusician alike. However, realization of this vision was impeded as the guitarist was twice arrested for narcotics possession. The arrests were widely publicized in newspapers, motivating the editors of *Swing Journal* to dress down Takayanagi in editorials, and possibly reinforcing their inclination to deny his band coverage. The specter of drugs plagued the organization: the 1963 all-night jam session that came to be immortalized on the *Ginparis Session* LP was a party simultaneously welcoming drummer Togashi Masahiko back from a period of incarceration for narcotics possession, and bidding farewell to Takayanagi, who was to leave the jazz world temporarily to begin drug rehab.[13]

By 1962 the collective had changed its name to New Century Music Workshop (Shin Seiki Ongaku Kenkyūjo), dubbed its performances "Jazz Seminars," and adopted stringent artistic and behavioral standards for its membership. Kanai Hideto says the Workshop was committed to bringing down the barriers that separate art from society. (A rare review of one of the Workshop's performances stated that "what the concert made me feel strongly was the players' indomitable will to synchronize [the acts of] living and performing music.")[14] As the group's principal conceptualist, Kanai encouraged musicians to think in societal terms and to contribute to humanity, as integral parts of society rather than as artists divorced from it. His basic philosophy remained unchanged when we chatted in 1995: musicians should be good people and should influence society in a positive manner. In keeping with this philosophy, the New Century Music Workshop discussed and accepted or rejected new members based on not only their musical abilities and commitment to their art but also on the strength of their personal characters. The Workshop established three fundamental artistic policies and three personal qualifications for its membership. The artistic policies demanded: "pursuit of the essence of original art"; "creative activity that engages and stimulates the audience, and which makes the audience understand the essence rather than the outer layers of music"; and attention

13. Bassist Kanai Hideto leads a Jazz Seminar in the early 1960s. Dr. Uchida Osamu (bottom left with glasses) documents the proceedings with his ever-ready tape recorder. Cramped quarters were the norm for this scruffling group. Photo used with permission of Dr. Uchida Osamu.

to the musical and personal development of young talent. In their personal characters members had to demonstrate a dedication to developing their own individual musical visions; a social consciousness that privileged their humanity over their musicianship; and a cooperative spirit and a willingness to contribute positively to the group.[15]

Aside from the New Century Music Workshop's socially committed philosophy—which reflected its solidarity with the post-Anpo spirit in other arts media—the pivotal participation of nonmusicians distinguished the movement. Uchida Osamu bought two tape recorders (one of which he kept in Tokyo, the other in Nagoya), with which he recorded performances for his own enjoyment and dubbed copies for musicians to study. Yoshida Mamoru, the proprietor of the Chigusa *jazu kissa* for thirty years, served as the Workshop's contact person and negotiated on the collective's behalf for work in the capital region and in Nagoya.[16] College students, artists, and bohemians packed the tiny Ginparis coffeehouse on Friday afternoons, transforming performances into "happenings." Although the released *Ginparis Session* actually sounds rather tame, Kanai insists that "no one could predict what would happen at those sessions." Pianist Yamashita Yōsuke recalled that the more bizarre experiments at the Ginparis sessions included playing stringless guitars and blowing saxophones with trumpet mouthpieces and trumpets with sax mouthpieces. "You couldn't laugh," Yamashita joked, "because it was 'Art.' "[17] Finally, an incident involving "fan participation" got the Workshop kicked out of the Ginparis for good in 1964: Kanai and Uchida both told me the story of a painter named Kageyama who, enthralled by the music, succeeded in urging his girlfriend to augment the performance with a nude dance.

After losing the regular Friday afternoon slot at the Ginparis, the Workshop splintered into various offshoots. Takayanagi founded his own group called Jazz Contemporary, though he and Kanai performed together briefly in an orchestra called King's Roar before parting ways. In the spring of 1966 King's Roar joined a Japanese performing arts troupe for an "expedition" to South America, Los Angeles, and Honolulu, where they performed only original compositions and Japanese folk and children's songs, with each member doubling on traditional instruments. In later years Kanai and Takayanagi performed together only sporadically, though their friendship apparently remained solid. After a decade of struggling to stay on the "front line," Kanai took the sixteen-piece King's Roar on a two-month tour of the USSR in 1976, but was forced to disband the orchestra immediately on its return because its survival was not economically feasible.[18] With smaller combos he recorded a series of acclaimed albums for the Three Blind Mice label in the seventies: *Q, Ode to Birds, What!* (a tribute to Mingus), and *Concierto de Aranjuez,* which contains an achingly beautiful arrangement of Joaquín Rodrigo's title piece. In the nineties Kanai manages to keep a busy performance schedule, leading the ten-piece Yokohama Jazz Orchestra and sitting in with smaller bands. Kanai is a jovial and spirited performer, shouting or continuously covering and uncovering his famous bald pate with a fedora as the music moves him. He makes the bass weep with a seemingly effortless technique. As of this writing only a CD distillation of *Concierto* and *What!* is in print, making it nearly impossible to hear the work of one of Japan's most important jazz conceptualists.

Takayanagi is only marginally better served in terms of available recordings, but enough exist to suggest his versatility and monumental stature as a guitarist and musical conceptualist. On the *Ginparis Session* LP his sharp tone and harmonic daring deconstruct "Greensleeves" in much the same manner that John Coltrane undermined the sentimentality of "My Favorite Things." In the years after the New Century Music Workshop disbanded, JoJo adopted a softer tone for the gently lyrical bossa nova sessions documented on *The Smile I Love.* But recordings of his New Direction Unit a few years later reveal a totally different concept: on the tour-de-force *Live Inde-*

14 & 15. Takayanagi Masayuki, the artistic conscience of Japan's avant-garde. Photos courtesy of Saitō Yasunori/JINYA Disc.

pendence (recorded in 1970) Takayanagi's brittle acoustic guitar belches in mysteriously controlled spasms on the darkly lyrical "Herdman's Pipe of Spain," while on "Mass Projection" he dispenses deceptively random shards of electronic sound, manipulating them adroitly through his amplifier. Although usually labeled "free jazz" because they seem to lack an identifiable harmonic structure, melodic reference point, and consistent rhythmic pulse, these performances were tightly controlled, disciplined, and attentively interactive. By contrast, a New Direction performance in the mid-seventies was likely to be a seemingly endless explosion of pure noise (as on *Inspiration and Power* and *April Is the Cruelest Month*), although the guitarist was also capable of teasing more subtle and identifiable textures from his rig, such as the snarling jungle cat sounds on "We Have Existed" (from *April*). A proponent of total spontaneity in music making, he often named his "compositions" or albums for the dates on which they were performed (for instance, the album *850113* was recorded on 13 January 1985). Takayanagi's restlessness and irreverent eclecticism continued throughout his career. In the years before his death from liver disease in 1991, he recorded with John Zorn, played telepathic duets with his protégé bassist

Ino Nobuyoshi, led a tango guitar ensemble called Loco Takayanagi y Los Pobres (Crazy Takayanagi and the Poor Boys), and performed solo noise ("Action Direct") concerts. "My most cherished conviction," he wrote with typical crypticism, "is that music does not yet exist."[19]

Takayanagi must have explored the entire sonic geography of his instrument: he often played the guitar with a violin bow or small metallic objects; sometimes it sounds like he barely touched the strings at all, but rather coaxed quirky textures from his amplifier. He was a classically trained guitarist of ample technique, who seems deliberately to have set out to unlearn standard methods of playing the instrument, in his quest for new textures, voicings, and phrasings. In exploring the guitaristic possibilities of the jazz avant-garde's disregard for traditional harmonic, rhythmic, and melodic structures, Jo-Jo had no obvious American model. Apparently Takayanagi Masayuki developed his conceptions earlier than, or at least independently of, his most obvious counterparts, Sonny Sharrock and Derek Bailey.[20] While the game of identifying "who did what first" is admittedly wearisome, in the context of the times it was quite significant for a Japanese jazz artist to attempt something that he or she had not heard an American doing already. Takayanagi and Kanai passed this exploratory spirit, the total antithesis of the reverence with which their generation approached the American jazz tradition, on to their disciples, among them Togashi Masahiko, the Hino brothers Terumasa and Motohiko, Kikuchi Masabumi, Satō Masahiko, Yamashita Yōsuke, and other future stars who would place Japan on the jazz map.

"Thrilling Live Performances"

In the wake of the Ginparis debacle, the remaining members of the New Century Music Workshop decided to open their own musician-run jazz club. Drummer Miyakawa Yōichi, Yoshida Mamoru, and a small group of musicians and fans pitched in to finance and refurbish the dilapidated basement of a Ginza building to create Jazz Gallery 8, which opened 26 July 1964. With performances in the afternoons and evenings before enthusiastic (if sparse) college audiences, Jazz Gallery 8 built a reputation as "Japan's Minton's House."[21] It struggled along for two years, offering young musicians a place to master the jazz language and perform experimental music. This underground jazz movement operated on the fringes of a jazz community that was already marginalized from Japan's entertainment mainstream. The jazz press was cautious, if not outright oblivious, of the movement, and few ventured to speculate on its potential aesthetic promise. The handful of coffeehouse owners who opened their places to the young avant-gardists usually only permitted after-hours performances, effectively limiting audience turnout and guaranteeing the obscurity of the movement's music. Certainly the grassroots effort to organize musicians and fans for the express purposes of reevaluating the jazz community's aesthetics, producing their own recitals, and managing their own performance spots was contrary to the modus operandi of an entertainment industry dominated by a handful of powerful companies which jealously gripped the reins of cultural production. In any case, music dubbed "experimental" or "inaccessible" was of little interest to a popular music industry absorbed with the marketing of "group sounds" (Beatles-based rock 'n roll), *enka*, and Japanese pops (*kayōkyoku*).[22] Those whose visions included jazz cared more about the importation of foreign talent rather than the promotion of native musicians.

The jazz underground's refusal to make artistic compromises won it few advocates in Japan's culture industry, but its lack of a charismatic leader, a celebrity on whom Japan's star-struck entertainment industry could fix its spotlight, seems to have been equally handicapping. Takayanagi's unorthodox approach to the guitar and his well-known history of drug problems, Kanai's soft-spoken, philosophical nature and dry humor, and Togashi Masahiko's sunglassed haughtiness did not make for star appeal. By the mid-1960s the jazz community openly craved a savior, someone to give it direction, to stir the mainstream from its complacency and lead the avant-garde out of its obscurity. Many fixed their hopes on Watanabe Sadao ("Nabe-sada"), who returned from the United States in November 1965. Literally as soon as he stepped off the airplane, the manufacturing of Japan's next big jazz celebrity commenced.

> *"Sadao is bad, man. Cat used to practice in his sleep. Walk around the hotels and shit."*
> . . . *"Sadao?" I said.*
> *"Watanabe," he said. "Ka-pow What-a-knobby."*[23]

Watanabe had made his name in the 1950s as a member of Akiyoshi's Cozy Quartet, the helm of which he inherited when she left for the States. Through Akiyoshi's good offices, he obtained a scholarship from the Hartford, Connecticut, Jazz Society for study at the Berklee College of Music starting in August 1962. But his real education came on the bandstand as a sideman with Chico Hamilton and Gary McFarland. Nabe-sada cited the pain of separation from his family, problems with U.S. immigration laws, and his irregular class attendance (due to frequent touring with Hamilton and McFarland) as reasons for his decision to forgo his final term at Berklee and return to Japan. Initially persuaded by American and Japanese friends to remain in the United States, he made his final decision only four days

16. Ultra-cool drum prodigy
Togashi Masahiko performs
at the 8th Yamaha Jazz Club
Concert, Nagoya, 4 July 1965.
Photo used with permission
of Dr. Uchida Osamu.

before returning to Japan for good. The saxophonist returned to a country
that all but touring American jazz stars regarded as a "tough environment
in which to play jazz." "There is no real work outside of jazz coffeehouses,"
bassist Arakawa Yasuo warned him. "The young musicians are doing their
best, but, unfortunately, our colleagues from the old days are in pretty
miserable shape."[24] A January 1966 article in Swing Journal concurred: "In
reality last year's jazz world did not seem very prosperous. It was also a year
in which the rainichi boom of the previous year (1964) slowed down a step;
and [judging] from the inquiries, questions, and letters directed to this
magazine from readers, it is easy to tell that right now there are many jazz
fans who are tired of waiting for the moment when Japanese jazzmen
engage in activity filled with a developed sense of self." The same article
expressed high expectations of Watanabe Sadao to relieve the jazz world's
malaise. In a remarkable turnaround, a mere one year later Swing Journal
was celebrating what it perceived as a substantial improvement in the domestic jazz community's fortunes, and attributing most of the credit to its
new star.[25]

Colleagues and protégés were inspired by Watanabe's tireless efforts to turn his homeland's jazz community around in 1966. It is worth noting that his experience was the exact opposite of Akiyoshi Toshiko's, whose disillusioned departure a few months earlier left many with thinly veiled bitterness. Watanabe found an eager audience that practically begged for his leadership, and he did not disappoint them. Announcing "I completely lost my [inferiority] complex" while in America, Nabe-sada heartened many when he assured them that "going to America enabled me to have the confidence that what I had been doing in Japan before was *not* a mistake."[26] Within days of his arrival he was making the rounds at jazz coffeehouses and inspiring energetic performances from his colleagues. With a working quartet consisting of New Century Music Workshop alumni (Kikuchi Masabumi [p], Suzuki Isao, then Ikeda Yoshio [b], and Togashi Masahiko [d]), the saxophonist nudged jazz back into the mainstream through monthly concerts, radio and television performances, and recordings of bossa, Beatles, and Burt Bacharach. Watanabe balanced his role as a performer with that of teacher. At the invitation of the Yamaha music company's Kawakami Gen'ichi, he and pianist Yagi Masao took the reins of the Yamaha Institute of Popular Music in February 1966. Borrowing liberally from his Berklee notes, Watanabe developed and taught courses on composition, harmonic theory, arranging, instrumental technique, and improvisation, and conducted the Institute's workshop orchestra.[27] It was a unique and unprecedented opportunity for Japanese musicians to receive a formal jazz education.

In hindsight, it would be difficult to discount the importance of Watanabe Sadao's high-profile campaign to resuscitate his nation's interest in jazz: he energized Japan's lethargic jazz community, bridged its generation gaps, piqued the interest of jazz fans old and new, and inspired musicians to develop their talents.[28] But it would likewise be remiss to attribute the jazz community's renewed energy exclusively to the efforts of one man. Although in terms of general popularity jazz was undeniably "losing ground" to rock and popular music,[29] for a number of reasons there was a vibrant hardcore jazz culture in Japan in the late 1960s, with a strong commitment to supporting and developing native musicians. One factor was the growing interest in jazz on college campuses, particularly among students involved in the late-sixties' political protest movements.[30] Compared to European countries, the appropriation of jazz by leftist intellectuals and students in Japan was relatively late. But in the early summer of 1969, pianist Yamashita Yōsuke, drummer Moriyama Takeo, and saxophonist Nakamura Seiichi expressed their solidarity with Waseda University students occupying and barricading their main campus, with an explosive set of music performed on the battleground (and later released as *Dancing Kojiki*).[31]

Members of the Zenkyoto ("all-campus joint struggle committee") movement, cheering on global revolutionary struggles such as the American civil rights movement and protesting Japanese complicity in the Vietnam War, regarded jazz as a "Third World expression" and a metaphor for freedom. Aware that detested "bourgeois" values had permeated their own upbringings, radical students attempted "to negate themselves as students" and identify rather with oppressed and underdeveloped peoples. To demonstrate solidarity with American black nationalism and pan-Africanism, student radicals liberally sprinkled the word *black* in their rhetoric and the titles of their arts and organizations. New Left activists found a haven or "liberated zone" in Tokyo's Shinjuku district, where experimental arts flourished, jazz prominent among them: poet Suwa Yū "jammed" with jazz musicians, while Yamashita Yōsuke lent extemporaneous piano to performances of Kara Jūrō's experimental play *John Silver* and other productions at the Red Tent. Although Hiraoka Masaaki's 1967 essay "Jazz Manifesto" claimed that "Jazz is still a virgin. It has yet to deal a hard blow against the traditional, the European, the elite, and the artistic," fellow critic Aikura Hisato disputed this contention: "The activity of Yamashita and his comrades throughout last year [1967] indicates that they are finally shedding that virgin consciousness" and taking truly revolutionary action.[32]

Students craving a funky, underground ambience gave *jazu kissa* a new lease on life and flocked to the growing number of live jazz clubs: a 1967 survey of 1500 jazz coffeehouse patrons confirmed that 42 percent were college students.[33] Following the demise of Jazz Gallery 8 in 1966, a small number of bohemian-style jazz nightclubs with a student clientele opened in Japan's major cities, offering a relatively low-cost and more visceral alternative to the upscale Ginza cabarets where swing remained king. The famed, faux-Greenwich Village hangout Pit-Inn in Shinjuku proclaimed its mission to serve the struggling young artist and the thrill-seeking young fan, with the mottoes "Thrilling Life Performances" and "Let's raise Japanese jazz!"[34] Unlike the cabarets, dance halls, and affluent nightclubs of previous eras, the new jazz clubs such as Pit-Inn and Tarō demanded studious, attentive listening from audiences and encouraged informal jam sessions, crucial to the maturation of musicians.[35] In response to the growing popularity of live domestic jazz, the recording industry began making more of an effort to document the music of Japanese musicians. In 1967 Columbia Records' TAKT subsidiary signed Watanabe Sadao and initiated the first sustained effort to record native artists since the demise of the late-fifties King Jazz Series.

It did not hurt the emerging interest in native talent that Japanese musicians faced quantitatively less competition from *rainichi* jazz tours. After Elvin Jones, Curtis Fuller, Tony Williams, and other American jazzmen were jailed for narcotics possession while in Japan, the Japanese government was increasingly reluctant to admit American jazz musicians. Miles Davis's manager Jack Whittemore, responding to news that a thirteen-concert, sold-out Davis tour had been canceled because the Japanese government would not grant the band visas, cited "unofficial guideposts" of government policy that would admit no musician with a record of convictions, "no matter how old or how minor." Whittemore went on to speculate that the "Japanese policy of exclusion has been broadened to include simple arrest without conviction."[36] The flood of American jazz artists thus slowed to a trickle. Conversely, the number of Japanese artists performing and studying abroad increased dramatically. The wide acclaim accorded to Japanese artists overseas was the kind of approval that Japan's jazz community had long coveted and sparked an unprecedented level of confidence in the domestic product.

It was rare for Japanese jazz artists to perform abroad, so the Shiraki Hideo Quintet's performance at the Berlin Jazz Festival in November 1965 (at the invitation of Joachim Berendt) was regarded as a momentous occasion.[37] What is intriguing about the tour is that Shiraki's band, regarded as the bluesiest, funkiest hard bop unit in Japan, was accompanied in Berlin by three female *koto* players and performed mostly Japanese folk tunes such as "Sakura Sakura." The band's novelty and artistry caused a sensation: "Applause is rather unusual at a rehearsal. The sons and daughters from the land of the rising sun received it," Barbara Rose wrote in the *Berliner Zeitung*. "The confrontation of Japanese tradition and occidental modernity is fascinating." Similarly, Horst Windelboth commented in the *Berlin Morgenpost* that "Shiraki and his musicians play jazz that reminds us of the masterpieces of Japanese painting: Tender, refined and like drawn with china ink." In the liner notes to the album commemorating Shiraki's visit, Yui Shōichi noted that "it is not without symbolism that this recording—with its splendid meeting of old Japan and modern jazz—was not done in our own country but in Germany. This country always showed a deep understanding for and interest in Japan."[38]

The precedent of performing native folk or Japanese-themed songs was honored in the coming years by future bands such as King's Roar and the Sharps and Flats. As the Sharps and Flats prepared a program of Japanese folk material for its Newport Jazz Festival appearance of 2 July 1967, bandleader Hara Nobuo told *Variety* magazine, "It's a dream come true . . . but my shoulders are very heavy. I'll be carrying the hopes of Japanese jazz." He aspired to "show the Japanese people that a Japanese band has the power to play with the best. And it could give encouragement to the many Japanese jazz musicians who are having difficulty." Hara hoped a program of Japanese folk songs would impress an American audience expecting a distinctive sound. Hara's organization made no money on the festival appearance and had to pay its own expenses. But Hara wanted the " 'moment of truth' that can only come from playing on the same program as his peers and subjecting the band to appraisal by America's top jazz critics and more savvy fans." In order to "rise to the same level of creativity as American bands," the Sharps and Flats would be better served by developing a new repertoire rather than by relying on its staples of Count Basie and Woody Herman swing tunes: "What better for a Japanese band than Japanese songs?" Hara's instincts apparently served him well, for the Sharps and Flats were a hit at the festival.[39]

Not all Japanese bands traveling abroad adopted this strategy: for instance, the Ōsaka New Orleans Rascals and the Waseda University High Society Orchestra stuck to more familiar repertoires for their U.S. tours, content to wow audiences with their facility in a music that was supposed to be foreign to them. Here is how the New Orleans publication *The Second Line* described the Rascals' two-week residence in the "birthplace" of jazz:

> The New Orleans Jazz Club wanted them to have a memorable arrival in New Orleans. There is no doubt that it succeeded in doing just that. Unknown to the Japanese group, the NOJC and friends in New Orleans had planned a musical welcome and motorcade back to town. . . . The reaction on the part of the visitors was heartwarming—one band member, pianist Satoshi Adachi, wept at the realization of the welcome planned for his countrymen. He said, "We are very surprised. We have been dreaming of New Orleans because New Orleans is the home of jazz and jazzmen are all brothers in this home of jazz. The clarinet-leader of the NEW ORLEANS RASCALS, Ryoichi Wawai, and one of the oldest members of the ODJC said, "it is a BIG, BIG, BIG, dream for our band to visit New Orleans; the music means so much to us. As I see it, the music (the blue and lonesome New Orleans jazz) is expressing destiny of human beings, slightness of man." They all seemed to love jazz more than anything else. . . . [A]lways whenever and wherever they appeared, they endeared themselves to the listeners. Their visit was one of excellent good will for both countries, for jazz, for various races and creeds.[40]

The New Orleans Rascals provide an interesting contrast to the so-called modern jazz groups, for their aesthetic aspirations were clearly different. The Ōsakans were clearly here to pay homage to—and maybe jam a bit with—their traditional jazz heroes. But Shiraki and Hara, products of the bebop and post-bop jazz movements of the forties and fifties, worked from a different artistic sensibility: they had lofty ambitions of creating something new that would earn esteem as a genuine innovation within the modern jazz idiom. Clearly, for them, a program of traditional Japanese songs would garner more attention and, it was hoped, respect for Japanese artists than a regurgitation of well-digested styles.

Akiyoshi Toshiko has remarked that in the late 1960s she too turned to what she called "my heritage" as a strategy for making her mark in jazz history. At that time, she was separated from and soon to be divorced from Charlie Mariano, and was scuffling to support herself and her daughter Monday Michiru with gigs at Greenwich Village clubs such as the Five Spot and Top of the Gate.[41] Realizing that as a player she was respected yet unlikely to leave much of a legacy, she considered quitting jazz altogether. But as she gained recognition as a composer following a 1967 Town Hall recital, Akiyoshi started believing that she could turn her Japanese ethnicity into an advantage that would set her apart from other artists and contribute something original to the music. In the documentary *Jazz Is My Native Language*, Akiyoshi recalled the personal and artistic concerns that led her to accentuate the "Japanese" in her music:

> The 1960s was a very difficult time for me, but it was also a very important time, because I had so much difficulty supporting my daughter and myself. I really had to take a look at who I was and what I was trying to do.... At least if you're an American it's *justified*, let's say, to be a jazz musician. Jazz is American music. And I thought, here I am, I'm a Japanese and a woman, and the woman part is not that important I think, but here I am Japanese and a jazz player and playing in New York. I never thought I was a bad player, but there are so many great players, too. And I look at it and then have to really think about where my position is, what my role will be. And somehow it looks kind of pathetic and comical, the fact that there is a Japanese little girl trying to play jazz . . . and I felt very insignificant. Did I do something, did I make any kind of revolution [in] the jazz world? At that time I thought to take that opportunity to just become a nice little woman who cleans the house and cooks. I think I was very tired, fighting the world since [I was] sixteen years old. Because at that time I wasn't really contributing anything [to jazz] and I thought I would quit. Lew [Tabackin, her second husband] kind of stopped me from giving up. He told me that I have some value.
>
> I decided that perhaps I would look upon my heritage, which . . . traditionally to be Japanese was a handicap to become a jazz player, because you were not American. But I decided that was a rather posi-

tive quality . . . I'd been playing long enough to have some experience at that time, and [I am] non-American, so I have a different heritage, and perhaps I can utilize this and infuse some of my heritage into jazz. Perhaps I can return something . . . perhaps I can build a library [of compositions] at least, and perhaps that is where my role [is].

Thus Akiyoshi and some of her former colleagues across the Pacific independently formulated similar solutions: the incorporation of explicitly "Japanese" elements into their music was the logical path for ethnic Japanese to pursue in order to be original in the jazz idiom.

We Now Create: Defining "Japanese Jazz"

"Japanese jazz" as a discursive category, which simultaneously asserted Japanese artistic originality and revolted against the hegemony of American standards of aesthetic innovation and expressive authenticity, was the culmination of the post-Anpo avant-garde's agitations, reaching its fullest articulation in the late sixties. Yet it was an idea of somewhat older pedigree, though such was rarely acknowledged. Hattori Ryōichi, Sano Tasuku, and Sugii Kōichi certainly aspired to the creation of an identifiably indigenous jazz style at the height of ultranationalism in the 1930s (although their efforts were rarely regarded as precursors of the new movement). Twenty years later, when King Records began selling its recordings of native artists overseas through a British corporation, a handful of critics began using the term "Japanese jazz" (*Nihonteki jazu*) to describe the contents of the King LPs: for better or worse, they contended, there was something essentially different about Japanese jazz. These critics made noticeably little effort, however, to define what made *Nihonteki jazu "Nihonteki."* Skeptics contended that if there was such a thing as a national style, it was distinguished by the relative ineptitude of native musicians compared to Americans. But as early as 1958 Yui Shōichi, the most prominent advocate of the concept in the late sixties, rejoined: "Something that uses the jazz idiom [yet] can be called 'Japanese jazz' is starting to sprout. We have come to a point now when Japanese jazz will soon be acknowledged by the world." Jazz critic Kawano Ryūji, in reply to Ishihara Yasuyuki's comment that Japanese musicians who wrote their own arrangements had stopped imitating Americans, asserted, "Generally Japanese jazz is thought to be jazzified Japanese folk songs, but if one thinks in terms of originality in jazz arranging, this can be said to be truly excellent Japanese jazz."[42]

Not everyone agreed that this was the proper way to discuss native jazz. "People say that we must create Japanese jazz," Kubota Jirō remarked. "This may seem at a glance to be the correct ideal, but I think it's really meaning-less. I say so because jazz is a music with an extremely distinctive shape. . . . [J]azz cannot be separated into Japanese jazz or Soviet jazz, because it possesses something more universal than that. So I think that saying 'we must create Japanese jazz' is relatively meaningless."[43] In response to Noguchi Hisamitsu's query regarding national differences in jazz, pianist Yagi Masao and composer/arranger Miho Keitarō both expressed empathy for that perspective but stopped short of endorsing the concept of Japanese jazz. "I think there's something Japanese about what Japanese play," Yagi stated. "When we saw what the French were doing, we felt that there was something relatively different about [their jazz]. [But] I think that they're not conscious of it themselves." "We don't have a consciousness of nationality, we don't make an issue of it," Miho insisted, "but when we heard French jazz we felt that there was something different from American jazz." Yet both musicians derided the idea of Japanese jazz. "Isn't Japan an assort-ment of American things and French things?" Miho asked. "Japanese peo-ple seem to like thinking of 'Japanese things' or 'Japanese jazz.'" "Some critics are saying that we should create a Japanese jazz, but I think that's foolish," Yagi scoffed, "and there are people who say things like, when you write jazz using ancient Japanese melodies, 'this is the birth of Japanese jazz!'"[44]

However, Miho's intriguingly "postmodern" perspective on Japan as an amalgamation of foreign cultures was the exception. Yui Shōichi and others maintained that Japan possessed an independent, core cultural identity, and for the first time since the war years, jazz musicians openly expressed this vision in their music. From the late 1950s there was noticeably renewed in-terest in "jazzing" Japanese folk material (min'yō), expanding considerably on Hattori's innovations. A 1958 Arts Festival featured a "Songs of Japan" segment as part of its "Japanese Jazz" program. Among the very few albums released by native artists from the late 1950s until the mid-1960s were a handful featuring Dixieland, Glenn Miller-style swing, or George Shearing-style "West Coast cool" treatments of Japanese pops and folk songs; there was even an album titled *Koto Jazz* (*O-koto no jazu*), with kotoist Yonekawa Toshiko backed by Okuda Munehiro's Blue Sky Orchestra. American jazz-men such as Tony Scott, Charlie Mariano, and Herbie Mann were arguably even more intrigued by the possibilities of a musical fusion than most Japanese were. Clarinetist Scott, who resided in Japan for some time in the late fifties and early sixties, recorded a minor classic of improvised music for Verve Records, *Music for Zen Meditation and Other Joys*, with *shakuhachi* player Yamamoto Hōzan and *koto* player Yuize Shin'ichi.[45] The results of such fusions could be stunning, as evidenced by the seamless integration of the elegant Japanese harp into the breakneck swing of drummer Shiraki Hideo's "Festival" (from *Hideo Shiraki in Festival*, 1961). The conservatory-trained percussionist's tom-toms evoke the thundering *taiko* drums so integral to Japanese festival music, while Shirane Kinuko's dexterous *koto* arpeggios contribute significantly to the overall swing of the piece (I have seen *koto* players' jaws drop on hearing it).

With the possible exception of *Hideo Shiraki in Festival*, such fusions were seldom greeted with critical enthusiasm; rather, critics consistently discounted them either as mere novelties or as overtly commercial attempts to attract listeners who preferred Japanese pops to "foreign" music. Few Japanese modernists showed interest in such experiments: Yagi confessed that traditional Japanese music felt "foreign" to his generation.[46] But "jazzing the (Japanese) classics" was not what Yui and Kawano meant by "Japanese jazz." Their definition (to the extent that they had one) suggested a much more recondite quality that was somehow recognizably "Japanese."

As noted earlier, for some Japanese bands performing overseas, musical fusions were deliberate strategies for constructing distinctive musical identities and thus winning over tough audiences. The belief that Japanese bands were most likely to be successful overseas if they stuck to material that was identifiably "Japanese" was more often than not confirmed by foreign audiences who expected originality, if not exoticism. "Jazzing" Japanese folk songs seemed to be a failsafe measure for deflecting accusations of excessive derivation. A significant shift in repertoire enabled Japanese musicians to adjust the aesthetic standards by which they were judged, to level the playing field, so to speak. Hara Nobuo conceded in our interview, "At Newport in 1967, I was thinking that I wanted to create 'Japanese jazz.' " Although he has since changed his thinking, and is more concerned with the assertion of "Hara's voice" rather than a national one, Hara's admission testifies to the growing concern in the late sixties with the creation of a style of jazz that expressed unmistakably quintessential "Japaneseness."

It was certainly not a concept readily embraced by all. Watanabe Sadao, the scene's acknowledged leader and a figure of significant celebrity by the late sixties, withheld his endorsement. The saxophonist repeatedly cited "originality" as the Japanese jazz musician's ultimate goal, but he viewed a national style as antithetical to that goal. "What is called 'Japan's own jazz' is vague," he said at a *Swing Journal* symposium in 1968. "For instance, even Charlie Mariano's 'Rock Garden of Ryōan Temple' has a real Japanese feeling. . . . But I don't feel that we should be playing just that kind of music." Watanabe exhorted players to develop recognizable individual styles that were not necessarily rooted in nationality or ethnicity. Two of his protégés, Kikuchi Masabumi and Satō Masahiko, expressed resentment over foreign expectations that their jazz "sound Japanese." (Although eventually Satō became a vocal advocate of a Japanese style.)[47]

It is interesting to note that even those who resisted the idea of a national style spoke in terms of a "Japanese rhythmic sense" or of a "Japanese feeling," indicating that they shared assumptions of Japanese exceptionalism with those who promoted the idea of a national style. There was considerable agreement that somehow Japanese played jazz differently from white and black Americans. Watanabe repeatedly faulted Japanese performers for a poor "rhythmic sense" resulting in a "non-swinging Japanese jazz."[48] Some discussants were careful to attribute such differences to environmental rather than racial or ethnic characteristics. Yet others who tended to treat ethnicity and national culture as deterministic, immutable categories took the additional step of celebrating the alleged differences between Japanese and American jazz as an embryonic national style; furthermore, prominent musicians in this circle, most notably Satō Masahiko and Togashi Masahiko, spoke of the creation of a Japanese jazz as the artist's responsibility.

Having first advanced the possibility of a Japanese jazz in the late fifties, Yui Shōichi began articulating a more fully conceived theory in the late sixties, as Japanese musicians were starting to attract unprecedented and favorable recognition at home and abroad. In a 1969 essay in *Jazz Critique,* Yui wrote:

> From Shiraki Hideo to Hara Nobuo, Japanese musicians invited to foreign jazz festivals, each with their own creativity, are using Japanese scales, *koto,* and *shakuhachi,* performing a unique jazz that other peoples cannot imitate, and garnering great acclaim. "We will not be accepted for imitating and playing the same things foreigners play," they say. "That made us painfully aware that Japanese musicians should create a Japanese jazz."
>
> Right now this is a new global trend that is coming to rule jazz. Even in America, blacks are aiming for black jazz, whites for white jazz; and in Europe, as well, in Spain and West Germany different national hues using the diction of jazz are being worked out. It is certainly reasonable that Japanese musicians are in a hurry to "create Japanese jazz."
>
> Now, thinking calmly, what in the world does the term "Japanese jazz" indicate? If it means jazzing [songs like] "Yagi-bushi" or "Sōran-bushi," [such attempts] have been tested since the early Shōwa period and they have all experienced merciless failure. They may have all been Japanese-Western compromises, but they have never been "Japanese."
>
> One hundred years after Meiji, the course of modernization that our nation has pursued has been accomplished only by abandoning pre-

cious Japanese traditions and taking in Western culture in large quantities. . . . [W]hat do we have to prove that we are real Japanese? Nothing. Right now there is no standard for "Japanese things." So aiming to "create a Japanese jazz" is significant talk.

Yui argued that Japanese should follow the example of black Americans, who had recently demonstrated renewed pride and interest in their "lost" African heritage, and search for a "clear solution" to the question "what is Japanese?"[49]

In a roundtable discussion to commemorate the second All Japanese Jazz Festival in 1969, Yui clarified his conception of Japanese jazz in an exchange with fellow critics Iwanami Yōzō, Ono Masaichirō, and Koyama Kiyoshi. "When one says 'Japanese jazz,'" Ono began, "one immediately thinks of jazz arrangements of Japanese folk songs, but Japanese jazz is the Japanese artist's expression of the Japanese heart through the Esperanto [universal language] of jazz. It is jazz that eats rice." Yui replied that "using scales from Japanese folk songs, or playing 'Yagi-bushi' with a four-beat rhythm" was not necessarily the only way to distinguish a national ethnicity in Japanese jazz. "The problem is," he went on, "what is Japanese?" Yui offered this answer to his own question:

When I listen to Akiyoshi Toshiko play the piano, I know that something comes out that is peculiar to Japanese, I know that it's not an American, but it's difficult to explain what that something is. I think that Takemitsu Tōru is the most Japanese of the great composers produced by Japan in the twentieth century, but what I like about his music is not, for instance, his use of the *biwa* or *shakuhachi*, but the fact that he has created music that really has the heart of Japanese people. If you ask what that is, in Takemitsu Tōru's case, it's his serious regard for "space" [*ma*]. Foreigners seem to have a sense of what is called "space," but not this. A temple bell always sings *"garan garan garan."* A Japanese temple's bell only makes one sound. The sound it makes reverberates and fades among the mountains. Before and after that there is a tremendous void, and if you're Japanese you feel that in your gut. Takemitsu Tōru's compositions call on that Japanese sympathy. . . . That [sense of space] is an element that must appear in various forms in Japanese jazz.

What impressed me as an example of a Japanese jazz performance in which that element appeared was Kikuchi Masabumi's piano solo on Charlie Mariano's composition "Rock Garden of Ryōan Temple" [from Mariano and Watanabe's 1967 LP *Iberian Waltz*]. *That* is a Japanese person's piano solo. Kikuchi's solo on this song has the so-called Japanese sense of "space," and constitutes a performance that the world's pianists probably couldn't imitate if you made them.[50]

Yui's emphasis on the amorphous concept of "space" echoed roughly contemporaneous neonationalist discourses within Japan's classical music community regarding the incorporation of "traditional" aesthetic principles. Composer Dan Ikuma, in particular, emphasized *ma* ("thinking in silences") as one principle on which a new national style would be based. Dan, a member of the self-described "nationalist" school of composers (including Akutagawa Yasushi and Mayuzumi Toshirō), expressed a vision that is echoed in Yui's formulations:

> It is not enough to write Japanese-sounding compositions using Western forms and harmonies. Those who have tried to do so have had no real or lasting success. The purpose of the composer, first of all, must be to write good music, and this we are not likely to have through mere rearrangement of traditional music for Western instruments. Something new, but at the same time fundamentally Japanese, must be created. . . . Western musical forms are based on Western ideals of logic and symmetry. These are not necessarily Eastern ideals. The East has its own ideals, and it is in relation to them that truly oriental musical forms must be evolved. In such forms will the Japanese Western-style music of the future be cast.[51]

Yui's definition of Japanese jazz was similar in that it went beyond previous conceptualizations of national style as a self-conscious combination of Japanese melodies and instrumentation with jazz harmonies and rhythms. Like composer Takemitsu Tōru, who has said, "I must not be trapped by traditional instruments any more than by all other kinds," Yui regarded Japanese jazz as not merely playing "Autumn Leaves" on the *koto,* but as a "living order that combines the fundamentally different musical phenomena of the West and Japan."[52] Yui contended that Japanese performers, even when working with Western instruments and Tin Pan Alley material, betray their ethnic identity by displaying a unique and unconscious sense of melodic construction, rhythm, and space. This "ethnicization" of jazz was, moreover, a universal phenomenon that Yui observed in the jazz of other nations. His theory of "jazz nationalism" thus maintained a faith in the much-proclaimed "universality" of jazz as a language, while incorporating nationalistic themes of fundamental ethnic difference and Japanese exceptionalism to distinguish Japanese jazz and accentuate its originality. As Yui wrote in liner notes for the CD reissue of the TAKT Jazz Series in 1996, "The movement for 'national [ethnic] independence' that surged through each country [in the sixties] became the motive power for what must be called 'jazz nationalism' [*jazu nashonarizumu*], 'to be free of America' [*Amerika banare*]."

Yui Shōichi was by no means the only person who expressed these views in the late sixties and early seventies. "I don't want to emphasize national ethnicity," keyboardist Satō Masahiko argued, "but I expect that the national ethnicity of Japanese must come out [in their music]." Openly advocating a "Japanese originality," he exhorted Japanese musicians to "create a music that only Japanese can play." In league with *shakuhachi* player Yamamoto Hōzan, Satō developed a performance workshop which he dubbed "Opening Untrodden Space" (19 August 1970), an attempt to "produce an untrodden space, which no one but Japanese musicians can discover."[53] Even veteran musicians hopped aboard the neonationalist bandwagon steered by their younger colleagues. As early as 1966, vibraphonist Sugiura Yōzō announced that "using Japanese instruments is not enough to produce Japanese jazz, so in addition to thoroughly studying Oriental scales I will create a Japanese rhythmic sense and chord work." Likewise, veteran tenor saxophonist Miyazawa Akira expressed a desire to develop a "rich tinge [of jazz] with a delicacy that only Japanese who have settled in Japan's climate [*fūdo*] can express. That is what I call originality." And although, as Yui would concede, Japanese jazz fans in general were reluctant to give their assent to the project, there were a few who joined in the clamor for a national style. For example, a Saitama college student, writing a review of Kikuchi Masabumi's LP *Dancing Mist,* exhorted native musicians to formulate "a new jazz concept . . . based on the Japanese skin sense [*hifu kankaku*]." By 1970, classical music critic Kurota Kyōichi believed he could proclaim the movement's success: "To say that Satō or Togashi's performances are so Japanese that foreigners cannot produce them is a vague way of putting it, but that is how I feel as a Japanese."[54]

What is striking about this discourse is the exclusivistic (or exclusionary) nature of its artistic ideal: a music that "only Japanese can play," that "foreigners cannot imitate." Such a stance represented no less than an attempt to alter the aesthetic standards by which Japanese jazz artists were judged by Japanese and Western listeners, and by which they judged themselves. After decades of playing by—and, in their own estimation, too often failing to measure up to—the aesthetic principles enshrined in a canon defined by Americans, Japanese jazz artists and aficionados were attempting to formulate a new aesthetic for judging their own work, one which did not entail comparisons with American achievements in the art. After all, whom could America offer to compare to Yamamoto Hōzan, whose bamboo flute improvisations represented for some an inimitable Japanese contribution to the idiom?[55] In the plaintive, shimmering tone of Yamamoto's *shakuhachi* could be heard the sound of revolution: no less than an artistic revolt against the hegemony of American jazz was afoot, coincident with the Japanese left's strident critiques of American-style industrial capitalism and imperialist brutality in Southeast Asia. The revolutionary spirit of the age was best conveyed by the album titles of two of its leading lights, Takayanagi Masayuki and Togashi Masahiko: *Independence* and *We Now Create*.[56]

Blues for the "Yellow Negro"

To be convincing and decisive, aesthetic revolution in the jazz community had to entail the discovery of a deeply expressive, *Japanese* artistic vernacular, analogous to the blues as a central, defining element of African American expressive culture. Japanese jazz aficionados read copiously the emerging black nationalist writings on jazz, especially those of Amiri Baraka (at that time known as LeRoi Jones), and monitored the activities of an Afrocentric jazz vanguard. Baraka's enormously influential and sweeping history of black American music, *Blues People* (1963), characterized blues as a "blood ritual" unavailable to nonblacks (and thus necessarily slighted by middle-class blacks attempting to be assimilated into the white mainstream):

> Blues as an autonomous music had been in a sense inviolable. There was no clear way into it, *i.e.*, its production, not its appreciation, except as concomitant with what seems to me to be the peculiar social, cultural, economic, and emotional experience of a black man in America. The idea of a white blues singer seems an even more violent contradiction of terms than the idea of a middle-class blues singer. The materials of blues were not available to the white American, even though some strange circumstance might prompt him to look for them. It was as if these materials were secret and obscure, and blues a kind of ethnohistoric rite as basic as blood.

In Baraka's theory, jazz, though most certainly rooted in blues, was still only an accessible dilution of the primary emotive vocabulary that reflected a peculiarly African American historical experience and sensibility:

> Jazz made it possible for the first time for something of the legitimate feeling of Afro-American music to be imitated successfully. . . . Or rather, jazz enabled *separate* and *valid* emotional expressions to be made that were based on older traditions of Afro-American music *that were clearly not a part of it*. The Negro middle class would not have a music if it were not for jazz. The white man would have no access to

blues. It was a music capable of reflecting not only the Negro and a black America but a white America as well. . . .

. . . The emergence of the white [jazz] player meant that Afro-American culture had already become the expression of a particular kind of American experience, and what is most important, that this experience was available intellectually, that it could be learned.

In *Blues People* and his groundbreaking 1961 essay "Jazz and the White Critic," Baraka contended that the only emotionally valid music was that which reflected the changing social and psychological realities of its creators: "This music cannot be completely understood (in critical terms) without some attention to the attitudes which produced it. It is the philosophy of Negro music that is most important, and this philosophy is only partially the result of the sociological disposition of Negroes in America. . . . The music is the result of the attitude, the stance. Just as Negroes made blues and other people did not because of the Negro's peculiar way of looking at the world."[57]

When Yui Shōichi posed the question "what is Japanese?" he was attempting to define the "peculiar way of looking at the world" that could be identified with his national culture. When he spoke of a "serious regard for 'space,' " or the temple bell "reverberat[ing] and fad[ing] among the mountains," which all Japanese felt in their "guts," or of Takemitsu Tōru's evocations of "Japanese sympathy," he was seeking the expression of a separate, identifiable, and essentialized identity for Japan akin to that which Baraka heard in the blues of black Americans. (It was also a hopelessly nostalgic, *rural* ideal, articulated at a time when Japanese were more likely to live in cities and go their whole lives without ever experiencing physical or aesthetic "space," or ever hearing a temple bell echo through the mountains.) I do not mean to suggest that Yui and others derived their conceptualizations, or their craving for "Japaneseness," from Baraka and fellow black nationalists, but I do think that they found confirmation of the propriety and rectitude of their quest in the increasingly politicized and racialized discourse on jazz in 1960s America. Baraka "proved" for many the relevance of historical experience and ethnic difference in studying the music, and he wrote with a sense of rage and passion, not to mention an eloquence, that few jazz aesthetes could convincingly equal. Baraka presented his panoramic view of the blues as more a history of a people than a history of a music. I would argue that the musicians and aficionados under scrutiny here were on a quest that they viewed as similar in scope and magnitude to that of the black nationalists. They sought a parallel emotive vocabulary as socially relevant, as historically indigenous, and as rich in depth of feeling as blues, a vernacular that communicated a singular Japanese experience the way blues was said to communicate a singular African American experience, and which rooted their future artistic explorations in a legitimate native tradition.

Japanese observers could witness implementation of these ideas in the activities of the Chicago-based Association for the Advancement of Creative Musicians (thanks to the jazz press's unabated zeal for covering the *honba*). On the one hand dedicated to the artist's self-reliance, the performance of original works, and the creation of performance opportunities and venues detached from white-dominated institutions, the AACM also sought to "assert black identity" through music, to "change the very nature of aesthetic understanding," and to cultivate an Afrocentric "aesthetic spiritualism" that strengthened community bonds for social action.[58] Attempts by Japanese groups such as the New Century Music Workshop to bypass standard entertainment channels, to produce original, spiritually infused music, and to foster social responsibility actually predate the AACM's 1965 foundation, but, again, Japan's avant-garde doubtless found validation in their Chicago counterparts' activities. It might appear at first glance that the Japanese represented a challenge to the AACM's Afrocentric posture: were Japanese, like Euro-Americans, not likewise guilty of "stealing" jazz and diluting the Africanisms that the AACM sought to rediscover? On the contrary, Japanese observers seem not only to have accepted the Afrocentric premises but to have launched sympathetic, parallel quests to recoup and identify what was "Japanese" in Japanese jazz. The Japanese search for "roots" need not impugn assertions of jazz's African character; in fact, it could serve the purpose of promoting a nonwhite solidarity.

The depth of Japanese interest in black nationalist discourse on jazz was such that jazz fans were as likely to read about the U.S. civil rights movement in music periodicals as in major newspapers. The "new pattern" for jazz criticism was informed by a sympathy for the politics of "Third World revolution," as exemplified in Aikura Hisato's *Perspectives of Contemporary Jazz* and Hiraoka Masaaki's *There Is No Other God but Jazz.*[59] At a time when particularly college-aged, neophyte jazz aficionados identified themselves with leftist radicalism, anti-war sentiment, and pro–civil rights politics, it was fashionable to affirm the basic affinities of the freedom-seeking "colored races" against the colonizing "white race." Today examples of racial prejudice and assertions of fundamental differences between Japanese and people of African descent are more well-publicized, particularly since Prime Minister Nakasone Yasuhiro's September 1986 suggestion that minorities bring down America's collective "intelligence level" made headlines. Historians, of course, are familiar with the nineteenth-century importation of social Darwinist concepts and Euro-American "scientific" racial hierarchies, which sank deep roots into Japanese intellectual circles. But historically speaking, discourses of racial difference are curiously flexible on demand. It was occasionally acknowledged that what Japanese and black people had in common was that they were not white. In the 1930s and early 1940s, for instance, the Japanese government promoted the idea of an "all-colored utopia," establishing contacts with radical black leaders such as Nation of Islam founder Elijah Mohammed and Robert Jordan (known in his day as "Harlem's Hitler"). One survey of images of Americans in postwar Japanese fiction found that "Negroes are always described favorably" because "both Negroes and Japanese feel suppressed by white peoples."[60]

One of the distinguishing traits of the postwar Japanese jazz community, in contrast to the social mainstream, was that the conventional racial hierarchy was inverted: the emerging consensus at the height of the "funky boom" favored black musicians as inherently bluesy and funky and thus superior players. That does not seem to have discouraged Japanese musicians and fans from trying to get funky themselves. The quandary was solved by a discursive loophole: Japanese, like people of African descent, were a "colored" race and therefore had more in common with black people than with white. "American whites have departed from copying Negroes and have created an excellent white jazz that only whites can play," *Swing Journal* declared on the eve of the "funky boom," "[but] the jazz that we Japanese create demonstrates a [closer] sensual affinity with Negro blues than white jazz does."[61] This passage is significant for two reasons: first, in keeping with the racial politics of the bebop revolution, it upholds "white jazz" and "black jazz" as legitimate, identifiable, and racially determined musical categories; second, it assumes a natural affinity between the "colored" races against the white race, an affinity that Japanese have alternately affirmed or denied throughout the twentieth century. In any case, these twin assumptions—that music can be classified by race, and that "colored" races have natural affinity—foreshadowed the racialist character of the more fully articulated neonationalist jazz discourse of the late 1960s. After all, if categories such as "white jazz" and "black jazz" were legitimate, then why not "Japanese jazz"?

Japanese and black Americans, Yui contended, shared a history of cultural humiliation in the face of white Euro-American accomplishments: "While we were catching up with European cultures," he said at 1971 conference in Warsaw,

> we were astonished at everything being upside-down from ours. We were ashamed, because we realized we had lived in the least advanced country for many years. Then what we did was to throw away our

traditional customs and instead we absorbed more advanced customs from overseas.

This reminds me of the Negro culture in the United States. Just two years after the Negro slaves were emancipated in the United States, Emperor Meiji became the Emperor of Japan. So, the Japanese people and Black American people started for the New World, of which they never knew, almost at the same time. In their musical tradition, both did not have a harmony conception. Moreover, the music they had was on the pentatonic scale. . . . And those two peoples had to abandon their old traditions, of which they were ashamed when they compared them to the old European traditions. Subconsciously, this historical coincidence has induced us to feel some affinities between the Japanese and American Black people.

That is why we Japanese can easily understand everything the American Black people are doing.[62]

If Japanese, whom the eminent poet Terayama Shūji (1935–1983) called "yellow Negroes," had a natural affinity and a shared history of humiliation and white oppression with other "colored" peoples, then did it not stand to reason that "yellow Negroes" had a deep emotive vocabulary analogous to African American blues, an artistic language of resistance to the subsuming and homogenizing forces of cultural imperialism?[63]

Prominent musicians in Japan's jazz avant-garde sought to answer that very question in the affirmative. It was altogether appropriate that the creation of "Japanese jazz" was a project undertaken primarily by the avant-garde (although we have seen that Dixieland, swing, and hard bop musicians took stabs at it), for in the estimation of authors like Frank Kofsky and Amiri Baraka, the "New Thing" was the music most in touch with the essence of the blues, in form, in sound, and in spirit. In the often tortured sounds of John Coltrane and Albert Ayler, people heard echoes of the black slave's field hollers, the lynching victim's cries, the sonic embodiment of millions of personalities warped by centuries of injustice and oppression. "In a sense, the music depends for its form on the same references as primitive blues forms," Baraka insisted. "Music and musician have been brought, in a manner of speaking, face to face, *without the strict and often grim hindrances of overused Western musical concepts;* it is only the overall musical intelligence of the musician which is responsible for shaping the music. It is, for many musicians, a terrifying freedom."[64] Avant-garde music, because of its disregard for "Western" standards of melodic beauty and symmetry of form, directly conveyed the most immediate and personal ideas and emotions of the artist. It thus made sense that Japanese avant-gardists (such as Yamashita Yōsuke, famous for his late-sixties "blue note studies," and Satō Masahiko, who spoke of "abandoning European modes of thinking" and incorporating "Oriental thought" into his trio music) would lead the quest for the blues of the "yellow Negro."[65] Success in such a quest would render the authenticating standards of American jazz superfluous, and promised finally to bring down the referential aesthetic. "Japanese jazz" would be a new and independent standard, one which only ethnic Japanese could define, meet, or fully appreciate.

For some jazz musicians, this quest necessitated the rediscovery and incorporation of indigenous folk and classical musics, with which most were at best unfamiliar and at worst indifferent. No doubt the immersion in *hōgaku* (a nineteenth-century category that essentially lumped all indigenous musics together) and *min'yō* confirmed for them the basic musical and spiritual affinity of Japanese with America's "blues people." As the American singer and activist Paul Robeson famously declared, pentatonic scales predominated folk music systems around the world, constituting the basic sonic components of Japanese and African American musics, among others. Robeson argued that his research confirmed the existence of "a world reservoir, a universal source of basic folk themes . . . , from which the entire folk music is derived and to which they have a direct or indirect tie." This "ancient body of world folk music" was linked by the universality of the pentatonic, "which belongs to no nation or race, [but] marks rather a stage of the development of the musical consciousness of mankind." The affinities of African-derived musics and Asian folk musics, as described by Robeson, have been a foundational article of faith among Asian American musician/activists such as Fred Ho (formerly Houn), Jon Jang, and Francis Wong, who prominently cite Robeson's influence on their conception of "sorrow songs." (Indeed these musicians quote Robeson's words as scripture, although like most quotes from scripture, they are selective: their political stances apparently necessitate highlighting the similarities between Asian and African musics, and ignoring Robeson's inclusion of Celtic, Icelandic, Russian, and other "white" musics in his theory.)[66]

The musicological kinship of Japanese musics to blues is further denoted by the importance of melismatic ornamentation and glissando in vocal and instrumental music, the instrumental mimicry of natural sounds and vocal timbres, the elasticity of form and meter, and the subservience of music to the demands of the verbal text. Like blues, Japanese folk music was often based in the "functional" communal work song, its rhythms thus rooted in the rhythms of manual labor. There are numerous examples of theatrical, folk, and classical musics in which percussion predominates: the music of fisherfolk in Okinawa and Amami is richly syncopated, with either consistent or occasional accents on "offbeats." Contrapuntal vocal lines ("call-and-response") are important to festival and dance musics, as they are in blues and southern American gospel. Finally, although classical musics favored *kata*, unalterable conventional patterns, there were folk forms in which improvisation played a role, such as the original *shakuhachi* hymns of itinerant Zen monks.[67] Once sensitized to these resemblances, jazz musicians found it not at all implausible that a Japanese analogue to blues existed and awaited rediscovery.

Yet this raises one of the more ironic aspects of "Japanese jazz" as a inherently *exclusionary* concept: even when these musicological affinities were acknowledged and indigenous musics rendered less alien, Japanese jazz musicians whose training consisted entirely of Western harmony, melody, and theory had to put as much effort into learning about their heritage as any foreigner did. Like Baraka's American Negro, Japanese purportedly had "a peculiar way of looking at the world," reflected in music. "It would be [quite] difficult for an American musician to learn to play Japanese music," pianist Imada Masaru insisted. "The problem is that the Americans have more to learn than the instrument itself. They have to learn the Japanese way of thinking, looking at life, and that sort of thing." But Yamashita admitted frustrations: "I keep asking myself why I have to play the piano, which represents Western culture and was developed with a different spiritual background. Why does the piano attract me? I realize when I listen to Oriental music that the piano is inconvenient and limited. So I love and hate it at the same time. I tried to learn how to play *shamisen* and to sing *kota* [sic]. I also tried to read books by [musicologist] Fumio Koizumi to learn authentic Japanese music. I am still trying to find an answer."[68] A Yamamoto Hōzan, fluent in *hōgaku* yet acclaimed as the representative of a national jazz style, was a virtual anomaly in postwar Japan. (Tsurumi Shunsuke and others have remarked that *foreign* students engaging in "reverse cultural borrowing" practically keep traditional music alive.)[69] Moreover, the musical fusions initiated by Charlie Mariano, Tony Scott, and Dave Brubeck (whose 1964 LP *Jazz Impressions of Japan* paired compositions with haiku in an attempt to convey "minute but lasting impressions, somewhat in the manner of classical haiku, wherein the . . . poem only *suggests* the feeling"), among others, indicate that despite the exclusionary rhetoric "playing Japanese" neither came naturally to Japanese nor was it ever beyond the capacity of foreigners. Finally, although representative recordings from the jazz neo-nationalists' heyday, such as Satō Masahiko's *Palladium* and *Transformation '69/'71* or Togashi Masahiko's *We Now Create*, make copious use of "space," so do contemporaneous recordings by the Art Ensemble of Chicago. Simply put, Japanese had no monopoly on pentatonic melodies, asymmetry, or space in their jazz. They created moving, personal, and exciting music, but the "Japanese" connections between Yamashita Yōsuke's pianistic thunderstorms, Watanabe Sadao's blithe pop-rock fusions, and Togashi Masahiko's quietly breathing meditations were too tenuous to be credible.

The Fate of "Japanese Jazz"

If neonationalist assertions of a unique national contribution to the jazz idiom remained unconvincing for most audiences, there was no denying that the jazz community as a whole had reached an important and heady stage in its history. As the 1960s came to a close, many believed that the decades-old project of "catching up" to and replicating American jazz had finally ended and the "dawn of Japanese jazz" was at hand. Freddy Santamaria's report "Du Swing chez les Samouraïs" in France's *Jazz Magazine* conceded that many Japanese musicians continued to work on replicating American achievements, but insisted that there was now a substantial number who were self-consciously "breaking away" from American influence and "blazing a difficult path that combines swinging rhythmic propulsion with folkloric contributions."[70]

The response to jazz musicians' new confidence and creative energy was encouraging. As a new decade dawned, recording industry and fan interest in domestic jazz was high enough to merit "boom" status, and bands such as the George Ōtsuka Trio, the Hino Terumasa Quintet, and Watanabe Sadao's ever-evolving jazz-bossa-pops quintet packed clubs and concert halls wherever they played.[71] As Japanese artists began incorporating electric instrumentation and rock rhythms into their jazz, they drew more attention from rock audiences previously uninterested in jazz. Hino and Watanabe, two artists in the forefront of electrification, became high-profile media stars who attracted more mainstream listeners to jazz: Hino as a teen idol, and Watanabe as the jazz ambassador on radio and television. "Crossover" or fusion music became increasingly popular in the seventies, propelling Watanabe and bands such as Native Son, T-Square, and Casiopea to stardom. Moreover, some observed that while the number of jazz clubs and coffeehouses in Japan's so-called "provincial regions" remained small, there was steady growth in the number of fan clubs, college bands, and jazz festivals. The inclusion of a jazz festival as part of the 1970 Ōsaka World Exposition of 1970, a major display of Japan's newfound affluence, was hailed by aficionados as a major coup and an ideal venue for demonstrating to the world Japan's hard-won prominence as a "jazz country" (*jazu kuni*). The Expo also provided the opportunity for Akiyoshi Toshiko's return and reconciliation with her homeland, ending a five-and-a-half year absence. Herself on the edge of a major breakthrough in her career, she lavished praise on the progress that jazz had made in Japan since her bitter departure. Finally, with numerous offers from around the world for professional and amateur Japanese bands to perform at festivals, and invitations for individuals to join the bands of luminaries such as Elvin Jones, Art Blakey, and Sonny Rollins, the international prestige of Japan's jazz community had never been higher. Guitarist Kawasaki Ryō and Ginparis alumni Kikuchi Masabumi and Hino Terumasa were able to settle and make respectable livings in the Big Apple, the world's most competitive jazz environment, while avant-garde trumpeter Oki Itaru made a name as an expatriate in Paris. The only thing that handicapped Japanese jazz musicians on the world stage, Santamaria concluded, was the difficulty of pronouncing their names.[72]

Predictably, perhaps, the enthusiasm for the domestic product and the concomitant interest in creating a national style waned substantially in the 1970s. By 1971 one writer claimed that the "Japanese jazz world as a whole is losing a clear sense of direction and purpose."[73] The same might be said of the nation as a whole, for high-profile political corruption, the student movement's failure to realize revolutionary change, and the substantial social, economic, and environmental consequences of the single-minded "high-speed growth" campaign haunted the population. In a 1977 *Down Beat* article Satō Masahiko surmised that the decline of student radicalism was an important determinant of the jazz community's fortunes in the seventies:

> During [the] 1970 jazz boom, underground jazz rose to an epochal height. At that time Japan was in the midst of opposing the 1970 Japan–U.S. Security Pact. The young Japanese confronted the established authority, applauding any movement that might lessen the strength of the established authority and supporting rock music and free style jazz.
> . . . Many newcomers appeared one after the other and the next epoch seemed to guarantee a ripening of jazz. But the time came when this enthusiastic period came to an end.
> The opposition movement against the 1970 Japan–U.S. Security Pact was effectively halted. The young people returned to the campus frustrated, and in due course graduated to employment in enterprises that supported the very power structure that they had regarded with enmity. They became "salary men" and lost their vitality to maintain a "jazz energy."

In Satō's estimation the "progress" made by native artists was overstated: "Although the critics claim that Japanese jazz has attained world standards, the actual achievements seem small." Nevertheless, he conceded, the jazz scene in the mid-seventies was at "its peak of prosperity. . . . Since 1970 . . . the jazz market has attracted a new generation of listeners by introducing commercial jazz, decorated to please the amateur listener."[74] Ultimately, Japanese jazz artists were not to lose the artistic and commercial victories they had accumulated in the late sixties.

While the idea of a national style noticeably lost momentum, it did not disappear entirely. Critic Yū Masahiko remarked on the "contemporary breakdown of Japanese jazz" by stating that concept was "an expression of the latent discriminatory consciousness that Japanese have," and concluded, "we must abandon the infiltrating concepts and fantasies about our own country's jazz that we have come to embrace."[75] But some refused to relinquish the ideal, and the popular culture seemed to encourage its continued survival. The 1970s witnessed the apex of "commercialised expression[s] of modern Japanese nationalism"; prolific treatises on the social, spiritual, psychological, linguistic, and physiological differences that defined a "Japanese essence" saturated the market and topped the best-seller lists. Peter Dale cites one survey's estimates that of the seven hundred titles published on the theme of Japanese identity between 1946 and 1978, 25 percent were published between 1976 and 1978.[76]

The work of two successful "representative" musicians, percussionist Togashi Masahiko and pianist Akiyoshi Toshiko, kept the ideal of a Japanese style of jazz in circulation. Togashi defended his ideal of a national style against a perceived backlash: "For several years now, putting the word 'Japanese' before the word 'jazz' has fallen in disfavor," he wrote in 1975, "but I would like once again to try to create 'Japanese jazz.' " In January 1970 Togashi suffered a major spinal injury that left him paralyzed from the waist down.[77] During his period of convalescence, he conceded that he had put much thought into his "destiny" as a Japanese who plays jazz. "I expect that there is something called a 'Japanese natural sense,' that foreigners see, that Japanese or anyone can hear, something from which one can take the feeling that this is a natural sense peculiar to Japanese," he ventured, "and I started noticing that something close to that was within my feelings toward my own music." Citing the inspiration he had derived from composer Takemitsu Tōru and from Akiyoshi Toshiko's composition "Kogun," Togashi announced his own artistic intentions: "Lately I have been thinking, isn't the Japanese heart [kokoro] something that can be created and expressed with jazz? In other words, I want to try to create a music so that Japanese, foreigners, or anybody who hears it can feel that 'this is something peculiar to Japanese people.' "[78]

Togashi's injury fundamentally reshaped his musical conception. As a conventional kit drummer he had always exemplified an unusual sensitivity to textures and colors, and had developed a readily identifiable and utterly personal rhythmic feel that owed more to the jarring, asymmetrical conception of pianist Thelonious Monk than to any jazz drummer. But, no longer able to play a conventional trap set, Togashi reinvented himself as a "percussionist," bringing his talents as a colorist to the forefront. He constructed a modified, multitextured battery of percussion instruments to augment the conventional kit. By the mid-seventies Togashi and his Experimental Sound Space Group had established a firm recorded legacy of music with a contemplative, ethereal flavor, "orientalized" through his extensive use of Asian wind and percussion instruments. But Togashi's efforts to construct a Japanese jazz did not stop at pillaging *hōgaku:* "I do not think that preserving the basis of tradition is the only path for establishing Japanese originality." Rather, he emphasized a unique and unconscious sense of rhythm and space as a distinguishing feature that ensured the Japanese identity of his jazz.

> In Oriental thought because there is existence [*yū*] there is nothingness [*mu*]. Because there is nothingness there is existence. . . . So by not playing a sound, you can make a combination of sounds, by making nothingness you create—totally different from Western thinking. So American and Japanese "concepts of space" are different.[79]
>
> Regarding my music, it's often written that one can feel a peculiar Japanese 'interval' [*ma*] or 'space' [*kūkan*], but in fact I'm not especially conscious that I'm creating such a thing; it's not an interval or space of which I have a theoretical grasp, it's not something I've completed studying. It's a condition that I first notice after it's been pointed out in writing, when I listen to it again myself. . . . These elements, the parts that I cannot explain theoretically, that is what I believe to be the Japanese natural sense.

Togashi added that there were fundamental rhythmic differences between American jazz and Japanese jazz: "Americans' jazz rhythmic sense is rough compared to that of Japanese. . . . My rhythmic sense is more complicated, I try to express the smallest parts in detail. No matter what I do, there's a side of me that can't become as rough as Americans' [rhythm]." He went on, "I would be happy if you listened to my 'Song for Myself' and could feel that it does not swing like American jazz, that it is fundamentally different." Togashi concluded, "I believe that the awareness that my music is fundamentally different from American jazz will become the basis on which the originality of Japanese jazz will be established."[80]

Togashi's cryptic explanations of Japanese jazz combined relatively concrete musicological analysis with mystic conceptions of "Japaneseness," in an attempt to win over a public that he believed had grown largely skeptical of a national style. But if the critical response to Akiyoshi Toshiko's ascendancy on the international stage is any indication, Togashi was preaching to the choir. For it was in Akiyoshi's oeuvre that Japanese jazz aficionados believed a true expression of the national essence had been achieved. The press hailed her for "communicating the Japanese heart to the world" and for expressing "the peculiar Japanese soul."[81]

Having moved from New York to Los Angeles in the summer of 1972, Akiyoshi and her second husband, tenor saxophonist/flautist Lew Tabackin, assembled a group of studio musicians for weekly rehearsals to perform Akiyoshi's ever-growing book of compositions. In early 1974 the sixteen-piece band started performing in public and recorded the classic album *Kogun*. The Akiyoshi-Tabackin Big Band was initially marketed to a Japanese audience, but with critic Leonard Feather's advocacy the band gained notoriety and soon rivaled the Mel Lewis–Thad Jones orchestra as the most popular and accomplished modern big band in the world. Featuring Akiyoshi's compositions exclusively, the orchestra almost single-handedly kept the big band genre vibrant in the 1970s: as Feather pointed out, even Duke Ellington and Akiyoshi's mentor Charles Mingus had not dared to perform their own works exclusively. The Akiyoshi-Tabackin band steadily accrued favorable recognition, and by 1978 had toppled the Lewis-Jones orchestra from first place in the *Down Beat* critics' poll Big Band category. By 1980 Akiyoshi had become the "Triple Crown Queen," the first woman and the first non-American to win in three categories (Big Band, Arranger, and Composer) in any jazz poll.

Akiyoshi's compositions represent a variety of styles, textures, and influences, but her "orientalized" pieces, featuring *taiko* drums, vocal textures from the *nō* theater, and Tabackin's eerily "oriental" flute work, have received the most attention in Japan and elsewhere. Although Akiyoshi had never publicly entered the debate about creating a national style of jazz, she made it clear that her music was in part an expression of her identity as a Japanese, and that her potential contribution to the music would entail the incorporation of her Japanese "language." Her composition "A-10-2059932"—her alien registration number—symbolized her refusal to forsake her Japanese citizenship. "Kogun" ("solitary soldier") was Akiyoshi's tribute to two soldiers, Onoda Hiro and Yokoi Shōichi, who were discovered hiding in the Philippines and Guam in the early 1970s, oblivious to the end of the Pacific War. The extended work "Minamata" drew attention to the plight of the victims of mercury poisoning in a fishing village not too distant from Akiyoshi's ancestral home. "Children of the Temple Ground" invoked images of religious festivals. In a body of work that she has often characterized as descriptive or "programmatic," Akiyoshi attempted to tell stories from her own personal experience and from the historical experiences of her homeland. As the principal representative of the "Japanese voice" in jazz, Akiyoshi became a well-known and respected figure in her homeland—a mere decade after a Japanese promoter, citing her anonymity among the Japanese public, turned down her application to tour Japan.[82]

Authenticating "Japanese Jazz"

It would be foolhardy to suggest that Akiyoshi's ascendancy completely erased either what Satō Masahiko called Japan's "inferiority complex" or widespread feelings that "jazz played by Japanese is not genuine."[83] Had she not received such enthusiastic praise from American musicians, fans, and critics, it is reasonable to assume from historical experience that Japanese aficionados would not have recognized her talents. Kurosawa's cinematic oeuvre was regarded as nothing special until his films won prizes in Europe; Ōe Kenzaburō's books did not appear on best-seller lists until he won the Nobel Prize in 1994 (after which I observed firsthand a rush on the bookstores, which could not keep Ōe's books in stock). Likewise, the Japanese jazz community continues to reserve special status for those talents of whom America approves. Nevertheless, the nation's jazz fans felt a sense of elation that a Japanese was duly recognized as an authentic jazz innovator. The jazz community's duty to country had been fulfilled, and jazz in Japan as a "progressing," evolutionary art had reached its final stage.

There is no question in my mind that Japanese artists were playing fresh, original music in the 1960s and 1970s. But it is fair to ask to what extent that music represented a national style or, put another way, to what extent the *idea* of a national style empowered them to erect alternative standards of authenticity. Most of the truly great jazz artists who emerged in this period developed their talents in the context of a burgeoning, politicized left-wing neonationalism that was flourishing in all of the arts. Artists in all media were reacting to what they perceived as the gradual and invidious erosion of Japan's aesthetic sensibilities, caused by the steady stream of American cultural imports. While these artists felt free to draw inspiration from a variety of cultural sources, their concern was to forge a "national cinema," a "national theater," a "national music," to assert a recognizably Japanese voice through art. It was no accident that this artistic neonationalism coincided with a national effort to attain affluence; indeed, much of the rhetoric of national "development" was echoed in these artistic movements. Just as patriotism was invoked to motivate the Japanese government, industry, and labor to pull off an "economic miracle," it was also invoked to motivate artists. Cultural nationalism provoked the jazz community to redouble its efforts to attain the long-cherished goal of parity with America's jazz legacy, and seemed to give jazz musicians the confidence they needed to emerge from the shadows of their American heroes, to take creative chances, and to proclaim their own aesthetic and spiritual standards.

The idea of "Japanese jazz" remains marginal but it is hardly dead. As recently as March 1999, the Japan Society's "Jazz from Japan" series presented a concert of Nakamura Akikazu's Trio Kokō ("innovative jazz performed on the shakuhachi and koto"), suggesting that the exoticism of the idea can still draw concert goers. In the liner notes to his maiden release with his multinational fusion ensemble Randooga, Satō Masahiko writes:

Since its birth jazz has evolved under the influence of other musical forms and by taking in a variety of modes of expression. These various musical influences include western classical music and modern and contemporary music as well as folk music of the Latin American countries, Brazil, India and the Arab world. When one considers how nearly universal these influences have been, it is therefore a little odd to think that one never hears of something from Japan (Japanese traditional music) having brought about a revolution in jazz.

This is perhaps due to formidable language problems, or to the closed nature of Japanese society, but it is perhaps more accurate to say that the biggest single factor has been the absence of a movement aiming to improve communication between traditional music and jazz, a movement willing to commit itself to jazz, while using the special characteristics of that traditional music.

Happily, I am a jazz musician, but at the same time I have accumulated considerable experience with traditional Japanese music through my activities as a composer, arranger and collaborator in many projects.

As a result of these experiments I have come to believe strongly that traditional music has the potential to make a major contribution to jazz at a time when some fear that it may have reached an evolutionary dead end.

By bringing musicians of different backgrounds together and using elements from traditional music within the jazz idiom, I have thought perhaps a new source of energy could be found. Now with this fantastic line-up of musicians [for this performance Randooga included Wayne Shorter, Ray Anderson, Alex Acuna, Umezu Kazutoki, and Nana Vasconcellos] I have the chance to try to bring this idea to life.

It has been very challenging to find a common means of expression that would allow musicians from outside of Japan to understand the special characteristics of traditional Japanese music, but I think we will manage to find the true intention of the music from between the lines of what may otherwise be inadequate scores, since all the players who have been kind enough to join me in Randooga are from the front ranks of their contemporaries.

If by the fusion of these different elements we may discover things that the composer himself never foresaw and thereby generate new musical excitement I will consider this to be a great success.[84]

There indeed is an undeniably *gagaku*-like texture to the music on Randooga's *Select Live under the Sky '90* (particularly "Seine Dragging Song"), suggesting that Satō's explorations of his country's musical heritage may yet yield undiscovered territories. Ironically, however, foreigners may be more intrigued by the possibilities of "Japanese jazz" than Japanese are. In the documentary *Tokyo Blues*, trumpeter Mike Price, a veteran of the Akiyoshi-Tabackin Orchestra who has resided in Japan since the early nineties, expresses a desire to incorporate traditional Japanese aesthetic principles into his jazz; *shakuhachi* player John Kaizan Neptune similarly regards "Japanese tradition" as a source of inspiration whose potential has yet to be fully discovered. John Zorn has also incorporated textures and imagery that evoke Japan into his own quirky vision (most notably on *Ganryū Island*, a sometimes comical 1984 duet with *tsugaru shamisen* master Satō Michihiro). Asian American jazz artists such as Mark Izu, Jon Jang, and Francis Wong have also sustained a significant movement in part by drawing on Asian musics and "sorrow songs" to produce what some regard as an identifiable ethnic style.

But I insist that national styles such as "Japanese jazz" are mere phantasms that artificially homogenize an unruly assemblage of highly individualistic artistic voices. The artists regarded as "representative" of Japanese jazz succeeded in forging strong individual styles, but Yamashita Yōsuke's blistering attack at the piano could not have been more different from Togashi Masahiko's meditative evocations of a primordial spiritualism, or from Watanabe Sadao's sunny excursions into Brazilian and African music. Yamashita no more represents a uniform, national or cultural approach to jazz than do Cecil Taylor or Sonny Rollins. As an artist Yamashita is free to use Japanese scales in his compositions, or to perform with the acclaimed postmodern *taiko* ensemble Kodō, but he is equally at liberty to incorporate Kurdish music into his work (as on his 1990s albums *Kurdish Dance, Dazzling Days,* and *Ways of Time*). Why would anyone try to label such an eclectic artist as representative of one nation's style? Just as the jazz aesthetic would have it, the individual voice conquered all attempts to essentialize or classify it. In sum, cultural nationalism may have motivated Japanese jazz artists to be more creatively assertive, but, happily, it did not overwhelm the individuality and distinctiveness of their respective artistic concepts.

If the idea of Japanese jazz failed ultimately to subsume the individual artistic visions of such talented musicians, it also failed to alter the aesthetic standards by which Japanese judged themselves. One advantage that national style promised was a new aesthetic, a self-referential standard of authenticity, which would render comparisons with American jazz meaningless. But no such aesthetic is in operation; perhaps the failure to fully develop and articulate such an aesthetic contributed to its ultimate demise. In the mid-1970s, well after the aesthetic revolution was to have taken place, Japanese musicians, critics, and fans were still expounding on what their jazz lacked when compared to American examples: for instance, stars such as Watanabe Sadao and George Ōtsuka argued that, although Japanese soloists could play with anyone in the world, there were still no great *bands* with distinctive sounds that could compare with, say, Weather Report.[85] There was always some way in which native jazz did not measure up, and the historical propensity to try to "measure up" to an external American referent remained firmly entrenched.

Ultimately, the unquestioned hegemony of the American jazz legacy has been proven in the marketplace. One reason that Japan became known as "jazz heaven" in the seventies was that its record companies produced more reissues of classic American albums (not to mention new recordings by Americans) than any other nation. By contrast, within a few years of their initial release, it became impossible to find copies of classic albums such as Satō Masahiko's *Palladium* or Togashi Masahiko's *We Now Create*. Each of these albums has been reissued on CD once in the 1990s, but each has been allowed to go out of print within two years. A two-year run is common for Japanese releases, but catalog titles on the Blue Note, Prestige, and Riverside labels, for instance, are *never* allowed to remain out of print. They appear dependably in increasingly opulent and reverential packaging: Sonny Clark's *Cool Struttin'* and Art Blakey's *Moanin'* perennially crowd native artists out of the racks. It is symbolic that in every record store I have ever been to in Japan, Japanese jazz artists' releases are placed together in a separate corner, at the end of the jazz section (although, as a collector of jazz by Japanese artists, I must concede the convenience of the practice). There may be no widely acknowledged national style, but marginality in record store racks is physical evidence of the assumed separateness of jazz "made in Japan." The hegemony of Clark and Blakey over Satō and Togashi is determined by the Japanese consumer: there is no malevolent imposition of taste by American companies or artists on Japanese audiences, but rather a decided preference among those audiences for what they feel to be the "genuine article," a preference which has been consistent throughout history and has fed the ambivalence toward the authenticity of native artists. In the average Japanese jazz aficionado's collection, the odd recording by a native artist remains as rare and exotic as it is in an American's collection. There can be no denying that thirty years after Japanese artists attempted to play the ethnic trump card in their own favor, being Japanese remains a commercial handicap for jazz artists in their own country.

POSTLUDE: J-JAZZ AND
THE FIN DE SIÈCLE BLUES

In January 1995 the late Yui Shōichi invited me to attend the annual *Swing Journal* Awards Ceremony, at which, I was stunned to note, record company executives took home all the prizes. Corporate "suits" walked on stage to accept album awards ostensibly going to Chick Corea and Ōnishi Junko. The only jazz artist who actually received an award was Pooh-san, pianist Kikuchi Masabumi, who flew in from New York to accept the annual Nanri Fumio Prize for significant artistry by a Japanese. When I asked Yui about these practices, he replied that *Swing Journal* bestows the awards directly to the recording companies to "get advertising." He personally disavowed this modus operandi, but that's how things are done.

Things started to make sense now. For months I had been struck by the fact that *SJ*, which reviews hundreds of new and reissued recordings each month, practically never gives a bad review. Jake Mori, a member of the magazine's editorial staff, concedes that its editorial policy rarely allows for worse than a three-and-a-half (out of five) star rating. He admitted feeling troubled that readers do not trust *SJ* reviews. But the problem is not unique to that publication. Uchida Kōichi, historian, vibraphonist, and publisher of the independent newsletter *Jazz World,* explains that positive reviews of a particular record company's releases result in substantial advertising revenue from said company. Furthermore, critics who write positive reviews are then offered jobs with those companies, writing liner notes for future releases: in other words, writing favorable reviews literally pays off for the critics. Isono Teruo, who worked for *SJ* for thirty years, admits partial responsibility for this state of affairs. He used to be a harsh critic—a trumpeter whose work he trashed once punched him in the face and broke his glasses—but as a member of the magazine's editorial staff he collected money from musicians who had scored well in *SJ* polls, thus setting a precedent of exchanging favorable attention for advertising revenue. He now disparages *SJ* as an "advertising magazine" that exists not for musicians but for recording and audio equipment companies. Jazz critics in Japan repeatedly express a yearning for the critical ideal we (theoretically) cherish in the United States: the honest evaluation of artistic products, with the purpose of educating consumers inundated with choices, independent of the marketing concerns of record companies. But they seem to think that they are powerless to change their situation. The bottom line is still the bottom line.

So wide-ranging are the tentacles of Japan's cultural industry that they have instigated "movements" that masquerade as artist-initiated. Evidence of the frequent usurpation of artistic initiative by corporate concerns abounds, perhaps nowhere more obviously than in Paddle Wheel Records' "Jazz Restoration in Japan" (*Nippon jazu ishin*). With great fanfare, Paddle Wheel proclaimed the Restoration in the spring of 1994, presenting as evidence a new recording of some of the nation's most promising young jazz stars. Like all proper cultural upheavals, the Jazz Restoration in Japan was announced via a grandiose "Declaration," penned (in both Japanese and English) by the eminent jazz critic Segawa Masahisa.

> It was in 1982 when a trumpeter by the name of Wynton Marsalis made his dramatic appearance in the American jazz scene and formed his own quintet with his older brother, Branford. Ever since, under the leadership of Wynton, a large number of young, talented jazzmen, mostly in their teens and 20s, made their debuts from all over the U.S., including New Orleans. They helped instill unprecedented vigor into the world of jazz. It is a well-known fact that these young lions are challenging the diverse directions of jazz by injecting straightforward four-beat acoustic sounds and experimenting with innovative new techniques. The long-awaited younger generation of jazzmen are finally emerging in Japan also. Leading young players got together in the U.S., including drummer Yoichi Kobayashi, who went to the U.S. twice during the 1980s to form "Good Fellas" with Vincent Herring . . . , drummer Masahiko Osaka who, while a student at Berklee Music School, toured the States with Delfeayo Marsalis and other musicians, and Makoto Kuriya who developed the unique X-Bar theory while studying in the U.S. After returning to Japan, they actively recruited new players, used them to form their own regular groups, and began to perform vigorously. Numerous talented new musicians emerged in Japan. . . . Almost concurrently, they all began to perform live. One young player after another based in Nagoya took part in the tandem quintet of Osaka [Masahiko] and Hara [Tomonao], and helped to stimulate jazz activities in the local areas. Yoichi Kobayashi, calling himself "Art Blakey of Japan," remains active by forming an all-rookie "Good Fellas, Japanese version." . . . Today's jazz restoration in Japan, led by

the young lions born after 1960, is about to enter a new phase: a full-fledged war.[1]

Clearly there is much hope and hype invested in the Jazz Restoration in Japan, which obscure its commercial and artistically conservative nature. In a promotional pamphlet, Kumagai Yoshihirō evoked the spirit of the 1960s neonationalist effort to develop an identifiable national style: "Some young musicians have said to me, 'At last, we feel that the era in which Japan learned jazz from America has ended. We want to go on to perform a jazz for Japanese, with a Japanese sensibility.' The young jazzmen who have come on the scene in the nineties are no longer catching up with 'American jazz.' . . . I think their jazz is fresh, hip, and energetic. On the night of 27 December 1993 [the date of the *Jam* recording], I witnessed the moment when 'Japanese jazz' was born."[2] Okazaki jazz fan Sugiura Shūichi is similarly enthusiastic, likening the Restoration to the effervescent American jazz culture of the 1950s and 1960s. Now that Japan is wealthy, he says, young Japanese can study the music seriously and still make a living, a situation conducive to revolutionary developments in the music to come. "You watch," he grinned, "this Japanese jazz is the *future*."

The Restoration must be explained in both commercial and artistic terms. On the one hand, the Jazz Restoration demonstrates the primacy of the culture industry in the creation—or, more appropriately, the manufacturing—of jazz music as commodified nostalgia in the contemporary world. Segawa, who has lent his considerable clout to publicize and support the Jazz Restoration, readily admits that it is as much a recording-industry-confected advertising campaign to attract younger audiences as it is an underground artistic upheaval. As a commercial campaign it is blatantly modeled on the U.S. "Young Lion" movement, which has effectively conferred an aura of aesthetic sophistication and respectability to the music industry in the 1980s and 1990s, while remaining profitable and satiating mass culture's lust for youthful models. It does appear to have worked. Young fashionably dressed and serious-minded native artists do seem to have generated a new audience for jazz in both the United States and Japan.

The most obvious Japanese example is that of pianist Ōnishi Junko; though not formally a member of Paddle Wheel's Restoration, her fame sets her whole generation aglow and her leadership of a workshop for young native musicians makes her emblematic. Backed by a multimillion yen promotional campaign that markets her as a jazz sex symbol and keeps her leggy image prominent in publications and record stores, she has appeared on the popular television talk show *Tetsuko's Room,* and her personal life is splattered in the headlines of trashy sports tabloids, where she is dubbed the "beautiful pianist" (*bijin pianisuto*). As a member of the Blue Note Records stable and the first Japanese to headline a prestigious weeklong gig at New York's Village Vanguard, she has brought considerable acclaim to her generation. The fans appreciate it: in what must be the most stunning upset ever in jazz circles, in 1995 *Swing Journal* readers voted Ōnishi "Most Popular Japanese Artist in History" and "Most Popular Jazzwoman in History," besting Akiyoshi Toshiko, Hino Terumasa, and Watanabe Sadao in the former category, and Billie Holiday, Sarah Vaughan, Ella Fitzgerald, and Mary Lou Williams in the latter.

For all the hype, Ōnishi happens to be a very talented and expansive artist: if her Vanguard date with Wynton Marsalis's rhythm team of Herlin Riley and Reginald Veal indicated her acceptance into the neoclassicist fold, she is more willing than many in that club to tackle the compositions and musical systems of Ornette Coleman and Charles Mingus. Her partnership with the leading avant-garde altoist Hayashi Eiichi suggests a breadth of musical vision rejected by many of her colleagues. Which brings us to the artistic aspects of such revivals: besides moving units, these movements aspire to "educate" their neophyte audiences, to inculcate (and ossify) a sense of jazz's core aesthetic values and stylistic traits. The aspiring neoclassicist is theoretically required to maintain "a careful balance between the modernist ideology of continuous innovation and an insistence on the priority of tradition,"[3] but the latter imperative invariably predominates. Despite the rhetoric about a new national style, the Restoration is essentially the Japanese version of a commercially viable American revivalist movement and thus an inherently conservative endeavor artistically.

It is worth noting in this regard the choice of words in Paddle Wheel's bilingual publicity campaign. It uses the English word *restoration* as a translation for the Japanese word *ishin*, which more properly means "renewal" or "renovation." The more literal choice for a Japanese equivalent for *restoration* would be *fukkō*, which in Japanese political tradition described the restoration of de facto imperial rule, the only truly legitimate authority, in the face of usurpation by courtiers and military strongmen. It is likely that *ishin* was chosen rather than *fukkō*, and the English *restoration* rather than *renewal*, because in general historical discourse the nineteenth-century political upheaval known in the West as the Meiji Restoration is called the *Meiji ishin* in Japanese. I would argue that the dissonance between *ishin* and *restoration* captures the essential paradox of the Jazz Restoration: *renewal* (*ishin*) implies not just retention but creative innovation,[4] whereas *restoration* (*fukkō*) suggests rectification, or the reassertion of an older, more legitimate order over a newer, illegitimate one. Rhetorically committed to taking the art of jazz into previously uncharted terrain (*ishin*), the Jazz Restoration in Japan comes off as little more than a conservative reaction against the avant-garde (*fukkō*), the principal aim of which is to re-enthrone and attract younger listeners to a particular style of jazz and a particular standard of authenticity (that of American jazz of the 1950s and 1960s). It is thus symbolic that the English word *restoration* is more descriptive of the movement's Americentric ideology and practice than the Japanese word *ishin* is.

The "restorationist" (as opposed to "renovationist") tendencies are clear in the Declaration itself: the legitimacy of the Restoration movement is asserted by locating its roots in "the birthplace of jazz," New Orleans; there is a not-so-subtle aversion to the "diverse directions of jazz," and an obvious preference for a "straightforward four-beat acoustic" mainstream.[5] Moreover, the Declaration unashamedly reinscribes the native artist as the "Japanese version" of an American model (Kobayashi as Japan's Blakey) and renews the emphasis on study and performance experience in the United States as a badge of legitimacy—most of the young jazz stars earned their credentials by studying at Boston's Berklee school (where year after year Japanese students consistently constitute some 10 percent of the student body).

Yet perhaps the last sentence ("Today's jazz restoration in Japan, led by the young lions born after 1960, is about to enter a new phase: a full-fledged war") is the most striking. I asked Segawa who the enemy was in this "full-fledged war," waged by youngsters whom Kumagai dubbed "courageous heroes" (*yūshi*). Being the consummate gentleman, Segawa demurred on the combative nature of the advertising campaign. Yet at other times in our conversation he freely derided what he called "Japanese peculiar comic jazz," a freely improvised music which "appeals to Europeans" yet, in his estimation, is not true to jazz's roots. It became clear that the 1960s avant-garde and 1970s fusion are the principal targets of the Restoration movement, both in America and Japan (although Segawa carefully exempts Yamashita Yōsuke, who "plays 'free' in a Japanese way, climaxing with the spirit of the *kamikaze*"). Thus, although Kumagai's rhetoric of *ishin* actually resounds with the revolutionary cultural nationalism of the 1960s avant-garde, the Restoration overtly rejects its music. As in any proper "restoration," the *more legitimate* order is being reinstituted. Wither *ishin*?

Given the historical tendency to view jazz played by Japanese as derivative and inauthentic, the Restoration leaves itself open to criticism as an "imitation" of a "copy." That is to say, it is a flagrant attempt to duplicate the economic success, fashion, and artistic agenda of the American Young Lions, who have enjoyed "unprecedented cultural acceptance as the first approved acoustic jazz musicians in decades" in their endeavor to re-create the pre-avant-garde jazz past.[6] I should make clear that there is nothing inherently *wrong* with playing repertoire music in an older style; in an art form such as jazz whose aesthetic worth has been so long denied, there is much yet to be learned and appreciated in the deep study of the classics. What is objectionable about the agenda of the revivalist movements in the United States and Japan is that they elevate the study and re-creation of previous musics to the level of the artist's principal obligation, and thereby make it that much harder for unorthodox musicians to be heard. Claiming to be the *only* legitimate heirs to the tradition and protectors of the spirit of jazz, neoclassicists paradoxically violate that tradition and spirit by refusing to question the boundaries of jazz as their forebears did, and by transforming the vital, sensual art of the speakeasy, dance hall, and bohemian dive into a fossilized museum piece. In the process of defining a jazz canon and pantheon, they deliberately exclude music that does not fit their rigid conception of jazz, not to mention artists who do not conform to their standards of legitimacy. "What distinguishes the neoclassicist attitude is not so much its habit of retrospection," Scott DeVeaux argues, "but rather its heavy-handed attempt to regulate the music of the present through an idealized representation of the past. History is a roll call of past masters . . . and the *responsibility* of the modern musician is to create music that lives up to and extends this legacy. All else—free jazz and fusion alike—is falsity and charlatanism. Neoclassicism saves its most pointed barbs for the kind of easy pluralism that would embrace all potential definitions for jazz, and therefore all potential outcomes for the narrative of its history." This ideology is best and most colorfully exemplified in a statement by the neoclassicists' primary spokesman in an essay entitled "What Jazz Is—and Isn't."

> [There are] those who profess an openness to everything—an openness that in effect just shows contempt for the basic values of the music and of our society. If everything is good, why should anyone subject himself to the pain of study? Their disdain for the specific knowledge that goes into jazz creation is their justification for saying that everything has its place. But their job should be to define that place—is it the toilet or the table?[7]

In Japan, more is being "restored" than merely the *music* from jazz's "golden age." There is also a reassertion of the practice of replicating American standards and privileging them as the most legitimate and authentic. The Restoration thus restores not only the music of the American 1950s but also the aesthetic practices of the Japanese 1950s. The faces have changed—Wynton Marsalis has replaced George Shearing and Charlie Parker—and so have some of the practices—drug use is scorned—but the fact remains that Japan's young musicians continue to look across the Pacific for artistic and ideological direction. To speak again in terms of "authenticating strategies," study at Berklee and apprenticeships in American bands are the 1980s and 1990s equivalent of the 1930s "Shanghai sojourn" or the 1960s attempt to forge a self-referential jazz aesthetic.

The commercial success of the Jazz Restoration might indicate that that latter effort failed miserably in its attempt to transform the ways that Japanese viewed their relationship to the music, but it is being perceived as a promising renaissance for what is now referred to as the "J-Jazz scene." A handful of Japanese—such as pianist Kikuchi Masabumi, trumpeter Hino Terumasa, guitarist Kawasaki Ryō, and pianist Ozone Makoto—had long ago compiled impressive enough résumés to settle permanently in New York City, the world's most competitive jazz market. (By 1982 jazz writer Iwanami Yōzō could answer his own question, "Can Japanese jazzmen make it in New York?" in the affirmative.) But with the more recent accomplishments of Ōnishi Junko and Jazz Restoration leaders Ōsaka Masahiko and Hara Tomonao (whose CD *Favorites* was released in the United States by Evidence), there is a sense that the international profile of Japanese jazz artists is reaching unprecedented heights.[8] I must also concede that the pride that contemporary J-Jazz engenders pays off handsomely for the researcher, as long-out-of-print recordings emerge from the vaults in digitalized form to sate those with historical curiosity. But the fact remains that the commercial victories of J-Jazz are predicated on American approval. Riding the coattails of the United States' self-appointed arbiters of jazz taste, young Japanese win that approval by demonstrating how deferential they can be to America's conceptions of jazz music, aesthetics, and racial politics. Hara Tomonao studied literally at the knee of Wynton Marsalis, and it is oddly disconcerting to hear not only Marsalis's dogma but his very tone replicated so precisely in Hara's horn. (Hara was duly rewarded for his devotion to the "true essence" of jazz by vaulting over perennial winner Hino Terumasa in the trumpet category of native artist polls.)

Another example of how firmly entrenched American-defined standards of authenticity remain in Japan is the case of vocalist and pianist Ayado Chie, who was all the rage when I visited my old haunts in 1998. Ayado is a diminutive dynamo with a surprisingly deep, throaty, resonant voice and sharp vibrato à la Nina Simone. Married to a black American and thus a U.S. resident for a number of years, she became an apprentice of Shirley Horn and sang with black church choirs throughout New York and the American South. Following her divorce, she returned to Japan, where her "black feeling and native pronunciation" as a jazz vocalist caught the ear of jazz impresario Uchida Osamu. When Dr. U brought her music to the attention of the jazz community, there were stunned reactions all around: "Is that person really a Japanese?!'"⁹ Ayado's story is more poignant because of a terminal illness that guarantees her ride to fame will be short. But the summer of 1998 was hers. My friends incessantly sought my stamp of approval for her performance: as an American "expert," it was clear that I was supposed to validate their belief that *someone had finally gotten it right*. They hammered home that what made her so good was that she did *not* sound Japanese, but rather just like an African American female singer. Ayado Chie is the Japanese jazz community's new "Great Yellow Hope."

Why is this happening now? Why is the nostalgic evocation of America's jazz past so prominent in mainstream jazz circles, especially at a time when Japan's own cultural capital abroad seems to be rising with the explosive popularity of *anime* among North American and European fans? At no previous time in the modern age has Japan been regarded as such an influential *producer* rather than as a voracious, imitative *consumer* of culture. It is tempting to tie the compulsion to reassert a derivative jazz aesthetic to Japan's "fin de siècle blues," the chronic malaise gripping the country since the "bubble economy" burst in the late 1980s, and to popular insecurity over the leadership role into which Japan was thrust by earlier successes. Author Ōe Kenzaburō gave voice to this anxiety in his speech "Japan, the Ambiguous, and Myself," delivered when he accepted the 1994 Nobel Price for Literature:

> My observation is that, after one hundred and twenty years of modernization since the opening of the country, present-day Japan is split between the two opposite poles of an ambiguity. I, too, as a writer, live with this polarization imprinted on me like a deep scar.
>
> This ambiguity, which is so powerful and penetrating that it splits both the state and its people, is evident in various ways. The modernization of Japan has drawn on learning from and imitating the West. Yet Japan is situated in Asia and has firmly maintained its traditional culture. This ambiguous orientation drove Japan into the position of an invader in Asia. On the other hand, the culture of modern Japan, though thoroughly open to the West, has long remained something obscure and inscrutable to the West, or at least a barrier to understanding by the West. What was more, Japan was isolated from other Asian countries, not only politically but also socially and culturally.
>
> What I call Japan's "ambiguity" in my lecture is a kind of chronic disease that has been prevalent throughout the modern age.

After over a century of following others, Japan itself has become a role model, a blueprint for economic development to emulate (or to avoid). Having attained an unprecedented degree of affluence, yet no longer motivated by a national campaign to fend off the Western invader or rescue its Asian neighbors, Japan must now define a future role for itself on the world stage. To assuage his citizens' fears and apprehensions, the late Prime Minister Obuchi Keizō offered the new slogan "wealth and virtue" (*fukoku yūtoku*, in contrast to the Meiji era slogan *fukoku kyōhei*, "wealthy nation, strong military"), but it is unlikely to convince either those insecure in their employment or those clamoring for redress of wartime sins. Anxiety and insecurity have moved many Japanese to express nostalgia for a past that they believe was simpler. It is indeed striking how strongly Japanese cherish their memories of their most difficult hour: the desolate times of the immediate postwar years, when Japan was under America's thumb.[10] The memories of the last time that Japan assumed an aggressive leadership role are still painful, and there is, perhaps, an understandable desire that someone else take the responsibility. Teleology can be quite comforting for a nation unsure of its next move.

But there are other, more localized, economic and aesthetic reasons why J-Jazz has turned its back on a self-referential standard of authenticity. While the term "J-Jazz" is sometimes used inclusively to encompass artists of all stylistic affiliations, more often it specifically denotes the young neo-classicists, thus in practice signifying the splintered nature of the contemporary jazz community. In the long shadows cast by the Restoration upstarts, toil the pioneers whose attempts to self-legitimate their art too often collect dust in record company vaults. Yamashita Yōsuke is the only avant-gardist to command anything resembling a popular following and a secure, consistent recording and performing career, but his popularity is based as much on his reputation as a humorous essayist as on his pianistic pyrotechnics. (I understand that many of his readers are oblivious to his musical stature.) Most avant-gardists of Yamashita's generation and younger regularly tour Europe,[11] but are fortunate to gig three days a month at home. According to saxophonist Hayasaka Sachi and bassist Nagata Toshiki, their band Stir Up! rarely recoups commuting expenses on some jobs. Pianist Itabashi Fumio concedes that gigging alone would not support him, so he supplements his income and sustains his independent Mix Dynamite label with a teaching job. Katayama Hiroaki lends his brawny tenor saxophone to pop, rock, and *enka* sessions as a studio musician to pay the bills.

In short, Japan's avant-garde exists in an entirely different aesthetic and economic universe from the J-Jazz mainstream. Popular taste being notoriously conservative, it is not likely that most consumers would choose bands with names like "Stir Up!" or "Mix Dynamite" to unwind after a hard day. But there is more to it than that, for even John Coltrane's more dissonant work continues to sell well. It seems that another reason for the avant-

17. Takase Aki's Oriental Express performing at Jazz Inn Lovely, Nagoya, 23 July 1994: Itaya Hiroshi (tb), Katayama Hiroaki (ts), Hayashi Eiichi (as), Igarashi Issei (tp); not pictured are Takase Aki (p), Ino Nobuyoshi (b), and Koyama Shōta (d). Photo courtesy of Sugiura Shūichi.

garde's alienation is that its art is premised on a quirky irreverence worlds apart from the "serious," studious, and awed demeanor of the revivalists. Reedist Umezu Kazutoki resembles a circus ringmaster as he performs in top hat and tails; Hayasaka Sachi emulates whale songs on her alto; Itabashi Fumio plays his own haunting and angular compositions, not the standards; Katayama Hiroaki romps extemporaneously with *ashtray* accompaniment. In my conversations with them, Hayasaka, Katayama, and Itabashi all expressed bored frustration with the hangups over tradition, ethnic ownership, and authenticity that they believe actually dissipate the jazz world; Katayama even ventured that Japan's jazz scene is more varied and interesting than New York's precisely because musicians in his circle have managed to liberate themselves and their music both from the demands of neoclassicism and the inevitable constraints of "national style." The saxophonist scoffed at my well-intentioned yet naive and misplaced expression of sympathy that he must "slum" in *enka* bands: Katayama set me straight that he just loves to play music, and brings something to and takes something from every session in which he participates. In any case, however, it seems that the avant-garde's relative lack of commercial success is partly due to its playful yet purposeful questioning of the very boundaries of jazz music, at a historical moment when it is much more lucrative to defend them—in spite of the fact that Ellington, Davis, Williams, Armstrong, Holiday, Coleman,

Coltrane, Mingus, and other stalwarts of the jazz canon earned their spots there precisely because of their disavowal of such boundaries.[12]

Nearly a century after its initial trans-Pacific voyage to East Asia, Japanese still explore and discuss their relationship to jazz music as some sort of enigma. The Disc Union record store's 1994 promotional pamphlet on "Japanese and Jazz" opened one of the latest expressions of this ongoing discourse thusly:

> In Japan (it is said) there are the singular cultures of *wabi* [poverty, simplicity] and *sabi* [rusticism]. Originally it seems to have been a stoic aesthetic valuing wretched, lonely conditions, finding ultimate beauty in sipping foul-tasting, bitter tea in a tiny straw-mat room. Jazz culture is a completely incompatible form of culture. In such a country as this, how is jazz expected to function? Must jazz performed by Japanese always be "jazz performed by Japanese"? Who in the world are Japanese who listen to jazz . . . ? The riddle of the Japanese-jazz relationship. A mutual love, wanting to go on loving.[13]

As long as ethnically and nationally defined notions of authenticity persist, Japanese can be expected to continue regarding their relationship to jazz as a riddle and to search for its answers.

But one need not add "Japan" to the equation to come up with a riddle; the riddle is jazz itself, a music that aspires to be both universal and particular. If, as the cliché goes, jazz is expressive of a quintessentially American character—the fast-paced rhythms, the tensions between the individual voice and the demands of the group, the spontaneity and improvisatory nature of life—it is equally expressive of the contradictions that plague U.S. life. In much the same way that American history is the tale of persistent inequities of race, class, and gender impeding realization of the nation's foundational ideals to develop and protect the individual capacities of all its citizens, jazz as a culture reneges on its promise to cultivate and value equally the visions of its individual artists. Indeed, the hierarchies of race, class, and gender that threaten the "American experiment" are inverted in the jazz culture to privilege some artists over others. Just as the mighty ideals of democratic practice are consistently curbed in American life, jazz's lofty expectations of artistic originality are often subordinated to the priority of racialized, nationalized, or commercialized notions of authenticity. The normalization of such notions too often prevents us from searching out and acknowledging the contributions non-(African) Americans have made to jazz music. The basic aesthetic principles of jazz—which include continual experimentation and innovation—are an unusable mockery if the music's social and sonic boundaries must be policed. One wonders, in our obsession with the "ethnic cleansing" of jazz's past, how much of its future we may have already missed.

Hino Terumasa has often stated that jazz is now a "universal" and "international" music that promises to mediate cultural differences: "Jazz is modern, a new genre—still in the making," he says. "The world is shrinking. No one can deny it. National boundaries are disintegrating. It's the prefect time for jazz. It transcends all barriers, whether they be political, cultural or economic. It started here [U.S.A.]. We can't forget that—to say thank you to America for giving us this beautiful gift. But now, jazz belongs to no one. At the same time it belongs to everyone, especially to musicians of great originality. It doesn't matter where one comes from. That's the beauty of jazz; it's universal." In another context Hino has said, "I think America and Japan respect each other's culture, and jazz is like a bridge between Japan and America, like a rainbow. I think it will continue to work that way, and that relationship between America and Japan will continue forever. And I'm looking forward to that."[14]

Hino's vision suggests that jazz has helped propel us into a postmodern utopia, where cultural globalization renders national identities, prejudice, and concomitant authenticities moot and anachronistic. It is a common, not entirely unfounded perspective. But when he made these comments Hino was jamming in elite company and had recently become the first Japanese to sign a record deal with the prestigious Blue Note label. He had achieved a level of acceptance in jazz circles that other non-Americans can barely imagine. But, though Hino's personal success may yet confer respect and legitimacy on others whose authenticity remains in question among Japanese, North American, and European aficionados, evidence abounds that many have yet to value jazz artists more for what they play than for who they are or where they come from. Globalization may very well have enfeebled national identities, but it has also unleashed a backlash that seeks reassertion of the national and the authentic, and jazz artists lacking the archetypical pedigree feel its sting.

One test of Hino's belief will be in future historical treatments of jazz: will those audacious enough to write yet another "history of jazz" feel compelled to include the stories and findings presented in this book, or in the work of S. Frederick Starr, Michael Kater, and others? Will they go beyond saying that jazz simply captivated the world, to acknowledge the debates jazz sparked and the symbolic associations it assumed in Japan and elsewhere? In short, will jazz histories be as "international" and all-embracing as Hino Terumasa believes jazz music to be? For that to happen, it seems, we will have to reconfigure our thinking about jazz, culture, race, and authenticity. Until then Hino's is a song of lovely sentiment as yet unsung.

NOTES

The following abbreviations are used for these instruments:
as = alto saxophone,
b = bass,
bj = banjo,
bs = baritone saxophone,
cel = cello,
cl = clarinet,
d = drums,
fl = flute,
g = guitar,
org = organ,
p = piano,
perc = percussion,
ss = soprano saxophone,
tb = trombone,
tp = trumpet,
ts = tenor saxophone,
v = violin,
vib = vibraphone,
vo = vocals.

Prelude: Plenty Plenty Soul

1. See also Gary Vercelli, "The Land of the Rising Sun," *Coda* 217 (1987–88): 10–11.
2. Aoki Tamotsu, "Murakami Haruki and Contemporary Japan," trans. Matthew Strecher, in *Contemporary Japan and Popular Culture*, ed. John Whittier Treat (Surrey: Curzon, 1996), 265–69. See also Ono Yoshie, *Jazu saishū shō*, ed. Kawamoto Saburō (Tokyo: Shin'ya Sōsho, 1998), 11–27; and Konishi Keita et al., eds., *Murakami Haruki no ongaku zukan* (Tokyo: Japan Mix, 1995).
3. Alan P. Merriam and Raymond W. Mack, "The Jazz Community," *Social Forces* 38 (Mar. 1960): 211–22. Portrayals of jazz musicians as fundamentally alienated from their audiences appear in Rogers E. M. Whitaker, "Spokesman with a Temperature—II," *New Yorker* 5 May 1945, 37; Howard S. Becker, "The Professional Dance Musician and His Audience," *American Journal of Sociology* 57 (Sept. 1951): 137, 141–44; Nat Hentoff, *The Jazz Life* (New York: Dial, 1961), 25; Richard A. Peterson, "Audiences—and All That Jazz," *Trans-action* Sept.–Oct. 1964: 31; Albert Goldman, *Freakshow: The Rocksoulbluesjazzsick-*

jewblackhumorsexpoppsych Gig and Other Scenes from the Counter-Culture (New York: Atheneum, 1971), 301; and Robert A. Stebbins, "Role Distance, Role Distance Behaviour, and Jazz Musicians," *British Journal of Sociology* 20 (1969): 406–15. For modifications of the concept of the "jazz community," see Robert A. Stebbins, "A Theory of the Jazz Community," *Sociological Quarterly* 9 (1968): 318–31; and Ronald M. Radano, "The Jazz Avant-Garde and the Jazz Community: Action and Reaction," *Annual Review of Jazz Studies* 3 (1985): 71–79.

4. Cornel West, *Race Matters* (Boston: Beacon Press, 1993), 105. See also Merriam and Mack, 220; Charles Nanry, "The Occupational Subculture of the Jazz Musician: Myth and Reality" (Ph.D. diss., Rutgers University, 1970), 338; Krin Gabbard, "Introduction: Writing the Other History," in *Representing Jazz,* ed. Krin Gabbard (Durham, N.C.: Duke University Press, 1995), 3; LeRoi Jones (Amiri Baraka), *Black Music* (New York: Morrow, 1967); Albert Murray, *Stomping the Blues* (New York: Vintage, 1976); William Howland Kenney, "Historical Context and the Definition of Jazz: Putting More of the History in 'Jazz History,' " in *Jazz among the Discourses,* ed. Krin Gabbard (Durham, N.C.: Duke University Press, 1995), 110–12; and David Meltzer, ed., *Reading Jazz* (San Francisco: Mercury House, 1993), 9. Spontaneity as "cultural stance" is the theme of Daniel Belgrad, *The Culture of Spontaneity: Improvisation and the Arts in Postwar America* (Chicago: University of Chicago Press, 1998).

5. See Edward Harvey, "Social Change and the Jazz Musician," *Social Forces* 46 (1967): 34–35; Donald Kennington and Danny L. Read, *The Literature of Jazz: A Critical Guide,* 2d ed. (Chicago: American Library Association, 1980), ix; and Eric Hobsbawm, *The Jazz Scene,* rev. ed. (New York: Pantheon, 1993), 210, 212.

6. John G. Russell's fascinating "Consuming Passions: Spectacle, Self-Transformation, and the Commodification of Blackness in Japan," *positions: east asia cultures critique* 6.1 (1998): 118–19, describes "the insatiable appetite for things black and the spectacle and vicarious pleasures their display offers," which render blackness "a site of resistance against Japanese social and behavioral norms and white cultural hegemony, [but] lacks any clear subversive direction or intent." Commodified and consumed blackness, Russell contends, supposedly enables Japanese to transform and liberate themselves expressively and sexually.

7. Gino Germani, *Marginality* (New Brunswick, N.J.: Transaction Books, 1980), 9.

8. Dick Hebdige, *Subculture: The Meaning of Style* (1979; London: Routledge, 1987), 18, 79.

9. Jack V. Buerkle and Danny Barker, *Bourbon Street Black: The New Orleans Black Jazzman* (New York: Oxford University Press, 1973), 188–89.

10. Sarah Spence, "A Marginal Introduction," in *Marginality: Voices from the Periphery,* ed. Murray McNeil, published in conjunction with the Comparative Literature Conference, California State University, Long Beach, 15 Mar. 1986, 5; Alan P. Merriam, *The Anthropology of Music* (Chicago: Northwestern University Press, 1964), 137, 144; and Hebdige, 17.

11. See Hidetoshi Katō, ed. and trans., *Japanese Popular Culture: Studies in Mass Communication and Culture Change* (Rutland, Vt. and Tokyo: Tuttle, 1959; Westport, Conn.: Greenwood Press, 1973); Hidetoshi Katō, ed., *Japan and Western Civilization: Essays on Comparative Culture* (Tokyo: University of Tokyo Press, 1984); Richard Gid Powers and Hidetoshi Katō, eds., *Handbook of Japanese Popular Culture* (Westport, Conn.: Greenwood Press, 1989); Louis Alvarez and Andrew Kolker, prods., *The Japanese Version,* VHS (Center for New American Media, 1991); Joseph J. Tobin, ed., *Re-Made in Japan: Everyday Life and Consumer Taste in a Changing Society* (New Haven, Conn.: Yale University Press, 1992); John A. Lent, ed., *Asian Popular Culture* (Boulder, Colo.: Westview Press, 1995); Lise Skov

and Brian Moeran, eds., *Women, Media and Consumption in Japan* (Surrey: Curzon, 1995); Treat, *Contemporary Japan and Popular Culture;* Mark Schilling, *The Encyclopedia of Japanese Pop Culture* (New York: Weatherhill, 1997); Sepp Linhart and Sabine Frühstück, eds., *The Culture of Japan as Seen through Its Leisure* (Albany: SUNY Press, 1998); D. P. Martinez, ed., *The Worlds of Japanese Popular Culture: Gender, Shifting Boundaries and Global Cultures* (Cambridge: Cambridge University Press, 1998); Timothy J. Craig, ed., *Japan Pop: Inside the World of Japanese Popular Culture* (Armonk, N.Y.: M. E. Sharpe, 2000); and Douglas Slaymaker, ed., *A Century of Popular Culture in Japan* (Lewiston, N.Y.: Edwin Mellen Press, 2000).

12. See, for example: Stuart Hall and Tony Jefferson, eds., *Resistance through Rituals: Youth Subcultures in Post-war Britain* (London: Hutchinson, 1976), 12; T. J. Jackson Lears, "*AHR* Forum: Making Fun of Popular Culture," *American Historical Review* Dec. 1992: 1420–21; Simon During, ed., *The Cultural Studies Reader* (London: Routledge, 1993), 7; and L. Gamman and M. Marshment, eds., *The Female Gaze: Women as Viewers of Popular Culture* (London: Women's Press, 1988), 2.

13. Burton W. Peretti, "Oral Histories of Jazz Musicians: The NEA Transcripts as Texts in Context," in Gabbard, *Jazz among the Discourses,* 122.

14. Phillip S. Hughes, "Jazz Appreciation and the Sociology of Jazz," *Journal of Jazz Studies* 1.2 (1974): 79.

15. Hughes, 92–93. Examples of the most important new historical, sociological, and musicological scholarship include: Kathy J. Ogren, *The Jazz Revolution* (New York: Oxford University Press, 1989); Ronald M. Radano, *New Musical Figurations: Anthony Braxton's Cultural Critique* (Chicago: University of Chicago Press, 1993); Paul Berliner, *Thinking in Jazz: The Infinite Art of Improvisation* (Chicago: University of Chicago Press, 1994); and Ingrid Monson, *Saying Something: Jazz Improvisation and Interaction* (Chicago: University of Chicago Press, 1996).

16. Michael H. Kater, *Different Drummers: Jazz in the Culture of Nazi Germany* (New York: Oxford University Press, 1992); and S. Frederick Starr, *Red & Hot: The Fate of Jazz in the Soviet Union,* rev. ed. (New York: Limelight Editions, 1994). See also Paul Oliver, "Jazz Is Where You Find It: The European Experience of Jazz," in *Superculture: American Popular Culture and Europe,* ed. C. W. E. Bigsby (London: Paul Elek, 1975), 140–51; Chris Goddard, *Jazz away from Home* (New York: Paddington, 1979); Erik Wiedemann, *Jazz i Denmark: ityverne, trediverne og fyrrerne* (Copenhagen: Gyldenal, 1985); Warren R. Pinckney Jr., "Jazz in India: Perspectives on Historical Development and Musical Acculturation," *Asian Music* 21.1 (1989–90): 35–77; William Minor, *Unzipped Souls: A Jazz Journey through the Soviet Union* (Philadelphia: Temple University Press, 1995); Mark Miller, *Such Melodious Racket: The Lost History of Jazz in Canada, 1914–1949* (Toronto: Mercury Press, 1998); and Kevin Whitehead, *New Dutch Swing* (New York: Billboard, 1998). I discuss the parochialism of jazz historiography and the potential benefits of expanding the jazz narrative's historical setting in "Multicultural Jazz: Expanding the Borders of Jazz History," paper presented at the 44th Annual Meeting of the Society for Ethnomusicology, Austin, Tex., 19 Nov. 1999.

17. See, for example, Noguchi Hisamitsu, "Nihon ni jazu ga haittekita koro (1)," *Jazu hihyō* [hereafter *JH*] 6 (1969): 22–25; Noguchi Hisamitsu, ed., "Nippon ni jazu ga haittekita koro (2)," *JH* 7 (1970): 126–32; Haruna Shizuo, "Nippon jazu ongaku zenshi (Nippon ni jazu ga haittekita koro)," *JH* 10 (1971): 136–41; and Matsuzaka Hiro, "Nihon no jazu sōshiki kara dainiji taisen made," *JH* 12 (1972): 8–69.

18. Ōshima Mamoru, "Concert Review—suingu jamu sesshon," *Swing Journal* [hereafter *SJ*] Feb. 1972: 199. Examples of historically themed concerts include: "Nanri Fumio Recital—

48 Years in Music" (30 Jan. 1973); "Jazz at the Nichigeki" (23–25 Dec. 1973 and 16–18 Aug. 1976); "Japanese Jazz—Part 1" (4 Feb. 1976), featuring Mizushima Sanae, Hatano Fukutarō's Orchestra ("Japan's first dance band"), the Columbia Jazz Band ("Japan's first full band"), Kami Kyōsuke's Corona Orchestra ("Japan's first symphonic jazz band"), and Matsumoto Shin's New Pacific Orchestra ("the first postwar band") (quoted in "Nippon no jazu tanjō wo saigen," *SJ* Feb. 1976: 230); "Gay Stars Jazz Again" concert series (1978); and Taniguchi Matashi's "The Jazz I Love" (21 Oct. 1979). The first of four Mocambo albums featuring Moriyasu Shōtarō was released in 1975. The Ginparis jam session LP was released in March 1972 and reissued in 1977. Albums from the late-fifties King Jazz Series were reissued starting in September 1973, and ten LPs from the late-sixties Takt series were released in August 1974.

19. Yui Shōichi, "Nippon popyurā ongaku shi," *Min'on*, thirty-five-part serial from Jan. 1975 until Dec. 1977; Segawa Masahisa, "Nippon no jazu shi," *SJ*, twenty-three-part serial from July 1975 to June 1977. The most oft-cited history is vibraphonist Uchida Kōichi's *Nihon no jazu shi: senzen, sengo* (Tokyo: Swing Journal, 1976). The retrospective *Bessatsu ichioku nin no Shōwa shi: Nihon no jazu—Jazz of Japan '82* (Tokyo: Mainichi Shinbunsha, 1982) contains a wealth of photographs and historical and biographical essays [hereafter cited as *Jazz of Japan '82*]. Segawa Masahisa, *Jazu de odotte: hakurai ongaku geinō shi* (Tokyo: Simul Shuppankai, 1983), and Ōmori Seitarō, *Nihon no yōgaku*, 2 vols. (Tokyo: Shinmon Shuppansha, 1986–87), are rich with anecdotes and prewar jazz lore. Honda Toshio's *Jazu* (Tokyo: Shin Nippon Shinsho, 1976) and *Modan Jazu* (Tokyo: Shin Nippon Shinsho, 1989) are popular histories arranged in a nonchronological manner. Hiraoka Masaaki's *Sengo Nippon no jazu shi* (Tokyo: Adin Shobō, 1977) is not at all the comprehensive postwar history suggested by the title, but rather a compilation of the author's reports on the contemporary scene from the short-lived magazine *Jazzland* (1975–76). Shimizu Toshihiko, Hiraoka Masaaki, and Okunari Tōru, *Nihon no jazu den* (Tokyo: Eipuriru Shuppan, 1977), details momentous postwar sessions and highlights, while Takahashi Ichirō and Sasaki Mamoru, *Jazu shifū—sengo sōsōki densetsu* (Tokyo: San'ichi Shobō, 1997), is a newer oral history.

20. Examples include: Yoshida Mamoru, *Yokohama jazu monogatari: "Chigusa" no 50 nen* (Yokohama: Kanagawa Shinbunsha, 1985); Uchida Osamu, *Jazu ga wakakatta koro* (Tokyo: Shōbunsha, 1984); Jatekku Bādo, comp., *Oretachi no jazu kyō seishun ki* (Tokyo: Jatekku Shuppan, 1991); Ōki Toshinosuke, *Jazu joifuru sutorīto* (Tokyo: JICC, 1991); Hayashi Junshin, Takagi Shōzō, and Azahara Noriyuki, *Tokyo shitamachi jazz dōri* (Tokyo: Wombat Press, 1992); Sugawara Shōji, *Jazu kissa "Beishii" no sentaku* (Tokyo: Kōdansha, 1993); Terajima Yasukuni, Ōnishi Yonehiro, and Noguchi Iori, *Kichijōji jazz monogatari* (Tokyo: Nippon Terebi, 1993); Kurita Eiji, *Roppongi jazu monogatari—Tales of Old Fashioned Jazzy Life in Roppongi* (Tokyo: Ensū Bukko, 1995); Okunari Tatsu, *Minna ga jazu ni akekureta* (Tokyo: San'ichi Shobō, 1997); and Nakayama Yasuki, *Suingu jānaru seishun roku (Ōsaka hen)* (Tokyo: Komichi Shobō, 1998).

21. Saitō Ren, *Shōwa no bansukingu tachi: jazu, minato, hōtō* (Tokyo: Music Magazine, 1983). Saitō's play, which won the twenty-fourth Kishida Prize in 1980, was a return to New Theater (*shingeki*) realism for the playwright, following his work with such avant-garde troupes as the Freedom Theater and Theater Center 68. Ueda Sakae, *Soshite, kaze ga hashirinukete itta (He Played Like a Breeze through Our Lives): tensai jazu pianisuto Moriyasu Shōtarō no shōgai* (Tokyo: Kōdansha, 1997). Biographical reference works include: the special issue of *JH* 25 (1977); Iwanami Yōzō, *Nihon no Jazumen* (Tokyo: Tairiku Shobō, 1982); and *Swing Journal shin sekai jazu jinmei jiten*, special ed., May 1988.

22. See Fukushima Teruhito's evolutionary account in "Nippon jazu gendaishi—kono jūnen ryūdō," *JH* 23 (1976): 12–20.

23. Sidney DeVere Brown, "Jazz in Japan: Its Sources and Development, 1925–1952," Proceedings, 1980 Annual Meeting, Southwest Conference on Asian Studies, New Orleans, 127–39 (German translation by Christian Schwandt published in *Japan: Ein Lesebuch*, ed. Peter Portner [Konkursbuch: University of Hamburg, 1986], 117–31); "New Orleans in Tokyo: Nanri Fumio (1910–1975)—Jazz Trumpet Virtuoso," Southwest Conference on Asian Studies, New Orleans, 3 Nov. 1989; "Toshiko Akiyoshi: The Meeting of East and West in Jazz," Southwest Conference on Asian Studies, Austin, Tex., 13 Oct. 1990; "California Origins of the Jazz Boom in Occupied Japan, 1945–1952," Conference on California and the Pacific Rim, University of the Pacific, Stockton, Calif., 30 April 1994 (copyright 1999); Eugene Enrico and Sidney D. Brown, *Jazz in Japan* (Early Music Television, University of Oklahoma, 1999). Elizabeth Ann Sesler-Beckman, "Jazz Is My Native Language: A Study of the Development of Jazz in Japan" (M.A. thesis, Tufts University, 1989); and Larry Richards, "Senzen no Nihon ni okeru jazu ongaku to sono gainen" (M.A. thesis, Tokyo Geijutsu Daigaku, 1992). Other English-language treatments include: Austrian Eckhart Derschmidt's "Thrilling Live Performances," *Resonance* 4.2 (Feb. 1996): 18–23, and "The Disappearance of the *Jazu-Kissa:* Some Considerations about Japanese 'Jazz-Cafés' and Jazz-Listeners," in Linhart and Frühstück, 303–15; Canadian Joe B. Moore's "Studying Jazz in Postwar Japan: Where to Begin?" *Japanese Studies* 18.3 (Dec. 1998): 265–80; and American Craig McTurk's 1999 documentary film *Tokyo Blues: Jazz and Blues in Japan*.

24. Merriam, *The Anthropology of Music*, 258. See also Bruno Nettl, *The Study of Ethnomusicology: Twenty-nine Issues and Concepts* (Urbana: University of Illinois Press, 1983), 131–33; and Anthony Seeger, "Styles of Musical Ethnography," in *Comparative Musicology and Anthropology of Music: Essays on the History of Ethnomusicology*, ed. Bruno Nettl and Philip V. Bohlman (Chicago: University of Chicago Press, 1991), 346.

25. Brief overviews of the Japanese popular music industry are available in English: see Linda Fujie, "Popular Music," in Powers and Katō, 197–220; Kawabata Shigeru, "The Japanese Record Industry," *Popular Music* 10.3 (1991): 327–45; and Mitsui Tōru, "Interactions of Imported and Indigenous Musics in Japan: A Historical Overview of the Music Industry," in *Whose Master's Voice? The Development of Popular Music in Thirteen Cultures*, ed. Alison J. Ewbank and Fouli T. Papageorgiou (Westport, Conn.: Greenwood Press, 1997), 152–74. Basic histories in Japanese are Kurata Yoshihiro, *Nihon rekōdo bunka shi* (Tokyo: Tokyo Shoseki, 1992), and Kawabata Shigeru, *Rekōdo gyōkai* (Tokyo: Kyōikusha, 1990).

26. Monson, 203.

1 The Japanese Jazz Artist and the Authenticity Complex

1. Art Ensemble of Chicago quoted in Soejima Teruto, "Nihonjin to jazu," *Jazu hihyō* [hereafter *JH*] 25 (1977): 30; see also Joe B. Moore, "Studying Jazz in Postwar Japan: Where to Begin?" *Japanese Studies* 18.3 (Dec. 1998): 265–66.

2. Quoted in Neil Tesser, "20 Questions: Branford Marsalis," *Playboy* Dec. 1993: 218; reprinted (in English with Japanese translation) in *Swing Journal* [hereafter *SJ*] April 1994: 70. Of course, jazz is not the only expressive art beholden to ethnonational standards of authenticity: Japanese have questioned the authenticity of non-Japanese *enka* singers, *nō* actors, and even *sumō* wrestlers.

3. "Nihonjin wa jazu o rikai shite inai?!" *SJ* April 1994: 72; Murakami Haruki, "Nihonjin ni jazu wa rikai dekiru noka: hitotsu no chisana Nichibei bunka massatsu ni tsuite no kōsatsu," *Gendai* Oct. 1994: 132–34.

4. Bailey quoted in Bill Moody, *The Jazz Exiles: American Musicians Abroad* (Reno: University of Nevada Press, 1993), 147, 152; The John Scofield Band, *Pick Hits Live* (Gramavision: R2 79405, 1988); and Miles Davis, with Quincy Troupe, *Miles: The Autobiography* (New York: Simon and Schuster, 1989), 269. See also John S. Wilson, *Jazz: The Transition Years, 1940–1960* (New York: Appleton-Century-Crofts, 1966), 138.

5. Michael Bourne, "Global Jazz Boosters Demand More U.S. Music," *Down Beat* Jan. 1980: 25.

6. Charley Gerard, *Jazz in Black and White: Race, Culture, and Identity in the Jazz Community* (Westport, Conn.: Praeger, 1998), 36; Ingrid Monson, *Saying Something: Jazz Improvisation and Interaction* (Chicago: University of Chicago Press, 1996), 202–3.

7. Anthony J. Palmer, "World Musics in Music Education: The Matter of Authenticity," *International Journal of Music Education* 19 (1992): 32–40; Edward M. Bruner, "Abraham Lincoln as Authentic Reproduction: A Critique of Postmodernism," *American Anthropologist* 96.2 (1994): 399–400; Peter Kivy, *Authenticities: Philosophical Reflections on Musical Performance* (Ithaca, N.Y.: Cornell University Press, 1995), 4–5, 108–15, 142; Joel Rudinow, "Race, Ethnicity, Expressive Authenticity: Can White People Sing the Blues?" *Journal of Aesthetics and Art Criticism* 52.1 (1994): 129. See also David Borgo, "Can Blacks Play Klezmer? Authenticity in American Ethnic Musical Expression," *Sonneck Society Bulletin* 24.2 (Summer 1998): 33–36.

8. Pierre Bourdieu, *Distinction: A Social Critique of the Judgment of Taste*, trans. Richard Nice (Cambridge: Harvard University Press, 1984), 28–29, 32, referencing José Ortega y Gasset, "La dehumanización del arte" (1925), in *Obras Completas*, vol. 3 (Madrid: Revista de Occidente, 1966), 355–56. The "humanized" arts are governed by what Bourdieu calls the "popular aesthetic" (43–44).

9. Irving Louis Horowitz, "Authenticity and Originality in Jazz: Toward a Paradigm in the Sociology of Music," *Journal of Jazz Studies* 1.1 (Oct. 1973): 57–58.

10. Billy Taylor, "Jazz: America's Classical Music," *Black Perspective in Music* 14.1 (1986): 21–25, reprinted in Robert Walser, ed., *Keeping Time: Readings in Jazz History* (New York: Oxford University Press, 1999), 327–32; and Robert G. O'Meally, *The Jazz Cadence of American Culture* (New York: Columbia University Press, 1998), 117–18.

11. John Gennari, "Jazz Criticism: Its Development and Ideologies," *Black American Literature Forum* 25 (1991): 466; Gene Lees, *Cats of Any Color: Jazz Black and White* (New York: Oxford University Press, 1994), 193; Gerard, xiv; Richard M. Sudhalter, *Lost Chords: White Musicians and Their Contribution to Jazz, 1915–1945* (New York: Oxford University Press, 1999), xv–xxii; and Ralph J. Gleason, "Can the White Man Sing the Blues?" *Jazz and Pop* Aug. 1968: 28.

12. Gerard, 3; Rickey Vincent, *Funk: The Music, the People, and the Rhythm of the One* (New York: St. Martin's Griffin, 1996), 5–7, 320; and Rudinow, 127.

13. Doc Cheatham and Wynton Marsalis quoted in "Jazz Musicians Discuss Racism in the Jazz World," reported by Dean Olsher, *All Things Considered*, National Public Radio, 10 Jan. 1996. See also James T. Jones IV, "Racism and Jazz: Same As It Ever Was . . . or Worse?" *Jazz Times* Mar. 1995: 52–61; and Lees, 190.

14. Morgenstern and Shepp quoted in Olsher; Leadbelly quoted in Gleason, 28; and Amiri Baraka, "The Great Music Robbery," in *The Music: Reflections on Jazz and Blues* (New York: Morrow, 1987), 328–32.

15. See Steve McClure, *Nippon Pop* (Tokyo: Tuttle, 1998), 92, 141.

16. Richard Cook and Brian Morton, *The Penguin Guide to Jazz on CD, LP and Cassette* (London: Penguin, 1994), 723, 55, 758, 558, 897; Keith Cahoon, "Popular Music in Japan," in *Japan: An Illustrated Encyclopedia* (Tokyo: Kōdansha Ltd.), 1287.

17. Jean Phillipe André, "Enthousiasme du public . . ." *Jazz Magazine* 388 (Dec. 1989): 43.

18. Tessa Morris-Suzuki, "The Invention and Reinvention of 'Japanese Culture,'" *Journal of Asian Studies* 54 (1995): 768, 776; Kōsaku Yoshino, *Cultural Nationalism in Contemporary Japan: A Sociological Inquiry* (London: Routledge, 1992), 28, 68; Peter N. Dale, *The Myth of Japanese Uniqueness* (London: Croom Helm, 1986), ii; and Marilyn Ivy, *Discourses of the Vanishing: Modernity, Phantasm, Japan* (Chicago: University of Chicago Press, 1995), 3–4. See also Tessa Morris-Suzuki, *Re-Inventing Japan: Time, Space, Nation* (Armonk, N.Y.: M. E. Sharpe, 1998).

19. Hidetoshi Katō, "Japanese Popular Culture Reconsidered," in *Handbook of Japanese Popular Culture*, ed. Richard Gid Powers and Hidetoshi Katō (Westport, Conn.: Greenwood Press, 1989), 315–16; Tsunoda Tadanobu, *Nihonjin no nō: nō no hataraki to tōzai no bunka* (Tokyo: Taishūkan, 1978). Tsunoda conceded that Japanese and Western brains are identical morphologically, but "differ in the hemispherical localisation of certain neurological functions" (Dale, 189). Other theories of Japanese sociobiological exceptionalism are reviewed in Ross Mouer and Yoshio Sugimoto, *Images of Japanese Society: A Study in the Social Construction of Reality* (London: KPI, 1986), 51–52.

20. See, for instance, bell hooks, *Yearning: Race, Gender, and Cultural Politics* (Boston: South End Press, 1990), 37; Yoshino, 28; Edward Said, *Culture and Imperialism* (New York: Vintage, 1993), xv, 336; and Morris-Suzuki, *Re-Inventing Japan*, 158.

21. Timothy D. Taylor, *Global Pop: World Music, World Markets* (New York: Routledge, 1996), 126. One caveat: I would say that Taylor's remark holds true for a certain segment of the "world music" public, but it seems clear to me that most consumers in this particular market prefer "modern," eclectic, and even techno-dance elements to traditional folk musics. More modern-sounding "world musics" seem to be much more accessible to the average listener.

22. Lise Skov, "Fashion Trends, Japonisme and Postmodernism, or 'What Is So Japanese about Comme Des Garçones?'" in *Contemporary Japan and Popular Culture*, ed. John Whittier Treat (Surrey: Curzon, 1996), 149, 151, 156–57.

23. Richard Ichirō Mayeda, "The Identity of Japanese Jazz," *The East* May 1972: 46; Elizabeth Ann Sesler-Beckman, "Jazz Is My Native Language: A Study of the Development of Jazz in Japan" (M.A. thesis, Tufts University, 1989), 95 (emphasis in original).

24. Yishane Lee, "From Taboo to Trend: Documentarian Traces Japan's Jazz Roots," *Japan Times* 31 Mar. 1998.

25. Koyama Kiyoshi, "Shimupojium—Nippon no jazu wo kangaeru," *SJ* May 1968: 78. Satō Masahiko similarly complained that the rest of the world demanded that "jazz from Japan should sound Japanese" (quoted in Koyama Kiyoshi, "Zoku: Nippon no jazu wo kangaeru," *SJ* Nov. 1968: 71).

26. Bourne, 27, states that "American musicians are idolized in Japan more than anywhere else in the world. But it's said that Japanese musicians who play jazz and other American musics are never more than imitators."

27. Eta Harich-Schneider, *A History of Japanese Music* (London: Oxford University Press, 1973), 547–48; William P. Malm, "Layers of Modern Music and Japan," *Asian Music* 4.2 (1973): 3; and Christine Yano, "The Floating World of Karaoke in Japan," *Popular Music and Society* 20.2 (Summer 1996): 12–13. In his *Japanese Music and Musical Instruments*

(Rutland, Vt.: Charles E. Tuttle, 1959), 172, William P. Malm describes this teaching method as "uninspired by Western standards," "unnecessarily tedious," and "constantly in danger of producing musical automatons."

28. D. P. Martinez, ed., *The Worlds of Japanese Popular Culture: Gender, Shifting Boundaries and Global Cultures* (Cambridge: Cambridge University Press, 1998), 11; see also Joseph J. Tobin, ed., *Re-Made in Japan: Everyday Life and Consumer Taste in a Changing Society* (New Haven, Conn.: Yale University Press, 1992), 4.

29. Sugino quoted in "Jazz in Japan: Have You Heard the Latest?" *Japan Update* 12 (Summer 1989): 21; Satō quoted in John Schofield, "Pianist Infuses Jazz with Japanese Spirit," *Wall Street Journal* 8 Oct. 1991: A20.

30. "What is Soul?" lyrics by George Clinton, *Funkadelic* (Westbound: WB 2000, 1971). See, for example, Bruno Nettl, "Thoughts on Improvisation: A Comparative Approach," *Musical Quarterly* 60.1 (1974): 1–19; Paul Berliner, *Thinking in Jazz: The Infinite Art of Improvisation* (Chicago: University of Chicago Press, 1994); Rolf Groesbeck, "Cultural Constructions of Improvisation in *Tāyampaka*, a Genre of Temple Instrumental Music in Kerala, India," *Ethnomusicology* 43.1 (1999): 1–30; and Bruno Nettl and Melinda Russell, eds., *In the Course of Performance* (Chicago: University of Chicago Press, 1998).

31. See William Bruce Cameron, "Sociological Notes on the Jam Session," *Social Forces* Dec. 1954: 179; and Horowitz, 59. Both depict this paradox as somehow unique to jazz, but I would argue that all artists face it to varying degrees.

32. Karel van Wolferen, *The Enigma of Japanese Power* (New York: Vintage, 1989), 379; Thomas R. H. Havens, *Artist and Patron in Postwar Japan* (Princeton, Princeton University Press, 1982), 20; Watanabe Mamoru, "Why Do the Japanese Like European Music?" *International Social Science Journal* 34 (1982): 662.

33. "Japanese jazz" is a translation of *Nihonteki jazu*, which means literally "Japanese-style jazz." Sometimes the term *Nihon no jazu* ("jazz of Japan") is used to connote the same concept, but more often than not the latter term simply refers to jazz played by Japanese, which (depending on the context) is different from "Japanese jazz."

34. Hillary Tann, "Tradition and Renewal in the Music of Japan," *Perspectives of New Music* 27.2 (1989): 44; and Judith Ann Herd, "The Neonationalist Movement: Origins of Japanese Contemporary Music," *Perspectives in New Music* 27.2 (1989): 119–20, 154. See also Havens, *Artist and Patron*, 16.

35. Yui Shōichi, personal communication quoted in Sesler-Beckman, 92 (emphasis mine).

36. Imada quoted in "Thirty Successful Years on the Jazz Beat in Japan: Mainstream Veteran Masaru Imada," *Keyboard* (Aug. 1985): 40; Inagaki quoted in "Jazz in Japan: Have You Heard the Latest?" 20, and from personal interview with the author.

37. "Jazz in Japan: Have You Heard the Latest?" 21.

2 The Soundtrack of Modern Life: Japan's Jazz Revolution

1. Charles Nanry, *The Jazz Text* (New York: D. Van Nostrand Co., 1979), 115; William Howard Kenney, *Chicago Jazz: A Cultural History, 1904–1930* (New York: Oxford University Press, 1993), xii–xiii.

2. Kikuchi Shigeya, "Nihon jazukai sōseiki no koro: ōrudo jazumen no omoide," in *Dikishiirando jazu nyūmon*, ed. Yui Shōichi (Tokyo: Arechi, 1975), 86.

3. Kikuchi, "Nihon jazukai sōseiki," 87; Yui Shōichi, "Nippon popyurā ongaku shi 5: Kikuchi

Shigeya-shi ga jazu to deatta koro," *Min'on* May 1975: 37. Kikuchi purchased some of the first jazz records ever made (probably Victor 18472 and 18457), recorded in 1918 and 1919.

4. *Gekkan gakufu* July 1920: 1. Since there is no other mention of a Tokyo Jazz Band, Larry Richards speculates that the men are models and no such band ever existed. Richards's research on this topic is presented in *"Jazu" ga Nihongo ni natta toki,* VHS, presented at the Fifth Annual Assembly of the Japanese Association for the Study of Popular Music, Nov. 1993.

5. The symbolic versatility of the word *jazz* has been noted by Alan P. Merriam, *The Anthropology of Music* (Chicago: Northwestern University Press, 1964), 241–44; Kathy Ogren, *The Jazz Revolution: Twenties America and the Meaning of Jazz* (New York: Oxford University Press, 1989), 7–8; Kenney, xiii; and Hosokawa Shūhei, "Seiyō ongaku no Nihonka, taishūka 24: 'Tokyo kōshinkyoku,'" *Music Magazine* Mar. 1991: 119.

6. Harris I. Martin, "Popular Music and Social Change in Prewar Japan," *Japan Interpreter* 7 (1972): 334.

7. Alessandro Portelli, "The Peculiarities of Oral History," *History Workshop* 12 (1981): 100; Paul Thompson, *The Voice of the Past: Oral History,* 2d ed. (Oxford: Oxford University Press, 1988), 139; Samuel Schrager, "What Is Social in Oral History?" *International Journal of Oral History* 4 (June 1983): 79.

8. Krin Gabbard, "Introduction: The Jazz Canon and Its Consequences," in *Jazz among the Discourses,* ed. Krin Gabbard (Durham: Duke University Press, 1995), 22n. A representative formalist definition of "jazz" is offered by Joachim Berendt, *The Jazz Book: From Ragtime to Fusion and Beyond,* rev. ed., trans. H. and B. Bredigkeit and Dan Morgenstern (Westport, Conn.: Lawrence Hill, 1981), 371–72, who admits that "the three basic elements of jazz temporarily achieve varying degrees of importance, and . . . the relationship between them is constantly changing." Alternative musicological definitions are discussed in Lee B. Brown, "The Theory of Jazz Music—'It Don't Mean a Thing . . .'" *Journal of Aesthetics and Art Criticism* 49 (1991): 115–27.

9. See Richard H. Mitchell, *Thought Control in Prewar Japan* (Ithaca, N.Y.: Cornell University Press, 1976), 30–31; Gregory Kasza, *The State and the Mass Media in Japan, 1918–1945* (Berkeley: University of California Press, 1988), xii–xiv.

10. Dan Ikuma, "The Influence of Japanese Traditional Music on the Development of Western Music in Japan," trans. Dorothy G. Britton, *The Transactions of the Asiatic Society of Japan,* 3d series, 8 (Dec. 1961): 203–4, refers to a "Japanese concept of art—including music—for literature's sake." See also Isabel K. F. Wong, "The Music of Japan," in *Excursions in World Music,* 2d ed. (Upper Saddle River, N.J.: Prentice Hall, 1997), 128–29.

11. Sidney DeVere Brown, "Jazz in Japan: Its Sources and Development, 1925–1952," Proceedings, 1980 Annual Meeting, Southwest Conference on Asian Studies, New Orleans, 129; Sidney Brown, interview in Elizabeth Ann Sesler-Beckman, "Jazz Is My Native Language: A Study of the Development of Jazz in Japan" (M.A. thesis, Tufts University, 1989), 144.

12. Richard C. Kraus, *Pianos and Politics in China: Middle-Class Ambitions and the Struggle over Western Music* (New York: Oxford University Press, 1989), 191, 195.

13. Reebee Garofalo, "Whose World, What Beat: The Transnational Music Industry, Identity, and Cultural Imperialism," *World of Music* 35.2 (1993): 17. Bruno Nettl, *The Western Impact on World Music: Change, Adaptation, and Survival* (New York: Schirmer Books, 1985), 26, suggests several possible adaptive "responses" of indigenous musics: consolidation ("the combination of style elements from diverse parts of a native repertory," i.e., "pan-Indian" or "Pan African" styles); diversification ("the combination into one performance context

of musics from the gamut of a non-Western repertory"); complete abandonment or "impoverishment" of a musical culture: artificial preservation ("the conscious separation of the older tradition from those aspects of culture that are being Westernized"); exaggeration of supposedly distinctive national traits; reintroduction of indigenous musics after a period of abandonment or impoverishment; and peaceful coexistence of styles.

14. The influence of Portuguese, Dutch, and Chinese musics in the sixteenth and seventeenth centuries is discussed by William P. Malm, "Music Cultures of Momoyama Japan," in *Warlords, Artists, and Commoners: Japan in the Sixteenth Century,* ed. George Elison and Bardwell L. Smith (Honolulu: University Press of Hawaii, 1981), 173–75.

15. Edward McCauley, *With Perry in Japan,* ed. Allan B. Cole (Princeton: Princeton University Press, 1942), 101; Francis L. Hawks, comp., *Narrative of an American Squadron to the China Seas and Japan, Performed in the Years 1852, 1853, and 1854, under the Command of Commodore M. C. Perry, United States Navy, by Order of the Government of the United States,* vol. 1 (Washington, D.C.: A. O. P. Nicholson, 1856), 376; and Pat Barr, *The Coming of the Barbarians* (London: Macmillan, 1967), plate 4.

16. Eric Walton Clemons, "The Role of African Americans in U.S. Navy Expeditions to Japan in the 1850s: A Lesson in Contradictions," *Conexoes* (East Lansing, Mich.: African Diaspora Research Project, Michigan State University) 3.2 (1991): 5–6. Eric Lott, *Love and Theft: Blackface Minstrelsy and the American Working Class* (New York: Oxford University Press, 1993), 3–4, explicates the "contradictory racial impulses at work" in the blackface minstrel show, reflecting a "white obsession with black (male) bodies which underlies white racial dread to our own day."

17. John Russell, "Race and Reflexivity: The Black Other in Contemporary Japanese Mass Culture," *Cultural Anthropology* Feb. 1991: 10; Clemons, 6. John Whiteoak, "From Jim Crow to Jazz: Imitation African-American Improvisatory Musical Practices in Pre-Jazz Australia," *Perfect Beat* (July 1993): 50–74, maintains that blackface minstrel shows performed by white American actors influenced "ragging" and improvisation among Australian musicians, but it is unclear if a similar process occurred in Japan.

18. One of the earliest reported African American musical performances in Japan was that of Fisk University's Louisiana Trio, a gospel group that toured Europe and performed for Queen Victoria. The trio performed in Tokyo on 26 May 1920. They later returned to Japan, where they were received so warmly that one member reportedly expressed a desire never to return to America. See Tsugawa Shuichi, *Jubirii shingāzu monogatari to kokujin reika shū* (Tokyo: Ongaku no Tomo Sha, 1960), 6–7.

19. Ury Eppstein, *The Beginnings of Western Music in Meiji Era Japan,* Studies in the History and Interpretation of Music 44 (Lewiston, N.Y.: Edwin Mellen Press, 1994), ii; and T. Fujitani, *Splendid Monarchy: Power and Pageantry in Modern Japan* (Berkeley: University of California Press, 1996), esp. chap. 3.

20. Inoue Musashi and Akiyama Tatsuhide, eds., *Nippon no yōgaku hyakunen shi* (Tokyo: Dai Ippōki, 1966), 262; Nagai Yoshikazu, *Shakō dansu to Nihonjin* (Tokyo: Shōbunsha, 1991), 20–21.

21. Quoted in Nomura Kōichi, "Occidental Music," *Japanese Music and Drama in the Meiji Era* (Tokyo: Ōbunsha, 1956), 466. See also William P. Malm, "The Modern Music of Meiji Japan," in *Tradition and Modernization in Japanese Culture,* ed. Donald H. Shively (Princeton, N.J.: Princeton University Press, 1971), 265–67; and Tsurumi Shunsuke, *A Cultural History of Postwar Japan, 1945–1980* (London: KPI Ltd., 1987), 79–80.

22. Malm, "The Modern Music of Meiji Japan," 269, 300. Mitsui Tōru, "Interactions of Imported and Indigenous Musics in Japan: A Historical Overview of the Music Industry,"

in *Whose Master's Voice? The Development of Popular Music in Thirteen Cultures*, ed. Alison J. Ewbank and Fouli T. Papageorgiou (Westport, Conn.: Greenwood Press, 1997), 153, offers a contrasting view, arguing that "the various stylized forms of indigenous music have never been seriously threatened per se by the impulse of Westernization." Eppstein maintains that Izawa's "compromise" was nothing of the sort, but rather "an indiscriminate study and adoption of Western musical principles, regardless of whether or not they fitted the Japanese environment, tradition and aesthetics." However, he detects such a "compromise" in *late* Meiji, with "new melody types, based on traditional tetrachords, . . . within a framework of European tonality, [which] signified a rejection of earlier musical internationalism in favour of a return to indigenous values" (ii–iii).

23. Sonobe Saburō, *Ongaku gojū nen* (Tokyo: Jiji Tsūshinsha, 1950), 33.

24. Horiuchi Keizō, *Jinta konokata* (Tokyo: Aoi Shobō, 1935), 20; Yui Shōichi, "Nippon popyurā ongaku shi 4: jinta kōbō shi," *Min'on* April 1975: 36–37. Horiuchi's essay provides not only the most in-depth musical analysis of *jinta* music, but also an unabashed nostalgia for these bands, which had their heyday during the Sino-Japanese War (1894–95) but declined following the Russo-Japanese War a decade later.

25. Horiuchi, *Jinta konokata*, 23–24; Horiuchi Keizō, *Ongaku Meiji hyakunen shi* (Tokyo: Ongaku no Tomo Sha, 1968), 119; Hayashi Kōjirō, "Chindonya," in *Taishū bunka jiten*, comp. Ishikawa Hiroyoshi, Tsuganesawa Toshihiro, et al. (Tokyo: Kobundō, 1994), 507 [hereafter cited as *TBJ*].

26. Sonobe, *Ongaku gojūnen shi*, 33; Uchida Kōichi, *Nihon no jazu shi: senzen, sengo* (Tokyo: Swing Journal, 1976), 31.

27. Tatsumi Mitsuyoshi, "Jazu ga fune ni notte yattekita," *Yokohama bunka jōhōshi* Sept. 1994: 1.

28. Burnet Hershey, "Jazz Latitude," *New York Times Book Review and Magazine*, 25 June 1922: 8–9, reprinted in Robert Walser, ed., *Keeping Time: Readings in Jazz History* (New York: Oxford University Press, 1999), 27.

29. Quoted in Uchida Kōichi, "Sōseiki wo ninatta jazu paionia tachi," in *Bessatsu ichioku nin no Shōwa shi: Nihon no jazu—Jazz of Japan '82*, comp. Mainichi Shinbunsha (Tokyo: Mainichi Shinbunsha, 1982), 56 [hereafter cited as *Jazz of Japan '82*].

30. Quoted in Uchida, *Nihon no jazu shi*, 18. In 1919 the Hatano band is said to have performed to great acclaim for President Woodrow Wilson at a YMCA convention in San Francisco. Wilson was in the Bay Area September 17–19, but *San Francisco Chronicle* descriptions of his itinerary do not confirm the story. The *Chronicle* did report that Hatano's ship, the *Chiyō-maru*, barely escaped attack by the German cruiser *Leipzig* by dimming its lights and sailing on to San Francisco (*San Francisco Chronicle* 1 Sept. 1914: 3).

31. Inoue and Akiyama, 409; Horiuchi Keizō, *Ongaku gojūnen shi* (Tokyo: Masu Shobō, 1942), 341, 357.

32. Grace Thompson Seton, "The Jazzing Japanese," *Metronome* July 1923: 52, 54; Hershey, 29, 27–28.

33. Hatano Fukutarō, who in 1921 led the Hatano Jazz Band at the Kagetsuen, described the music they played for dancers: "At the Kagetsuen we played fox trot, one-step, and two-step scores, which I'd bought in America, as they were. Nobody knew anything about adlibbing [improvisation] yet" (quoted in Uchida, *Nihon no jazu shi*, 30).

34. Nagai, 56–59; Kami Kyōsuke, "Ano koro no jazu 8: hatsu no kippusei dansu hōru," *Tokyo shinbun*, evening ed., 12 Oct. 1957: 5. Takashima Tateo opened Cottage as a bar in the Naniwa development in 1922, but converted it to a dance hall in 1924.

35. Albert Murray, *Stomping the Blues* (New York: Vintage, 1976), 116. Ogren, too, contends,

"Dancing remained a central feature of participatory music creation," and cites James P. Johnson, Danny Barker, and Pops Foster, among others, who admitted that dancers affected their own performances (for better or worse) (40).

36. Matsuzaka Hiro, ed., "Nihon no jazu sōshiki kara dainiji taisen made," *Jazu hihyō* [hereafter *JH*] 12 (1972): 17; Nakazawa Mayumi, "Nihonjin ga jazu o kuchizunda hi," *Ushio* Dec. 1981: 195.

37. Quoted in Yui Shōichi, "Nippon popyurā ongaku shi 6: Nihon no jazu sōseiki to Masuda kyōdai," *Min'on* June 1975: 37. The youngest Masuda brother, Sadanobu, believes that the family started playing jazz when his oldest brother Katsunobu returned from America, "around 1920." Masuda Sadanobu, "Jazu ga haittekita koro," in *Jazu of Japan*, '82, 62.

38. Matsuzaka, 19; Kami Kyōsuke, "Ano koro no jazu 16: okanemochi mo majieta bando," *Tokyo shinbun* 23 Oct. 1957, evening ed.: 5. Kami described Dōmoto as "the spitting image of the collegian that appears in the movies," but regretted the trumpeter's lack of ambition: "If he had not been wealthy, I think he would have become Japan's [Bix] Beiderbecke."

39. Quoted in Yui, "Masuda kyōdai," 37.

40. Yui, "Masuda kyōdai," 36; Honda Toshio, *Rongu ierō rōdo: jazu sankan joō no nagai michinori—Akiyoshi Toshiko* (Tokyo: Ikkōsha, 1984), 179; Uchida, *Nihon no jazu shi*, 58. In 1923 *Metronome*'s correspondent observed: "There is no doubt that the coming of the Prince of Wales and the festivities planned for his visit caused a spread of jazz among the upper class of society, and, of course, quickly and joyously throughout the middle classes" (Seton, 53).

41. Ōmori Seitarō, *Nihon no yōgaku*, vol. 1 (Tokyo: Shinmon Shuppansha, 1986), 136; Mitsui, 156–57.

42. Ōya Sōichi, "Ōsaka wa Nippon no Beikoku da," *Ōsaka Mainichi shinbun*, Dec. 1929, reprinted in *Ōya Sōichi zenshū*, vol. 2 (Tokyo: Sōyōsha, 1981), 146–48. Ōsaka's prominence as a center of mass entertainment is discussed by Jeffrey E. Hanes in "Taishū bunka/ka'i bunka/minshū bunka: senkanki no Nihon no toshi ni okeru kindai seikatsu," in *Toshi no kūkan, toshi no shintai*, ed. Yoshimi Shun'ya (Tokyo: Keisō Shobō, 1996), 107–9, and in "Media Culture in Taishō Osaka," in *Japan's Competing Modernities: Issues in Culture and Democracy 1900–1930*, ed. Sharon Minichiello (Honolulu: University of Hawaii Press, 1998), 267–87. Ōsaka's importance in jazz history is mentioned in Sōgensha Henshūbu, *Ōsaka monoshiri jiten* (Ōsaka: Sōgensha, 1994), 66–67.

43. The description *kenchiku kakuteru* appears in Kitao Ryōnosuke, *Kindai Ōsaka* (Ōsaka: Sōgensha, 1932), 286; Hanes, "Taishū bunka/ka'i bunka/minshū bunka," 123.

44. Ōsaka-shi Shakaibu Chōsaka, ed., *Yoka seikatsu no kenkyū*. Rōdō Chōsa Hōkoku 19 (Kyōto: Kobundō, 1923), 64, 65, 67, 68.

45. Ishikawa Hiroyoshi, *Goraku no senzen shi* (Tokyo: Tokyo shoseki, 1981), 125, 136; Shinshū Ōsaka-shi Shi Hensan Iinkai, *Shinshū Ōsaka-shi shi*, vol. 6 (Ōsaka City, 1994), 832–33. A photo of Ōsaka's famous Cafe Paulista appears in Okamoto Ryōichi, ed., *Furusato no omoide shashinshū Meiji Taishō Shōwa Ōsaka*, vol. 1 (Tokyo: Kokusho Kankōkai, 1985), 65.

46. Quoted in *Zoku: Minami-ku shi* (Ōsaka City, 1982), 591. This is clearly a continuation of the ceremonial practice of *kaomise* ("showing the faces") at the opening of a new *kabuki* season, in which actors under contract to Dōtonbori theaters would arrive by boat at nighttime to the cheers of throngs lining the riverbank and standing on the bridges. See Donald Shively, "The Social Environment of Tokugawa Kabuki," reprinted in *Japanese Aesthetics and Culture: A Reader*, ed. Nancy G. Hume (Albany: SUNY Press, 1995), 211.

47. Hershey, 27; William R. Pfeiffer, *Filipino Music: Indigenious* [sic], *Folk, Modern* (Dumaguete City, R.P.: Silliman Music Foundation 1976), 156; Ōmori, vol. 1, 144–45.

48. Hattori Ryōichi, *Boku no ongaku jinsei* (Tokyo: Chūō Bungeisha, 1983), 72; Maeno Kōzō quoted in Ōmori, vol. 1, 149. Filipinos may also have been the first to make records with labels bearing the word *jazu*. Two Filipino groups, the Carl's Show Jazz Band and the Philippine Jazz Band, recorded "St. Louis Blues" and "I Want to Be Happy Honolulu," respectively, in November 1923. The same year, a Filipino group known as the Nittō Jazz Band recorded "Walla Walla." These records sound very much like the Chicago-style jazz of the 1920s. See Kurata Yoshihiro, *Nihon rekōdo bunka shi* (Tokyo: Tokyo Shoseki, 1992), 139; Larry Richards, "Senzen no Nihon ni okeru jazu ongaku to sono gainen" (M.A. thesis, Tokyo Geijutsu Daigaku, 1992), 24–25; and Segawa Masahisa, liner notes, *A History of King Jazz Recordings: Pioneer* [sic] *of Japanese Jazz—New Edition* (King: KICJ 192, 1994), 6–7. "Walla Walla" and the Ōsaka Shōchiku Jazz Band's 1925 recording of "Song of India" appear on this CD.

49. Tyler Stovall, *Paris Noir: African Americans in the City of Light* (Boston: Houghton Mifflin, 1996), 26, states, "Unlike many expatriates who came to Paris to learn from the French, African American musicians journeyed to Paris as teachers, and found many willing pupils." See also Paul Oliver, "Jazz Is Where You Find It: The European Experience of Jazz," in *Superculture: American Popular Culture and Europe*, ed. C. W. E. Bigsby (London: Paul Elek, 1975), 141; and S. Frederick Starr, *Red & Hot: The Fate of Jazz in the Soviet Union*, rev. ed. (New York: Limelight Editions, 1994), 38–39, 62–63.

50. "Kon'yū hōsō sareru banjō, piano gassō," *Yomiuri shinbun* 16 Feb. 1925, photocopy from the collection of Larry Richards.

51. Vidi Conde quoted in Ōmori, vol. 1, 166; Segawa Masahisa, "Coromubia jazu songu no shuyaku tachi," liner notes, *Orijinaru genban ni yoru Nihon no jazu songu senzen hen* (Nippon Columbia: SZ-7011–15, 1976), 14; and Segawa Masahisa, *Jazu de odotte: hakurai ongaku geinō shi* (Tokyo: Simul Shuppankai, 1983), 55–56.

52. Uchida, *Nihon no jazu shi*, 335; Kami Kyōsuke, "Ano koro no jazu 11: Tenkatsu Ichiza no Hawaiian gakudan," *Tokyo shinbun*, evening ed., 17 Oct. 1957: 5. The itinerary of the Tenkatsu Ichiza's U.S. tour is recounted in Ishikawa Gashō, *Shōkyokusai Tenkatsu* (Tokyo: Tōgensha, 1968), 182–201. Magician Shōkyokusai Ten'ichi (1853–1912) founded the troupe in the late 1800s, but after his death leadership passed on to his wife Shōkyokusai Tenkatsu (1886–1944), who was dubbed "the 'Mary Pickford' of Japan" ("24 Japanese Actors Arrive in This City," *San Francisco Chronicle* 10 Mar. 1924: 13). See also "Shōkyokusai Tenkatsu," *Nihon josei jinmei jiten* (Tokyo: Nihon tosho sentā, 1993), 546.

53. Quoted in Ōmori, vol. 1, 166; Kami wrote about Okunesu with assurance of his own authority, but as is the case with his account of the Masudas, it is unclear what his personal connection was. He claimed that Okunesu was moved to tears by the expressions of appreciation he received from his pupils. Kami Kyōsuke, "Ano koro no jazu 12: shikagoha chokuden no dekishii," *Tokyo shinbun*, evening ed., 18 Oct. 1957: 5.

54. "I have the oldest relationship to jazz music." Ida Ichirō, "Nippon jazu ongaku sokumen shi 1: Mitsukoshi kangen gakudan jidai," *Varaeti* Dec. 1938: 4. I thank Larry Richards for bringing Ida's serialized account, which previous historians had neglected, to my attention. See also Uchida, "Sōseiki," 56.

55. Ida Ichirō, "Nippon jazu ongaku sokumen shi 3: Takarazuka shōjo kageki no jazu sōdō zengo," *Varaeti* April 1939: 18–19. On the popularity of the Takarazuka theater, see Jennifer Robertson, *Takarazuka: Sexual Politics and Popular Culture in Modern Japan* (Berkeley: University of California Press, 1998).

56. Ida Ichirō, "Nippon jazu ongaku sokumen shi 4: Ōsaka Shōchiku gakugekidan jidai," *Varaeti* May 1939: 14; Uchida, *Nihon no jazu shi*, 44–45.

57. Ida Ichirō, "Nippon jazu ongaku sokumen shi 5: Harada Jun-shi to no ikisatsu," *Varaeti* July 1939: 25.

58. Kami Kyōsuke, "Ano koro no jazu 14: Ōsaka o doron shite Tokyo de kōhyō," *Tokyo shinbun*, evening ed., 21 Oct. 1957: 5; Kikuchi, "Nihon jazukai sōseiki," 90; Uchida, *Nihon no jazu shi*, 49; Segawa Masahisa, "Nanri Fumio to Nihon jazu shakaishi josetsu," *Jazz* Nov. 1975: 77.

59. Segawa, *Jazu de odotte*, 5. Maeno quoted in Uchida, *Nihon no jazu shi*, 49.

60. Nakazawa, "Nihonjin ga jazu wo kuchizunda hi," 209.

61. "Awatadashii Ōsaka eki no machiai de namidagumashii mokutō, sakariba mo hanamachi mo oto naku, itaru tokoro gōgai o ubaiau," *Ōsaka Mainichi shinbun* 25 Dec. 1926: 3; "Shin'nen shogishiki subete gotoritome," *Ōsaka Asahi shinbun*, evening ed., 26 Dec. 1926: 3; and "Ryōan torishimari," *Ōsaka Mainichi shinbun* 26 Dec. 1926: 2.

62. "Keu no unmei o mae ni dansu hōru jihai," *Ōsaka Asahi shinbun* 25 Dec. 1927: 5. I was unable to find reports in either of the Ōsaka dailies of the March 1927 restrictions. Social dance was still the province of expatriates and self-styled "cosmopolitans," which further supports Ōbayashi Sōshi's contemporary observation that Ōsaka "mass culture" was effectively segmented into "class cultures," distinct subcultures with distinct entertainment tastes and budgets. See Ōbayashi Sōshi, *Minshū goraku no jissai kenkyū: Ōsaka-shi no minshū goraku chōsa* (Ōsaka: Ōhara Shakai Kenkyūjo, 1922), 75–77; and Hanes, "Taishū bunka/ka'i bunka/minshū bunka," 106, 120, 125.

63. *Tanizaki Jun'ichirō zenshū* 22 (Tokyo: Chūō Kōronsha, 1959), 197; translation from Edward Seidensticker, *Tokyo Rising: The City since the Great Earthquake* (New York: Knopf, 1990), 57, 63.

64. Ida Ichirō, "Nippon jazu ongaku sokumen shi 8," *Varaeti* Oct. 1939: 18. The band members at this time were Ashida Mitsuru (as), Obata Mitsuyuki (tp), Taniguchi Matashi (tb), Katō Kazuo (d), Taira Shigeo (p), and Ida Ichirō (bj, v).

65. Matsuzaka, 23.

66. Ida, "Sokumen shi 8," 19.

67. Richards, 26.

68. The Columbia recording (N16855), cut in March 1928, featured Keiō's Red and Blue Jazz Band. Victor's version (50460) was arranged by Ida Ichirō. See Mitsui, 159.

69. Uenoda Setsuo, *Japan and Jazz: Sketches and Essays on Japanese City Life* (Tokyo: Taiheiyōsha, 1930), 33. Excerpts also published as Uenoda Setsuo, "Jazz Songs of Japan," *Trans-Pacific* 26 Sept. 1929: 6. Filmmaker Kurosawa Akira (1910–1998) characterized late-Taishō popular songs as "gloomy, full of glorification of despair." *Something Like an Autobiography*, trans. Audie E. Bock (New York: Vintage, 1982), 32. See also Marta E. Savigliano, "Tango in Japan and the World Economy of Passion," in *Re-Made in Japan: Everyday Life and Consumer Taste in a Changing Society*, ed. Joseph J. Tobin (New Haven: Yale University Press, 1992), 235–52.

70. Sales figures for "Tokyo March" (lyrics by Saijō Yaso, 1929) and the explosion of record sales (quickly outstripping instrument sales) are discussed in "Rekōdo dairyūkō, 'Tokyo kōshinkyoku' sanjūman mai," *Ōsaka Asahi shinbun* 18 Oct. 1929, reprinted in Uchikawa Yoshimi, comp., *Shōwa nyūzu jiten*, vol. 2 (Tokyo: Mainichi Communications, 1990), 657.

71. Martin, 342; Kōdansha, comp., *Shūkan Yearbook nichiroku 20 seiki 1929*, 14 July 1998: 2–5; and Mitsui, 160.

72. Uenoda, 31–33. See also Ishikawa, *Goraku no senzen shi*, 157.

73. "Min'yō e no kōkaijō to kōgi," *Yomiuri shinbun* 4 Aug. 1929: 4; see also Kurata 158–61. Since its inception in August 1926, state radio excluded commercials and restricted entertainment, and rather focused on news, weather, and "practical knowledge." Popular music was even more restricted, with Western classics, *hōgaku*, and (later) military songs receiving the lion's share of airplay. In the interwar period radio was less crucial to the diffusion of jazz and popular music than it would be in the immediate postwar era. See Gregory J. Kasza, "Democracy and the Founding of Japanese Public Radio," *Journal of Asian Studies* 45 (Aug. 1986): 748; and Mitsui, 165.

74. Quoted in Satō Mieko, *Rikutsu janai yo, kibun da ya: jazu doramā Jimii Harada hachijūsan sai no shōgai* (Tokyo: Tōrin Shuppansha, 1996), 22–23.

75. Ōya Sōichi, "Kindai bi to yaban bi," in *Ōya Sōichi zenshū*, vol. 2, 27.

76. *Madamu to nyōbō*, dir. Gosho Heinosuke, Shōchiku, 1931. Joseph L. Anderson and Donald Richie, *The Japanese Film*, rev. ed. (Princeton, N.J.: Princeton University Press, 1982), 73, describe the soundtrack's creation: "In shooting the film there were no re-recording or dubbing facilities, so that everything had to be recorded at the same time on the final track. All the background sound, plus the jazz band so important to the plot, had to be recorded during shooting . . . For exterior scenes the orchestra would often have to find a place for itself among trees and bushes, blowing and fiddling away under the dialogue."

77. Ōmori, vol. 1, 194–95; Matsuzaka, 43; and J. L. Anderson, "Spoken Silents in the Japanese Cinema; or, Talking to Pictures: Essaying the *Katsuben*, Contextualizing the Texts," in *Reframing Japanese Cinema: Authorship, Genre, History*, ed. Arthur Noletti Jr. and David Desser (Bloomington: Indiana University Press, 1992), 291. Kurosawa Akira's brother Heigo was a popular *benshi* who committed suicide after losing his job to talkies (Kurosawa, 84–86).

78. Matsuzaka, 48.

79. William Bruce Cameron, "Sociological Notes on the Jam Session," *Social Forces* Dec. 1954: 177–78.

80. Kitao, 401–3, 405.

81. Ishikawa, *Goraku no senzen shi*, 130.

82. *Chabuya* are poorly documented. Sketchy accounts can be found in Honmoku Ayumi Kenkyūkai, *Honmoku no ayumi* (Yokohama: Hirai Insatsujo, 1986), 68; Hanzawa Masatoki, "Chabuya," in *Kanagawa-ken hyakka jiten*, ed. Kanagawa-ken Hyakka Jiten Kankōkai (Tokyo: Yamato Shobō, 1983), 572; Yoshida Mamoru, "Daremo shiranai Nihon jazu shi (1)," *Waseda Jazz* 2 (Jan. 1974): 13–14; Ishii Mitsutarō, et al., eds., *Yokohama kindaishi sōgō nenpyō* (Yokohama: Yūrindō, 1989), 291, 449, 493, 560; Saitō Ren, *Shōwa no bansukingu tachi: jazu, minato, hōtō* (Tokyo: Music Magazine, 1983), 47; and Satō, *Rikutsu janai yo*, 23.

83. "Chabuya shisatsu no Jo hakushi ikkō," *Yokohama bōeki shinpō*, 26 June 1931: 3.

84. Liza Dalby, *Geisha* (New York: Vintage, 1983), 77, notes that geisha at the Pontochō Kaburenjō in Kyōto were trained in Western social dancing as early as 1915. A photograph of dancing Okazaki geisha appears in "Jazu de odotte," *Me de miru Shōwa, Vol. 1: gannen—20 nen* (Tokyo: Asahi Shinbunsha, 1973), 46–47.

85. Seton, 52.

86. Ōya Sōichi, "Ōsaka no Tokyo-ka to Tokyo no Ōsaka-ka," *Ōsaka Asahi shinbun* 27 Mar. 1930, reprinted in *Ōya Sōichi zenshū*, vol. 2, 143–45.

87. Quoted in Uchida, *Nihon no jazu shi*, 103.

88. Nagai, 83. Tamaki Shinkichi, "Shakō dansu jūnen no omoide," *The Modern Dance* June

1936: 19, commemorated Nichibei (formerly Tokyo Dance School) as Tokyo's first commercial dance hall. It opened with about twenty taxi dancers and the Al Candara Jazz Band, a Filipino band imported from Shanghai.

89. Survey from *Modan dansu* Jan. 1937, reprinted in Nagai, 108. See also Uchida, *Nihon no jazu shi*, 99–102.

90. Kagetsuen founder Hiraoka Shizuko opened Florida (under the name Tameike Dance Hall) in 1928, with deserters from Ida Ichirō's Cherryland Dance Orchestra on stage. See Tsuda Matatarō, " 'Florida' o kataru" (pamphlet from reopening party following a fire), Oct. 1932, reprinted in Segawa, *Jazu de odotte*, 104. See also Kikuchi Shigeya, "Nihon jazu ongaku zenshi 10: Bōrurūmu Furorida no maki," *Dansu to ongaku* April 1956: 16.

91. The survey is quoted in Shigeta Tadayasu, *Fūzoku keisatsu no riron to jissai* (Tokyo: Nankōsha, 1934), 177. In addition to 789 female dancers, it also listed 18 male and 3 female dance instructors, 147 musicians, and 125 males and 70 females otherwise employed by dance halls. "It's said that one month's income can be as much as ¥200, but the average is sixty or seventy."

92. Burton Crane, "Coda on Japan," *Metronome* Jan. 1937: 17. Bands that worked at Florida included Joe Cavalero and the Hawaiian Serenadors (1928–1929); Wayne Coleman's orchestra (1930); France's Mulan Rouge Tango Orchestra (1932); and the A. L. King jazz band (1935–1936).

93. Kikuchi, "Nihon jazu ongaku zenshi 10," 17.

94. Quoted in Uchida, *Nihon no jazu shi*, 103–4. Students' economic worries are discussed in Henry D. Smith II, *Japan's First Student Radicals* (Cambridge, Mass.: Harvard University Press, 1972), 265, and Byron K. Marshall, "Growth and Conflict in Japanese Higher Education, 1905–1930," in *Conflict in Modern Japanese History: The Neglected Tradition*, ed. Tetsuo Najita and J. Victor Koschmann (Princeton, N.J.: Princeton University Press, 1982), 284–87.

95. Satō, *Rikutsu janai yo*, 23; and Horiuchi, *Ongaku Meiji hyakunen shi*, 196.

96. Yoshida Mamoru, quoted in "Jazu no taishūka: jazu kissa no ayumi," *JH* 12 (1972): 68. Yoshida's use of the terms "upper class" and "masses" here is vague. He has described his clientele as consisting mostly of musicians, college students, and salaried white collar workers, whose education and training distinguish them from urban and rural laborers more commonly known as "the masses," among whom jazz was less appealing than vernacular pop songs. Incidentally, in spite of Yoshida's protestations about the high cost, he was nevertheless a frequent patron of dance halls and *chabuya*. See Ōtani Ichirō, *Noge sutōri* (Yokohama: Kanagawa Sankei Shinbun, 1986), 8.

97. Hashizume Shin'ya and Satō Kenji, "Kissaten," *TBJ*, 189; Kata Kōji, "Miruku hōru," *TBJ*, 771; Ishikawa, *Goraku no senzen shi*, 135–36; Yoshida Mamoru, *Yokohama jazu monogatari: "Chigusa" no 50 nen* (Yokohama: Kanagawa Shinbunsha, 1985), 16–19; Yoshida, "Daremo shiranai Nihon jazu shi (1)," 5–7; "Jazu no taishūka," 64. Jazz coffeehouses in Ōsaka and other cities outside of the capital region are invariably omitted in these histories.

98. "All of Rio's records are imported!" Ad for Maison Rio, *Dansu to ongaku* Oct. 1937. With such high duty rates, imported records sold for ¥3 to ¥8 and domestic records for around ¥1. "Jazu no taishūka," 66; Yoshida Mamoru, "Rekōdo tatta hyakumai de 'Chigusa' wa hajimatta," *Oretachi no jazu kyōseishunki*, 69; Yoshida Mamoru, "Ano koro no Yokohama," *JH* 54 (1986): 312; and Mitsui, 158.

99. "Jazu no taishūka," 68; Yoshida, *Yokohama jazu monogatari*, 19–20; Miyama Toshiyuki and Segawa Masahisa, "Talk Session: Jazz 1940s in Japan," *JH* 80 (1994): 250. Representative ads for Duet, Brown Derby, and Maison Rio appear in 1937 issues of *Dansu to*

ongaku. A representative gossip column about taxi dancers and sign girls is "Dansā uwasa banashi," *Dansu to ongaku* Jan. 1938: 48–49.

100. Quoted in Noguchi Hisamitsu, ed., "Nihon ni jazu ga haittekita koro 1," *JH* 6 (1969): 25.
101. Kitahara Tetsuo, ed., *Jazu ongaku*, ARS Ongaku Daikōza, vol. 9 (Tokyo: ARS, 1936).
102. See the bibliography for titles and publication dates. My thanks to Larry Richards for sharing the fruits of his own research on music magazines. See also Yui Shōichi, "Nippon popyurā ongaku shi 21: senzen no jazu no bunken Shioiri Kamesuke no 'Jazu ongaku,'" *Min'on* Sept. 1976: 33.
103. Noguchi Hisamitsu, "Nippon ni okeru jazu hyōron no senkusha: Nogawa Kōbun-shi no omoide," *JH* 12 (1972): 79.
104. Kikuchi, "Nihon jazukai sōseiki," 93, comments on the paucity of instructional materials.
105. Horiuchi, *Ongaku Meiji hyakunen shi*, 195.
106. Quoted in Matsuzaka, 51.
107. Segawa, "Coromubia," 16. By 1931 the wage system was gone, and musicians were paid per song recorded.
108. The Florida Boys' personnel was: Kikuchi Shigeya (p), Watanabe Ryō (b), Tsunoda Takashi (g, bj), Tanaka Kazuo (d), Taniguchi Matashi (tb), Tommy Misman and Ashida Mitsuru (as), Matsumoto Shin (ts), Nanri Fumio and Kikkawa Masashi (tp), and Moriyama Hisashi (tp, vo).
109. Uchida, *Nihon no jazu shi*, 87–88.
110. Kami Kyōsuke, "Ano koro no jazu 29: tobeichū ni bunken ya gakufu o shūshū," *Tokyo shinbun*, evening ed., 7 Nov. 1957: 5; Kami Kyōsuke, "Ano koro no jazu 30: hatsu no shinfonikku jazu," *Tokyo shinbun*, evening ed., 8 Nov. 1957: 5. Kami was acclaimed as the "Japanese Paul Whiteman" in Claude Lapham, "Popular Japanese Music," *Asia* 37 (Dec. 1937): 860.
111. Kami Kyōsuke and Matsuoka Hideo, "Kono hito to: ongaku hitosuji ni," *Mainichi shinbun* 25 Dec. 1970: 5; 26 Dec. 1970: 5.
112. Taniguchi Matashi, "Toronbon to ayunda watakushi no jazu jinsei (saishū kai)," *Jazurando* Dec. 1975: 117–18.
113. The story is recounted in Shiozawa Sanenobu, "Nanri Fumio monogatari 2," *Swing Journal* [hereafter *SJ*] Oct. 1956: 43–44; Nanri Fumio and Segawa Masahisa, "My Opinion," *SJ* June 1971: 217; and Uchida, *Nihon no jazu shi*, 110–11.
114. Steven B. Elworth, "Jazz in Crisis, 1948–1958: Ideology and Representation," in Gabbard, *Jazz among the Discourses*, 61.
115. "Japanese Jazz Writers Get an American Radio Hearing," *Newsweek* 26 June 1937: 30; Segawa, "Coromubia," 17.
116. Burton Crane, "The Reminiscences of Burton Crane" (New York: Oral History Research Office, Columbia University, 1961), 4, 13–14.
117. Kikuchi Shigeya, "Nihon jazu zenshi 14," *Dansu to ongaku*, Oct. 1956: 19; Mizushima Sanae, "Nihon no jazu hensen shi—mukashi o furikaette," *Jazz* Nov. 1975: 79–80; Shimizu Kimiko, interview in Uchida, *Nihon no jazu shi*, 114. Kikuchi was even more impressed by Williams's accompanist Segure, whose "rhythmic countermelody style" dazzled him. Following their extended Asian tour Roger Segure achieved recognition by writing arrangements for Andy Kirk, Jimmie Lunceford, and Louis Armstrong, and Williams went on to enjoy modest fame in the United States as a singer with Bunny Berigan, Armstrong, and Teddy Wilson, before dying prematurely sometime in the 1950s.
118. Rose McKee, 1935 communication, quoted in George Yoshida, *Reminiscing in Swingtime:*

Japanese Americans in American Popular Music, 1925–1960 (San Francisco: National Japanese American Historical Society, 1997), 62. Alice Kawahata (as she prefers her name to be pronounced) is still alive in Los Angeles. See Norikoshi Takao, *Alice: The Story of Kawahata Fumiko* (Tokyo: Kōdansha, 1999).

119. Hata Toyokichi, "Jazzu ongaku," *Chūō kōron* May 1928: 31. Hata added disparaging comments about the "amateur" (in both senses of the word) bands playing jazz in Tokyo in the late 1920s (32).

120. Dorinne K. Kondo, *Crafting Selves: Power, Gender, and Discourses of Identity in a Japanese Workplace* (Chicago: University of Chicago Press, 1990), 11, notes the fascination that many Japanese who "adhere to an eminently biological definition of Japaneseness" feel when encountering someone who is virtually a "living oxymoron, someone who [is] both Japanese and not Japanese."

121. Nakano Tadaharu and the Columbia Rhythm Boys, "Tsukiyo no sanpo" ("Side by Side") (Nippon Columbia: 29781, 1938); Taft Beppu, "St. Louis Blues" (Nippon Columbia: 27994, 1934). These recordings appear together on Columbia's collection *Orijinaru genban ni yoru Nippon no jazu songu (senzen hen)*.

122. Yoshida, *Reminiscing in Swingtime*, 41–116, provides detailed biographies of each artist as well as rare photographs, posters, and concert programs that testify to their popularity. Their story is also told in Brown, "California Origins of the Jazz Boom in Occupied Japan, 1945–1952."

123. Saitō's story is recounted in Uchida, *Nihon no jazu shi*, 66–67. Japanese dance halls in Shanghai are discussed in Ōmori, vol. 1, 169–70.

124. My "Jammin' on the Jazz Frontier: The Japanese Jazz Community in Interwar Shanghai," *Japanese Studies* 19.1 (May 1999): 5–16, discusses in greater depth theories of the symbolic contours and transformative effects of the "frontier," as well as the effects of Saitō Ren's *Shanghai Advance Kings* franchise on popular memories of the Shanghai experience.

125. Randall Gould, "Where Races Mingle but Never Merge," *Christian Science Monitor*, weekly magazine section, 24 June 1936: 4. The term *frontier* seems even more appropriate since the publication of Frederic Wakeman's *The Shanghai Badlands: Wartime Terrorism and Urban Crime, 1937–1941* (Cambridge: Cambridge University Press, 1996), which describes how "illicit pleasures . . . were both a momentary escape from unbearable social tensions and a constant reminder of a cleaved city festering under foreign domination." Like other frontiers (as zones of cultural interaction and conflict), Shanghai was characterized by lawlessness, nightly shootings, and a tense "triangular relationship between the foreign settlement, the Japanese military, and the puppet regime" (1).

126. Frederic Wakeman Jr. and Wen-hsin Yeh, eds., *Shanghai Sojourners* (Berkeley: Institute of East Asian Studies, 1992), 6–7; Frederic Wakeman Jr., *Policing Shanghai: 1927–1937* (Berkeley: University of California Press, 1995), xv, 11. Even women who were not prostitutes were employed in the "sexual marketplace," selling their companionship as hostesses, waitresses, and taxi dancers.

127. Gould, 4; Marie-Claire Bergeré, " 'The Other China': Shanghai from 1919 to 1949," in *Shanghai: Revolution and Development in an Asian Metropolis*, ed. Christopher Howe (Cambridge: Cambridge University Press, 1981), 22.

128. Such a view confirms the findings of historians who argue that mass media and popular entertainment were deeply implicated in the colonial enterprise. See in particular Miriam Silverberg, "Remembering Pearl Harbor, Forgetting Charlie Chaplin, and the

Case of the Disappearing Western Woman: A Picture Story," *positions: east asia cultures critique* 1.1 (1993): 25; Louise Young, *Japan's Total Empire: Manchuria and the Culture of Wartime Imperialism* (Berkeley: University of California Press, 1998), 68–78; and Robertson, chap. 3.

129. Hershey, 28; Wakeman, *Policing Shanghai,* 107; John Pal, *Shanghai Saga* (London: Jarrolds, 1963), 76.

130. Ernest O. Hauser, *Shanghai: City for Sale* (New York: Harcourt, Brace, 1940), 261–62. For an equally entertaining description of Shanghai night life, see *All about Shanghai and Environs: A Standard Guide Book* (Shanghai: The University Press, 1934–35), 73, republished as *All about Shanghai: A Standard Guidebook* (Hong Kong: Oxford University Press, 1983).

131. The first "dance hall girls" in Shanghai in the 1920s were said to be mostly White Russians fleeing the Russian Revolution: "In jaded Shanghai, ever on the alert for a new sensation, much addicted to the pleasures of the senses, the voluptuous Russian girl was an immediate success" (Marc T. Greene, "Shanghai Cabaret Girl," *Literary Digest* 23 Oct. 1937: 25). Chinese dancers (*wunü*) were hired in greater numbers in the 1930s. By the end of the 1930s there were 2,500 to 5,000 taxi dancers in Shanghai (Wakeman, *Policing Shanghai,* 108).

132. Claude Lapham, "Looking at Japanese Jazz," *Metronome* June 1936: 14; Claude Lapham, "China Needs American Bands," *Metronome* July 1936: 13, 37.

133. See S. James Staley, "Is It True What They Say about China?" *Metronome* Dec. 1936: 17+; and Crane, "Coda on Japan."

134. Weatherford was the epitome of the globe-trotting "jazz exile." He was married to a Japanese and spent several years in East Asia and Europe before settling in India before World War II. He died in Calcutta in April 1945, leaving very few recordings. See Warren R. Pinckney Jr., "Jazz in India: Perspectives on Historical Development and Musical Acculturation," *Asian Music* 21.1 (1989–90): 37.

135. Quoted in Nanri and Segawa, "My Opinion," 216–17.

136. Quoted in Saitō, *Shōwa no bansukingu tachi,* 35.

137. Saitō, *Shōwa no bansukingu tachi,* 24; Uchida, *Nihon no jazu shi,* 69.

138. Quoted in Saitō, *Shōwa no bansukingu tachi,* 24.

139. Matsuzaka, 29.

140. Quoted in Nanri and Segawa, "My Opinion," 217.

141. One Chinese writer described the tension at the beginning of the 1930s: "With three of their provinces forcibly taken away from them, it would be against human nature for the Chinese in Shanghai to love their Japanese neighbors as before. Similarly, elated by the unexpected success in Manchuria [in 1931], the Japanese in Shanghai would have to be angels before they would not be stirred to emulating the example of their compatriots." Hsü Shuhsi, *Japan and Shanghai* (Shanghai: Kelly and Walsh, 1938), 11–12.

142. Mizushima, 78–79; Takeichi Yoshihisa, "Sayōnara Mizushima Sanae," *SJ* April 1978: 66–67.

143. Quoted in Nanri and Segawa, "My Opinion," 217.

144. Nanri Fumio, interview in Uchida, *Nihon no jazu shi,* 75–76.

145. See Saitō, *Shōwa no bansukingu tachi,* 252; Uchida, *Nihon no jazu shi,* 76.

146. Benedict Anderson, *Imagined Communities: Reflections on the Origin and Spread of Nationalism,* 2d ed. (London: Verso, 1991), 22–36.

1. "Ihaku, kachō fujin tōtō, furin koi no steppu," *Tokyo Asahi shinbun*, 8 Nov. 1933: 7.

2. Mori's novel (*Dansu hōru ero kyōraku jidai*) is cited in Nagai Yoshikazu, *Shakō dansu to Nihonjin* (Tokyo: Shōbunsha, 1991), 113–14, 117; see also Uchida Kōichi, *Nihon no jazu shi: senzen, sengo* (Tokyo: Swing Journal, 1976), 130–33. The social ills of the day are discussed in Margit Nagy, "Middle-Class Working Women during the Interwar Years," in *Recreating Japanese Women*, ed. Gail Bernstein (Berkeley: University of California Press, 1991), 199, 210–11.

3. Dick Hebdige, *Subculture: The Meaning of Style* (1979; London: Routledge, 1987), 92–93.

4. These themes are discussed in Tetsuo Najita and H. D. Harootunian, "Japanese Revolt against the West: Political and Cultural Criticism in the Twentieth Century," in *The Cambridge History of Japan*, vol. 6: *The Twentieth Century*, ed. Peter Duus (Cambridge: Cambridge University Press, 1988), 734; and H. Paul Varley, *Japanese Culture*, 3d ed. (Honolulu: University of Hawaii Press, 1984), 254.

5. See Paul Oliver, "Jazz Is Where You Find It: The European Experience of Jazz," in *Superculture: American Popular Culture and Europe*, ed. C. W. E. Bigsby (London: Paul Elek, 1975), 140; E. J. Hobsbawm, *Nations and Nationalism since 1780: Programme, Myth, Reality* (Cambridge: Cambridge University Press, 1990), 131, which describes the early twentieth century as "the apogee of nationalism"; Erik Levi, *Music in the Third Reich* (New York: St. Martin's Press, 1994), 120; and S. Frederick Starr, *Red & Hot: The Fate of Jazz in the Soviet Union*, rev. ed. (New York: Limelight Editions, 1994), 54–106.

6. See Edward Seidensticker, *Tokyo Rising: The City since the Great Earthquake* (New York: Knopf, 1990), 90; J. Thomas Rimer, ed., *Culture and Identity: Japanese Intellectuals during the Interwar Years* (Princeton, N.J.: Princeton University Press, 1990), x; and Richard H. Mitchell, *Thought Control in Prewar Japan* (Ithaca, N.Y.: Cornell University Press, 1976), 30.

7. In fact, the aesthetic standards and musicological criteria that are invoked nowadays to distinguish jazz from other musics serve in part to write Whiteman out of the dominant evolutionary narrative of jazz history. As Bernard Gendron, "Jamming at Le Boeuf: Jazz and the Paris Avant-Garde," *Discourse* 12.1 (1989–90) notes, Whiteman's "nominal jazz [did] not fit into the trajectory leading to modern jazz or give a sense to its aesthetics," and thus has been eliminated from the jazz canon (14). Criticisms of Whiteman usually characterize his music as "watered-down jazz, jazz that lacks both the drive and earthiness of the music created by jazzmen; [it] lacks the improvisatory element." See Peter Clayton and Peter Gammond, *The Guiness Jazz Companion* (Middlesex: Guiness, 1989), 232.

8. Gangstarr, "Jazz Thing," *Mo' Better Blues* (CBS: 46792, 1990).

9. Charles Nanry, *The Jazz Text* (New York: 1979), 120. The irony of regarding symphonic jazz as watered-down "white jazz" is that the black composer James Reese Europe (1881–1919) pioneered this style. See Ronald G. Welburn, "James Reese Europe and the Infancy of Jazz Criticism," *Black Music Research Journal* 7 (1987): 35–43; and John Gennari, "Jazz Criticism: Its Development and Ideologies," *Black American Literature Forum* 25 (1991): 470–71.

10. Neil Leonard, *Jazz and the White Americans: The Acceptance of a New Art Form* (Chicago: University of Chicago Press, 1962), 4, neatly characterizes Whiteman's symphonic jazz as the "synthesis" resulting from "a pattern of Hegelian derivation" in which classical music and its aesthetic values represent the thesis and black jazz the antithesis. As a synthesis,

Whiteman's music could be widely accepted by a mainstream public unprepared for the racial and rhythmic implications of "real" jazz. Yet "in their own moderate ways symphonic jazz advocates found in their music something of the same thing that real jazz enthusiasts found in theirs—an expression of revolt and a fresh source of morality" (77). For an intriguing contrast to Leonard's study, see James Lincoln Collier, *The Reception of Jazz in America: A New View*, I.S.A.M. Monographs 27 (Brooklyn, N.Y.: Institute for Studies in American Music, 1988), which challenges the conventional wisdom that jazz was appreciated and accepted as an art in Europe before it was in America.

11. Paul Whiteman, with Mary Margaret McBride, *Jazz, Popular Culture in America 1800–1925* (1926; New York: Arno Press, 1974), 155.

12. Kami Kyōsuke, "Ano koro no jazu 30: hatsu no shinfonikku jazu," *Tokyo shinbun*, evening ed., 8 Nov. 1957: 5.

13. Pōru Howaitoman, *Jazo: Howaitoman cho*, trans. Natsukawa Tarō (Tokyo: Inakasha, 1929); Hata Toyokichi, "Jazzu ongaku," *Chūō kōron* May 1928: 27.

14. Gennari, 466, argues that the French intellectuals who made jazz criticism "respectable" in the 1930s—Hugues Panassié, Charles Delauney, and Rober Goffin—were guided by a "primitivist credo [that] drew on a tradition reaching back to Jean Jacques Rousseau's admiration of the 'savage's innate goodness.' . . . [T]he ideal primitive man for Panassié and his compatriots—the noblest of all savages—was Louis Armstrong." The consensus of this group was that black jazz musicians were better than white ones "because of their unique ability to achieve a trance state while they were playing," and because their alleged inability to read music facilitated "their unadorned, uncompromising, instinctual approach" to music making.

15. Yui Shōichi repeats an oft-cited remark that in the interwar period "nearly all Japanese thought as I did, that 'jazz dance music' was white American music" (quoted in Yui Shōichi, Bob Belden, and Ogawa Takao, "Taidan: umi o watatta ongaku—jazu de kataru nichibei taishū bunka shi," *Chūō kōron* May 1995: 242). But the "black roots" of jazz were acknowledged. Unuma Naoki, "Jazu," *Modango jiten* (Tokyo: Seibundō, 1930), 247, defined "jazz" as the music of *kuronbō* ("darkies").

16. Architect Kon Wajirō was one writer who attempted to create a scientific method for studying modern customs (*gendai fūzoku*), and even dubbed his field of inquiry "modernologio" (*kōgengaku*). See Kon Wajirō, "Gendai fūzoku," in *Nihon fūzoku shi kōza* (Tokyo: Yūyama Kakuban, 1929), 3–6, 42. This topic is addressed in Miriam Silverberg, "Concerning the Japanese Ethnography of Modernity," *Journal of Asian Studies* 51 (Feb. 1992): 30–54.

17. Nomura Kōichi, "Jazu ongaku raisan," *Ongaku sekai* Oct. 1929: 24–25.

18. Narita Ryūichi, "Toshi no seikatsu kakumei," in *Taishō no engeki to toshi*, ed. Taishō Engeki Kenkyukai (Tokyo: Musashino Shobō, 1991), 138. Seidensticker, 5, emphasizes the earthquake in the shift from the cultural centrality of the "low city" (*shitamachi*) to the "high city" ("the western hilly districts").

19. Minami Hiroshi and Shakai Shinri Kenkyūjo, eds., *Taishō bunka 1905–1927* (1965; Tokyo: Keisō Shobō, 1987), 353.

20. Yamano Haruo, "Kantō dai shinsai go no shakai jōsei," in *Taishō demokurashii*, ed. Kinbara Samon, Kindai Nippon no Kiseki 4 (Tokyo: Yoshikawa Hiroshi Bunkan, 1994), 216.

21. Iwamoto Kenji, *Nihon eiga to modanizumu, 1920–1930* (Tokyo: Libro, 1991), 6–7, discusses the differing connotations of the terms *kindaishugi* (modernism) and *modanizumu* (modernism).

22. Eric Hobsbawm, *The Age of Extremes: A History of the World, 1914–1991* (New York: Pan-

theon, 1994), 181; Norman F. Cantor, *Twentieth-Century Culture: Modernism to Deconstruction* (New York: Peter Lang, 1988), 4–6; Gennari, 462; and Tyrus Miller, *Late Modernism: Politics, Fiction, and the Arts between the World Wars* (Berkeley: University of California Press, 1999), 13.

23. Miriam Silverberg, "Constructing a New Cultural History of Prewar Japan," in *Japan in the World*, ed. Masao Miyoshi and H. D. Harootunian (Durham, N.C.: Duke University Press, 1993), 116, argues that Japanese *modanizumu* was more than another importation, but was rather distinct from European modernism because it incorporated elements of emperor worship and ultranationalism.

24. Satō Takeshi, "Modanizumu to Amerikaka: senkyūhyaku-nijū nendai o chūshin toshite," in *Nihon modanizumu no kenkyū: shisō, seikatsu, bunka*, ed. Minami Hiroshi (Tokyo: Burēn Shuppan, 1982), 18–20, 25; Jeffrey E. Hanes, "Taishū bunka/ka'i bunka/minshū bunka: senkanki no Nihon no toshi ni okeru kindai seikatsu," in *Toshi no kūkan, toshi no shintai*, ed. Yoshimi Shun'ya (Tokyo: Keisō Shobō, 1996), 99–100.

25. Murobuse Kōshin, *Gaitō no shakaigaku* (Tokyo: Inakasha, 1929), 33; Ōya Sōichi, *Modan sō to modan sō* (Tokyo: Daihōkaku Shobō, 1930), 191.

26. Hobsbawm, *Age of Extremes*, 184.

27. Hosokawa Shūhei, "Seiyō ongaku no Nihonka, taishūka 24: 'Tokyo kōshinkyoku,'" *Music Magazine* Mar. 1991: 119; and Unuma, 247. Constructions of modernity in nonjazz popular songs are discussed in Christine R. Yano, "Defining the Modern Nation in Japanese Popular Song, 1914–1932," in *Japan's Competing Modernities: Issues in Culture and Democracy 1900–1930*, ed. Sharon Minichiello (Honolulu: University of Hawaii Press, 1998), 247–64.

28. On images of the *moga* (and the alleged irrelevance of the *mobo*), see Barbara Hamill, "Modan gāru no jidaiteki imi," *Gendai no esupuri* 188: *Nihon modanizumu*, ed. Minami Hiroshi (1983): 84–85; Barbara Hamill Satō, "The *Moga* Sensation: Perceptions of the *Modan Gāru* in Japanese Intellectual Circles during the 1920s," *Gender & History* 5.3 (1993): 370; and Miriam Silverberg, "The Modern Girl as Militant," in Bernstein, 254.

29. Silverberg, "The Modern Girl as Militant," 239. Silverberg denies the existence of the *moga* as anything other than a "highly commodified cultural construct crafted by journalists" (240); she rather redefines them as "Modern Girls" who were "militant," who "transgressed by crossing boundaries erected by class, gender, and culture" and by performing nontraditional roles as "consumers, producers, legal subjects, and political activists" (254–55).

30. Uenoda Setsuo, *Japan and Jazz: Sketches and Essays on Japanese City Life* (Tokyo: Taiheiyōsha, 1930), 16; Inage Sofū, "Seibi no junka," *Nihon hyōron* Jan. 1917: 136, cited and translated in Donald Roden, "Taishō Culture and the Problem of Gender Ambivalence," in Rimer, *Culture and Identity*, 47.

31. Gendron, 18.

32. Nishigaki Tetsuo, "Jazu to jazu," *Ongaku shinchō* April 1930: 10. For discussion of how jazz figured within aesthetic hierarchies, see Lawrence Levine, "Jazz and American Culture," in *The Unpredictable Past: Explorations in American Cultural History* (New York: Oxford University Press, 1993), 172–88.

33. Shioiri Kamesuke, "Modānizumu no ongaku: jazu!" *Ongaku sekai* Oct. 1929: 27–28. The fears of classical musicians are discussed in Leonard, *Jazz and the White Americans*, 31.

34. Hata, "Jazzu ongaku," 24.

35. Tokunaga Masatarō, "Nippon jazu ongaku undō shōshi," *Ongaku shinchō* April 1930: 7.

This essay can be characterized as the first "history" of jazz in Japan, primarily through a genealogy of bands.

36. Horiuchi Keizō, "Ragutaimu no kenkyū," *Ongaku kai* Oct. 1920: 15. I am grateful to Larry Richards for bringing this source to my attention.

37. Horiuchi Keizō, "Jazu geijutsu no kandan," *Ongaku shinchō* Jan. 1925: 17. In *Jinta konokata* (Tokyo: Aoi Shobō, 1935), 78–79, Horiuchi described the JOAK Jazz Band: "Of course they were not very good [compared to foreign bands], but I had peace of mind that the members could read and therefore would not give an unmusical performance."

38. Horiuchi, *Jinta konokata*, 75–77; and Horiuchi, "Jazu geijutsu no kandan," 16. Whiteman himself promoted this image of himself as having transformed "the discordant Jazz" through "the art of scoring," as the program notes to his 1924 premiere of *Rhapsody in Blue* (quoted in Walser, 40) indicate.

39. Horiuchi Keizō, "Ryūkōka wa shinpo suru," *Yomiuri shinbun* 14 Aug. 1929: 4; 15 Aug. 1929: 4.

40. Shioiri Kamesuke, *Jazu ongaku* (Tokyo: Keibunkan, 1929), 10, 74; Shioiri, "Modānizumu no ongaku: jazu!" 28. Shioiri cited Henry O. Osgood's *So This Is Jazz*, Alfred Von Baresel's *Das neue Jazzbuch*, and Paul von Bernhard's *Jazz* as his only research sources.

41. Kawabata Yasunari, "Asakusa Kurenaidan," in *Kawabata Yasunari zenshū*, vol. 2 (Tokyo: Shinchōsha, 1960), 31; Ōya Sōichi, "Modan sō to modan sō," *Chūō kōron* Feb. 1929: 181; Hata, "Jazzu ongaku," 21; and Kiyozawa Kiyoshi, "Amerika tsūshin: spiido kuni Amerika," *Chūō kōron* Nov. 1929: 203, 212.

42. Quoted in Hosokawa Shūhei, "Seiyō ongaku no Nihonka, taishūka 32: jazu bungaku," *Music Magazine* Nov. 1991: 153. The series ("Sekai dai tokai sentan jazu bungaku" in Japanese) featured works by Japanese and Western authors that "tied city names to musical terms."

43. Kathy Ogren, *The Jazz Revolution* (New York: Oxford University Press, 1989), 154.

44. Horiuchi Keizō, preface in Shioiri, *Jazu ongaku*, 5.

45. Matsuyama Sueyoshi, "Jazu mandan," *Ongaku sekai* Oct. 1929: 42; Horiuchi Keizō, "Jazu riyū," *Ongaku sekai* Oct. 1929: 19; Murashima Yoriyuki, *Kanraku no ōkyō kafe* (Tokyo: Bunka Seikatsu Kenkyūkai, 1929), 199; Uenoda, *Japan and Jazz*, 30; advertisement for Shioiri's *Jazu ongaku*, *Ongaku sekai*, May 1931.

46. Ogren, 140.

47. "Dai Tokyo no jazo—The Jazz-Band of Tokyo," *Asahigraph* 2 Nov. 1927: 7.

48. Larry Richards, "Senzen no Nihon ni okeru jazu ongaku to sono gainen" (M.A. thesis, Tokyo Geijutsu Daigaku, 1992), 50; Hosokawa Shūhei, "Seiyō ongaku no Nihonka, taishūka 31: sōon," *Music Magazine* Oct. 1991: 127–29.

49. Shioiri, "Modānizumu no ongaku: jazu!" 27–28. Regarding the association of jazz with mechanization in America, Ogren 144, writes, "Jazz rhythms, in particular syncopation, joined mechanization as a cause of the hectic tempo of the twenties." See also Levine, "Jazz and American Culture," 179.

50. David Meltzer, ed., *Reading Jazz* (San Francisco: Mercury House, 1993), 4, 26; James Clifford, *The Predicament of Culture: Twentieth-Century Ethnography, Literature, and Art* (Cambridge: Harvard University Press, 1988), 198n.

51. Horiuchi, "Jazu riyū," 19; Murobuse, 136–38.

52. Y. Kawabata, 31–33; Roden 50.

53. Y. Kawabata, 33, translated in Seidensticker, 79.

54. Jennifer Robertson, *Takarazuka: Sexual Politics and Popular Culture in Modern Japan* (Berkeley: University of California Press, 1998), 55–57.

55. Murobuse, 133–34; Murashima, 195–96. The eroticized *jokyū* is discussed in Miriam Silverberg, "The Cafe Waitress Serving Modern Japan," in *Mirror of Modernity: Invented Traditions of Modern Japan*, ed. Stephen Vlastos (Berkeley: University of California Press, 1998), 208–25.

56. See Donald H. Shively, "Popular Culture," in *Cambridge History of Japan*, vol. 4: *Early Modern Japan*, ed. John Whitney Hall (Cambridge: Cambridge University Press, 1991), 742–43, 748–49; and Ono Takeo, *Yoshiwara, Shimabara* (Tokyo: Kyōikusha, 1978), 32.

57. James C. Scott, *Domination and the Arts of Resistance: Hidden Transcripts* (New Haven: Yale University Press, 1990), 2–4, defines "public transcript" as the "public performance of the subordinate [which], out of prudence, fear, and the desire to curry favor, [is] shaped to appeal to the expectations of the powerful . . . , a shorthand way of describing the open interaction between subordinates and those who dominate." In contrast, the "hidden transcript" denotes "discourse that takes place 'offstage,' beyond direct observation by powerholders."

58. Hata Toyokichi, "Shakō dansu," *Chūō kōron* Sept. 1928: 150.

59. Tsuji Katsumi, *Shōgyō kōkoku zuan dai shūsei*, Shōwa modan āto 4: kōkoku (1936; Tokyo: MPC, 1989); and James Fraser, Steven Heller, and Seymour Chwast, *Japanese Modern: Graphic Design between the Wars* (San Francisco: Chronicle, 1996). Both collections are rich in the iconography of modernism, particularly images of *mobo* and *moga* drinking alcohol and smoking cigarettes. The use of jazz iconography in advertising illustrates Dick Hebdige's point about the appropriation of the superficial aspects of subcultures by the hegemonic culture.

60. Jeffrey E. Hanes, "Advertising Culture in Interwar Japan," *Japan Foundation Newsletter* 23.4 (Jan. 1996): 11. See Regal Pomade ad in Tsuji, 10; and ads featuring black caricatures, jazz instruments, or the word *jazu* in Fraser, Heller, and Chwast, 32, 64, 90, 92, 113.

61. Najita and Harootunian, 711.

62. "Hyōgo-ken, genjūna torishimari kisoku o kōfu," *Tokyo Asahi shinbun* 6 Nov. 1928, reprinted in Uchikawa Yoshimi, ed., *Shōwa nyūzu jiten*, vol. 1 (Tokyo: Mainichi Communications, 1990), 393.

63. Quoted in Haruko Taya Cook and Theodore F. Cook, *Japan at War: An Oral History* (New York: New Press, 1992), 62.

64. "Keishichō mo kuiki seigen nado torishimari kisoku o jisshi," *Tokyo Asahi shinbun* 10 Nov. 1928, reprinted in Uchikawa, *Shōwa nyūzu jiten*, vol. 1, 393. Tokyo's code ("Budōjō torishimari kisoku [Keishichō rei #16])" is reprinted in Minami Hiroshi and Shakai Shinri Kenkyūjo, eds., *Shōwa bunka 1925–1945* (Tokyo: Keisō Shobō, 1987), 165–66; and in Nagai, 84–86.

65. Nagai, 83–84.

66. Kitao Ryōnosuke, *Kindai Ōsaka* (Ōsaka: Sōgensha, 1932), 413. I thank Jeff Hanes for bringing this source to my attention.

67. Kitao, 403–4.

68. Kitao, 407, 411, 413–14.

69. Funabashi Yōji, "Jazukai no dōkō o ronjite gakushi shokun ni atau," *Dansu to ongaku* April 1935: 38–39.

70. Nagai, 125–26.

71. Shigeta Tadayasu, *Fūzoku keisatsu no riron to jissai* (Tokyo: Nankōsha, 1934), 178–80. Minami, *Shōwa bunka*, 162, characterizes Shigeta's book as a "relatively liberal theory for policing customs." See also Nagai, 135–36.

72. Shigeta, 169, 178.

73. Najita and Harootunian, 717, 734, 743; Miles Fletcher, *The Search for a New Order: Intellectuals and Fascism in Prewar Japan* (Chapel Hill: University of North Carolina Press, 1982), 156–57; and Sidney DeVere Brown, "Jazz in Japan: Its Sources and Development, 1925–1952," Proceedings, 1980 Annual Meeting, Southwest Conference on Asian Studies, New Orleans, 133.

74. Leslie Pincus, *Authenticating Culture in Imperial Japan: Kuki Shūzō and the Rise of National Aesthetics* (Berkeley: University of California Press, 1996), 216, citing George Mosse, "Introduction: Towards a General Theory of Fascism," in *International Fascism: New Thoughts and New Approches* (London: Sage Publications, 1979).

75. "As Japanese life became remade in the image of the West through the penetration of Western consumer capitalism and the commodification of daily life, the distinctiveness of Japanese cultural identity was recovered through the construction of a traditional aesthetic expressed in the longing for the tastes and styles of an earlier period before the 'invasion' of Western consumer culture and in the valorization of the tastes and styles of the Japanese countryside. . . . [M]any in Japan lamented not so much the loss of a traditional way of life, but the disappearance of a traditional aesthetic." Jason G. Karlin, "Gendering Modernity: Taste, Style, and Aestheticism in Early-Twentieth-Century Japan," unpublished paper presented at 46th Annual Meeting of Midwest Conference on Asian Affairs, Northern Illinois University, 28 Sept. 1997, 1, 27.

76. Kuki Shūzō, " 'Iki' no kōzō," in *Kuki Shūzō zenshū*, vol. 1, ed. Amano Teiyū, Omodaka Hisayuki, and Satō Akio (Tokyo: Iwanami Shoten, 1981), 46, translated and cited in Pincus, 196. Pincus defines *iki* as "an elusive sense of style . . . [and] a rarefied blend of sobriety and audacity . . . which circulated in the erotically charged atmosphere of the Edo pleasure quarters, the Kabuki theaters, and the popular arts of the late Tokugawa period" (2).

77. Ōya, "Modan sō to modan sō," 181.

78. The irony is that the cultural practices of the eighteenth and nineteenth centuries that Kuki and others valorized in the twentieth were regarded as subversive of the Tokugawa moral cosmology because of their focus on the body. As Harry Harootunian, "Late Tokugawa Thought and Culture," in *Cambridge History of Japan*, vol. 5: *The Nineteenth Century*, ed. Marius B. Jansen (Cambridge: Cambridge University Press, 1989), 173, notes, "Late Tokugawa cultural practice seemed to converge upon the body, making public what hitherto had remained private. . . . [T]he content of the playful culture invariably focused on the activities of the body." "Bodily imagery in both verbal and illustrated texts signified a different kind of social reality with an inverted scale of priorities for the Edo townsmen. It was an order that had as its head the genitalia or anus and as its heart the stomach" (176).

79. Muromachi Jirō, "Jazu myūjikku ni taisuru ikkōsatsu," *Dansu to ongaku* April 1935: 20–21.

80. Kevin Doak, *Dreams of Difference: The Japan Romantic School and the Crisis of Modernity* (Berkeley: University of California Press, 1994), xvi, xxviii–xxix.

81. "Saikin no dansukai wo kentō suru zadankai," *Modern Dance* March 1936: 23, quoted in Nagai, 141.

82. Gendron, 21; Oliver, 147. See also Levine, "Jazz in American Culture," 182–83.

83. Clifford, 197; Tyler Stovall, *Paris Noir: African Americans in the City of Light* (Boston: Houghton Mifflin, 1996), 32. See also Gendron, 9, and Oliver, 140. Clifford adds: "The black body in Paris of the twenties was an ideological artifact. Archaic Africa (which came to Paris by way of the future—that is, America) was sexed, gendered, and invested with 'magic' in specific ways. Standard poses adopted by 'La Bakaire,' like Léger's designs and

costumes, evoked a recognizable 'Africanity'—the naked form emphasizing pelvis and buttocks, a segmented stylization suggesting a strangely mechanical vitality" (197–98).

84. Hata, "Jazzu ongaku," 22–23. In contemporary usage the word *kuronbō* is usually regarded as the equivalent of *nigger,* or at best a "cute and endearing" term "connoting emotional immaturity and less than full adult status" (John Russell, "Race and Reflexivity: The Black Other in Contemporary Japanese Mass Culture," *Cultural Anthropology* Feb. 1991: 8, 22n). However, Ronald Toby informs me that the word has been in use for centuries and neither had perennially pejorative connotations nor referred exclusively to people of African descent.

85. Nogawa Kōbun, *Gendaijin no ongaku—jazu* (Tokyo: Hibakusha, 1949), 10; Shioiri, "Modānizumu no ongaku: jazu!" 27–28.

86. Fujiura Kō, "Jazu nashi ni wa kurasenai," *Demos* May 1949: 39, 41; Noguchi Hisamitsu, "Jazu no kiki," *Ondori tsūshin* 7.5 (1951): 47; Honda Toshio, "Jazu wa jidai o han'ei suru," *Ongaku no sekai* (May 1981): 26; Noguchi Hisamitsu, "Jazu wa ryūkōbyō ka?" *Bungei shunjū* 31.14 (1953): 213.

87. Noguchi, "Jazu wa ryūkōbyō ka?" 213; Nogawa, *Gendaijin no ongaku—jazu,* 11; Mayuzumi Toshirō, "Jazu to minzokusei," *Fīru hāmoni* April 1950: 25.

88. Carol Gluck and Stephen R. Graubard, eds., *Showa: The Japan of Hirohito* (New York: Norton, 1992), xxviii–xxix.

89. Nogawa, *Gendaijin no ongaku—jazu,* 9–10.

90. "Yo wa masa ni jazu nekkyō jidai, nami ni noru bandoman ya kashu," *Mainichi shinbun,* evening ed., 2 Aug. 1953: 4; Sonobe Saburō, *Enka kara jazu e no Nihon shi* (Tokyo: Wakōsha, 1954), 168; and Minami Hiroshi, "Jazu no kōzai," *Fujin kōron* April 1954: 130, 132.

91. Uenoda, *Japan and Jazz,* 31.

4 "Jazz for the Country's Sake": Toward a New Cultural Order in Wartime Japan

1. Quoted in Nakazawa Mayumi, "The Conversation: Noriko Awaya," *Tokyo Journal* Oct. 1994: 39. The story is recounted in Hattori Ryōichi, *Boku no ongaku jinsei* (Tokyo: Chūō Bungeisha, 1983), 197. Yoshitake Teruko, *Burūsu no joō: Awaya Noriko* (Tokyo: Bungei Shunjū, 1989), 229, relates a similar story of a police officer calling Awaya "un-Japanese" (*hikokumin*) for refusing to wear the obligatory drab clothes.

2. Donald Shively, "Bakufu versus Kabuki," *Harvard Journal of Asiatic Studies* 18 (1955): 326–56, describes how government censorship transformed *kabuki* from an unruly circus of prostitutes to a refined (if bawdy) dramatic art.

3. See, for example, Honda Toshio, *Jazu* (Tokyo: Shin Nippon Shinsho, 1976), 13–24, and *Modan Jazu* (Tokyo: Shin Nippon Shinsho, 1989), 127–41; Sidney DeVere Brown, "Jazz in Japan: Its Sources and Development, 1925–1952," Proceedings, 1980 Annual Meeting, Southwest Conference on Asian Studies, New Orleans, 133–36; Takahashi Ichirō and Sasaki Mamoru, *Jazu shifū—sengo sōsōki densetsu* (Tokyo: San'ichi Shobō, 1997), 215–16; and Gregory Kasza, *The State and the Mass Media in Japan, 1918–1945* (Berkeley: University of California Press, 1988), 256–57. The most cursory treatment I have seen is at "Nihon no jazu shi," http://jp.jazzcentralstation.com/jcsjp/station/jazzdest/japan/history.html.

4. Quoted in Matsuzaka Hiro, ed., "Nihon no jazu sōshiki kara dainiji taisen made," *Jazu hihyō* [hereafter *JH*] 12 (1972): 58–59.

5. See Ian Buruma, *The Wages of Guilt* (New York: Farrar Strauss Giroux, 1994); George L. Hicks, *Japan's War Memories: Amnesia or Concealment?* (Aldershot: Ashgate, 1997); and Carol Gluck, "The Past in the Present," in *Postwar Japan as History,* ed. Andrew Gordon (Berkeley: University of California Press, 1993), 79–85.

6. John Dower, *Japan in War and Peace: Selected Essays* (New York: New Press, 1995), 51. See also Richard H. Mitchell, *Thought Control in Prewar Japan* (Ithaca, N.Y.: Cornell University Press, 1976), 180–82; Ienaga Saburō, *The Pacific War, 1931–1945* (New York: Pantheon, 1978), 204–28; Hashikawa Bunsō, "The 'Civil Society' Ideal and Wartime Resistance," trans. Robert Wargo, in *Authority and the Individual in Japan: Citizen Protest in Historical Perspective,* ed. J. Victor Koschmann (Tokyo: University of Tokyo Press, 1978), 128–42; Andrew Barshay, *State and Intellectual in Imperial Japan: The Public Man in Crisis* (Berkeley: University of California Press, 1989); and Ben-ami Shillony, *Politics and Culture in Wartime Japan* (New York: Oxford University Press, 1981), 126.

7. Jacques Maritain, *The Responsibility of the Artist* (New York: Scribner's, 1960), 72–73, states that "*Art for the social group*" is "warped and bent to the service of a master who is not its only genuine master, namely the work, its true object, in the service of which it achieves its own inalienable freedom. . . . [I]t becomes, thus inevitably, propaganda art. . . . An artist who yields to this craving for regimentation fails by the same token in his gifts, in his calling and in his proper virtue" (original emphasis retained).

8. *Kokumin no ongaku* is discussed in Inoue Musashi and Akiyama Tatsuhide, eds., *Nihon no yōgaku hyakunen shi* (Tokyo: Dai Ippōki, 1966), 410. Kasza, *The State and the Mass Media in Japan,* 257, describes the "National Music" movement as one which "started in the early 1930s as a response by traditional artists to the invasion of Western popular music. Arrangements were written for a full orchestra, a concession to current Western tastes, but most instruments used were the traditional ones. . . . The new form was very well received."

9. Quoted in Hattori, *Boku no ongaku jinsei,* 140; "Wakare no burūsu" (Nippon Columbia: 29834A, 1937). This was not the first "blues" by a Japanese: Taniguchi Matashi recorded "Memory Blues" in 1936, and Hattori's "Foggy Crossroads" ("Kiri no jūjiro" [Nippon Columbia: 29266B, 1937]) was recorded by Moriyama Hisashi earlier, as well. See also Mitsui Tōru, "Interactions of Imported and Indigenous Musics in Japan: A Historical Overview of the Music Industry," in *Whose Master's Voice? The Development of Popular Music in Thirteen Cultures,* ed. Alison J. Ewbank and Fouli T. Papageorgiou (Westport, Conn.: Greenwood Press, 1997), 155, for Shimamura Hogetsu's 1935 comment that Japanese should write compositions that were "identifiably Japanese."

10. See my "Nipponism in Japanese Painting 1937–45," *Wittenberg Review* 1.1 (spring 1990): 64–69; Darrell William Davis, *Picturing Japaneseness: Monumental Style, National Identity, Japanese Film* (New York: Columbia University Press, 1996), 10; Kevin M. Doak, *Dreams of Difference: The Japan Romantic School and the Crisis of Modernity* (Berkeley: University of California Press, 1994); and Donald Richie, "The Occupied Arts," in *The Confusion Era: Art and Culture of Japan during the Allied Occupation, 1945–1952,* ed. Mark Sandler (Seattle: Arthur M. Sackler Gallery, Smithsonian Institution, and the University of Washington Press, 1997), 12–13.

11. See Davis, 2, 10; Miriam Silverberg, "Constructing a New Cultural History of Prewar Japan," in *Japan in the World,* ed. Masao Miyoshi and H. D. Harootunian (Durham, N.C.: Duke University Press, 1993), 116; Jeffrey E. Hanes, "Advertising Culture in Interwar Japan," *Japan Foundation Newsletter* 23.4 (Jan. 1996): 11; and Akira Kurosawa, *Something Like an Autobiography,* trans. Audie E. Bock (New York: Vintage, 1982), 148. E. J. Hobs-

bawm, *Nations and Nationalism since 1780: Programme, Myth, Reality* (Cambridge: Cambridge University Press, 1990), 141–42, notes the role of mass media (cinema, press, and radio) in nationalist expression: "National symbols [could be made] part of the life of every individual."

12. Segawa Masahisa, "Coromubia jazu songu no shuyaku tachi," liner notes, *Orijinaru genban ni yoru Nihon no jazu songu senzen hen* (Nippon Columbia: SZ-7011–15, 1976), 22. For an overview of Hattori's career at Columbia, listen to the three-CD set *Hattori Ryōichi—boku no ongaku jinsei* (Nippon Columbia: CA-2740–2742, 1989).

13. "Japanese Jazz Writers Get an American Radio Hearing," *Newsweek* 26 June 1937: 30.

14. Hattori, *Boku no ongaku jinsei,* 149. Larry Richards has noted that Hattori's "blues" had little musicological relation to most American blues: the melody contains no "blue notes" and the structure is modeled on W. C. Handy's "non-blues" composition "St. Louis Blues," rather than the standard twelve-bar blues (Hattori, *Boku no ongaku jinsei,* 143). "At any rate, in this Japanese blues [mistakenly] assumed a completely separate character from the original blues." Richards, "Senzen no Nihon ni okeru jazu ongaku to sono gainen" (M.A. thesis, Tokyo Geijutsu Daigaku, 1992), 34–37. Handy indeed altered the folk blues he heard and marketed it as sheet music. But I would argue that blues is more than a structure, as indicated by artists such as Blind Blake, Mississippi John Hurt, John Lee Hooker, and Little Milton, who have refused to limit themselves structurally.

15. Segawa, "Coromubia," 24. "Yamadera no oshō-san" (Nippon Columbia: 29300A, 1937).

16. From article in *Hōchi shinbun,* evening ed., 24 Sept. 1937, quoted in Nakazawa Mayumi, "'Dinah' wa mō kikoenai—Nihon no jazu: senchū hen," *Ushio* 281 (Sept. 1982): 186, and in Kurata Yoshihiro, *Nihon rekōdo bunka shi* (Tokyo: Tokyo Shoseki, 1992), 197–98.

17. Yui Shōichi, "Nippon popyurā ongaku shi 34: Nippon no jazu to wa nanika ni taisuru mosaku," *Min'on* Nov. 1977: 33; Mitsui, 162.

18. "China Tango" (Nippon Columbia: 30202A, 1939), composed and arranged by Hattori Ryōichi, lyrics by Fujiura Kō, performed by Nakano Tadaharu.

19. Sano quoted in Nakazawa, "'Dinah' wa mō kikoenai," 185. See also Segawa Masahisa, "Nihon no jazu shi 17," *Swing Journal* [hereafter *SJ*] Dec. 1976: 319; and Sano Hiromi, *Sano Tasuku: ongaku to sono shōgai* (Tokyo: San'ichi Shobō, 1997), 100–101. Several of these songs appear on the 10-LP anthology *Orijinaru genban ni yoru Nippon no jazu-popyurā shi* (Nippon Victor: SJ-8003, 1976).

20. "Uta wa sekai o meguru," *A History of King Jazz Recordings: Pioneer* [sic] *of Japanese Jazz—New Edition* (King: KICJ 192, 1994).

21. Unless otherwise noted, all information on Sugii Kōichi's life comes from Segawa Masahisa, "SP jidai no jazu," liner notes, *A History of King Jazz Recordings* (*Nippon jazu taikei: Kingu rekōdo sōgyō 60 shūnen kikaku*) (King: KICJ 6001–6010, 1991), 40–41.

22. Eleven of Sugii Kōichi's contributions to the King Salon Music Series have been reissued on the CD *Pioneers of Japanese Jazz* (King: KICJ 192, 1994), as well as on *A History of King Jazz Recordings.*

23. Spiritual Mobilization is discussed in Thomas R. H. Havens, *Valley of Darkness: The Japanese People and World War Two* (New York: Norton, 1978), 13–14, 25.

24. Quoted in Nagai Yoshikazu, *Shakō dansu to Nihonjin* (Tokyo: Shōbunsha, 1991), 147.

25. Nagai, 149.

26. From unnamed dance periodicals cited in Uchida Kōichi, *Nihon no jazu shi: senzen, sengo* (Tokyo: Swing Journal, 1976), 134.

27. Yoshida Mamoru, "Jazu kissa gojūnen," *Bessatsu ichioku nin no Shōwa shi: Nihon no jazu—Jazz of Japan '82* (Tokyo: Mainichi Shinbunsha, 1982), 156–57 [hereafter cited as *Jazz of*

Japan '82]; Ōtani Ichirō, *Noge sutōri* (Yokohama: Kanagawa Sankei Shinbun, 1986), 6; Yoshida Mamoru, *Yokohama jazu monogatari: "Chigusa" no 50 nen* (Yokohama: Kanagawa Shinbunsha, 1985), 34, 36; and "Jazu no taishūka: jazu kissa no ayumi," *JH* 12 (1972): 67.

28. "Koyoi kagiri no steppu," *Tokyo Asahi shinbun* 1 Nov. 1940: 7; and Nagai, 160. Curiously, social dancing continued at the Yokohama *chabuya*, which remained open throughout most of the war, illustrating the haphazard nature of social control measures enacted by the wartime state. See Yoshida, "Daremo shiranai Nihon jazu shi," *Waseda Jazz* 3 (June 1975): 14.

29. *Chikaki yori*, Feb. 1938; translated and cited in Hashikawa, 139.

30. Arnold Perris, *Music as Propaganda: Art to Persuade, Art to Control* (Westport, Conn.: Greenwood Press, 1985), 3.

31. See Roland L. Warren, "The Nazi Use of Music as an Instrument of Social Control," *Journal of Abnormal Psychology* 38 (1943): 96–100. Regarding the functionality of music from a cross-cultural perspective, Bruno Nettl, *The Study of Ethnomusicology: Twenty-nine Issues and Concepts* (Urbana: University of Illinois Press, 1983), 151, writes that "in the literate societies the function of aesthetic enjoyment ranks high, as does entertainment. . . . Music as an activity that contributes to the integration of society appears highest in cultures 'under siege,' that is, confronted by imminent change as a result of forced contact with other cultures."

32. Hellmut Lehmann-Haupt, *Art under a Dictatorship* (New York: Oxford University Press, 1954), xviii. "Instrumentalist" versus "transformative" theories of art are discussed in Sylvia Harvey, *May '68 and Film Culture* (London: BFI Publishing, 1980), 45–86.

33. Toshio Iritani, *Group Psychology of the Japanese in Wartime* (London: Kegan Paul International, 1991), 168.

34. "Shinmin no michi," published in English as "The Way of Subjects," *Japan Times Advertiser* Aug. 1941; reprinted in David J. Lu, *Japan: A Documentary History* (Armonk, N.Y.: M. E. Sharpe, 1997), 438.

35. Quoted in Nakazawa, " 'Dinah' wa mō kikoenai," 183; see also "Bungei mo shindō: zen bunkamen no renraku ni noridasu," *Tokyo Asahi shinbun* 12 Dec. 1940: 7.

36. For instance, membership in the Japan Literary Patriotic Association (founded in May 1942) was not obligatory, "but most of Japan's 3,100 novelists, playwrights, critics, and poets chose to join in, either out of patriotism or out of fear that non-membership would damage their publication prospects" (Shillony, 116).

37. "Haki seyo, Beiei no gakufu: ongaku bunkyō no kessen daini dan," *Asahi shinbun* 16 June 1943: 3.

38. Quoted in Robert King Hall, ed., and John Owen Gauntlett, trans., *Kokutai No Hongi: Cardinal Principles of the National Entity of Japan* (Newton, Mass.: Crofton, 1974), 95, 94 (emphasis mine). The psychological aspects of and motivations for apostasy (*tenkō*) are discussed in Richard H. Mitchell, *Thought Control in Prewar Japan* (Ithaca, N.Y.: Cornell University Press, 1976), 142–47.

39. "Jazu ongaku torishimarijō no kenkai," originally published in *Shuppan keisatsuhō* 138 (July 1941), reprinted in *Gendaishi shiryō*, vol. 41: *Masu media tōsei 2*, ed. Uchikawa Yoshimi (Tokyo: Misuzu Shobō, 1975), 347–54. Subsequent quotations are cited with page numbers in the text. I am grateful to Larry Richards for bringing this document to my attention.

40. This last remark about *hōgaku*, and others cited later, is quite different from the "New Japanese Music" and "National Music" that Kasza, *The State and the Mass Media in Japan*, 257, describes as an attempt to revive indigenous classical musics. Hosokawa Shūhei also notes in his "In Search of the Sound of Empire: Tanabe Hisao and the Foundation of Japanese Ethnomusicology," *Japanese Studies* 18.1 (May 1998): 5–19, that ethnomusicolo-

gists such as Tanabe, who devoted themselves to the study of Asian musics to discover the cultural unity of the continent, advocated *hōgaku* as a perfect wartime art because it exemplified appropriate moral principles. The discrepancy seems to indicate the artistic and social distance between classical, traditional, and popular music communities, for advocates of light music were adamant that *hōgaku* would not accomplish spiritual mobilization goals.

41. Shillony, 138–41; Havens, *Valley of Darkness*, 30; and Hall and Gauntlett, 178–79. See also William M. Tsutsui, *Manufacturing Ideology: Scientific Management in Twentieth-Century Japan* (Princeton: Princeton University Press, 1998), esp. chap. 3.

42. Hall and Gauntlett, 183.

43. "'Hotaru no hikari' wa sashitsukaenai, Beiei ongaku tsuihō," *Tokyo Nichinichi shinbun* 31 Dec. 1941, reprinted in Uchikawa Yoshimi, ed. *Shōwa nyūzu jiten*, vol. 7 (Tokyo: Mainichi Communications, 1994), 324.

44. Horiuchi Keizō, "Dai tōa sensō ni sho suru ongaku bunka no shinro," *Ongaku no tomo* Jan. 1942: 10–11, 12–14. *Ongaku no tomo* was the product of the September 1941 consolidation of three music magazines, *Gekkan gakufu*, *Ongaku kurabu*, and *Ongaku sekai*. In that same month, some twenty music periodicals were consolidated to a handful. The wartime consolidation of the press was ordered to save paper and to facilitate the control of information. The new music magazines' editorial policies were based on the Information Bureau's policy that stated, "From now on, Japanese will not be allowed to perform the enemy's works, whether they be pure music or light music" (quoted in Nakazawa, "'Dinah' wa mō kikoenai," 188).

45. A transcript of the symposium's proceedings is reprinted in Takeuchi Yoshimi, *Kindai no chōkoku* (Tokyo: Chikuma Sōsho 285, 1983), in which the Moroi quotations appear on pages 38 and 213. I quote the English translations in Minamoto Ryōen, "The Symposium on 'Overcoming Modernity,'" trans. James Heisig, *Rude Awakenings: Zen, the Kyoto School, and the Question of Nationalism*, ed. James W. Heisig and John C. Maraldo (Honolulu: University of Hawaii Press, 1995), 208–9. Minamoto adds, "I find it surprising that readers of the symposium did not make more of [Moroi's approach]. Perhaps the ideological lens through which they were filtering its contents was too thick for its subtleties." Moroi's biography appears in *Shin ongaku jiten: jinmei* (Tokyo: Ongaku no Tomo sha, 1983), 636.

46. Reyes and Tanaka quoted in Nakazawa, "'Dinah' wa mō kikoenai," 188, 190–91. The SLMO personnel was Tanaka Kazuo (d), Francisco "Kiko" Reyes (p), Tsunoda Takashi (g), Raymond Conde (cl), Nanri Fumio (tp), Watanabe Hiroshi (ts), and Shin'ya Isaburō (1910–1966) (b).

47. John Morris, *Traveler from Tokyo* (New York: Sheridan, 1944), 208; also cited in Shillony, 144.

48. "Keiongaku," *Tokyo Asahi shinbun*, evening ed., 4 Oct. 1942: 1; and "Rekōdo no tekisei," *Tokyo Asahi shinbun*, evening ed., 14 April 1942: 2. Kurosawa recalled using a sequence from Sousa's "Semper Fidelis" in his 1944 film *The Most Beautiful*, but Home Ministry censors "sat through the sequence without labeling it 'British-American'" (134).

49. "Machi kara mo ie kara mo Beiei ongaku o issō: seiri onban, senjo shu o shitei," *Mainichi shinbun* 14 Jan. 1943: 3; and "Beiei ongaku ni tsuihō rei," *Tokyo Asahi shinbun* 14 Jan. 1943: 3. See also Mitsui, 163.

50. "Haki seyo, Beiei no gakufu," 3; and "Tekikoku no gakufu haiki," *Ongaku bunka shinbun* 1 July 1943, reprinted in Inoue and Akiyama, 559.

51. Another émigré Filipino jazzman, trombonist Teodoro D. Jansarin, refused to accept

Japanese citizenship and in 1944 was incarcerated for three months in Yokohama on suspicion of spying. See Nakazawa, " 'Dinah' wa mō kikoenai," 190; Uchida, *Nihon no jazu shi*, 138; and Satō Mieko, *Rikutsu janai yo, kibun da ya: jazu doramā Jimii Harada hachijūsan sai no shōgai* (Tokyo: Tōrin Shuppansha, 1996), 62. For examples of the frequently comical replacement of English words with "ersatz native equivalents," see Havens, *Valley of Darkness*, 30–31; Shillony, 148–50; and " 'Tekiseigo,' 'Tekisei ongaku' no tsuihō: haigaishugi senden no chingenshō, zokushutsu," *Shōwa Day by Day: Shōwa nimannichi no zen kiroku*, vol. 6 (Tokyo: Kōdansha, 1999), 206–7.

52. "Coronbia ga Nitchiku ni kaishō," *Ongaku bunka shinbun*, 10 Feb. 1943, reprinted in Inoue and Akiyama, 556–57.

53. Yoshida, *Yokohama jazu monogatari*, 252; and Yoshida, "Daremo shiranai Nihon jazu shi (2)," 14.

54. Kamiyama Keizō, *Nihon no ryūkōka* (Tokyo: Hayakawa Shobō, 1965), 155–57; I quote the English translation from Iritani, 174. Actually, "Auld Lang Syne," "Home Sweet Home," and "Last Rose of Summer" were exempted from the ban because they were deemed sufficiently Japanified. See " 'Hotaru no hikari' wa sashitsukaenai, Beiei ongaku tsuihō," 324; and "Taihai ongaku o tsuihō," *Ongaku no tomo* (March 1943): 93.

55. Naniwa Ayayoshi, "Amerikanizumu no hatan," *Chūō kōron* April 1943: 70–80. Anti-Semitism is discussed in Shillony, 156–71, and David Goodman and Masanori Miyazawa, *Jews in the Japanese Mind: The History and Uses of a Cultural Stereotype* (New York: Free Press, 1995).

56. "The Philippines: Islands Endeavor to Rid Themselves of Obnoxious U.S. Influence," *Nippon Times Weekly* 14.1 (1 Jan. 1943): 51. I thank Greg Guelcher for bringing this source to my attention.

57. Kobayashi Hitoshi, "Beiei ongaku no tsuihō," *Shūhō* 328 (1943), reprinted in *Jazz of Japan* '82, 77, 79; and in Yoshitake, 225–27.

58. Morita Masayoshi, "Ongaku bunka ni okeru Beiei to no tatakai," *Ongaku* Jan. 1943, reprinted in Inoue and Akiyama, 555.

59. Ara Ebisu [sic], "Teki Beiei no onban," *Ongaku chishiki* Nov. 1944: 18–19.

60. Morita, 555.

61. Maruyama Tetsuo and Wada Hajime, "Taidan: tekibei omi ongaku no seitai," *Ongaku chishiki* Dec. 1944: 12. Wada Hajime had played with Hatano Fukutarō, Ida Ichirō, and Awaya Noriko (whom he later married and divorced) before the war. In this article he comments harshly on jazz, but he continued playing Japanese songs in a jazz manner throughout the war as a member of the NHK orchestra.

62. Maruyama and Wada, 9–10.

63. "Keiongaku no kakumei," *Ongaku bunka* June 1944, reprinted in Inoue and Akiyama, 565.

64. Satō Kunio, "Nippon keiongaku no hōkō," *Ongaku no tomo* April 1943: 33; Maruyama and Wada, 12.

65. See Donald Keene's groundbreaking "Japanese Writers and the Greater East Asia War" (1964), reprinted in *Appreciations of Japanese Culture* (Tokyo: Kōdansha, 1971), 300–321; Atkins, "Nipponism," 68–69; Shillony, 116–17; Joseph L. Anderson and Donald Richie, *The Japanese Film*, rev. ed. (Princeton, N.J.: Princeton University Press, 1982), 126; Dower, *Japan in War and Peace*, 35, 51; and Steve Rabson, *Righteous Cause or Tragic Folly: Changing Views of War in Modern Japanese Poetry* (Ann Arbor: Center for Japanese Studies, University of Michigan, 1998). The ballet (which premiered March 1944) is mentioned in Havens, *Valley of Darkness*, 149.

66. Yamada Kōsaku, "Kokumin ongaku sōzō no sekimu," *Ongaku bunka* Dec. 1943: 2.

67. *Ongaku bunka* was the product of a second round of consolidation in the music press, subsuming seven music periodicals, in order to provide "correct leadership on the music front" and "contribute to the elevation of the music culture of Greater East Asia" ("Sōkan no hōkoku," *Ongaku bunka* Dec. 1943: 1).

68. Yamada, "Kokumin ongaku sōzō no sekimu," 3–4; Horiuchi Keizō, "Gakudan senkyō," *Ongaku bunka* Dec. 1943: 28–29; and "Ikan ni shite ongaku o Beiei gekimetsu ni yakuta-taseruka," *Ongaku bunka* Dec. 1943: 36–42.

69. Quoted in *Fifty Years of Light and Dark: The Hirohito Era* (Tokyo: Mainichi Newspapers, 1975), 148.

70. Yoshida, *Yokohama jazu monogatari*, 36–37; Miyama Toshiyuki and Segawa Masahisa, "Talk Session: Jazz 1940s in Japan," *JH* 80 (1994): 254; Yui Shōichi, "Boku no wakarashi koro," *SJ* Aug. 1959: 33; and Segawa Masahisa, "Boku no wakarashi koro," *SJ* Dec. 1959: 65. Banned jazz records commanded prices ranging from ¥10 to several hundred yen on the wartime black market (see Ara, 18). Serious collectors like Yoshida, Yui, and Kawano Ryūji were able to protect their thousands of 78 RPM records from the police, but not from the Allied air raids. See Kawano Ryūji, "Jazu hyōronka no wakaki hi no omoide," *SJ* Feb. 1959: 31.

71. Satō Kunio, "Ongaku goraku no gunjunsei," *Ongaku no tomo* Mar. 1943: 56.

72. "Comfort bands" are discussed in Ōmori Seitarō, *Nihon no yōgaku*, vol. 1 (Tokyo: Shinmon Shuppansha, 1986), 255–60; and Uchida, *Nihon no jazu shi*, 145–48. Sano, 102–38, provides a lengthy account of a five-week Southeast Asian tour sponsored by the *Asahi* newspaper.

73. Recounted in Hattori, *Boku no ongaku jinsei*, 199–200; and Yoshitake, 224.

74. Australian Major Charles Hughes Cousens, U.S. Captain Ted Wallace Ince, and Philippines Lt. Norman Reyes were "hired" at salaries commensurate to their ranks to produce and broadcast "Zero Hour." Although they were courted with rooms at the Daiichi Hotel and trips to the Yokohama *chabuya*, the three POWs remained discreetly intransigent, often sabotaging their own scripts to dupe their non-English-speaking supervisors and egging the Allies on. See Masayo Duus, *Tokyo Rose: Orphan of the Pacific*, trans. Peter Duus (Tokyo: Kōdansha, 1979), 74–76; and Ikeda Norizane, *Hinomaru awā* (Tokyo: Chūō Kōronsha, 1979), 16–20. For a concise English-language account of NHK overseas transmissions, see Namikawa Ryō, "Overseas Broadcasting by Japan during World War II (Abridged)," *NHK senji kaigai hōsō*, ed. Kaigai Hōsō Kenkyū Group (Tokyo: Hara Shobō, 1982), 453–69.

75. "Zero Hour" script, quoted in Namikawa, 460. Contrary to popular belief, there was no single "Tokyo Rose." A number of Japanese-American women were in NHK's employ, taking turns behind the microphone on shows such as "Zero Hour." Ironically, Iva Toguri d'Aquino, the woman who was tried and convicted of treason as "Tokyo Rose," was one of the few Japanese Americans stranded in Japan during the war who did not renounce her U.S. citizenship. She was given amnesty in 1977. See Duus, 63; and Namikawa, 461–63.

76. Nakazawa, " 'Dinah' wa mō kikoenai," 193.

77. Only two record companies were still active at war's end, and the number of record stores in Japan plummeted from a prewar high of around four thousand to about five hundred stores during the war. See Ōmori, vol. 1, 268; and Kurata, 218.

78. The Sunday Promenade Concert band included leader Watanabe Ryō (b), Tsunoda Takashi (g), Francisco Reyes (p), Hashimoto Jun, Ashida Mitsuru, Matsumoto Shin (reeds), Obata

Mitsuyuki (tp), Raymond Conde (cl), and Tanaka Kazuo (d). The New Order Rhythm Orchestra included conductor Kami Kyōsuke, Kikuchi Shigeya (p), Taniguchi Matashi (tb), and Sano Tasuku (reeds). Practically all of Japan's biggest jazz stars were involved.

79. Shibata Yoshi, the "jazz liaison" at NHK during the war, claimed that a British POW taken at Singapore was enlisted to rewrite the song lyrics (Uchida, *Nihon no jazu shi*, 151). Moriyama Hisashi, in a 1 Aug. 1985 interview with Sidney Brown (for which I have the transcript), declined to comment on possible charges of treason brought against him by the Allies for his extensive participation in the broadcasts. Tib Kamayatsu was captured as a POW in China in 1945 and taught English to Chinese children. See George Yoshida, ed., *Nikkei Music Makers: The Swing Era*, National Japanese American Historical Society Calendar #7, 1995.

80. Nakazawa, " 'Dinah' wa mō kikoenai," 192; and *Jazz of Japan '82*, 67.

81. Quoted in Maejima Susumu, "Still Jazzing It up after All These Years," *Asahi Evening News*, 8 Feb. 1995: 6.

82. "Keiongaku no gakki hensei tenkan," *Ongaku bunka* April 1944: 26. A study committee chaired by Horiuchi Keizō reiterated the new light music policy, dubbed the "revolution in light music," at its 10–11 May 1944 meeting. See "Keiongaku no kakumei," 565.

83. "Kessen hijō sochi to ongaku," *Ongaku bonka* April 1944: 26; Iritani, 173.

84. S. Frederick Starr, *Red & Hot: The Fate of Jazz in the Soviet Union*, rev. ed. (New York: Limelight Editions, 1994), 175, 170, 189, 192, 203.

85. Erik Levi, *Music in the Third Reich* (New York: St. Martin's, 1994), 120, 121–22; Michael H. Kater, *Different Drummers: Jazz in the Culture of Nazi Germany* (New York: Oxford University Press, 1992), 52–53, 57, 202.

86. Perris, 4, describes this prejudice as applied to music: "To link the beloved art of music with the devices of deception and with the presentation of controlled information that intentionally misleads is distasteful. . . . The concept of a state which controls artists is also offensive to citizens of the Western democracies, who believe that the making of art should be left to artists, according to the principle of free speech, perhaps colored by the nineteenth-century view of the artist's will as paramount and inviolable. We judge that extramusical controls must ultimately inhibit the work of the composer and diminish the quality of his work. Can an artistic mind function if it is bound to the strictures of a political ideology?"

5 Bop, Funk, Junk, and That Old Democracy Boogie: The Jazz Tribes of Postwar Japan

1. George Kawaguchi, "Watakushi no rirekisho 20: hadena shō ni nekkyō," *Nihon keizai shinbun* 21 Aug. 1993: 12.

2. The most comprehensive treatment in English of this pivotal moment from the Japanese perspective is John W. Dower, *Embracing Defeat: Japan in the Wake of World War II* (New York: W. W. Norton/The New Press, 1999). See also Kōsaku Yoshino, *Cultural Nationalism in Contemporary Japan: A Sociological Inquiry* (London: Routledge, 1992), 32–36; Aoki Tamotsu, *Nihon bunka ron no hen'yō* (Tokyo: Chūō Kōron sha, 1990), 58; Shūichi Katō, "Japanese Writers and Modernization," in *Changing Japanese Attitudes toward Modernization*, ed. Marius B. Jansen (1965; Rutland, Vt.: Charles E. Tuttle, 1982), 441–42; H. D. Harootunian, "America's Japan/Japan's Japan," in *Japan in the World*, ed. Masao Miyoshi and H. D. Harootunian (Durham, N.C.: Duke University Press, 1992), 200–203; and

Kevin Doak, *Dreams of Difference: The Japan Romantic School and the Crisis of Modernity* (Berkeley: University of California Press, 1994), 133.

3. J. Thomas Rimer, "High Culture in the Shōwa Period," in *Showa: The Japan of Hirohito,* ed. Carol Gluck and Stephen R. Graubard (New York: W. W. Norton, 1992), 272, touches on this problem in his analysis of "high culture" (particularly painting and Western classical music).

4. Dower, *Embracing Defeat,* 439. See Etō Jun, *Ochiba no hakiyose: haisen, senryō, ken'etsu to bungaku* (Tokyo: Bungei Shunjūsha, 1981). Etō's views are rebuffed by Jay Rubin, "From Wholesomeness to Decadence: The Censorship of Literature under the Allied Occupation," *Journal of Japanese Studies* 11.1 (1985): 71–103.

5. Isoi Gijin, *We Had Those Occupation Blues,* trans. Steven Karpa (Saratoga: R & E Publishers, 1988), 59, 75.

6. Marlene J. Mayo, "The War of Words Continues: American Radio Guidance in Occupied Japan," in *The Occupation of Japan: Arts and Culture,* ed. Thomas W. Burkman, MacArthur Memorial Foundation Symposium (Norfolk, Va.: General Douglas MacArthur Foundation, 1988), 52, 68; *GHQ bunsho no yoru senryōki hōsō shi nenpyō* (Tokyo: N H K Hōsō Bunka Chōsa Kenkyūjo, 1987), 100. See also Kyoko Hirano, *Mr. Smith Goes to Tokyo: Japanese Cinema under the Occupation,* Smithsonian Studies in the History of Film and Television, series ed. Charles Musser (Washington, D.C.: Smithsonian Institute Press, 1992), 5; and Marilyn Ivy, "Formations of Mass Culture," in *Postwar Japan as History,* ed. Andrew Gordon (Berkeley: University of California Press, 1993), 245.

7. See, for example, Uchida Osamu, *Jazu ga wakakatta koro* (Tokyo: Shōbunsha, 1984), 9; Honda Toshio, *Modan jazu* (Tokyo: Shin Nippon Shinsho, 1989), 139; Watanabe Sadao, *Boku jishin no tame no jazu,* ed. Iwanami Yōzō (Tokyo: Arachi Shuppansha, 1969), 18; Uchida Kōichi, *Nihon no jazu shi: senzen, sengo* (Tokyo: Swing Journal, 1976), 160; Sidney Brown, "California Origins of the Jazz Boom in Occupied Japan, 1945–1952," Conference on California and the Pacific Rim, University of the Pacific, Stockton, Calif., 30 April 1994 (copyright 1999), 12; Stephen I. Thompson, "American Country Music in Japan," *Popular Music and Society* 16.3 (Fall 1992): 32–33; and Takahashi Ichirō and Sasaki Mamoru, *Jazu shifū—sengo sōsōki densetsu* (Tokyo: San'ichi Shobō, 1997), 211–12. Similar epiphanies were also recounted in my interviews with Dr. Uchida Osamu, Akiyoshi Toshiko, Hara Nobuo, Tsukahara Aiko, Inagaki Jirō, and Kanai Hideto.

8. Office of Strategic Services, Research and Analysis Branch, "Civil Affairs Guide: Radio Broadcasting in Japan" (R&A #2537 file), 18 April 1945, 13.

9. General Headquarters, Supreme Commander for the Allied Powers [hereafter G H Q / S C A P], *History of the Nonmilitary Activities of the Occupation of Japan, 1945 through 1951,* vol. 33: *Radio Broadcasting,* 1, 8. The contents of Iokibe Makoto, ed., *The Occupation of Japan: U.S. Planning Documents, 1942–45* (Bethesda, Md.: Congressional Information Service, 1987), include nothing related to arts or media other than motion pictures, radio (public information programming only), and museums. See also Donald Richie, "The Occupied Arts," in *The Confusion Era: Art and Culture of Japan during the Allied Occupation, 1945–1952,* ed. Mark Sandler (Seattle: Arthur M. Sackler Gallery, Smithsonian Institution, and the University of Washington Press, 1997), 11–12.

10. Robert Trumbull, "A Report from Tokyo," *New York Times* 21 Oct. 1945: B8; Radio Culture Research Institute, B C J [N H K], "Summarized Result of Program Rating Surveys," #1–6, Oct. 1950, cited in G H Q / S C A P, 19; and Mayo, 68–69.

11. Hirano, 154–65; Joseph L. Anderson and Donald Richie, *The Japanese Film,* rev. ed. (Princeton, N.J.: Princeton University Press, 1982), 175–77; Mitsui Tōru, "Interactions of

Imported and Indigenous Musics in Japan: A Historical Overview of the Music Industry," in *Whose Master's Voice? The Development of Popular Music in Thirteen Cultures*, ed. Alison J. Ewbank and Fouli T. Papageorgiou (Westport, Conn.: Greenwood Press, 1997), 166; Herbert Passin, "The Occupation—Some Reflections," in Gluck and Graubard, 119. Passin's personal impressions of the Occupation are also recounted in his "The Legacy of the Occupation of Japan," Occasional Papers of the East Asian Institute (New York: Columbia University Press, 1968).

12. Brown, "California Origins of the Jazz Boom in Occupied Japan," 13, cites a notice in the 7 May 1950 *Nippon Times* about a CIE program in Yokohama on 16 May featuring records by Kid Ory, Albert Ammons, and Muggsy Spanier, with commentary by Capt. R. D. Conally, 8th Army Information Center, and Nippon Victor's Kōno Ryūji.

13. "Jazz Program on 'Voice' to Get World Booking," *New York Times* [hereafter cited as *NYT*] 2 April 1956: 17; Felix Belair Jr., "United States Has Secret Sonic Weapon—Jazz," *NYT* 6 Nov. 1955: 1+; Robert Alden, "Hands of U.S. Tied in Asia 'Cold War,'" *NYT* 11 June 1956: 11; Hal Davis, "Appeal of Jazz Cited," *NYT* 21 Nov. 1955: 6; "Remote Lands to Hear Old Democracy Boogie," *NYT* 18 Nov. 1955: 16. See also John S. Wilson, *Jazz: The Transition Years, 1940–1960* (New York: Appleton-Century-Crofts, 1966), 111–14; S. Frederick Starr, *Red & Hot: The Fate of Jazz in the Soviet Union*, rev. ed. (New York: Limelight Editions, 1994), 210, 243–44; and Warren R. Pinckney Jr., "Jazz in India: Perspectives on Historical Development and Musical Acculturation," *Asian Music* 21.1 (1989–90): 38.

14. "Jazzu," *Time* 8 Aug. 1949: 40. See also Takatoshi Kyōgoku, "Jazz with a Classical Tint Rules Japan," *Down Beat* 1 Dec. 1948: 15.

15. John Dower, *War without Mercy: Race and Power in the Pacific War* (New York: Pantheon, 1986), 308. See also Uchida, *Nihon no jazu shi*, 167–68; Uchida Kōichi, "Shinchūgun kyanpu no jazu & shō: RAA no hassoku," *Jazz World* 187 (Sept. 1994): 9; Uchida Kōichi, "Shinchūgun kyanpu no jazu & shō: RAA no shōchō," *Jazz World* 188 (Oct. 1994): 10; Minami Hiroshi and Shakai Shinri Kenkyūkai, eds., *Shōwa bunka 1945–1989* (Tokyo: Keisō Shobō, 1990), iii–iv; Takahashi and Sasaki, 202–6, 219–23; Nagai Yoshikazu, *Shakō dansu to Nihonjin* (Tokyo: Shōbunsha, 1991), 163–70; and Dower, *Embracing Defeat*, 127–31.

16. Thompson, 32–33.

17. Nogawa Kōbun, "Nippon no jazu ensōka," *Ongaku geijutsu* Nov. 1951: 48.

18. George Kawaguchi quoted in Kawasaki Hiroshi, *EM kurabu monogatari* (Tokyo: Shichōsha, 1992), 42–43. The poem originally ran in the poetry journal *Gendaishi techō* (Feb.–Aug. 1992), complementing Kawasaki's 1988 TBS radio documentary *Bye Bye EM Club* and a 1987 concert ("Bye Bye EM Club Concert: Yokosuka Jazz Dreams") to commemorate the historical and cultural importance of enlisted men's clubs, most of which have been demolished or fallen into disrepair. The book also contains ghostly photographs of the abandoned club facilities.

19. Masao Manbo, "He Blows High . . . He Blows Low!" *Japan Times* 4 Mar. 1948, quoted in George Yoshida, *Reminiscing in Swingtime: Japanese Americans in American Popular Music, 1925–1960* (San Francisco: National Japanese American Historical Society, 1997), 112; Fujika quoted in Kawasaki, 54.

20. Hashimoto Jun, quoted in Uchida, *Nihon no jazu shi*, 161.

21. Raymond Conde (cl), Francisco Reyes (p), Nanri Fumio (tp), Shin'ya Isaburō (b), Tsunoda Takashi (g), and Iiyama Shigeo (d). Iiyama eventually founded the Swing Club, a service which bought instruments from American GIs, loaned them to Japanese musicians, and booked bands at American clubs.

22. Uchida, *Nihon no jazu shi*, 173. Ōmori Seitarō, *Nihon no yōgaku*, vol. 2 (Tokyo: Shinmon Shuppansha, 1987), 94–95, lists tunes for which so-called stock arrangements were widely circulated in postwar Japan.

23. Uchida, *Nihon no jazu shi*, 173–76; "Jazu bando kakuzuke shinsa," *Gendai fūzoku shi nenpyō: Shōwa 20-nen (1945)–Shōwa 60-nen (1985)*, ed. Seso Fūzoku Kanrakukai (Tokyo: Kawade Shobō Shinsha, 1986), 26; "Jazu ensōka to kakusuke shinsa iinkai," *Showa Day by Day: Shōwa nimannichi no zenki*, vol. 18 (Tokyo: Kōdansha, 1989), 313.

24. Les Brown's orchestra came to Japan in 1950 and the Swing Jamboree in December 1951 to entertain U.S. forces. Although they did not perform for Japanese audiences, they did mingle and jam with Japanese musicians. The Jamboree included Howard McGhee (tp), J. J. Johnson (tb), Rudy Williams (ts), Skeeter Best (g), Charlie Rice (d), Oscar Pettiford (b), and guest pianist Lt. Norbert de Coteaux. Akiyoshi describes studying with Les Brown's pianist Jeff Clarkson, and partying with the Swing Jamboree, in *Jazu to ikiru* (Tokyo: I Wanami Shinsho, 1996), 76–77, 82–85. A photograph of Pettiford and Johnson with Akiyoshi and jazz critic/drummer Kubota Jirō at a sukiyaki party appears in "Nippon no jazu to tomo ni," *Swing Journal* [hereafter *SJ*] June 1971: 48.

25. Uchida Kōichi, "Higeki no tensai pianisuto Moriyasu Shōtarō no densetsu," *SJ* April 1975, *Jazu piano hyakka* (special issue), 196; Ueda Sakae, *Soshite, kaze ga hashirinukete itta (He Played Like a Breeze through Our Lives): tensai jazu pianisuto Moriyasu Shōtarō no shōgai* (Tokyo: Kōdansha, 1997), 278, 302–3. I thank Akiyoshi for spelling de Coteaux's name for me! She denies Uchida's assertion (*Nihon no jazu shi*, 241) that de Coteaux introduced her to the music of her principal influence, Bud Powell. She recalls hearing Powell for the first time on WVTR. See also Honda Toshio, *Rongu ierō rōdo: jazu sankan joō no nagai michinori— Akiyoshi Toshiko* (Tokyo: Ikkōsha, 1984), 128–29.

26. Araki arranged "A.P.O. 500" and "Rock Romondo," and composed "Boogie in C," "Tokyo Riff," and "A Night in Pakistan" for the Victor Hot Club session. The Victor Hot Club was actually Nanri Fumio's Hot Peppers: Nanri Fumio (tp), Ōno Tadaosa (ts), Mori Tōru (tb), Matsui Hachirō (p), Matsuda Takayoshi (b), and Tanaka Kazuo (d). Uchida Kōichi characterizes the performance as a bop session with "Dixieland solos" (*Nihon no jazu shi*, 202). The session's output was reissued on *Kōgane jidai no Victor Hot Club* (Nippon Victor: 1180-M, 1973) and *Orijinaru genban ni yoru Nippon no jazu-popyurā shi (sengo hen)* (Nippon Victor: SJ-8005, 1977).

27. The recording session, released as *Jazz Beat: Midnight Jazz Session* (Nippon Victor: JV-5006, 1959), was conducted at the end of Araki's tenure as a Ford Foundation research fellow on 10 June 1959. It was held at the Video Hall in Tokyo and featured Araki's experimental overdubbing to produce a four-alto saxophone choir. See *SJ* July 1959: 51; and Yoshida, *Reminiscing in Swingtime*, 112–15.

28. Hawes's presence in Yokohama was first reported in *SJ* Nov. 1953: 5. See also Yoshida Mamoru, "Hōzu, Peppā no omoide," *Jazu hihyō* [hereafter *JH*] 66 (1989): 44.

29. Hampton Hawes and Don Asher, *Raise Up Off Me* (1972; New York: Da Capo, 1979), 61–63; Toshiko, 98–100. Akiyoshi credits a Japanese whose name she does not recall for bringing Peterson and Philips to see her gig at Tennessee, though Hawes wrote that he brought Peterson to see her play.

30. "Toshiko Akiyoshi," *Jazz Profiles*, National Public Radio, 7 June 1998; see also Akiyoshi, *Jazu to ikiru*, 104.

31. Quoted in John S. Wilson, liner notes for *Everybody Likes Hampton Hawes: Vol. 3, The Trio* (Contemporary: C-3523, 1956). Among the classic trilogy of trio albums Hawes recorded

immediately after his discharge, only the first LP's liner notes even mention that he was in Japan and played with native musicians.

32. *SJ* Nov. 1953: 5; "Jazu būmu," *Gendai fūzoku shi nenpyō*, 74.

33. "Keiongaku bangumi, kaisetsusha, disukujokkii ninki tōhyō chūkan seiseki happyō," *SJ* July 1959: 21; Nogawa Kōbun, "Takamaru rekōdo shūshūnetsu," *SJ* Oct. 1952: 4; and Linda Fujie, "Popular Music," in *Handbook of Japanese Popular Culture*, ed. Richard Gid Powers and Hidetoshi Katō (Westport, Conn.: Greenwood Press, 1989), 205. The growth of postwar mass culture is described in Laura E. Hein, "Growth Versus Success: Japan's Economic Policy in Historical Perspective," in Gordon, 110; and Minami Hiroshi and Shakai Shinri Kenkyūjo, eds., *Shōwa bunka 1945–1989* (Tokyo: Keisō Shobō, 1990), 278–80. An alternative view is provided by Ivy, "Formations of Mass Culture," 246–47, who contends that "culture was detached from mass consumption" until 1955, making local communities the locus for cultural life and causing "a resurgence of small-scale popular forms and practices."

34. Krupa quoted in *Down Beat* 18 June 1952, cited in Bruce H. Klauber, *World of Gene Krupa: That Legendary Drummin' Man* (Ventura, Calif.: Pathfinder Publishing, 1990), 85. See also *SJ* June 1952: 1–4. The rock-throwing incident is mentioned in "Konsāto jazu no uramomote," *SJ* July 1959: 15. A JATP concert recording from the 1953 Japan tour is available as *Jazz at the Philharmonic in Tokyo: Live at the Nichigeki* (Pablo: 2620104, 1990). Other jazz stars on the bill were Flip Phillips, Charlie Shavers, Bill Harris, J. C. Herd, Herb Ellis, Willie Smith, and Raymond Tania. For details and photos of Armstrong's visit and Nanri's "trumpeters' party," see *SJ* Jan. 1954; *Asahi shinbun*, evening ed., 3 Dec. 1953: 2; and *Bessatsu ichioku nin no Shōwa shi: Nihon no jazu—Jazz of Japan '82* (Tokyo: Mainichi Shinbunsha, 1982), 91 [hereafter cited as *Jazz of Japan '82*].

35. "Yokohama monogatari," *Yokohama bunka jōhōshi* Dec. 1991: 3. See also Sonobe Saburō, *Ongaku gojū nen* (Tokyo: Jiji Tsūshinsha, 1950), 283; Dower, *Embracing Defeat*, 172–77; and Mitsui, 163.

36. *Nippon Times* 15 Oct. 1946, 30 May 1947, and 13 March 1947, all cited in Brown, "California Origins of the Jazz Boom in Occupied Japan," 13–15.

37. *Nippon Times* 4 Feb. 1947, 25 March 1948, 4 June 1948, and 7 June 1947, all cited in Brown, "California Origins of the Jazz Boom in Occupied Japan," 14–15; and Haruna Shizuo, "Shōdo, odoriba yūkyō roku," *Dansu to ongaku* Feb. 1972: 27.

38. Ichimura Jōji, "Nōson dansu fūkei," *Modan dansu* July 1949: 46–47; William Kelly, "Regional Japan: The Price of Prosperity and the Benefits of Dependency," in Gluck and Graubard, 218–21; *Nippon Times* 13 May 1947, cited in Brown, "California Origins of the Jazz Boom in Occupied Japan," 14.

39. "Hakkan no ji," *SJ* April 1947. See also "Sōkan 25 shūnen kinen tokubetsu kikaku—bakushō zadankai: ima da kara hanasō Nippon no jazu shi," *SJ* June 1971: 93–94; and "Nippon no jazu to tomo ni," 42–43.

40. *SJ* Oct. 1950: 5. See also Ishihara Yasuyuki, "Nippon hotto kurabu hassoku, zakki," *JH* 12 (1972): 86–88; and "Jazu bangumi hōsō ni kyōryoku shita nikkei beihei," *Showa Day by Day*, vol. 18, 313. The formation of the Nagoya Hot Club in 1952 is described by Uchida Osamu in "Dokutā Uchida no jazu ni kanpai! 6: LP ni kantan shi konsāto o," *Chūnichi shinbun*, evening ed., 2 July 1986: 6, and "Dokutā Uchida no jazu ni kanpai! 7: LP hatsu kōkai ni Kuroyama no hito no nami," *Chūnichi shinbun*, evening ed., 7 July 1986: 10. Kyōto's New Jazz Society sponsored recitals, lecture series, and jam sessions at the American Culture Center (*SJ* Nov. 1958: 51; May 1960: 17, 30). Ōsaka had its New Orleans

Alligator Club and Modern Jazz Group (*SJ* Oct. 1957: 38; July 1958: 109), and even Fukui had a Hot Club (*SJ* Oct. 1958: 113).

41. Sagara Senkichi, "JAZZ: dare ga tame ni jazu wa naru," *Chūō kōron* Sept. 1954: 183, 187; Eta Harich-Schneider, "The Last Remnants of a Mendicant Musicians' Guild: The *Goze* in Northern Honshu (Japan)," *International Folk Music Journal* 11 (1959): 57; Minami Hiroshi, "Jazu no kōzai," *Fujin kōron* April 1954: 132; and Tanikawa Shuntarō, "Nagara-zoku no tanoshimi," cited and translated in David W. Plath, *The After Hours: Modern Japan and the Search for Enjoyment* (Berkeley: University of California Press, 1964), 131. Nogawa Kōbun noted that the rise of interest in jazz among Japanese youth was in contrast to the trend in the United States ("Rivaibaru to jazu fan," *SJ* April 1953: 3).

42. "Konsāto jazu no uraomote," *SJ* July 1959: 19–20; "Jazu kissa no shin'ya eigyō fukannō," *SJ* Aug. 1964: 59. The article does not explain the reasoning behind the ordinance.

43. Stephen Prince, *The Warrior's Camera: The Cinema of Akira Kurosawa* (Princeton, N.J.: Princeton University Press, 1991), 73, 85–86.

44. Anderson and Richie, 193–94, discuss the teen sex genre. *Jazzy Girls* and *Youthful Jazz Girls*, both starring George Kawaguchi, are cited in Leonard Feather, *The Encyclopedia of Jazz* (New York: Horizon, 1960), 297. Jiji Tsūshinsha, *Japan Motion Picture Almanac 1957* (Tokyo: Council of Motion Picture Industry of Japan, 1957), 113, lists *Jazu musume kanpai*, starring Eri Chiemi and Yukimura Izumi. As of this writing I have been unable to locate and view these films, but the titles alone speak volumes.

45. Krin Gabbard, *Jammin' at the Margins: Jazz and the American Cinema* (Chicago: University of Chicago Press, 1996), 9; Mark Schilling, *The Encyclopedia of Japanese Pop Culture* (New York: Weatherhill, 1997), 315, 71; and Shimazaki Seisuke, "Taiyōzoku," in *Taishū bunka jiten*, comp. Ishikawa Hiroyoshi, Tsuganesawa Toshihiro, et al. (Tokyo: Kobundō, 1994), 467 [hereafter cited as *TBJ*]. In 1959 Ithiel de Sola Pool, "Forward," *Japanese Popular Culture: Studies in Mass Communication and Cultural Change*, ed. and trans. Hidetoshi Katō (Rutland, Vt., and Tokyo: Tuttle, 1959; Westport, Conn.: Greenwood Press, 1973), 11, noted postwar Japan's fascination with such rebels: "The heroes are often radical and nihilistic, the heroines victims of outmoded customs. The outcomes are varied." See also descriptions of decadent "cultures of defeat" in Dower, *Embracing Defeat*, 26, 121–67.

46. George Kawaguchi, "Watashi no rireki sho 2: Nihon jazu no kusawake," *Nihon keizai shinbun* 2 Aug. 1993: 12; "Watashi no rireki sho 3: senretsu na tenchi no inshō," *Nihon keizai shinbun* 3 Aug. 1993: 12; "Watashi no rireki sho 4: baiorin te ni tokkun," *Nihon keizai shinbun* 4 Aug. 1993: 12. I thank the late Koyama Hachirō for recommending this source to me.

47. George Kawaguchi, "Watashi no rireki sho 19: Nihon jazu no kusawake," *Nihon keizai shinbun* 20 Aug. 1993: 12; Uchida, *Nihon no jazu shi*, 223; and Kubota Jirō, "Ninki zetchō no Biggu Foa o miru! Excited Moved and Thrilled by Big Four," *SJ* July 1953: 10. The most recent reissue of recordings by the original Big Four is *Nippon jazu sōseiki (The Legendary Japanese Jazz Scene) vol. 1—George Kawaguchi and The Big 4* (Paddle Wheel: KICJ 232, 1995).

48. "Yo wa masa ni jazu nekkyō jidai, nami ni noru bandoman ya kashu," *Mainichi shinbun*, evening ed., 2 Aug. 1953: 4; *SJ* April 1954: 24; *SJ* Nov. 1955: 30; Uchida, *Nihon no jazu shi* 224. The "Torys era" Big Four (with Ueda Gō on bass) appears on the LP *Jazz at the Torys* (King: LKB-7, 1957).

49. *The Official Crazy Cats Graffiti: Hey! We've Got the Musekinin Soul of the 60's* (Tokyo: Treville, 1993), 25, 31, 55, 72; Schilling, 153; Yano Seiichi, "Kurējii kyattsu," *TBJ* 219.

50. Tom Frank, "Alternative to What?" in *Sounding Off: Music as Subversion / Resistance / Revo-*

lution, ed. Ron Sakolsky and Fred Wei-han Ho (Brooklyn: Autonomedia, 1995), 109–13; Dick Hebdige, *Subculture: The Meaning of Style* (1979; London: Routledge, 1987), 92–99.

51. Quoted in Ueda, 25.

52. Imada quoted in "Thirty Successful Years on the Jazz Beat in Japan: Mainstream Veteran Masaru Imada," *Keyboard* (Aug. 1985): 41.

53. William Bruce Cameron, "Sociological Notes on the Jam Session," *Social Forces* Dec. 1954: 177–78.

54. For instance, Scott DeVeaux writes: "For all its chaotic diversity of style and expression and for all the complexity of its social origins, jazz is presented as a coherent whole, and its history as a skillfully contrived and easily comprehended narrative. . . . Again and again, present day musicians, whether neo-classicist or avant-garde, invoke the past, keeping before the public's eye the idea that musics as diverse as those of King Oliver and the Art Ensemble of Chicago are in some fundamental sense *the same* music" ("Constructing the Jazz Tradition: Jazz Historiography," *Black American Literature Forum* 25 [fall 1991]: 525, 530). See also Robert Walser, ed., *Keeping Time: Readings in Jazz History* (New York: Oxford University Press, 1999), 151.

55. Will Friedwald, liner notes, *Masters of Jazz Vol. 2: Bebop's Greatest Hits* (Rhino: 72469, 1996), 3; Gillespie quoted in "Beyond the Cool," *Time* 27 June 1960: 56; Monk quoted in liner notes for Ornette Coleman, *Beauty Is a Rare Thing: The Complete Atlantic Recordings* (Rhino: 71410, 1993), 16.

56. DeVeaux, "Constructing the Jazz Tradition," 538–41, 549; Scott DeVeaux, *The Birth of Bebop* (Berkeley: University of California Press, 1997), 27; Armstrong quoted in " 'Bop Will Kill Business Unless It Kills Itself First'—Louis Armstrong," *Down Beat* 7 April 1948: 2. See also Daniel Belgrad, *The Culture of Spontaneity: Improvisation and the Arts in Postwar America* (Chicago: University of Chicago Press, 1998), esp. chap. 8.

57. Nogawa Kōbun et al., "Nyū jazu no chishiki," *Rekōdo geijutsu* Sept. 1952: 94; Isono Teruo, "1592 [sic] nen ni katsuyaku shita sutātachi," *SJ* Feb. 1953: 20.

58. Honda Toshio, *Jazu* (Tokyo: Shin Nippon Shinso, 1976), 47; Uchida, *Nihon no jazu shi*, 202; Kawasaki, 52; and Ōmori, vol. 2, 29–31. Bebop method books were indeed a rarity, but jazz critic Maki Yoshio claimed to have found one entitled *How to Play Bop* by Van Alexander. (I have had no luck locating this book myself.) Maki recalled lending the book to pianist Moriyasu Shōtarō (Uchida, *Nihon no jazu shi*, 228–29).

59. Charles Nanry, *The Jazz Text* (New York: D. Van Nostrand, 1979), 166, contends that V-Discs provide a glimpse of the changes in popular music that occurred during the period of the recording ban, including the so-called "bebop revolution."

60. Hayama Jirō, "Dance Band Review—Yokohama ni arawareta nyū fēsu Kuramubēku Nain," *SJ* Feb.–Mar. 1949: 4, the first review of Clambake 9 (CB 9), stated that they sounded like "amateurs" but had a strong rhythm section and could possibly "go to the top of Japan's swing world." A later review appears in *SJ* Dec. 1949: 19. "1950 no suingu," *SJ* Jan. 1950: 7, states that "1949 should be remembered as the year that bop was first played in Japan." The original lineup was: Mawatari Yoshikazu (ts), Ebihara Keiichirō (as), Tanabe Akira (cl), Kitazawa Tatsuo (ts), Ohara Shigetoku (b), Shimizu Jun (d), Hirazawa Shin'ichi (g), Arimoto Yoshitaka (tp), and Terada Tsunesaburō (p). CB 9 recorded for *Jazz on Flame: Jazz Cavalcade in Japan* (Discomate: DSP-3008–10, 1976). See also Yoshida Mamoru, *Yokohama jazu monogatari: "Chigusa" no 50 nen* (Yokohama: Kanagawa Shinbunsha, 1985), 77, 84.

61. *SJ* Dec. 1949: 19; *SJ* Jan. 1950: 21; *SJ* Feb. 1950: 20; *SJ* Aug. 1950: 23. Gramercy 6's

original lineup was: Teraoka Shinzō (p), Arai Noboru (g), Kubota Jirō (d), Asahara Tetsuo (b), Atsumo Yūjirō (ts), Oida Toshio (vo).

62. For an account of the contestation and eventual compromise between "the progressives and the 'moldy figs,'" see DeVeaux, "Constructing the Jazz Tradition," 538–40; Bernard Gendron, "'Moldy Figs' and Modernists: Jazz at War (1942–1946)," in Jazz among the Discourses, ed. Krin Gabbard (Durham: Duke University Press, 1995), 31–56; and Nogawa Kōbun, "Bappu—dikishiirando sutairu no ongaku sen," SJ May 1950: 10+.

63. Nogawa Kōbun, Gendaijin no ongaku—jazu (Tokyo: Hibakusha, 1949), 11; Akutagawa Yasushi, quoted in Nogawa et al., "Nyū jazu," 95; Jimmy Araki quoted in Sonoda Toshiaki, "Jazu yo dansu ni kaereru?" SJ Aug. 1950: 3; Nanri Fumio quoted in SJ Aug. 1950: 8; and Noguchi Hisamitsu, "Jazu no kiki," Ondori tsūshin 7.5 (1951): 46.

64. Sakurai Yōko, "Kissaten meguri (2)—Yūraku-chō Combo no maki," Music Life (Aug. 1953): 37; Uchida Osamu, "Dokutā Uchida no jazu ni kanpai! 16: Nagoya ni mo jazu kissa ga ōpun," Chūnichi shinbun, evening ed., 28 July 1986: 4. See also Aikura Hisato, "'Mainichi ga jazuyōbi' datta hibi ni," Modan jazu kanshō (Tokyo: Kadokawa Bunko, 1981), 7–16. Tokyo's Combo closed in June 1955, and Nagoya's Combo shut down in the late sixties, but Chigusa was still open as of the summer of 1998.

65. Yoshida, Yokohama jazu monogatari, 56; Oda Satoru, Sake to bara no hibi (Nagoya: Efe Shuppan, 1993), 34–35; and "Japanese Jazz," New York Times Magazine 11 April 1954: 57.

66. Albert Goldman, Freakshow: The Rocksoulbluesjazzsickjewblackhumorsexpoppsych Gig and Other Scenes from the Counter-Culture (New York: Atheneum, 1971), 293; and Amiri Baraka (LeRoi Jones), Blues People: Negro Music in White America (1963; New York: Quill, 1999), 202, 188.

67. "Fukumen zadankai: mayaku to jazu," SJ Aug. 1956: 8–12; "Wareware wa mayaku ga hitsuyō nanoka? aete myūjishan shoshi ni tou," SJ Nov. 1960: 16–17. Philly Joe Jones and Persip were arrested in Kōbe while participating in the "Four Drummers" tour (Asahi shinbun 9 Jan. 1965; SJ Feb. 1965: 62); George Kawaguchi, Togashi Masahiko, and Shiraki Hideo filled in for them during their incarceration. Curtis Fuller, on tour with the Jazz Messengers, was arrested 25 January 1965 (SJ Mar. 1965). Elvin Jones, participating in another all-start drummer package, was arrested in November 1966 (SJ Jan. 1967: 112).

68. See Tsukuda Norio, "Hiropon," in Nippon senryō kenkyū jiten, ed. Shisō no Kagaku Kenkyūkai (Tokyo: Tokuma shoten, 1978), 120–21; Miyata Shinpei, "Hiropon," TBJ 656; Haruko Taya Cook and Theodore F. Cook, Japan at War: An Oral History (New York: New Press, 1992), 190–91; and Dower, Embracing Defeat, 108.

69. Harry Shapiro, Waiting for the Man: The Story of Drugs and Popular Music (New York: William Morrow, 1988), 65; Nat Hentoff, The Jazz Life (New York: Dial Press, 1961), 86, 93; and Baraka, Blues People, 201–2.

70. Quoted in Terayama Shūji and Yugawa Reiko, eds., Jazu o tanoshimu hon (Tokyo: Kubo Shoten, 1961), 244–51. Uchida, Nihon no jazu shi, 208, 226, briefly describes the addictions of Shimizu and Sleepy Matsumoto.

71. Uchida Osamu, "Dokutā Uchida no jazu ni kanpai! 18: jisatsu mo kangaeta tensai Togashi shōnen," Chūnichi shinbun 30 July 1986: 6; Sugiura's comeback reported in SJ Aug. 1965: 93, and Sept. 1965: 92.

72. Neil Leonard, Jazz: Myth and Religion (New York: Oxford University Press, 1987), 39.

73. Uchida, "Higeki no tensai pianisuto Moriyasu Shōtarō no densetsu," 196. Raymond Knabner wrote in a personal correspondence, "I witnessed with my own eyes Japanese musicians writ[ing] and copy[ing] music, while listening to an American record with allegro." The term "cocktail bop" to describe Shearing's music is from Richard Cook and

Brian Morton, *The Penguin Guide to Jazz on CD, LP and Cassette* (London: Penguin, 1994), 1168.

74. Kubota Jirō, "Four Sounds . . . soshite Nippon no jazu," *SJ* March 1954: 14–15, 17.

75. Leonard, *Jazz: Myth and Religion*, 39, 118–35.

76. Yoshida Mamoru, "Shinshun hōdan: Moriyasu Shōtarō no maboroshi o akasu!" *Jazz* Jan. 1976: 62–63.

77. Two tracks ("I Want to Be Happy" and "It's Only a Paper Moon") were issued the year after Moriyasu's death on the EP *Shotaro Moriyasu Memorial* (Rockwell: ME 503, 1956). The complete recordings were most recently available as a two-CD collection, *The Historic Mocambo Session '54* (Rockwell/Polydor: POCJ-1878/9, 1990).

78. Miyazawa Akira, "Moriyasu Shōtarō no shi o itamu," *SJ* Nov. 1955: 23.

79. Quoted in Takahashi and Sasaki, 37–38. See also Oda, 37–39.

80. "Kōun hirotta 'jūsannichi no kinyō' jazu pianisuto midasarete beimoku e shōkai," *Asahi shinbun* 14 Nov. 1953: 3; Kubota Jirō, "J.A.T.P. rainichi ga unda jazu no Shinderera Akiyoshi Toshiko," *SJ* Dec. 1953: 33; "Shinderera Akiyoshi Toshiko shōgaku shikin kakutoku no keii," *SJ* Jan. 1956: 19; *SJ* Mar. 1956: 26; Segami Yasuo, "Nippon no jazu shi—Toshiko no shojo rokuon hiwa," *SJ* April 1972: 208–9; Akiyoshi, *Jazu to ikiru* 100–102. The ten-inch LP *The Amazing Toshiko Akiyoshi* (Norgran: MGN 22, 1954) was released in the United States (but not in Japan), earning a three-star review in *Down Beat*. Akiyoshi was accompanied by Ray Brown (b), J. C. Herd (d), and Herb Ellis (g).

81. *Down Beat* 18 April 1956: 41; *Mademoiselle* Jan. 1958: 69; *Toshiko Akiyoshi and Leon Sash at Newport* (Verve: MGV8236, 1957); *The Toshiko Trio* (Storyville: STLP 912, 1956). Akiyoshi's *What's My Line* appearance is shown in *Jazz Is My Native Language: A Portrait of Toshiko Akiyoshi*, VHS, prod. Renée Cho (Rhapsody Films, 1983).

82. Brian Priestley, *Mingus: A Critical Biography* (New York: Da Capo Press, 1982), 134. Akiyoshi wrote home about her tenure in Mingus's band in *SJ* Aug. 1962: 46–47.

83. Quoted in Leonard Feather, "Tokyo Blues," *Down Beat* 10 Sept. 1964: 21. The significance of the Blakey tour is discussed by Honda, *Modan jazu*, 9–16; and in "1961 dai kaiko," *JH* 65 (1989): 133–57. A complete list of foreign jazz artists who performed in Japan from 1945 to March 1988 appears in *Swing Journal shin sekai jazu jinmei jiten*, special ed., May 1988: 478–500. A photographic record of the early sixties *rainichi* rush was compiled by Miura Kōdai in his *JAZZ in Japan, 1963–1974* (Tokyo: Nishida Shoten, 1991).

84. Quoted in Dave Jampel, "Hampton's Asiatic-Harlem Band Hits Pioneer Note in East-West Integration," *Variety* 17 April 1963: 56; "Kotoshi no Nippon jazukai sōkessan," *SJ* Jan. 1964: 26; "Musical Mentor to a Japanese Star: Carl Jones, Chiemi Eri are big hit in Far East," *Ebony* Aug. 1962: 73–78. Hampton took the Japanese singer Hoshino Miyoko back on tour in the States with him for ten months. She sang American standards in kimono and appeared on the cover of *Jet* (see *SJ* July 1964: 58; and "Ura kara mita Amerika jazu kai," *SJ* Sept. 1964: 120–24).

85. Quoted in Feather, "Tokyo Blues," 22.

86. The difficulties of keeping a band together are discussed in Kubota Jirō, "Shūgō risan ron," *SJ* May 1955: 21; "Bando no menbā wa kōshite idō suru," *SJ* April 1957: 34–37.

87. *SJ* Jan. 1955: 25; Fukuda Ichirō, "1957 nen no bano tenbō," *SJ* Mar. 1957: 38; *SJ* Jan. 1957: 63. For years the conventional wisdom in the recording industry had been that jazz by Japanese would not sell (*SJ* Aug. 1953: 31).

88. "Konsāto jazu no uraomote," 17–19. See also article in *Mainichi shinbun* 8 Dec. 1953, reprinted in Mainichi Shinbunsha, comp., *Shōwa zen kiroku* (Tokyo: Mainichi Shinbunsha, 1989), 537.

89. "Shinu, Shinu, Shinu," *Time* 12 Sept. 1960: 60; Donald C. Cannalte, "Tokyo's Coffee Musicales," *New York Times* 12 Aug. 1956: B28. The decline of *jazu kissa* is described in Eckhart Derschmidt, "The Disappearance of the *Jazu-Kissa:* Some Considerations about Japanese 'Jazz-Cafés' and Jazz-Listeners," in *The Culture of Japan as Seen through Its Leisure,* ed. Sepp Linhart and Sabine Frühstück (Albany, N.Y.: SUNY Press, 1998), 303–15; and in my unpublished manuscript "Yokohama Jazz Story: Chigusa and the 'Hometown of Japanese Jazz,' " presented at Midwest Conference on Asian Affairs, St. Louis, 15 Oct. 1995, and at the Ph.D. Kenkyūkai, International House of Japan, Tokyo, 10 April 1995.

90. Kawano Ryūji, "Jazu no chōshū ni tsuite," *Ongaku geijutsu* Oct. 1957: 38; Ōhashi Kyosen, "Nippon no jazukai: 1958 nen no jazukai kaisō," *SJ* Dec. 1958: 27; Saijō quoted in "Round a Table Talk about 'KING JAZZ SERIES,' " *SJ* Jan. 1958: 75. The single best overview of the series is *A History of King Jazz Recordings (Nippon jazu taikei: Kingu rekōdo sōgyō 60 shūnen kikaku),* 10 CDs (King: KICJ 6001–6010, 1992).

91. Yamaya Kiyoshi, interviewed by Segawa Masahisa, liner notes, *Modern Jazz Composer's Corner* (Toshiba EMI: TOCT-9212, 1995).

92. Review of *Midnight in Tokyo,* vol. 1 (London: LTZ 15124, 1958) in *The Gramophone* Aug. 1958: 126.

93. Charlie Mariano, "Jazz in Japan," *Jazz* May–June 1964: 10, 29. Oda Satoru confessed his frustrations about having to play pop instead of jazz in *SJ* Oct. 1963: 60.

94. Akiyoshi Toshiko, "Sakanna kitaō no jazu," *SJ* Aug. 1964: 135; "Nippon jazukai shindan," *SJ* July 1961: 51; "Meet the Toshiko Mariano Quartet," *SJ* Jan. 1961: 30; "Nyūsu hairaito: kokoku o satta Toshiko Mariano," *SJ* April 1965: 65.

95. One writer commented that although musicians seemed to prefer modern jazz, the accessible BG-style combo was more marketable in the cabarets that employed so many jazz musicians in this period. "Band Box—Yamada Ichirō to shikkusu furēmusu," *SJ* June 1955: 32.

96. Matsumoto quoted in Kubota Jirō, "Danwa shitsu—Matsumoto Hidehiko," *SJ* May 1958: 54. Ted Gioia, *West Coast Jazz: Modern Jazz in California, 1945–1960* (New York: Oxford University Press, 1992), 362, states that West Coast jazz "had a strong compositional emphasis; it delighted in counterpoint; it had a cooler demeanor than Bird and Dizzy's bebop; the drummers were not so dominating as Roach and Blakey; the horn players were not so heavily rooted in the bebop vocabulary as Stitt and Rollins. The West Coast sound was cleanly articulated, the execution fluid and polished." By contrast, David H. Rosenthal, *Hard Bop: Jazz and Black Music 1955–1965* (New York: Oxford University Press, 1992), 27, describes East Coast hard bop as an amalgam of bebop, black gospel, funk, and rhythm and blues. I say "imagined dichotomy" here because there was considerable transgression of the East-West boundaries, by artists as diverse as Charles Mingus, Harold Land, Eric Dolphy, and Ornette Coleman. In 1959 George Crater problematized the distinction: "If an east coast musician is playing jazz on the west coast, is he an east coast jazz musician playing east coast jazz on the west coast or is he an east coast jazz musician playing west coast jazz on the west coast or is he a west coast jazz musician playing east coast jazz?" ("The West Coast Scene," *Down Beat* 12 Nov. 1959: 15).

97. Quoted in John Schofield, "Pianist Infuses Jazz with Japanese Spirit," *Wall Street Journal* 8 Oct. 1991: A20.

98. Kubota Jirō, "Band Reviews: Akiyoshi Toshiko to kōjii kuintetto," *SJ* June 1954: 18; Kubota, "Four Sounds," 15.

99. Quoted in Richard Gehman, "Jazz over Tokyo," *Saturday Review* 14 Mar. 1959: 76.

100. "Gaikokujin kara mita Nippon no jazukai," *SJ* Oct. 1964: 26–31.

101. Joachim Ernst Berendt, "Jazz in Japan," trans. Ernest Borneman, *Down Beat* 6 Dec. 1962: 15–16. Berendt's remarks are supported by the favorable critical reaction to Coleman and other avant-gardists' music in *Swing Journal*. There was nothing even remotely like the hostile debates that Coleman's music generated in *Down Beat* and other American jazz magazines.

102. Feather, "Tokyo Blues," 23; and Leonard Feather, "Jazz Conquers Japan," *Ebony* Oct. 1964: 134.

103. Gruntz quoted in "Japan Has Almost Everything—Except Jazz Soloists," *Down Beat* 9 May 1963: 8; Berendt, "Jazz in Japan," 15, 16; Mariano, 10.

104. "Gaikokujin kara mita Nippon no jazukai," 26.

105. Kubota Takashi, "Kansai jazukai no tenbō," *SJ* June 1960: 26. The "funky boom" was also known as the "black people [kokujin] boom." See "Negro Acts Big on Japan Junkets," *Variety* 15 Feb. 1961: 62.

106. "Nippon no uesuto kōsuto: Kansai jazukai no tenbō," *SJ* Aug. 1960: 34.

107. Oda Makoto, "Third Generation Intellectual," *Atlas* 3.2 (Feb. 1962): 106, cited in Plath, 190; Nakano Yoshio, "Mohaya 'sengo' dewanai," *Bungei shunjū* Feb. 1956; Nakano Yoshio, " 'Sengo' e no ketsubetsu," *Sekai* Aug. 1956: 8.

108. Ōkura Ichitarō, "Nippon no biggu bando tenbō," *SJ* Nov. 1959: 15. MacArthur quotation from U.S. Senate, Hearings before the Committee on Armed Services and the Committee on Foreign Relations, *Military Situation in the Far East*, May 1951, part 1, 312; also quoted in Sheila K. Johnson, *American Attitudes toward Japan, 1941–1975* (American Enterprise Institute for Public Policy Research, 1975), 52, and Dower, *Embracing Defeat*, 550–51.

6 Our Thing: Defining "Japanese Jazz"

1. "45th Annual Readers Poll," *Down Beat* Dec. 1980: 17; Leonard Feather, "Toshiko's Triple," *Melody Maker* 5 Dec. 1981: 27. Akiyoshi continued to win in all three categories in both the readers' and international critics' polls until 1982. She consistently placed second or third in similar polls in *Jazz Journal International*.

2. Mark Gardner, "Jazz Is Alive and Living in Japan," *Melody Maker* 16 Jan. 1971: 28; Yui Shōichi, "Jazu rekōdo tenkoku—Nippon: '74 no tenbō to keishō," *Swing Journal Maboroshi no meiban dokuhon*, special ed., April 1974: 290; and Maurice Gourgues, "Made in Japan," *Jazz Magazine* 233 (May–June 1975): 37.

3. Haruhiko Fukuhara, "The Great Jazz Boom," *Jazz Journal International* Oct. 1978: 33, 36; Bruce Ingram, " 'Frisco FMer Jazzes It Up with Live Broadcast to Japan," *Variety* 1 July 1988: 45. See also Alex Abramoff, "Japanese Develop Domestic Jazz amid Flourishing Import Scene," *Billboard* 9 July 1977: 70; and Takako Mizuoka, "Tremendous Activity on the Recording Scene," *Jazz Journal International* Oct. 1978: 40–41.

4. Carol Gluck, "The Idea of Showa," *Showa: The Japan of Hirohito*, ed. Carol Gluck and Stephen R. Graubard (New York: Norton, 1992), 5, argues that the Shōwa boom occurred "during the years widely identified as a break with the earlier postwar decades."

5. " '72 Jazz Scene in Japan," *SJ* April 1972: 102–3.

6. Marilyn Ivy, "Formations of Mass Culture," in *Postwar Japan as History*, ed. Andrew Gordon (Berkeley: University of California Press, 1993), 253–54. Ivy attributes the term *micromass* to Fujioka Wakao, *Sayonara, taishū: kansei jidai o dō yomu ka* (Tokyo: PHP Kenkyūjo, 1984).

7. See Minami Hiroshi, "The Introspection Boom: Wither the National Character," *Japan*

Interpreter 8 (1973): 160–75; Aoki Tamotsu, *"Nihon bunka ron" no hen'yō* (Tokyo: Chūō kōron sha, 1990), 82; and Kōsaku Yoshino, *Cultural Nationalism in Contemporary Japan: A Sociological Inquiry* (London: Routledge, 1992), 36.

8. The terms *avant-garde, free jazz,* and *out music* encompass a variety of styles that emerged in the early 1960s under the leadership of such pioneers as Cecil Taylor, Ornette Coleman, John Coltrane, and Sun Ra. These artists and their followers eschewed functional tonality, harmonic structures, and steady rhythmic pulses that had been basic to previous styles of jazz. Many commentators have regarded avant-garde music as an expression of 1960s black nationalism. See, for example, Frank Kofsky, *Black Nationalism and the Revolution in Music* (New York: Pathfinder Press, 1970); Ekkehard Jost, *Free Jazz* (Graz, Austria: Universal Edition, 1974); Valerie Wilmer, *As Serious as Your Life: The Story of the New Jazz* (Westport, Conn.: L. Hill, 1977); John Litweiler, *The Freedom Principle: Jazz after 1958* (New York: William Morrow, 1984); John Gray, comp., *Fire Music: A Bibliography of the New Jazz, 1959–1990* (New York: Greenwood, 1991); Francis Davis, *Outcats: Jazz Composers, Instrumentalists, and Singers* (New York: Oxford University Press, 1992); and David G. Such, *Avant-Garde Jazz Musicians: Performing 'Out There'* (Iowa City, University of Iowa Press, 1993).

9. The political drama of Anpo (often romanticized as "Ampo") is discussed in George R. Packard III, *Protest in Tokyo: The Security Treaty Crisis of 1960* (Princeton, N.J.: Princeton University Press, 1966). Regarding the junctures between avant-garde and nativist movements in the arts in the 1960s and 1970s, see Thomas R. H. Havens, *Artist and Patron in Postwar Japan* (Princeton, N.J.: Princeton University Press, 1982); Judith Ann Herd, "The Neonationalist Movement: Origins of Japanese Contemporary Music," *Perspectives in New Music* 27.2 (1989): 119–20; David G. Goodman, *Japanese Drama and Culture in the 1960s: The Return of the Gods* (Armonk, N.Y.: M. E. Sharpe, 1988); and David Desser, *Eros Plus Massacre* (Bloomington: Indiana University Press, 1988). Goodman and Desser's respective studies of post–New Theater and New Wave film locate the impetus for those movements in the frustration of the so-called Anpo protests of 1960. Goodman's study, in particular, focuses on the development of a politicized avant-garde art that was at once revolutionary and traditionalistic. Avant-garde theater, produced by "the disgruntled graduates of the Security Treaty struggle," rejected the modernist concern with realism that New Theater (*shingeki*) advocated, and attempted to "reestablish contact with the postmodern imagination that had been taboo since shingeki's rupture with kabuki" (10, 15).

10. See Terui Akira, "Haikei, Nippon no jazu o ai suru mina sama e," *Bessatsu ichioku nin no Shōwa shi: Nihon no jazu—Jazz of Japan '82* (Tokyo: Mainichi Shinbunsha, 1982), 162–63 [hereafter cited as *Jazz of Japan '82*]; "Jazu Nippon rettō 55 nenban," *Jazu hihyō* [hereafter *JH*] 35 (1980): 30; "Jazu Nippon rettō 95 nenban," *JH*, special ed. (Jan. 1995): 13.

11. *SJ* Dec. 1960: 51.

12. *Ginparis Session June 26, 1963* (Three Blind Mice: TBM-9, 1972; TBM-2509, 1977; ART Union/DIW: ART-CD-8, 1986). See also Uchida Osamu, "Maboroshi no Ginpari sesshon futatabi," *SJ* Dec. 1977: 180–83; " 'Maboroshi' no Ginpari sesshon," *Jazz of Japan '82*, 130; Uchida Osamu, *Jazu ga wakakatta koro* (Tokyo: Shōbunsha, 1984), 126–50. See also Uchida Kōichi, *Nihon no jazu shi: senzen, sengo* (Tokyo: Swing Journal, 1976), 305–7; Yoshida Mamoru, " 'Mimizu no tawagoto—Ginpari sesshon' ga TBM kara hatsubai sareta node, ano koro ga natsukashiku natte," *JH* 29 (1978): 150–53, which reprints an original membership list from Dec. 1962. (In 1992 Uchida donated these tapes to the city of Okazaki, and they currently are preserved in the Okazaki Mindscape Museum. Although the tapes are being transferred to digital audio tape for future public use, my requests in

1994 and 1998 for access to these tapes—supported with recommendations from Dr. Uchida himself and Okazaki's Diet representative—have been rebuffed. Analysis of the contents will thus have to wait for a later date.)

13. Uchida, "Maboroshi no Ginpari sesshon futatabi," 183; Yoshida, "Mimizu no tawagoto," 150; *SJ* June 1961: 57; and Shimizu Toshihiko, Hiraoka Masaaki, and Okunari Tōru, *Nihon no jazu den* (Tokyo: Eipuriru Shuppan, 1977), 77. Takayanagi was chastised in "Wareware wa mayaku ga hitsuyō nanoka? aete myūjishan shoshi ni tou," *SJ* Nov. 1960: 16–17; and "Futatabi mayaku ni tsuite," *SJ* Mar. 1962: 24–25.

14. *SJ* Dec. 1962: 59.

15. Quoted in Takayanagi Masayuki and Tamai Shinji, "Takayanagi Masayuki—Ginpari no densetsu nante tsumaranai," *JH* 22 (1975): 89–90. See also Yoshida Mamoru, *Yokohama jazu monogatari: "Chigusa" no 50 nen* (Yokohama: Kanagawa Shinbunsha, 1985), 138–39.

16. Live jazz performances, rare enough in Tokyo, were even more so in provincial cities like Nagoya. But with the intercession of Yoshida Mamoru and Uchida Osamu (who lived in nearby Okazaki), the New Century Music Workshop performed several all-night sessions at Kuno Jirō's Nagoya coffeehouse Combo. See Uchida Osamu, "Dokutā Uchida no jazu ni kanpai! 21: wasure enu taiken Nagoya ensōkai," *Chūnichi shinbun*, evening ed., 6 Aug. 1986: 6.

17. Yamashita made his comments at a concert entitled "Tribute to Jo-Jo (Takayanagi Masayuki)" at TUC Jazz Court in Tokyo, 27 Jan. 1995. See also Takayanagi and Tamai, 91.

18. *SJ* Feb. 1966: 93; *SJ* Jan. 1972: 207; and *SJ* July 1976: 242.

19. Takayanagi Masayuki and Ino Nobuyoshi, *Reason for Being* (Jinya Disc: B-02/LMCD-1287, 1992).

20. Eckhart Derschmidt, "Thrilling Live Performances," *Resonance* 4.2 (Feb. 1996): 19, makes a similar assertion. See also Alan Cummings, "Undiscovered Country: Shooting Star and Supernova," *Avant* Winter 1997: 40–41.

21. *SJ* Sept. 1964: 63; "Jazz Sessions at the Tokyo: katsuyaku suru Nippon no jazu," *SJ* Sept. 1966: 122. Minton's Playhouse was the Harlem club at which bebop pioneers Dizzy Gillespie, Charlie Parker, and Theolonious Monk developed their music in informal jam session contexts in the early 1940s. See also Yoshida, *Yokohama jazu monogatari*, 140–55; and Takayanagi and Tamai, 94–96.

22. One of the most famous examples of 1960s Japanese pops was Sakamoto Kyū's "Ue o muite arukō," which was a number-one hit in the United States under the title "Sukiyaki" in 1963. For more on 1960s popular music see, for example, Linda Fujie, "Popular Music," in *Handbook of Japanese Popular Culture*, ed. Richard Gid Powers and Hidetoshi Katō (Westport, Conn.: Greenwood Press, 1989), 207; Steve McClure, "Japanese Pop Music: A Beginner's Guide," *Mangajin* 36 (June 1994): 15; and Tsurumi Shunsuke, *Sengo Nippon no taishu bunka shi: 1945–1980* (Tokyo: Iwanami shoten, 1984), 149–66.

23. Richie Vitale, quoted in Adam Gussow, *Mister Satan's Apprentice: A Blues Memoir* (New York: Pantheon, 1998), 188.

24. Watanabe Sadao, *Boku jishin no tame no jazu*, ed. Iwanami Yōzō (Tokyo: Arachi Shuppansha, 1969), 125–31, 139; "Watanabe Sadao no miyage banashi," *SJ* Jan. 1966: 120; and "1965 nendo naigai jazukai o kaiko suru," *SJ* Dec. 1965: 79.

25. "Editor's Choice," *SJ* Jan. 1966: 116; "1966 nendo naigai jazukai kaiko," *SJ* Jan. 1967: 88–93.

26. "Watanabe Sadao no miyage banashi," 122.

27. *SJ* Feb. 1966: 90; and Max E. Lash, "Japan's First Jazz School," *Down Beat* 15 May 1969: 40–41.

28. "The sole point of contact between the [older and younger] generations of jazz musicians is the world-class altoist Watanabe Sadao." Segawa Masahisa, "Watanabe Sadao to Nippon no modan jazu," *SJ: Modan jazu dokuhon '67*, special ed., Nov. 1967: 86.
29. Honda Toshio, "Jazz Losing Ground in Japan: DJ Honda," *Billboard* 29 July 1967: 29.
30. "Karejji jazu no katsudō sakan," *SJ* Nov. 1966: 104. Surprisingly little has been written on the 1960s student culture in Japan. For an in-depth analysis of the structures and strategies of student movements, see Patricia G. Steinhoff, "Student Conflict," in *Conflict in Japan*, ed. Ellis S. Krauss, Thomas P. Rohlen, and Patricia G. Steinhoff (Honolulu: University of Hawai'i Press, 1984), 174–213.
31. *Dancing Kojiki* (Sadaneri Shobō: DANC-3, 1995) documents this "expression of a passionate age." See also Yū Masahiko, "Japan," *Swing Journal: Modan jazu dokuhon '70*, special ed., Nov. 1969: 101; Yui Shōichi, "Ningen dokyumento—Yamashita Yōsuke," in *Jazz of Japan '82*, 149; and Shimizu, Hiraoka, and Okunari, 133–35, which incorrectly states that the event occurred in 1967.
32. Muto Ichiyo, "The Birth of the Women's Liberation Movement," in *The Other Japan* (New Edition), ed. Joe Moore (Armonk, N.Y.: M. E. Sharpe, 1997), 171; Muto Ichiyo and Inoue Reiko, "Beyond the New Left (Part 2—II): In Search of a Radical Base in Japan," *AMPO Japan-Asia Quarterly Review* 17.4 (1985): 51; Hiraoka Masaaki, "Jazu ni totte Nippon rokujū nendai shisō to wa nanika," *JH* 7 (1970): 93; Uchida Osamu, "Jazu wa Ginza kara Shinjuku e," in *Shinjuku Pittoin*, ed. Aikura Hisato et al. (Tokyo: Shōbunsha, 1985), 181–82; Aikura Hisato, *Jazu kara no aisatsu* (Tokyo: Ongaku no Tomo Sha, 1968), 88, 93; and Derschmidt, "Thrilling Live Performances," 19.
33. "Honshi tokubetsu seron chōsa: jazu kissatsū no seikatsu to iken," *SJ: Modan jazu dokuhon '67*, special ed., Nov. 1967: 284. See also Ono Yasuhiko, "Vol. 5: Jinbōchō hen—'60 nendaimatsu, 'demo ni sanka suru' wakamono kara gakuseishō o atsukatta 'Hibiki' no Ōki ōnā wa Erubin no sōru burazā," *Tokyo jazu kissa monogatari*, Ad Lib, comp. (Tokyo: Ad Lib, 1989), 119–34.
34. Pit-Inn opened as a jazz coffeehouse in February 1966, but was remodeled as a Greenwich-Village-style hangout to become "Japan's first real jazz club" in late 1968 (quoted in *SJ* Dec. 1968: 124). The mottos appear in advertisements in *SJ* Oct. 1966: 95, and Sept. 1967: 209. See also Derschmidt, "Thrilling Live Performances," 19; and Aikura et al., *Shinjuku Pittoin*, 9–12.
35. The popularity of jam sessions (or "jazz sessions") at Tokyo jazz spots such as Pit-Inn, Five Spot (in Jiyūgaoka), Marunouchi Hotel Sakura Room, Tarō (Shinjuku), Jazz Gallery 8 (Ginza), and Satin Doll (Yotsuya) is discussed in *SJ* May 1966: 94; and "Jazz Sessions at the Tokyo: katsuyaku suru Nippon no jazu," *SJ* Aug. 1966: 88–91; Sept. 1966: 122–24.
36. Quoted in "Japanese Wreck Tour by Miles Davis Group," *Down Beat* 20 Feb. 1969; see also Lash, 40.
37. Prior to the Shiraki Hideo Quintet's appearance in Berlin, only a few Japanese had performed as solo guests at overseas jazz festivals. Akiyoshi Toshiko performed at the Newport Jazz Festival in 1957 and 1958; "Sleepy" Matsumoto at the Monterey Jazz Festival in September 1963; vocalist Hirota Mieko at Newport in 1965; and Watanabe Sadao at the Chicago *Down Beat* Festival in August 1965. See Uchida, *Nihon no jazu shi*, 326–27.
38. The quintet (Hino Terumasa [t], Muraoka Takeru [ts], Sera Yuzuru [p], Kurita Hachirō [b], Shiraki Hideo [d] and *koto* trio (Shirane Kuniko, Nosaka Keiko, and Miyamoto Sachiko) recorded the Japanese folk songs while in Berlin, becoming the first working Japanese jazz band to record for a foreign label (*SJ* July 1968: 131). The LP was released in West Germany as *Japan Meets Jazz* (Saba/MPS: SB 15064ST, 1968) and in Japan as *Matsuri no*

gensō—Berurin no Shiraki Hideo kuintetto (MPS/Columbia: Y5-2320-MP). All quotes are from the LP's liner notes.

39. Hara quoted in Dave Jampel, "Japanese Jazzmen Invading Newport: Bandleader Nobuo Hara Seeks 'Moment of Truth' at Wein's Fest Classic," *Variety* 14 June 1967: 50. The performance was recorded and released as *Sharps and Flats in Newport* (Nippon Columbia: XMS-10019, 1969). In *Modan jazu* (Tokyo: Shin Nippon Shinsho, 1989), 198–99, Honda Toshio, who accompanied and reported on the Sharps and Flats concert at Newport, speculated that "the average American's thinking is that Japanese orchestras should play Japanese songs."

40. S. G. Nirts, "Osaka New Orleans Rascals Visit New Orleans," *The Second Line* July–Aug. 1966: 95–96, 101; see also *SJ* Sept. 1966: 95. High Society toured the United States in February and March 1967, performing original arrangements by Maeda Norio at twenty college campuses on the West Coast (*SJ* Mar. 1967: 99).

41. Akiyoshi's late-sixties travails were candidly reported by Yukiko Erwin in "Nippon o satta tensai no josei ongakuka—haha toshite sakkyokuka toshite kunō suru Akiyoshi Toshiko no naimen," *Ushio* 87 (Sept. 1967): 378–86.

42. Yui Shōichi, "Jazu fesutivaru in Japan: senkyūhyaku gojūhachi nendo Suingu Jānaru ōru sutāsu o kiku," *SJ* Dec. 1958: 85; Kawano quoted in Kawano Ryūji, Shima Yukio, and Ishihara Yasuyuki, "Zadankai: S.J. ōru sutāzu 'jazu in Japan,'" *SJ* Jan. 1958: 60.

43. Quoted in Kubota Jirō and Takura Kōji, "Taidan: jazu no tanoshisa," *Ongaku geijutsu* Oct. 1957: 40.

44. Quoted in Noguchi Hisamitsu et al., "Zadankai: Nippon ni okeru modan jazu no genjō to shōrai," *Ongaku geijutsu* Nov. 1959: 17–18.

45. "Ensōkai meguri," *SJ* Dec. 1958: 70; *O-koto no jazu* referenced in *SJ* Jan. 1959: 51; "Gagakunized Jazz," *Newsweek* 28 Sept. 1964: 89; and Charlie Mariano and Watanabe Sadao, "Chāri no mita Nippon no jazu," *SJ* Aug. 1967: 103. Recordings include The Dixie Kings, *Dikishii Nippon min'yō* (King: SKG-27, 1963); Ono Shigenori and the Blue Coats, *Guren Mirā sutairu—Nippon no mūdo* (Nippon Victor: SJL-5088, 1964), and *Guren Mirā sutairu ni yoru Nippon no senritsu* (Nippon Columbia: PS-5070, 1965); *Jazz of the Four Seasons* (Polydor: SLJ-59, 1964), featuring Inomata Takeshi and the Westliners, Sawada Shungo's Double Beats, and the Fujita Masaaki Quintet; and Tony Scott, *Music for Zen Meditation and Other Joys* (Verve: V6-8634, 1964). See also Segawa Masahisa, "Nippon no jazu to sono rekōdo," *Swing Journal: Jazu rekōdo no subete*, special ed., May 1966: 96–99; and Elizabeth Ann Sesler-Beckman, "Jazz Is My Native Language: A Study of the Development of Jazz in Japan" (M.A. thesis, Tufts University, 1989), 26.

46. Yagi quoted in Noguchi, "Nippon ni okeru modan jazu no genjō to shōrai," 17.

47. Quoted in Koyama Kiyoshi, "Shimupojium—Nippon no jazu o kangaeru," *SJ* May 1968: 78–79; and Koyama Kiyoshi, "Zoku: Nippon no jazu o kangaeru," *SJ* Nov. 1968: 71.

48. Watanabe, *Boku jishin no tame no jazu*, 135.

49. Yui Shōichi, "Nipponteki jazu," *JH* 6 (July 1969): 28–29.

50. Quoted in "Zadankai: 'Nippon no jazu' o kataru," *'69 All Japan Jazz Festival—19th Swing Journal Poll Winners* (Tokyo: Swing Journal, 1969), 25–28.

51. Dan Ikuma, "The Influence of Japanese Traditional Music on the Development of Western Music in Japan," trans. Dorothy G. Britton, *The Transactions of the Asiatic Society of Japan*, 3d series, 8 (Dec. 1961): 201, 216–17.

52. Takemitsu Tōru, quoted in Akiyama Kuniharu, "Japan," in *Dictionary of Contemporary Music*, ed. John Vinton (New York: E. P. Dutton, 1974), 365, and in Havens, *Artist and Patron*, 183–84.

53. Quoted in Koyama, "Zoku: Nippon no jazu o kangaeru," 71; *SJ* Aug. 1970: 159.

54. Sugiura quoted in "Editor's Choice," *SJ* Jan. 1966: 118; Miyazawa quoted in "SJ Post," *SJ* Mar. 1970: 157; Yui Shōichi, "Nippon popyurā ongaku shi 34," 32; Okabe Yoshihirō (Iwatsuki, Saitama), review in *SJ* Oct. 1971: 286; and Kurota quoted in "Shinshun tokubetsu zadankai—1970 nendai no jazu wo kataru," 93. The richly nationalistic implications of the term *fūdo* (used in Miyazawa's quotation) are discussed in Tessa Morris-Suzuki, *Re-Inventing Japan: Time, Space, Nation* (Armonk, N.Y.: M. E. Sharpe, 1998), 56–58, 115–117.

55. See "Jazukai jidai no ninaite Yamamoto Hōzan," *SJ* May 1968: 200–201. Yamamoto's jazz albums include: *New Jazz in Japan* (Nippon Columbia: YS-10022, 1968), and *Beautiful Bamboo Flute* (Philips: FX-8510, 1971), both with Hara Nobuo's Sharps and Flats; *Ginkai (Silver World)* (Philips: BT-5319, 1970); *Hozan, Friesen + 1* (Next Wave: 25PJ-1002, 1980); and *Again and Again* (JVC: SGS-38, 1985).

56. Takayanagi Masayuki, *Independence: Tread on New Ground* (Teichiku/Union: UPS-2010-J, 1969); and Togashi Masahiko Quintet, *We Now Create: Music for Strings, Winds, and Percussions* (Nippon Victor/World: SMJX 10065, 1969).

57. Amiri Baraka (LeRoi Jones), *Blues People: Negro Music in White America* (1963; New York: Quill, 1999), 148–49, 155 (emphasis mine, except for "valid"); and Baraka, "Jazz and the White Critic," reprinted in *Black Music* (New York: William Morrow, 1968), 14, 17. See also Segawa Masahisa, "Watanabe Sadao to Nihon no modan jazu," *Swing Journal modan jazu dokuhon '67*, special ed., Nov. 1967: 91; and Aikura, *Jazu kara no aisatsu*, 95.

58. See Ronald M. Radano, *New Musical Figurations: Anthony Braxton's Cultural Critique* (Chicago: University of Chicago Press, 1993), chap. 3 (quotations from 77, 81, 100); and Leslie Rout, "AACM: New Music (!) New Ideas (?)," *Journal of Popular Culture* 1.2 (fall 1967): 128–40.

59. See Hiraoka Masaaki, *Sengo Nippon no jazu shi* (Tokyo: Adin Shobō, 1977), 15; Iwashiro Yutaka, "Kokujin jazu no minzokusei ni tsuite" *JH* 2 (Nov. 1967): 40–47; and John G. Russell, "Consuming Passions: Spectacle, Self-Transformation, and the Commodification of Blackness in Japan," *positions: east asia cultures critique* 6.1 (1998): 120.

60. Kenichi Adachi, "The Image of Americans in Contemporary Japanese Fiction," *Japanese Popular Culture: Studies in Mass Communication and Cultural Change*, ed. and trans. Hidetoshi Katō (1959; Westport, Conn.: Greenwood Press, 1973), 59. Regarding allegations of wartime collaboration between black radicals and Japanese, see Erdmann D. Beynon, "The Voodoo Cult among Negro Migrants in Detroit," *American Journal of Sociology* 43 (1938): 897, 904; Roi Ottley, *New World A-Coming: Inside Black America* (Boston: Houghton-Mifflin, 1943), 332, 337; C. Eric Lincoln, *The Black Muslims in America* (Boston: Beacon, 1961), 26; Faith Berry, *Langston Hughes: Before and Beyond Harlem* (Westport, Conn.: Lawrence Hill, 1983), 196–97; John Dower, *War without Mercy: Race and Power in the Pacific War* (New York: Pantheon, 1986), 174; and Waldo Heinrichs, *Threshold of War* (New York: Oxford University Press, 1988), 124. Regarding Nakasone's comments, see John G. Russell, "Re-thinking the Japanese Image of Blacks," *IHJ Bulletin* 10.4 (1990): 1.

61. "Suingu Jānaru ōru sutāzu Eikoku de hatsubai saru!!" *SJ* Nov. 1958: 15.

62. Shōichi Yui, "Jazz in Japan," *Jazz Forum* 17 (June 1971): 43–44.

63. Terayama quoted in Yui Shōichi, Terayama Shūji, Yamashita Yōsuke, and Adachi Motohiko, "Wareware ni totte jazu to wa nanika?" *Ongaku geijutsu* Aug. 1968: 26.

64. Baraka, *Blues People*, 226–27 (emphasis mine). See also Michael J. Budds, *Jazz in the Sixties: The Expansion of Musical Resources and Techniques* (Iowa City: University of Iowa Press, 1990), 116–27.

65. Yamashita's "blue note studies" are obliquely mentioned in Yui, "Ningen dokyumento,"

147–48; Satō quoted in Freddy Santamaria, "Du Swing chez les Samouraïs," *Jazz Maga-zine* 173 (Dec. 1969): 65. Togashi Masahiko and Soejima Teruto discuss the universal nature of blues in "Taidan: burūsu wa sorezore no minzoku no uta dearu," *JH* 10 (1971): 28–36.

66. Robeson, quoted in Foner, 444, 437, 446. See also liner notes for Fred Houn and the Afro-Asian Music Ensemble, *We Refuse to Be Used and Abused* (Soul Note: 121167, 1988).

67. Examples abound in the series *Japanese Traditional Music (Nihon no dentō ongaku)* (King: KICH 2001–2010, 1991), and *Music of Japanese People (Nihon no minzoku ongaku)* (King: KICH 2021–2030, 1991), particularly in two volumes from the latter series: *Japanese Dance Music* (KICH 2022) and *Music of Okinawa* (KICH 2025).

68. Imada quoted in "Thirty Successful Years on the Jazz Beat in Japan: Mainstream Veteran Masaru Imada," *Keyboard* (Aug. 1985): 40; Yamashita quoted in "Conflict and Harmony at the Fringes of Jazz: Avant-garde Pianist Yosuke Yamashita," *Keyboard* (Aug. 1985): 42.

69. Tsurumi Shunsuke, *A Cultural History of Postwar Japan 1945–1980* (London: KPI Ltd., 1987), 82–83. Alienation of Japanese from traditional musics is addressed in Linda Fujie, "Effects of Urbanization on *Matsuri-Bayashi* in Tokyo," *Yearbook for Traditional Music* 15 (1983): 38–44; and William P. Malm, "The Modern Music of Meiji Japan," *Tradition and Modernization in Japanese Culture*, ed. Donald H. Shively (Princeton, N.J.: Princeton University Press, 1971), 300.

70. Yū Masahiko, "Nippon no jazu: sono ryūsei wo sasaeru hitotachi," *Swing Journal: Jazu rekōdo hyakka*, special ed., April 1970: 368; and Santamaria, 46.

71. "All Japan Jazz Festival," *SJ* July 1969: 57; "Jazz '69 in Japan: '69 naigai jazukai o kaiko suru," *SJ* Dec. 1969: 71.

72. *SJ* Jan. 1971: 211; "Jazz '71 in Japan," *SJ* Dec. 1971: 58; and Santamaria, 65. The Expo '70 Jazz Festival was temporarily canceled in August 1969, but revived on a smaller scale after several Japanese jazz aficionados, fearing that the world jazz community would doubt "Japan's commitment to jazz," lobbied for its reinstatement. See *SJ* Oct. 1969: 142; and *SJ* Jan. 1970: 153.

73. Yamashita Toshiichirō, "Concert Review—1971 samā jazu fesutibaru," *SJ* Oct. 1971: 279.

74. Satō Masahiko quoted in "Around the World: Random Impressions of the International Jazz Scene: Japan," *Down Beat* 10 Feb. 1977: 18, 43.

75. Yū Masahiko, "Jazz in '73: Nippon no jazu—genjō daha no teian," *SJ* April 1973: 113.

76. Peter N. Dale, *The Myth of Japanese Uniqueness* (London: Croom Helm, 1986), 14–15. The survey (conducted by the Nomura Sōgō Kenkyūjo) confirmed that the "*nihonjinron* have become a force in society conditioning the way Japanese regard themselves."

77. The nature of Togashi's injury is an open secret in the jazz community: insiders are privy to the story and have shared it with me, but virtually no one writes about it publicly (the only disclosure I have read in print is Ono Yoshie's reference to "romantic entanglements" in *Jazu saishū shō*, 137), so I will honor that practice here.

78. Togashi Masahiko, "Nippon no jazutte nan darō," *SJ* April 1975: 114–15.

79. Togashi Masahiko, "Hatashite donaki tabitachi ni mukete," *JH* 17 (1974): 125.

80. Togashi, "Nippon no jazutte nan darō," 115–16. The influence of language, work patterns, and history on the "Japanese sense of rhythm" is explored by ethnomusicologist Fujii Tomoaki, *Minzoku to rizumu*, Minzoku Ongaku Sōsho 8 (Tokyo Shoseki, 1990), 27–35.

81. Iwanami Yōzō, "Nippon no kokoro o sekai ni tsutaeru Toshiko," *SJ* Oct. 1974: 242; *SJ* April 1974: 211.

82. Chris Albertson, liner notes, *Desert Lady Fantasy* (Columbia: CK 57856, 1994); Honda

Toshio, *Rongu ierō rōdo: jazu sankan joō no nagai michinori—Akiyoshi Toshiko* (Tokyo: Ik-kōsha, 1984), 161.

83. Satō quoted in "Around the World: Random Impressions of the International Jazz Scene," 43.

84. Liner notes for Satō Masahiko/Randooga, *Select Live under the Sky '90* (Epic: ESCA 5171, 1990).

85. Segawa Masahisa, "Nippon no jazu ni kakeru mono," *JH* 18 (1974): 26–31; Yui Shōichi, Watanabe Sadao, and George Ōtsuka, "Nippon no jazu no genjō to tenbō," *SJ* April 1974: 116; and "Kongetsu no jazumen: Hino Motohiko," *SJ* Aug. 1975: 227.

Postlude: J-Jazz and the Fin de Siècle Blues

1. Segawa Masahisa, "Declaration: The Jazz Restoration in Japan," liner notes, *The Jazz Restoration in Japan/Jam* (Paddle Wheel: KICJ 209, 1994); published in Japanese as "Nihon jazu ishin sengen," *Nihon jazu ishin '94*, King/Paddlewheel pamphlet included in *Swing Journal* [hereafter *SJ*] April 1994: 2.

2. Kumagai Yoshihirō, "Dentō o ikashita henkaku ga tanomoshii! 'Manabu' jidai wa owatta...," *Nihon jazu ishin '94*, 3.

3. Scott DeVeaux, "Constructing the Jazz Tradition: Jazz Historiography," *Black American Literature Forum* 25 (fall 1991): 551.

4. See Tetsuo Najita, *Japan: The Intellectual Foundations of Modern Japanese Politics* (Chicago: University of Chicago Press, 1974), 44–45, 67.

5. DeVeaux, "Constructing the Jazz Tradition," 550–51, notes that "mainstream" is a favorite term, coined by opponents of the jazz avant-garde, for designating "any body of music neither so conservative as to deny the possibility or desirability of further development, nor so radical as to send that development in uncontrollable directions." But, he concludes, "the concept of the mainstream insists that the essence of jazz is to be found not on the cutting edge, but well back within the tradition."

6. Steven B. Elworth, "Jazz in Crisis, 1948–1958: Ideology and Representation," in *Jazz among the Discourses*, ed. Krin Gabbard (Durham, N.C.: Duke University Press, 1995), 61, 58.

7. DeVeaux, "Constructing the Jazz Tradition," 551 (emphasis mine); and Wynton Marsalis, "What Jazz Is—and Isn't," *New York Times* 31 July 1988: 21, reprinted in Robert Walser, ed., *Keeping Time: Readings in Jazz History* (New York: Oxford University Press, 1999), 335. See also Tamara E. Livingston, "Music Revivals: Towards a General Theory," *Ethnomusicology* 43.1 (1999): 66–85.

8. Iwanami Yōzō, "Nihon no jazumen wa Nyū Yōku de katsuyaku dekiru ka," *Imateki jazu dangi* (Tokyo: Arachi, 1982), 155–60; Uchida Osamu, "East Meets West: Japanese Jazz Jam in Washington D.C.," *SJ* June 1997: 54–55; and Masahiko Osaka and Tomonao Hara Quintet, *Favorites* (Evidence: ECD, 22134, 1995).

9. Uchida Osamu and Koyama Kiyoshi, liner notes for Ayado Chie, *For All We Know* (Ewe: EWCD 0005, 1998).

10. See Gavan McCormack, "From Number One to Number Nothing: Japan's *Fin de Siècle* Blues," *Japanese Studies* 18.1 (May 1998): 31–44; Ōe Kenzaburō, "The Nobel Lecture: Japan, the Ambiguous, and Myself," reprinted at http://www2.passagen.se/tvs/tidning/nobeloo.html; Kawakatsu Heita, "Toward a Country of Wealth and Virtue," *Japan Echo* 26.2 (April 1999), http://www.japanecho.co.jp/docs/html/260214.htm; and John W. Dower, *Embracing Defeat: Japan in the Wake of World War II* (Norton New Press, 1999), 28.

11. See France's festival J'Asie (Jazz Japon d'Aujourd'hui, http://www.jazzmagazine.com/oJT/japon.htm).

12. My thinking here has been influenced by Herman Gray's discussion of contemporary debates over innovation and canonization in his "Jazz as Cultural Practice and the Politics of Diversity," delivered at "Conference on Living and Working with Cultural Plurality: Communities and Their Institutions," sponsored by the Program for the Study of Cultural Values and Ethics, University of Illinois at Urbana-Champaign, 30 Oct. 1992. See also David Meltzer, ed., *Reading Jazz* (San Francisco: Mercury House, 1993), 28–29.

13. "Tokushū: Nihonjin to jazu," *What's New,* vol. 2, ed. Numada Jun (Tokyo: Disc Union, 1994), 15 Aug. 1994: 1 (ellipsis in original).

14. Hino's comments from Susan Boulmetis, "Jazz: Where East Jams with West," *Japan Society Newsletter* Mar. 1993: 7, and Craig McTurk's documentary *Tokyo Blues: Jazz and Blues in Japan* (1999).

REFERENCES

Interviews

Akiyoshi Toshiko, 5 February 1996, by telephone from New York City.
Anzai Takeshi, 14 July 1994, Waseda University, Tokyo.
Jodie Christian, 18 January 1999, at his home, Chicago, Ill.
Raymond Conde, 28 Feb. 1995, Shin-bashi Daiichi Hotel, Tokyo.
Daitoku Toshiyuki, 12 July 1994, Naru, Ochanomizu, Tokyo.
Tomoko Ōno Farnham, 18 Jan. 1995, Shibuya, Tokyo.
Jimmy Harada, 9 Dec. 1994, Saiseria, Shinbashi, Tokyo.
Hara Nobuo and Tsukahara Aiko, 11 April 1995, at their home, Hiro-o, Tokyo.
Hayasaka Sachi and Nagata Toshiki, 15 July 1994, Paper Moon, Ikebukuro, Tokyo.
Hinata Toshifumi, 15 Nov. 1994, Akasaka-mitsuke, Tokyo.
Igarashi Issei, 23 July 1994, Jazz Inn Lovely, Nagoya.
Inagaki Jirō and Inagaki Masayuki, 12 April 1995, Soul Media Corp., Yotsuya, Tokyo.
Isono Teruo, 2 May 1995, Radio Nippon, Azabudai, Tokyo.
Itabashi Fumio, 20 Aug. 1994, Airegin, Yokohama.
Kanai Hideto, 27 April 1995, Pronto coffeehouse, Tsurumi, Yokohama.
Kaneko Yasunori, 9 Oct. 1994, Yokohama Jazz Promenade.
Katayama Hiroaki, 23 July 1994, Jazz Inn Lovely, Nagoya.
Jerry Miner, 11 Oct. 1995, at his home, Urbana, Ill.
Jake Mori, 10 April 1995, *Swing Journal* offices, Shiba-kōen, Tokyo.
Mori Yasumasa, Little Darlin' Oldies Live House, Yokohama, 3 May 1994.
Phil Morrison, by correspondence, July 1996; by telephone, October 1998.
Nagao Masashi, 5 May 1995, at his home, Hiyoshi, Yokohama.
Oda Satoru, 14 Jan. 1995, Birdland, Roppongi, Tokyo.
Oida Toshio, 27 April 1995, Donpa coffeehouse, Roppongi, Tokyo.
Ōno Takanori, 20 Oct. 1994, Tōhō Gakuen, Kunitachi City, Tokyo.
Daniel J. Perrino, 2 July 1993, University of Illinois Union, Urbana, Ill.
Tom Pierson, 15 Sept. 1994, Amano coffeehouse, Ikenoue, Tokyo.
Segawa Masahisa, 22 Aug. 1994, Shibuya, Tokyo.
Shima Yukio, 7 Nov. 1994, Tokyo.
Sugita Kuniko, 31 Mar. 1995, Pacifico Yokohama, Yokohama.
Sugiura Hitomi and Sugiura Shūichi, 20 July 1994, at their home, Okazaki.
Taira Shigeo, 20 Feb. 1995, near his home in Midori-ku, Yokohama.
Uchida Kōichi, 10 Nov. 1994; 10 Jan. 1995, at his home, Tokyo.
Dr. Uchida Osamu, 23 July 1994, Donna Lee, Nagoya; 29 Nov. 1994, Nagoya; 10 Feb. 1995, New Dug, Shinjuku, Tokyo.

Ueda Sakae, 17 Nov. 1994, at my home, Yokohama.
Yamaoka Miki, 17 Jan. 1995, Tokyo Prince Hotel.
Yasumi Takashi, 6 July 1994, Akasaka-mitsuke, Tokyo.
George Yoshida, 14 July 1995, at his home, El Cerrito, California.
Yoshida Mamoru, 17 May 1994, Chigusa, Yokohama.
Yui Shōichi, 12 Sept. 1994, at his home, Tokyo.

Periodicals and Newspapers

(all Japanese unless otherwise indicated)
Ad Lib (Sept. 1973–)
Billboard (USA)
Chūnichi shinbun
Chūō kōron
The Daily Yomiuri
The Dance (Feb. 1932–Jan. 1934)
Dansu to ongaku (April 1935–April 1938)
Down Beat (USA)
Ebony (USA)
Gekkan gakufu (Jan. 1912–Dec. 1941)
The Japan Times (*Nippon Times*)
Jazu hihyō (June 1967–)
Jazurando (Aug. 1975–Dec. 1976)
Jazz (June 1969–April 1977); later *Jazu magajin* (June 1977–Jan. 1988)
Jazz Journal International (UK)
Jazz Life (Nov. 1977–)
Jazz Magazine (France)
Jazz World (Mar. 1979–)
Kanagawa shinbun
Mainichi shinbun
Melody Maker (UK)
The Metronome (USA)
Min'on
The Modern Dance (Feb. 1933–Sept. 1938); later known as *Varaeti* (*Variety*, Oct. 1938–Aug. 1940) and *Dansu to ongaku* (1949–)
Music Life
New York Times (USA)
Ongaku bunka (Dec. 1943–Nov. 1944)
Ongaku geijutsu (1943–)
Ongaku no tomo (Dec. 1941–; known as *Ongaku chishiki*, Dec. 1943–Jan. 1945)
Ongaku sekai (Jan. 1929–Oct. 1941)
Ongaku shinchō (1924–?)
Rekōdo bunka (Nov. 1941–)
San Francisco Chronicle (USA)
Shakō dansu (Jan. 1933–April 1934)
Swing Journal (April 1947–)
Tokyo Asahi shinbun

Variety (USA)

Yokohama bunka jōhōshi (Dec. 1991–)

Yomiuri shinbun

Japanese Sources

Ad Lib. Tokyo jazu kissa monogatari. Tokyo: Ad Lib, 1989.

Aikura, Hisato. Jazu kara no aisatsu. Tokyo: Ongaku no Tomo Sha, 1968.

——. Modan jazu kanshō. 1963. Tokyo: Kakugawa bunko, 1981.

Aikura, Hisato, et al., eds. Shinjuku Pittoin. Tokyo: Shōbunsha, 1985.

Akiyoshi, Toshiko. Jazu to ikiru. Tokyo: Iwanami Shinsho, 1996.

Aoki, Tamotsu. "Nihon bunka ron" no hen'yō. Tokyo: Chūō Kōronsha, 1990.

Arc Shuppan, comp. Jazu no jiten. Tokyo: Fuyutatsusha, 1983, 1987.

Asahi Shinbunsha, comp. Me de miru Shōwa. 2 vols. Tokyo: Asahi Shinbunsha, 1973.

Awaya, Noriko. Sake, uta, otoko, waga hōrōki. Tokyo: Chōbunsha, 1969.

Etō, Jun. Ochiba no hakiyose: haisen, senryō, ken'etsu to bungaku. Tokyo: Bungei Shunjūsha, 1981.

Fujii, Tomoaki, ed. Minzoku to rizumu. Minzoku ongaku sōsho 8. Tokyo: Tokyo Shoseki, 1990.

Fukushima, Teruhito. "Nippon jazu gendaishi—kono jūnen ryūdō." Jazu hihyō 23 (1976): 12–20.

Hanes, Jeffrey E. "Taishū bunka/ka'i bunka/minshū bunka: senkanki no Nihon no toshi ni okeru kindai seikatsu." In Toshi no kūkan, toshi no shintai, ed. Yoshimi Shun'ya. Tokyo: Keisō Shobō, 1996. 91–136.

Hanzawa, Masatoki. "Chabuya." In Kanagawa-ken hyakka jiten, ed. Kanagawa-ken Hyakka Jiten Kankōkai. Tokyo: Yamato Shobō, 1983.

Hata, Toyokichi. "Jazzu ongaku." Chūō kōron May 1928: 21–33.

——. "Shakō dansu." Chūō kōron Sept. 1928: 149–62.

Hattori, Raymond. "Nihon no jazu shingā no rekishi." In Jazu songu no utaikata. (English title: How to Sing Jazz Songs). Tokyo: Shinkō Gakufu Shuppansha, 1959. 9–25.

Hattori, Ryōichi. Boku no ongaku jinsei. Tokyo: Chūō Bungeisha, 1982.

Hayashi, Junshin, Takagi Shōzō, and Azahara Noriyuki. Tokyo shitamachi jazz dōri. Tokyo: Wombat Press, 1992.

Hayatsu, Toshihiko. Aroha! Mere Hawaii—Nihon Hawaii ongaku, budō shi. Tokyo: Sankurieito, 1987.

Hino, Terumasa. Nyū Yōku ekusupuresu. Tokyo: Kōdansha, 1985.

Hiraoka, Masaaki. Sengo Nihon no jazu shi. Tokyo: Adin Shobō, 1977.

Honda, Toshio. Jazu. Tokyo: Shin Nippon Shinsho, 1976.

——. "Jazu wa jidai o han'ei suru." Ongaku no sekai May 1981: 22–26.

——. Modan jazu. Tokyo: Shin Nippon Shinsho, 1989.

——. Rongu ierō rōdo: jazu sankan joō no nagai michi nori—Akiyoshi Toshiko. Tokyo: Ikkōsha, 1984.

Honmoku Ayumi Kenkyūkai. Honmoku no ayumi. Yokohama: Hirai Insatsujo, 1986.

Horiuchi, Keizō. Jinta konokata. Tokyo: Aoi Shobō, 1935.

——. Ongaku gojūnen shi. Tokyo: Masu Shobō, 1942.

——. Ongaku Meiji hyakunen shi. Tokyo: Ongaku no Tomo Sha, 1968.

Hosokawa, Shūhei. "Seiyō ongaku no Nihonka, taishūka." Music Magazine. Sixty-one-part serial from April 1989 to April 1994.

Ida, Ichirō. "Nihon jazu ongaku sokumen shi." Varaeti. Nine-part serial from Dec. 1938 to Jan. 1940.

Ikeda, Norizane. *Hinomaru awā.* Tokyo: Chūkō Shinsho, 1979.

Inoue, Musashi, and Akiyama Tatsuhide, eds. *Nihon no yōgaku hyakunen shi.* Tokyo: Dai Ippōki Shuppan, 1966.

Ishii, Mitsutarō, et al., eds. *Yokohama kindaishi sōgō nenpyō.* Yokohama: Yūrindō, 1989.

Ishikawa, Gashō. *Shōkyokusai Tenkatsu.* Tokyo: Tōgensha, 1968.

Ishikawa, Hiroyoshi. *Goraku no senzen shi.* Tokyo: Tokyo Shoseki, 1981.

——, et al., comps. *Taishū bunka jiten.* Tokyo: Kobundō, 1994.

Iwamoto, Kenji. *Nihon eiga to modanizumu.* Tokyo: Libro, 1991.

Iwanami, Yōzō. *Nihon no jazumen.* Tokyo: Tairiku Shobō, 1982.

——. "Nihon no jazumen wa Nyū Yōku de katsuyaku dekiruka." In *Konnichi teki jazu dangi.* Tokyo: Arachi, 1982. 155–60.

Jatekku Bādo, comp. *Oretachi no jazu kyō seishun ki.* Tokyo: Jatekku Shuppan, 1991.

"Jazu ongaku torishimari jō no kenkai." In *Gendaishi shiryō 41: masu media tōsei 2*, ed. Uchikawa Yoshimi. Tokyo: Misuzu Shobō, 1975. 347–54.

Kaigai Hōsō Kenkyū Gurūpu, ed. *NHK senji kaigai hōsō.* Tokyo: Hara Shobō, 1982.

Kami, Kyōsuke. "Ano koro no jazu." *Tokyo shinbun*, evening edition. Thirty-seven-part serial from 3 Oct. to 16 Nov. 1957.

Kami, Kyōsuke, and Muraoka Hideo. "Kono hito to." *Mainichi shinbun.* Eight-part serial from 23 Dec. 1970 to 31 Dec. 1970.

Kamiyama, Keizō. *Nihon no ryūkōka.* Tokyo: Hayakawa Shobō, 1965.

Kanagawa-ken Hyakka Jiten Kankōkai, ed. *Kanagawa-ken hyakka jiten.* Tokyo: Yamato Shobō, 1983.

Kanai, Hideto. "Jazu hyōron." Manuscript in author's possession.

——. "Kanai Hideto no jazu wa nani zoya to wa nani zoya." Manuscript in author's possession.

Katō, Hidetoshi, Inoue Tadashi, Takada Masatoshi, and Hosotsuji Keiko. *Shōwa nichijō seikatsu shi. Vol. 1: mobo, moga kara yamiichi made.* Tokyo: Kadokawa Shoten, 1985.

Kawabata, Shigeru. *Rekōdo gyōkai.* 6th ed. Tokyo: Kyōikusha, 1990.

Kawabata, Yasunari. *Kawabata Yasunari zenshū.* Vol. 2. Tokyo: Shinchōsha, 1960.

Kawaguchi, George. "Watashi no rirekisho" *Nihon keizai shinbun.* Thirty-part serial from 1 Aug. 1993 to 31 Aug. 1993.

Kawaguchi, Yōko. "Jazu no juyō: Nihon ni okeru jazu no kachi o motomete." B.A. thesis, Hyōgo Kyōiku Daigaku, 1991.

Kawano, Norio. *Jazu no hon.* Tokyo: Aokisha, 1977.

Kawasaki, Hiroshi. *EM kurabu monogatari.* Tokyo: Shichōsha, 1992.

Kikuchi, Shigeya. "Nihon jazukai sōseiki no koro—ōrudo jazumen no omoide." In *Dikishiirando jazu nyūmon*, ed. Yui Shōichi. Tokyo: Arachi, 1975. 79–95.

——. "Nihon no jazu no zenshi." *Dansu to ongaku.* 15-part serial from Feb. 1955 to Nov. 1956.

Kitahara, Tetsuo. *Jazu ongaku.* ARS Ongaku Daikōza vol. 9. Tokyo: ARS, 1936.

Kitao, Ryōnosuke. *Kindai Ōsaka.* Ōsaka: Sōgensha, 1932.

Kōdansha, comp. *Shōwa Day by Day: Shōwa nimannichi no zen kiroku.* 19 vols. Tokyo: Kōdansha, 1989–91.

——. *Shūkan Yearbook nichiroku 20 seiki 1929.* 14 July 1998.

Kon, Wajirō. "Gendai fūzoku." In *Nihon fūzoku shi kōza.* Tokyo: Yūyama Kakuban, 1929. 1–42.

Konishi Keita et al., eds. *Murakami Haruki no ongaku zukan.* Tokyo: Japan Mix, 1995.

Koyama, Kiyoshi. "Jazu no sengo myūjishan tachi no seishun." *Yokohama bunka jōhōshi* 8 Aug. 1993: 1–7.

Kurata, Yoshihiro. *Nihon rekōdo bunkashi.* Rev. ed. Tokyo: Tokyo Shoseki, 1992.

Kurita, Eiji. *Roppongi jazu monogatari—Tales of Old Fashioned Jazzy Life in Roppongi*. Tokyo: Ensō Bukko, 1995.

Maeda, Ichirō. *Jazu no rekishi to sono sakuhin: Afuro Amerika ongaku no genryū*. Kumamoto Shōka Daigaku Kaigai Jijō Kenkyūjo Kenkyū Sōsho 12. Kumamoto: Sōgensha, 1984.

Mainichi Shinbunsha. *Bessatsu ichi oku nin no Shōwa shi: Nihon no jazu—Jazz of Japan '82*. Tokyo: Mainichi Shinbunsha, 1982.

———. *Shōwa shi zen kiroku*. Tokyo: Mainichi Shinbunsha, 1989.

Matsuzaka, Hiro, ed. "Nihon no jazu sōshiki kara dainiji taisen made." *Jazu hihyō* 12 (1972): 8–69.

Minami, Hiroshi, ed. *Gendai no esupuri* 188: *Nippon modanizumu—ero guro nansensu* (Mar. 1983).

———, ed. *Nihon modanizumu no kenkyū: shisō, seikatsu, bunka*. Tokyo: Burēn Shuppan, 1982.

Minami, Hiroshi, and Shakai Shinri Kenkyūjo, eds. *Shōwa bunka 1945–1989*. Tokyo: Keisō Shobō, 1990.

———, eds. *Shōwa bunka 1925–1945*. Tokyo: Keisō Shobō, 1987.

———, eds. *Taishō bunka 1905–1927*. 1965. Tokyo: Keisō Shobō, 1988.

Miura, Kōdai. *Jazz in Japan, 1963–1974: Miura Kōdai dai shashin shū*. Tokyo: Nishida Shoten, 1991.

Morita, Yūko. *Abe Kaoru 1949–1978*. Tokyo: Bun'yūsha, 1994.

Murakami, Haruki. "Nihonjin ni jazu wa rikai dekirunoka." *Gendai* October 1994: 124–35.

Murashima, Yoriyuki. *Kanraku no ōkyō kafe*. Tokyo: Bunka Seikatsu Kenkyūkai, 1929.

Murobuse, Kōshin. *Gaitō no shakaigaku*. Tokyo: Inakasha, 1929.

Nagai, Yoshikazu. *Shakō dansu to Nihonjin*. Tokyo: Shōbunsha, 1991.

Nakamura, Fuyuo. *Jazu supotto yori ai o komete*. Tokyo: Seinen Shokan, 1982.

Nakayama, Yasuki. *Suingu jānaru seishun roku (Ōsaka hen)*. Tokyo: Komichi Shobō, 1998.

Nakazawa, Mayumi. " 'Dinah' wa mō kikoenai—Nihon no jazu: senchū hen." *Ushio* 281 (Sept. 1982): 180–201.

———. "Nihonjin ga jazu o kuchizusanda hi." *Ushio* 271 (Dec. 1981): 180–211.

NHK Hōsō Bunka Chōsa Kenkyūjo, ed. *GHQ bunsho ni yoru senryōki hōsō shi nenpyō*. Tokyo: NHK, 1987.

Nogawa, Kōbun. *Gendaijin no ongaku "jazu."* Tokyo: Hakubisha, 1949.

Norikoshi, Takao. *Alice: The Story of Kawahata Fumiko*. Tokyo: Kōdansha, 1999.

Ōbayashi, Sōshi. *Minshū goraku no jissai kenkyū: Ōsaka-shi no minshū goraku chōsa*. Ōsaka: Ōhara Shakai Kenkyūjo, 1922.

Oda, Satoru. *Sake to bara no hibi*. Nagoya: Efue Shuppan, 1993.

The Official Crazy Cats Graffiti: Hey! We've Got the Musekinin Soul of the 60's. Tokyo: Treville, 1993.

Okamoto, Ryōichi, ed. *Furusato no omoide shashinshū Meiji Taishō Shōwa Ōsaka*. Tokyo: Kokusho Kankōkai, 1985.

Okazaki Mindscape Museum, ed. *Jazu no machikado: Uchida Osamu jazu korekushon*. Okazaki: Okazaki Mindscape Museum, 1996.

Ōki, Toshinosuke. *Jazu joifuru sutorīto*. Tokyo: JICC, 1991.

Okunari, Tatsu. *Minna ga jazu ni akekureta*. Tokyo: San'ichi Shobō, 1997.

Ōmori, Seitarō. *Nihon no yōgaku*. 2 vols. Tokyo: Shinmon Shuppansha, 1986–87.

Ono, Takeo. *Yoshiwara, Shimabara*. Tokyo: Kyōikusha, 1978.

Ono, Yoshie. *Jazu saishū shō*. Ed. Kawamoto Saburō. Tokyo: Shin'ya Sōsho, 1998.

Ōsaka-shi Shakaibu Chōsaka, ed. *Yoka seikatsu no kenkyū*. Rōdō chōsa hōkoku 19. Kyōto: Kobundō, 1923.

Ōsaka toshi kyōkai. *Zoku Minami-ku shi.* Ōsaka: Ōsaka Toshi Kyōkai, 1982.

Ōya, Sōichi. *Modan sō to modan sō.* Tokyo: Daihōkaku Shobō, 1930.

——. *Ōya Sōichi zenshū.* Vol. 2. Eds. Aochi Shin and Inoue Yasushi. Tokyo: Soyosha, 1981.

Richards, Larry B. "Senzen no Nihon ni okeru jazu ongaku to sono gainen." M.A. thesis, Tokyo Geijutsu Daigakuin, 1992.

Saitō, Ren. *Shōwa no bansukingu tachi: jazu, minato, hōtō.* Tokyo: Music Magazine, 1983.

Sano, Hiromi. *Sano Tasuku: ongaku to sono shōgai.* Tokyo: San'ichi Shobō, 1997.

Satō, Mieko. *Rikutsu janai yo, kibun da yo: jazu doramā Jimii Harada hachijūsan sai no shōgai.* Tokyo: Tōrin Shuppansha, 1996.

Segawa, Masahisa. *Jazu de odotte: hakurai geinō shi.* Tokyo: Simul Press, 1983.

——. "Nihon jazu ishin sengen." *Nihon jazu ishin '94.* King/Paddlewheel pamphlet included in *Swing Journal* April 1994.

——. "Nippon no jazu shi." *Swing Journal.* Twenty-three-part serial from July 1975 to June 1977.

Seso Fūzoku Kansatsukai, comp. *Gendai fūzokushi nenpyō: Shōwa 20 nen (1945)–Shōwa 60 nen (1985).* Tokyo: Kawade Shobō, 1986.

Shigeta, Tadayasu. *Fūzoku keisatsu no riron to jissai.* Tokyo: Nankōsha, 1934.

Shimizu, Toshihiko, Hiraoka Masaaki, and Okunari Tōru. *Nihon no jazu den.* Tokyo: Eipuriru Shuppan, 1977.

Shin ongaku jiten: jinmei. Tokyo: Ongaku no Tomo Sha, 1983.

Shinshū Ōsaka Shishi Hensan Iinkai. *Shinshū Ōsaka shishi.* Vol. 6. Ōsaka, 1994.

Shioiri, Kamesuke. *Jazu ongaku.* Tokyo: Keibunkan, 1929.

Shisō no Kagaku Kenkyūkai, eds. *Nippon senryō kenkyū jiten.* Tokyo: Tokuma Shoten, 1978.

Shūkan Asahi, comp. *1945–1971: Amerika to no nijūroku nen.* Tokyo: Shinbyōsha, 1972.

Sōgensha, ed. *Ōsaka monoshiri jiten.* Ōsaka: Sōgensha, 1994.

Somayama, Kōichi. "Nippon no jazu." *Ongaku jiten.* Tokyo: Heibonsha, 1960, 1964. 1262–64.

Sonobe, Saburō. *Enka kara jazu e no Nihon shi.* Tokyo: Wakōsha, 1954.

——. *Ongaku gojūnen.* Tokyo: Jiji Tsūshinsha, 1950.

Sugawara, Shōji. *Jazu kissa "Beishii" no sentaku.* Tokyo: Kōdansha, 1993.

Taishō Engeki Kenkyūkai, eds. *Taishō no engeki to toshi.* Tokyo: Musashino Shobō, 1991.

Takahashi, Ichirō, and Sasaki Mamoru. *Jazu shifū—sengo sōsōki densetsu.* Tokyo: San'ichi Shobō, 1997.

Takeuchi, Yoshimi. *Kindai no chōkoku.* Tokyo: Chikuma Sōsho 285, 1983.

Taniguchi, Matashi, with Segawa Masahisa. "Toronbon to ayunda watakushi no jazu jinsei." *Jazurando.* Five-part serial from Aug. 1975 to Dec. 1975.

Tatsumi, Mitsuyoshi. "Jazu wa fune ni notte yattekita." *Yokohama bunka jōhōshi* 31 (Sept. 1994): 1–6.

Terajima, Yasukuni, Ōnishi Yonehiro, and Noguchi Iori. *Kichijōji jazz monogatari.* Tokyo: Nippon Terebi, 1993.

Terayama, Shūji, and Yugawa Reiko, eds. *Jazu o tanoshimu hon.* Tokyo: Kubo Shoten, 1961.

Tokunaga, Masatarō. "Nihon jazu ongaku undō shōshi." *Ongaku shinchō* April 1930: 7–9.

"Tokushū—'hajimaru' Yokohama no ongaku 'jazz.'" *Yokohama bunka jōhōshi* Dec. 1991: 2–9.

"Tokushū—Nihonjin to jazu." *What's New* 15 Aug. 1994: 1–19.

Tsugawa, Shuichi. *Jubirii shingāzu monogatari to kokujin reika.* Tokyo: Ongaku no Tomo Sha, 1960.

Tsuji, Katsumi, ed. *Sangyō kōkoku zuan dai shūsei.* Shōwa Modan Aato 4: *Kōkoku,* 1936. Tokyo: MPC, 1989.

Tsurumi, Shunsuke. *Sengo Nippon no taishū bunka shi: 1945–1980.* Tokyo: Iwanami Shoten, 1984.

Uchida, Kōichi. *Nihon no jazu shi, senzen, sengo.* Tokyo: Swing Journal, 1976.
Uchida, Osamu. "Dokutā Uchida no jazu ni kanpai!" *Chūnichi shinbun,* evening ed. Twenty-four-part serial from 23 June to 13 Aug. 1986.
——. "Dokutā Uchida no jazu wa tomodachi." *Chūnichi shinbun,* evening ed. Thirty-part serial from 8 May to 19 July 1989.
——. *Jazu ga wakakatta koro.* Tokyo: Shōbunsha, 1984.
Uchikawa, Yoshimi, ed. *Shōwa nyūzu jiten.* Vols. 1 and 2. Tokyo: Mainichi Communications, 1990.
——. *Taishō nyūzu jiten.* Vol. 7. Tokyo: Mainichi Communications, 1989.
Ueda, Sakae. *Soshite, kaze ga hashirinukete itta (He Played Like a Breeze through Our Lives): tensai jazu pianisuto Moriyasu Shōtarō no shōgai.* Tokyo: Kōdansha, 1997.
Uekusa, Jin'ichi. *Uekusa Jin'ichi no geijutsushi.* Uekusa Jin'ichi Kurabu Series. Tokyo: Shōbunsha, 1994.
Unuma, Naoki. *Modango jiten* (Tokyo: Seibundō, 1930).
Waka, Moritarō. *Nihon seikatsu bunkashi, Vol. 9: shiminteki seikatsu no tenkai.* Tokyo: Kawade Shobō, Shinsha, 1986.
Watanabe, Sadao. *Boku jishin no tame no jazu,* ed. Iwanami Yōzō. Tokyo: Arachi, 1969.
Yamano, Haruo. "Kantō daishinsai go no shakai jōsei." In *Taishō demokurashii,* ed. Kinbara Samon. Kindai Nihon no Kiseki 4. Tokyo: Yoshikawa Hiroshi Bunkan, 1994. 201–24.
Yamato, Akira. *Jazu koko ga kikidokoro.* Tokyo: Ongaku no Tomo Sha, 1984.
Yoshida, Mamoru. "Daremo shiranai Nippon jazu shi." *Waseda Jazz* 2 (Jan. 1974): 1–22; 3 (June 1975): 1–19.
——. *Yokohama jazu monogatari—"Chigusa" no 50 nen.* Yokohama: Kanagawa Shinbunsha, 1985.
Yoshiga Noboru et al., comps. *Nihon josei jinmei jiten.* Tokyo: Nihon Tosho Sentā, 1993.
Yoshitake, Teruko. *Burūsu no joō: Awaya Noriko.* Tokyo: Bungei Shunjū, 1989.
Yui, Shōichi. "Burū Nōto ga Nihon ni yattekita koro." In *Burū Nōto sainyūmon* (English title: *More from Blue Note),* ed. Namekata Hitoshi. Tokyo: Komichi Shobō, 1994. 63–74.
——. *A History of Jazz* (Japanese title: *Jazu rekishi monogatari*). Tokyo: Swing Journal, 1972.
——. *Ikiteiru jazu shi.* Tokyo: Shinkō Music, 1988.
——. "Nippon popyura ongaku shi." *Min'on.* Thirty-five-part serial from Jan. 1975 until Dec. 1977.
——. "Zadankai: 'Nihon no jazu' o kataru." *'69 All Japan Jazz Festival: 19th Swing Journal Poll Winners.* Tokyo: Swing Journal, 1969.

Western Language Sources

Adorno, Theodor W. *Prisms.* 1967. Trans. Samuel and Shierry Weber. Cambridge, Mass.: MIT Press, 1981.
Anderson, Benedict. *Imagined Communities: Reflections on the Origin and Spread of Nationalism.* 2nd ed. London: Verso, 1991.
Anderson, J. L. "Spoken Silents in the Japanese Cinema; or, Talking to Pictures: Essaying the *Katsuben,* Contextualizing the Texts." In *Reframing Japanese Cinema: Authorship, Genre, History,* ed. Arthur Noletti Jr. and David Desser. Bloomington: Indiana University Press, 1992.
Anderson, Joseph L., and Donald Richie. *The Japanese Film: Art and Industry.* Rev. ed. Princeton, N.J.: Princeton University Press, 1982.
Atkins, E. Taylor. "Can Japanese Sing the Blues? 'Japanese Jazz' and the Problem of Authen-

ticity." In *Japan Pop: Inside the World of Japanese Popular Culture*, ed. Timothy J. Craig. Armonk, N.Y.: M. E. Sharpe, 2000. 27–59.

——. "Jammin' on the Jazz Frontier: The Japanese Jazz Community in Interwar Shanghai." *Japanese Studies* 19.1 (May 1999): 5–16.

——. "Multicultural Jazz: Expanding the Borders of Jazz History." Paper presented at the 44th Annual Meeting of the Society for Ethnomusicology, Austin, Tex., 19 Nov. 1999, and at the American Studies Association Annual Meeting, Detroit, Mich., 13 Oct. 2000.

——. "Nipponism in Japanese Painting, 1937–45." *Wittenberg Review* 1.1 (1990): 61–76.

——. "This Is Our Music: Authenticating Japanese Jazz, 1920–1980." Ph.D. dissertation, University of Illinois at Urbana-Champaign, 1997.

——. "The War on Jazz, or Jazz Goes to War: Toward a New Cultural Order in Wartime Japan." *positions: east asia cultures critique* 6.2 (fall 1998): 345–92.

Baraka, Amiri (LeRoi Jones). *Black Music*. New York: Morrow, 1967.

——. *Blues People: Negro Music in White America*. New York: Morrow, 1963; with new introduction, Quill, 1999.

——, and Amina Baraka. *The Music: Reflections on Jazz and Blues*. New York: William Morrow, 1987.

Barr, Pat. *The Coming of the Barbarians*. London: Macmillan, 1967.

Barshay, Andrew. *State and Intellectual in Imperial Japan: The Public Man in Crisis*. Berkeley: University of California Press, 1989.

Belgrad, Daniel. *The Culture of Spontaneity: Improvisation and the Arts in Postwar America*. Chicago: University of Chicago Press, 1998.

Benjamin, Walter. "The Work of Art in the Age of Mechanical Reproduction." In *Illuminations*, ed. Hannah Arendt. New York: Schoken, 1969. 217–52.

Bergeré, Marie-Claire. " 'The Other China': Shanghai from 1919 to 1949." In *Shanghai: Revolution and Development in an Asian Metropolis*, ed. Christopher Howe. Cambridge: Cambridge University Press, 1981. 1–34.

Berliner, Paul. *Thinking in Jazz: The Infinite Art of Improvisation*. Chicago: University of Chicago Press, 1994.

Bernstein, Gail, ed. *Recreating Japanese Women: 1600–1945*. Berkeley: University of California Press, 1991.

Berry, Faith. *Langston Hughes: Before and Beyond Harlem*. Westport: Lawrence Hill, 1983.

Beynon, Erdmann D. "The Voodoo Cult among Negro Migrants in Detroit." *American Journal of Sociology* 43 (1938): 894–907.

Blum, Stephen, Philip Bohlman, and Daniel M. Neuman, eds. *Ethnomusicology and Modern Music History*. Urbana, Ill.: University of Illinois Press, 1991.

Borgo, David. "Can Blacks Play Klezmer? Authenticity in American Ethnic Musical Expression." *Sonneck Society Bulletin* 24.2 (Summer 1998): 33–36.

Boulmetis, Susan. "Jazz: Where East Jams with West." *Japan Society Newsletter* Mar. 1993: 6–7.

Bourdieu, Pierre. *Distinction: A Social Critique of the Judgement of Taste*. Trans. Richard Nice. Cambridge: Harvard University Press, 1984.

Breuilly, John. *Nationalism and the State*. 2d ed. Chicago: University of Chicago Press, 1994.

Brown, Lee B. "The Theory of Jazz Music—'It Don't Mean a Thing . . .' " *Journal of Aesthetics and Art Criticism* 49 (1991): 115–27.

Brown, Sidney DeVere. "California Origins of the Jazz Boom in Occupied Japan, 1945–1952." Paper presented at the Conference on California and the Pacific Rim, University of the Pacific, Stockton, Calif., 30 April 1994.

——. "Jazz in Japan: Its Sources and Development, 1925–1952." Proceedings, 1980 Annual

Meeting, Southwest Conference on Asian Studies, New Orleans, 127–39. German translation by Christian Schwandt published in *Japan: Ein Lesebuch,* ed. Peter Portner. Konkursbuch: University of Hamburg Press, 1986. 117–31.

——. "New Orleans in Tokyo: Nanri Fumio (1910–1975)—Jazz Trumpet Virtuoso." Southwest Conference on Asian Studies, New Orleans, 3 Nov. 1989.

——. "Toshiko Akiyoshi: The Meeting of East and West in Jazz." Southwest Conference on Asian Studies, Austin, Tex. 13 Oct. 1990.

Bruyninckx, Walter. *Seventy Years of Recorded Jazz, 1917–1987.* Mechelen, Belgium. Published by the author, 1978–90.

Budds, Michael J. *Jazz in the Sixties: The Expansion of Musical Resources and Techniques.* Iowa City: University of Iowa Press, 1990.

Buerkle, Jack V., and Danny Barker. *Bourbon Street Black: The New Orleans Black Jazzman.* New York: Oxford University Press, 1973.

Burkman, Thomas W., ed. *The Occupation of Japan: Arts and Culture.* Proceedings of the Sixth Symposium of The MacArthur Memorial Foundation. Norfolk, Va.: General Douglas MacArthur Foundation, Old Dominion University, 1988.

Cameron, William Bruce. "Sociological Notes on the Jam Session." *Social Forces* (Dec. 1954): 177–82.

Cantor, Norman F. *Twentieth-Century Culture: Modernism to Deconstruction.* New York: Peterling, 1988.

Chevigny, Paul. *Gigs: Jazz and the Cabaret Laws in New York City.* New York: Routledge, 1991.

Clayton, Peter, and Peter Gammond. *The Guiness Jazz Companion.* Middlesex: Guiness, 1989.

Clemons, Eric Walton. "The Role of African Americans in U.S. Navy Expeditions to Japan in the 1850s: A Lesson in Contradictions." *Conexoes* 3.2 (1991): 5–6. East Lansing, Mich.: African Diaspora Research Project, Michigan State University, 1991.

Clifford, James. *The Predicament of Culture: Twentieth-Century Ethnography, Literature and Art.* Cambridge: Harvard University Press, 1988.

Close, Albert B. "Japanese Jazz Discography (1948–1953)." *Record Research* 76 (May 1966): 8+.

Collier, James Lincoln. *The Reception of Jazz in America: A New View.* I.S.A.M. Monographs 27. Brooklyn, N.Y.: Institute for Studies in American Music, 1988.

Cook, Haruko Taya, and Theodore F. Cook. *Japan at War: An Oral History.* New York: New Press, 1992.

Cook, Richard, and Brian Morton. *The Penguin Guide to Jazz on CD, LP and Cassette.* London: Penguin, 1994.

Crane, Burton. "The Reminiscences of Burton Crane." Occupation of Japan Project. New York: Oral History Research Office, Columbia University, 1961.

Cummings, Alan. "Undiscovered Country: Shooting Star and Supernova." *Avant* Winter 1997: 40–41.

Dahl, Linda. *Stormy Weather: The Music and Lives of a Century of Jazzwomen.* New York: Pantheon, 1984.

Dalby, Liza. *Geisha.* New York: Vintage, 1983.

Dale, Peter N. *The Myth of Japanese Uniqueness.* London: Croom Helm, 1986.

Dan, Ikuma. "The Influence of Japanese Traditional Music on the Development of Western Music in Japan." Trans. Dorothy G. Britton. *Transactions of the Asiastic Society of Japan* (3d series) 8 (Dec. 1961): 201–17.

Daniels, Douglas Henry. "Oral History, Masks, and Protocol in the Jazz Community." *Oral History Review* 15 (spring 1987): 143–64.

Davis, Darrell William. *Picturing Japaneseness: Monumental Style, National Identity, Japanese*

References 337

Film. Film and Culture Series, ed. John Belton. New York: Columbia University Press, 1996.

Davis, Miles, and Quincy Troupe. *Miles: The Autobiography.* New York: Simon and Schuster, 1989.

Derschmidt, Eckhart. "The Disappearance of the *Jazu-Kissa:* Some Considerations about Japanese 'Jazz-Cafés' and Jazz-Listeners." In *The Culture of Japan as Seen through Its Leisure,* eds. Sepp Linhart and Sabine Frühstück. Albany, N.Y.: SUNY Press, 1998. 303–15.

——. "Thrilling Live Performances." *Resonance* 4.2 (Feb. 1996): 18–23.

Desser, David. *Eros Plus Massacre: An Introduction to the Japanese New Wave Cinema.* Bloomington: Indiana University Press, 1988.

DeVeaux, Scott. *The Birth of Bebop.* Berkeley: University of California Press, 1997.

——. "Constructing the Jazz Tradition: Jazz Historiography," *Black American Literature Forum* 25 (fall 1991): 525–60.

Doak, Kevin M. *Dreams of Difference: The Japan Romantic School and the Crisis of Modernity.* Berkeley: University of California Press, 1994.

——. "Ethnic Nationalism and Romanticism in Early Twentieth-Century Japan." *Journal of Japanese Studies* 22.1 (1996): 77–103.

Dower, John W. *Embracing Defeat: Japan in the Wake of World War II.* New York: Norton/New Press, 1999.

——. *Japan in War and Peace: Selected Essays.* New York: New Press, 1995.

——. *War without Mercy: Race and Power in the Pacific War.* New York: Pantheon, 1986.

During, Simon, ed. *The Cultural Studies Reader.* London: Routledge, 1993.

Duus, Masayo. *Tokyo Rose: Orphan of the Pacific.* Trans. Peter Duus. Tokyo: Kōdansha, 1979.

Eppstein, Ury. *The Beginnings of Western Music in Meiji Era Japan.* Studies in the History and Interpretation of Music 44. Lewiston: Edwin Mellen Press, 1994.

Erlmann, Veit. "The Politics and Aesthetics of Transnational Musics." *The World of Music* 35.2 (1993): 3–15.

Feather, Leonard. *The Encyclopedia of Jazz.* New York: Horizon, 1960.

Fletcher, Miles. *The Search for a New Order: Intellectuals and Fascism in Prewar Japan.* Chapel Hill: University of North Carolina Press, 1982.

Foner, Philip S., ed. *Paul Robeson Speaks: Writings, Speeches, Interviews 1918–1974.* Secaucus, N.J.: Citadel Press, 1978.

Fraser, James, Steven Heller, and Seymour Chwast, *Japanese Modern: Graphic Design between the Wars.* San Francisco: Chronicle, 1996.

Fujitani, T. *Splendid Monarchy: Power and Pageantry in Modern Japan.* Berkeley: University of California Press, 1996.

Gabbard, Krin. *Jammin' at the Margins: Jazz and the American Cinema.* Chicago: University of Chicago Press, 1996.

——, ed. *Jazz among the Discourses.* Durham, N.C.: Duke University Press, 1995.

——, ed. *Representing Jazz.* Durham, N.C.: Duke University Press, 1995.

Garofalo, Reebee. "Whose World, What Beat: The Transnational Music Industry, Identity, and Cultural Imperialism." *The World of Music* 35.2 (1993): 16–32.

Gendron, Bernard. "Jamming at Le Boeuf: Jazz and the Paris Avant-Garde." *Discourse* 12.1 (1989–90): 3–27.

General Headquarters, Supreme Commander for the Allied Powers. *History of the Nonmilitary Activities of the Occupation of Japan, 1945 through 1951.* Vol. 33: Radio Broadcasting.

Gennari, John. "Jazz Criticism: Its Development and Ideologies." *Black American Literature Forum* 25 (fall 1991): 449–521.

Gerard, Charley. *Jazz in Black and White: Race, Culture, and Identity in the Jazz Community.* Westport, Conn.: Praeger, 1998.

Germani, Gino. *Marginality.* New Brunswick, N.J.: Transaction Books, 1980.

Gillespie, Luke O. "Literacy, Orality, and the Parry-Lord 'Formula': Improvisation and the Afro-American Jazz Tradition." *International Review of the Aesthetics and Sociology of Music* 22 (Dec. 1991): 147–64.

Gleason, Ralph J. "Can the White Man Sing the Blues?" *Jazz and Pop* Aug. 1968: 28–29.

Gluck, Carol, and Stephen R. Graubard, eds. *Showa: The Japan of Hirohito.* New York: W. W. Norton, 1992.

Goddard, Chris. *Jazz away from Home.* New York: Paddington, 1979.

Goldman, A. *Freakshow: The Rocksoulbluesjazzsickjewblackhumorsexpoppsych Gig and Other Scenes from the Counter-Culture.* New York: Atheneum, 1971.

Goodman, David. *Japanese Drama and Culture in the 1960s: The Return of the Gods.* Armonk, N.Y.: M. E. Sharpe, 1988.

Goodman, David, and Masanori Miyazawa. *Jews in the Japanese Mind: The History and Uses of a Cultural Stereotype.* New York: Free Press, 1995.

Gordon, Andrew. *Postwar Japan as History.* Berkeley: University of California Press, 1993.

Gray, Herman. "Jazz as Cultural Practice and the Politics of Diversity." Paper delivered at Conference on "Living and Working with Cultural Plurality: Communities and Their Institutions." Program for the Study of Cultural Values and Ethics, University of Illinois at Urbana-Champaign, 30 Oct. 1992.

Grele, Ronald J., ed. *Envelopes of Sound: The Art of Oral History.* 2d ed. New York: Praeger, 1991.

Groesbeck, Rolf. "Cultural Constructions of Improvisation in *Tāyampaka*, a Genre of Temple Instrumental Music in Kerala, India." *Ethnomusicology* 43.1 (1999): 1–30.

Gussow, Adam. *Mister Satan's Apprentice: A Blues Memoir.* New York: Pantheon, 1998.

Hall, Robert King, ed., and John Owen Gauntlett, trans. *Kokutai No Hongi: Cardinal Principles of the National Entity of Japan.* Newton, Mass.: Crofton, 1974.

Hall, Stuart. "Ethnicity: Identity and Difference." *Radical America.* 23.4 (1989): 9–20.

Hanes, Jeffrey E. "Advertising Culture in Interwar Japan." *Japan Foundation Newsletter* 23.4 (Jan. 1996): 8–12.

Harich-Schneider, Eta. *A History of Japanese Music.* London: Oxford University Press, 1973.

Harootunian, Harry D. "Late Tokugawa Thought and Culture." In *The Cambridge History of Japan.* Vol. 5: *The Nineteenth Century,* ed. Marius B. Jansen. Cambridge: Cambridge University Press, 1989. 168–258.

Harvey, Sylvia. *May '68 and Film Culture.* London: BFI Publishing, 1980.

Hashikawa, Bunsō, "The 'Civil Society' Ideal and Wartime Resistance." Trans. Robert Wargo. In *Authority and the Individual in Japan: Citizen Protest in Historical Perspective,* ed. J. Victor Koschmann. Tokyo: University of Tokyo Press, 1978.

Hauser, Ernest O. *Shanghai: City for Sale.* New York: Harcourt, Brace, 1940.

Havens, Thomas R. H. *Artist and Patron in Postwar Japan.* Princeton: Princeton University Press, 1982.

———. *Valley of Darkness: The Japanese People and World War Two.* New York: W. W. Norton, 1978.

Hawes, Hampton, and Don Asher. *Raise Up Off Me.* 1972. New York: Da Capo, 1979.

Hawks, Francis L., comp. *Narrative of an American Squadron to the China Seas and Japan, Performed in the Years 1852, 1853, and 1854, under the Command of Commodore M. C. Perry, United States Navy, by Order of the Government of the United States.* Vol. 1. Washington, D.C.: A. O. P. Nicholson, 1856.

Hebdige, Dick. *Subculture: The Meaning of Style.* 1979. London: Routledge, 1987.

Heinrichs, Waldo. *Threshold of War.* New York: Oxford University Press, 1988.

Hentoff, Nat. *The Jazz Life.* New York: Dial, 1961.

Herd, Judith Ann. "The Neonationalist Movement: Origins of Japanese Contemporary Music." *Perspectives of New Music* 27.2 (1989): 118–63.

Herzog zu Mecklenburg, Carl Gregor. *International Jazz Bibliography: Jazz Books From 1919 to 1968.* Graz, Austria: Universal Edition, 1969, 1970 Supplement. Graz, Austria: Universal Edition, 1971, 1971–73 Supplement. Graz, Austria: Universal Edition, 1975.

Hicks, George L. *Japan's War Memories: Amnesia or Concealment?* Aldershot: Ashgate, 1997.

Hirano, Kyoko. *Mr. Smith Goes to Tokyo: Japanese Cinema under the Occupation.* Smithsonian Studies in the History of Film and Television. Series ed. Charles Musser. Washington: Smithsonian Institution Press, 1992.

Hobsbawm, Eric J. *The Age of Extremes: A History of the World, 1914–1991.* New York: Pantheon, 1994.

——. *The Jazz Scene.* Rev. ed. New York: Pantheon, 1993.

——. *Nations and Nationalism since 1780: Programme, Myth, Reality.* Cambridge: Cambridge University Press, 1990.

Hodeir, André. *Jazz—Its Evolution and Essence.* Trans. David Noakes. New York: Grove Press, 1956.

hooks, bell. *Yearning: Race, Gender, and Cultural Politics.* Boston: South End Press, 1990.

Horowitz, Irving Louis. "Authenticity and Originality in Jazz: A Paradigm in the Sociology of Music." *Journal of Jazz Studies* October 1973: 57–64.

Hosokawa, Shūhei. "East of Honolulu: Hawaiian Music in Japan from the 1920s to the 1940s." *Perfect Beat* July 1994: 51–67.

——. "In Search of the Sound of Empire: Tanabe Hisao and the Foundation of Japanese Ethnomusicology." *Japanese Studies* 18.1 (May 1998): 5–19.

Hsü, Shushi. *Japan and Shanghai.* Political and Economic Studies 4. Shanghai: Kelly and Walsh, 1938.

Hudson, John C. "Theory and Methodology in Comparative Frontier Studies." In *The Frontier: Comparative Studies,* ed. David Harry Miller and Jerome O. Steffen. Norman: University of Oklahoma Press, 1977.

Hughes, Phillip S. "Jazz Appreciation and the Sociology of Jazz." *Journal of Jazz Studies* June 1974: 79–96.

Hume, Nancy G. *Japanese Aesthetics and Culture: A Reader.* Albany: SUNY Press, 1995.

Hunt, Lynn, ed. *The New Cultural History.* Berkeley: University of California Press, 1989.

Ienaga, Saburō. *The Pacific War, 1931–1945.* New York: Pantheon, 1978.

Inomata, Takeshi. "The Course of Jazz (Popular) Music History in Japan." *Percussive Notes* 22.4 (1984): 49–50.

Iokibe, Makoto, ed. *The Occupation of Japan: U.S. Planning Documents, 1942–1945.* Bethesda, Md.: Congressional Information Service, 1987.

Iritani, Toshio. *Group Psychology of the Japanese in Wartime.* London: Kegan Paul International, 1991.

Isoi, Gijin. *We Had Those Occupation Blues.* Trans. Steven Karpa. Saratoga, Calif.: R & E Publishers, 1988.

Ivy, Marilyn. *Discourses of the Vanishing: Modernity, Phantasm, Japan.* Chicago: University of Chicago Press, 1995.

Jansen, Marius B., ed. *Changing Japanese Attitudes toward Modernization.* 1965. Rutland, Vt.: Charles E. Tuttle, 1982.

"Japanese Radio Themes." State Dept. papers, 22 Feb. 1943.

"Jazz in Japan: Have You Heard the Latest?" *Japan Update* 12 (summer 1989): 17–21.

Johnson, Sheila K. *American Attitudes toward Japan, 1941–1975.* American Enterprise Institute for Public Policy Research, 1975.

Karlin, Jason G. "Gendering Modernity: Taste, Style, and Aestheticism in Early Twentieth Century Japan." Paper presented at 46th Annual Meeting of Midwest Conference on Asian Affairs, Northern Illinois University, 28 Sept. 1997.

Kartomi, Margaret J., and Stephen Blum, eds. *Music-Cultures in Contact: Convergences and Collisions.* Basel, Switzerland: Gordon and Breach, 1994.

Kasza, Gregory J. "Democracy and the Founding of Japanese Public Radio." *Journal of Asian Studies* 45 (Aug. 1986): 745–67.

——. *The State and the Mass Media in Japan, 1918–1945.* Berkeley: University of California Press, 1988.

Kater, Michael H. *Different Drummers: Jazz in the Culture of Nazi Germany.* New York: Oxford University Press, 1992.

Katō, Hidetoshi, ed. *Japanese Popular Culture: Studies in Mass Communication and Cultural Change.* Westport, Conn.: Greenwood, 1973.

Kawabata, Shigeru. "The Japanese Record Industry." *Popular Music* 10.3 (1991): 327–45.

Keene, Donald. "Japanese Writers and the Greater East Asia War." Reprinted in *Appreciations of Japanese Culture.* Tokyo: Kōdansha, 1971. 300–321.

Kenney, William Howland. *Chicago Jazz: A Cultural History, 1904–1930.* New York: Oxford University Press, 1993.

Kennington, Donald, and Danny L. Read. *The Literature of Jazz: A Critical Guide.* Rev. ed. Chicago: American Library Association, 1980.

Kivy, Peter. *Authenticities: Philosophical Reflections on Musical Performance.* Ithaca, N.Y.: Cornell University Press, 1995.

Klauber, Bruce H. *World of Gene Krupa: That Legendary Drummin' Man.* Ventura, Calif.: Pathfinder, 1990.

Kondo, Dorinne K. *Crafting Selves: Power, Gender, and Discourses of Identity in a Japanese Workplace.* Chicago: University of Chicago Press, 1990.

Kraus, Richard C. *Pianos and Politics in China: Middle-Class Ambitions and the Struggle over Western Music.* New York: Oxford University Press, 1989.

Kurabayashi, Yoshimasa, and Yoshihiro Matsuda. *Economic and Social Aspects of the Performing Arts in Japan: Symphony Orchestras and Opera.* Tokyo: Kinokuniya, 1988.

Kurosawa, Akira. *Something Like an Autobiography.* Trans. Audie Bock. New York: Alfred A. Knopf, 1982.

Lees, Gene. *Cats of Any Color: Jazz Black and White.* New York: Oxford University Press, 1994.

Lehmann-Haupt, Hellmut. *Art under a Dictatorship.* New York: Oxford University Press, 1954.

Lent, John A. *Asian Popular Culture.* Boulder, Colo.: Westview Press, 1995.

Leonard, Neil. *Jazz: Myth and Religion.* New York: Oxford University Press, 1987.

——. *Jazz and the White Americans: The Acceptance of a New Art Form.* Chicago: University of Chicago Press, 1962.

Lethbridge, H. J. *All about Shanghai: A Standard Guidebook.* 1934–35. Hong Kong: Oxford University Press, 1983.

Levi, Erik. *Music in the Third Reich.* New York: St. Martin's, 1994.

Levine, Lawrence. "AHR Forum—The Folklore of Industrial Society: Popular Culture and Its Audiences." *American Historical Review* 97 (Dec. 1992): 1369–1430.

——. *Highbrow/Lowbrow: The Emergence of Cultural Hierarchy in America.* Cambridge: Harvard University Press, 1988.

——. "Jazz and American Culture." In *The Unpredictable Past: Explorations in American Cultural History*. New York: Oxford University Press, 1993. 172–88.

Lewis, Alan. "The Social Interpretation of Modern Jazz." *Canadian University Music Review* 2 (1981): 138–65.

Lincoln, C. Eric. *The Black Muslims in America*. Boston: Beacon, 1961.

Littlewood, Ian. *The Idea of Japan: Western Images, Western Myths*. Chicago: Ivan R. Dee, 1996.

Litweiler, John. *The Freedom Principle: Jazz after 1958*. New York: William Morrow, 1984.

Livingston, Tamara E. "Music Revivals: Towards a General Theory." *Ethnomusicology* 43.1 (1999): 66–85.

Lomax, Alan. *Mister Jelly Roll: The Fortunes of Jelly Roll Morton, New Orleans Creole and "Inventor of Jazz."* New York: Grove, 1950.

Lott, Eric. *Love and Theft: Blackface Minstrelsy and the American Working Class*. New York: Oxford University Press, 1993.

Lu, David J. *Japan: A Documentary History*. Armonk, N.Y.: M. E. Sharpe, 1997.

Mabuchi, Usaburō, and Yamaguti [sic] Osamu, eds. *Music Cultures in Interaction: Cases between Asia and Europe*. Tokyo: Academia Music Ltd., 1994.

Mainichi Daily Newspapers, ed. *Fifty Years of Light and Dark: The Hirohito Era*. Tokyo: Mainichi Newspapers, 1975.

Malm, William P. *Japanese Music and Musical Instruments*. Rutland, Vt. Charles E. Tuttle, 1959.

——. "Layers of Modern Music and Japan." *Asian Music* 4.2 (1973): 3–6.

——. "The Modern Music of Meiji Japan." In *Tradition and Modernization in Japanese Culture*, ed. Donald H. Shively. Princeton, N.J.: Princeton University Press, 1971.

——. "Music Cultures of Momoyama Japan." In *Warlords, Artists, and Commoners: Japan in the Sixteenth Century*, eds. George Elison and Bardwell L. Smith. Honolulu: University Press of Hawaii, 1981. 163–85.

——. *Music Cultures of the Pacific, the Near East, and Asia*. 2d ed. Englewood Cliffs, N.J.: Prentice-Hall, 1977.

——. "Some of Japan's Musics and Musical Principles." In *Musics of Many Cultures: An Introduction*, ed. Elizabeth May. Berkeley: University of California Press, 1980. 46–62.

Martin, Harris I. "Popular Music and Social Change in Prewar Japan." *Japan Interpreter* 7.3–4 (1972): 332–52.

Martinez, D. P., ed. *The Worlds of Japanese Popular Culture: Gender, Shifting Boundaries, and Global Cultures*. Cambridge: Cambridge University Press, 1998.

Mayeda, Richard Ichirō. "The Identity of Japanese Jazz." *The East* 8.5 (May 1972): 45–49.

McClure, Steve. "Japanese Pop Music: A Beginner's Guide." *Mangajin* June 1994: 14+.

——. *Nippon Pop*. Tokyo: Tuttle, 1998.

McIntosh, Tom. "Reflections on Jazz and the Politics of Race." *boundary 2* 22.2 (summer 1995): 25–35.

McNeil, Murray, ed. *Marginality: Voices from the Periphery*. Published in conjunction with the Comparative Literature Conference, California State University, Long Beach, 15 Mar. 1986.

Meltzer, David, ed. *Reading Jazz*. San Francisco: Mercury House, 1993.

Merod, Jim. "Jazz as a Cultural Archive." *boundary 2* 22.2 (summer 1995): 1–18.

Merriam, Alan P. *The Anthropology of Music*. Evanston, Ill.: Northwestern University Press, 1964.

——, and Raymond W. Mack. "The Jazz Community." *Social Forces* (Mar. 1960): 211–22.

Miller, Mark. *Jazz in Canada: Fourteen Lives*. Toronto: University of Toronto Press, 1982.

——. *Such Melodious Racket: The Lost History of Jazz in Canada, 1914–1949.* Toronto: Mercury Press, 1998.

Miller, Tyrus. *Late Modernism: Politics, Fiction, and the Arts between the World Wars.* Berkeley: University of California Press, 1999.

Minami, Hiroshi. "The Introspection Boom: Wither the National Character." *Japan Interpreter* 8 (1973): 160–75.

Minamoto, Ryōen. "The Symposium on 'Overcoming Modernity.'" Trans. James Heisig. In *Rude Awakenings: Zen, the Kyoto School, and the Question of Nationalism,* eds. James W. Heisig, and John C. Maraldo. Honolulu: University of Hawaii Press, 1995: 197–229.

Mingus, Charles. *Beneath the Underdog: His World as Composed by Mingus.* Ed. Nel King. 1971. New York: Vintage, 1991.

Minichiello, Sharon A., ed. *Japan's Competing Modernities: Issues of Culture and Democracy, 1900–1930.* Honolulu: University of Hawaii Press, 1998.

Minor, William. *Unzipped Souls: A Jazz Journey through the Soviet Union.* Philadelphia: Temple University Press, 1995.

Mitchell, Richard H. *Thought Control in Prewar Japan.* Ithaca, N.Y.: Cornell University Press, 1976.

Mitsui, Tōru. "Interactions of Imported and Indigenous Musics in Japan: A Historical Overview of the Music Industry." In *Whose Master's Voice? The Development of Popular Music in Thirteen Cultures,* eds. Alison J. Ewbank and Fouli T. Papageorgiou. Westport, Conn.: Greenwood Press, 1997. 152–74.

Miyoshi, Masao, and H. D. Harootunian, eds. *Japan in the World.* Durham, N.C.: Duke University Press, 1993.

Modleski, Tania, ed. *Studies in Entertainment: Critical Approaches to Mass Culture.* Bloomington: Indiana University Press, 1986.

Monson, Ingrid. *Saying Something: Jazz Improvisation and Interaction.* Chicago: University of Chicago Press, 1996.

Montgomery, John D. *Traveler from Tokyo.* New York: Sheridan, 1944.

Moody, Bill. *The Jazz Exiles: American Musicians Abroad.* Reno: University of Nevada Press, 1993.

Moore, Joe B. "Studying Jazz in Postwar Japan: Where to Begin?" *Japanese Studies* 18.3 (Dec. 1998): 265–80.

Morgenstern, Dan. *The Jazz Story: An Outline History of Jazz.* New York: New York Jazz Museum, 1973.

Morris-Suzuki, Tessa. "The Invention and Reinvention of 'Japanese Culture.'" *Journal of Asian Studies* 54.3 (1995): 759–80.

——. *Re-inventing Japan: Time, Space, Nation.* Armonk, N.Y.: M. E. Sharpe, 1998.

Mouer, Ross, and Yoshio Sugimoto. *Images of Japanese Society: A Study in the Social Construction of Reality.* London: KPI, 1986.

Mukerji, Chandra, and Michael Schudson, eds. *Rethinking Popular Culture: Contemporary Perspectives in Cultural Studies.* Berkeley: University of California Press, 1991.

Murray, Albert. *Stomping the Blues.* New York: Vintage, 1976.

Muto, Ichiyo. "The Birth of the Women's Liberation Movement." In *The Other Japan,* ed. Joe Moore. Armonk, N.Y.: M. E. Sharpe, 1997. 147–71.

——, and Inoue Reiko. "Beyond the New Left (Part 2—II): In Search of a Radical Base in Japan." *AMPO Japan-Asia Quarterly Review* 17.4 (1985): 51–57.

Najita, Tetsuo. *Japan: The Intellectual Foundations of Modern Japanese Politics.* Chicago: University of Chicago Press, 1974.

Najita, Tetsuo, and H. D. Harootunian. "Japanese Revolt against the West: Political and Cultural Criticism in the Twentieth Century." In *The Cambridge History of Japan*. Vol. 6: *The Twentieth Century*, ed. Peter Duus. Cambridge: Cambridge University Press, 1988. 711–74.

Najita, Tetsuo, and J. Victor Koschmann, eds. *Conflict in Modern Japanese History: The Neglected Tradition*. Princeton, N.J.: Princeton University Press, 1982.

Nanry, Charles. *The Jazz Text*. New York: D. Van Nostrand, 1979.

Naremore, James, and Patrick Brantlinger, eds. *Modernity and Mass Culture*. Bloomington: Indiana University Press, 1991.

Nettl, Bruno. *Eight Urban Musical Cultures*. Urbana: University of Illinois Press, 1978.

——. *The Study of Ethnomusicology: Twenty-nine Issues and Concepts*. Urbana: University of Illinois Press, 1983.

——. "Thoughts on Improvisation: A Comparative Approach." *Musical Quarterly* 60.1 (1974): 1–19.

——. *The Western Impact on World Music: Change, Adaptation, and Survival*. New York: Schirmer Books, 1985.

Nettl, Bruno, and Philip V. Bohlman, eds. *Comparative Musicology and Anthropology of Music*. Chicago: University of Chicago Press, 1991.

Nettl, Bruno, Charles Capwell, Philip V. Bohlman, Isabel K. F. Wong, and Thomas Turino. *Excursions in World Music*. 2d ed. Upper Saddle River, N.J.: Prentice Hall, 1997.

Ogren, Kathy J. *The Jazz Revolution*. New York: Oxford University Press, 1989.

Ohtani, Kimiko, and Tokumaru Yoshiko. "Ethnomusicology in Japan since 1970." *Yearbook for Traditional Music* 15 (1983): 155–59.

Oliver, Paul. "Jazz Is Where You Find It: The European Experience of Jazz." In *Superculture: American Popular Culture and Europe*, ed. C. W. E. Bigsby. London: Paul Elek, 1975. 140–51.

O'Meally, Robert, ed. *The Jazz Cadence of American Culture*. New York: Columbia University Press, 1998.

Ottley, Roi. *New World A-Coming: Inside Black America*. Boston: Houghton-Mifflin, 1943.

Packard, George R., III. *Protest in Tokyo: The Security Treaty Crisis of 1960*. Princeton, N.J.: Princeton University Press, 1966.

Pal, John. *Shanghai Saga*. London: Jarrolds, 1963.

Palmer, Anthony J. "World Musics in Music Education: The Matter of Authenticity." *International Journal of Music Education* 19 (1992): 32–40.

Passin, Herbert. "The Legacy of the Occupation in Japan." Occasional Papers of the East Asian Institute. New York: Columbia University, 1968.

Perris, Arnold. *Music as Propaganda: Art to Persuade, Art to Control*. Contributions to the Study of Music and Dance 8. Westport, Conn.: Greenwood Press, 1985.

Pfeiffer, William R. *Filipino Music: Indigenous* [sic], *Folk, Modern*. Dumaguete City, R.P.: Silliman Music Foundation, 1976.

Pinckney, Warren R., Jr. "Jazz in India: Perspectives on Historical Development and Musical Acculturation." *Asian Music* 21.1 (fall/winter 1989–90): 35–77.

Pincus, Leslie. *Authenticating Culture: Kuki Shūzō and the Rise of National Aesthetics*. Berkeley: University of California Press, 1996.

Placksin, Sally. *American Women in Jazz, 1900 to the Present: Their Words, Lives, and Music*. N.p.: Wideview Books, 1982.

Plath, David W. *The After Hours: Modern Japan and the Search for Enjoyment*. Berkeley: University of California Press, 1964.

Portelli, Alessandro. "The Peculiarities of Oral History," *History Workshop* 12 (1981): 96–107.

Powers, Richard Gid, and Hidetoshi Katō, eds. *Handbook of Japanese Popular Culture.* New York and Westport: Greenwood Press, 1989.

Prince, Stephen. *The Warrior's Camera: The Cinema of Akira Kurosawa.* Princeton, N.J.: Princeton University Press, 1991.

Rabson, Steve. *Righteous Cause or Tragic Folly: Changing Views of War in Modern Japanese Poetry.* Ann Arbor: Center for Japanese Studies, University of Michigan, 1998.

Radano, Ronald M. "The Jazz Avant-Garde and the Jazz Community: Action and Reaction." *Annual Review of Jazz Studies* 3 (1985): 71–79.

—. *New Musical Figurations: Anthony Braxton's Cultural Critique.* Chicago: University of Chicago Press, 1993.

Research and Analysis Branch, Office of Strategic Services. "Civil Affairs Guide: Radio Broadcasting in Japan." R & A #2537, 18 April 1945.

Rimer, J. Thomas, ed. *Culture and Identity: Japanese Intellectuals during the Interwar Years.* Princeton, N.J.: Princeton University Press, 1990.

Robertson, Jennifer. *Takarazuka: Sexual Politics and Popular Culture in Modern Japan.* Berkeley: University of California Press, 1998.

Rosenthal, David H. *Hard Bop: Jazz and Black Music 1955–1965.* New York: Oxford University Press, 1992.

Rout, Leslie. "AACM: New Music (!) New Ideas (?)." *Journal of Popular Culture* 1.2 (fall 1967): 128–40.

Rubin, Jay. "From Wholesomeness to Decadence: The Censorship of Literature under the Allied Occupation." *Journal of Japanese Studies* 11.1 (1985): 71–103.

Rudinow, Joel. "Race, Ethnicity, Expressive Authenticity: Can White People Sing the Blues?" *Journal of Aesthetics and Art Criticism* 52.1 (1994): 127–37.

Russell, John G. "Consuming Passions: Spectacle, Self-Transformation, and the Commodification of Blackness in Japan." *positions: east asia cultures critique* 6.1 (1998): 113–77.

—. "Race and Reflexivity: The Black Other in Contemporary Japanese Mass Culture." *Cultural Anthropology* Feb. 1991: 3–25.

—. "Re-thinking the Japanese Image of Blacks." *IHJ Bulletin* 10 (autumn 1990): 1–5.

Said, Edward. *Culture and Imperialism.* New York: Vintage, 1993.

Sandler, Mark, ed. *The Confusion Era: Art and Culture of Japan during the Allied Occupation, 1945–1952.* Seattle and London: Arthur M. Sackler Gallery, Smithsonian Institution, and University of Washington Press, 1997.

Santiago, Francisco. *The Development of Music in the Philippines.* 1931. Quezon City: University of the Philippines, 1957.

Satō, Barbara Hamill. "The *Moga* Sensation: Perceptions of the *Modan Gāru* in Japanese Intellectual Circles During the 1920s." *Gender and History* 5.3 (1993): 363–81.

Schilling, Mark. *The Encyclopedia of Japanese Pop Culture.* New York: Weatherhill, 1997.

Schrager, Samuel. "What Is Social in Oral History?" *International Journal of Oral History* 4 (June 1983): 76–98.

Scott, James C. *Domination and the Arts of Resistance.* New Haven, Conn.: Yale University Press, 1990.

Seidensticker, Edward. *Tokyo Rising: The City since the Great Earthquake.* New York: Knopf, 1990.

Sesler-Beckman, Elizabeth. "Jazz Is My Native Language: A Study of the Development of Jazz in Japan." M.A. thesis, Tufts University, 1989.

Shapiro, Harry. *Waiting for the Man: The Story of Drugs and Popular Music.* New York: William Morrow, 1988.

Shillony, Ben-ami. *Politics and Culture in Wartime Japan*. Oxford: Clarendon Press, 1981.

Shively, Donald H. "Bakufu versus Kabuki." *Harvard Journal of Asiatic Studies* 18 (1955): 326–56.

——. "Popular Culture." In *The Cambridge History of Japan*. Vol. 4: *Early Modern Japan*, ed. John Whitney Hall. Cambridge: Cambridge University Press, 1991. 706–69.

Silverberg, Miriam. "The Cafe Waitress Serving Modern Japan." In *Mirror of Modernity: Invented Traditions of Modern Japan*, ed. Stephen Vlastos. Berkeley: University of California Press, 1998). 208–25.

——. "Constructing the Japanese Ethnography of Modernity." *Journal of Asian Studies* 51 (Feb. 1992): 30–54.

——. "Remembering Pearl Harbor, Forgetting Charlie Chaplin, and the Case of the Disappearing Western Woman: A Picture Story," *positions: east asia cultures critique* 1.1 (1993): 24–76.

Skvorecky, Josef. *Talkin' Moscow Blues: Essays about Literature, Politics, Movies, and Jazz*. Hopewell, N.J.: Ecco Press, 1990.

Slaymaker, Douglas, ed. *A Century of Popular Culture in Japan*. Lewiston, N.Y.: Edwin Mellen Press, 2000.

Smith II, Henry D. *Japan's First Student Radicals*. Cambridge, Mass.: Harvard University Press, 1972.

Springer, Robert. *Authentic Blues: Its History and Its Themes*. Trans. André J. M. Prévos and Robert Springer. Studies in the History and Interpretation of Music 47. Lewiston, N.Y.: Edwin Mellen Press, 1995.

Starr, S. Frederick. *Red & Hot: The Fate of Jazz in the Soviet Union*. Rev. ed. New York: Limelight, 1994.

Stebbins, Robert A. "Role Distance, Role Distance Behaviour, and Jazz Musicians." *British Journal of Sociology* 20 (1969): 406–15.

——. "A Theory of the Jazz Community." *Sociological Quarterly* 9 (1968): 318–31.

Steinhoff, Patricia G. "Student Conflict." In *Conflict in Japan*, ed. Ellis S. Krauss, Thomas P. Rohlen, and Patricia G. Steinhoff. Honolulu: University of Hawaii Press, 1984: 174–213.

Stovall, Tyler. *Paris Noir: African Americans in the City of Light*. Boston: Houghton Mifflin, 1996.

Strinati, Dominc. *An Introduction to Theories of Popular Culture*. London: Routledge, 1995.

Such, David G. *Avant-Garde Musicians: Performing "Out There."* Iowa City: University of Iowa Press, 1993.

Sudhalter, Richard M. *Lost Chords: White Musicians and Their Contribution to Jazz, 1915–1945*. New York: Oxford University Press, 1999.

Sugimoto, Yoshio. *An Introduction to Japanese Society*. Cambridge: Cambridge University Press, 1997.

Supreme Commander for the Allied Powers, General Headquarters. *History of the Nonmilitary Activities of the Occupation of Japan, 1945 through 1951*. Vol. 33: *Radio Broadcasting*.

Tanizaki, Jun'ichirō. *Naomi*. (Japanese title: *Chijin no Ai*.) Trans. Anthony H. Chambers. Tokyo: Charles E. Tuttle, 1985.

Tann, Hillary. "Tradition and Renewal in the Music of Japan." *Perspectives of New Music* 27.2 (1989): 44–47.

Taylor, Paul Christopher. ". . . So Black and Blue: Response to Rudinow." *Journal of Aesthetics and Art Criticism* 53.3 (1995): 313–16.

Taylor, Timothy D. *Global Pop: World Musics, World Markets*. New York: Routledge, 1997.

Thompson, Paul. *The Voice of the Past: Oral History*. 2d ed. Oxford: Oxford University Press, 1988.

Thompson, Stephen I. "American Country Music in Japan." *Popular Music and Society* 16.3 (fall 1992): 31–38.

Tobin, Joseph J. *Re-made in Japan: Everyday Life and Consumer Taste in a Changing Society*. New Haven, Conn.: Yale University Press, 1992.

Treat, John Whittier, ed. *Contemporary Japan and Popular Culture*. Surrey: Curzon, 1996.

Trilling, Lionel. *Sincerity and Authenticity: The Charles Eliot Norton Lectures, 1969–1970*. Cambridge: Harvard University Press, 1972.

Tsutsui, William M. *Manufacturing Ideology: Scientific Management in Twentieth-Century Japan*. Princeton, N.J.: Princeton University Press, 1998.

Turner, Frederick Jackson. "The Significance of the Frontier in American History," *Annual Report of the American Historical Association for the Year 1893*. Washington, D.C.: Government Printing Office, 1894.

Uenoda, Setsuo. *Japan and Jazz: Sketches and Essays on Japanese City Life*. Tokyo: Taiheiyōsha, 1930.

———. "Jazz Songs of Japan." *Trans-Pacific* 26 (Sept. 1929): 6.

Ulanov, Barry. "Jazz: Issues of Identity." *Musical Quarterly* (April 1979): 245–56.

Varley, H. Paul. *Japanese Culture*. 3d ed. Honolulu: University of Hawaii Press, 1984.

Vercelli, Gary. "The Land of the Rising Sun." *Coda* 217 (1987–88): 10–11.

Vincent, Rickey. *Funk: The Music, the People, and the Rhythm of The One*. New York: St. Martin's Griffin, 1996.

Wakeman, Frederic, Jr. *Policing Shanghai 1927–1937*. Berkeley: University of California Press, 1995.

———. *The Shanghai Badlands: Wartime Terrorism and Urban Crime, 1937–1941*. Cambridge: Cambridge University Press, 1996.

Wakeman, Frederic, Jr., and Wen-hsih Yeh, eds. *Shanghai Sojourners*. Berkeley: Institute of East Asian Studies, 1992.

Walser, Robert, ed. *Keeping Time: Readings in Jazz History*. New York: Oxford University Press, 1999.

Weber, David J., and Jane M. Rausch, eds. *Where Cultures Meet: Frontiers in Latin American History*. Jaguar Books on Latin America 6. Wilmington, Del.: Scholarly Resources, Inc., 1994.

West, Cornel. *Race Matters*. Boston: Beacon Press, 1993.

Whiteman, Paul, and Mary Margaret McBride. *Jazz*. 1926. Popular Culture in America 1800–1925. New York: Arno, 1974.

Whiteoak, John. "From Jim Crow to Jazz: Imitation African-American Improvisatory Musical Practices in Pre-Jazz Australia." *Perfect Beat* (July 1993): 50–74.

Wilson, John S. *Jazz: The Transition Years, 1940–1960*. New York: Appleton-Century-Crofts, 1966.

Wolfskill, George, and Stanley Palmer, eds. *Essays on Frontiers in World History*. Austin, Tex.: University of Texas Press, 1981.

Yamanouchi, Hisaaki. *The Search for Authenticity in Modern Japanese Literature*. Cambridge: Cambridge University Press, 1978.

Yano, Christine R. "The Floating World of Karaoke in Japan." *Popular Music and Society* (summer 1996): 1–17.

Yoshida, George, ed. *Nikkei Music Makers: The Swing Era*. National Japanese American Historical Society Calendar #7, 1995.

———. *Reminiscing in Swingtime: Japanese Americans in American Popular Music, 1925–1960*. San Francisco: National Japanese American Historical Society, 1997.

Yoshimi, Shun'ya. "The Condition of Cultural Studies in Japan." *Japanese Studies* 18.1 (May 1998): 65–72.
Yoshino, Kosaku. *Cultural Nationalism in Contemporary Japan*. London: Routledge, 1992.
Young, Louise. *Japan's Total Empire: Manchuria and the Culture of Wartime Imperialism*. Berkeley: University of California Press, 1998.
Yui, Shōichi. "Jazz in Japan." *Jazz Forum* 17 (June 1972): 43–45.

Radio/Television Broadcasts

Ayado Chie, interview with Koyama Kiyoshi. *Jazu kurabu*, NHK-FM, 24 May 1998.
"Ellington's World." *Duke Ellington Centennial Radio Project*, Public Radio International, 4 June 1999.
Ningen dokyumento—Hattori Ryōichi monogatari. FNN-TV, Jan. 1994.
Olsher, Dean. "Jazz Musicians Discuss Racism in the Jazz World." *All Things Considered*, National Public Radio, 10 Jan. 1996.
Shin Nihon tanbō—oyaji ni sasageru jazu. NHK-TV, 8 Jan. 1995.
"Toshiko Akiyoshi." *Jazz Profiles*, National Public Radio, 7 June 1998.
Yoshida Mamoru Tribute, *Welcome to the Jazz World*, Jazz World 8 (satellite), 4 Nov. 1994.

Filmography

Arashi o yobu otoko. Dir. Inoue Umeji. Nikkatsu, 1957.
Culture Shock: The Devil's Music. PBS Video, 2000.
Ikiru. Dir. Kurosawa Akira. Tōhō, 1952.
The Japanese Version. VHS. Prod. Louis Alvarez and Andrew Kolker. Center for New American Media, 1991.
Jazu daimyō. Dir. Okamoto Kihachi. Daiei, 1986.
"Jazu" ga Nihongo ni natta toki. VHS. Prod. Larry Richards. Presented at Fifth Annual Assembly of the Japanese Association for the Study of Popular Music. Nov. 1993.
Jazz in Japan. Prod. Eugene Enrico and Sidney D. Brown. Early Music Television, University of Oklahoma, 1999.
Jazz Is My Native Language: A Portrait of Toshiko Akiyoshi. VHS. Prod. Renée Cho. Rhapsody Films, 1983.
Madamu to nyōbō. Dir. Gosho Heinosuke. Shōchiku Home Video, 1931.
Shanhai bansukingu. Dir. Kushida Kazumi. Nippon Eiga, 1987.
Tokyo Blues: Jazz and Blues in Japan. Prod. Craig McTurk, 1999.
Yoidore tenshi (Drunken Angel). Dir. Kurosawa Akira. Tōhō, 1948.

Performances/Events/Happenings

Akiyoshi Toshiko (solo piano), Kaikō Kinen Kaikan, Yokohama Jazz Promenade, 9 Oct. 1994.
Akiyoshi Toshiko Jazz Orchestra, NHK Studios, 22 Aug. 1994.
Akiyoshi Toshiko Trio, Hikawa Maru, Yokohama Jazz Promenade, 10 Oct. 1993.
Akiyoshi Toshiko Trio, Landmark Hall, Yokohama Jazz Promenade, 9 Oct. 1994.
Asakusa Jazz Band Contest (13th Annual), Asakusa Kōkaidō Hall, Tokyo, 20 Mar. 1994.
Charlie Byrd Trio, Asahi Beer Lobby Concert vol. 22, Tokyo, 8 June 1994.

The Cozy Corners, Bird, Shin-Yokohama, 6 July 1994.
Daitoku Toshiyuki Trio, Jazz House Naru, Ochanomizu, Tokyo, 12 July 1994.
Fujika Kōji Quintet, Birdland, Roppongi, Tokyo, 28 July 1998.
Jim Hall Quartet, Blue Note Tokyo, 19 Sept. 1994.
Hara Nobuo Sharps and Flats, Hikawa Maru, Yokohama Jazz Promenade, 10 Oct. 1993.
Hara Tomonao Quartet, Tōhō Gakuen, Kumitachi City, 20 Oct. 1994.
Jimmy Harada + 3, Saiseria, Ginza, Tokyo, 9 Dec. 1994.
Hayashi Eiichi and Ōnuma Shirō, Dolphy, Yokohama, 15 June 1994.
Hayasaka Sachi and Stir Up!, Airegin, Yokohama, 23 June 1994.
Hayasaka Sachi and Stir Up!, Landmark Hall, Yokohama Jazz Promenade, 9 Oct. 1994.
Hayasaka Sachi and Stir Up!, "2.26," Buddy, Ekoda, Tokyo, 26 Feb. 1995.
High Society Big Band rehearsal, Waseda University, Tokyo, 14 July 1994.
Hino Motohiko, "It's There," Valentine, Roppongi, Tokyo, 12 Aug. 1994.
Hino Terumasa Quartet, Shinjuku Pit-Inn, Tokyo, 28 Dec. 1994.
"A History of Jazz Vol. II: The Battle Royal in Kannai Hall '94," Yokohama, 16 Sept. 1994.
Honda Toshio and Honda Toshiyuki, "Talk and Jazz: Yokohama Jazz Story," Forum Yokohama, 23 Oct. 1994.
Hot Club of Japan (monthly meeting), Pioneer Bldg., Tokyo, 9 Mar. 1995.
Igarashi Issei Quintet, Body and Soul, Minami Aomori, Tokyo, 9 Nov. 1994.
Itabashi Fumio, Hayashi Eiichi, and Katayama Hiroaki, Airegin, Yokohama, 20 Aug. 1994.
Itabashi Fumio Mix Dynamite Quintet, Airegin, Yokohama Jazz Promenade, 10 Oct. 1993.
Itō Kimiko, "A History of Jazz Vol. 1: Standards My Way," Kannai Hall, Yokohama, 24 Sept. 1993.
Izunuma Eitarō, Dolphy, Yokohama, 26 June 1994.
Jazz Restoration in Japan Jam (CD release party), TUC Music Inn, Tokyo, 26 Aug. 1994.
Junior High Jazz Band, Kannai Hall, Yokohama Jazz Promenade, 10 Oct. 1993.
Karashima Fumio Trio, Kaikō Kinen Kaikan, Yokohama Jazz Promenade, 9 Oct. 1994.
George Kawaguchi New Big Four, Kaikō Kinen Kaikan, Yokohama Jazz Promenade, 10 Oct. 1993.
George Kawaguchi New Big Four, Kaikō Kinen Kaikan, Yokohama Jazz Promenade, 9 Oct. 1994.
Bob Kenmotsu 5, First, Hinodechō, Yokohama, 21 Mar. 1995.
Kikuchi Akinori, Shinjuku Pit-Inn, Tokyo, 7 Sept. 1994.
The Meters, Club Cuattro, Shibuya, Tokyo, 9 Oct. 1993.
Mine Kōsuke Quintet, Kaikō Kinen Kaikan, Yokohama Jazz Promenade, 9 Oct. 1994.
Moriyama Takeo Group, Aketa no Mise, Nishi-Ogikubo, Tokyo, 4 Nov. 1994.
Moriyama Takeo Quartet, Rag, Kyōto, 15 July 1998.
Mori Yasumasa (Elvis impersonator), Little Darlin' Oldies Live House, Yokohama, 3 May 1994.
Mt. Fuji Jazz Festival (Horace Silver, J. J. Johnson, Lou Donaldson, US3), 28 Aug. 1994.
Nakakawa Yoshihiro and His Dixie Dix, Kaikō Kinen Kaikan, Yokohama Jazz Promenade, 9 Oct. 1994.
Noguchi Hisamitsu, "Music Funeral" (ongaku sōshiki), 16 June 1994.
Oida Toshio 50th Anniversary Recital, Yūhōto Hoken Hall, Tokyo, 21 Feb. 1995.
Ōnishi Junko, Landmark Hall, Yokohama, 22 June 1994.
Ōno Tomoko (Farnham), J Live House, Shinjuku, Tokyo, 12 Jan. 1995.
George Ōtsuka We Three, Roppongi Pit-Inn, Tokyo, 6 Jan. 1995.
Maceo Parker and Roots Revisited, Blue Note Tokyo, 26 Sept. 1994.
Reunion of musicians who performed in U.S. Armed Service Club, Tokyo Kaikan, 30 Oct.

1994 (Yoda Teruo and Six Lemons, Raymond Conde and Gay Septet with Oda Satoru, others).

Max Roach Quartet, Blue Note Tokyo, 23 Nov. 1994.

Sonny Rollins, Kanagawa Kenmin Hall, Yokohama, 29 May 1994.

Sugihara Jun Sextet, with Oda Satoru, Birdland, Roppongi, Tokyo, 14 Jan. 1995.

Sugiura Yōzō, Kanai Hideto, and Masui Shigeru, "3 for Duke," Jazzmen Club, Yokohama, 5 May 1995.

Suzuki Shōji and Rhythm Ace, Kaikō Kinen Kaikan, Yokohama Jazz Promenade, 9 Oct. 1994.

Swing Journal Awards Ceremony (performance by Kikuchi Masabumi and Mine Kōsuke), Tokyo Prince Hotel, 17 Jan. 1995.

Takase Aki Septet, Jazz Inn Lovely, Nagoya, 23 July 1994.

Togashi Masahiko (solo concert), Salon de Thé Samouar, Yokohama, 30 Jan. 1994.

Tokyo New Jazz Festival '94 (Shibusashirazu, Hayashi-Katayama "de-ga-show," w.r.u.), Kichi-jōji Baus Theater, Kunitachi City, 26 Nov. 1994.

Tribute to "Jo-Jo" (Takayanagi Masayuki), tuc Jazz Court, Tokyo, 27 Jan. 1998.

Umezu Kazutoki and Nazo, Yamate Goethe-za, Yokohama Jazz Promenade, 9 Oct. 1994.

Yamano Big Band Contest (25th Annual), Nippon Seinenkan, Tokyo, 13 Aug. 1994.

Yamashita Yōsuke, Hayasaka Sachi, and Horikoshi Akira, Airegin, Yokohama, 1 May 1994.

Yamashita Yōsuke New York Trio, Landmark Hall, Yokohama, 28 Nov. 1993.

Yokohama Bayside Jazz Special '94: Drum Battle of Big 3 (George Kawaguchi, Inomata Take-shi, Jimmy Takeuchi), Kannai Hall, Yokohama, Mar. 1994.

DISCOGRAPHY

This cannot be a comprehensive listing of recordings by Japanese artists, but rather is a list of recordings collected and/or consulted for this study. I have also included several entries to which I have not yet had an opportunity to listen, but which are generally regarded as important or are cited in the text. Historical significance, availability, financial resources, and personal taste influenced my decisions in building this collection. Whenever possible, I have included both original issue numbers and most recent reissue numbers. Each artist's works are listed chronologically by recording date.

Abe, Kaoru. *Last Date.* DIW: 335, 1989.
——. *Solo Live at Gaya,* vols. 1–10. DIW: 371–380, 1990–91.
Akiyoshi, Toshiko. *The Amazing Toshiko Akiyoshi.* Norgran: MGN-22, 1954; Verve: POCJ-2580, 1998.
——. *The Toshiko Trio.* Storyville: STLP-912, 1956.
——. *Toshiko Mariano Quartet.* Candid: CS 9012, 1961.
——. *Toshiko Meets Her Old Pals.* King: SKC-3, 1961.
——. *Timestream: Toshiko Plays Toshiko.* Nippon Crown: CRCJ-9137, 1997.
Toshiko Akiyoshi Jazz Orchestra. *Wishing Peace.* Ken Music: 27KEN-001, 1989.
——. *Carnegie Hall Concert.* Columbia: CK 48805, 1992.
——. *Desert Lady/Fantasy.* Columbia: CK 57856, 1994.
Toshiko Akiyoshi–Lew Tabackin Big Band. *Road Time.* RCA:CPL2-2242, 1976.
——. *Salted Ginko Nuts.* BMG Victor: RVJ-6031, 1979; BMG/Baystate: B20D-47005, 1989.
——. *The Toshiko Akiyoshi–Lew Tabackin Big Band.* Novus: 3106, 1991.
Araki, James. *Jazz Beat: Midnight Jazz Session.* Nippon Victor: JV-5006, 1959.
Awaya, Noriko. *Wakare no burūsu.* Nippon Columbia: COCA-12042, 1994.
Ayodo, Chie. *Only You.* R-9690100, 1996.
——. *For All We Know.* Ewe: EWCD 0005, 1998.
Casiopea. *Live Anthology Fine.* Pioneer: PICL-1097, 1994.
The Dixie Kings. *Dikishii Nippon min'yō.* King: SKG-27, 1963.
Hara, Nobuo, and Sharps and Flats. *Sharps and Flats in Newport.* Nippon Columbia: XMS-10019, 1969.
——. *Big Band Boss 3.* Nobuo Hara Music Office: NH101, 1995.
Hara, Nobuo, and Sharps and Flats with Yamamoto Hōzan. *New Jazz in Japan.* Nippon Columbia: YS-10022, 1968.
——. *Beautiful Bamboo Flute.* Philips: FX-8510, 1971.
Harada, Jimmy, and Old Boys, with Yoshida Hideko. *Shōwa no bansukingu tachi.* Nippon Victor: SJX-30244, 1984.

Hattori, Ryōichi. *Hattori Ryōichi—boku no ongaku jinsei.* Nippon Columbia: CA-2740–2742, 1989.

Hayasaka, Sachi, and Stir Up! *Straight to the Core.* Three Blind Mice: TBM 5034, 1990.

——. *2.26.* Enja: CRCJ-1044, 1994; ENJ-8014, 1994.

Hayashi, Eiichi, and Katayama Hiroaki. *dé-ga-show!* Omagatoki: SC-7108, 1994.

High Society Orchestra. *Seven Steps to Heaven.* 1992.

Hino, Motohiko. *Ryūhyō (Sailing Ice).* Three Blind Mice: TBM 2561, 1976.

——. *Hip Bone.* Fun House: FHCF-2190, 1994.

Hino, Terumasa. *The Best.* Somethin' Else: TOCJ-5549, 1993.

Hino, Terumasa, and Kikuchi Masabumi. *Hino-Kikuchi Quintet.* Takt: XMS-10011, 1969; Nippon Columbia/Takt: COCY-80430, 1996.

——. *Acoustic Boogie.* Blue Note: 7743 8 36259, 1995.

Igarashi, Issei. *Camel.* deep blue: TFCC-88404, 1994.

Hino, Terumasa, Kikuchi Masabumi, and Togashi Masahiko. *Triple Helix.* Enja: ENJ-8056, 1993.

Ino, Nobuyoshi, and Lester Bowie. *Duet.* King/Paddlewheel: KICJ 8079, 1994.

Itabashi, Fumio. *Mix Dynamite Trio On Stage: Live at Body and Soul.* Mix Dynamite: MD-002, 1994.

——. *The Mix Dynamite Yū.* Omagatoki: OMCZ-1010, 1996.

——, with Yahiro Tomohiro. *Jigazō sakuhin I.* Mix Dynamite: MD-001, 1994.

The Jazz Restoration in Japan. *Jam (Nippon jazu ishin jamu).* Paddle Wheel: KICJ 209, 1994.

Kanai, Hideto. *Q.* Three Blind Mice: TBM-6, 1971.

——. *Ode to Birds.* Three Blind Mice: TBM 2545.

——. *Concierto de Aranjuez.* Three Blind Mice: TBM 5012, 1989 (combines tracks from the original *Concierto de Aranjuez* [TBM 5012] and *What!* [TBM 5015]).

Katayama, Hiroaki. *So-kana.* Omagatoki: SC-7106, 1992.

——. *Instant Groove: Katayama Hiroaki Live at the 7th Floor.* Natya: W101, 1998.

Kawaguchi, George. *Jazz at the Torys.* King: LKB-7, 1957.

——. *The Legendary Japanese Jazz Scene Vol. 1: George Kawaguchi and The Big Four.* Paddle Wheel: KICJ 232, 1995.

Kikuchi, Masabumi. *Attached.* NEC Avenue: A29C-1024, 1989.

——. *Tethered Moon.* Evidence: ECD 22071, 1993.

Maeda, Norio, Miho Keitarō, and Yamaya Kiyoshi. *Modern Jazz Composer's Corner.* Toshiba EMI: JSP-1001, 1960; TOCT-9212, 1995.

Maeda, Norio, and Wind Breakers. *Kurofune.* Toshiba EMI: PCDZ-1298B, 1994.

Matsumoto, Hidehiko ("Sleepy"). *Jazz Progression.* Universal: U-1001, 1958.

Mine, Dick. *Dikku Mine jazu bōkaru besuto—"suingu shinakerya imi nai ne."* Teichiku: BH-1544, n.d.

Mine, Kōsuke. *Mine.* Three Blind Mice: TBM 2501, 1970.

——. *Major to Minor.* Verve: POCJ-1195, 1993.

Miyama, Toshiyuki, and New Herd. *Perspective: New Herd.* Nippon Columbia: JPS-5178, 1969.

Miyazawa, Akira. *My Piccolo.* Next Wave: EJD-3080, 1981.

Modern Jazz All Stars of Japan. *Battle of Funky (Fankii no kyōen).* Toshiba: JSP-1009, 1961; TOCJ-9213, 1995.

Moriyama, Takeo. *Mana.* Tokuma Japan Communications: TKCA-70494, 1994.

——. *Over the Rainbow (Niji no achira ni).* Tokuma Japan Communications: TKCA-70495, 1994.

Moriyasu, Shōtarō. *Shotaro Moriyasu Memorial.* Rockwell: ME 503, 1956.

——. *The Historic Mocambo Session '54 (Maboroshi no Mocanbo sesshon)*. Polydor/Rockwell. Vol. I: MP-2490, 1975; vol. 2: MP-2491, 1975; vol. 3: MP-2492, 1976; vol. 4: MPF-1070, 1977; POCJ-1878/9, 1990 (complete set on 2 CDS).

Oida, Toshio. *The Legendary Japanese Jazz Scene Vol. 2: Oida Toshio*. Paddle Wheel: KICJ 233, 1995.

Ōnishi, Junko. *Live at the Village Vanguard*. Somethin' Else: TOCJ-5570, 1995.

——. *Live at the Village Vanguard Volume II*. Somethin' Else: TOCJ-5572, 1997.

——. *Self Portrait*. Somethin' Else: TOCJ-8001, 1998.

——, with Jazz Workshop. *Pandora*. Somethin' Else: TOCJ-5597-99, 1998.

Ono, Shigenori, and the Blue Coats. *Guren Mirā sutairu—Nippon no mūdo*. Nippon Victor: SJL-5088, 1964.

——. *Guren Mirā sutairu ni yoru Nippon no senritsu*. Nippon Columbia: PS-5070, 1965.

Original cast. *Shanhai bansukingu—besuto serekushon*. Apollon: BY32-38, 1987.

Ōtsuka, George. *Page 2*. Nippon Columbia/Takt: XMS-10002-CT, 1968.

Satō Masahiko. *Palladium*. Toshiba Express: EP-8004, 1969; TOCT-9363, 1996.

——. *Transformation '69/'71*. Toshiba Express: ETP-9041, 1971; TOCT-9734, 1996.

Satō Masahiko, and Randooga. *Select Live under the Sky '90*. Epic/Sony: ESCA 5171, 1990.

Shiraki, Hideo Quintet. *Hideo Shiraki in Festival (Matsuri no gensō)*. Teichiku: SL3002, 1961; Teichiku/Baybridge: TECW-20735, 1998.

——. *Japan Meets Jazz*. Saba/MPS: 15064ST, 1968.

Soul Media. *Funky Best Groove*. Nippon Columbia: COCY-80751, 1997.

Swing Journal All Stars. *Swing Journal All-Star Bands*. King: LKB-2, 1956.

——. *The Swing Journal Critic Poll, 1958*. King: LKB-14, 1958.

——. *Readers Idea: Far East Coast Jazz*. King: SKC-2, 1960.

——. *Swing Journal All Stars '67*. Takt: JAZZ-4, 1967.

——. *Swing Journal All Stars '68*. Nippon Columbia/Takt: COCY-80435, 1968.

——. *All Japan Jazz Festival '69*. Nippon Columbia: PSS1005-6, 1969.

Takahashi, Tatsuya, and the Tokyo Union. *Scandanavian Suite*. Three Blind Mice: TBM 1005, 1977.

Takase, Aki. *Oriental Express*. Omagatoki: SC-7109, 1995; Enja: ENJ-9101, 1997.

Takase, Aki, with David Murray. *Blue Monk*. Enja: ENJ-7039, 1994.

Takayanagi, Masayuki. *Independence: Tread on New Ground*. Teichiku/Union: UPS 2010-J, 1969; TECP-18772.

——. *The Smile I Love*. Jinya Disc: B-03/LMCD-1313, 1992.

——. *Call in Question*. Selfportrait/PSF: PSFD-41, 1994.

——. *Live Independence*. Selfportrait/PSF: PSFD-57, 1995.

——. *April Is the Cruellest Month*. ESP: 3032, 1975; April-Disk: AP-1, n.d.

——. *850113: Takayanagi's Angry Waves Live*. Aketa's Disk: AD-23, n.d.

Takayanagi, Masayuki, with Ino Nobuyoshi. *Reason for Being*. Jinya Disc: B-02/LMCD-1287, 1992.

Togashi, Masahiko. *We Now Create: Music for Strings, Winds, and Percussions*. Nippon Victor: SMJX-10065, 1969; VICJ-23007, 1990.

——. *Spiritual Nature*. East Wind/Nippon Phonogram: EW-8013, 1975; PHCE-4133, 1994.

——. *Three Masters (Donaueschinger Musiktage/1980, Jazz of Japan, Vol. 1)*. Next Wave/Nippon Phonogram: 25PJ-1006, 1980.

Togashi, Masahiko, with Yamashita Yōsuke. *Kizashi*. Next Wave/Nippon Phonogram: 25PJ-1001, 1980; PHCE-4132, 1994.

Tominaga, Haru, and Toshiba Recording Orchestra. *Jazu goto wa utachi (Koto Sings Jazz)*. Toshiba: JPO 1143, 1961.

Various artists. *Jazz Message from Tokyo*. King: LKB-4, 1957.

———. *Jazz of the Four Seasons*. Polydor: SLJ-59, 1964.

———. *Ginparis Session June 26, 1963*. Three Blind Mice: TBM-9, 1972; ART Union/DIW: ART-CD-8, 1986.

———. *1947–1962 Jazz in Japan*. 2 LPS. Victor: SJV-1158-9, 1972.

———. *Kōgane jidai no Victor Hot Club*. Victor: 1180-M, 1973.

———. *Inspiration and Power 14 Free Jazz Festival 1*. Trio: PA-3006-7, 1973; Vivid Sound: VSCD-302-3, 1992.

———. *Jazz on Flame: Jazz Cavalcade in Japan*. Discomate: DSP-3008-10, 1976.

———. *Orijinaru genban ni yoru Nippon no jazu-popyurā shi (senzen hen)*. Victor: SJ-8003, 1976.

———. *Orijinaru genban ni yoru Nippon no jazu songu (senzen hen)*. Nippon Columbia: SZ-7011-15, 1976.

———. *Orijinaru genban ni yoru Nippon no jazu-popyurā shi (sengo hen)*. Victor: SJ-8005, 1977.

———. *The Famous Sound of Three Blind Mice*. Vol. 1: TBM CD 9001, 1988; Vol. 2: TBM CD 9002, 1988; Vol. 3: TBM CD 9003, 1989.

———. *Nihon no ryūkōkashi taikei*. 66 CDS. Daicel Chemical Industries, 1990.

———. *A History of King Jazz Recordings* (Japanese title: *Nippon jazu taikei: Kingu rekōdo sōgyō 60 shūnen kikaku*). King: KICJ 6001-6010, 1992.

———. *All Star Series No. 3: "Modern Jazz."* King: KICJ 2113, 1993.

———. *Midnight in Tokyo*. Vol. 1: King: WWLJ-7094, 1994; vol. 3: King: KICJ 2114, 1993; WWLJ-7095, 1994.

———. *Pioneer* [sic] *of Japanese Jazz—New Edition (Nippon jazu taikei serekuto shinpen SP Jidai no jazu)*. King: KICJ 192, 1994.

———. *Senji kayō*. King: KICX 8428, 1997.

Watanabe, Kazumi. *Mobo I & II*. Gramavision: R2 79417, 1984.

Watanabe, Kazumi, with Ozone Makoto. *Dandyism*. domo: POCJ-1412, 1998.

Watanabe, Kazumi, with Resonance Vox. *Resonance Vox*. domo: POCH-1250, 1993.

Watanabe, Sadao. *Jazz and Bossa*. Takt-1, 1967; Nippon Columbia/Takt: COCY-80418, 1996.

———. *Sadao Plays Bacharach and Beatles*. Takt: XMS-10010, 1969; Nippon Columbia/Takt: COCY-80502, 1997.

———. *Parker's Mood—Live at Bravas Club '85*. Elektra: 69475, 1986.

———. *Selected*. Elektra: 32P2-2302, 1988.

Watanabe, Sadao, and Charlie Mariano. *Iberian Waltz*. Takt: JAZZ-7, 1967; Nippon Columbia/Takt: COCY-80419, 1996.

———. *We Got a New Bag (Sadao and Charlie Again)*. 1968; Nippon Columbia/Takt: COCY-80503, 1997.

Yagi, Masao. *Plays Thelonious Monk*. King: SKC-1, 1960.

Yamamoto, Hōzan, and Kikuchi Masabumi. *Ginkai (Silver World)*. Philips: BT-5319, 1970; PHCE-4134, 1994.

———. *Chiasma*. MPS: 1976; POCJ-2552, 1998.

———. *Dazzling Days*. Verve: 521 303, 1993.

———. *Ways of Time*. Verve: POCJ-1250, 1994.

Yamashita, Yōsuke. *Dancing Kojiki*. Sadaneri Shobō: DANC-3, 1995.

———. *Complete Frasco Recordings*. 1998.

———, with Kodō and Panja Ensemble. *Kodō vs Yosuke Yamashita in Live*. Denon: C38-7900, 1986.

Additional Recordings (Non-Japanese Artists)

Adderley, Julian "Cannonball." *Nippon Soul.* Riverside: RLP-9477, 1963; OJC 435, 1990.

———. *Cannonball in Japan.* Capitol: B21 Y-93560, 1967; CDP 7935602, 1990.

Blakey, Art, and the Jazz Messengers. *Tokyo 1961.* Somethin' Else: CJ32-5503.

Brubeck, Dave, Quartet. *Jazz Impressions of Japan.* Columbia: PC 9012, 1964; Sony: SRCS 9367, 1998.

Ellington, Duke. *The Far East Suite.* RCA-Victor: LPM/LSP-3782, 1967; Bluebird: 66551, 1995.

Funkadelic. *Funkadelic.* Westbound: WB-2000, 1971.

Hawes, Hampton. *The Trio, Vol. 1.* Contemporary: C-3505, 1955; OJC 316, 1987.

———. *Everybody Likes Hampton Hawes: Vol. 3, The Trio.* Contemporary: 3523, 1956; OJC 421, 1990.

———. *The Trio, Vol. 2.* Contemporary: C-3515, 1956; OJC 318, 1987.

Houn, Fred, and the Afro-Asian Music Ensemble. *We Refuse to Be Used and Abused.* Soul Note: 121167, 1988.

Jang, Jon, Octet. *Island: The Immigrant Suite No. 1.* Soul Note: 121303, 1995.

Jang, Jon, Octet, and the Pan Asian Arkestra. *Tiananmen!* Soul Note: 121223, 1993.

Jazz at the Philharmonic. *Jazz at the Philharmonic in Tokyo: Live at the Nichigeki.* Pablo: 2620104, 1990.

Mingus, Charles (with Miyama Toshiyuki and His New Herd). *Charles Mingus with Orchestra.* Nippon Columbia: NCB 7008, 1971; Denon: 8565, 1990.

Pierson, Tom. *Planet of Tears.* Auteur: 1229, 1996.

———. *II.* Auteur: 1171, 1993.

———. *III.* Auteur: 1194, 1994.

Scofield, John. *Pick Hits: The John Scofield Band Live.* Gramavision R2 79405, 1990.

Scott, Tony. *Music for Zen Meditation and Other Joys.* Verve: V6-8634, 1965; 314 521 444, 1997.

Silver, Horace. *The Tokyo Blues.* Blue Note: 84110, 1962; CDP 53355, 1996.

Sun Ra Arkestra. *Live at Pit-Inn, Tokyo, Japan.* DIW: 824, 1988.

Tacuma, Jamaaladeen. *Music World.* Gramavision: R2 79437, 1986.

Various artists. *Exotic Japan: Orientalism in Occupied Japan.* Audi-Book: AB129, 1996.

Zorn, John, and Satō Michihiro. *Ganryū Island.* Tzadik: TZ 7319, 1998.

To acquaint myself with indigenous Japanese musics I relied on selected volumes from two 10-CD series: *Japanese Traditional Music (Nihon no dentō ongaku)* (King: KICH 2001-2010, 1991) and *Music of Japanese People (Nihon no minzoku ongaku)* (King: KICH 2021-2030, 1991). Both collections are beautifully packaged and thoroughly annotated in both Japanese and English.

INDEX

Abe Kaoru, 16, 19
Acuna, Alex, 261
Adderley, Julian "Cannonball," 21, 209
Aikura Hisato, 225, 237, 250
Akagi Kei, 27
Akiyoshi Toshiko, 3, 19, 138, 168, 177, 179, 182, 183–84, 195, 201, 202, 205–6, 207–9, 212–13, 214, 215, 217, 222, 224, 226, 234, 236, 240–41, 245, 255–56, 257, 259–60, 268. *See also* Cozy Quartet
Akutagawa Yasushi, 38, 246
Allen, Steve, 208
American Federation of Musicians, 177, 198
Ammons, Gene, 198
Anderson, Benedict, 90
Anderson, Ray, 261
Anpo (U.S.-Japan Security Treaty) protests, 225, 230, 241, 256
Anthony, Ray, 187
Anzai, Takeshi, 35
Araki, Jimmy, 180, 181, 182, 200
Armstrong, Louis, 25, 33, 82, 87, 99, 174, 186, 196, 197
Art Ensemble of Chicago, 19–20, 22, 32, 254
Ashida Mitsuru, 60–61, 70, 78
Asmanians, 187, 193
Association for the Advancement of Creative Musicians (AACM), 250
Authenticity, 7, 15–16, 23, 27, 75, 78, 81–82, 88, 91, 119, 131, 167–69, 183, 204, 225–26, 241, 260, 263–64, 270–71, 273, 275–76; definitions, 23–25; Japan's authenticity complex, 11, 22, 37–38, 42, 236, 263–64; racial/ethnic notions of, 10–12, 17–18, 20, 25, 27, 34, 38, 123, 196, 203–4, 206, 216, 217–18, 273, 275; strategies of

authentication, 12, 36–38, 41, 88–90, 91, 138–39, 161–62, 169, 195–96, 201, 203–4, 224–26, 238–41, 243, 253, 263–64, 271
Awaya Noriko, 81, 127–28, 132
Ayado Chie, 271–72
Ayler, Albert, 252

Bacharach, Burt, 236
Bailey, Derek, 233
Bailey, Donald "Duck," 21
Baldwin, James, 216
Bands: bands-for-hire, 53, 57; department store youth troupes, 53–57; early jazz bands, 57, 60; jinta, 52–53; ocean liner salon orchestras, 53–54, 59; studio bands, 76–78, 212. *See also* Filipino jazz bands; *and under names of individual bands*
Baraka, Amiri (LeRoi Jones), 7, 26, 27, 42, 201, 216, 248–49, 252, 254
Barker, Danny, 8
Basie, Count, 75, 133, 174, 187, 239
Beatles, 234, 236
Bebop, 36, 162, 167–68, 175, 176, 179–80, 181–82, 186, 195, 196–202, 205–6, 211, 239–40, 251
Bebop Ace, 198
Bechet, Sidney, 17
Beiderbecke, Bix, 99
Benton, Walter, 179, 183, 206
Beppu, Taft, 81, 82
Berendt, Joachim, 215, 216, 217, 238
Berklee College of Music, 34, 37, 88, 207–8, 234, 236, 266, 269, 271
Big Four, 165–66, 184, 192–94, 228. *See also* Kawaguchi, George
Blakey, Art, 36, 209, 227, 256, 263, 266, 269

Hōgaku (traditional music). *See* Music: traditional (*hōgaku*)
Holiday, Billie, 19, 82, 268, 274
Holman, Bill, 211
Home Ministry (Naimushō), 63, 139, 142, 147, 150, 153, 175, 187
Honda, Helen, 81
Honda Toshio, 15, 124
Horiuchi Keizō, 74, 104–7, 109, 143, 147–48, 155
Hosokawa Shūhei, 108–9
Hot Club of Japan, 7, 188
Hughes, Phillip S., 13–14

Ichiban Octet, 179, 183, 198, 207
Ida Ichirō, 61–65, 66, 91, 103–4, 177
Iemoto system, 33–36
Iiyama Shigeo, 176
Ikeda Yoshio, 236
Imada Masaru, 40, 196, 254
Imperialism, 30, 49; Japanese in East Asia, 68, 84–85, 89–90, 113; and music, 49–50. *See also* Jazz: as cultural imperialism
Imperial Rule Assistance Association (IRAA), 142
Improvisation, 35, 49, 52, 59–60, 61, 65, 69, 104–5, 134, 177, 212, 226, 236
Inada, Betty, 81, 151
Inagaki Jirō, 41–41, 175, 180, 186, 200, 214
Inage Sōfu, 102–3
Ino Nobuyoshi, 1, 27, 232–33
Inoue Umeji, 191
Ishihara Yasuyuki, 241
Ishihara Yūjirō, 191–92
Isoi Gijin, 170, 171
Isono Teruo, 41, 174, 179, 265
Itabashi Fumio, 41, 273–74
Ivy, Marilyn, 223
Iwami Kiyoshi, 206
Iwanami Yōzō, 245, 271
Izawa Shūji, 52
Izu, Mark, 262
Izumi Kimio, 72

Jam sessions, 69–70, 71, 182–84, 196, 202, 211, 216, 237. *See also* Ginparis sessions; Mocambo sessions
James, Harry, 172

Jang, Jon, 253, 262
Japan Musician's Union, 177, 210
Japanese American jazz artists, 81–82, 91, 151, 158, 180, 183
Japanese jazz (national style), 12, 17, 30–32, 39–41, 126, 131, 132–39, 144, 154, 160–62, 169, 224–26, 241–55, 257–60, 261–63, 267, 268, 274; as "light music" (*kei-ongaku*), 131, 134, 138, 144–46, 153–54, 160; *ma* (space, interval) in, 40, 245–46, 249, 254–55, 258; rhythmic sense, 41, 215, 244, 258; as strategy of authentication, 36–38, 169, 224–26, 238–40, 243, 253, 263–64. *See also* Jazz in Japan
Jazu kissa. *See* Jazz coffeehouses (*jazu kissa*)
Jazz: aesthetic prejudice against, 62, 81, 100, 103–6; as art, 6, 188–89, 190, 197, 199–201; in cinema, 48, 68, 191–92; criticism, 76, 188, 250, 265–66; as cultural capital, 11; as cultural imperialism, 29, 125, 263–64; debates on, 67, 94–97, 99–100, 107, 110, 121, 123–26; as democratic propaganda, 171–74; and freedom, 25, 43, 124, 237; history and historiography, 13–14, 47, 196–97, 199–200, 269–70, 276; and modernity, 67, 97, 103, 107–10, 112–13, 120, 121, 123–26, 145, 152, 167; and racial politics, 26–27, 97–98, 251; and radicalism, 121–22, 236–37, 250, 256; and social dance, 3, 56, 70–71, 116–17, 188, 199–200; as symbol, 46, 47, 67, 97, 107–10, 112–13, 120, 121, 123–26, 152–53, 167, 171, 190–91, 237, 276; as universal, 22, 25, 38, 96, 121, 124, 169, 245, 246–47, 261, 275–76. *See also* Bebop; Improvisation; Jazz in Japan
Jazz Academy, 227–29. *See also* New Century Music Workshop (Shin Seiki Ongaku Kenkyūjo)
Jazz at the Philharmonic (JATP), 186, 207
Jazz coffeehouses (*jazu kissa*), 4, 6–7, 15, 68, 74–75, 140, 141, 149–50, 151, 184, 190, 195, 197, 200, 210–11, 212, 215, 216, 227, 233–34, 235, 236, 237, 255
Jazz community, in Japan: definition, 6, 277–78 n.3; sociological characteristics, 4–9, 168–69, 200, 201–2, 218, 251; stylistic segmentation of, 6–7, 197–98, 199, 200, 202, 223–24

E. Taylor Atkins is Assistant Professor of History at Northern
Illinois University.

Library of Congress Cataloging-in-Publication Data
Atkins, E. Taylor.
Blue Nippon : authenticating jazz in Japan / E. Taylor Atkins.
Includes bibliographical references, discography, and index.
ISBN 0-8223-2710-4 (cloth : alk. paper).
ISBN 0-8223-2721-X (pbk. : alk. paper)
1. Jazz—Japan—History and criticism. I. Title.
ML3509.J3 A85 2001   781.65'0952—dc21   2001023019